Enterprise JavaBeans™

Related titles from O'Reilly

THIRD EDITION

Enterprise JavaBeans™

Richard Monson-Haefel

O'REILLY®

Beijing · Cambridge · Farnham · Köln · Paris · Sebastopol · Taipei · Tokyo

Enterprise JavaBeans™, Third Edition
by Richard Monson-Haefel

Copyright © 2001, 2000, 1999 O'Reilly & Associates, Inc. All rights reserved.
Printed in the United States of America.

Published by O'Reilly & Associates, Inc., 101 Morris Street, Sebastopol, CA 95472.

Editor:	Mike Loukides
Production Editor:	Rachel Wheeler
Cover Designer:	Hanna Dyer
Interior Designer:	Melanie Wang

Printing History:

June 1999:	First Edition.
March 2000:	Second Edition.
September 2001:	Third Edition.

ISBN: 0-596-00226-2
[M]

For my wife and best friend,
Hollie

Table of Contents

Preface

Author's Note

In the winter of 1997, I was consulting on an e-commerce project that was using Java RMI. Not surprisingly, the project failed because Java RMI didn't address performance, scalability, failover, security, or transactions, all of which are vital in a production environment. Although the outcome of that project is not unique to Java RMI—I have seen the same thing happen with CORBA—the timing of the project was especially interesting. Enterprise JavaBeans™ was first introduced by Sun Microsystems at around that time, and had Enterprise JavaBeans (EJB) been available earlier, that same project probably would have succeeded.

At the time I was working on that ill-fated Java RMI project, I was also writing a column for *JavaReport Online* called "The Cutting Edge." The column covered what were then new Java technologies such as the Java Naming and Directory Interface™ (JNDI) and the JavaMail™ API. I was actually looking for a new topic for the third installment of "The Cutting Edge" when I discovered the first public draft of Enterprise JavaBeans, Version 0.8. I had originally heard about this technology in 1996, but this was the first time that public documentation had been made available. Having worked on CORBA, Java RMI, and other distributed object technologies, I knew a good thing when I saw it and immediately began writing an article about this new technology.

That seems like eons ago. Since I published that article in March 1998, literally hundreds of articles on EJB have been written, and several books on the subject have come and gone. This book, now in its third edition, has kept pace with three versions of the EJB specification in as many years. As the newest version of the specification takes flight, and a slew of new books on the subject debut, I can't help but remember the days when the words "Enterprise JavaBeans" drew blank looks from just about everyone. I'm glad those days are over.

What Is Enterprise JavaBeans?

When Java™ was first introduced in the summer of 1995, most of the IT industry focused on its graphical user interface characteristics and the competitive advantage it offered in terms of distribution and platform independence. Those were interesting times. The applet was king, and only a few of us were attempting to use it on the server side. In reality, we spent about half of our time coding and the other half trying to convince management that Java was not a fad.

Today, the focus has broadened considerably: Java has been recognized as an excellent platform for creating enterprise solutions, specifically for developing distributed server-side applications. This shift has much to do with Java's emerging role as a universal language for producing implementation-independent abstractions for common enterprise technologies. The JDBC™ API is the first and most familiar example. JDBC (Java Database Connectivity) provides a vendor-independent Java interface for accessing SQL relational databases. This abstraction has been so successful that it's difficult to find a relational database vendor that doesn't support JDBC. Java abstractions for enterprise technologies have expanded considerably to include JNDI for abstracting directory services, JTA (Java Transaction API) for abstracting access to transaction managers, JMS (Java Message Service) for abstracting access to different message-oriented middleware products, and more.

Enterprise JavaBeans, first introduced as a draft specification in late 1997, has since established itself as one of the most important Java enterprise technologies provided by Sun Microsystems. EJB provides an abstraction for component transaction monitors (CTMs), which represent the convergence of two technologies: traditional transaction-processing (TP) monitors (such as CICS, TUXEDO, and Encina), and distributed object services (such as CORBA, DCOM, and native Java RMI). Combining the best of both technologies, component transaction monitors provide a robust, component-based environment that simplifies distributed development while automatically managing the most complex aspects of enterprise computing, such as object brokering, transaction management, security, persistence, and concurrency.

Enterprise JavaBeans defines a server-side component model that allows business objects to be developed and moved from one brand of EJB container to another. A component (i.e., an enterprise bean) presents a simple programming model that allows the developer to focus on its business purpose. An EJB server is responsible for making the component a distributed object and for managing services such as transactions, persistence, concurrency, and security. In addition to defining the bean's business logic, the developer defines the bean's runtime attributes in a way that is similar to choosing the display properties of visual widgets. The transactional, persistence, and security behaviors of a component can be defined by choosing from a list of properties. The end result is that EJB makes developing distributed-component systems that are managed in a robust transactional environment much easier. For developers and corporate IT shops that have struggled with the complexities of delivering mission-critical, high-performance distributed systems using CORBA, DCOM, or Java RMI, EJB provides a far simpler and more productive platform on which to base development efforts.

When Enterprise JavaBeans 1.0 was finalized in 1998, it quickly become a de facto industry standard. Many vendors announced their support even before the specification was finalized. Since that time, EJB has been enhanced twice. The specification was first updated in 1999, to Version 1.1, which was covered in the second edition of this book. The most recent revision to the specification, Version 2.0, is covered by this, the third edition of *Enterprise JavaBeans*. This edition also covers EJB 1.1, which is for the most part a subset of the functionality offered by EJB 2.0.

Products that conform to the EJB standard have come from every sector of the IT industry, including the TP monitor, CORBA ORB, application server, relational database, object database, and web server industries. Some of these products are based on proprietary models that have been adapted to EJB; many more wouldn't even exist without EJB.

In short, Enterprise JavaBeans 2.0 and 1.1 together provide a standard distributed-component model that greatly simplifies the development process and allows beans developed and deployed on one vendor's EJB server to be easily deployed on a different vendor's EJB server. This book will provide you with the foundation you need to develop vendor-independent EJB solutions.

Who Should Read This Book?

This book explains and demonstrates the fundamentals of the Enterprise JavaBeans 2.0 and 1.1 architectures. Although EJB makes distributed computing much simpler, it is still a complex technology that requires a great deal of time and study to master. This book provides a straightforward, no-nonsense explanation of the underlying technology, Java classes and interfaces, component model, and runtime behavior of Enterprise JavaBeans. It includes material that is backward-compatible with EJB 1.1 and provides special notes and chapters when there are significant differences between 1.1 and 2.0.

Although this book focuses on the fundamentals, it's not a "dummies" book. Enterprise JavaBeans is an extremely complex and ambitious enterprise technology. While using EJB may be fairly simple, the amount of work required to truly understand and master EJB is significant. Before reading this book, you should be fluent in the Java language and have some practical experience developing business solutions. Experience with distributed object systems is not a must, but you will need some experience with JDBC (or at least an understanding of the basics) to follow the examples in this book. If you are unfamiliar with the Java language, I recommend *Learning Java™* by Patrick Niemeyer and Jonathan Knudsen; this book was formerly *Exploring Java™* (O'Reilly). If you are unfamiliar with JDBC, I recommend

Database Programming with JDBC™ and Java™ by George Reese (O'Reilly). If you need a stronger background in distributed computing, I recommend *Java™ Distributed Computing* by Jim Farley (O'Reilly).

Organization

Here's how the book is structured. The first three chapters are largely background material, placing Enterprise JavaBeans 2.0 and 1.1 in the context of related technologies and explaining at the most abstract level how the EJB technology works and what makes up an enterprise bean. Chapters 4 through 13 go into detail about developing enterprise beans of various types. Chapters 14 and 15 could be considered advanced topics, except that transactions (Chapter 14) are essential to everything that happens in enterprise computing, and design strategies (Chapter 15) help you deal with a number of real-world issues that influence bean design. Chapter 16 describes in detail the XML deployment descriptors used in EJB 2.0 and 1.1, and Chapter 17 gives an overview of Java™ 2, Enterprise Edition (J2EE), which includes servlets, JavaServer Pages™ (JSP), and EJB. Finally, the three appendices provide some reference information that should be useful to you.

Chapter 1, *Introduction*
> This chapter defines component transaction monitors and explains how they form the underlying technology of the Enterprise JavaBeans component model.

Chapter 2, *Architectural Overview*
> This chapter defines the architecture of the Enterprise JavaBeans component model and examines the difference between the three basic types of enterprise beans: entity beans, session beans, and message-driven beans.

Chapter 3, *Resource Management and the Primary Services*
> This chapter explains how the EJB-compliant server manages an enterprise bean at runtime.

Chapter 4, *Developing Your First Enterprise Beans*
> This chapter walks the reader through the development of some simple enterprise beans.

Chapter 5, *The Client View*
> This chapter explains in detail how enterprise beans are accessed and used by a remote client application.

Chapter 6, *EJB 2.0 CMP: Basic Persistence*
> This chapter provides an explanation of how to develop basic container-managed entity beans in EJB 2.0.

Chapter 7, *EJB 2.0 CMP: Entity Relationships*
> This chapter picks up where Chapter 6 left off, expanding your understanding of container-managed persistence to complex bean-to-bean relationships.

Chapter 8, *EJB 2.0 CMP: EJB QL*

This chapter addresses the Enterprise JavaBeans Query Language (EJB QL), which is used to query EJBs and to locate specific entity beans in EJB 2.0 container-managed persistence.

Chapter 9, *EJB 1.1 CMP*

This chapter covers EJB 1.1 container-managed persistence, which is supported in EJB 2.0 for backward compatibility. Read this chapter only if you need to support legacy EJB applications.

Chapter 10, *Bean-Managed Persistence*

This chapter covers the development of bean-managed persistence beans including when to store, load, and remove data from the database.

Chapter 11, *The Entity-Container Contract*

This chapter covers the general protocol between an entity bean and its container at runtime and applies to both container-managed persistence in EJB 2.0 and 1.1 and bean-managed persistence.

Chapter 12, *Session Beans*

This chapter shows how to develop stateless and stateful session beans.

Chapter 13, *Message-Driven Beans*

This chapter shows how to develop message-driven beans in EJB 2.0.

Chapter 14, *Transactions*

This chapter provides an in-depth explanation of transactions and describes the transactional model defined by Enterprise JavaBeans.

Chapter 15, *Design Strategies*

This chapter provides some basic design strategies that can simplify your EJB development efforts and make your EJB system more efficient.

Chapter 16, *XML Deployment Descriptors*

This chapter provides an in-depth explanation of the XML deployment descriptors used in EJB 1.1 and 2.0.

Chapter 17, *Java 2, Enterprise Edition*

This chapter provides an overview of J2EE v1.3 and explains how EJB 2.0 fits into this new platform.

Appendix A, *The Enterprise JavaBeans API*

This appendix provides a quick reference to the classes and interfaces defined in the EJB packages.

Appendix B, *State and Sequence Diagrams*

This appendix provides diagrams that clarify the life cycle of enterprise beans at runtime.

Appendix C, *EJB Vendors*

This appendix provides information about the vendors of EJB servers.

Software and Versions

This book covers Enterprise JavaBeans Versions 2.0 and 1.1, including all optional features. It uses Java language features from the Java 1.2 platform and JDBC. Because the focus of this book is on developing vendor-independent Enterprise Java-Beans components and solutions, I have stayed away from proprietary extensions and vendor-dependent idioms. Any EJB-compliant server can be used with this book, but you should be familiar with your server's specific installation, deployment, and runtime-management procedures to work with the examples.

EJB 2.0 and 1.1 have a lot in common, but when they differ, chapters or sections within a chapter that are specific to each version are clearly marked. Feel free to skip version-specific sections that do not concern you. Unless indicated, the source code in this book has been written for both EJB 2.0 and 1.1.

Examples developed in this book are available from *ftp://ftp.oreilly.com/pub/examples/ java/ejb/*. The examples are organized by chapter.

Example Workbooks

Although EJB applications themselves are portable, the manner in which you install and run EJB products varies widely from one vendor to the next. For this reason it is nearly impossible to cover all the EJB products available, so I have chosen a radical but effective way to address these differences: workbooks.

To help you deploy the book examples in different EJB products, I will publish several free workbooks that you can use along with this book to run the examples on specific commercial and noncommercial EJB servers. The workbook for a specific product will address that product's most advanced server. So, for example, if the vendor supports EJB 2.0, the examples in the workbook will address EJB 2.0 features. If, on the other hand, the vendor supports only EJB 1.1, the examples in the workbook will be specific to EJB 1.1.

Although I plan to publish workbooks for several different EJB servers, at least two workbooks will be made available immediately. These workbooks will be available free online (in PDF format) at *http://www.oreilly.com/catalog/entjbeans3/* or *http:// www.titan-books.com.*

Conventions

The following typographical conventions are used in this book:

Italic
> Used for filenames and pathnames, hostnames, domain names, URLs, and email addresses. *Italic* is also used for new terms where they are defined.

Constant width

Used for code examples and fragments, XML elements and tags, and SQL commands, table names, and column names. Constant width is also used for class, variable, and method names and for Java keywords used within the text.

Constant width bold

Used for emphasis in some code examples.

Constant width italic

Used to indicate text that is replaceable. For example, in *BeanName*PK, you would replace *BeanName* with a specific bean name.

 Indicates a tip, suggestion, or general note.

 Indicates a warning or caution.

An Enterprise JavaBean consists of many parts; it's not a single object, but a collection of objects and interfaces. To refer to an enterprise bean as a whole, we use its business name in Roman type, followed by the acronym EJB. For example, we will refer to the Customer EJB when we want to talk about the enterprise bean in general. If we put the name in a constant-width font, we are referring explicitly to the bean's remote interface; thus, CustomerRemote is the remote interface that defines the business methods of the Customer EJB.

Comments and Questions

Please address comments and questions concerning this book to the publisher:

O'Reilly & Associates, Inc.
101 Morris Street
Sebastopol, CA 95472
(800) 998-9938 (in the United States or Canada)
(707) 829-0515 (international or local)
(707) 829-0104 (fax)

There is a web page for this book, which lists errata, examples, and any additional information. You can access this page at:

http://www.oreilly.com/catalog/entjbeans3/

To comment on or ask technical questions about this book, send email to:

bookquestions@oreilly.com

For more information about books, conferences, software, Resource Centers, and the O'Reilly Network, see the O'Reilly web site at:

http://www.oreilly.com

The author maintains a web site for the discussion of EJB and related distributed computing technologies at *http://www.jmiddleware.com*. jMiddleware.com provides news about this book as well as code tips, articles, and an extensive list of links to EJB resources.

Acknowledgments

While there is only one name on the cover of this book, the credit for its development and delivery is shared by many individuals. Michael Loukides, my editor, was pivotal to the success of every edition of this book. Without his experience, craft, and guidance, this book would not have been possible. Other people at O'Reilly & Associates, including Rachel Wheeler, Rob Romano, Kyle Hart, and many others, were also very important to the success of this book.

Many expert technical reviewers helped ensure that the material was technically accurate and true to the spirit of Enterprise JavaBeans. Of special note are Greg Nyberg of ObjectPartners, Hemant Khandelwal of Pramati, Kyle Brown of IBM, Robert Castaneda of CustomWare, Joe Fialli of Sun Microsystems, Anil Sharma and Priyank Rastogi of Pramati, Seth White of BEA, Evan Ireland and Meyer Tanuan of Sybase, David Chappell of David Chappell & Associates, Jim Farley, author of *Java™ Distributed Computing* (O'Reilly), and Prasad Muppirala of BORN Information Services. They contributed greatly to the technical accuracy of this book and brought a combination of industry and real-world experience to bear, helping to make this one of the best books on Enterprise JavaBeans published today.

I would also like to thank everyone in the community who provided valuable feedback by reviewing this book while it was being written at *http://oreilly.techrev.org*, including (in alphabetical order): Dion Almaer, Jim Archer, Stephen Davies, John De la Cruz, Tom Gullo, Marty Harvey, Hai Hoang, Meeraj Kunnumpurath, Tom Larson, Bjarne Rasmussen, rgparker (name unknown), Larry Seltzer, and Curt Smith.

Special thanks also go to Sriram Srinivasan of BEA, Anne Thomas of Sun Microsystems, Ian McCallion of IBM Hursley, Tim Rohaly of jGuru.com, James D. Frentress of ITM Corp., Andrzej Jan Taramina of Accredo Systems, Marc Loy, coauthor of *Java™ Swing* (O'Reilly), Don Weiss of Step 1, Mike Slinn of The Dialog Corporation, and Kevin Dick of Kevin Dick & Associates. The contributions of these technical experts were critical to the technical and conceptual accuracy of earlier editions of this book. Others I would like to thank include Maggie Mezquita, Greg Hartzel, John Klug, and Jon Jamsa of BORN Information who all suffered though the first draft of the first edition so long ago to provide valuable feedback.

Thanks also to Vlad Matena and Mark Hapner of Sun Microsystems, the primary architects of Enterprise JavaBeans; Linda DeMichiel, EJB 2.0 specification lead; and Bonnie Kellett, J2EE Program Manager—they were all willing to answer several of my most complex questions. Thanks to all the participants in the EJB-INTEREST mailing list hosted by Sun Microsystems for their interesting and sometimes controversial, but always informative, postings over the past four years.

Finally, I extend the most sincere gratitude to my wife, Hollie, for supporting and assisting me through the three years of painstaking research and writing that were required to produce three editions of this book. Without her unfailing support and love, this book would not have been completed.

CHAPTER 1

Introduction

This book is about Enterprise JavaBeans 2.0 and 1.1, which are the third and second versions of the Enterprise JavaBeans specification. Just as the Java platform has revolutionized the way we think about software development, Enterprise JavaBeans has revolutionized the way we think about developing mission-critical enterprise software. It combines server-side components with distributed object technologies and asynchronous messaging to greatly simplify the task of application development. It automatically takes into account many of the requirements of business systems, including security, resource pooling, persistence, concurrency, and transactional integrity.

This book shows you how to use Enterprise JavaBeans to develop scalable, portable business systems. But before we can start talking about EJB itself, we'll need a brief introduction to the technologies addressed by EJB, such as component models, distributed objects, component transaction monitors (CTMs), and asynchronous messaging. It's particularly important to have a basic understanding of component transaction monitors, the technology that lies beneath EJB. In Chapters 2 and 3, we'll start looking at EJB itself and see how enterprise beans are put together. The rest of this book is devoted to developing enterprise beans for an imaginary business and discussing advanced issues.

It is assumed that you're already familiar with Java; if you're not, *Learning Java™*, by Patrick Niemeyer and Josh Peck (O'Reilly), is an excellent introduction. This book also assumes that you're conversant in the JDBC API, or at least in SQL. If you're not familiar with JDBC, see *Database Programming with JDBC™ and Java™* by George Reese (O'Reilly).

One of Java's most important features is platform independence. Since it was first released, Java has been marketed as "write once, run anywhere." While the hype has gotten a little heavy-handed at times, code written with Sun's Java programming language is remarkably platform independent. Enterprise JavaBeans isn't just platform independent—it's also implementation independent. If you've worked with JDBC, you know a little about what this means. Not only can the JDBC API run on a Windows machine or on a Unix machine, it can also access relational databases of many different vendors (DB2, Oracle, Sybase, SQLServer, etc.) by using different JDBC drivers. You don't have to code to a particular database implementation—just change JDBC drivers and you change databases. It's the same with EJB. Ideally, an EJB component, an enterprise bean, can run in any application server that implements the EJB specification.* This means that you can develop and deploy your EJB business system in one server, such as Orion or BEA's WebLogic, and later move it to a different EJB server, such as Pramati, Sybase EAServer, IBM's WebSphere, or an open source project such as OpenEJB, JOnAS, or JBoss. Implementation independence means that your business components are not dependent on the brand of server, which gives you many more options before, during, and after development and deployment.

Setting the Stage

Before defining Enterprise JavaBeans more precisely, let's set the stage by discussing a number of important concepts: distributed objects, business objects, component transaction monitors, and asynchronous messaging.

Distributed Objects

Distributed computing allows a business system to be more accessible. Distributed systems allow parts of the system to be located on separate computers, possibly in many different locations, where they make the most sense. In other words, distributed computing allows business logic and data to be reached from remote locations. Customers, business partners, and other remote parties can use a business system at any time from almost anywhere. The most recent development in distributed computing is *distributed objects*. Distributed object technologies such as Java RMI, CORBA, and Microsoft's .NET allow objects running on one machine to be used by client applications on different computers.

Distributed objects evolved from a legacy form of three-tier architecture used in transaction processing (TP) monitor systems such as IBM's CICS and BEA's TUXEDO. These systems separate the presentation, business logic, and database into three distinct tiers (or layers). In the past, these legacy systems were usually composed of a "green screen" or dumb terminal for the presentation tier (first tier), COBOL or PL/1 applications as the middle tier (second tier), and some sort of database, such as DB2, as the backend (third tier). The introduction of distributed objects in recent years has given rise to a new form of three-tier architecture. Distributed object technologies make it possible to replace the procedural COBOL and PL/1 applications on the middle tier with business objects. A three-tier distributed-business-object architecture might have a sophisticated graphical or web-based interface on the first tier, business

---

* Provided that the bean components and EJB servers comply with the specification, and no proprietary functionality is used in development.

objects on the middle tier, and a relational or some other database on the backend. More complex architectures often have many tiers: different objects reside on different servers and interact to get the job done. Creating these *n*-tier architectures with Enterprise JavaBeans is relatively easy.

Server-Side Components

Object-oriented languages, such as Java, C++, and Smalltalk, are used to write software that is flexible, extensible, and reusable—the three axioms of object-oriented development. In business systems, object-oriented languages are used to improve development of GUIs, to simplify access to data, and to encapsulate the business logic. The encapsulation of business logic into *business objects* is a fairly recent focus in the information-technology industry. Business is fluid, which means that a business's products, processes, and objectives evolve over time. If the software that models the business can be encapsulated into business objects, it becomes flexible, extensible, and reusable, and therefore evolves as the business evolves.

A server-side component model may define an architecture for developing *distributed business objects* that combine the accessibility of distributed object systems with the fluidity of objectified business logic. Server-side component models are used on the middle-tier application servers, which manage the components at runtime and make them available to remote clients. They provide a baseline of functionality that makes it easy to develop distributed business objects and assemble them into business solutions.

Server-side components can also be used to model other aspects of a business system, such as presentation and routing. The Java servlet, for example, is a server-side component that is used to generate HTML and XML data for the presentation layer of a three-tier architecture. EJB 2.0 message-driven beans, which are discussed later in this book, are server-side components that are used to consume and process asynchronous messages.

Server-side components, like other components, can be bought and sold as independent pieces of executable software. They conform to a standard component model and can be executed without direct modification in a server that supports that component model. Server-side component models often support attribute-based programming, which allows the runtime behavior of the component to be modified when it is deployed, without having to change the programming code in the component. Depending on the component model, the server administrator can declare a server-side component's transactional, security, and even persistence behavior by setting these attributes to specific values.

As an organization's services, products, and operating procedures evolve, server-side components can be reassembled, modified, and extended so that the business system reflects those changes. Imagine a business system as a collection of server-side components that model concepts such as customers, products, reservations, and warehouses. Each component is like a Lego™ block that can be combined with other components to build a business solution. Products can be stored in the warehouse or delivered to a customer; a customer can make a reservation or purchase a product. You can assemble components, take them apart, use them in different combinations, and change their definitions. A business system based on server-side components is fluid because it is objectified, and it is accessible because the components can be distributed.

Component Transaction Monitors

A new breed of software called *application servers* has recently evolved to manage the complexities associated with developing business systems in today's Internet world. An application server is often made up of some combination of several different technologies, including web servers, object request brokers (ORBs), message-oriented middleware (MOM), databases, and so forth. An application server can also focus on one technology, such as distributed objects. Application servers that are based on distributed objects vary in sophistication. The simplest are ORBs, which facilitate connectivity between the client applications and the distributed objects. ORBs allow client applications to locate and use distributed objects easily. However, ORBs have frequently proven to be inadequate in high-volume transactional environments. They provide a communication backbone for distributed objects but fail to provide the kind of robust infrastructure that is needed to handle larger user populations and mission-critical work. In addition, ORBs provide a fairly crude server-side component model that places the burden of handling transactions, concurrency, persistence, and other system-level considerations on the shoulders of the application developer. These services are not automatically supported in an ORB. Application developers must explicitly access these services (if they are available) or, in some cases, develop them from scratch.

Early in 1999, Anne Manes[*] coined the term *component transaction monitor* (CTM) to describe the most sophisticated distributed object application servers. CTMs evolved as a hybrid of traditional TP monitors and ORB technologies. They implement robust server-side component models that make it easier for developers to create, use, and deploy business systems. CTMs provide an infrastructure that can automatically manage transactions, object distribution, concurrency, security, persistence, and resource management. They are capable of handling huge user populations and mission-critical work but also provide value to smaller systems because they are easy to use. CTMs are the ultimate application servers. Other terms for these kinds of technology include object transaction monitor (OTM), component transaction server, distributed component server, and COMware. This book uses the term

---

[*] At the time that Ms. Manes coined the term, she worked for the Patricia Seybold Group under the name Anne Thomas. Ms. Manes is now the Director of Business Strategy for Sun Microsystems, Sun Software division.

"component transaction monitor" because it embraces the three key characteristics of this technology: the use of a component model, the focus on transactional management, and the resource and service management typically associated with monitors.

Enterprise JavaBeans Defined

Sun Microsystems' definition of Enterprise JavaBeans is:

> The Enterprise JavaBeans architecture is a component architecture for the development and deployment of component-based distributed business applications. Applications written using the Enterprise JavaBeans architecture are scalable, transactional, and multi-user secure. These applications may be written once, and then deployed on any server platform that supports the Enterprise JavaBeans specification.[*]

That's a mouthful, but it's not atypical of how Sun defines many of its Java technologies—have you ever read the definition of the Java language itself? It's about twice as long. This book offers a shorter definition of EJB:

> Enterprise JavaBeans is a standard server-side component model for component transaction monitors.

We have already set the stage for this definition by briefly defining the terms "distributed objects," "server-side components," and "component transaction monitors." To provide you with a complete and solid foundation for learning about Enterprise Java-Beans, this chapter will now expand on these definitions.

If you already have a clear understanding of distributed objects, transaction monitors, CTMs, and asynchronous messaging, feel free to skip the rest of this chapter and move on to Chapter 2.

Distributed Object Architectures

EJB is a component model for component transaction monitors, which are based on distributed object technologies. Therefore, to understand EJB you need to understand how distributed objects work. Distributed object systems are the foundation for modern three-tier architectures. In a three-tier architecture, as shown in Figure 1-1, the presentation logic resides on the client (first tier), the business logic resides on the middle tier (second tier), and other resources, such as the database, reside on the backend (third tier).

All distributed object protocols are built on the same basic architecture, which is designed to make an object on one computer look like it's residing on a different computer. Distributed object architectures are based on a network communication layer that is really very simple. Essentially, there are three parts to this architecture: the business object, the skeleton, and the stub.

---

[*] Sun Microsystems' *Enterprise JavaBeans™ Specification, v2.0*, Copyright 2001 by Sun Microsystems, Inc.

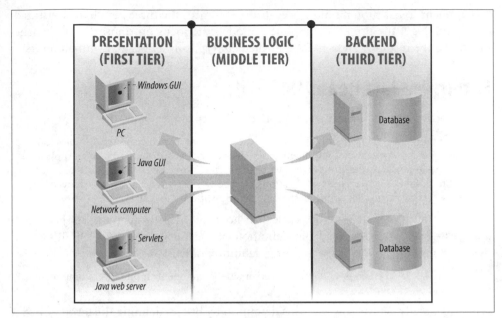

PRESENTATION
(FIRST TIER)

BUSINESS LOGIC
(MIDDLE TIER)

BACKEND
(THIRD TIER)

Windows GUI

PC

Java GUI

Network computer

Servlets

Java web server

Database

Database

Figure 1-1. Three-tier architecture

The *business object* resides on the middle tier. It's an instance of an object that models the state and business logic of some real-world concept, such as a person, order, or account. Every business object class has matching stub and skeleton classes built specifically for that type of business object. So, for example, a distributed business object called Person would have matching Person_Stub and Person_Skeleton classes. As shown in Figure 1-2, the business object and skeleton reside on the middle tier, and the stub resides on the client.

The *stub* and the *skeleton* are responsible for making the business object on the middle tier look as if it is running locally on the client machine. This is accomplished through some kind of *remote method invocation* (RMI) protocol. An RMI protocol is used to communicate method invocations over a network. CORBA, Java RMI, and Microsoft .NET all use their own RMI protocols.* Every instance of the business object on the middle tier is wrapped by an instance of its matching skeleton class. The skeleton is set up on a port and IP address and listens for requests from the stub, which resides on the client machine and is connected via the network to the skeleton. The stub acts as the business object's surrogate on the client and is responsible for communicating requests from the client to the business object through the skeleton. Figure 1-2 illustrates the process of communicating a method invocation from the client to the server object and back. The stub and the skeleton hide the

---

* The acronym RMI isn't specific to Java RMI. This section uses the term RMI to describe distributed object protocols in general. Java RMI is the Java language version of a distributed object protocol.

communication specifics of the RMI protocol from the client and the implementation class, respectively.

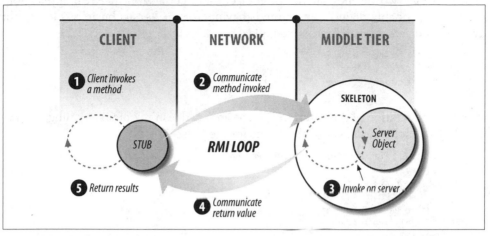

Figure 1-2. RMI loop

The business object implements a public interface that declares its business methods. The stub implements the same interface as the business object, but the stub's methods do not contain business logic. Instead, the business methods on the stub implement whatever networking operations are required to forward the request to the business object and receive the results. When a client invokes a business method on the stub, the request is communicated over the network by streaming the name of the method invoked, and the values passed in as parameters, to the skeleton. When the skeleton receives the incoming stream, it parses the stream to discover which method is requested, then invokes the corresponding business method on the business object. Any value that is returned from the method invoked on the business object is streamed back to the stub by the skeleton. The stub then returns the value to the client application as if it had processed the business logic locally.

Rolling Your Own Distributed Object

The best way to illustrate how distributed objects work is to show how you can implement a distributed object yourself, with your own distributed object protocol. This will give you some appreciation for what a true distributed object protocol like CORBA does. Actual distributed object systems such as DCOM, CORBA, and Java RMI are, however, much more complex and robust than the simple example we will develop here. The distributed object system we develop in this chapter is only illustrative; it is not a real technology, nor is it part of Enterprise JavaBeans. The purpose is to provide you with some understanding of how a more sophisticated distributed object system works.

Here's a very simple distributed business object called PersonServer that implements the Person interface. The Person interface captures the concept of a person business object. It has two business methods: getAge() and getName(). In a real application, we would probably define many more behaviors for the Person business object, but two methods are enough for this example:

```
public interface Person {
    public int getAge() throws Throwable;
    public String getName() throws Throwable;
}
```

The implementation of this interface, PersonServer, doesn't contain anything surprising. It defines the business logic and state for the Person:

```
public class PersonServer implements Person {
    int age;
    String name;

    public PersonServer(String name, int age){
        this.age = age;
        this.name = name;
    }
    public int getAge(){
        return age;02.    }
    public String getName(){
        return name;
    }
}
```

Now we need some way to make the PersonServer available to a remote client. That's the job of the Person_Skeleton and Person_Stub. The Person interface describes the concept of a person independent of implementation. Both the PersonServer and the Person_Stub implement the Person interface because they are both expected to support the concept of a person. The PersonServer implements the interface to provide the actual business logic and state; the Person_Stub implements the interface so that it can look like a Person business object on the client and relay requests back to the skeleton, which in turn sends them to the object itself. Here's what the stub looks like:

```
import java.io.ObjectOutputStream;
import java.io.ObjectInputStream;
import java.net.Socket;

public class Person_Stub implements Person {
    Socket socket;

    public Person_Stub() throws Throwable {
        /* Create a network connection to the skeleton.
           Use "localhost" or the IP Address of the skeleton
           if it's on a different machine. */
        socket = new Socket("localhost",9000);
    }
```

```java
        public int getAge() throws Throwable {
            // When this method is invoked, stream the method name to the skeleton.
            ObjectOutputStream outStream =
                new ObjectOutputStream(socket.getOutputStream());
            outStream.writeObject("age");
            outStream.flush();
            ObjectInputStream inStream =
                new ObjectInputStream(socket.getInputStream());
            return inStream.readInt();
        }
        public String getName() throws Throwable {
            // When this method is invoked, stream the method name to the skeleton.
            ObjectOutputStream outStream =
                new ObjectOutputStream(socket.getOutputStream());
            outStream.writeObject("name");
            outStream.flush();
            ObjectInputStream inStream =
                new ObjectInputStream(socket.getInputStream());
            return (String)inStream.readObject();
        }
    }
```

When a method is invoked on the Person_Stub, a String token is created and
streamed to the skeleton. The token identifies the method that was invoked on the
stub. The skeleton parses the method-identifying token, invokes the corresponding
method on the business object, and streams back the result. When the stub reads the
reply from the skeleton, it parses the value and returns it to the client. From the client's perspective, the stub processes the request locally. Now let's look at the skeleton:

```java
import java.io.ObjectOutputStream;
import java.io.ObjectInputStream;
import java.net.Socket;
import java.net.ServerSocket;

public class Person_Skeleton extends Thread {
    PersonServer myServer;

    public Person_Skeleton(PersonServer server){
        // Get a reference to the business object that this skeleton wraps.
        this.myServer = server;
    }
    public void run(){
        try {
            // Create a server socket on port 9000.
            ServerSocket serverSocket = new ServerSocket(9000);
            // Wait for and obtain a socket connection from the stub.
            Socket socket = serverSocket.accept();
            while (socket != null){
                // Create an input stream to receive requests from the stub.
                ObjectInputStream inStream =
                    new ObjectInputStream(socket.getInputStream());
                // Read the next method request from the stub. Block until the
                // request is sent.
```

```
                String method = (String)inStream.readObject();
                // Evaluate the type of method requested.
                if (method.equals("age")){
                    // Invoke the business method on the server object.
                    int age = myServer.getAge();
                    // Create an output stream to send return values back to
                    // the stub.
                    ObjectOutputStream outStream =
                        new ObjectOutputStream(socket.getOutputStream());
                    // Send results back to the stub.
                    outStream.writeInt(age);
                    outStream.flush();
                } else if(method.equals("name")){
                    // Invoke the business method on the server object.
                    String name = myServer.getName();
                    // Create an output stream to send return values back to
                    // the stub.
                    ObjectOutputStream outStream =
                        new ObjectOutputStream(socket.getOutputStream());
                    // Send results back to the stub.
                    outStream.writeObject(name);
                    outStream.flush();
                }
            }
        } catch(Throwable t) {t.printStackTrace();System.exit(0); }
    }
    public static void main(String args [] ){
        // Obtain a unique Person instance .
        PersonServer person = new PersonServer("Richard", 36);
        Person_Skeleton skel = new Person_Skeleton(person);
        skel.start();
    }
}
```

The Person_Skeleton routes requests received from the stub to the business object, PersonServer. Essentially, the Person_Skeleton spends all its time waiting for the stub to stream it a request. Once a request is received, it is parsed and delegated to the corresponding method on the PersonServer. The return value from the business object is then streamed back to the stub, which returns it as if it was processed locally.

Now that we've created all the machinery, let's look at a simple client that makes use of the Person:

```
public class PersonClient {
    public static void main(String [] args){
        try {
            Person person = new Person_Stub();
            int age = person.getAge();
            String name = person.getName();
            System.out.println(name+" is "+age+" years old");
        } catch(Throwable t) {t.printStackTrace();}
    }
}
```

This client application shows how the stub is used on the client. Except for the instantiation of the Person_Stub at the beginning, the client is unaware that the Person business object is actually a network proxy to the real business object on the middle tier. In Figure 1-3, the RMI loop diagram is changed to represent the RMI process as applied to our code.

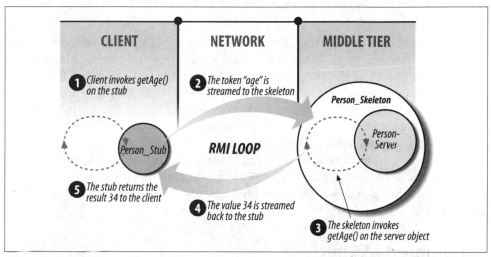

Figure 1-3. RMI loop with Person business object

As you examine Figure 1-3, notice how the RMI loop was implemented by our distributed Person object. RMI is the basis of distributed object systems and is responsible for making distributed objects *location transparent*. Location transparency means that a server object's actual location—usually on the middle tier—is unknown and unimportant to the client using it. In this example, the client could be located on the same machine or on a different machine very far away, but the client's interaction with the business object is the same. One of the biggest benefits of distributed object systems is location transparency. Although transparency is beneficial, you cannot treat distributed objects as local objects in your design because of the performance differences. This book will provide you with good distributed object design strategies that take advantage of transparency while maximizing the distributed system's performance.

When this book talks about the stub on the client, we will often refer to it as a *remote reference* to the business object. This allows us to talk more directly about the business object and its representation on the client.

Distributed object protocols such as CORBA, DCOM, and Java RMI provide much more infrastructure for distributed objects than the Person example. Most implementations of distributed object protocols provide utilities that automatically generate the appropriate stubs and skeletons for business objects. This eliminates custom development of these constructs and allows much more functionality to be included in the stub and skeleton.

Even with automatic generation of stubs and skeletons, the Person example hardly scratches the surface of a sophisticated distributed object protocol. Real-world protocols such as Java RMI and CORBA IIOP provide error- and exception-handling, parameter-passing, and other services such as the passing of transaction and security context. In addition, distributed object protocols support much more sophisticated mechanisms for connecting the stub to the skeleton. The direct stub-to-skeleton connection in the Person example is fairly primitive.

Real distributed object protocols, like CORBA, also provide an object request broker, which allows clients to locate and communicate with distributed objects across the network. ORBs are the communication backbone, the switchboard, for distributed objects. In addition to handling communications, ORBs generally use a naming system for locating objects and many other features such as reference passing, distributed garbage collection, and resource management. However, ORBs are limited to facilitating communication between clients and distributed business objects. While they may support services like transaction management and security, use of these services is not automatic. With ORBs, most of the responsibility for creating system-level functionality or incorporating services falls on the shoulders of the application developer.

Component Models

The term "component model" has many different interpretations. Enterprise Java-Beans specifies a *server-side* component model. Using a set of classes and interfaces from the javax.ejb package, developers can create, assemble, and deploy components that conform to the EJB specification.

The original JavaBeans™ is also a component model, but it's not a server-side component model like EJB. In fact, other than sharing the name "JavaBeans," these two component models are completely unrelated. In the past, a lot of the literature referred to EJB as an extension of the original JavaBeans, but this is a misrepresentation. The two APIs serve very different purposes, and EJB does not extend or use the original JavaBeans component model.

JavaBeans is intended to be used for *intra*process purposes, while EJB is designed for *inter*process components. In other words, the original JavaBeans was not intended for distributed components. JavaBeans can be used to solve a variety of problems, but it is primarily used to build clients by assembling visual (GUI) and nonvisual widgets. It's an excellent component model, possibly the best one ever devised for intraprocess development, but it's not a server-side component model. EJB, on the other hand, is explicitly designed to address issues involved with managing distributed business objects in a three-tier architecture.

Given that JavaBeans and Enterprise JavaBeans are completely different, why are they both called component models? In this context, a component model defines a set of contracts between the component developer and the system that hosts the component. The contracts express how a component should be developed and packaged. Once a component is defined, it becomes an independent piece of software that can be distributed and used in other applications. A component is developed for a specific purpose but not a specific application. In the original JavaBeans, a component might be a push button or a spreadsheet that can be used in any GUI application according to the rules specified in the original JavaBeans component model. In EJB, a component might be a customer business object that can be deployed in any EJB server and used to develop any business application that needs a customer business object. Other types of Java component models include servlets, JSP pages (JSPs), and applets.

Component Transaction Monitors

The CTM industry grew out of both the ORB and TP monitor industries. The CTM is really a hybrid of these two technologies that provides a powerful, robust distributed object platform. To better understand what a CTM is, we will examine the strengths and weakness of TP monitors and ORBs.

Transaction Processing Monitors

Transaction processing (TP) monitors have been evolving for about 30 years (CICS, the Customer Information Control System, was introduced in 1968) and have become powerful, high-speed server platforms for mission-critical applications. Some TP products, such as CICS and TUXEDO, may be familiar to you. TP monitors are operating systems for business applications written in languages such as COBOL. It may seem strange to call a TP monitor an "operating system," but because it controls an application's entire environment, it's a fitting description. TP monitor systems automatically manage the entire environment in which a business application runs, including transactions, resource management, and fault tolerance. The business applications that run in TP monitors are written in procedural programming languages (e.g., COBOL and C) that are often accessed through *network messaging* or *remote procedure calls* (RPCs). Messaging allows a client to send a message to a TP monitor requesting that some application be run with certain parameters. It's similar in concept to the Java event model. Messaging can be synchronous or asynchronous, meaning that the sender may or may not be required to wait for a response. RPC, which is the ancestor of RMI, is a distributed mechanism that allows clients to invoke procedures on applications in a TP monitor as though the procedures were executed locally. The primary difference between RPC and RMI is that RPC is used for *procedure*-based applications and RMI is used for distributed *object* systems. With RMI, methods can be invoked on a specific object identity; i.e., a specific business entity. In RPC, a client can call procedures on a specific type of application, but there is no concept of object identity. RMI is object-oriented; RPC is procedural.

TP monitors have been around for a long time, so the technology behind them is as solid as a rock; that is why they are used in many mission-critical systems today. But TP monitors are not object-oriented. Instead, they work with procedural code that can perform complex tasks but has no sense of identity. Accessing a TP monitor through RPC is like executing a static method; there's no such thing as a unique object. In addition, because TP monitors are based on procedural applications and not on objects, the business logic in a TP monitor is not as flexible, extensible, or reusable as business objects in a distributed object system.

Object Request Brokers

Distributed object systems allow unique objects that have state and identity to be accessed across a network. Distributed object technologies like CORBA and Java RMI grew out of RPC with one significant difference: when you invoke a distributed object method, it's on an object instance, not an application procedure. Distributed objects are usually deployed on some kind of ORB, which is responsible for helping client applications find distributed objects easily.

ORBs, however, do not define an "operating system" for distributed objects. They are simply communications backbones that are used to access and interact with unique remote objects. When you develop a distributed object application using an ORB, all the responsibility for concurrency, transactions, resource management, and fault tolerance falls on your shoulders. These services may be supported by an ORB, but the application developer is responsible for incorporating them into the business objects. In an ORB, there is no concept of an operating system in which system-level functionality is handled automatically. The lack of implicit system-level infrastructure places an enormous burden on the application developer. Developing the infrastructure required to handle concurrency, transactions, security, persistence, and everything else needed to support large user populations is a Herculean task that few corporate development teams are equipped to accomplish.

CTMs: The Hybrid of ORBs and TP Monitors

As the advantages of distributed objects became apparent, the number of systems deployed using ORBs increased rapidly. ORBs support distributed objects by employing a somewhat crude server-side component model that allows distributed objects to be connected to a communication backbone, but they don't implicitly support transactions, security, persistence, and resource management. These services must be explicitly accessed through APIs by the distributed object, resulting in more complexity and, frequently, more development problems. In addition, resource-management strategies such as instance swapping, resource pooling, and activation may not be supported at all. These types of strategies make it possible for a distributed object system to scale, improving performance and throughput and reducing latency. Without automatic support for resource management, application developers must implement homegrown resource-management solutions, which requires a very sophisticated understanding of distributed object systems. ORBs fail to address the complexities of managing a component in a high-volume, mission-critical environment, an area in which TP monitors have always excelled.

With three decades of TP-monitor experience, it wasn't long before companies such as IBM and BEA began developing a hybrid of ORBs and TP-monitor systems, which we refer to as component transaction monitors (CTMs). These types of application servers combine the fluidity and accessibility of distributed object systems based on ORBs with the robust "operating system" of a TP monitor. CTMs provide a comprehensive environment for server-side components by automatically managing concurrency, transactions, object distribution, load balancing, security, and resource management. While application developers still need to be aware of these facilities, they don't have to explicitly implement them when using a CTM.

The basic features of a CTM are distributed objects, an infrastructure that includes transaction management and other services, and a server-side component model. CTMs support these features in varying degrees; choosing the most robust and feature-rich CTM is not always as critical as choosing one that best meets your needs. Very large and robust CTMs can be enormously expensive and may be overkill for smaller projects. CTMs have come out of several areas, including the relational database, application server, web server, CORBA ORB, and TP monitor industries. Each vendor offers products that reflect their particular area of expertise. However, when you're getting started, choosing a CTM that supports the Enterprise JavaBeans component model may be much more important than any particular feature set. Because Enterprise JavaBeans is implementation independent, choosing an EJB CTM provides the business system with the flexibility to scale to larger CTMs as needed. We will discuss the importance of EJB as a standard component model for CTMs later in this chapter.

Analogies to Relational Databases

This chapter spends a lot of time talking about CTMs because they are essential to the definition of EJB. The discussion of CTMs is not over, but to make things as clear as possible before proceeding, we will use relational databases as an analogy for CTMs.

Relational databases provide a simple development environment for application developers, in combination with a robust infrastructure for data. As an application developer using a relational database, you might design the table layouts, decide which columns are primary keys, and define indexes and stored procedures, but you don't develop the indexing algorithm, the SQL parser, or the cursor-management system. These types of system-level functionality are left to the database vendor; you simply choose the product that best fits your needs. Application developers are concerned with how business data is organized, not how the database engine works. It would be a waste of resources for an application developer to write a relational database from scratch when vendors such as Microsoft and Oracle already provide them.

Distributed business objects, if they are to be effective, require the same system-level management from CTMs as business data requires from relational databases. System-level functionality like concurrency, transaction management, and resource management is necessary if the business system is going to be used for large user populations or mission-critical work. It is unrealistic and wasteful to expect application developers to reinvent this system-level functionality when commercial solutions already exist.

CTMs are to business objects what relational databases are to data. CTMs handle all the system-level functionality, allowing the application developer to focus on the business problems. With a CTM, application developers can focus on the design and development of the business objects without having to waste thousands of hours developing the infrastructure in which the business objects operate.

CTMs and Server-Side Component Models

CTMs require that business objects adhere to the server-side component model implemented by the vendor. A good component model is critical to the success of a development project because it defines how easily an application developer can write business objects for the CTM. The component model is a contract that defines the responsibilities of the CTM and the business objects. With a good component model, a developer knows what to expect from the CTM, and the CTM understands how to manage the business object. Server-side component models are great at describing the responsibilities of the application developer and CTM vendor.

Server-side component models are based on a specification. As long as the component adheres to the specification, it can be used by the CTM. The relationship between the server-side component and the CTM is like the relationship between a CD-ROM and a CD player. As long as the component (CD-ROM) adheres to the player's specifications, you can play it.

A CTM's relationship with its component model is also similar to the relationship the railway system has with trains. The railway system manages the train's environment, providing alternate routes for load balancing, multiple tracks for concurrency, and a traffic-control system for managing resources. The railway provides the infrastructure on which trains run. Similarly, a CTM provides server-side components with the entire infrastructure needed to support concurrency, transactions, load balancing, etc.

Trains on the railway are like server-side components: they all perform different tasks but they do so using the same basic design. The train focuses on performing a task, such as moving cars, not on managing the environment. For the engineer, the person driving the train, the interface for controlling the train is fairly simple: a brake and a throttle. For the application developer, the interface to the server-side component is similarly limited.

Different CTMs may implement different component models, just as different railways have different kinds of trains. The differences between the component models vary, like railway systems having different track widths and different controls, but the fundamental operations of CTMs are the same. They all ensure that business objects are managed so that they can support large populations of users in mission-critical situations. This means that resources, concurrency, transactions, security, persistence, load balancing, and distribution of objects can be handled automatically, limiting the application developer to a simple interface. This allows the application developer to focus on the business logic instead of the enterprise infrastructure.

Microsoft's .NET Framework

Microsoft was the first vendor to ship a CTM. Originally called the Microsoft Transaction Server (MTS), it was later renamed COM+. Microsoft's COM+ is based on the Component Object Model (COM), originally designed for use on the desktop but eventually pressed into service as a server-side component model. For distributed access, COM+ clients use the Distributed Component Object Model (DCOM).

When MTS was introduced in 1996, it was exciting because it provided a comprehensive environment for business objects. With MTS, application developers could write COM components without worrying about system-level concerns. Once a business object was designed to conform to the COM model, MTS (and now COM+) would take care of everything else, including transaction management, concurrency, and resource management.

Recently, COM+ has become part of Microsoft's new .NET Framework. The core functionality provided by COM+ services remains essentially the same in .NET, but the way it appears to a developer has changed significantly. Rather than writing components as COM objects, .NET Framework developers build applications as *managed objects*. All managed objects, and in fact all code written for the .NET Framework, depends on a Common Language Runtime (CLR). For Java-oriented developers, the CLR is much like a Java virtual machine (VM), and a managed object is analogous to an instance of a Java class; i.e., to a Java object.

Although the .NET Framework provides many interesting features, as an open standard, it falls short. The COM+ services in the .NET Framework are Microsoft's proprietary CTM, which means that using this technology binds you to the Microsoft platform. This may not be so bad, because .NET promises to work well, and the Microsoft platform is pervasive. In addition, the .NET Framework's support for the Simple Object Access Protocol (SOAP) will enable business objects in the .NET world to communicate with objects on any other platform written in any language. This can potentially make business objects in .NET universally accessible, a feature that is not easily dismissed.

If, however, your company is expected to deploy server-side components on a non-Microsoft platform, .NET is not a viable solution. In addition, the COM+ services in the .NET Framework are focused on stateless components; there's no built-in support for persistent transactional objects. Although stateless components can offer higher performance, business systems need the kind of flexibility offered by CTMs that include stateful and persistent components.

EJB and CORBA CTMs

Until the fall of 1997, non-Microsoft CTMs were pretty much nonexistent. Promising products from IBM, BEA, and Hitachi were on the drawing board, while MTS was already on the market. Although the non-MTS designs were only designs, they all had one thing in common: they used CORBA as a distributed object service.

Most non-Microsoft CTMs were focused on what was at the time the more open standard of CORBA, so they could be deployed on non-Microsoft platforms and support non-Microsoft clients. CORBA is both language and platform independent, so CORBA CTM vendors could provide their customers with more implementation options.* The problem with CORBA CTM designs was that they all had different server-side component models. In other words, if you developed a component for one vendor's CTM, you couldn't turn around and use that same component in another vendor's CTM. The component models were too different.

With Microsoft's MTS far in the lead by 1997 (it had already been around for a year), CORBA-based CTM vendors needed a competitive advantage. One problem CTMs faced was a fragmented CORBA market in which each vendor's product was different from the next. A fragmented market didn't benefit anyone, so the CORBA CTM vendors needed a standard around which to rally. Besides the CORBA protocol, the most obvious standard needed was a component model, which would allow clients and third-party vendors to develop their business objects to one specification that would work in any CORBA CTM. Microsoft was, of course, pushing their component model as a standard—which was attractive because MTS was an actual working product—but Microsoft didn't support CORBA. The Object Management Group (OMG), the same people who developed the CORBA standard, were defining an alternative server-side component model. This model held promise because it was sure to be tailored to CORBA, but the OMG was slow in developing a standard—too slow for the evolving CTM market.†

---

* The recent introduction of SOAP brings into question the future of the CORBA Internet Inter-Operability Protocol (IIOP). It's obvious that these two protocols are competing to become the standard language-independent protocol for distributed computing. IIOP has been around for several years and is therefore far more mature, but SOAP may quickly catch up by leveraging lessons learned in the development of IIOP.

† CORBA's CTM component model, the CORBA Component Model (CCM), was eventually released. It has seen lackluster acceptance in general, and was forced to adopt Enterprise JavaBeans as part of its component model just to be viable and interesting.

In 1997, Sun Microsystems was developing the most promising standard yet for server-side components: Enterprise JavaBeans. Sun offered some key advantages. First, Sun was respected and was known for working with vendors to define Java-based and vendor-agnostic APIs for common services. Sun had a habit of adopting the best ideas in the industry and then making the Java implementation an open standard—usually successfully. The Java database connectivity API, called JDBC, was a perfect example. Based largely on Microsoft's ODBC, JDBC offered vendors a more flexible model for plugging in their own database access drivers. In addition, developers found the JDBC API much easier to work with than ODBC. Sun was doing the same thing in its newer technologies, such as the JavaMail API and the Java Naming and Directory Interface (JNDI). These technologies were still being defined, but the collaboration among vendors was encouraging, and the openness of the APIs was attractive.

Although CORBA offered an open standard, it attempted to standardize low-level facilities such as security and transactions. Vendors could not justify rewriting existing products such as TUXEDO and CICS to the CORBA standards. EJB got around that problem by saying that how you implement the low-level services doesn't matter; all that matters is that all the facilities are applied to the components according to the specification—a much more palatable solution for existing and prospective CTM vendors. In addition, the Java language offered some pretty enticing advantages, not all of them purely technical. First, Java was a hot and sexy technology, and simply making your product Java-compatible seemed to boost your exposure in the market. Java was more or less platform independent, and component models defined in the Java language had definite marketing and technical benefits.

As it turned out, Sun had not been idle after it announced Enterprise JavaBeans. Sun's engineers had been working with several leading vendors to define a flexible and open standard to which vendors could easily adapt their existing products. This was a tall order because vendors had various kinds of servers, including web servers, relational database servers, application servers, and early CTMs. It's likely that no one wanted to sacrifice their architecture for the common good, but eventually the vendors agreed on a model that was flexible enough to accommodate different implementations yet solid enough to support real mission-critical development. In December of 1997, Sun Microsystems released the first draft specification of Enterprise JavaBeans, EJB 1.0, and vendors have been flocking to the server-side component model ever since.

Benefits of a Standard Server-Side Component Model

So what does it mean to be a standard server-side component model? Quite simply, it means that you can develop business objects using the Enterprise JavaBeans component model and expect them to work in any CTM that supports the complete EJB specification. This is a pretty powerful statement, because it largely eliminates the biggest problem faced by potential customers of CORBA-based CTM products: fear of vendor "lock-in." With a standard server-side component model, customers can commit to using an EJB-compliant CTM with the knowledge that they can migrate to a better CTM if one becomes available. Obviously, care must be taken when using proprietary extensions developed by vendors, but this is nothing new. Even in the relational database industry—which has been using the SQL standard for a couple of decades—optional proprietary extensions abound.

Having a standard server-side component model has benefits beyond implementation independence. A standard component model provides a vehicle for growth in the third-party products. If numerous vendors support EJB, creating add-on products and component libraries is more attractive to software vendors. The IT industry has seen this type of cottage industry grow up around other standards, such as SQL; hundreds of add-on products can now be purchased to enhance business systems whose data is stored in SQL-compliant relational databases. Report-generating tools and data-warehouse products are typical examples. The GUI component industry has also seen the growth of its own third-party products. A healthy market for component libraries already exists for GUI component models such as Microsoft's ActiveX and Sun's original JavaBeans component model.

Many third-party products for Enterprise JavaBeans exist today. Add-on products for credit card processing, legacy database access, and other business services have been introduced for various EJB-compliant systems. These types of products make development of EJB systems simpler and faster than the alternatives, making the EJB component model attractive to corporate IS and server vendors alike. The market is growing for prepackaged EJB components in several domains, including sales, finance, education, web-content management, collaboration, and other areas.

EJB 2.0: Asynchronous Messaging

In addition to supporting RMI-based distributed business objects, Enterprise Java-Beans 2.0 supports advanced asynchronous messaging. Asynchronous messaging is an important distributed computing paradigm that has become an important part of EJB.

An asynchronous messaging system allows two or more applications to exchange information in the form of messages. A message, in this case, is a self-contained package of business data and network-routing headers. The business data contained in a message can be anything—depending on the business scenario—and usually contains information about some business transaction. In enterprise messaging systems, messages inform an application of some event or occurrence in another system.

Messages are transmitted from one application to another on a network using message-oriented middleware (MOM). MOM products ensure that messages are properly distributed among applications. In addition, MOM usually provides fault tolerance, load balancing, scalability, and transactional support for enterprises that need to reliably exchange large quantities of messages.

MOM vendors use different message formats and network protocols for exchanging messages, but the basic semantics are the same. An API is used to create a message, give it a payload (application data), assign it routing information, and then send the message. The same API is used to receive messages produced by other applications.

In all modern enterprise-messaging systems, applications exchange messages through virtual channels called *destinations*. When you send a message, it's addressed to a destination, not to a specific application. Any application that subscribes or registers an interest in that destination may receive that message. In this way, the applications that receive messages and those that send messages are decoupled. Senders and receivers are not bound to each other in any way and may send and receive messages as they see fit.

Enterprise JavaBeans 2.0 integrates the functionality of MOM into its component model for CTMs. This integration extends the EJB platform's "operating system" so that it supports both RMI and asynchronous messaging. EJB 2.0 supports asynchronous messaging through the Java Message Service and a new kind of component called the message-driven bean.

Java Message Service

Each MOM vendor implements its own networking protocols, routing, and administration facilities, but the basic semantics of the developer API provided by different MOMs are the same. It's this similarity in APIs that makes the Java Message Service (JMS) possible.

JMS is a vendor-agnostic Java API that can be used with many different MOM vendors. JMS is very similar to JDBC in that an application developer can reuse the same API to access many different systems. If a vendor provides a compliant service provider for JMS, the JMS API can be used to send messages to and receive messages from that vendor. For example, you can use the same JMS API to send messages with Progress' SonicMQ as with IBM's MQSeries.

Message-driven beans

All JMS vendors provide application developers with the same API for sending and receiving messages, and sometimes they provide a component model for developing routers that can receive and send messages. These component models, however, are proprietary and not portable across MOM vendors.

Enterprise JavaBeans 2.0 introduces a new kind of component, called a *message-driven bean*, which is a kind of standard JMS bean. It can receive and send asynchronous JMS messages, and because it's co-located with other kinds of RMI beans (i.e., entity and session beans) it can also interact with RMI components.

Message-driven beans in EJB 2.0 act as an integration point for an EJB application, allowing other applications to send asynchronous messages that can be captured and processed by the application. This is an extremely important feature that will allow EJB applications to better integrate with legacy and other proprietary systems.

Message-driven beans are also transactional and require all the infrastructure associated with other RMI-based transactional server-side components. Like other RMI-based components, message-driven beans are considered business objects, which fulfill the important role of routing and interpreting requests and coordinating the application of those requests against other RMI-based components, namely enterprise beans. Message-driven beans are a good fit for the CTM landscape and are an excellent addition to the EJB platform.

Titan Cruises: An Imaginary Business

To make things a little easier, and more fun, we will discuss all the concepts in this book in the context of one imaginary business, a cruise line called Titan. A cruise line makes a particularly interesting example because it incorporates several different businesses: it has ship cabins that are similar to hotel rooms, it serves meals like a restaurant, it offers various recreational opportunities, and it needs to interact with other travel businesses.

This type of business is a good candidate for a distributed object system because many of the system's users are geographically dispersed. Commercial travel agents, for example, who need to book passage on Titan ships will need to access the reservation system. Supporting many—possibly hundreds—of travel agents requires a robust transactional system to ensure that agents have access and that reservations are completed properly.

Throughout this book, we will build a fairly simple slice of Titan's EJB system that focuses on the process of making a reservation for a cruise. This will give us an opportunity to develop Ship, Cabin, TravelAgent, ProcessPayment, and other enterprise beans. In the process, you will need to create relational database tables for persisting data used in the example. It is assumed that you are familiar with relational database management systems and that you can create tables according to the SQL statements provided. EJB can be used with any kind of database or legacy application, but relational databases seem to be the most commonly understood database, so we have chosen this as the persistence layer.

What's Next?

To develop business objects using EJB, you have to understand the life cycle and architecture of EJB components. This means understanding conceptually how EJB's components are managed and made available as distributed objects. Developing an understanding of the EJB architecture is the focus of the next two chapters.

CHAPTER 2

Architectural Overview

As you learned in Chapter 1, Enterprise JavaBeans is a component model for component transaction monitors, which are the most advanced type of business application servers available today. To effectively use Enterprise JavaBeans, you need to understand the EJB architecture, so this book includes two chapters on the subject. This chapter explores the core of EJB: how enterprise beans are distributed as business objects. Chapter 3 explores the services and resource-management techniques supported by EJB.

To be truly versatile, the EJB component design had to be smart. For application developers, assembling enterprise beans is simple, requiring little or no expertise in the complex system-level issues that often plague three-tier development efforts. While EJB makes the process easy for application developers, it also provides system developers (the people who write EJB servers) with a great deal of flexibility in how they support the EJB specification.

The similarities among different CTMs allow the EJB abstraction to be a standard component model for all of them. Each vendor's CTM is implemented differently, but they all support the same primary services and similar resource-management techniques. These services and techniques are covered in more detail in Chapter 3, but some of the infrastructure for supporting them is addressed in this chapter.

The Enterprise Bean Component

Enterprise JavaBeans server-side components come in three fundamentally different types: *entity, session,* and *message-driven beans*. Both session and entity beans are RMI-based server-side components that are accessed using distributed object protocols. The message-driven bean, which is new to EJB 2.0, is an asynchronous server-side component that responds to JMS asynchronous messages.

A good rule of thumb is that entity beans model business concepts that can be expressed as nouns. For example, an entity bean might represent a customer, a piece of equipment, an item in inventory, or even a place. In other words, entity beans model real-world objects; these objects are usually persistent records in some kind of database. Our hypothetical cruise line will need entity beans that represent cabins, customers, ships, etc.

Session beans are an extension of the client application and are responsible for managing processes or tasks. A Ship bean provides methods for doing things directly to a ship but doesn't say anything about the context under which those actions are taken. Booking passengers on the ship requires that we use a Ship bean, but it also requires a lot of things that have nothing to do with the ship itself: we'll need to know about passengers, ticket rates, schedules, and so on. A session bean is responsible for this kind of coordination. Session beans tend to manage particular kinds of activities, such as the act of making a reservation. They have a lot to do with the relationships between different enterprise beans. A TravelAgent session bean, for example, might make use of a Cruise, a Cabin, and a Customer—all entity beans—to make a reservation.

Similarly, message-driven beans in EJB 2.0 are responsible for coordinating tasks involving other session and entity beans. The major difference between a message-driven bean and a session bean is how they are accessed. While a session bean provides a remote interface that defines which methods can be invoked, a message-driven bean does not. Instead, the message-driven bean subscribes to or listens for specific asynchronous messages to which it responds by processing the message and managing the actions other beans take in response to those messages. For example, a ReservationProcessor message-driven bean would receive asynchronous messages—perhaps from a legacy reservation system—from which it would coordinate the interactions of the Cruise, Cabin, and Customer beans to make a reservation.

The activity a session or message-driven bean represents is fundamentally transient: you start making a reservation, you do a bunch of work, and then it's finished. The session and message-driven beans do not represent things in the database. Obviously, session and message-driven beans have lots of side effects on the database: in the process of making a reservation, you might create a new Reservation by assigning a Customer to a particular Cabin on a particular Ship. All of these changes would be reflected in the database by actions on the respective entity beans. Session and message-driven beans like TravelAgent and ReservationProcessor, which are responsible for making a reservation on a cruise, can even access a database directly and perform reads, updates, and deletes to data. But there's no TravelAgent or ReservationProcessor record in the database—once the bean has made the reservation, it waits to process another.

What makes the distinction between the different types of beans difficult to understand is that it's extremely flexible. The relevant distinction for Enterprise JavaBeans is that an entity bean has persistent state; session and message-driven beans model interactions but do not have persistent state.

Classes and Interfaces

A good way to understand the design of enterprise beans is to look at how you'd go about implementing one. To implement entity and session enterprise beans, you need to define the component interfaces,* a bean class, and a primary key:

Remote interface

> The remote interface defines the bean's business methods that can be accessed from applications outside the EJB container: the business methods a bean presents to the outside world to do its work. It enforces conventions and idioms that are well suited for distributed object protocols. The remote interface extends javax.ejb.EJBObject, which in turn extends java.rmi.Remote. It is used by session and entity beans in conjunction with the remote home interface.

Remote home interface

> The home interface defines the bean's life-cycle methods that can be accessed from applications outside the EJB container: the life-cycle methods for creating new beans, removing beans, and finding beans. It enforces conventions and idioms that are well suited for distributed object protocols. The home interface extends javax.ejb.EJBHome, which in turn extends java.rmi.Remote. It is used by session and entity beans in conjunction with the remote interface.

EJB 2.0: Local interface

> The local interface for an enterprise bean defines the bean's business methods that can be used by other beans co-located in the same EJB container: the business methods a bean presents to other beans in the same address space. It allows beans to interact without the overhead of a distributed object protocol, which improves their performance. The local interface extends javax.ejb.EJBLocalObject. It is used by session and entity beans in conjunction with the local home interface.

EJB 2.0: Local home interface

> The local home interface defines the bean's life-cycle methods that can be used by other beans co-located in the same EJB container: that is, the life-cycle methods a bean presents to other beans in the same address space. It allows beans to interact without the overhead of a distributed object protocol, which improves their performance. The local home interface extends javax.ejb.EJBLocalHome. It is used by session and entity beans in conjunction with the local interface.

Bean class

> The session and entity bean classes actually implement the bean's business and life-cycle methods. Note that the bean class for session and entity beans usually does not implement any of the bean's component interfaces directly. However, it

---

* There are basically two kinds of component interfaces: remote and local. The remote interfaces are supported by both EJB 2.0 and 1.1, while the local component interfaces are new in EJB 2.0 and are not supported by EJB 1.1.

must have methods matching the signatures of the methods defined in the remote and local interfaces and must have methods corresponding to some of the methods in both the remote and local home interfaces. If this sounds perfectly confusing, it is. The book will clarify this as we go along. An entity bean must implement `javax.ejb.EntityBean`; a session bean must implement `javax.ejb.SessionBean`. The `EntityBean` and `SessionBean` extend `javax.ejb.EnterpriseBean`.

The message-driven bean in EJB 2.0 does not use any of the component interfaces, because it is never accessed by method calls from other applications or beans. Instead, the message-driven bean contains a single method, `onMessage()`, which is called by the container when a new message arrives. The message-driven bean does not have a component interface as does the session and entity beans; it only needs only the bean class to operate. The message-driven bean class implements the `javax.ejb.MessageDrivenBean` and `javax.jms.MessageListener` interfaces. The JMS `MessageListener` interface is what makes a message-driven bean specific to JMS, instead of some other protocol. EJB 2.0 requires the use of JMS, but future versions may allow other messaging systems. The `MessageDrivenBean`, like the `EntityBean` and the `SessionBean`, extends the `javax.ejb.EnterpriseBean` interface.

Primary key

The primary key is a very simple class that provides a pointer into the database. Only entity beans need a primary key. The only requirement for this class is that it implements `java.io.Serializable`.

EJB 2.0 adds the crucial distinction between remote and local interfaces. Local interfaces provide a way for beans in the same container to interact efficiently; calls to methods in the local interface don't involve RMI; the methods in the local interfaces don't need to declare that they throw `RemoteException`, and so on. An enterprise bean isn't required to provide a local interface if you know when you're developing the bean that it will interact only with remote clients. Likewise, an enterprise bean doesn't need to provide a remote interface if you know it will be called only by enterprise beans in the same container. You can provide either a local or a remote component interface, or both.

The complexity—particularly all the confusion about classes implementing the methods of an interface but not implementing the interface itself—comes about because enterprise beans exist in the middle between some kind of client software and some kind of database. The client never interacts with a bean class directly; it always uses the methods of the entity or session bean's component interfaces to do its work, interacting with stubs that are generated automatically. (For that matter, a bean that needs the services of another bean is just another client: it uses the same stubs, rather than interacting with the bean class directly.)

Although the local component interfaces (local and local home) in EJB 2.0 represent session and entity beans in the same address space and do not use distributed object protocols, they still represent a stub or a proxy to the bean class. While there is no network between co-located beans, the stubs allow the container to monitor the interactions between the beans and apply security and transactions as appropriate.

It's important to note that EJB 2.0's message-driven bean doesn't have any component interfaces, but it may become the client of other session or entity beans and interact with those beans through their component interfaces. The entity and session beans with which the message-driven bean interacts may be co-located, in which case it uses their local component interfaces, or they may be located in a different address space and EJB container, in which case the remote component interfaces are used.

There are also many interactions between an enterprise bean and its server. These interactions are managed by a *container*, which is responsible for presenting a uniform interface between the bean and the server. (Many people use the terms "container" and "server" interchangeably, which is understandable because the difference between them isn't clearly defined.) The container is responsible for creating new instances of beans, making sure they are stored properly by the server, and so on. Tools provided by the container's vendor do a tremendous amount of work behind the scenes. At least one tool takes care of creating the mapping between entity beans and records in the database. Other tools generate code based on the component interfaces and the bean class itself. The code generated does things like create the bean, store it in the database, and so on. This code (in addition to the stubs) is what actually implements the component interfaces, and it is the reason the bean class doesn't have to do so.

Naming conventions

Before going on, let's establish some conventions. When we speak about an enterprise bean as a whole—its component interfaces, bean class, and so forth—we will call it by its common business name, followed by the acronym "EJB." For example, an enterprise bean that is developed to model a cabin on a ship will be called the "Cabin EJB." Notice that we don't use a constant-width font for "Cabin." This is because we are referring to all the parts of the bean (the component interfaces, bean class, etc.) as a whole, not just to one particular part, such as the remote interface or bean class. The term *enterprise bean* or *bean* denotes any kind of bean, including entity, session, and message-driven beans. *Entity bean* denotes an entity-type enterprise bean; *session bean* denotes a session-type enterprise bean; and *message-driven bean* denotes a message driven–type enterprise bean. It's popular to use the acronym EJB for enterprise bean, a style adopted in this book.

We will also use suffixes to distinguish between local component interfaces and remote component interfaces. When we are talking about the remote interface of the Cabin EJB we will combine the common business name with the word *Remote*. For example, the remote interface for the Cabin EJB is called the CabinRemote interface. In EJB 2.0, the local component interface of the Cabin EJB would be the CabinLocal interface. The home interfaces follow the convention by adding the word *Home* to the mix. The remote and local home interfaces for the Cabin EJB would be `CabinHomeRemote` and `CabinHomeLocal`, respectively. The bean class is always the common business name followed by the word *Bean*. For example, the Cabin EJB's bean class would be named `CabinBean`.

The remote interface

Having introduced the machinery, let's look at how to build an entity or stateful enterprise bean with remote component interfaces. In this section, we will examine the Cabin EJB, an entity bean that models a cabin on a cruise ship. Let's start with its remote interface.

We'll define the remote interface for a Cabin bean using the `CabinRemote` interface, which defines business methods for working with cabins. All remote-interface types extend the `javax.ejb.EJBObject` interface:

```
import java.rmi.RemoteException;

public interface CabinRemote extends javax.ejb.EJBObject {
    public String getName() throws RemoteException;
    public void setName(String str) throws RemoteException;
    public int getDeckLevel() throws RemoteException;
    public void setDeckLevel(int level) throws RemoteException;
}
```

These are methods for naming the cabin and methods for setting the cabin's deck level; you can probably imagine lots of other methods that you'd need, but this is enough to get started. All of these methods declare that they throw `RemoteException`, which is required of all methods on remote component interfaces, but not EJB 2.0's local component interfaces. EJB requires the use of Java RMI-IIOP conventions with remote component interfaces, although the underlying protocol can be CORBA IIOP, Java Remote Method Protocol (JRMP), or some other protocol. Java RMI-IIOP will be discussed in more detail in the next chapter.

The remote home interface

The remote home interface defines life-cycle methods used by clients of entity and session beans for locating enterprise beans. The remote home interface extends `javax.ejb.EJBHome`. We'll call the home interface for the Cabin bean `CabinHomeRemote` and define it like this:

```
import java.rmi.RemoteException;
import javax.ejb.CreateException;
import javax.ejb.FinderException;

public interface CabinHomeRemote extends javax.ejb.EJBHome {
    public CabinRemote create(Integer id)
        throws CreateException, RemoteException;
    public CabinRemote findByPrimaryKey(Integer pk)
        throws FinderException, RemoteException;
}
```

The create() method is responsible for initializing an instance of our bean. If your application needs them, you can provide other create() methods with different arguments.

In addition to findByPrimaryKey(), you are free to define other methods that provide convenient ways to look up Cabin beans—for example, you might want to define a method called findByShip() that returns all the cabins on a particular ship. Find methods like these are used in entity beans but not in session beans and obviously not in message-driven beans.

EJB 2.0: The bean class

Now let's look at an actual entity bean. Here's the code for the CabinBean; it's a sparse implementation, but it will show you how the pieces fit together:

```
import javax.ejb.EntityContext;

public abstract class CabinBean implements javax.ejb.EntityBean {

    public Integer ejbCreate(Integer id){
        setId(id);
        return null;
    }
    public void ejbPostCreate(Integer id){
        // do nothing
    }

    public abstract String getName();
    public abstract void setName(String str);

    public abstract int getDeckLevel();
    public abstract void setDeckLevel(int level);

    public abstract Integer getId();
    public abstract void setId(Integer id);

    public void setEntityContext(EntityContext ctx){
        // not implemented
    }
    public void unsetEntityContext(){
        // not implemented
    }
    public void ejbActivate(){
        // not implemented
    }
    public void ejbPassivate(){
        // not implemented
    }
    public void ejbLoad(){
        // not implemented
    }
    public void ejbStore(){
        // not implemented
```

```
        }
    public void ejbRemove(){
        // not implemented
    }
}
```

Notice that the CabinBean class is declared as abstract, as are several of its methods that access or update the EJB's persistent state. Also notice that there are no instance fields to hold the state information these methods access. This is because we are working with a container-managed entity bean, which has its abstract methods implemented by the container system automatically—this will be explained in detail later in the book. EJB 2.0 container-managed entity beans are the only beans that are declared as abstract with abstract accessor methods. You won't see abstract classes and methods with other types of entity beans, session beans, or message-driven beans.

EJB 1.1: The bean class

Here's the code for the CabinBean in EJB 1.1:

```
import javax.ejb.EntityContext;

public class CabinBean implements javax.ejb.EntityBean {

    public Integer id;
    public String name;
    public int deckLevel;

    public Integer ejbCreate(Integer id){
        setId(id);
        return null;
    }
    public void ejbPostCreate(Integer id){
        // do nothing
    }

    public String getName(){
        return name;
    }
    public void setName(String str){
        name = str;
    }

    public int getDeckLevel(){
        return deckLevel;
    }
    public void setDeckLevel(int level){
        deckLevel = level;
    }
    public Integer getId(){
        return id;
    }
    public void setId(Integer id){
        this.id = id;
```

```
        }
        public void setEntityContext(EntityContext ctx){
            // not implemented
        }
        public void unsetEntityContext(){
            // not implemented
        }
        public void ejbActivate(){
            // not implemented
        }
        public void ejbPassivate(){
            // not implemented
        }
        public void ejbLoad(){
            // not implemented
        }
        public void ejbStore(){
            // not implemented
        }
        public void ejbRemove(){
            // not implemented
        }
    }
```

EJB 2.0 and 1.1: The bean class

The set and get methods for the cabin's name and deck level are the CabinBean's business methods; they match the business methods defined by the EJB's remote interface, CabinRemote. The CabinBean class has state and business behavior that models the concept of a cabin. The business methods are the only methods visible to the client application; the other methods are visible only to the EJB container or the bean class itself. For example, the setId()/getId() methods are defined in the bean class but not in the remote interface, which means they cannot be called by the entity bean's client. The other methods are required by the EJB component model and are not part of the bean class's public business definition.

The ejbCreate() and ejbPostCreate() methods initialize the instance of the bean class when a new cabin record is to be added to the database. The last seven methods in the CabinBean are defined in the javax.ejb.EntityBean interface. These methods are life-cycle callback methods. The EJB container invokes these callback methods on the bean class when important life-cycle events occur. The ejbRemove() method, for example, notifies an entity bean that its data is about to be deleted from the database. The ejbLoad() and ejbStore() methods notify the bean instance that its state is being read or written to the database. The ejbActivate() and ejbPassivate() methods notify the bean instance that it is about to be activated or deactivated, a process that conserves memory and other resources. setEntityContext() provides the bean with an interface to the EJB container that allows the bean class to get information about itself and its surroundings. unsetEntityContext() is called by the EJB container to notify the bean instance that it is about to be dereferenced for garbage collection.

All these callback methods provide the bean class with *notifications* of when an action is about to be taken, or was just taken, on the bean's behalf by the EJB server. These notifications simply inform the bean of an event; the bean doesn't have to do anything about it. The callback notifications tell the bean where it is during its life cycle, when it is about to be loaded, removed, deactivated, and so on. Most of the callback methods pertain to persistence, which can be done automatically for the bean class by the EJB container. Because the callback methods are defined in the javax.ejb. EntityBean interface, the entity bean class must implement them, but it isn't required to do anything meaningful with the methods if it doesn't need to. Our bean, the CabinBean, won't need to do anything when these callback methods are invoked, so these methods are empty implementations. Details about these callback methods, when they are called, and how a bean should react to them are covered in Chapter 11.

The primary key

The primary key is a pointer that helps locate data that describes a unique record or entity in the database; it is used in the findByPrimaryKey() method of the home interface to locate a specific entity. Primary keys are defined by the bean developer and must be some type of serializable object. The Cabin EJB uses a simple java.lang. Integer type as its primary key. Its also possible to define custom primary keys, called *compound primary keys*, which represent complex primary keys consisting of several different fields. Primary keys are covered in detail in Chapter 11.

What about session beans?

CabinBean is an entity bean, but a session bean wouldn't be all that different. It would extend SessionBean instead of EntityBean and would have an ejbCreate() method that would initialize the bean's state, but no ejbPostCreate(). Session beans do not have an ejbLoad() or ejbStore() method, because session beans are not persistent. While session beans have a setSessionContext() method, they do not have an unsetSessionContext() method. Session beans do have ejbActivate() and ejbPassivate() methods, which are used by stateful session beans to manage conversational state. Finally, session beans would provide an ejbRemove() method, which would be called to notify the bean that the client no longer needs it. However, this method wouldn't tell the bean that its data was about to be removed from the database, because a session bean doesn't represent data in the database.

Session beans don't have a primary key. That's because session beans are not persistent themselves, so there is no need for a key that maps to the database. Session beans are covered in detail in Chapter 12.

EJB 2.0: What about message-driven beans?

Remote, local, and home interfaces would not be defined for a message-driven bean, because message-driven beans do not have component interfaces. Instead, the message-driven bean would define only a few callback methods and no business methods.

The callback methods include the ejbCreate() method, which is called when the bean class is first created; the ejbRemove() method, called when the bean instance is about to be discarded from the system (usually when the container doesn't need it any longer); the setMessageDrivenBeanContext(); and the onMessage() method. The onMessage() method is called every time a new asynchronous message is delivered to the message-driven bean. The message-driven bean doesn't define the ejbPassivate()/ejbActivate() or ejbLoad()/ejbStore() methods because it doesn't need them.

Message-driven beans don't have a primary key, for the same reason that session beans don't. They are not persistent, so there is no need for a key to the database. Message-driven beans are covered in detail in Chapter 13.

Deployment Descriptors and JAR Files

Much of the information about how beans are managed at runtime is not addressed by the interfaces and classes discussed previously. You may have noticed, for example, that we didn't talk about how beans interact with security, transactions, naming, and other services common to distributed object systems. As you know from prior discussions, these types of primary services are handled automatically by the EJB container, but the EJB container still needs to know how to apply the primary services to each bean class at runtime. To do this, we use *deployment descriptors*.

Deployment descriptors serve a function very similar to property files. They allow us to customize the behavior of software (enterprise beans) at runtime without having to change the software itself. Property files are often used with applications, but deployment descriptors are specific to an enterprise bean. Deployment descriptors are also similar in purpose to property sheets used in Visual Basic and PowerBuilder. Where property sheets allow us to describe the runtime attributes of visual widgets (background color, font size, etc.), deployment descriptors allow us to describe runtime attributes of server-side components (security, transactional context, etc.). Deployment descriptors allow certain runtime behaviors of beans to be customized without altering the bean class or its interfaces.

When a bean class and its interfaces have been defined, a deployment descriptor for the bean is created and populated with data about the bean. Frequently, integrated development environments (IDEs) that support development of Enterprise Java-Beans will allow developers to graphically set up the deployment descriptors using visual utilities like property sheets. After the developer has set all the properties for a bean, the deployment descriptor is saved to a file. Once the deployment descriptor is completed and saved to a file, the bean can be packaged in a JAR file for deployment.

JAR (Java ARchive) files are ZIP files that are used specifically for packaging Java classes (and other resources such as images) that are ready to be used in some type of application. JARs are used for packaging applets, Java applications, JavaBeans, web applications (servlets and JSPs), and Enterprise JavaBeans. A JAR file containing one or more enterprise beans includes the bean classes, component interfaces, and supporting classes for each bean. It also contains one deployment descriptor, which is used for all the beans in the JAR file. When a bean is deployed, the JAR file's path is given to the container's deployment tools, which read the JAR file.

When the JAR file is read at deployment time, the container tools read the deployment descriptor to learn about the bean and how it should be managed at runtime. The deployment descriptor tells the deployment tools what kind of beans are in the JAR file (session, entity, or message-driven), how they should be managed in transactions, who has access to the beans at runtime, and other runtime attributes of the beans. The person who is deploying the bean can alter some of these settings, such as transactional and security access attributes, to customize the bean for a particular application. Many container tools provide property sheets for graphically reading and altering the deployment descriptor when the bean is deployed. These graphical property sheets are similar to those used by bean developers.

The deployment descriptors help the deployment tools add beans to the EJB container. Once the bean is deployed, the properties described in the deployment descriptors will continue to be used to tell the EJB container how to manage the bean at runtime.

When Enterprise JavaBeans 1.0 was released, serializable classes were used for the deployment descriptor. Starting with Enterprise JavaBeans 1.1, the serializable deployment descriptor classes used in EJB 1.0 were dropped in favor of a more flexible file format based on the eXtensible Markup Language (XML). The XML deployment descriptors are text files structured according to a standard EJB Document Type Definition (DTD) that can be extended so the type of deployment information stored can evolve as the specification evolves. Chapter 16 provides a detailed description of XML deployment descriptors. The following sections provide a brief overview of XML deployment descriptors.

EJB 2.0: Deployment descriptor

The following deployment descriptor might be used to describe the Cabin bean in EJB 2.0:

```
<!DOCTYPE ejb-jar PUBLIC "-//Sun Microsystems, Inc.//DTD EnterpriseJavaBeans 2.0//EN"
"http://java.sun.com/dtd/ejb-jar_2_0.dtd">

<ejb-jar>
    <enterprise-beans>
        <entity>
            <ejb-name>CabinEJB</ejb-name>
            <home>com.titan.CabinHomeRemote</home>
            <remote>com.titan.CabinRemote</remote>
            <local-home>com.titan.CabinHomeLocal</local-home>
            <local>com.titan.CabinLocal</local>
            <ejb-class>com.titan.CabinBean </ejb-class>
            <persistence-type>Container</persistence-type>
            <prim-key-class>java.lang.Integer</prim-key-class>
```

```
            <reentrant>False</reentrant>
        </entity>
    </enterprise-beans>
</ejb-jar>
```

EJB 1.1: Deployment descriptor

The following deployment descriptor might be used to describe the Cabin bean in EJB 1.1:

```
<!DOCTYPE ejb-jar PUBLIC "-//Sun Microsystems, Inc.//DTD EnterpriseJavaBeans 1.1//EN"
"http://java.sun.com/j2ee/dtds/ejb-jar_1_1.dtd">

<ejb-jar>
    <enterprise-beans>
        <entity>
            <ejb-name>CabinEJB</ejb-name>
            <home>com.titan.CabinHomeRemote</home>
            <remote>com.titan.CabinRemote</remote>
            <ejb-class>com.titan.CabinBean</ejb-class>
            <persistence-type>Container</persistence-type>
            <prim-key-class>java.lang.Integer</prim-key-class>
            <reentrant>False</reentrant>
        </entity>
    </enterprise-beans>
</ejb-jar>
```

EJB 2.0 and 1.1: Elements of the XML deployment descriptor

The deployment descriptor for a real bean would have a lot more information. This example simply illustrates the type of information you'll find in an XML deployment descriptor.

The first element in any XML document is `<!DOCTYPE>`. This element describes the organization that defined the DTD for the XML document, the DTD's version, and a URL location of the DTD. The DTD describes how a particular XML document is structured.

All the other elements in the XML document are specific to EJB. They do not represent all the elements used in deployment descriptors, but they illustrate the types of elements that are used. Here's what the elements mean:

`<ejb-jar>`
> The root of the XML deployment descriptor. All other elements must be nested below this one. It must contain one `<enterprise-beans>` element and may contain other optional elements.

`<enterprise-beans>`
> Contains declarations for all the enterprise beans described by this XML document. It may contain `<entity>`, `<session>`, or `<message-driven>` (EJB 2.0) elements, which describe entity, session, and message-driven enterprise beans, respectively.

`<entity>`

Describes an entity bean and its deployment information. There must be one of these elements for every entity bean described by the XML deployment descriptor. The `<session>` element is used in the same way to describe a session bean. The `<message-driven>` element is different as it does not define any component interfaces.

`<ejb-name>`

The descriptive name of the enterprise bean. This is the name we use for the enterprise bean in conversation, when talking about the bean component as a whole.

`<home>`

The fully qualified class name of the remote home interface. This interface defines the life-cycle behaviors (create, find, remove) of the enterprise bean to its clients outside the container system.

`<remote>`

The fully qualified class name of the remote interface. This interface defines the enterprise bean's business methods to its clients outside the container system.

EJB 2.0: `<local-home>`

The fully qualified class name of the local home interface. This interface defines the life-cycle behaviors (create, find, remove) of the enterprise bean to other co-located enterprise beans.

EJB 2.0: `<local>`

The fully qualified class name of the local interface. This interface defines the enterprise bean's business methods to other co-located enterprise beans.

`<ejb-class>`

The fully qualified class name of the bean class. This class implements the business methods of the bean.

`<prim-key-class>`

The fully qualified class name of the enterprise bean's primary key. The primary key is used to find the bean data in the database.

The last two elements in the deployment descriptor, the `<persistence-type>` and `<reentrant>` elements, express the persistence strategy and concurrency policies of the entity bean. These elements are explained in more detail later in the book.

As you progress through this book, you will be introduced to the elements that describe concepts we have not covered yet, so don't worry about knowing all of the elements you might find in a deployment descriptor at this time.

EJB Objects and EJB Home

The entity and session beans both declare the component interfaces that their clients will use to access them. In EJB 2.0 and 1.1, clients outside the container system, like servlets or Java applications, will always use the enterprise bean's remote component interfaces. In EJB 2.0, clients that are other enterprise beans in the same container system will usually use local component interfaces to interact. This section explains in logical terms how the component interfaces are connected to instances of the bean class at runtime.

While this discussion will help you understand entity and session beans, it doesn't apply to EJB 2.0's message-driven beans at all, because they do not declare component interfaces. Message-driven beans are a very different kind of animal, and a full description of these beans is left to Chapter 13.

Now that you have a basic understanding of some of the enterprise beans parts (component interfaces, bean class, and deployment descriptor) it's time to talk a little more precisely about how these parts come together inside an EJB container system. Unfortunately, we can't talk as precisely as we'd like. There are a number of ways for an EJB container to implement these relationships; we'll show some of the possibilities. Specifically, we'll talk about how the container implements the component interface of entity and session beans, so that clients, either applications outside the container or other co-located enterprise beans can interact with and invoke methods on the bean class.

The two missing pieces are the EJB object itself and the EJB home. You will probably never see the EJB home and EJB object classes because their class definitions are proprietary to the vendor's EJB implementation and are generally not made public. This is good because it represents a separation of responsibilities along areas of expertise. As an application developer, you are intimately familiar with how your business environment works and needs to be modeled, so you will focus on creating the applications and beans that describe your business. System-level developers, the people who write EJB servers, don't understand your business, but they do understand how to develop CTMs and support distributed objects. It makes sense for system-level developers to apply their skills to the mechanics of managing distributed objects but leave the business logic to you, the application developer. Let's talk briefly about the EJB object and the EJB home so you understand the missing pieces in the big picture.

The EJB object

This chapter has said a lot about a bean's remote and local interfaces, which extend the `EJBObject` and, for EJB 2.0, the `EJBLocalObject` interfaces, respectively. Who implements these interfaces? Clearly, the stub does: we understand that much. But what about the server side?

On the server side, an EJB object is an object that implements the remote and/or local (EJB 2.0) interfaces of the enterprise bean. The EJB object wraps the enterprise bean instance—that is, an instance of the enterprise bean class you've created (in our example, the `CabinBean`)—on the server and expands its functionality to include `javax.ejb.EJBObject` and/or `javax.ejb.EJBLocalObject` behavior.

You will have noticed that "and/or" is used a lot when talking about which interface the EJB object implements. That's because enterprise beans in EJB 2.0 can declare either the local interface, remote interface, or both! Local interfaces don't apply to EJB 1.1, so if you are working with that version, ignore references to them; they are relevant only to EJB 2.0 container systems.

In EJB 2.0, regardless of which interfaces the bean implements, we can think of the EJB object as implementing both. In reality, there may be a special EJB object for the remote interface and another special EJB object for the local interface of each enterprise bean; that depends on the how the vendor chooses to implement it. For our purposes, the term EJB object will be used to talk about the implementation of either the local or remote interfaces, or both. The functionality of these interfaces is so similar from the EJB object's perspective that discussing separate EJB object implementations isn't necessary.

The EJB object is generated by the utilities provided by the vendor of your EJB container and is based on the bean classes and the information provided by the deployment descriptor. The EJB object wraps the bean instance and works with the container to apply transactions, security, and other system-level operations to the bean at runtime. Chapter 3 talks more about the EJB object's role with regard to system-level operations.

A vendor can use a number of strategies to implement the EJB object. Figure 2-1 illustrates three possibilities using the CabinRemote interface. The same implementation strategies apply to the CabinLocal and javax.ejb.EJBLocalObject interfaces.

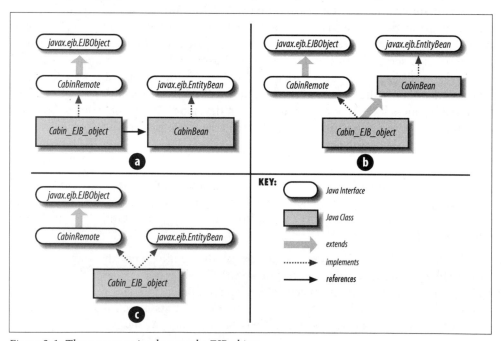

Figure 2-1. Three ways to implement the EJB object

In Figure 2-1(a), the EJB object is a classic wrapper because it holds a reference to the bean class and delegates the requests to the bean. Figure 2-1(b) shows that the EJB object class actually extends the bean class, adding functionality specific to the EJB container. In Figure 2-1(c), the bean class is no longer included in the model. In this case, the EJB object has both the proprietary implementation required by the EJB container and bean class method implementations that were copied from the bean class's definition.

The EJB object design shown in Figure 2-1(a) is perhaps the most common. Throughout this book, particularly in the next chapter, we will explain how EJB works with the assumption that the EJB object wraps the bean class instance as depicted in Figure 2-1(a). But the other implementations are used; it shouldn't make a difference which one your vendor has chosen. The bottom line is that you never really know much about the EJB object: its implementation is up to the vendor. Knowing that the EJB object exists answers a lot of questions about how enterprise beans are structured. The information that a client (including other enterprise beans) needs to know about an enterprise bean is described by the remote and home interfaces.

The EJB home

The EJB home is a lot like the EJB object. It's another class that's generated automatically when you install an enterprise bean in a container. It implements all the methods defined by the home interfaces (local and/or remote) and is responsible for helping the container manage the bean's life cycle. Working closely with the EJB container, the EJB home is responsible for locating, creating, and removing enterprise beans. This may involve working with the EJB server's resource managers and instance pooling and persistence mechanisms, the details of which are hidden from the developer.

For example, when a create method is invoked on a home interface, the EJB home creates an instance of the EJB object that references a bean instance of the appropriate type. Once the bean instance is associated with the EJB object, the instance's matching ejbCreate() method is called. In the case of an entity bean, a new record is inserted into the database. With session beans, the instance is simply initialized. Once the ejbCreate() method has completed, the EJB home returns a remote or local reference (i.e., a stub) for the EJB object to the client. The client can then begin to work with the EJB object by invoking business methods using the stub. The stub relays the methods to the EJB object; in turn, the EJB object delegates those method calls to the bean instance.

In EJB 2.0, how does the EJB home know which type of EJB object reference (local or remote) to return? It depends on which home interface is being used. If the client invokes a create() method on the remote home interface, the EJB home will return a remote interface reference. If the client is working with a local home interface, the EJB home will return a reference implementing the local interface. EJB 2.0 requires

that the return type of remote home interface methods be remote interfaces and that
the return type of local home interface methods be local interfaces:

```
// The Cabin EJB's remote home interface
public interface CabinHomeRemote extends javax.ejb.EJBHome {
    public CabinRemote create(Integer id)
        throws CreateException, RemoteException;
    public CabinRemote findByPrimaryKey(Integer pk)
        throws FinderException, RemoteException;
}


// The Cabin EJB's local home interface
public interface CabinHomeLocal extends javax.ejb.EJBHome {
    public CabinLocal create(Integer id)
        throws CreateException;
    public CabinLocal findByPrimaryKey(Integer pk)
        throws FinderException;
}
```

Figure 2-2 illustrates the architecture of EJB with the EJB home and EJB object
implementing the home interface and remote or local interface, respectively. The
bean class is also shown as being wrapped by the EJB object.

Throughout this book, we will consider the EJB object and EJB home as constructs
that support both the remote and local component interfaces. In reality, we have no
idea how the vendor chose to implement the EJB object and EJB home, since they
are only logical constructs and may not have equivalent software counterparts. It's
important to remember that "EJB object" and "EJB home" are simply terms to
describe the EJB container's responsibilities for supporting the component interfaces. We have chosen to give them a more concrete description in this book purely
for instructional purposes; the EJB object and EJB home implementations discussed
throughout this book are to be considered illustrative and *not* a true representation
of how these terms may be implemented.

Deploying a bean

The EJB objects and EJB homes are automatically generated during the deployment
process. After the files that define the bean (the component interfaces and the bean
classes) have been packaged into a JAR file, the bean is ready to be deployed; that is,
it can be added to an EJB container so it can be accessed as a distributed component. During the deployment process, tools provided by the EJB container vendor
generate the EJB object and EJB home classes by examining the deployment descriptor and the other interfaces and classes in the JAR file.

Using Enterprise Beans

Let's look at how a client would work with an enterprise bean to do something useful. We'll start with the Cabin EJB defined earlier. A cabin is a thing or place whose

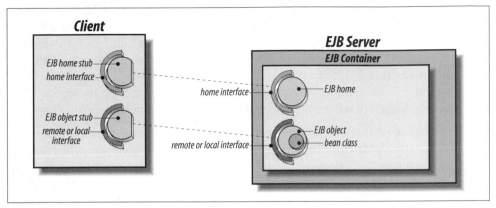

Figure 2-2. EJB architecture

description is stored in a database. To make the example a little more real, imagine that there are other entity beans: Ship, Cruise, Ticket, Customer, Employee, and so on.

Getting Information from an Entity Bean

Imagine that a GUI client needs to display information about a particular cruise, including the cruise name, the ship name, and a list of cabins. Using the cruise ID obtained from a text field, we can use some of our beans to populate the GUI with data about the requested cruise. Here's what the code would look like:

```
CruiseHomeRemote cruiseHome = ... use JNDI to get the home
// Get the cruise ID from a text field.
String cruiseID = textFields1.getText();
// Create an EJB primary key from the cruise ID.
Integer pk = new Integer(cruiseID);
// Use the primary key to find the cruise.
CruiseRemote cruise = cruiseHome.findByPrimaryKey(pk);
// Set text field 2 to show the cruise name.
textField2.setText(cruise.getName());
// Get a remote reference to the ship that will be used
// for the cruise from the cruise bean.
ShipRemote ship = cruise.getShip();
// Set text field 3 to show the ship's name.
textField3.setText(ship.getName());

// Get all the cabins on the ship.
Collection cabins = ship.getCabins();
Iterator cabinItr = cabins.iterator();

// Iterate through the enumeration, adding the name of each cabin
// to a list box.
while( cabinItr.hasNext())
    CabinRemote cabin = (CabinRemote)cabinItr.next();
    listBox1.addItem(cabin.getName());
}
```

Let's start by getting a remote reference to the EJB home for an entity bean that represents a cruise. We are using a remote reference instead of a local one, because the client is a GUI Java application located outside the EJB container. In EJB 1.1, we don't have a choice because only remote component interfaces are supported. It's not shown in the example, but references to the EJB home are obtained using JNDI. JNDI is a powerful API for locating resources, such as remote objects, on networks. It's a little too complicated to talk about here, but it will be covered in subsequent chapters.

We read a cruise ID from a text field, use it to create a primary key, and use that primary key together with the EJB home to get a `CruiseRemote` reference, which implements the business methods of our bean. Once we have the appropriate Cruise EJB, we can ask the Cruise EJB to give us a remote reference to a Ship EJB that will be used for the cruise. We can then get a `Collection` of remote Cabin EJB references from the Ship EJB and display the names of the Cabin EJBs in the client.

Entity beans model data and behavior. They provide a reusable and consistent interface to data in the database. The behavior used in entity beans is usually focused on applying business rules that pertain directly to changing data. In addition, entity beans can model relationships with other entities. A ship, for example, has many cabins. We can get a list of cabins owned by the ship by invoking the `ship.getCabins()` method.

Modeling Workflow with Session Beans

Entity beans are useful for objectifying data and describing business concepts that can be expressed as nouns, but they're not very good at representing a process or a task. A Ship bean provides methods and behavior for doing things directly to a ship, but it does not define the context under which these actions are taken. The previous example retrieved data about cruises and ships; we could also have modified this data. With enough effort, we could have figured out how to book a passenger—perhaps by adding a Customer EJB to a Cruise EJB or adding a customer to a list of passengers maintained by the ship. We could try to shove methods for accepting payment and other tasks related to booking into our GUI client application, or even into the Ship or Cabin EJBs, but that's a contrived and inappropriate solution. We don't want business logic in the client application—that's why we went to a multitier architecture in the first place. Similarly, we don't want this kind of logic in our entity beans that represent ships and cabins. Booking passengers on a ship or scheduling a ship for a cruise are the types of activities or functions of the business, not the Ship or the Cabin bean, and are therefore expressed in terms of a process or task.

Session beans act as agents for the client managing business processes or tasks; they're the appropriate place for business logic. A session bean is not persistent like an entity bean; nothing in a session bean maps directly into a database or is stored between sessions. Session beans work with entity beans, data, and other resources to control *workflow*. Workflow is the essence of any business system, because it expresses how entities interact to model the actual business. Session beans control tasks and resources but do not themselves represent data.

 Although the term "workflow" is frequently used to describe the management of business processes that may span several days with lots of human intervention, that is not the definition used in this book. The term workflow in this book describes the interactions of beans within a single transaction, which takes only a few seconds to execute.

The following code demonstrates how a session bean, designed to make cruise-line reservations, might control the workflow of other entity and session beans to accomplish this task. Imagine that a piece of client software, in this case a user interface, obtains a remote reference to a TravelAgent session bean. Using the information entered into text fields by the user, the client application books a passenger on a cruise:

```
// Get the credit card number from the text field.
String creditCard = textField1.getText();
int cabinID = Integer.parseInt(textField2.getText());
int cruiseID = Integer.parseInt(textField3.getText());

// Create a new Reservation session passing in a reference to a
// customer entity bean.
TravelAgent travelAgent = travelAgentHome.create(customer);

// Set cabin and cruise IDs.
travelAgent.setCabinID(cabinID);
travelAgent.setCruiseID(cruiseID);

// Using the card number and price, book passage.
// This method returns a Ticket object.
TicketDO ticket = travelAgent.bookPassage(creditCard, price);
```

This is a fairly *coarse-grained* abstraction of the process of booking a passenger: most of the details are hidden from the client. Hiding the *fine-grained* details of workflow is important because it provides us with more flexibility in how the system evolves and how clients are allowed to interact with the EJB system.

The following listing shows some of the code included in the TravelAgentBean. The bookPassage() method actually works with three entity beans, the Customer, Cabin, and Cruise EJBs, and another session bean, the ProcessPayment EJB. The ProcessPayment EJB provides several methods for making a payment, including check, cash, and credit card. In this case, we are using the ProcessPayment session to make a credit card purchase of a cruise ticket. Once payment has been made, a serializable TicketDO object is created and returned to the client application.

```
public class TravelAgentBean implements javax.ejb.SessionBean {
    public CustomerRemote customer;
    public CruiseRemote cruise;
```

```
    public CabinRemote cabin;

    public void ejbCreate(CustomerRemote cust){
        customer =cust;
    }
    public TicketDO bookPassage(CreditCardDO card,double price)
        throws IncompleteConversationalState {
        if (customer == null ||cruise == null ||cabin == null){
            throw new IncompleteConversationalState();
        }
        try {
            ReservationHomeRemote resHome = (ReservationHomeRemote)
                getHome("ReservationHome",ReservationHomeRemote.class);
            ReservationRemote reservation =
                resHome.create(customer,cruise,cabin,price,new Date());
            ProcessPaymentHomeRemote ppHome = (ProcessPaymentHomeRemote)
                getHome("ProcessPaymentHome",ProcessPaymentHomeRemote.class);

            ProcessPaymentRemote process = ppHome.create();
            process.byCredit(customer,card,price);

            TicketDO ticket = new TicketDO(customer,cruise,cabin,price);
            return ticket;
        }catch(Exception e){
            throw new EJBException(e);
        }
    }

    // More business methods and callback methods follow
}
```

This example leaves out some details, but it demonstrates the difference in purpose between a session bean and an entity bean. Entity beans represent the behavior and data of a business object, while session beans model the workflow of beans. The client application uses the TravelAgent EJB to perform a task using other beans. For example, the TravelAgent EJB uses a ProcessPayment EJB and a Reservation EJB in the process of booking passage. The ProcessPayment EJB processes the credit card, and the Reservation EJB records the actual reservation in the system. Session beans can also be used to read, update, and delete data that can't be adequately captured in an entity bean. Session beans don't represent records or data in the database like entity beans, but they can access data in the database.

All of the work performed by the TravelAgent session bean could have been coded in the client application. Having the client interact directly with entity beans is a common but troublesome design approach because it ties the client directly to the details of the business tasks. This is troublesome for two reasons: any changes in the entity beans and their interaction require changes to the client, and it's very difficult to reuse the code that models the workflow.

Session beans are coarse-grained components that allow clients to perform tasks without being concerned with the details that make up the task. This allows developers to

---

update the session bean, possibly changing the workflow, without impacting the client code. In addition, if the session bean is properly defined, other clients that perform the same tasks can reuse it. The ProcessPayment session bean, for example, can be reused in many areas besides reservations, including retail and wholesale sales. For example, the ship's gift shop could use the ProcessPayment EJB to process purchases. As a client of the ProcessPayment EJB, the TravelAgent EJB doesn't care how ProcessPayment works; it's only interested in the ProcessPayment EJB's coarse-grained interface, which validates and records charges.

Moving workflow logic into a session bean also helps to thin down the client applications and reduce network traffic and connections. Excessive network traffic is actually one of the biggest problems in distributed object systems. Excessive traffic can overwhelm the server and clog the network, hurting response times and performance. Session beans, if used properly, can substantially reduce network traffic by limiting the number of requests needed to perform a task. In distributed objects, every method invocation produces network traffic. Distributed objects communicate requests using an RMI loop. This requires that data be streamed between the stub and skeleton with every method invocation. With session beans, the interaction of beans in a workflow is kept on the server. One method invocation on the client application results in many method invocations on the server, but the network sees only the traffic produced by one method call on the session bean. In the TravelAgent EJB, the client invokes bookPassage(), but on the server, the bookPassage() method produces several method invocations on the component interfaces of other enterprise beans. For the network cost of one method invocation, the client gets several method invocations.*

In addition, session beans reduce the number of network connections needed by the client. The cost of maintaining many network connections can be very high, so reducing the number of connections each client needs improves the performance of the system as a whole. When session beans are used to manage workflow, the number of connections that each client has to the server may be substantially reduced, which improves the EJB server's performance. Figure 2-3 compares the network traffic and connections used by a client that uses only entity beans to those used by a client that uses session beans.

Session beans also limit the number of stubs used on the client, which saves the client memory and processing cycles. This may not seem like a big deal, but without the use of session beans, a client might be expected to manage hundreds or even thousands of remote references at one time. In the TravelAgent EJB, for example, the bookPassage() method works with several remote references, but the client is exposed only to the remote reference of the TravelAgent EJB.

---

* In EJB 2.0, the bookPassage() method might have used the local component interfaces of the other enterprise beans, because they are much more efficient.

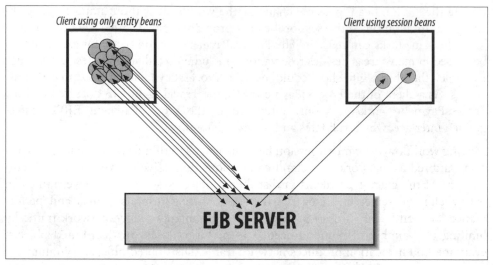

Figure 2-3. Session beans reduce network traffic and thin down clients

Stateless and stateful session beans

Session beans can be either *stateful* or *stateless*. Stateful session beans maintain *conversational state* when used by a client. Conversational state is not written to a database; it's state that is kept in memory while a client uses a session. Maintaining conversational state allows a client to carry on a conversation with an enterprise bean. As each method on the enterprise bean is invoked, the state of the session bean may change, and that change can affect subsequent method calls. The TravelAgent session bean, for example, may have many more methods than the bookPassage() method. The methods that set the cabin and cruise IDs are examples. These set methods are responsible for modifying conversational state. They convert the IDs into remote references to Cabin and Cruise EJBs that are later used in the bookPassage() method. Conversational state is kept for only as long as the client application is actively using the bean. Once the client shuts down or releases the TravelAgent EJB, the conversational state is lost forever. Stateful session beans are not shared among clients; they are dedicated to the same client for the life of the enterprise bean.

Stateless session beans do not maintain any conversational state. Each method is completely independent and uses only data passed in its parameters. The Process-Payment EJB is a perfect example of a stateless session bean. The ProcessPayment EJB doesn't need to maintain any conversational state from one method invocation to the next. All the information needed to make a payment is passed into the byCreditCard() method. Stateless session beans provide higher performance in terms of throughput and resource consumption than entity and stateful session beans because only a few stateless session bean instances are needed to serve hundreds and possibly thousands of clients. Chapter 12 talks more about the use of stateless session beans.

EJB 2.0: Accessing EJB with Message-Driven Beans

Message-driven beans are integration points for other applications interested in working with EJB applications. Java applications or legacy systems that need to access EJB applications can send messages via JMS to message-driven beans. The message-driven beans can then process those messages and perform the required tasks using other entity and session beans.

In many ways, message-driven beans fulfill the same role as session beans by managing the workflow of entity and session beans to complete a given task. The task to be completed is initiated by an asynchronous message sent by an application using JMS. Unlike session beans, which respond to business methods invoked on their component interfaces, a message-driven bean responds to asynchronous messages delivered to the bean through its onMessage() method. Since the messages are asynchronous, the client that sends them doesn't expect or wait for a reply. The messaging client simply sends the message and forgets about it.

As an example, we can recast the TravelAgent EJB developed earlier as the ReservationProcessor EJB, a message-driven bean:

```
public class ReservationProcessorBean implements javax.ejb.MessageDrivenBean,
    javax.jms.MessageListener {

    public void onMessage(Message message) {
        try {
            MapMessage reservationMsg = (MapMessage)message;

            Integer customerPk = (Integer)reservationMsg.getObject("CustomerID");
            Integer cruisePk = (Integer)reservationMsg.getObject("CruiseID");
            Integer cabinPk = (Integer)reservationMsg.getObject("CabinID");
            double price = reservationMsg.getDouble("Price");

            CreditCardDO card = getCreditCard(reservationMsg);
            CustomerRemote customer = getCustomer(customerPk);
            CruiseLocal cruise = getCruise(cruisePk);
            CabinLocal cabin = getCabin(cabinPk);

            ReservationHomeLocal resHome = (ReservationHomeLocal)
                jndiContext.lookup("java:comp/env/ejb/ReservationHome");
            ReservationLocal reservation =
                resHome.create(customer,cruise,cabin,price,new Date());

            Object ref = jndiContext.lookup("java:comp/env/ejb/ProcessPaymentHome");
            ProcessPaymentHomeRemote ppHome = (ProcessPaymentHomeRemote)
                PortableRemoteObject.narrow(ref,ProcessPaymentHomeRemote.class);

            ProcessPaymentRemote process = ppHome.create();
            process.byCredit(customer,card,price);

            TicketDO ticket = new TicketDO(customer,cruise,cabin,price);
        } catch(Exception e) {
```

```
                    throw new EJBException(e);
            }
        }
    // More helper methods and callback methods follow
    }
```

Notice that all the information about the reservation is obtained from the message delivered to the message-driven bean. JMS messages can take many forms, one of which is javax.jms.MapMessage form used in this example, which carries name-value pairs. Once the information is obtained from the message and the enterprise bean references are obtained, the reservation is processed as it was in the session bean. The only difference is that a TicketDO is not returned to the caller; message-driven beans don't have to respond to the caller because the process is asynchronous.

Message-driven beans, like stateless session beans, do not maintain any conversational state. The processing of each new message is independent from the previous messages. The message-driven bean is explained in detail in Chapter 13.

The Bean-Container Contract

The environment that surrounds the beans on the EJB server is often referred to as the *container*. The container is more a concept than a physical construct. Conceptually, the container acts as an intermediary between the bean and the EJB server. It manifests and manages the EJB objects and EJB homes for a particular type of bean and helps these constructs to manage bean resources and apply primary services such as transactions, security, concurrency, naming, and so forth at runtime. Conceptually, an EJB server may have many containers, each of which may contain one or more types of enterprise beans. As you will discover a little later, the container and the server are not clearly different constructs, but the EJB specification defines the component model in terms of the container's responsibilities, so we will follow that convention here.

Enterprise bean components interact with the EJB container through a well-defined component model. The EntityBean, SessionBean, and MessageDrivenBean (EJB 2.0) interfaces are the bases of this component model. As we learned earlier, these interfaces provide callback methods that notify the bean class of life-cycle events. At runtime, the container invokes the callback methods on the bean instance when appropriate life-cycle events occur. When the container is about to write an entity bean instance's state to the database, for example, it first calls the bean instance's ejbStore() method. This provides the bean instance with an opportunity to do some cleanup on its state just before it's written to the database. The ejbLoad() method is called just after the bean's state is populated from the database, providing the bean developer with an opportunity to manage the bean's state before the first business method is called.* Other callback methods can be used by the bean class in a similar

---

* The ejbLoad() and ejbStore() behavior illustrated here is for container-managed persistence. With bean-managed persistence, the behavior is slightly different. This distinction is examined in detail in Chapter 11.

fashion. EJB defines when these various callback methods are invoked and what can be done within their contexts. This provides the bean developer with a predictable runtime component model.

While all the callback methods are declared in bean interfaces, a meaningful implementation of the methods is not mandatory. In other words, the method body of any or all of the callback methods can be left empty in the bean class. Beans that implement one or more callback methods are usually more sophisticated and access resources that are not managed by the EJB system. Enterprise beans that wrap legacy systems often fall into this category. The only exception to this is the onMessage() method, which is defined in the MessageDrivenBean interface. This method must have a meaningful implementation if the message-driven bean is to do anything useful.

javax.ejb.EJBContext is an interface that is implemented by the container and is also part of the bean-container contract. Entity beans use a subclass of javax.ejb. EJBContext called javax.ejb.EntityContext. Session beans use a subclass called javax.ejb.SessionContext. Message-driven beans use the subclass javax.ejb. MessageDrivenContext. These EJBContext types provide the bean with information about its container, the client using the enterprise bean, and the bean itself. They also provide other functionality that is described in more detail in Chapters 11, 12, and 13. The important thing about the EJBContext types is that they provide the enterprise bean with information about the world around it, which the enterprise bean can use while processing requests from clients and callback methods from the container.

In addition to EJBContext, EJB 1.1 and 2.0 have expanded the enterprise bean's interface with the container to include a JNDI name space, called the *environment naming context*, which provides the bean with a more flexible and extensible bean-container interface. The JNDI environment naming context is discussed in detail in Chapters 11 and 12.

The Container-Server Contract

The container-server contract is not defined by the Enterprise JavaBeans specification. It was left undefined to facilitate maximum flexibility for vendors defining their EJB server technologies. Other than isolating the beans from the server, the container's responsibility in the EJB system is a little vague. The EJB specification defines only the bean-container contract, not the container-server contract. It is difficult to determine, for example, exactly where the container ends and the server begins when it comes to resource management and other services.

In the first few generations of EJB servers this ambiguity has not been a problem, because most EJB server vendors also provide EJB containers. Since the vendor provides both the container and the server, the interface between the two can remain proprietary. In future generations of the EJB specification, however, some work may be done to define the container-server interface and delimit the responsibilities of the container.

One advantage of defining a container-server interface is that it allows third-party vendors to produce containers that can plug into any EJB server. If the responsibilities of the container and server are clearly defined, vendors who specialize in the technologies that support these different responsibilities can focus on developing the containers or servers that best match their core competencies. The disadvantage of a clearly defined container-server interface is that the plug-and-play approach could impact performance. The high level of abstraction that would be required to clearly separate the container interface from the server would naturally lead to looser binding between these large components, which could result in lower performance. The following rule of thumb best describes the advantages and disadvantages associated with a container-server interface: the tighter the integration, the better the performance; the higher the abstraction, the greater the flexibility. The biggest deterrent to defining a container-server interface is that it would require the definition of low-level facilities, which was one of the problems established CTM vendors had with CORBA. The ability to implement low-level facilities such as transactions and security as they see fit is one of EJB's biggest attractions for vendors.[*]

Many EJB-compliant servers actually support several different kinds of middleware technologies. It's quite common, for example, for an EJB server to support the vendor's proprietary CTM model as well as EJB, servlets, web-server functionality, a JMS provider, and other server technologies. Defining an EJB container concept is useful for clearly distinguishing the part of the server that supports EJB from all the other services it provides.

This said, we could define the responsibilities of containers and servers based on current implementations of the EJB specification. In other words, we could examine how current vendors are defining the container in their servers and use this as a guide. Unfortunately, the responsibilities of the container in each EJB server largely depend on the core competency of the vendor in question. Database vendors, for example, implement containers differently from TP-monitor vendors. The strategies for assigning responsibilities to the container and server are so varied that discussing them separately won't really help you understand the overall architecture. Instead, this book addresses the architecture of the EJB system as though the container and server were one component and refers to them collectively as the EJB server or container.

Summary

This chapter covered a lot of ground, describing the basic architecture of an EJB system. At this point, you should understand that beans are business object components. The home interfaces define life-cycle methods for creating, finding, and destroying beans, and the remote and local interfaces define the public business

---

[*] Of all the commercial and open source EJB servers available today, only one, OpenEJB, has experimented with defining a container-server interface. OpenEJB is an open source EJB container system that I developed.

methods of the bean. Message-driven beans do not have component interfaces. The bean class is where the state and behavior of the bean are implemented.

There are three basic kinds of beans: entity, session, and message-driven. Entity beans are persistent and represent a person, place, or thing. Session beans are extensions of the client and embody a process or a workflow that defines how other beans interact. Session beans are not persistent, receiving their state from the client, and they live only as long as the client needs them. Message-driven beans in EJB 2.0 are integration points that allow other applications to interact with EJB applications using JMS asynchronous messaging. Message-driven beans, like stateless session beans, are not persistent and do not maintain conversational state.

The EJB object and EJB home are conceptual constructs that delegate method invocations to session and entity beans from the client and help the container to manage the enterprise bean at runtime. The clients of entity and session beans do not interact with the instances of the bean class directly. Instead, the client software interacts with stubs, which are connected to the EJB object and EJB home. The EJB object implements the remote and/or local interface and expands the bean class's functionality. The EJB home implements the home interface and works closely with the container to create, locate, and remove beans.

Beans interact with their containers through the well-defined bean-container contract. This contract provides callback methods, the EJBContext, and the JNDI environment naming context. The callback methods notify the bean class that it is involved in a life-cycle event. The EJBContext and JNDI environment naming context provide the bean instance with information about its environment. The container-server contract is not well defined and remains proprietary at this time. Future versions of EJB may specify the container-server contract.

CHAPTER 3
Resource Management and the Primary Services

Chapter 2 discussed the basic architecture of Enterprise JavaBeans, including the relationship between the bean class, the component interfaces, the EJB object and EJB home, and the EJB container. These architectural components define a common model for distributed server-side components in component transaction monitors.

One of the reasons why CTMs are such great distributed object platforms is that they do more than just distribute objects: they also manage the resources used by distributed objects. CTMs are designed to manage thousands, even millions, of distributed objects simultaneously. To be this robust, CTMs must be very smart resource managers, managing how distributed objects use memory, threads, database connections, processing power, and more. EJB recognizes that some of the resource-management techniques employed by CTMs are very common, and it defines interfaces that help developers create beans that can take advantage of these common practices.

EJB CTMs are also great distributed object brokers. Not only do they help clients locate the distributed objects they need, but they also provide many services that make it much easier for a client to use the objects correctly. CTMs commonly support six primary services: concurrency, transaction management, persistence, object distribution, naming, and security. These services provide the kind of infrastructure that is necessary for a successful three-tier system.

With the introduction of message-driven beans in EJB 2.0, Enterprise JavaBeans goes beyond most CTMs by expanding the platform's responsibilities to include managing asynchronous messaging components. CTMs have historically been responsible only for managing RMI-based distributed objects. While the method of access is different for message-driven beans, EJB is still responsible for managing the primary services for message-driven beans just as it does for session and entity beans.

This chapter discusses both the resource-management facilities and the primary services that are available to Enterprise JavaBeans.

Resource Management

One of the fundamental benefits of using EJB servers is that they are able to handle heavy workloads while maintaining a high level of performance. A large business system with many users can easily require thousands of objects—even millions of objects—to be in use simultaneously. As the number of interactions among these objects increases, concurrency and transactional concerns can degrade the system's response time and frustrate users. EJB servers increase performance by synchronizing object interactions and sharing resources.

There is a relationship between the number of clients and the number of distributed objects that are required to service them. As client populations increase, the number of distributed objects and resources required increases. At some point, the increase in the number of clients will impact performance and diminish throughput. EJB explicitly supports two mechanisms that make it easier to manage large numbers of beans at runtime: instance pooling and activation.

Instance Pooling

The concept of pooling resources is nothing new. A commonly used technique is to pool database connections so that the business objects in the system can share database access. This trick reduces the number of database connections needed, which reduces resource consumption and increases throughput. Pooling and reusing database connections is less expensive than creating and destroying connections as needed. Most EJB containers also apply resource pooling to server-side components; this technique is called *instance pooling*. Instance pooling reduces the number of component instances, and therefore resources, needed to service client requests. It is also less expensive to reuse pooled instances than to frequently create and destroy instances.

As you already know, EJB clients of session and entity beans interact with these types of enterprise beans through the remote and, for EJB 2.0, local interfaces that are implemented by EJB objects. Client applications never have direct access to the actual session or entity bean. Instead, they interact with EJB objects, which wrap bean instances. Similarly, JMS clients in EJB 2.0 never interact with message-driven beans directly. They send messages that are routed to the EJB container system. The EJB container then delivers these messages to the proper message-driven instance.

Instance pooling leverages indirect access to enterprise beans to provide better performance. In other words, since clients never access beans directly, there's no fundamental reason to keep a separate copy of each enterprise bean for each client. The server can keep a much smaller number of enterprise beans around to do the work, reusing each enterprise bean instance to service different requests. Although this sounds like a resource drain, when done correctly, it greatly reduces the resources actually required to service all the client requests.

The entity bean life cycle

To understand how instance pooling works for RMI components (session and entity beans), let's examine the life cycle of an entity bean. EJB defines the life cycle of an entity bean in terms of its relationship to the instance pool. Entity beans exist in one of three states:

No state
> When a bean instance is in this state, it has not yet been instantiated. We identify this state to provide a beginning and an end for the life cycle of a bean instance.

Pooled state
> When an instance is in this state, it has been instantiated by the container but has not yet been associated with an EJB object.

Ready state
> When a bean instance is in this state, it has been associated with an EJB object and is ready to respond to business method invocations.

Overview of state transitions

Each EJB vendor implements instance pooling for entity beans differently, but all instance-pooling strategies attempt to manage collections of bean instances so that they are quickly accessible at runtime. To create an instance pool, the EJB container creates several instances of a bean class and then holds onto them until they are needed. As clients make business-method requests, bean instances from the pool are assigned to the EJB objects associated with the clients. When the EJB object doesn't need the instance any more, it's returned to the instance pool. An EJB server maintains instance pools for every type of bean deployed. Every instance in an instance pool is *equivalent*—they are all treated equally. Instances are selected arbitrarily from the instance pool and assigned to EJB objects as needed.

Soon after the bean instance is instantiated and placed in the pool, it's given a reference to a javax.ejb.EJBContext provided by the container. The EJBContext provides an interface that the bean can use to communicate with the EJB environment. This EJBContext becomes more useful when the bean instance moves to the Ready state. Enterprise beans also have a JNDI context called the environment naming context. The function of the environment naming context is not critical to this discussion and will be addressed in more detail later in the chapter.

When a client uses an EJB home to obtain a remote or local reference to a bean, the container responds by creating an EJB object. Once created, the EJB object is assigned a bean instance from the instance pool. When a bean instance is assigned to an EJB object, it officially enters the Ready state. From the Ready state, a bean instance can receive requests from the client and callbacks from the container. Figure 3-1 shows the sequence of events that results in an EJB object wrapping a bean instance and servicing a client.

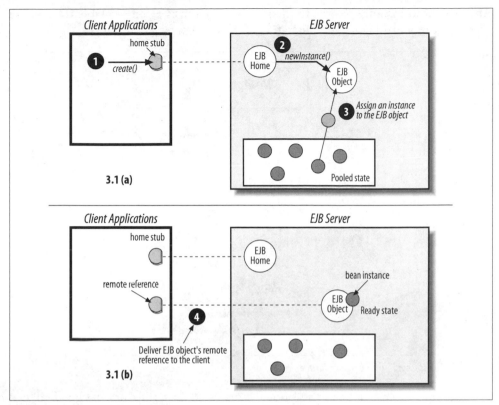

Figure 3-1. A bean moves from the instance pool to the Ready state

When a bean instance moves into the Ready state, the EJBContext takes on new meaning. The EJBContext provides information about the client that is using the bean. It also provides the instance with access to its own EJB home and EJB object, which is useful when the bean needs to pass references to itself to other enterprise beans, or when it needs to create, locate, or remove beans of its own class. So the EJBContext is not a static class; it is an interface to the container, and its state changes as the instance is assigned to different EJB objects.

When the client is finished with a bean's remote reference, either the remote reference passes out of scope or one of the bean's remove methods is called.[*] Once a bean has been removed or is no longer in scope, the bean instance is disassociated from the EJB object and returned to the instance pool. Bean instances can also be returned to the instance pool during lulls between client requests. If a client request is received and no bean instance is associated with the EJB object, an instance is retrieved from the pool and assigned to the EJB object. This is called *instance swapping*.

---

[*] The EJBHome, EJBLocalHome, EJBObject, and EJBLocalObject interfaces all define methods that can be used to remove a bean.

After the bean instance returns to the instance pool, it is again available to service a new client request. Figure 3-2 illustrates the life cycle of a bean instance.

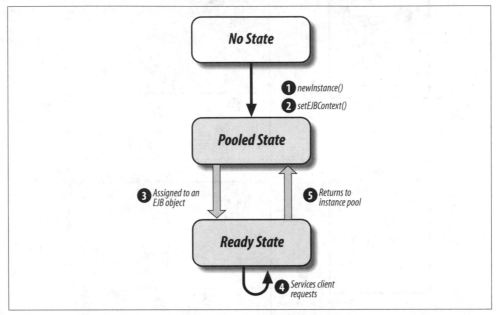

Figure 3-2. Life cycle of a bean instance

The number of instances in the pool fluctuates as instances are assigned to EJB objects and returned to the pool. The container can also manage the number of instances in the pool, increasing the count when client activity increases and lowering the count during less active periods.

Instance swapping

Stateless session beans offer a particularly powerful opportunity to leverage instance pooling. A stateless session bean does not maintain any state between method invocations. Every method invocation on a stateless session bean operates independently, performing its task without relying on instance variables. This means that any stateless session instance can service requests for any EJB object of the proper type, allowing the container to swap bean instances in and out between method invocations made by the client.

Figure 3-3 illustrates this type of instance swapping between method invocations. In Figure 3-3(a), instance A is servicing a business method invocation delegated by EJB object 1. Once instance A has serviced the request, it moves back to the instance pool (Figure 3-3(b)). When a business method invocation on EJB object 2 is received, instance A is associated with that EJB object for the duration of the operation (Figure 3-3(c)). While instance A is servicing EJB object 2, another method invocation is received by EJB object 1 from the client and is serviced by instance B (Figure 3-3(d)).

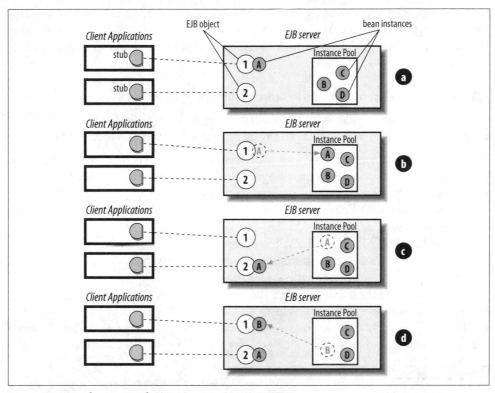

Figure 3-3. Stateless session beans in a swapping strategy

Using this swapping strategy allows a few stateless session bean instances to serve hundreds of clients. This is possible because the amount of time it takes to perform most method invocations is substantially shorter than the pauses between method invocations. The periods in a bean instance's life when it is not actively servicing the EJB object are unproductive; instance pooling minimizes these inactive periods. When a bean instance is finished servicing a request for an EJB object, it is immediately made available to any other EJB object that needs it. This allows fewer stateless session instances to service more requests, which decreases resource consumption and improves performance.

Stateless session beans are declared stateless in the deployment descriptor. Nothing in the class definition of a session bean is specific to being stateless. Once a bean class is deployed as stateless, the container assumes that no conversational state is maintained between method invocations. So a stateless bean can have instance variables, but because bean instances can be servicing several different EJB objects, they should not be used to maintain conversational state.

Implementations of instance pooling vary, depending on the vendor. One way that instance pooling implementations often differ is in how instances are selected from the pool. Two of the common strategies are FIFO (first in, first out) and LIFO (last in, first out). The FIFO strategy places instances in a queue, where they wait in line to service EJB objects. LIFO uses a stack strategy, where the last bean that was added to the stack is the first bean assigned to the next EJB object. Figure 3-3 uses a LIFO strategy.

EJB 2.0: Message-driven beans and instance pooling

Message-driven beans, like stateless session beans, do not maintain state specific to a client request, which makes them an excellent component for instance pooling.

In most EJB containers, each type of message-driven bean has its own instance pool that is used to service incoming messages. Message-driven beans subscribe to a specific message destination, which is a kind of address used when sending and receiving messages. When a JMS client sends an asynchronous message to a specific destination, the message is delivered to the EJB containers of message-driven beans that subscribe to that destination. The EJB container will first determine which message-driven bean subscribes to that destination, then choose an instance of that type from the instance pool to process the message. Once the message-driven bean instance has finished processing the message (when the onMessage() method returns), the EJB container will return the instance to its instance pool. An EJB container can process hundreds, possibly thousands, of messages concurrently by leveraging instance pools. Figure 3-4 illustrates how client requests are processed by an EJB container.

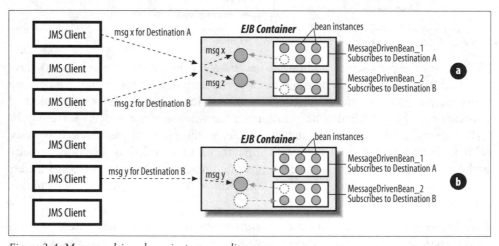

Figure 3-4. Message-driven bean instance pooling

In Figure 3-4, the top JMS client delivers a message to Destination A and the bottom JMS client delivers a message to Destination B. The EJB container chooses an instance of MessageDrivenBean_1 to process the message intended for Destination A and an instance of MessageDrivenBean_2 to process the message intended for Destination B. The bean instances are removed from the pool and assigned and used to process the messages.

A moment later, the middle JMS client sends a message to Destination B. At this point, the first two messages have already been processed and the container is returning the instances to their respective pools. As the new message comes in, the container chooses a new instance of MessageDrivenBean_2 to process the message.

Message-driven beans are always deployed to process messages from a specific destination. In the above example, instances of MessageDrivenBean_1 process messages only for Destination A, while instances of MessageDrivenBean_2 process messages only for Destination B. Several messages for the same destination can be processed at the same time. If, for example, a hundred messages for Destination A all arrived at the same time from a hundred different JMS clients, the EJB container would simply choose a hundred instances of MessageDrivenBean_1 to process the incoming messages; each instance is assigned a message.

The ability to concurrently process messages makes message-driven beans extremely powerful enterprise beans, on the same level as session and entity beans. They are truly first-class components and are an important addition to the Enterprise Java-Beans platform.

The Activation Mechanism

Unlike other enterprise beans, stateful session beans maintain state between method invocations. This is called *conversational state* because it represents the continuing conversation with the stateful session bean's client. The integrity of this conversational state needs to be maintained for the life of the bean's service to the client. Stateful session beans, unlike stateless session, entity, and message-driven beans, do not participate in instance pooling. Instead, activation is used with stateful session beans to conserve resources. When an EJB server needs to conserve resources, it can evict stateful session beans from memory. This reduces the number of instances maintained by the system. To passivate the bean and preserve its conversational state, the bean's state is serialized to a secondary storage and maintained relative to its EJB object. When a client invokes a method on the EJB object, a new stateful instance is instantiated and populated from the passivated secondary storage.

Passivation is the act of disassociating a stateful bean instance from its EJB object and saving its state. Passivation requires that the bean instance's state be held relative to its EJB object. After the bean has been passivated, it is safe to remove the bean instance from the EJB object and evict it from memory. Clients are completely unaware of the deactivation process. Remember that the client uses the bean's remote reference, which is implemented by an EJB object, and therefore does not directly communicate with the bean instance. As a result, the client's connection to the EJB object can be maintained while the bean is passivated.

Activating a bean is the act of restoring a stateful bean instance's state relative to its EJB object. When a method on the passivated EJB object is invoked, the container automatically instantiates a new instance and sets its fields equal to the data stored during passivation. The EJB object can then delegate the method invocation to the bean as normal. Figure 3-5 shows activation and passivation of a stateful bean. In Figure 3-5(a), the bean is being passivated. The state of instance B is read and held relative to the EJB object it was serving. In Figure 3-5(b), the bean has been passivated and its state preserved. Here, the EJB object is not associated with a bean instance. In Figure 3-5(c), the bean is being activated. A new instance, instance C, has been instantiated and associated with the EJB object and is in the process of having its state populated with the state held relative to the EJB object.

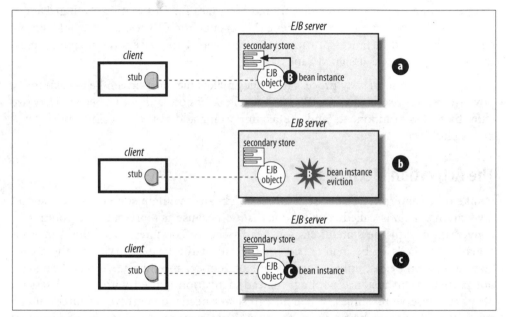

Figure 3-5. The passivation and activation processes

The exact mechanism for activating and passivating stateful beans is up to the vendor, but each stateful bean is serializable and thus provides at least one way of temporarily preserving its state. While some vendors take advantage of the Java serialization mechanism, the exact mechanism for preserving the conversational state is not specified. As long as the mechanism employed follows the same rules as Java serialization with regard to transitive closure of serializable objects, any mechanism is legal. Because Enterprise JavaBeans also supports other ways of saving a bean's state, the transient property is not treated the same when activating a passivated bean as it is in Java serialization. In Java serialization, transient fields are always set back to the initial value for that field type when the object is deserialized. Integers are set to zero, Booleans to false, object references to null, and so on. In EJB, transient fields are not necessarily set back to their initial values but can maintain their original values, or any arbitrary value, after being activated. Care should be taken when using transient fields, since their state following activation is implementation specific.

The activation process is supported by the life-cycle callback methods discussed in Chapter 2. The ejbActivate() and ejbPassivate() methods, respectively, notify the stateful bean instance that it is about to be activated or passivated. The ejbActivate() method is called immediately following the successful activation of a bean instance and can be used to reset transient fields to an initial value if necessary. The ejbPassivate() method is called immediately prior to passivation of the bean instance. These two methods are especially helpful if the bean instance maintains connections to resources that need to be manipulated or freed prior to passivation and reobtained following activation. Because the stateful bean instance is evicted from memory, open connections to resources are not maintained. The exceptions are remote references to other beans and the SessionContext, which must be maintained with the serialized state of the bean and reconstructed when the bean is activated. EJB also requires that the references to the JNDI environment context, component interfaces, and the UserTransaction bean be maintained through passivation.

Unlike stateful beans, entity beans do not have conversational state that needs to be serialized; instead, the state of each entity bean instance is persisted directly to the database. Entity beans do, however, leverage the activation callback methods (ejbActivate() and ejbPassivate()) to notify the instance when it's about to be swapped in or out of the instance pool. The ejbActivate() method is invoked immediately after the bean instance is swapped into the EJB object, and the ejbPassivate() method is invoked just before the instance is swapped out.

Primary Services

Many value-added services are available for distributed applications. The OMG (the CORBA governing body), for example, has defined 13 services for use in CORBA-compliant ORBs. This book looks at seven value-added services that are called the *primary services*, because they are required to complete the Enterprise JavaBeans platform. The primary services include concurrency, transactions, persistence, distributed objects, asynchronous messaging (EJB 2.0), naming, and security.

The seven primary services are not new concepts; the OMG defined interfaces for these services that are specific to the CORBA platform some time ago. In most traditional CORBA ORBs, services are add-on subsystems that are explicitly utilized by the application code. This means that the server-side component developer has to write code to use primary service APIs right alongside their business logic. The use of primary services becomes complicated when they are used in combination with resource-management techniques because the primary services are themselves complex. Using them in combination only compounds the problem.

As more complex component interactions are required, coordinating these services becomes a difficult task, requiring system-level expertise unrelated to the task of writing the application's business logic. Application developers can become so mired in the system-level concerns of coordinating various primary services and resource-management mechanisms that their main responsibility, modeling the business, is all but forgotten.

EJB servers automatically manage all the primary services. This relieves the application developers from the task of mastering these complicated services. Instead, developers can focus on defining the business logic that describes the system and leave the system-level concerns to the EJB server. The following sections describe each of the primary services and explain how they are supported by EJB.

Concurrency

The issue of concurrency is important to all the bean types, but it has a different meaning when applied to EJB 2.0 message-driven beans than it does with the RMI-based session and entity beans. This is because of the difference in context: with RMI-based beans, concurrency refers to multiple clients accessing the same bean simultaneously; with message-driven beans, concurrency refers to the processing of multiple asynchronous messages simultaneously. For this reason, we will discuss the importance of concurrency as a primary service separately for these different types of beans.

Concurrency with session and entity beans

Session beans do not support concurrent access. This makes sense if you consider the nature of both stateful and stateless session beans. A stateful bean is an extension of one client and serves only that client. It doesn't make sense to make stateful beans concurrent if they are used only by the clients that created them. Stateless session beans don't need to be concurrent because they don't maintain state that needs to be shared. The scope of the operations performed by a stateless bean is limited to the scope of each method invocation. No conversational state is maintained.

Entity beans represent data in the database that is shared and needs to be accessed concurrently. Entity beans are shared components. In Titan's EJB system, for example, there are only three ships: *Paradise*, *Utopia*, and *Valhalla*. At any given moment the Ship entity bean that represents the *Utopia* might be accessed by hundreds of clients. To make concurrent access to entity beans possible, the EJB container needs to protect the data represented by the shared bean, while allowing many clients to access the bean simultaneously.

In a distributed object system, problems arise when you attempt to share distributed objects among clients. If two clients are both using the same EJB object, how do you keep one client from writing over the changes of the other? If, for example, one client reads the state of an instance just before a different client makes a change to the same instance, the data the first client read becomes invalid. Figure 3-6 shows two clients sharing the same EJB object.

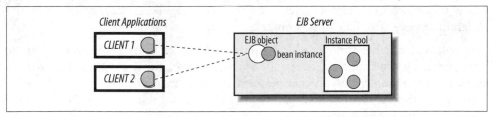

Figure 3-6. Clients sharing access to an EJB object

EJB has addressed the dangers associated with concurrency in entity beans by implementing a simple solution: EJB, by default, prohibits concurrent access to bean instances. In other words, several clients can be connected to one EJB object, but only one client thread can access the bean instance at a time. If, for example, one of the clients invokes a method on the EJB object, no other client can access that bean instance until the method invocation is complete. In fact, if the method is part of a larger transaction the bean instance cannot be accessed at all, except within the same transactional context, until the entire transaction is complete.

Since EJB servers handle concurrency automatically, a bean's methods do not have to be made thread-safe. In fact, the EJB specification prohibits use of the synchronized keyword. Prohibiting the use of the thread synchronization primitives prevents developers from thinking that they control synchronization and enhances the performance of bean instances at runtime. In addition, EJB explicitly prohibits beans from creating their own threads. In other words, as a bean developer, you cannot create a thread within a bean. The EJB container has to maintain complete control over the bean to properly manage concurrency, transactions, and persistence. Allowing the bean developer to create arbitrary threads would compromise the container's ability to track what the bean is doing and thus would make it impossible for the container to manage the primary services.

Reentrance. When talking about concurrency in entity beans, we need to discuss the related concept of *reentrance*. Reentrance is when a thread of control attempts to reenter a bean instance. In EJB, entity-bean instances are nonreentrant by default, which means that loopbacks are not allowed. Before I explain what a loopback is, it is important that you understand a very fundamental concept in EJB: entity and session beans interact using each other's remote references and do not interact directly. In other words, when bean A operates on bean B, it does so the same way an application client would, by using B's remote or local interface as implemented by an EJB object. This allows the EJB container to interpose between method invocations from one bean to the next to apply security and transaction services.

While most bean-to-bean interactions in EJB 2.0 take place using local interfaces of co-located enterprise beans, occasionally beans may interact using remote interfaces. Remote interfaces enforce complete location transparency. When interactions between beans take place using remote references, the beans can be relocated—possibly to a different server—with little or no impact on the rest of the application.

Regardless of whether remote or local interfaces are used, from the perspective of the bean servicing the call, all clients are created equal. Figure 3-7 shows that, from a bean's point of view, only clients perform business method invocations. When a business method is invoked on a bean instance, it cannot tell the difference between a remote application client and a bean client.

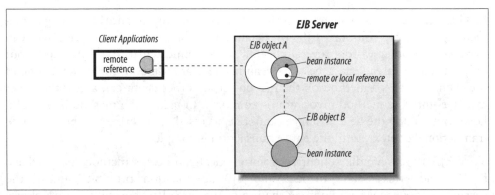

Figure 3-7. Beans access each other through EJB objects

A *loopback* occurs when bean A invokes a method on bean B that then attempts to make a call back to bean A. Figure 3-8 shows this type of interaction. In Figure 3-8, client 1 invokes a method on bean A. In response to the method invocation, bean A invokes a method on bean B. At this point, there is no problem because client 1 controls access to bean A and bean A is the client of bean B. If, however, bean B attempts to call a method on bean A, it is blocked because the thread has already entered bean A. By calling its caller, bean B is performing a loopback. This is illegal by default, because EJB doesn't allow a thread of control to reenter a bean instance.

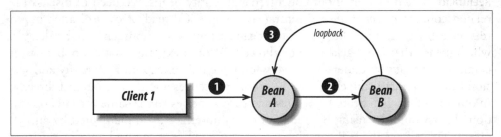

Figure 3-8. A loopback scenario

The nonreentrance policy is applied differently to session beans and entity beans. Session beans can never be reentrant, and they throw an exception if a loopback is attempted. The same is true of a nonreentrant entity bean. Entity beans can be configured in the deployment descriptor to allow reentrance at deployment time.

Making an entity bean reentrant, however, is discouraged by the specification. Reentrance is not relevant to EJB 2.0's message-driven beans because they do not respond to RMI calls, as session and entity beans do.

As discussed previously, client access to a bean is synchronized so that only one client can access any given bean at one time. Reentrance addresses a thread of control—initiated by a client request—that attempts to reaccess a bean instance. The problem with reentrant code is that the EJB object—which intercepts and delegates method invocations on the bean instance—cannot differentiate between reentrant code and multithreaded access within the same transactional context. (You'll read more about transactional context in Chapter 14.) If you permit reentrance, you also permit multithreaded access to the bean instance. Multithreaded access to a bean instance can result in corrupted data because threads impact each other's work when they try to accomplish their separate tasks.

It's important to remember that reentrant code is different from a bean instance that simply invokes its own methods at an instance level. In other words, method foo() on a bean instance can invoke its own public, protected, default, or private methods directly as much as it wants. Here is an example of intra-instance method invocation that is perfectly legal:

```
public HypotheticalBean extends EntityBean {
    public int x;

    public double foo() {
        int i = this.getX();
        return this.boo(i);
    }
    public int getX() {
        return x;
    }
    private double boo(int i) {
        double value = i * Math.PI;
        return value;
    }
}
```

In the previous code fragment, the business method, foo(), invokes another business method, getX(), and then a private method, boo(). The method invocations made within the body of foo() are intra-instance invocations and are not considered reentrant.

EJB 2.0: Concurrency with message-driven beans

Concurrency in message-driven beans refers to the processing of more then one message at a time. As mentioned earlier, concurrent processing of messages makes message-driven beans a powerful asynchronous component model. If message-driven beans could process only a single message at time, they would be practically useless in a real-world application because they couldn't handle heavy message loads.

Many JMS clients may send messages to the same destination at once. The ability of a message-driven bean to process all the messages simultaneously is concurrency. As Figure 3-9 illustrates, if three messages are delivered to a specific destination from three different clients at the same time, three instances of a single message-driven bean that subscribes or listens to that destination can be used to process the messages simultaneously. This is concurrent processing.

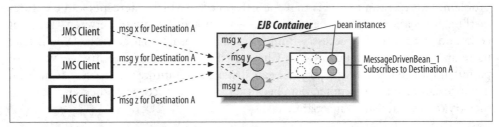

Figure 3-9. Concurrent processing with message-driven beans

There is actually a lot more to concurrent processing in message-driven beans. For example, topic and queue type destinations are processed differently, although the basic value of concurrent processing is the same. This book will explore the details behind the topic and queue type destinations in Chapter 13.

Transactions

Component transaction monitors were developed to bring the robust, scalable transactional integrity of traditional TP monitors to the dynamic world of distributed objects. Enterprise JavaBeans, as a server-side component model for CTMs, provides robust support for transactions for all the bean types (session, entity, and message-driven).

A *transaction* is a unit-of-work or a set of tasks that are executed together. Transactions are atomic; in other words, all the tasks in a transaction must be completed together for the transaction to be considered a success. In the previous chapter, we used the TravelAgent bean to describe how a session bean controls the interactions of other beans. Here is a code snippet showing the bookPassage() method described in Chapter 2:

```
public TicketDO bookPassage(CreditCardDO card,double price)
    throws IncompleteConversationalState {
    if (customer == null ||cruise == null ||cabin == null) {
        throw new IncompleteConversationalState();
    }
    try {
        ReservationHomeRemote resHome = (ReservationHomeRemote)
            getHome("ReservationHome",ReservationHomeRemote.class);
        ReservationRemote reservation =
            resHome.create(customer,cruise,cabin,price,new Date());
```

```
        ProcessPaymentHomeRemote ppHome = (ProcessPaymentHomeRemote)
            getHome("ProcessPaymentHome",ProcessPaymentHomeRemote.class);

        ProcessPaymentRemote process = ppHome.create();
        process.byCredit(customer,card,price);

        TicketDO ticket = new TicketDO(customer,cruise,cabin,price);
        return ticket;
    } catch(Exception e) {
        throw new EJBException(e);
    }
}
```

The bookPassage() method consists of two tasks that must be completed together: the creation of a new Reservation EJB and the processing of the payment. When the TravelAgent EJB is used to book a passenger, the charges to the passenger's credit card and the creation of the reservation must both be successful. It would be inappropriate for the ProcessPayment EJB to charge the customer's credit card if the creation of a new Reservation EJB fails. Likewise, you can't make a reservation if the customer credit card is not charged. An EJB server monitors the transaction to ensure that all the tasks are completed successfully.

Transactions are managed automatically, so as a bean developer you don't need to use any APIs to explicitly manage a bean's involvement in a transaction. Simply declaring the transactional attribute at deployment time tells the EJB server how to manage the bean at runtime. EJB does provide a mechanism that allows beans to manage transactions explicitly, if necessary. Setting the transactional attributes during deployment is discussed in Chapter 14, as is explicit management of transactions and other transactional topics.

Persistence

Entity beans represent the behavior and data associated with real-world people, places, or things. Unlike session and message-driven beans, entity beans are persistent, which means that the state of an entity is stored permanently in a database. This allows entities to be durable, so that both their behavior and their data can be accessed at any time without concern that the information will be lost because of a system failure.

When a bean's state is automatically managed by a persistence service, the container is responsible for synchronizing the entity bean's instance fields with the data in the database. This automatic persistence is called *container-managed* persistence. When a bean is designed to manage its own state, as is often the case when dealing with legacy systems, it is called *bean-managed* persistence.

Each vendor gets to choose the exact mechanism for implementing container-managed persistence, but the vendor's implementation must support the EJB callback methods and transactions. The most common mechanisms used in persistence by EJB vendors are *object-to-relational* persistence and *object database* persistence.

Object-to-relational persistence

Object-to-relational persistence is perhaps the most common persistence mechanism used in EJB servers today. Object-to-relational persistence involves mapping entity bean state to relational database tables and columns.

In Titan's system, the CabinBean models the business concept of a ship's cabin. The CabinBean defines three fields: a String of type name, an int of type deckLevel, and an Integer of type id.

In EJB 2.0, the abbreviated definition of the CabinBean looks like this:

```
public abstract class CabinBean implements javax.ejb.EntityBean {

    public abstract String getName();
    public abstract void setName(String str);

    public abstract int getDeckLevel();
    public abstract void setDeckLevel(int level);

    public abstract Integer getId();
    public abstract void setId(Integer id);

}
```

In EJB 2.0, the abstract accessor methods represent the entity bean's container-managed fields, which we will just call fields. When an entity bean is deployed, the container will implement these virtual fields for the bean, so it is convenient to think of the abstract accessor methods as describing persistent fields. For example, when we are talking about the state represented by the setName()/getName() abstract accessor method, we will refer to it as the name field. Similarly, the getId()/setId() is the id field, and the getDeckLevel()/setDeckLevel() is the deckLevel field.

In EJB 1.1, the CabinBean definition looks like this:

```
public class CabinBean implements javax.ejb.EntityBean {

    public int id;
    public String name;
    public int deckLevel;

}
```

With object-to-relational database mapping, the fields of an entity bean correspond to columns in a relational database. The Cabin's name field, for example, maps to the column labeled NAME in a table called CABIN in Titan's relational database. Figure 3-10 shows a graphical depiction of this type of mapping.

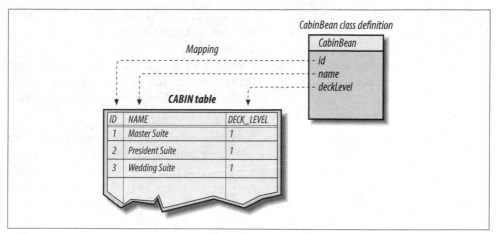

Figure 3-10. Object-to-relational mapping of entity beans

Really good EJB systems provide wizards or administrative interfaces for mapping relational database tables to the fields of entity-bean classes. Using these wizards, mapping entities to tables is a fairly straightforward process and is usually performed at deployment time. Figure 3-11 shows Pramati Application Server's object-to-relational mapping wizard.

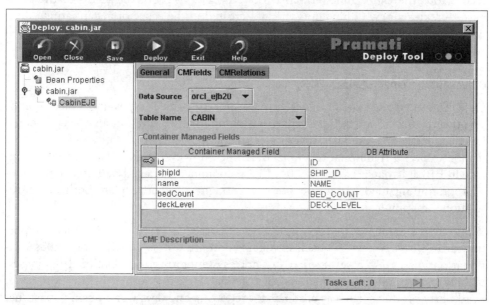

Figure 3-11. Pramati object-to-relational mapping wizard

Once a bean's fields are mapped to the relational database, the container takes over the responsibility of keeping the state of an entity-bean instance consistent with the corresponding tables in the database. This process is called *synchronizing* the state of the bean instance. In the case of `CabinBean`, bean instances at runtime will map one-to-one to rows in the `CABIN` table of the relational database. When a change is made to a Cabin EJB, it is written to the appropriate row in the database. Frequently, bean types will map to more than one table. These are more complicated mappings, often requiring an SQL join. Good EJB deployment tools should provide wizards that make multitable mappings fairly easy.

In addition, EJB 2.0 container-managed persistence defines entity-bean relationship fields, which allow entity beans to have one-to-one, one-to-many, and many-to-many relationships with other beans. Entity beans can maintain collections of other entity beans or single references. The persistence of entity beans in EJB 2.0 is a great deal more complex and powerful than was supported in previous versions of the specification. The new EJB 2.0 container-managed persistence model is covered in Chapters 6, 7, and 8.

In addition to synchronizing the state of an entity, EJB provides mechanisms for creating and removing entities. Calls to the EJB home to create and remove entities will result in a corresponding insertion or deletion of records in the database. Because each entity stores its state in a database table, new records (and therefore bean identities) can be added to tables from outside the EJB system. In other words, inserting a record into the `CABIN` table—whether done by EJB or by direct access to the database—creates a new Cabin entity. It's not created in the sense of instantiating a Java object, but rather in the sense that the data that describes a Cabin entity has been added to the system.

Object database persistence

Object-oriented databases are designed to preserve object types and object graphs and therefore are a much better match for components written in an object-oriented language such as Java. They offer a cleaner mapping between entity beans and the database than a traditional relational database. However, this is more of an advantage in EJB 1.1 than it is in EJB 2.0. EJB 2.0 container-managed persistence provides a programming model that is expressive enough to accommodate both object-to-relational mapping and object databases.

While object databases perform well when it comes to very complex object graphs, they are still fairly new to business systems and are not as widely accepted as relational databases. As a result, they are not as standardized as relational databases, making it more difficult to migrate from one database to another. In addition, fewer third-party products (such as products for reporting and data warehousing) exist that support object databases.

Several relational databases support extended features for native object persistence. These databases allow some objects to be preserved in relational database tables like other data types and offer some advantages over other databases.

Legacy persistence

EJB is often used to put an object wrapper on legacy systems, systems that are based on mainframe applications or nonrelational databases. Container-managed persistence in such an environment requires a special EJB container designed specifically for legacy data access. Vendors might, for example, provide mapping tools that allow beans to be mapped to IMS, CICS, b-trieve, or some other legacy application.

Regardless of the type of legacy system used, container-managed persistence is preferable to bean-managed persistence. With container-managed persistence, the bean's state is managed automatically, which is more efficient at runtime and more productive during bean development. Many projects, however, require that beans obtain their states from legacy systems that are not supported by the EJB vendor. In these cases, developers must use bean-managed persistence, which means that the developer doesn't use the automatic persistence service of the EJB server. Chapters 6–11 describe container-managed and bean-managed persistence in detail.

Distributed Objects

Three main distributed object services are available today: CORBA IIOP, Java RMI, and Microsoft's .NET. Each of these platforms uses a different RMI network protocol, but they all accomplish basically the same thing: location transparency. Microsoft's .NET platform, which relies on DCOM, is used in the Microsoft Windows environment and is currently not supported by other operating systems. Its tight integration with Microsoft products makes it a good choice for Microsoft-only systems. This may change with the growing support for SOAP (Simple Object Access Protocol), an XML-based protocol that is quickly becoming popular and offers interoperability with non-Microsoft applications. CORBA IIOP is neither operating-system specific nor language specific and has traditionally been considered the most open distributed object service of the three. It's an ideal choice when integrating systems developed in multiple programming languages. Java RMI is a Java language abstraction or programming model for any kind of distributed object protocol. In the same way that the JDBC API can be used to access any SQL relational database, Java RMI is intended to be used with almost any distributed object protocol. In practice, Java RMI has traditionally been limited to the Java Remote Method Protocol (JRMP)—known as Java RMI over JRMP—which can be used only between Java applications. Recently, an implementation of Java RMI over IIOP (Java RMI-IIOP), the CORBA protocol, has been developed. Java RMI-IIOP is a CORBA-compliant version of Java RMI, which allows developers to leverage the simplicity of the Java RMI programming model while taking advantage of the platform- and language-independent CORBA protocol, IIOP.[*]

---

[*] Java RMI-IIOP is interoperable with CORBA ORBs that support the CORBA 2.3.1 specification. ORBs that support an older specification cannot be used with Java RMI-IIOP because they do not implement the object-by-value portion of the 2.3.1 specification.

When we discuss the component interfaces and other EJB interfaces and classes used on the client, we are talking about the client's view of the EJB system. The *EJB client view* doesn't include the EJB objects, the EJB container, instance swapping, or any of the other implementation specifics. As far as a remote client is concerned, a bean is defined by its remote interface and home interface. Everything else is invisible. As long as the EJB server supports the EJB client view, any distributed object protocol can be used. EJB 2.0 requires that every EJB server support Java RMI-IIOP, but it doesn't limit the protocols an EJB server can support to just Java RMI-IIOP.

Regardless of the protocol used, the server must support Java clients using the Java EJB client API, which means that the protocol must map to the Java RMI-IIOP programming model. Using Java RMI over DCOM seems a little far-fetched, but Java RMI over SOAP is possible. Figure 3-12 illustrates the Java language EJB API supported by different distributed object protocols.

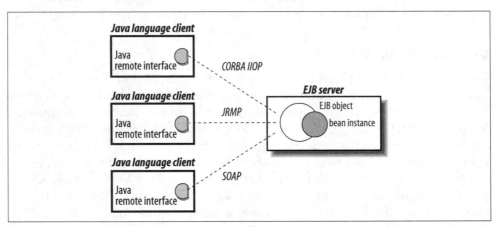

Figure 3-12. Java EJB client view supported by various protocols

EJB also allows servers to support access to beans by clients written in languages other than Java. An example of this is the EJB-to-CORBA mapping defined by Sun.* This document describes the CORBA Interface Definition Language (IDL) that can be used to access enterprise beans from CORBA clients. A CORBA client can be written in any language, including C++, Smalltalk, Ada, and even COBOL. The mapping also includes details about supporting the Java EJB client view as well as details on mapping the CORBA naming system to EJB servers and distributed transactions across CORBA objects and beans. Eventually, an EJB-to-SOAP mapping may be defined that will allow SOAP client applications written in languages such as Visual Basic, Delphi, and PowerBuilder to access beans. Figure 3-13 illustrates the possibilities for accessing an EJB server from different distributed object clients.

---

* Sun Microsystems' *Enterprise JavaBeans™ to CORBA Mapping, Version 1.1*, by Sanjeev Krishnan. Copyright 1999 by Sun Microsystems.

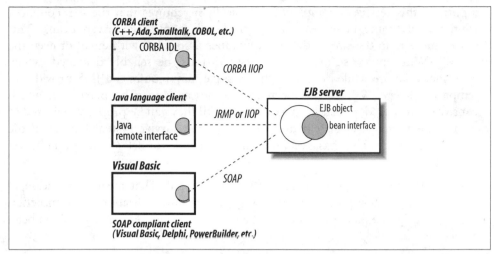

Figure 3-13. EJB accessed from different distributed clients

As a mature, platform- and language-independent distributed object protocol, CORBA is currently regarded by many as the superior of the three protocols discussed here. For all its advantages, however, CORBA suffers from some limitations. Pass-by-value, a feature easily supported by Java RMI-IIOP, was only recently introduced in the CORBA 2.3 specification and is not well supported by vendors. Another limitation of CORBA has to do with casting remote proxies. In Java RMI-JRMP, you can cast or widen a proxy's remote interface to a subtype or supertype of the interface, just like any other object. This is a powerful feature that allows remote objects to be polymorphic. In Java RMI-IIOP, you have to call a special narrowing method to change the interface of a proxy to a subtype, which is cumbersome.*

However, JRMP has its own limitations. While JRMP may be a more natural fit for Java-to-Java distributed object systems, it lacks inherent support for both security and transactional services—support that is a part of the CORBA IIOP specification. This limits the effectiveness of JRMP in heterogeneous environments where security and transactional contexts must be passed between systems.

EJB 2.0: Asynchronous Enterprise Messaging

Prior to EJB 2.0, support for asynchronous enterprise messaging and specifically the Java Message Service was not considered a primary service because it wasn't necessary in order to have a complete EJB platform. However, with the introduction of message-driven beans in EJB 2.0, asynchronous enterprise messaging has become so important that it has been elevated to the status of a primary service.

---

* Some vendors actually support native casting in Java clients without the need for the RemotePortableObject. narrow( ) method—it is not technically that difficult—but the EJB specification requires the use and support of the narrow( ) method in the remote client API.

Support for this service is complex, but basically it requires that the EJB container system reliably route messages from JMS clients to message-driven beans. This involves more than the simple delivery semantics associated with email or even the JMS API. With enterprise messaging, messages must be reliably delivered, which means that a failure while delivering the message may require the JMS provider to attempt redelivery.* What's more, enterprise messages may be persistent, which means they are stored to disk or to a database until they can be properly delivered to their intended clients. Persistent messages also must survive system failures; if the EJB server crashes, these messages must still be available for delivery when the server comes back up.

Most importantly, enterprise messaging is transactional. That means if a message-driven bean fails while processing a message, that failure will abort the transaction and force the EJB container to redeliver the message to another message-driven bean instance.

In addition to message-driven beans, stateless session beans and entity beans can also send JMS messages. Sending messages can be as important to Enterprise Java-Beans as delivery of messages to message-driven beans—support for both facilities tends to go hand in hand.

It's interesting to note that the semantics of supporting message-driven beans requires tight coupling between the EJB container system and the JMS message router, so that many EJB container systems will support a limited number of JMS providers. This means that message-driven beans can't consume messages from any arbitrary JMS provider or MOM product. Only the JMS providers supported explicitly by the EJB vendor will be able to deliver messages to message-driven beans.†

Naming

All distributed object services use a naming service of some kind. Java RMI-JRMP and CORBA use their own naming services. All naming services do essentially the same thing, regardless of how they are implemented: they provide clients with a mechanism for locating distributed objects or resources.

To accomplish this, a naming service must provide two things: object binding and a lookup API. *Object binding* is the association of a distributed object with a natural language name or identifier. The CabinHomeRemote object, for example, might be bound to the name "CabinHomeRemote" or "room." A binding is really a pointer or an index to a specific distributed object, which is necessary in an environment that

---

* Most EJB vendors will place a limit on the number of times a message can be redelivered. If redelivery occurs too many times, the message might be placed in a "dead message" repository, where it can be reviewed by an administrator.

† This may change as the Java Connector API evolves to better support asynchronous communication systems such as JMS, which could make JMS providers more of a plugable service for EJB platforms.

manages hundreds of different distributed objects. A *lookup API* provides the client with an interface to the naming system. Simply put, lookup APIs allow clients to connect to a distributed service and request a remote reference to a specific object.

Enterprise JavaBeans mandates the use of JNDI as a lookup API on Java clients. JNDI supports just about any kind of naming and directory service. A directory service is an advanced naming service that organizes distributed objects and other resources—printers, files, application servers, etc.—into hierarchical structures and provides more sophisticated management features. With directory services, metadata about distributed objects and other resources is also available to clients. The metadata provides attributes that describe the object or resource and can be used to perform searches. For example, you can search for all the laser printers that support color printing in a particular building.

Directory services also allow resources to be linked virtually, which means that a resource can be located anywhere you choose in the directory-services hierarchy. JNDI allows different types of directory services to be linked together so that a client can move between various types of services seamlessly. For example, it's possible for a client to follow a directory link in a Novell NetWare directory into an EJB server, allowing the server to be integrated more tightly with other resources of the organization it serves.

Java client applications can use JNDI to initiate a connection to an EJB server and to locate a specific EJB home. The following code shows how the JNDI API might be used to locate and obtain a reference to the EJB home `CabinHomeRemote`:

```
javax.naming.Context jndiContext = new javax.naming.InitialContext(properties);
Object ref = jndiContext.lookup("CabinHomeRemote");
CabinHomeRemote cabinHome = (CabinHome)
    PortableRemoteObject.narrow(ref, CabinHomeRemote.class);

Cabin cabin = cabinHome.create(382, "Cabin 333",3);
cabin.setName("Cabin 444");
cabin.setDeckLevel(4);
```

The properties passed into the constructor of `InitialContext` tell the JNDI API where to find the EJB server and what JNDI service provider (driver) to load. The `Context.lookup()` method tells the JNDI service provider the name of the object to return from the EJB server. In this case, we are looking for the home interface to the Cabin EJB. Once we have the Cabin EJB's home interface, we can use it to create new cabins and access existing cabins.

There are many different kinds of directory and naming services; EJB vendors can choose the one that best meets their needs, but all EJB 2.0 platforms must support the CORBA naming service in addition to any other directory services they choose to support.

Enterprise JavaBeans requires the use of the `PortableRemoteObject.narrow()` method to cast remote references obtained from JNDI into the `CabinHomeRemote` interface type. This is addressed in more detail in Chapters 4 and 5 and is not essential to the content covered here—the use of this facility is not required when enterprise beans use the local component interfaces of other co-located enterprise beans.

Security

Enterprise JavaBeans servers can support as many as three kinds of security: authentication, access control, and secure communication. Only access control is specifically addressed by Enterprise JavaBeans.

Authentication

> Simply put, authentication validates the identity of the user. The most common kind of authentication is a simple login screen that requires a username and a password. Once users have successfully passed through the authentication system, they are free to use the system. Authentication can also be based on secure ID cards, swipe cards, security certificates, and other forms of identification. While authentication is the primary safeguard against unauthorized access to a system, it is fairly crude because it doesn't police an authorized user's access to resources within the system.

Access control

> Access control (a.k.a. authorization) applies security policies that regulate what a specific user can and cannot do within a system. Access control ensures that users access only those resources for which they have been given permission. Access control can police a user's access to subsystems, data, and business objects, or it can monitor more general behavior. Certain users, for example, may be allowed to update information while others are allowed only to view the data.

Secure communication

> Communication channels between a client and a server are frequently the focus of security concerns. A channel of communication can be secured by physical isolation (e.g., via a dedicated network connection) or by encrypting the communication between the client and the server. Physically securing communication is expensive, limiting, and pretty much impossible on the Internet, so we will focus on encryption. When communication is secured by encryption, the messages passed are encoded so that they cannot be read or manipulated by unauthorized individuals. This normally involves the exchange of cryptographic keys between the client and the server. The keys allow the receiver of the message to decode the message and read it.

Most EJB servers support secure communication—usually through the Secure Socket Layer (SSL) protocol—and some mechanism for authentication, but Enterprise JavaBeans specifies only access control in its server-side component models. Authentication may be specified in subsequent versions, but secure communication will probably never be specified because it is independent of the EJB specification and the distributed object protocol.

Although authentication is not specified in EJB, it is often accomplished using the JNDI API. In other words, a client using JNDI can provide authenticating information using the JNDI API to access a server or resources in the server. This information is frequently passed when the client attempts to initiate a JNDI connection to the EJB server. The following code shows how the client's password and username are added to the connection properties used to obtain a JNDI connection to the EJB server:

```
properties.put(Context.SECURITY_PRINCIPAL, userName );
properties.put(Context.SECURITY_CREDENTIALS, userPassword);

javax.naming.Context jndiContext = new javax.naming.InitialContext(properties);
Object ref= jndiContext.lookup("CabinHomeRemote");
CabinHomeRemote cabinHome = (CabinHome)
    PortableRemoteObject.narrow(ref, CabinHomeRemote.class);
```

EJB specifies that every client application accessing an EJB system must be associated with a security identity. The security identity represents the client as either a user or a role. A user might be a person, security credential, computer, or even a smart card. Normally, the user is a person whose identity is assigned when she logs in. A role represents a grouping of identities and might be something like "manager," which is a group of user identities that are considered managers at a company.

When a remote client logs on to the EJB system, it is associated with a security identity for the duration of that session. The identity is found in a database or directory specific to the platform or EJB server. This database or directory is responsible for storing individual security identities and their memberships to groups.

Once a remote client application has been associated with a security identity, it is ready to use beans to accomplish some task. The EJB server keeps track of each client and its identity. When a client invokes a method on a component interface, the EJB server implicitly passes the client's identity with the method invocation. When the EJB object or EJB home receives the method invocation, it checks the identity to ensure that the client is allowed to invoke that method.

Role-driven access control

In Enterprise JavaBeans, the security identity is represented by a java.security. Principal object. As a security identity, the Principal acts as a representative for users, groups, organizations, smart cards, etc. to the EJB access-control architecture. Deployment descriptors include tags that declare which logical roles are allowed to access which bean methods at runtime. The security roles are considered logical roles because they do not directly reflect users, groups, or any other security identities in a specific operational environment. Instead, security roles are mapped to real-world user groups and users when the bean is deployed. This allows a bean to be portable; every time the bean is deployed in a new system, the roles can be mapped to the users and groups specific to that operational environment.

Here is a portion of the Cabin EJB's deployment descriptor that defines two security roles, ReadOnly and Administrator:

```
<security-role>
    <description>
        This role is allowed to execute any method on the bean
        and to read and change any cabin bean data.
    </description>
    <role-name>
        Administrator
    </role-name>
</security-role>

<security-role>
    <description>
        This role is allowed to locate and read cabin info.
        This role is not allowed to change cabin bean data.
    </description>
    <role-name>
        ReadOnly
    </role-name>
</security-role>
```

The role names in this descriptor are not reserved or special names with predefined meanings; they are simply logical names chosen by the bean assembler. In other words, the role names can be anything you want as long as they are descriptive.[*]

How are roles mapped into actions that are allowed or forbidden? Once the <security-role> tags are declared, they can be associated with methods in the bean using <method-permission> tags. Each <method-permission> tag contains one or more <method> tags, which identify the bean methods associated with one or more logical roles identified by the <role-name> tags. The <role-name> tags must match the names defined by the <security-role> tags shown earlier:

```
<method-permission>
    <role-name>Administrator</role-name>
    <method>
        <ejb-name>CabinEJB</ejb-name>
        <method-name>*</method-name>
    </method>
</method-permission>
<method-permission>
    <role-name>ReadOnly</role-name>
    <method>
        <ejb-name>CabinEJB</ejb-name>
        <method-name>getName</method-name>
    </method>
    <method>
        <ejb-name>CabinEJB</ejb-name>
```

---

[*] For a complete understanding of XML, including specific rules for tag names and data, see *Learning XML* by Erik Ray (O'Reilly).

```
        <method-name>getDeckLevel</method-name>
    </method>
    <method>
        <ejb-name>CabinEJB</ejb-name>
        <method-name>findByPrimaryKey</method-name>
    </method>
</method-permission>
```

In the first `<method-permission>`, the Administrator role is associated with all methods on the Cabin EJB, which is denoted by specifying the wildcard character (*) in the `<method-name>` of the `<method>` tag. In the second `<method-permission>`, the ReadOnly role is limited to accessing only three methods: getName(), getDeckLevel(), and findByPrimaryKey(). Any attempt by a ReadOnly role to access a method that is not listed in the `<method-permission>` will result in an exception. This kind of access control makes for a fairly fine-grained authorization system.

Since a single XML deployment descriptor can describe more than one enterprise bean, the tags used to declare method permissions and security roles are defined in a special section of the deployment descriptor This allows several beans to share the same security roles. The exact location of these tags and their relationship to other sections of the XML deployment descriptor will be covered in more detail in Chapter 16.

When the bean is deployed, the person deploying the bean will examine the `<security-role>` information and map each logical role to a corresponding user group in the operational environment. The deployer need not be concerned with what roles go to which methods; he can rely on the descriptions given in the `<security-role>` tags to determine matches based on the description of the logical role. This unburdens the deployer, who may not be a developer, from having to understand how the bean works in order to deploy it.

Figure 3-14 shows the same enterprise bean deployed in two different environments (labeled X and Z). In each environment, the user groups in the operational environment are mapped to their logical equivalent roles in the XML deployment descriptor so that specific user groups have access privileges to specific methods on specific enterprise beans.

As you can see from the figure, the ReadOnly role is mapped to those groups that should be limited to the get accessor methods and the find method. The Administrator role is mapped to those user groups that should have privileges to invoke any method on the Cabin EJB.

The access control described here is implicit; once the bean is deployed, the container takes care of checking that users access only those methods for which they have permission. This is accomplished by propagating the security identity, the Principal, with each method invocation from the client to the bean. When a client invokes a method on a bean, the client's Principal is checked to see if it is a member of a role mapped to that method. If it's not, an exception is thrown and the client is

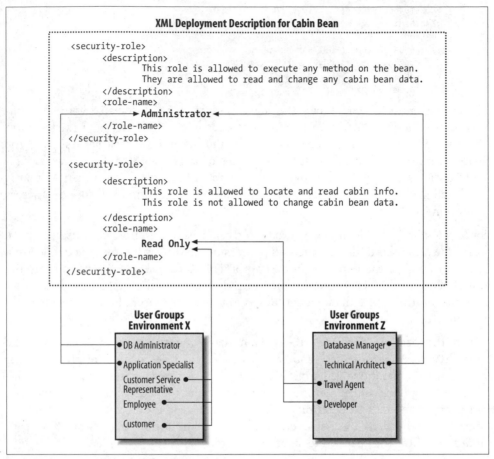

Figure 3-14. Mapping roles in the operational environment to logical roles in the deployment descriptor

denied permission to invoke the method. If the client is a member of a privileged role, the method is invoked.

If a bean attempts to access any other enterprise beans while servicing a client, it will pass along the client's security identity for access-control checks by the other beans. In this way, a client's Principal is propagated from one bean invocation to the next, ensuring that its access is controlled whether or not it invokes a bean method directly. In EJB 2.0, this propagation can be overridden by specifying that the enterprise bean executes under a different security identity, called the *runAs* security identity, which is discussed later in this chapter.

EJB 2.0: Unchecked methods

In EJB 2.0, a set of methods can be designated as *unchecked*, which means that the security permissions are not checked before the method is invoked. An unchecked method can be invoked by any client, no matter what role it is using. To designate a method or methods as unchecked, use the `<method-permission>` element and replace the `<role-name>` element with an empty `<unchecked>` element:

```
<method-permission>
    <unchecked/>
    <method>
        <ejb-name>CabinEJB</ejb-name>
        <method-name>*</method-name>
    </method>
    <method>
        <ejb-name>CustomerEJB</ejb-name>
        <method-name>findByPrimaryKey</method-name>
    </method>
</method-permission>
<method-permission>
    <role-name>administrator</role-name>
    <method>
        <ejb-name>CabinEJB</ejb-name>
        <method-name>*</method-name>
    </method>
</method-permission>
```

This declaration tells us that all the methods of the Cabin EJB, as well as the Customer EJB's `findByPrimaryKey()` method, are unchecked. Although the second `<method-permission>` element gives the administrator permission to access all the Cabin EJB's methods, this declaration is overridden by the unchecked method permission. Unchecked method permissions always override all other method permissions.

EJB 2.0: The runAs security identity

In addition to specifying the `Principals` that have access to an enterprise bean's methods, the deployer can also specify the runAs `Principal` for the entire enterprise bean. The runAs security identity was originally specified in EJB 1.0 but was abandoned in EJB 1.1. It has been reintroduced in EJB 2.0 and modified so that it is easier for vendors to implement.

While the `<method-permission>` elements specify which `Principals` have access to the bean's methods, the `<security-identity>` element specifies under which `Principal` the method will run. In other words, the runAs `Principal` is used as the enterprise bean's identity when it tries to invoke methods on other beans—this identity isn't necessarily the same as the identity that's currently accessing the bean.

For example, the following deployment descriptor elements declare that the `create()` method can be accessed only by `JimSmith` but that the Cabin EJB always runs under the `Administrator` security identity:

```
<enterprise-beans>
...
    <entity>
        <ejb-name>EmployeeService</ejb-name>
```

```
        ...
        <security-identity>
            <run-as>
                <role-name>Administrator</role-name>
            </run-as>
        </security-identity>
        ...
    </entity>
...
</enterprise-beans>
<assembly-descriptor>
<security-role>
    <role-name>Administrator</role-name>
</security-role>
<security-role>
    <role-name>JimSmith</role-name>
</security-role>
...
<method-permission>
    <role-name>JimSmith</role-name>
    <method>
        <ejb-name>CabinEJB</ejb-name>
        <method-name>create</method-name>
    </method>
</method-permission>
...
</assembly-descriptor>
```

This kind of configuration is useful when the enterprise beans or resources accessed in the body of the method require a `Principal` that is different from the one used to gain access to the method. For example, the `create()` method might call a method in enterprise bean X that requires the `Administrator` security identity. If we want to use enterprise bean X in the `create()` method, but we want only Jim Smith to create new cabins, we would use the `<security-identity>` and `<method-permission>` elements together to give us this kind of flexibility: the `<method-permission>` for `create()` would specify that only Jim Smith can invoke the method, and the `<security-identity>` element would specify that the enterprise bean always runs under the `Administrator` security identity. To specify that an enterprise bean will execute under the caller's identity, the `<security-identity>` role contains a single empty element, the `<use-caller-identity>` element. For example, the following declarations specify that the Cabin EJB always executes under the caller's identity, so if Jim Smith invokes the `create()` method, the bean will run under the `JimSmith` security identity:

```
<enterprise-beans>
...
    <entity>
        <ejb-name>CabinEJB</ejb-name>
        ...
        <security-identity>
            <use-caller-identity/>
        </security-identity>
        ...
```

```
        </entity>
    ...
    </enterprise-beans>
```

Figure 3-15 illustrates how the runAs Principal can change in a chain of method invocations. Notice that the runAs Principal is the Principal used to test for access in subsequent method invocations.

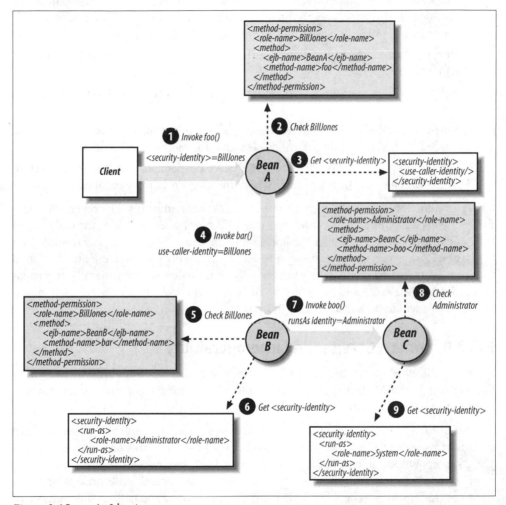

Figure 3-15. runAs Identity

Here's what's going on in this figure:

1. The client, who is identified as BillJones, invokes the method foo() on enterprise bean A.

2. Before servicing the method, enterprise bean A checks to see if BillJones is included in the <method-permission> elements for foo(). It is.

3. The `<security-identity>` of enterprise bean A is declared as `<use-caller-identity>`, so the `foo()` method executes under the caller's `Principal`; in this case, it's `BillJones`.

4. While `foo()` is executing, it invokes method `bar()` on enterprise bean B using the `BillJones` security identity.

5. Enterprise bean B checks the `foo()` method's `Principal` (`BillJones`) against the allowed identities for method `bar()`. `BillJones` is included in the `<method-permission>` elements, so the method `bar()` is allowed to execute.

6. Enterprise bean B specifies the `<security-identity>` to be the runAs `Principal` of `Administrator`.

7. While `bar()` is executing, enterprise bean B invokes the method `boo()` on enterprise bean C.

8. Enterprise bean C checks whether `bar()`'s runAs `Principal` (`Administrator`) is included in the `<method-permission>` elements for method `boo()`. It is.

9. The `<security-identity>` for enterprise bean C specifies a runAs `Principal` of `System`, which is the identity under which the `boo()` method executes.

This protocol applies equally to entity and stateless session beans. However, message-driven beans have only a runAs identity; they will never execute under the caller identity, because there is no "caller." Message-driven beans process asynchronous JMS messages. These messages are not considered calls, and the JMS clients that send them are not associated with the messages. With no caller security identity to propagate, message-driven beans must always have a runAs security identity specified and will always execute under that runAs `Principal`.

EJB 2.0: Primary Services and Interoperability

Interoperability is a vital part of EJB 2.0. The new specification includes the required support for Java RMI-IIOP for remote method invocation and provides for transaction, naming, and security interoperability.

The EJB 2.0 specification requires vendors to provide an implementation of Java RMI that uses the CORBA 2.3.1 IIOP protocol. The goal of this requirement is that J2EE servers will be able to interoperate, so that J2EE components (enterprise beans, applications, servlets and JSPs) in one J2EE server can access enterprise beans in a different J2EE server. The Java RMI-IIOP specification standardizes the transfer of parameters, return values, and exceptions as well as the mapping of interfaces and value objects to the CORBA IDL.

Vendors may support protocols other than Java RMI-IIOP, as long as the semantics of the RMI interfaces adhere to the types allowed in RMI-IIOP. This constraint ensures that a client's view of EJB is consistent, regardless of the protocol used in remote invocations.

Transaction interoperability between containers for two-phase commits is an optional but important feature of EJB 2.0. It ensures that transactions started by a J2EE web component propagate to enterprise beans in other containers through the implicit propagation mechanism described in the CORBA Object Transaction Service (OTS) v1.2 specification. The EJB 2.0 specification details how two-phase commits are handed across EJB containers as well as how transactional containers interact with non-transactional containers.

The new specification also addresses the need for an interoperable naming service for looking up enterprise beans. It specifies CORBA CosNaming as the interoperable naming service, defining how the service must implement the IDL interfaces of beans in the CosNaming module and how EJB clients use the service over IIOP.

EJB 2.0 provides security interoperability by specifying how EJB containers establish trust relationships and how containers exchange security credentials when J2EE components access enterprise beans across containers. EJB containers are required to support the Secure Sockets Layer (SSL 3.0) protocol and the related IETF standard Transport Layer Security (TLS 1.0) protocol for secure connections between clients and enterprise beans.

What's Next?

The first three chapters of this book gave you a foundation on which to develop Enterprise JavaBeans components and applications. You should have a better understanding of CTMs and the EJB component model.

Beginning with Chapter 4, you will develop your own beans and learn how to apply them in EJB applications.

Developing Your First Enterprise Beans

Choosing and Setting Up an EJB Server

One of the most important features of EJB is that enterprise beans work with containers from different vendors. However, that doesn't mean that selecting a server and installing your enterprise beans on that server are trivial processes.[*]

The EJB server you choose should provide a utility for deploying an enterprise bean. It doesn't matter whether the utility is command-line oriented or graphical, as long as it does the job. The deployment utility should allow you to work with prepackaged enterprise beans, i.e., enterprise beans that have already been developed and archived in a JAR file. Finally, the EJB server should support an SQL-standard relational database that is accessible using JDBC. For the database, you should have privileges sufficient for creating and modifying a few simple tables in addition to normal read, update, and delete capabilities. If you have chosen an EJB server that does not support an SQL-standard relational database, you may need to modify the examples to work with the product you are using.

This book does not say very much about how to install and deploy enterprise beans. That task is largely server-dependent. I'll provide some general ideas about how to organize JAR files and create deployment descriptors, but for a complete description of the deployment process, you'll have to refer to your vendor's documentation or look at the workbook for your vendor.

This chapter provides you with your first opportunities to use a workbook. Throughout the rest of this book, you will see *callouts* that direct you to exercises in the workbook. A callout will look something like the following:

📖 Workbook Exercise 4.2, A Simple Session Bean

---

[*] To help you work with different vendors' products, I have created free workbooks for specific EJB servers. See the Preface for more information about these workbooks and how to obtain them.

As was mentioned in the Preface, the workbooks can be downloaded in PDF format from *http://www.oreilly.com/catalog/entjbeans3/* or *http://www.titan-books.com*—some workbooks may even be available in paper book form and can be ordered directly from *http://www.titan-books.com.*

Setting Up Your Java IDE

To get the most from this chapter, it helps to have an IDE that has a debugger and allows you to add Java files to its environment. Several Java IDEs—such as Web-Gain's Visual Cafe, IBM's VisualAge, Borland's JBuilder, and Sun's Forte—fulfill this simple requirement. Some EJB products, such as IBM's WebSphere, are tightly coupled with an IDE that makes life a lot easier when it comes to writing, deploying, and debugging your applications.

Once you have an IDE set up, you need to include the Enterprise JavaBeans package, `javax.ejb`. You also need the JNDI packages, including `javax.naming`, `javax.naming.directory`, and `javax.naming.spi`. In addition, you will need the `javax.rmi` and `javax.jms` packages. All these packages can be downloaded from Sun's Java site (*http://www. javasoft.com*) in the form of ZIP or JAR files. They may also be accessible in the subdirectories of your EJB server, normally under the *lib* directory.

Developing an Entity Bean

There seems to be no better place to start than the Cabin EJB, which we have been examining throughout the previous chapters. The Cabin EJB is an entity bean that encapsulates the data and behavior associated with a cruise ship cabin in Titan's business domain.

Cabin: The Remote Interface

When developing an entity bean, we first want to define the enterprise bean's remote interface. The remote interface defines the enterprise bean's business purpose; the methods of this interface must capture the concept of the entity. We defined the remote interface for the Cabin EJB in Chapter 2; here, we add two new methods for setting and getting the ship ID and the bed count. The ship ID identifies the ship to which the cabin belongs, and the bed count tells how many people the cabin can accommodate:

```
package com.titan.cabin;

import java.rmi.RemoteException;

public interface CabinRemote extends javax.ejb.EJBObject {
    public String getName() throws RemoteException;
    public void setName(String str) throws RemoteException;
```

```
public int getDeckLevel() throws RemoteException;
public void setDeckLevel(int level) throws RemoteException;
public int getShipId() throws RemoteException;
public void setShipId(int sp) throws RemoteException;
public int getBedCount() throws RemoteException;
public void setBedCount(int bc) throws RemoteException;
}
```

The CabinRemote interface defines four properties: the name, deckLevel, shipId, and bedCount. *Properties* are attributes of an enterprise bean that can be accessed by public set and get methods. The methods that access these properties are not explicitly defined in the CabinRemote interface, but the interface clearly specifies that these attributes are readable and changeable by a client.

Notice that we have made the CabinRemote interface a part of a new package named com.titan.cabin. Place all the classes and interfaces associated with each type of bean in a package specific to the bean.* Because our beans are for the use of the Titan cruise line, we placed these packages in the com.titan package hierarchy. We also created directory structures that match package structures. If you are using an IDE that works directly with Java files, create a new directory somewhere called *dev* (for development) and create the directory structure shown in Figure 4-1. Copy the CabinRemote interface into your IDE and save its definition to the *cabin* directory. Compile the CabinRemote interface to ensure that its definition is correct. The *CabinRemote.class* file, generated by the IDE's compiler, should be written to the *cabin* directory, the same directory as the *CabinRemote.java* file. The rest of the Cabin bean's classes will be placed in this same directory.

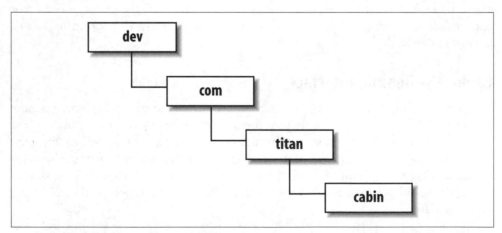

Figure 4-1. Directory structure for the Cabin bean

---

* The examples, which can be downloaded from *http://www.oreilly.com/catalog/entjbeans3/*, provide a good guide for how to organize your code. The code is organized in a directory structure that's typical for most products. The workbooks provide additional help for organizing your development projects and will point out any vendor-specific requirements.

CabinHome: The Remote Home Interface

Once we have defined the remote interface of the Cabin EJB, we have defined the remote view of this simple entity bean. Next, we need to define the Cabin EJB's remote home interface, which specifies how the enterprise bean can be created, located, and destroyed by remote clients; in other words, the Cabin EJB's life-cycle behavior. Here is a complete definition of the `CabinHomeRemote` home interface:

```
package com.titan.cabin;

import java.rmi.RemoteException;
import javax.ejb.CreateException;
import javax.ejb.FinderException;

public interface CabinHomeRemote extends javax.ejb.EJBHome {

    public CabinRemote create(Integer id)
        throws CreateException, RemoteException;

    public CabinRemote findByPrimaryKey(Integer pk)
        throws FinderException, RemoteException;
}
```

The `CabinHomeRemote` interface extends the `javax.ejb.EJBHome` and defines two life-cycle methods: `create()` and `findByPrimaryKey()`. These methods create and locate remote references to Cabin EJBs. Remove methods (for deleting enterprise beans) are defined in the `javax.ejb.EJBHome` interface, so the `CabinHomeRemote` interface inherits them.

CabinBean: The Bean Class

We have now defined the complete client-side API for creating, locating, removing, and using the Cabin EJB. Now we need to define `CabinBean`, the class that provides the implementation on the server for the Cabin EJB. The `CabinBean` class is an entity bean that uses container-managed persistence, so its definition will be fairly simple.

In addition to the callback methods discussed in Chapters 2 and 3, we must also define accessor methods for the `CabinRemote` interface and an implementation of the create method defined in the `CabinHomeRemote` interface.

Throughout this book we will show both the EJB 2.0 and EJB 1.1 code when they are different. In many cases the component interfaces are the same, but the bean class code and XML deployment descriptors will be different. This is the case with the Cabin EJB, so two code listings are shown for the bean class: the first is for EJB 2.0, and the second is for EJB 1.1. EJB 2.0 readers should ignore the EJB 1.1 listing and EJB 1.1 readers should ignore the EJB 2.0 code listing.

EJB 2.0: The CabinBean class

Here is the complete definition of the CabinBean class in EJB 2.0:

```
package com.titan.cabin;

import javax.ejb.EntityContext;

public abstract class CabinBean implements javax.ejb.EntityBean {

    public Integer ejbCreate(Integer id){
        this.setId(id);
        returns null;
    }
    public void ejbPostCreate(Integer id){

    }
    public abstract void setId(Integer id);
    public abstract Integer getId();

    public abstract void setShipId(int ship);
    public abstract int getShipId();

    public abstract void setName(String name);
    public abstract String getName();

    public abstract void setBedCount(int count);
    public abstract int getBedCount();

    public abstract void setDeckLevel(int level);
    public abstract int getDeckLevel();

    public void setEntityContext(EntityContext ctx) {
        // Not implemented.
    }
    public void unsetEntityContext() {
        // Not implemented.
    }
    public void ejbActivate() {
        // Not implemented.
    }
    public void ejbPassivate() {
        // Not implemented.
    }
    public void ejbLoad() {
        // Not implemented.
    }
    public void ejbStore() {
        // Not implemented.
    }
    public void ejbRemove() {
        // Not implemented.
    }
}
```

The CabinBean class can be divided into four sections for discussion: declarations for the container-managed fields, the ejbCreate()/ejbPostCreate() methods, the callback methods, and the remote-interface implementations.

The CabinBean defines several abstract accessor methods that appear in pairs. For example, setName() and getName() are a pair of abstract accessor methods. These methods are responsible for setting and getting the entity bean's name field. When the bean is deployed, the EJB container automatically implements all the abstract accessor methods so that the bean state can be synchronized with the database. These implementations map the abstract accessor methods to fields in the database. Although all the abstract accessor methods have corresponding methods in the remote interface, CabinRemote, it's not necessary that they do so. Some accessor methods are for the entity bean's use only and are never exposed to the client through the remote or local interfaces.

It's customary in EJB 2.0 to consider the abstract accessor methods as providing access to virtual fields and to refer to those fields by their method names, less the get or set prefix. For example, the getName()/setName() abstract accessor methods define a virtual *container-managed persistence* (CMP) field called name (the first letter is always changed to lowercase). The getDeckLevel()/setDeckLevel() abstract accessor methods define a virtual CMP field called deckLevel, and so on.

The name, deckLevel, shipId, and bedCount virtual CMP fields represent the Cabin EJB's persistent state. They will be mapped to the database at deployment time. These fields are also publicly available through the entity bean's remote interface. Invoking the getBedCount() method on a CabinRemote EJB object at runtime causes the container to delegate that call to the corresponding getBedCount() method on the CabinBean instance. Unlike the matching methods in the remote interface, the abstract accessor methods do not throw RemoteExceptions.

There is no requirement that CMP fields must be exposed. The id field is another container-managed field, but its abstract accessor methods are not exposed to the client through the CabinRemote interface. This field is the primary key of the Cabin EJB; it's the entity bean's index to its data in the database. It's bad practice to expose the primary key of an entity bean because you don't want client applications to be able to change that key.

EJB 1.1: The CabinBean class

Here is the complete definition of the CabinBean class in EJB 1.1:

```
package com.titan.cabin;

import javax.ejb.EntityContext;

public class CabinBean implements javax.ejb.EntityBean {

    public Integer id;
```

```java
public String name;
public int deckLevel;
public int shipId;
public int bedCount;

public Integer ejbCreate(Integer id) {
    this.id = id;
    return null;
}
public void ejbPostCreate(Integer id) {
    // Do nothing. Required.
}
public String getName() {
    return name;
}
public void setName(String str) {
    name = str;
}
public int getShipId() {
    return shipId;
}
public void setShipId(int sp) {
    shipId = sp;
}
public int getBedCount() {
    return bedCount;
}
public void setBedCount(int bc) {
    bedCount = bc;
}
public int getDeckLevel() {
    return deckLevel;
}
public void setDeckLevel(int level ) {
    deckLevel = level;
}

public void setEntityContext(EntityContext ctx) {
    // Not implemented.
}
public void unsetEntityContext() {
    // Not implemented.
}
public void ejbActivate() {
    // Not implemented.
}
public void ejbPassivate() {
    // Not implemented.
}
public void ejbLoad() {
    // Not implemented.
}
public void ejbStore() {
```

```
    // Not implemented.
}
public void ejbRemove() {
    // Not implemented.
}
}
```

Declared fields in a bean class can be *persistent* fields or *property* fields. These categories are not mutually exclusive. Persistent field declarations describe the fields that will be mapped to the database. A persistent field is often a property (in the JavaBeans sense): any attribute that is available using public set and get methods. Of course, a bean can have any fields that it needs; they need not all be persistent, or properties. Fields that aren't persistent won't be saved in the database. In CabinBean, all the fields are persistent.

The id field is persistent, but it is not a property. In other words, id is mapped to the database but cannot be accessed through the remote interface.

The name, deckLevel, shipId, and bedCount fields are also persistent fields. They will be mapped to the database at deployment time. These fields are also properties, because they are publicly available through the remote interface.

EJB 2.0 and 1.1: The callback methods

In the case of the Cabin EJB, there was only one create() method, so there is only one corresponding ejbCreate() method and one ejbPostCreate() method. When a client invokes the create() method on the remote home interface, it is delegated to a matching ejbCreate() method on the entity bean instance. The ejbCreate() method initializes the fields; in the case of the CabinBean, it sets the name field.

The ejbCreate() method always returns the primary key type; with container-managed persistence, this method returns the null value. It's the container's responsibility to create the primary key. Why does it return null? Simply put, this convention makes it easier for a bean-managed enterprise bean (i.e., an enterprise bean that explicitly manages its own persistence) to extend a container-managed enterprise bean. This functionality is valuable for EJB vendors who support container-managed persistence beans by extending them with bean-managed persistence bean implementations—it's a technique that is more common in EJB 1.1. Bean-managed persistence beans, which are covered in Chapter 10, always return the primary key type.

Once the ejbCreate() method has executed, the ejbPostCreate() method is called to perform any follow-up operations. The ejbCreate() and ejbPostCreate() methods must have signatures that match the parameters and (optionally) the exceptions of the home interface's create() method. The ejbPostCreate() method is used to perform any postprocessing on the bean after it is created, but before it can be used by the client. Both methods will execute, one right after the other, when the client invokes the create() method on the remote home interface.

The `findByPrimaryKey()` method is not defined in container-managed bean classes. Instead, find methods are generated at deployment and implemented by the container. With bean-managed entity beans, find methods must be defined in the bean class. In Chapter 10, when you develop bean-managed entity beans, you will define the find methods in the bean classes you develop.

The `CabinBean` class implements `javax.ejb.EntityBean`, which defines seven callback methods: `setEntityContext()`, `unsetEntityContext()`, `ejbActivate()`, `ejbPassivate()`, `ejbLoad()`, `ejbStore()`, and `ejbRemove()`. The container uses these callback methods to notify the `CabinBean` of certain events in its life cycle. Although the callback methods are implemented, the implementations are empty. The `CabinBean` is simple enough that it doesn't need to do any special processing during its life cycle. When we study entity beans in more detail in Chapters 6 through 11, we will take advantage of these callback methods.

The Deployment Descriptor

You are now ready to create a deployment descriptor for the Cabin EJB. The deployment descriptor performs a function similar to a properties file. It describes which classes make up a enterprise bean and how the enterprise bean should be managed at runtime. During deployment, the deployment descriptor is read and its properties are displayed for editing. The deployer can then modify and add settings as appropriate for the application's operational environment. Once the deployer is satisfied with the deployment information, she uses it to generate the entire supporting infrastructure needed to deploy the enterprise bean in the EJB server. This may include resolving enterprise bean references, adding the enterprise bean to the naming system, and generating the enterprise bean's EJB object and EJB home, persistence infrastructure, transactional support, and so forth.

Although most EJB server products provide a wizard for creating and editing deployment descriptors, we will create ours directly so that the enterprise bean is defined in a vendor-independent manner.[*] This requires some manual labor, but it gives you a much better understanding of how deployment descriptors are created. Once the deployment descriptor is finished, the enterprise bean can be placed in a JAR file and deployed on any EJB-compliant server of the appropriate version.

An XML deployment descriptor for every example in this book has already been created and is available from the download site.

The following sections offer a quick peek at the EJB 2.0 and 1.1 deployment descriptors for the Cabin EJB, so you can get a feel for how an XML deployment descriptor is structured and the type of information it contains.

---

[*] The workbooks show you how to use the vendors' tools for creating deployment descriptors.

EJB 2.0: The Cabin EJB's deployment descriptor

In EJB 2.0, the deployment descriptor looks like this:

```
<!DOCTYPE ejb-jar PUBLIC "-//Sun Microsystems, Inc.//DTD Enterprise
JavaBeans 2.0//EN" "http://java.sun.com/dtd/ejb-jar_2_0.dtd">

<ejb-jar>
    <enterprise-beans>
        <entity>
            <ejb-name>CabinEJB</ejb-name>
            <home>com.titan.cabin.CabinHomeRemote</home>
            <remote>com.titan.cabin.CabinRemote</remote>
            <ejb-class>com.titan.cabin.CabinBean</ejb-class>
            <persistence-type>Container</persistence-type>
            <prim-key-class>java.lang.Integer</prim-key-class>
            <reentrant>False</reentrant>
            <abstract-schema-name>Cabin</abstract-schema-name>
            <cmp-field><field-name>id</field-name></cmp-field>
            <cmp-field><field-name>name</field-name></cmp-field>
            <cmp-field><field-name>deckLevel</field-name></cmp-field>
            <cmp-field><field-name>shipId</field-name></cmp-field>
            <cmp-field><field-name>bedCount</field-name></cmp-field>
            <primkey-field>id</primkey-field>
            <security-identity><use-caller-identity/></security-identity>
        </entity>
    </enterprise-beans>
    <assembly-descriptor>
    ...
    </assembly-descriptor>
</ejb-jar>
```

EJB 1.1: The Cabin EJB's deployment descriptor

In EJB 1.1, the deployment descriptor looks like this:

```
<!DOCTYPE ejb-jar PUBLIC "-//Sun Microsystems, Inc.//DTD Enterprise
JavaBeans 1.1//EN" "http://java.sun.com/j2ee/dtds/ejb-jar_1_1.dtd">

<ejb-jar>
    <enterprise-beans>
        <entity>
            <ejb-name>CabinEJB</ejb-name>
            <home>com.titan.cabin.CabinHomeRemote</home>
            <remote>com.titan.cabin.CabinRemote</remote>
            <ejb-class>com.titan.cabin.CabinBean</ejb-class>
            <persistence-type>Container</persistence-type>
            <prim-key-class>java.lang.Integer</prim-key-class>
            <reentrant>False</reentrant>
            <cmp-field><field-name>id</field-name></cmp-field>
            <cmp-field><field-name>name</field-name></cmp-field>
            <cmp-field><field-name>deckLevel</field-name></cmp-field>
            <cmp-field><field-name>shipId</field-name></cmp-field>
            <cmp-field><field-name>bedCount</field-name></cmp-field>
```

```
            <primkey-field>id</primkey-field>
        </entity>
    </enterprise-beans>
    <assembly-descriptor>
    ...
    </assembly-descriptor>
</ejb-jar>
```

EJB 2.0 and 1.1: Defining the XML elements

The `<!DOCTYPE>` element describes the purpose of the XML file, its root element, and the location of its DTD. The DTD is used to verify that the document is structured correctly. This element is discussed in detail in Chapter 16. One important distinction between EJB 2.0 and EJB 1.1 is that they use different DTDs for deployment descriptors. EJB 2.0 specifies the `ejb-jar_2_0.dtd`, while EJB 1.1 specifies the `ejb-jar_1_1.dtd`.

The rest of the XML elements are nested one within another and are delimited by beginning and ending tags. The structure is not complicated. If you have done any HTML coding, you should already understand the format. An element always starts with a *<name_of_tag>* tag and ends with a *</name_of_tag>* tag. Everything in between—even other elements—is part of the enclosing element.

The first major element is the `<ejb-jar>` element, which is the root of the document. All the other elements must lie within this element. Next is the `<enterprise-beans>` element. Every bean declared in an XML file must be included in this section. This file describes only the Cabin EJB, but we could define several beans in one deployment descriptor.

The `<entity>` element shows that the beans defined within this tag are entity beans. Similarly, a `<session>` element describes session beans; since the Cabin EJB is an entity bean, we don't need a `<session>` element. In addition to a description, the `<entity>` element provides the fully qualified class names of the remote interface, home interface, bean class, and primary key. The `<cmp-field>` elements list all the container-managed fields in the entity bean class. These are the fields that will persist in the database and be managed by the container at runtime. The `<entity>` element also includes a `<reentrant>` element that can be set as True or False depending on whether the bean allows reentrant loopbacks or not.

EJB 2.0 specifies a name, which is used in EJB QL (Query Language) to identify the entity bean. This isn't important right now. The 2.0 deployment descriptor also specifies the `<security-identity>` as `<use-caller-identity/>`, which simply means the bean will propagate the calling client's security identity when it accesses resources or other beans. This was covered in detail in Chapter 3.

The section of the XML file after the `<enterprise-beans>` element is enclosed by the `<assembly-descriptor>` element, which describes the security roles and transaction attributes of the bean. This section of the XML file is the same for both EJB 2.0 and EJB 1.1 in this example:

```
<ejb-jar>
    <enterprise-beans>
    ...
    <enterprise-beans>
    <assembly-descriptor>
        <security-role>
            <description>
                This role represents everyone who is allowed full access
                to the Cabin EJB.
            </description>
            <role-name>everyone</role-name>
        </security-role>

        <method-permission>
            <role-name>everyone</role-name>
            <method>
                <ejb-name>CabinEJB</ejb-name>
                <method-name>*</method-name>
            </method>
        </method-permission>

        <container-transaction>
            <method>
                <ejb-name>CabinEJB</ejb-name>
                <method-name>*</method-name>
            </method>
            <trans-attribute>Required</trans-attribute>
        </container-transaction>
    </assembly-descriptor>
</ejb-jar>
```

It may seem odd to separate the `<assembly-descriptor>` information from the `<enterprise-beans>` information, since it clearly applies to the Cabin EJB, but in the scheme of things it's perfectly natural. A single XML deployment descriptor can describe several beans, which might all rely on the same security roles and transaction attributes. To make it easier to deploy several beans together, all this common information is grouped in the `<assembly-descriptor>` element.

There is another (perhaps more important) reason for separating information about the bean itself from the security roles and transaction attributes. Enterprise Java-Beans defines the responsibilities of different participants in the development and deployment of beans. We don't address these development roles in this book because they are not critical to learning the fundamentals of EJB. For now, it's enough to know that the person who develops the beans and the person who assembles the beans into an application have separate responsibilities and therefore deal with separate parts of the XML deployment descriptor. The bean developer is responsible for everything within the `<enterprise-beans>` element; the bean assembler is responsible for everything within the `<assembly-descriptor>`. Throughout this book you will play both roles, developing the beans and assembling them. Other roles you will fill are that of the deployer, who is the person who actually loads the enterprise beans into the EJB container; and the administrator, who is responsible for tuning the EJB server and managing it at runtime. In real projects, all these roles may be filled by one or two people, or by several different individuals or even teams.

The `<assembly-descriptor>` contains the `<security-role>` elements and their corresponding `<method-permission>` elements, which were described in Chapter 3 under the section "Security." In this example, there is one security role, everyone, which is mapped to all the methods in the Cabin EJB using the `<method-permission>` element. (The * in the `<method-name>` element means "all methods.") As already mentioned, for EJB 2.0 you'll have to specify a security identity; in this case, it's the caller's identity.

The `<container-transaction>` element declares that all the methods of the Cabin EJB have a Required transaction attribute, which means that all the methods must be executed within a transaction. Transaction attributes are explained in more detail in Chapter 14. The deployment descriptor ends with the closing tag of the `<ejb-jar>` element.

Copy the Cabin EJB's deployment descriptor into the same directory as the class files for the Cabin EJB files (*Cabin.class*, *CabinHome.class*, *CabinBean.class*, and *CabinPK. class*) and save it as *ejb-jar.xml*. You have now created all the files you need to package your Cabin EJB. Figure 4-2 shows all the files that should be in the *cabin* directory.

cabin.jar: The JAR File

The JAR file is a platform-independent file format for compressing, packaging, and delivering several files together. Based on the ZIP file format and the ZLIB compression standards, the JAR (Java archive) tool and packages were originally developed to make downloads of Java applets more efficient. As a packaging mechanism, however, the JAR file format is a very convenient way to "shrink-wrap" components and other software for delivery to third parties. The original JavaBeans component architecture depends on JAR files for packaging, as does Enterprise JavaBeans. The goal in using the JAR file format in EJB is to package all the classes and interfaces associated with a bean, including the deployment descriptor, into one file.

Creating the JAR file for deployment is easy. Position yourself in the *dev* directory that is just above the *com/titan/cabin* directory tree, and execute the following command:

```
\dev % jar cf cabin.jar com/titan/cabin/*.class META-INF/ejb-jar.xml

F:\..\dev>jar cf cabin.jar com\titan\cabin\*.class META-INF\ejb-jar.xml
```

You might have to create the *META-INF* directory first and copy *ejb-jar.xml* into that directory. The *c* option tells the *jar* utility to create a new JAR file that contains the files indicated in subsequent parameters. It also tells the *jar* utility to stream the

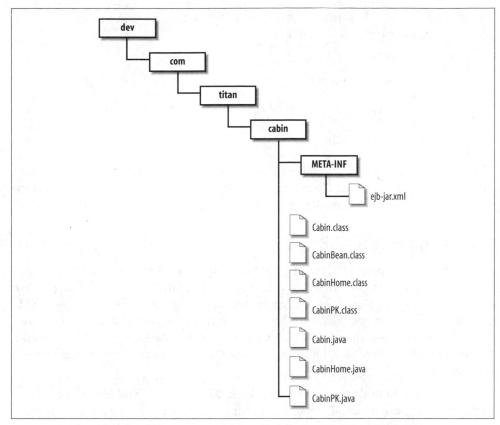

Figure 4-2. The Cabin EJB files

resulting JAR file to standard output. The *f* option tells *jar* to redirect the standard output to a new file named in the second parameter (*cabin.jar*). It's important to get the order of the option letters and the command-line parameters to match. You can learn more about the *jar* utility and the java.util.zip package in *Java™ in a Nutshell* by David Flanagan, or *Learning Java™* by Pat Niemeyer and Jonathan Knudsen (both published by O'Reilly).

The *jar* utility creates the file *cabin.jar* in the *dev* directory. If you're interested in looking at the contents of the JAR file, you can use any standard ZIP application (WinZip, PKZIP, etc.), or you can use the command *jar tvf cabin.jar*.

Creating a CABIN Table in the Database

One of the primary jobs of a deployment tool is mapping entity beans to databases. In the case of the Cabin EJB, we must map its id, name, deckLevel, shipId, and bedCount container-managed fields to some data source. Before proceeding with deployment, you need to set up a database and create a CABIN table. You can use the following standard SQL statement to create a `CABIN` table that will be consistent with the examples provided in this chapter:

```
create table CABIN
(
    ID int primary key NOT NULL,
    SHIP_ID int,
    BED_COUNT int,
    NAME char(30),
    DECK_LEVEL int
)
```

This statement creates a `CABIN` table that has five columns corresponding to the container-managed fields in the `CabinBean` class. Once the table is created and connectivity to the database is confirmed, you can proceed with the deployment process.

Deploying the Cabin EJB

Deployment is the process of reading the bean's JAR file, changing or adding properties to the deployment descriptor, mapping the bean to the database, defining access control in the security domain, and generating any vendor-specific classes needed to support the bean in the EJB environment. Every EJB server product has its own deployment tools, which may provide a graphical user interface, a set of command-line programs, or both. Graphical deployment "wizards" are the easiest deployment tools to use.

A deployment tool reads the JAR file and looks for the *ejb-jar.xml* file. In a graphical deployment wizard, the deployment descriptor elements are presented in a set of property sheets similar to those used to customize visual components in environments such as Visual Basic, PowerBuilder, JBuilder, and Symantec Café. Figure 4-3 shows the deployment wizard used in the J2EE 1.3 SDK (Reference Implementation) server.

The J2EE Reference Implementation's deployment wizard has fields and panels that match the XML deployment descriptor. You can map security roles to user groups, set the JNDI lookup name, map the container-managed fields to the database, etc.

Different EJB deployment tools provide varying degrees of support for mapping container-managed fields to a data source. Some provide very robust and sophisticated graphical user interfaces, while others are simpler and less flexible. Fortunately, mapping the `CabinBean`'s container-managed fields to the `CABIN` table is a fairly straightforward process. The documentation for your vendor's deployment tool will show you how to create this mapping. Once you have finished the mapping, you can complete the deployment of the Cabin EJB and prepare to access it from the EJB server.

Creating a Client Application

Now that the Cabin EJB has been deployed in the EJB server, we want to access it from a remote client. When we say remote, we are usually talking about either a client

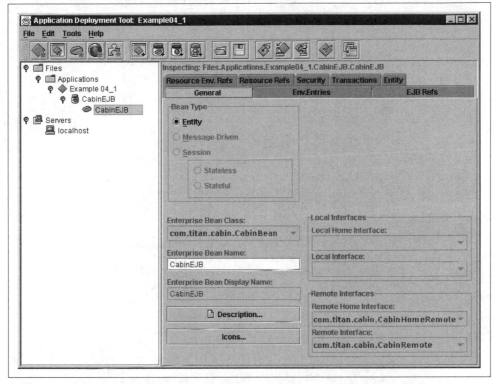

Figure 4-3. J2EE 1.3 SDK Reference Implementation's deployment wizard

application that is located on a different computer or a different process on the same computer. In this section, we will create a remote client that will connect to the EJB server, locate the EJB remote home for the Cabin EJB, and create and interact with several Cabin EJBs. The following code shows a Java application that is designed to create a new Cabin EJB, set its name, deckLevel, shipId, and bedCount properties, and then locate it again using its primary key:

```java
package com.titan.cabin;

import com.titan.cabin.CabinHomeRemote;
import com.titan.cabin.CabinRemote;

import javax.naming.InitialContext;
import javax.naming.Context;
import javax.naming.NamingException;
import java.rmi.RemoteException;
import java.util.Properties;
import javax.rmi.PortableRemoteObject;

public class Client_1 {
    public static void main(String [] args) {
        try {
```

```
            Context jndiContext = getInitialContext();
            Object ref = jndiContext.lookup("CabinHomeRemote");
            CabinHomeRemote home = (CabinHomeRemote)
                PortableRemoteObject.narrow(ref,CabinHomeRemote.class);
            CabinRemote cabin_1 = home.create(new Integer(1));
            cabin_1.setName("Master Suite");
            cabin_1.setDeckLevel(1);
            cabin_1.setShipId(1);
            cabin_1.setBedCount(3);

            Integer pk = new Integer(1);

            CabinRemote cabin_2 = home.findByPrimaryKey(pk);
            System.out.println(cabin_2.getName());
            System.out.println(cabin_2.getDeckLevel());
            System.out.println(cabin_2.getShipId());
            System.out.println(cabin_2.getBedCount());

        } catch (java.rmi.RemoteException re){re.printStackTrace();}
        catch (javax.naming.NamingException ne){ne.printStackTrace();}
        catch (javax.ejb.CreateException ce){ce.printStackTrace();}
        catch (javax.ejb.FinderException fe){fe.printStackTrace();}
    }

    public static Context getInitialContext()
        throws javax.naming.NamingException {

        Properties p = new Properties();
        // ... Specify the JNDI properties specific to the vendor.
        return new javax.naming.InitialContext(p);
    }
}
```

To access an enterprise bean, a client starts by using the JNDI package to obtain a directory connection to a bean's container. JNDI is an implementation-independent API for directory and naming systems. Every EJB vendor must provide directory service that is JNDI-compliant. This means that they must provide a JNDI service provider, which is a piece of software analogous to a driver in JDBC. Different service providers connect to different directory services—not unlike JDBC, where different drivers connect to different relational databases. The getInitialContext() method contains logic that uses JNDI to obtain a network connection to the EJB server.

The code used to obtain the JNDI Context differs depending on which EJB vendor you use. Consult your vendor's documentation to find out how to obtain a JNDI Context appropriate to your product. For example, the code used to obtain a JNDI Context in WebSphere might look something like the following:

```
    public static Context getInitialContext()
        throws javax.naming.NamingException {

        java.util.Properties properties = new java.util.Properties();
        properties.put(javax.naming.Context.PROVIDER_URL, "iiop:///");
```

```
        properties.put(javax.naming.Context.INITIAL_CONTEXT_FACTORY,
            "com.ibm.ejs.ns.jndi.CNInitialContextFactory");
        return new InitialContext(properties);
    }
```

The same method developed for BEA's WebLogic Server would be different:

```
    public static Context getInitialContext()
        throws javax.naming.NamingException {

        Properties p = new Properties();
        p.put(Context.INITIAL_CONTEXT_FACTORY, "weblogic.jndi.WLInitialContextFactory");
        p.put(Context.PROVIDER_URL, "t3://localhost:7001");
        return new javax.naming.InitialContext(p);
    }
```

Once a JNDI connection is established and a context is obtained from the getInitialContext() method, the context can be used to look up the EJB home of the Cabin EJB.

The Client_1 application uses the PortableRemoteObject.narrow() method:

```
    Object ref = jndiContext.lookup("CabinHome");
    CabinHome home = (CabinHomeRemote)
        PortableRemoteObject.narrow(ref,CabinHomeRemote.class);
```

The PortableRemoteObject.narrow() method was first introduced in EJB 1.1 and continues to be used on remote clients in EJB 2.0. It is needed to support the requirements of RMI over IIOP. Because CORBA supports many different languages, casting is not native to CORBA (some languages don't have casting). Therefore, to get a remote reference to CabinHomeRemote, we must explicitly narrow the object returned from lookup(). This has the same effect as casting and is explained in more detail in Chapter 5.

The name used to find the Cabin EJB's EJB home is set by the deployer using a deployment wizard like the one pictured earlier. The JNDI name is entirely up to the person deploying the bean; it can be the same as the bean name set in the XML deployment descriptor or something completely different.

Creating a new Cabin EJB

Once we have a remote reference to the EJB home, we can use it to create a new Cabin entity:

```
    CabinRemote cabin_1 = home.create(new Integer(1));
```

We create a new Cabin entity using the create(Integer id) method defined in the remote home interface of the Cabin EJB. When this method is invoked, the EJB home works with the EJB server to create a Cabin EJB, adding its data to the database. The EJB server then creates an EJB object to wrap the Cabin EJB instance and returns a remote reference to the EJB object to the client. The cabin_1 variable then contains a remote reference to the Cabin EJB we just created.

We don't need to use the PortableRemoteObject.narrow() method to get the EJB object from the home reference, because it was declared as returning the CabinRemote type; no casting was required. We don't need to explicitly narrow remote references returned by findByPrimaryKey() for the same reason.

With the remote reference to the EJB object, we can update the name, deckLevel, shipId, and bedCount of the Cabin EJB:

```
CabinRemote cabin_1 = home.create(new Integer(1));
cabin_1.setName("Master Suite");
cabin_1.setDeckLevel(1);
cabin_1.setShipId(1);
cabin_1.setBedCount(3);
```

Figure 4-4 shows how the relational database table we created should look after executing this code. It should contain one record.

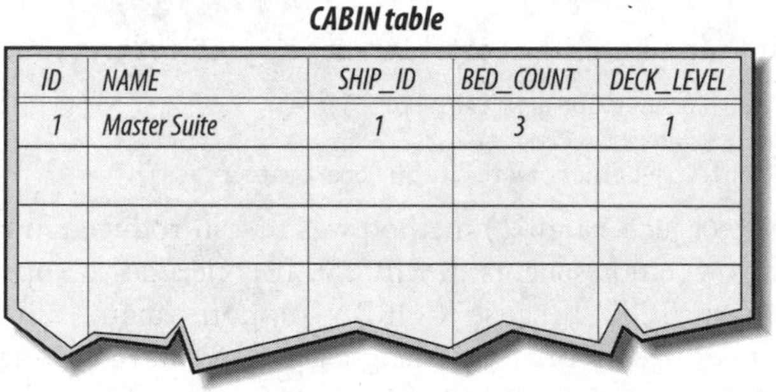

CABIN table

ID	NAME	SHIP_ID	BED_COUNT	DECK_LEVEL
1	Master Suite	1	3	1

Figure 4-4. CABIN table with one cabin record

After an entity bean has been created, a client can locate it using the findByPrimaryKey() method in the home interface. First, we create a primary key of the correct type—in this case, Integer. When we invoke the finder method on the home interface using the primary key, we get back a remote reference to the EJB object. We can now interrogate the remote reference returned by findByPrimaryKey() to get the Cabin EJB's name, deckLevel, shipId, and bedCount:

```
Integer pk = new Integer(1);

CabinRemote cabin_2 = home.findByPrimaryKey(pk);
System.out.println(cabin_2.getName());
System.out.println(cabin_2.getDeckLevel());
System.out.println(cabin_2.getShipId());
System.out.println(cabin_2.getBedCount());
```

You are now ready to create and run the Client_1 application against the Cabin EJB you deployed earlier. Compile the client application and deploy the Cabin EJB into the container system. Then run the Client_1 application.

📖 Workbook Exercise 4.1, A Simple Entity Bean

When you run the `Client_1` application, your output should look something like the following:

```
Master Suite
1
1
3
```

Congratulations! You just created and used your first entity bean. Of course, the client application doesn't do much. Before going on to create session beans, create another client that adds some test data to the database. Here we'll create `Client_2`, as a modification of `Client_1` that populates the database with a large number of cabins for three different ships:

```
package com.titan.cabin;

import com.titan.cabin.CabinHomeRemote;
import com.titan.cabin.CabinRemote;

import javax.naming.InitialContext;
import javax.naming.Context;
import javax.naming.NamingException;
import javax.ejb.CreateException;
import java.rmi.RemoteException;
import java.util.Properties;
import javax.rmi.PortableRemoteObject;

public class Client_2 {

    public static void main(String [] args) {
        try {
            Context jndiContext = getInitialContext();

            Object ref = jndiContext.lookup("CabinHomeRemote");
            CabinHomeRemote home = (CabinHomeRemote)
                PortableRemoteObject.narrow(ref,CabinHomeRemote.class);
            // Add 9 cabins to deck 1 of ship 1.
            makeCabins(home, 2, 10, 1, 1);
            // Add 10 cabins to deck 2 of ship 1.
            makeCabins(home, 11, 20, 2, 1);
            // Add 10 cabins to deck 3 of ship 1.
            makeCabins(home, 21, 30, 3, 1);

            // Add 10 cabins to deck 1 of ship 2.
            makeCabins(home, 31, 40, 1, 2);
            // Add 10 cabins to deck 2 of ship 2.
            makeCabins(home, 41, 50, 2, 2);
            // Add 10 cabins to deck 3 of ship 2.
            makeCabins(home, 51, 60, 3, 2);

            // Add 10 cabins to deck 1 of ship 3.
            makeCabins(home, 61, 70, 1, 3);
            // Add 10 cabins to deck 2 of ship 3.
```

```
                makeCabins(home, 71, 80, 2, 3);
                // Add 10 cabins to deck 3 of ship 3.
                makeCabins(home, 81, 90, 3, 3);
                // Add 10 cabins to deck 4 of ship 3.
                makeCabins(home, 91, 100, 4, 3);

                for (int i = 1; i <= 100; i++){
                    Integer pk = new Integer(i);
                    CabinRemote cabin = home.findByPrimaryKey(pk);
                    System.out.println("PK = "+i+", Ship = "+cabin.getShipId()
                        + ", Deck = "+cabin.getDeckLevel()
                        + ", BedCount = "+cabin.getBedCount()
                        + ", Name = "+cabin.getName());
                }

            } catch (java.rmi.RemoteException re) {re.printStackTrace();}
              catch (javax.naming.NamingException ne) {ne.printStackTrace();}
              catch (javax.ejb.CreateException ce) {ce.printStackTrace();}
              catch (javax.ejb.FinderException fe) {fe.printStackTrace();}
        }

        public static javax.naming.Context getInitialContext()
            throws javax.naming.NamingException{
        Properties p = new Properties();
        // ... Specify the JNDI properties specific to the vendor.
        return new javax.naming.InitialContext(p);
        }

        public static void makeCabins(CabinHomeRemote home, int fromId,
                                    int toId, int deckLevel, int shipNumber)
            throws RemoteException, CreateException {

        int bc = 3;
        for (int i = fromId; i <= toId; i++) {
            CabinRemote cabin = home.create(new Integer(i));
            int suiteNumber = deckLevel*100+(i-fromId);
            cabin.setName("Suite "+suiteNumber);
            cabin.setDeckLevel(deckLevel);
            bc = (bc==3)?2:3;
            cabin.setBedCount(bc);
            cabin.setShipId(shipNumber);
            }
        }
    }
```

Create and run the Client_2 application against the Cabin EJB you deployed earlier. Client_2 produces a lot of output that lists all the new Cabin EJBs you just added to the database:

```
PK = 1, Ship = 1, Deck = 1, BedCount = 3, Name = Master Suite
PK = 2, Ship = 1, Deck = 1, BedCount = 2, Name = Suite 100
PK = 3, Ship = 1, Deck = 1, BedCount = 3, Name = Suite 101
PK = 4, Ship = 1, Deck = 1, BedCount = 2, Name = Suite 102
```

```
PK = 5, Ship = 1, Deck = 1, BedCount = 3, Name = Suite 103
PK = 6, Ship = 1, Deck = 1, BedCount = 2, Name = Suite 104
PK = 7, Ship = 1, Deck = 1, BedCount = 3, Name = Suite 105
...
```

You now have 100 cabin records in your CABIN table, representing 100 cabin entities in your EJB system. This provides a good set of test data for the session bean we will create in the next section and for subsequent examples throughout the book.

Developing a Session Bean

Session beans act as agents to the client, controlling workflow (the business process) and filling the gaps between the representation of data by entity beans and the business logic that interacts with that data. Session beans are often used to manage interactions between entity beans and can perform complex manipulations of beans to accomplish certain tasks. Since we have defined only one entity bean so far, we will focus on a complex manipulation of the Cabin EJB rather than the interactions of the Cabin EJB with other entity beans. The interactions of entity beans within session beans will be explored in greater detail in Chapter 12.

Client applications and other beans use the Cabin EJB in a variety of ways. Some of these uses were predictable when the Cabin EJB was defined, but many were not. After all, an entity bean represents data—in this case, data describing a cabin. The uses to which we put that data will change over time—hence the importance of separating the data itself from the workflow. In Titan's business system, for example, we may need to list and report on cabins in ways that were not predictable when the Cabin EJB was defined. Rather than change the Cabin EJB every time we need to look at it differently, we will obtain the information we need using a session bean. Changing the definition of an entity bean should be done only within the context of a larger process—for example, a major redesign of the business system.

In Chapters 1 and 2, we talked hypothetically about a TravelAgent EJB that was responsible for the workflow of booking a passage on a cruise. This session bean will be used in client applications accessed by travel agents throughout the world. In addition to booking tickets, the TravelAgent EJB provides information about which cabins are available on the cruise. In this chapter, we will develop the first implementation of this listing behavior in the TravelAgent EJB. The listing method we develop in this example is admittedly very crude and far from optimal. However, this example is useful for demonstrating how to develop a very simple stateless session bean and how these session beans can manage other beans. In Chapter 12, we will rewrite the listing method. The "list cabins" behavior developed here will be used by travel agents to provide customers with a list of cabins that can accommodate their needs. The Cabin EJB does not directly support this kind of list, nor should it. The list we need is specific to the TravelAgent EJB, so it's the TravelAgent EJB's responsibility to query the Cabin EJB and produce the list.

You will need to create a development directory for the TravelAgent EJB, as we did for the Cabin EJB. We will name this directory *travelagent* and nest it below the */dev/com/titan* directory, which also contains the *cabin* directory (see Figure 4-5).

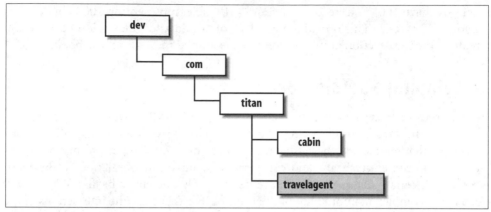

Figure 4-5. Directory structure for the TravelAgent EJB

You will be placing all the Java files and the XML deployment descriptor for the TravelAgent EJB into this directory.

TravelAgentRemote: The Remote Interface

As before, we start by defining the remote interface so that our focus is on the business purpose of the bean, rather than its implementation. Starting small, we know that the TravelAgent EJB will need to provide a method for listing all the cabins available with a specified bed count for a specific ship. We'll call that method listCabins(). Since we need only a list of cabin names and deck levels, we'll define listCabins() to return an array of Strings. Here's the remote interface for TravelAgentRemote:

```
package com.titan.travelagent;

import java.rmi.RemoteException;
import javax.ejb.FinderException;

public interface TravelAgentRemote extends javax.ejb.EJBObject {

    // String elements follow the format "id, name, deck level"
    public String [] listCabins(int shipID, int bedCount)
        throws RemoteException;
}
```

TravelAgentHomeRemote: The Remote Home Interface

The second step in the development of the TravelAgent EJB bean is to create the remote home interface. The remote home interface for a session bean defines the create methods that initialize a new session bean for use by a client.

Find methods are not used in session beans; they are used with entity beans to locate persistent entities for use on a client. Unlike entity beans, session beans are not persistent and do not represent data in the database, so a find method would not be meaningful; there is no specific session to locate. A session bean is dedicated to a client for the life of that client (or less). For the same reason, we don't need to worry about primary keys—since session beans don't represent persistent data, we don't need a key to access that data.

```
package com.titan.travelagent;

import java.rmi.RemoteException;
import javax.ejb.CreateException;

public interface TravelAgentHomeRemote extends javax.ejb.EJBHome {
    public TravelAgentRemote create()
        throws RemoteException, CreateException;
}
```

In the case of the TravelAgent EJB, we need only a simple create() method to get a reference to the bean. Invoking this create() method returns the TravelAgent EJB's remote reference, which the client can use for the reservation process.

TravelAgentBean: The Bean Class

Using the remote interface as a guide, we can define the TravelAgentBean class that implements the listCabins() method. The following code contains the complete definition of TravelAgentBean for this example:

```
package com.titan.travelagent;

import com.titan.cabin.CabinRemote;
import com.titan.cabin.CabinHomeRemote;
import java.rmi.RemoteException;
import javax.naming.InitialContext;
import javax.naming.Context;
import java.util.Properties;
import java.util.Vector;
import javax.rmi.PortableRemoteObject;
import javax.ejb.EJBException;


public class TravelAgentBean implements javax.ejb.SessionBean {

    public void ejbCreate() {
    // Do nothing.
    }
    public String [] listCabins(int shipID, int bedCount) {

        try {
            javax.naming.Context jndiContext = new InitialContext();
            Object obj = jndiContext.lookup("java:comp/env/ejb/CabinHomeRemote");
```

```
        CabinHomeRemote home = (CabinHomeRemote)
            PortableRemoteObject.narrow(obj,CabinHomeRemote.class);

        Vector vect = new Vector();
        for (int i = 1; ; i++) {
            Integer pk = new Integer(i);
            CabinRemote cabin;
            try {
                cabin = home.findByPrimaryKey(pk);
            } catch(javax.ejb.FinderException fe) {
                break;
            }
            // Check to see if the bed count and ship ID match.
            if (cabin.getShipId() == shipID &&
                cabin.getBedCount() == bedCount) {
                String details = i+","+cabin.getName()+","+cabin.getDeckLevel();
                vect.addElement(details);
            }
        }

        String [] list = new String[vect.size()];
        vect.copyInto(list);
        return list;

    } catch(Exception e) {throw new EJBException(e);}
}

private javax.naming.Context getInitialContext()
    throws javax.naming.NamingException {
    Properties p = new Properties();
    // ... Specify the JNDI properties specific to the vendor.
    return new javax.naming.InitialContext(p);
}

public void ejbRemove(){}
public void ejbActivate(){}
public void ejbPassivate(){}
public void setSessionContext(javax.ejb.SessionContext cntx){}
}
```

Examining the listCabins() method in detail, we can address the implementation in pieces, starting with the use of JNDI to locate the CabinHomeRemote:

```
javax.naming.Context jndiContext = new InitialContext();

Object obj = jndiContext.lookup("java:comp/env/ejb/CabinHomeRemote");

CabinHomeRemote home = (CabinHomeRemote)
    javax.rmi.PortableRemoteObject.narrow(obj, CabinHomeRemote.class);
```

Beans are clients to other beans, just like client applications. This means that they must interact with other beans in the same way that client applications interact with beans. In order for one bean to locate and use another bean, it must first locate and obtain a reference to the bean's EJB home. This is accomplished using JNDI in exactly the same way we used JNDI to obtain a reference to the Cabin EJB in the `Client_1` and `Client_2` applications we developed earlier.

All beans have a default JNDI context called the environment naming context, which was discussed briefly in Chapter 3. The default context exists in the name space (directory) called `"java:comp/env"` and its subdirectories. When the bean is deployed, any beans it uses are mapped into the subdirectory `"java:comp/env/ejb"`, so that bean references can be obtained at runtime through a simple and consistent use of the JNDI default context. We'll come back to this shortly when we take a look at the deployment descriptor for the TravelAgent EJB.

As you learned in Chapter 2, enterprise beans in EJB 2.0 may have remote and/or local component interfaces. However, to keep things simple with this first set of examples, we are working with only the remote component interfaces—Chapter 5 will explain how this example may have been implemented with local interfaces.

Once the remote EJB home of the Cabin EJB is obtained, we can use it to produce a list of cabins that match the parameters passed. The following code loops through all the Cabin EJBs and produces a list that includes only those cabins with the ship and bed count specified:

```
Vector vect = new Vector();
for (int i = 1; ; i++) {
    Integer pk = new Integer(i);
    CabinRemote cabin;
    try {
        cabin = home.findByPrimaryKey(pk);
    } catch(javax.ejb.FinderException fe){
        break;
    }
    // Check to see if the bed count and ship ID match.
    if (cabin.getShipId() == shipID && cabin.getBedCount() == bedCount) {
        String details = i+","+cabin.getName()+","+cabin.getDeckLevel();
        vect.addElement(details);
    }
}
```

This method simply iterates through all the primary keys, obtaining a remote reference to each Cabin EJB in the system and checking whether its `shipId` and `bedCount` match the parameters passed. The `for` loop continues until a `FinderException` is thrown, which will probably occur when a primary key that isn't associated with a bean is used. (This isn't the most robust code possible, but it will do for now.) Following this block of code, we simply copy the `Vector`'s contents into an array and return it to the client.

While this is a very crude approach to locating the right Cabin EJBs—we will define a better method in Chapter 12—it is adequate for our current purposes. The purpose of this example is to illustrate that the workflow associated with this listing behavior is not included in the Cabin EJB, nor is it embedded in a client application. Workflow logic, whether it's a process like booking a reservation or obtaining a list, is placed in a session bean.

The TravelAgent EJB's Deployment Descriptor

The TravelAgent EJB uses an XML deployment descriptor similar to the one used for the Cabin entity bean. The following sections contain the *ejb-jar.xml* file used to deploy the TravelAgent bean in EJB 2.0 and 1.1, respectively. In Chapter 12, you will learn how to deploy several beans in one deployment descriptor, but for now the TravelAgent and Cabin EJBs are deployed separately.

EJB 2.0: Deployment descriptor

In EJB 2.0, the deployment descriptor for the TravelAgent EJB looks like this:

```
<!DOCTYPE ejb-jar PUBLIC "-//Sun Microsystems, Inc.//DTD Enterprise
JavaBeans 2.0//EN" "http://java.sun.com/dtd/ejb-jar_2_0.dtd">
<ejb-jar>
    <enterprise-beans>
        <session>
            <ejb-name>TravelAgentEJB</ejb-name>
            <home>com.titan.travelagent.TravelAgentHomeRemote</home>
            <remote>com.titan.travelagent.TravelAgentRemote</remote>
            <ejb-class>com.titan.travelagent.TravelAgentBean</ejb-class>
            <session-type>Stateless</session-type>
            <transaction-type>Container</transaction-type>
            <ejb-ref>
                <ejb-ref-name>ejb/CabinHomeRemote</ejb-ref-name>
                <ejb-ref-type>Entity</ejb-ref-type>
                <home>com.titan.cabin.CabinHomeRemote</home>
                <remote>com.titan.cabin.CabinRemote</remote>
            </ejb-ref>
            <security-identity><use-caller-identity/></security-identity>
        </session>
    </enterprise-beans>
    <assembly-descriptor>
    ...
    </assembly-descriptor>
</ejb-jar>
```

EJB 1.1: Deployment descriptor

In EJB 1.1, the TravelAgent EJB's deployment descriptor looks like this:

```
<!DOCTYPE ejb-jar PUBLIC "-//Sun Microsystems, Inc.//DTD Enterprise
JavaBeans 1.1//EN" "http://java.sun.com/j2ee/dtds/ejb-jar_1_1.dtd">
<ejb-jar>
    <enterprise-beans>
        <session>
            <ejb-name>TravelAgentEJB</ejb-name>
            <home>com.titan.travelagent.TravelAgentHomeRemote</home>
```

```
            <remote>com.titan.travelagent.TravelAgentRemote</remote>
            <ejb-class>com.titan.travelagent.TravelAgentBean</ejb-class>
            <session-type>Stateless</session-type>
            <transaction-type>Container</transaction-type>
            <ejb-ref>
                <ejb-ref-name>ejb/CabinHome</ejb-ref-name>
                <ejb-ref-type>Entity</ejb-ref-type>
                <home>com.titan.cabin.CabinHomeRemote</home>
                <remote>com.titan.cabin.CabinRemote</remote>
            </ejb-ref>
        </session>
    </enterprise-beans>
    <assembly-descriptor>
    ...
    </assembly-descriptor>
</ejb-jar>
```

EJB 2.0 and 1.1: Defining the XML elements

The only significant difference between the 2.0 and 1.1 deployment descriptors is the name of the DTD and the addition of a <security-identity> element in EJB 2.0, which simply propagates the caller's identity.

Other than the <session-type> and <ejb-ref> elements, the TravelAgent EJB's XML deployment descriptor should be familiar: it uses many of the same elements as the Cabin EJB's. The <session-type> element can be Stateful or Stateless, to indicate which type of session bean is used. In this case we are defining a stateless session bean.

The <ejb-ref> element is used at deployment time to map the bean references used within the TravelAgent EJB. In this case, the <ejb-ref> element describes the Cabin EJB, which we already deployed. The <ejb-ref-name> element specifies the name that must be used by the TravelAgent EJB to obtain a reference to the Cabin EJB's home. The <ejb-ref-type> tells the container what kind of bean it is, Entity or Session. The <home> and <remote> elements specify the fully qualified interface names of the Cabin's home and remote bean interfaces.

When the bean is deployed, the <ejb-ref> will be mapped to the Cabin EJB in the EJB server. This is a vendor-specific process, but the outcome should always be the same. When the TravelAgent EJB does a JNDI lookup using the context name "java: comp/env/ejb/CabinHomeRemote", it will obtain a remote reference to the Cabin EJB's home. The purpose of the <ejb-ref> element is to eliminate network specific and implementation specific use of JNDI to obtain remote bean references. This makes a bean more portable, because the network location and JNDI service provider can change without impacting the bean code or even the XML deployment descriptor.

However, as you will learn in Chapter 5, with EJB 2.0 it's always preferable to use local references instead of remote references when beans access each other within the same server. Local references are specified using the <ejb-local-ref> element, which looks just like the <ejb-ref> element.

The `<assembly-descriptor>` section of the deployment descriptor is the same for both EJB 2.0 and EJB 1.1:

```
<assembly-descriptor>
    <security-role>
        <description>
            This role represents everyone who is allowed full access
            to the Cabin EJB.
        </description>
        <role-name>everyone</role-name>
    </security-role>

    <method-permission>
        <role-name>everyone</role-name>
        <method>
            <ejb-name>TravelAgentEJB</ejb-name>
            <method-name>*</method-name>
        </method>
    </method-permission>

    <container-transaction>
        <method>
            <ejb-name>TravelAgentEJB</ejb-name>
            <method-name>*</method-name>
        </method>
        <trans-attribute>Required</trans-attribute>
    </container-transaction>
</assembly-descriptor>
```

Deploying the TravelAgent EJB

Once you've defined the XML deployment descriptor, you are ready to place the TravelAgent EJB in its own JAR file and deploy it into the EJB server.

To make your TravelAgent EJB available to a client application, you need to use the deployment utility or wizard of your EJB server. The deployment utility reads the JAR file to add the TravelAgent EJB to the EJB server environment. Unless your EJB server has special requirements, it is unlikely that you will need to change or add any new attributes to the bean. You will not need to create a database table for this example, since the TravelAgent EJB is using the Cabin EJB and is not itself persistent. However, you will need to map the `<ejb-ref>` element in the TravelAgent EJB's deployment descriptor to the Cabin EJB. You EJB server's deployment tool will provide a mechanism for doing this. Deploy the TravelAgent EJB and proceed to the next section.

Use the same process to JAR the TravelAgent EJB as was used for the Cabin EJB. Shrink-wrap the TravelAgent EJB class and its deployment descriptor into a JAR file and save the file to the *com/titan/travelagent* directory:

```
\dev % jar cf cabin.jar com/titan/travelagent/*.class META-INF/ejb-jar.xml

F:\..\dev>jar cf cabin.jar com\titan\travelagent\*.class META-INF\ejb-jar.xml
```

You might have to create the *META-INF* directory first, and copy *ejb-jar.xml* into that directory. The TravelAgent EJB is now complete and ready to be deployed. Next, use your EJB container's proprietary tools to deploy the TravelAgent EJB into the container system.

Creating a Client Application

To show that our session bean works, we'll create a simple client application that uses it. This client simply produces a list of cabins assigned to ship 1 with a bed count of 3. Its logic is similar to the client we created earlier to test the Cabin EJB: it creates a context for looking up TravelAgentHomeRemote, creates a TravelAgent EJB, and invokes listCabins() to generate a list of the cabins available. Here's the code:

```
import com.titan.cabin.CabinHomeRemote;
import com.titan.cabin.CabinRemote;

import javax.naming.InitialContext;
import javax.naming.Context;
import javax.naming.NamingException;
import javax.ejb.CreateException;
import java.rmi.RemoteException;
import java.util.Properties;
import javax.rmi.PortableRemoteObject;

public class Client_3 {
    public static int SHIP_ID = 1;
    public static int BED_COUNT = 3;

    public static void main(String [] args) {
        try {
            Context jndiContext = getInitialContext();

            Object ref = jndiContext.lookup("TravelAgentHomeRemote");
            TravelAgentHomeRemote home = (TravelAgentHomeRemote)
                PortableRemoteObject.narrow(ref,TravelAgentHomeRemote.class);

            TravelAgentRemote travelAgent = home.create();

            // Get a list of all cabins on ship 1 with a bed count of 3.
            String list [] = travelAgent.listCabins(SHIP_ID,BED_COUNT);

            for(int i = 0; i < list.length; i++){
                System.out.println(list[i]);
            }

        } catch(java.rmi.RemoteException re){re.printStackTrace();}
            catch(Throwable t){t.printStackTrace();}
    }
    static public Context getInitialContext() throws Exception {
        Properties p = new Properties();
        // ... Specify the JNDI properties specific to the vendor.
```

```
        return new InitialContext(p);
    }
}
```

When you have successfully run Client_3, the output should look like this:

```
1,Master Suite          ,1
3,Suite 101             ,1
5,Suite 103             ,1
7,Suite 105             ,1
9,Suite 107             ,1
12,Suite 201             ,2
14,Suite 203             ,2
16,Suite 205             ,2
18,Suite 207             ,2
20,Suite 209             ,2
22,Suite 301             ,3
24,Suite 303             ,3
26,Suite 305             ,3
28,Suite 307             ,3
30,Suite 309             ,3
```

You have now successfully created the first piece of the TravelAgent session bean—a method that obtains a list of cabins by manipulating the Cabin EJB entity.

📖 Workbook Exercise 4.2, A Simple Session Bean

CHAPTER 5

The Client View

Developing the Cabin EJB and the TravelAgent EJB should have raised your confidence, but it also should have raised a lot of questions. So far, we have glossed over most of the details involved in developing, deploying, and accessing these enterprise beans. In this chapter and the ones that follow, we will slowly peel away the layers of the Enterprise JavaBeans onion to expose the details of EJB application development.

This chapter focuses specifically on the client's view of entity and session beans. Message-driven beans are not covered in this chapter—they are covered in detail in Chapter 13. The client, whether it is an application or another enterprise bean, doesn't work directly with the beans in the EJB system. Instead, clients interact with a set of interfaces that provide access to beans and their business logic. These interfaces consist of the JNDI API and an EJB client-side API. JNDI allows us to find and access enterprise beans regardless of their location on the network; the EJB client-side API is the set of interfaces and classes developers use on the client to interact with enterprise beans.

The best approach to this chapter is to read about several features of the client view and then follow the workbook examples to see those features in action. This will provide you with hands-on experience and a much clearer understanding of the concepts. Have fun, experiment, and you'll be sure to understand the fundamentals.

Locating Beans with JNDI

In Chapter 4, the client application started by creating an InitialContext, which it then used to get a remote reference to the homes of the Cabin and TravelAgent EJBs. The InitialContext is part of a larger API called the Java Naming and Directory Interface (JNDI). We use JNDI to look up an EJB home in an EJB server just like you might use a phone book to find the home number of a friend or business associate.

JNDI is a standard Java optional package that provides a uniform API for accessing a wide range of services. In this respect, it is somewhat similar to JDBC, which provides uniform access to different relational databases. Just as JDBC lets you write code that doesn't care whether it's talking to an Oracle database or a Sybase database, JNDI lets you write code that can access different directory and naming services, such as LDAP, Novell NetWare NDS, Sun Solaris NIS+, CORBA Naming Service, and the naming services provided by EJB servers. EJB servers are required to support JNDI by organizing beans into a directory structure and providing a JNDI driver, called a *service provider*, for accessing that directory structure. Using JNDI, an enterprise can organize its beans, services, data, and other resources in a large virtual-directory structure, which can provide a powerful mechanism for binding together disparate systems.

Two of JNDI's greatest features are that it is virtual and dynamic. JNDI is virtual because it allows one directory service to be linked to another through simple URLs. The URLs in JNDI are analogous to HTML links. Clicking on a link in HTML allows a user to load the contents of a web page. The new web page can be downloaded from the same host as the starting page or from a completely different web site—the location of the linked page is transparent to the user. Likewise, using JNDI, you can drill down through directories to files, printers, EJB home objects, and other resources using links that are similar to HTML links. The directories and subdirectories can be located in the same host or can be physically hosted at different locations. The user doesn't know or care where the directories are actually located. As a developer or administrator, you can create virtual directories that span a variety of services over many different physical locations.

JNDI is dynamic because it allows the JNDI drivers (a.k.a. service providers) for specific types of directory services to be loaded at runtime. A driver maps a specific kind of directory service into the standard JNDI class interfaces. When a link to a different directory service is chosen, the driver for that type of directory service is automatically loaded from the directory's host, if it is not already resident on the user's machine. Automatically downloading JNDI drivers makes it possible for a client to navigate across arbitrary directory services without knowing in advance what kinds of services it is likely to find.

JNDI allows the application client to view the EJB server as a set of directories, like directories in a common filesystem. After the client application locates and obtains a remote reference to the EJB home using JNDI, the client can use the EJB home to obtain an EJB object reference to an enterprise bean. In the TravelAgent EJB and the Cabin EJB with which you worked in Chapter 4, you used the method getInitialContext() to get a JNDI InitialContext object, which looked like this:

```
public static Context getInitialContext()
    throws javax.naming.NamingException {

    Properties p = new Properties();
    // ... Specify the JNDI properties specific to the vendor.
    return new javax.naming.InitialContext(p);
}
```

An *initial context* is the starting point for any JNDI lookup—it's similar in concept to the root of a filesystem. The way you create an initial context is peculiar, but not fundamentally difficult. You start with a properties table of type `Properties`. This is essentially a hash table to which you add various values that determine the kind of initial context you get.

Of course, as mentioned in Chapter 4, this code will change depending on how your EJB vendor has implemented JNDI. For example, with the Pramati Application Server, `getInitialContext()` might look something like this:

```
public static Context getInitialContext() throws Exception {
    Hashtable p = new Hashtable();
    p.put(Context.INITIAL_CONTEXT_FACTORY,
        "com.pramati.naming.client.PramatiClientContextFactory");
    p.put(Context.PROVIDER_URL, "rmi://127.0.0.1:9191");
    return new InitialContext(p);
}
```

For a more detailed explanation of JNDI, see O'Reilly's *Java™ Enterprise in a Nutshell* by David Flanagan, Jim Farley, William Crawford, and Kris Magnusson.

The Remote Client API

Enterprise bean developers are required to provide a bean class, component interfaces, and, for entity beans, a primary key. Only the component interfaces and primary key class are visible to the client; the bean class is not. The component interfaces and primary key contribute to the client-side API in EJB.

In EJB 1.1, all clients, whether they are in the same container system or not, must use the *Remote Client API*, which means they must use the remote interface, the remote home interface, and Java RMI in all their interactions. In EJB 2.0, remote clients still must use the Remote Client API, but enterprise beans that are located in the same EJB container system have the option of using the *Local Client API*. The Local Client API provides local component interfaces and avoids the restrictions and overhead of the Remote Client API.

This section examines in more detail the remote component interfaces and the primary key, as well as other Java types that make up EJB's remote client-side API, which is used in both EJB 2.0 and EJB 1.1. This will provide you with a better understanding of how the remote client-side API is used and its relationship with the bean class on the EJB server. At the end of this chapter, in the section "EJB 2.0: The Local Client API," we will examine the use of local component interfaces for EJB 2.0 readers.

Java RMI-IIOP

Enterprise JavaBeans 2.0 and 1.1 define an enterprise bean's remote interfaces in terms of Java RMI-IIOP, which enforces compliance with CORBA. This means that the underlying protocol used by remote clients to access enterprise beans can be anything the vendor wants as long as it supports the types of interfaces and arguments that are compatible with Java RMI-IIOP. EJB 1.1 required only that the wire protocol used by vendors utilize types that were compatible with Java RMI-IIOP. In other words, the interface types and values used in remote references had to be compliant with the types allowed for Java RMI-IIOP. This ensured that early Java RMI-IIOP adopters were supported and made for a seamless transition for other vendors who wanted to use real Java RMI-IIOP in EJB 2.0. In EJB 2.0, vendors can still offer other Java RMI-IIOP–compatible protocols, but in addition to any proprietary protocols they support, they must also support the CORBA IIOP 1.2 protocol as defined in the CORBA 2.3.1 specification.

To comply with Java RMI-IIOP types, EJB vendors have to restrict the definition of interfaces and arguments to types that map nicely to IIOP 1.2. These restrictions are really not all that bad, and you probably won't even notice them while developing your beans, but it's important to know what they are. The next few sections discuss the Java RMI-IIOP programming model for both EJB 2.0 and EJB 1.1. Note that EJB 2.0's local component interfaces are not Java RMI interfaces and do not have to support IIOP 1.2 or use types compliant with the Java RMI-IIOP protocol.

Java RMI return types, parameters, and exceptions

The supertypes of the remote home interface and remote interface, javax.ejb.EJBHome and javax.ejb.EJBObject, both extend java.rmi.Remote. As Remote interface subtypes, they are expected to adhere to the Java RMI specification for Remote interfaces.

Return types and parameters. The remote component interfaces must follow several guidelines, some of which apply to the return types and parameters that are allowed. There are two kinds of return and parameter types: *declared* types, which are checked by the compiler; and *actual* types, which are checked by the runtime. The types that may be used in Java RMI are actual types. To be compatible with Java RMI, the actual types used in the java.rmi.Remote interfaces must be primitives, String types, java.rmi.Remote types, or serializable types. java.rmi.Remote types and serializable types do not have to explicitly implement java.rmi.Remote and java.io.Serializable. For example, the java.util.Collection type, which does not explicitly extend java.io.Serializable, is a perfectly valid return type for a remote finder method, provided that the concrete class implementing Collection, the actual type, does implement java.io.Serializable.

Java RMI has no special rules regarding declared return types or parameter types. At runtime, a type that is not a java.rmi.Remote type is assumed to be serializable; if it is not, an exception is thrown. The actual type passed cannot be checked by the compiler, it must be checked at runtime.

Here is a list of the types that can be passed as parameters or returned in Java RMI:

Primitives
> byte, boolean, char, short, int, long, double, float

Java serializable types
> Any class that implements or any interface that extends java.io.Serializable

Java RMI remote types
> Any class that implements or any interface that extends java.rmi.Remote

Serializable objects are passed by copy (a.k.a., passed by value), not by reference, which means that changes in a serialized object on one tier are not automatically reflected on the others. Objects that implement Remote, like TravelAgentRemote or CabinRemote, are passed as *remote references*, which are a little different. A remote reference is a Remote interface implemented by a distributed object stub. When a remote reference is passed as a parameter or returned from a method, it is the stub that is serialized and passed by value, not the object server remotely referenced by the stub. In Chapter 12, the home interface for the TravelAgent EJB is modified so that the create() method takes a reference to a Customer EJB as its only argument:

```
public interface TravelAgentHomeRemote extends javax.ejb.EJBHome {
    public TravelAgentRemote create(CustomerRemote customer)
        throws RemoteException, CreateException;
}
```

The customer argument is a remote reference to a Customer EJB that is passed into the create() method. When a remote reference is passed or returned in Enterprise JavaBeans, the EJB object stub is passed by copy. The copy of the EJB object stub points to the same EJB object as the original stub. This results in both the enterprise bean instance and the client having remote references to the same EJB object. Thus, changes made on the client using the remote reference will be reflected when the enterprise bean instance uses the same remote reference. Figures 5-1 and 5-2 show the difference between a serializable object and a remote reference argument in Java RMI.

Exceptions. The Java RMI specification states that every method defined in a Remote interface must throw the java.rmi.RemoteException. The RemoteException is used when problems occur with distributed object communications, such as a network failure or inability to locate the object server. In addition, Remote interface types can throw any application-specific exceptions (exceptions defined by the application developer) that are necessary. The following code shows the remote interface to the TravelAgent EJB discussed in Chapter 2. This remote interface is similar to the one defined in Chapter 4. TravelAgentRemote has several remote methods, including bookPassage(). The bookPassage() method can throw a RemoteException (as required) in addition to an application exception, IncompleteConversationalState:

```
public interface TravelAgentRemote extends javax.ejb.EJBObject {

    public void setCruiseID(int cruise)
        throws RemoteException, FinderException;
```

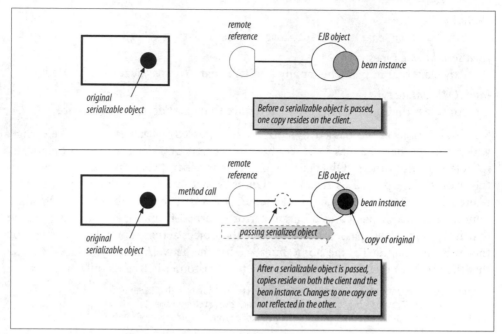

Figure 5-1. Serializable arguments in Java RMI

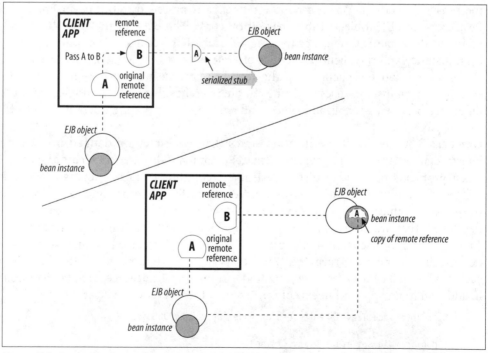

Figure 5-2. Remote reference arguments in Java RMI

```
    public int getCruiseID() throws RemoteException;

    public void setCabinID(int cabin)
        throws RemoteException, FinderException;
    public int getCabinID() throws RemoteException;

    public int getCustomerID() throws RemoteException;

    public Ticket bookPassage(CreditCardRemote card, double price)
        throws RemoteException,IncompleteConversationalState;

    public String [] listAvailableCabins(int bedCount)
        throws RemoteException;

}
```

Java RMI-IIOP type restrictions

In addition to the Java RMI programming model discussed earlier, Java RMI-IIOP imposes additional restrictions on the remote interfaces and value types used in the Remote Client API. These restrictions are born of limitations inherit in the Interface Definition Language (IDL) upon which CORBA IIOP 1.2 is based. The exact nature of these limitations is outside the scope of this book. Here are two of the restrictions; the others, like IDL name collisions, are so rarely encountered that it wouldn't be constructive to mention them:[*]

- Method overloading is restricted; a remote interface may not directly extend two or more interfaces that have methods with the same name (even if their arguments are different). A remote interface may, however, overload its own methods and extend a remote interface with overloaded method names. Overloading is viewed, here, as including overriding. Figure 5-3 illustrates both of these situations.

- Serializable types must not directly or indirectly implement the java.rmi.Remote interface.

Explicit narrowing using PortableRemoteObject

In Java RMI-IIOP, remote references must be explicitly narrowed using the javax.rmi.PortableRemoteObject.narrow() method. The typical practice in Java is to cast the reference to the more specific type:

```
javax.naming.Context jndiContext;
...
CabinHomeRemote home = (CabinHomeRemote)jndiContext.lookup("CabinHomeRemote");
```

---

[*] To learn more about CORBA IDL and its mapping to the Java language, consult "The Common Object Request Broker: Architecture and Specification" and "The Java Language to IDL Mapping," both available at the OMG web site (*http://www.omg.org*).

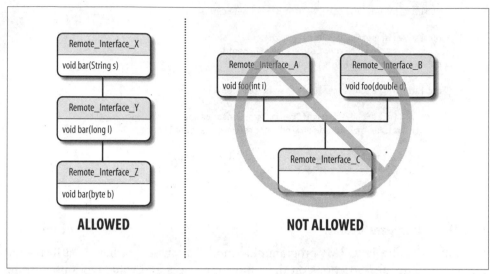

Figure 5-3. Overloading rules for remote interface inheritance in Java RMI-IIOP

The `javax.naming.Context.lookup()` method returns an `Object`. In EJB 2.0's Local Client API, we can assume that it is legal to cast the return argument. However, the Remote Client API must be compatible with Java RMI-IIOP, which means that clients must adhere to limitations imposed by the IIOP 1.2 protocol. To accommodate all languages, many of which have no concept of casting, IIOP 1.2 does not support stubs that implement multiple interfaces. The stub returned in IIOP implements only the interface specified by the return type of the remote method that was invoked. If the return type is `Object`, as is the remote reference returned by the `lookup()` method, the stub will implement only methods specific to the `Object` type.

Of course, some means for converting a remote reference from a more general type to a more specific type is essential in an object-oriented environment, so Java RMI-IIOP provides a mechanism for explicitly narrowing references to a specific type. The `javax.rmi.PortableRemoteObject.narrow()` method abstracts this narrowing to provide narrowing in IIOP as well as other protocols. Remember that while the Remote Client API requires that you use Java RMI-IIOP reference and argument types, the wire protocol need not be IIOP 1.2. Other protocols besides IIOP may also require explicit narrowing. The `PortableRemoteObject` abstracts the narrowing process so that any protocol can be used.

To narrow the return argument of the `Context.lookup()` method to the appropriate type, we must explicitly ask for a remote reference that implements the interface we want:

```
import javax.rmi.PortableRemoteObject;
...
javax.naming.Context jndiContext;
...
```

```
Object ref = jndiContext.lookup("CabinHomeRemote");
CabinHomeRemote home = (CabinHomeRemote)
    PortableRemoteObject.narrow(ref, CabinHomeRemote.class);
```

When the `narrow()` method has successfully executed, it returns a stub that implements the `Remote` interface specified. Because the stub is known to implement the correct type, you can then use Java's native casting to narrow the stub to the correct `Remote` interface. The `narrow()` method takes two arguments: the remote reference that is to be narrowed and the type to which it should be narrowed. The definition of the `narrow()` method is:[*]

```
package javax.rmi;

public class PortableRemoteObject extends java.lang.Object {

    public static java.lang.Object narrow(java.lang.Object narrowFrom,
        java.lang.Class narrowTo)
        throws java.lang.ClassCastException;
    ...
}
```

The `narrow()` method needs to be used only when a remote reference to an EJB home or EJB object is returned without a specific `Remote` interface type. This occurs in six circumstances:

1. When a remote EJB home reference is obtained using the `javax.naming.Context.lookup()` method:

    ```
    Object ref = jndiContext.lookup("CabinHomeRemote");
    CabinHomeRemote home = (CabinHomeRemote)
        PortableRemoteObject.narrow(ref, CabinHomeRemote.class);
    ```

2. When a remote EJB object reference is obtained from a `Collection` or `Enumeration` returned by a remote home interface finder method:

    ```
    ShipHomeRemote shipHome = ... // get ship home
    Enumeration enum = shipHome.findByCapacity(2000);
    while(enum.hasMoreElements()){
        Object ref = enum.nextElement();
        ShipRemote ship = (ShipRemote)
            PortableRemoteObject.narrow(ref, ShipRemote.class);
        // do something with Ship reference
    }
    ```

3. When a remote EJB object reference is obtained using the `javax.ejb.Handle.getEJBObject()` method:

    ```
    Handle handle = .... // get Handle
    Object ref = handle.getEJBObject();
    CabinRemote cabin = (CabinRemote)
    PortableRemoteObject.narrow(ref,CabinRemote.class);
    ```

---

[*] Other methods included in the `PortableRemoteObject` class are not important to EJB application developers. They are intended for Java RMI developers.

4. When a remote EJB home reference is obtained using the javax.ejb.HomeHandle.getEJBHome() method:

```
HomeHandle homeHdle = ... // get home Handle
EJBHome ref = homeHdle.getEJBHome();
CabinHomeRemote home = (CabinHomeRemote)
    PortableRemoteObject.narrow(ref, CabinHomeRemote.class);
```

5. When a remote EJB home reference is obtained using the javax.ejb.EJBMetaData.getEJBHome() method:

```
EJBMetaData metaData = homeHdle.getEJBMetaData();
EJBHome ref = metaData.getEJBHome();
CabinHomeRemote home = (CabinHomeRemote)
    PortableRemoteObject.narrow(ref, CabinHomeRemote.class);
```

6. When a wide remote EJB object type is returned from any business method. Here is a hypothetical example:

```
// Officer extends Crewman
ShipRemote ship = // get Ship remote reference
CrewmanRemote crew = ship.getCrewman("Burns", "John", "1st Lieutenant");
OfficerRemote burns = (OfficerRemote)
    PortableRemoteObject.narrow(crew, OfficerRemote.class);
```

The PortableRemoteObject.narrow() method is not required when the remote type is specified in the method signature. This is true of the create methods and find methods in remote home interfaces that return a single bean. For example, the create() and findByPrimaryKey() methods defined in the CabinHomeRemote interface (Chapter 4) do not require the use of the narrow() method because these methods already return the correct EJB object type. Business methods that return the correct type do not need to use the narrow() method either, as the following code illustrates:

```
/* The CabinHomeRemote.create() method specifies
 * the CabinRemote interface as the return type,
 * so explicit narrowing is not needed.*/
CabinRemote cabin = cabinHome.create(12345);

/* The CabinHomeRemote.findByPrimaryKey() method specifies
 * the CabinRemote interface as the return type,
 * so explicit narrowing is not needed.*/
CabinRemote cabin = cabinHome.findByPrimaryKey(12345);

/* The ShipRemote.getCrewman() business method specifies
 * the CrewmanRemote interface as the return type,
 * so explicit narrowing is not needed.*/
CrewmanRemote crew = ship.getCrewman("Burns", "John", "1st Lieutenant");
```

The Remote Home Interface

The remote home interface provides life-cycle operations and metadata for the bean. When you use JNDI to access a bean, you obtain a remote reference, or stub, to the bean's EJB home, which implements the remote home interface. Every bean type may have one home interface, which extends the javax.ejb.EJBHome interface.

Here is the EJBHome interface:

```
public interface javax.ejb.EJBHome extends java.rmi.Remote {
    public abstract EJBMetaData getEJBMetaData()
        throws RemoteException;
    public HomeHandle getHomeHandle()     // new in 1.1
        throws RemoteException;
    public abstract void remove(Handle handle)
        throws RemoteException, RemoveException;
    public abstract void remove(Object primaryKey)
        throws RemoteException, RemoveException;
}
```

Removing beans

The EJBHome.remove() methods are responsible for deleting an enterprise bean. The argument is either the javax.ejb.Handle of the enterprise bean or, if it's an entity bean, its primary key. The Handle will be discussed in more detail later, but it is essentially a serializable pointer to a specific enterprise bean. When either of the EJBHome.remove() methods are invoked, the remote reference to the enterprise bean on the client becomes invalid: the stub to the enterprise bean that was removed no longer works. If for some reason the enterprise bean can't be removed, a RemoveException is thrown.

The impact of the EJBHome.remove() on the enterprise bean itself depends on the type of bean. For session beans, the EJBHome.remove() methods end the session's service to the client. When EJBHome.remove() is invoked, the remote reference to the session bean becomes invalid, and any conversational state maintained by the session bean is lost. The TravelAgent EJB you created in Chapter 4 is stateless, so no conversational state exists (you'll read more about this in Chapter 12).

When a remove() method is invoked on an entity bean, the remote reference becomes invalid, and any data it represents is actually deleted from the database. This is a far more destructive activity, because once an entity bean is removed, the data it represents no longer exists. The difference between using a remove() method on a session bean and using remove() on an entity bean is similar to the difference between hanging up on a telephone conversation and actually killing the caller on the other end. Both end the conversation, but the methods are a little different.

The following code fragment is taken from the main() method of a client application that is similar to the clients we created to exercise the Cabin and TravelAgent EJBs. It shows that you can remove enterprise beans using a primary key (for entity beans only) or a Handle. Removing an entity bean deletes the entity from the database; removing a session bean results in the remote reference becoming invalid. Here's the code:

```
Context jndiContext = getInitialContext();

// Obtain a list of all the cabins for ship 1 with bed count of 3.

Object ref = jndiContext.lookup("TravelAgentHomeRemote");
```

```
TravelAgentHomeRemote agentHome = (TravelAgentHomeRemote)
    PortableRemoteObject.narrow(ref,TravelAgentHomeRemote.class);

TravelAgentRemote agent = agentHome.create();
String list [] = agent.listCabins(1,3);
System.out.println("1st List: Before deleting cabin number 30");
for(int i = 0; i < list.length; i++){
    System.out.println(list[i]);
}

// Obtain the home and remove cabin 30. Rerun the same cabin list.

ref = jndiContext.lookup("CabinHomeRemote");
CabinHomeRemote c_home = (CabinHomeRemote)
    PortableRemoteObject.narrow(ref, CabinHomeRemote.class);

Integer pk = new Integer(30);
c_home.remove(pk);
list = agent.listCabins(1,3);
System.out.println("2nd List: After deleting cabin number 30");
for (int i = 0; i < list.length; i++) {
    System.out.println(list[i]);
}
```

First, the application creates a list of cabins, including the cabin with the primary key 30. Then it removes the Cabin EJB with this primary key and creates the list again. The second time the iteration is performed, cabin 30 will not be listed; the listCabin() method will be unable to find a cabin with a primary key equal to 30 because the bean and its data are no longer in the database. Your output should look something like this:

```
1st List: Before deleting cabin number 30
1,Master Suite                  ,1
3,Suite 101                     ,1
5,Suite 103                     ,1
7,Suite 105                     ,1
9,Suite 107                     ,1
12,Suite 201                     ,2
14,Suite 203                     ,2
16,Suite 205                     ,2
18,Suite 207                     ,2
20,Suite 209                     ,2
22,Suite 301                     ,3
24,Suite 303                     ,3
26,Suite 305                     ,3
28,Suite 307                     ,3
29,Suite 309                     ,3
30,Suite 309                     ,3
2nd List: After deleting cabin number 30
1,Master Suite                  ,1
3,Suite 101                     ,1
5,Suite 103                     ,1
7,Suite 105                     ,1
9,Suite 107                     ,1
```

```
12,Suite 201                    ,2
14,Suite 203                    ,2
16,Suite 205                    ,2
18,Suite 207                    ,2
20,Suite 209                    ,2
22,Suite 301                    ,3
24,Suite 303                    ,3
26,Suite 305                    ,3
28,Suite 307                    ,3
29,Suite 308                    ,3
```

Bean metadata

EJBHome.getEJBMetaData() returns an instance of javax.ejb.EJBMetaData that describes the remote home interface, remote interface, and primary key classes and indicates whether the enterprise bean is a session or entity bean.* This type of metadata is valuable to Java tools such as IDEs that have wizards or other mechanisms for interacting with an enterprise bean from a client's perspective. A tool could, for example, use the class definitions provided by the EJBMetaData with Java reflection to create an environment in which deployed enterprise beans can be "wired" together by developers. Of course, information such as the JNDI names and URLs of the enterprise beans is also needed.

Most application developers rarely use the EJBMetaData. Knowing that it's there, however, is valuable when you need to create automatic code generators or some other automatic facility. In those cases, familiarity with the Reflection API is necessary.† The following code shows the interface definition for EJBMetaData. Any class that implements the EJBMetaData interface must be serializable; it cannot be a stub to a distributed object. This allows IDEs and other tools to save the EJBMetaData for later use:

```
public interface javax.ejb.EJBMetaData {
    public abstract EJBHome getEJBHome();
    public abstract Class getHomeInterfaceClass();
    public abstract Class getPrimaryKeyClass();
    public abstract Class getRemoteInterfaceClass();
    public abstract boolean isSession();
}
```

The following code shows how the EJBMetaData for the Cabin EJB could be used to get more information about the enterprise bean. Notice that there is no way to get the bean class using the EJBMetaData; the bean class is not part of the client API and therefore doesn't belong to the metadata. Here's the code:

```
Context jndiContext = getInitialContext();

Object ref = jndiContext.lookup("CabinHomeRemote");
```

---

* Message-driven beans in EJB 2.0 don't have component interfaces and can't be accessed by Java RMI-IIOP.

† The Reflection API is outside the scope of this book, but it is covered in *Java™ in a Nutshell*, by David Flanagan (O'Reilly).

```
CabinHomeRemote c_home = (CabinHomeRemote)
    PortableRemoteObject.narrow(ref, CabinHomeRemote.class);

EJBMetaData meta = c_home.getEJBMetaData();

System.out.println(meta.getHomeInterfaceClass().getName());
System.out.println(meta.getRemoteInterfaceClass().getName());
System.out.println(meta.getPrimaryKeyClass().getName());
System.out.println(meta.isSession());
```

This application creates output like the following:

```
com.titan.cabin.CabinHomeRemote
com.titan.cabin.CabinRemote
com.titan.cabin.CabinPK
false
```

In addition to providing the class types of the enterprise bean, the EJBMetaData makes available the remote EJB home for the bean. Once we get the remote EJB home from the EJBMetaData, we can obtain references to the remote EJB object and perform other functions. In the following code, we use the EJBMetaData to get the primary key class, create a key instance, obtain the remote EJB home, and get a remote reference to the EJB object for a specific cabin entity from the EJB home:

```
Object primKeyType = meta.getPrimaryKeyClass();
if(primKeyType instanceof java.lang.Integer){
    Integer pk = new Integer(1);

    Object ref = meta.getEJBHome();
    CabinHomeRemote c_home2 = (CabinHomeRemote)
        PortableRemoteObject.narrow(ref,CabinHomeRemote.class);

    CabinRemote cabin = c_home2.findByPrimaryKey(pk);
    System.out.println(cabin.getName());
}
```

The HomeHandle

The HomeHandle is accessed by calling the EJBHome.getHomeHandle() method. This method returns a javax.ejb.HomeHandle object that provides a serializable reference to an enterprise bean's remote home. The HomeHandle allows a remote home reference to be stored and used later. It is similar to the javax.ejb.Handle and is discussed in more detail a little later.

Creating and finding beans

In addition to the standard javax.ejb.EJBHome methods that all remote home interfaces inherit, remote home interfaces also include special *create* and *find* methods for the bean. We have already talked about create and find methods, but a little review will solidify your understanding of the remote home interface's role in the Remote

Client API. The following code shows the remote home interface defined for the Cabin EJB:

```
public interface CabinHomeRemote extends javax.ejb.EJBHome {
    public CabinRemote create(Integer id)
        throws CreateException, RemoteException;

    public CabinRemote findByPrimaryKey(Integer pk)
        throws FinderException, RemoteException;
}
```

Create methods throw a `CreateException` if something goes wrong during the creation process; find methods throw a `FinderException` if there is an error. Since these methods are defined in an interface that subclasses `Remote`, they must also declare that they throw the `RemoteException`.

The create and find methods are specific to each enterprise bean, so it is up to the bean developer to define the appropriate create and find methods in the remote home interface. `CabinHomeRemote` currently has only one create method, which creates a cabin with a specified ID, and one find method, which looks up an enterprise bean given its primary key. However, it is easy to imagine methods that would create and find a cabin with particular properties—for example, a cabin with three beds, or a deluxe cabin with blue wallpaper.

Only entity beans have find methods; session beans do not. Entity beans represent unique identifiable data within a database and therefore can be found. Session beans, on the other hand, do not represent data: they are created to serve a client application and are not persistent, so there is nothing to find. A find method for a session bean would be meaningless.

In EJB 2.0, the create methods were expanded so that a method name could be used as suffix. In other words, all create methods may take the form create<*SUFFIX*>(). For example, the Customer EJB might define a remote home interface with several create methods, each of which takes a different `String` type parameter but has a different method names:

```
public interface CustomerHome extends javax.ejb.EJBHome {

    public CustomerRemote createWithSSN(Integer id, String socialSecurityNumber)
        throws CreateException, RemoteException;

    public CustomerRemote createWithPIN(Integer personalIdNumber)
        throws CreateException, RemoteException;

    public CustomerRemote createWithBLN(Integer id, String businessLicenseNumber)
        throws CreateException, RemoteException;

    public Customer findByPrimaryKey(Integer id)
        throws FinderException, RemoteException;
}
```

While the use of a suffix in the create method names in EJB 2.0 is allowed, it is not required. EJB 1.1 doesn't support the use of suffixes in create method names.

The create and find methods defined in the remote home interfaces are straightforward and can be easily employed by the client. The create methods on the home interface have to match the ejbCreate() and ejbPostCreate() methods on the bean class. The create(), ejbCreate(), and ejbPostCreate() methods match when they have the same parameters, when the arguments are of the same type and in the same order, and when their method names are the same. This way, when a client calls the create method on the home interface, the call can be delegated to the corresponding ejbCreate() and ejbPostCreate() methods on the bean instance.

The find methods in the home interface work similarly for bean-managed entities in EJB 2.0 and 1.1. Every find<SUFFIX>() method in the home interface must correspond to an ejbFind<SUFFIX>() method in the bean itself. Container-managed entities do not implement ejbFind() methods in the bean class; the EJB container supports find methods automatically. You will discover more about how to implement the ebjCreate(), ejbPostCreate(), and ejbFind() methods in the bean in Chapters 6 through 11.

EJB 2.0: Home methods

In addition to find and create methods, the home interface of EJB 2.0 entity beans may also define *home methods*. The home method is a business method that can be invoked on the home interface (local or remote) and is not specific to one bean instance. For example, the Cabin EJB could define a home method that returns the number of Cabins on a specific deck level:

```
public interface CabinHomeRemote extends javax.ejb.EJBHome {
    public CabinRemote create(Integer id)
        throws CreateException, RemoteException;

    public CabinRemote findByPrimaryKey(Integer pk)
        throws FinderException, RemoteException;

    public int getDeckCount(int level) throws RemoteException;
}
```

Any method defined in the home interface that is not a create or find method is assumed to be a home method and should have a corresponding ejbHome() method in the bean class, as shown here:

```
public class CabinBean implements javax.ejb.EntityBean{
    public int ejbHomeGetDeckCount(int level){
        // implement logic to determine deck count
    }
    ...
}
```

Clients can use home methods from the enterprise bean's home interface. The client does not have to get a reference to a specific EJB object:

```
Object ref = jndiContext.lookup("CabinHome");
CabinHomeRemote home = (CabinHomeRemote)
    PortableRemoteObject.narrow(ref, CabinHomeRemote.class);

int count = home.getDeckCount(2);
```

Home methods are only available to entity beans and not session beans. They can be used for generic business logic that applies changes across a group of entity beans or obtains information that is not specific to any one entity bean. Home methods are discussed in more detail in Chapter 11.

The Remote Interface

The business methods of an enterprise bean can be defined by the remote interface provided by the enterprise bean developer. The javax.ejb.EJBObject interface, which extends the java.rmi.Remote interface, is the base class for all remote interfaces.

The following code is the remote interface for the TravelAgent bean we developed in Chapter 4:

```
public interface TravelAgentRemote extends javax.ejb.EJBObject {

    public String [] listCabins(int shipID, int bedCount)
        throws RemoteException;
}
```

Figure 5-4 shows the TravelAgentRemote interface's inheritance hierarchy.

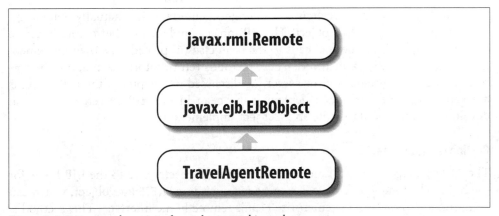

Figure 5-4. Enterprise bean interface inheritance hierarchy

Remote interfaces are focused on the business problem and do not include methods for system-level operations such as persistence, security, concurrency, or transactions.

System-level operations are handled by the EJB server, which relieves the client developer of many responsibilities. All remote interface methods for beans must throw, at the very least, a java.rmi.RemoteException, which identifies problems with distributed communications. In addition, methods in the remote interface can throw as many custom exceptions as needed to indicate abnormal business-related conditions or errors in executing the business method. You will learn more about defining custom exceptions in Chapters 12 and 14.

📖 Workbook Exercise 5.1, The Remote Component Interfaces

EJBObject, Handle, and Primary Key

All remote interfaces extend the javax.ejb.EJBObject interface, which provides a set of utility methods and return types. These methods and return types are valuable in managing the client's interactions with beans. Here is the definition for the EJBObject interface:

```
public interface javax.ejb.EJBObject extends java.rmi.Remote {
    public abstract EJBHome getEJBHome()
        throws RemoteException;
    public abstract Handle getHandle()
        throws RemoteException;
    public abstract Object getPrimaryKey()
        throws RemoteException;
    public abstract boolean isIdentical(EJBObject obj)
        throws RemoteException;
    public abstract void remove()
        throws RemoteException, RemoveException;
}
```

When the client obtains a reference to the remote interface, it is actually obtaining a remote reference to an EJB object. The EJB object implements the remote interface by delegating business method calls to the bean class; it provides its own implementations for the EJBObject methods. These methods return information about the corresponding bean instance on the server. As discussed in Chapter 2, the EJB object is automatically generated when deploying the bean in the EJB server, so the bean developer doesn't need to write an EJBObject implementation.

Getting the EJBHome

The EJBObject.getEJBHome() method returns a remote reference to the EJB home for the bean. The remote reference is returned as a javax.ejb.EJBHome object, which can be narrowed to the specific enterprise bean's remote home interface. This method is useful when an EJB object has left the scope of the remote EJB home that manufactured it. Because remote references can be passed as references and returned from methods, like any other Java object, a remote reference can quickly find itself in a completely different part of the application from its remote home. The following code is contrived, but it illustrates how a remote reference can move out of the scope of its home and how getEJBHome() can be used to get a new reference to the EJB home at any time:

```
public static void main(String [] args) {
    try {
        Context jndiContext = getInitialContext();
        Object ref = jndiContext.lookup("TravelAgentHomeRemote");
        TravelAgentHomeRemote home = (TravelAgentHomeRemote)
            PortableRemoteObject.narrow(ref,TravelAgentHomeRemote.class);

        // Get a remote reference to the bean (EJB object).
        TravelAgentRemote agent = home.create();
        // Pass the remote reference to some method.
        getTheEJBHome(agent);

    } catch (java.rmi.RemoteException re){re.printStackTrace();}
      catch (Throwable t){t.printStackTrace();}
}

public static void getTheEJBHome(TravelAgentRemote agent)
    throws RemoteException {

    // The home interface is out of scope in this method,
    // so it must be obtained from the EJB object.
    Object ref = agent.getEJBHome();
    TravelAgentHomeRemote home = (TravelAgentHomeRemote)
        PortableRemoteObject.narrow(ref,TravelAgentHomeRemote.class);
    // Do something useful with the home interface.
}
```

Primary key

EJBObject.getPrimaryKey() returns the primary key for an entity bean. This method is supported only by EJB objects that represent entity beans. Entity beans represent specific data that can be identified using this primary key. Session beans represent tasks or processes, not data, so primary keys are meaningless for this type of bean. To better understand the nature of a primary key, we need to look beyond the boundaries of the client's view into the EJB container's layer, which was introduced in Chapters 2 and 3.

The EJB container is responsible for the persistence of entity beans, but the exact mechanism for persistence is up to the vendor. To locate an instance of a bean in a persistent store, the data that makes up the entity must be mapped to some kind of unique key. In relational databases, data is uniquely identified by one or more column values that can be combined to form a primary key. In an object-oriented database, the key wraps an object ID (OID) or some kind of database pointer. Regardless of the mechanism—which isn't really relevant from the client's perspective—the unique key for an entity bean's data is encapsulated by the primary key, which is returned by the EJBObject.getPrimaryKey() method.

The primary key can be used to obtain remote references to entity beans using the findByPrimaryKey() method. From the client's perspective, the primary key object can be used to identify a unique entity bean. Understanding the context of a primary key's uniqueness is important, as the following code shows:

```
Context jndiContext = getInitialContext();

Object ref = jndiContext.lookup("CabinHomeRemote");
CabinHomeRemote home = (CabinHomeRemote)
    PortableRemoteObject.narrow(ref,CabinHomeRemote.class);

CabinRemote cabin_1 = home.create(101);
Integer pk = (Integer)cabin_1.getPrimaryKey();
CabinRemote cabin_2 = home.findByPrimaryKey(pk);
```

In this code, the client creates a Cabin EJB, retrieves its primary key, and then uses the key to get a new reference to the same Cabin EJB. Thus, we have two variables, cabin_1 and cabin_2, which are remote references to EJB objects. These both reference the same Cabin bean, with the same underlying data, because they have the same primary key.

The primary key must be used for the correct bean in the correct container. While this seems fairly obvious, the primary key's relationship to a specific container and home interface is important. The primary key can be guaranteed to return the same entity only if it is used within the container that produced the key. As an example, imagine that a third-party vendor sells the Cabin EJB as a product. The vendor sells the Cabin EJB to both Titan and a competitor. Both companies deploy the entity bean using their own relational databases with their own data. An Integer primary key with value of 20 in Titan's EJB system will not map to the same Cabin entity in the competitor's EJB system. Both cruise companies have a Cabin bean with a primary key equal to 20, but they represent different cabins for different ships. The Cabin EJBs come from different EJB containers, so their primary keys are not equivalent.[*] Every entity EJB object has a unique identity within its EJB home. If two EJB objects have the same home and same primary key, they are considered identical.

A primary key must implement the java.io.Serializable interface. This means that the primary key, regardless of its form, can be obtained from an EJB object, stored on the client using the Java serialization mechanism, and deserialized when needed. When a primary key is deserialized, it can be used to obtain a remote reference to the same entity bean using findByPrimaryKey(), provided that the key is used on the right remote home interface and container. Preserving the primary key using serialization might be useful if the client application needs to access specific entity beans at a later date.

---

[*] This is, of course, not true if both Cabin EJBs use the same database, which is common in a clustered scenario.

The following code shows a primary key that is serialized and then deserialized to reobtain a remote reference to the same bean:

```
// Obtain cabin 101 and set its name.
Context jndiContext = getInitialContext();

Object ref = jndiContext.lookup("CabinHomeRemote");
CabinHomeRemote home = (CabinHomeRemote)
    PortableRemoteObject.narrow(ref, CabinHomeRemote.class);

Integer pk_1 = new Integer(101);
CabinRemote cabin_1 = home.findByPrimaryKey(pk_1);
cabin_1.setName("Presidential Suite");

// Serialize the primary key for cabin 101 to a file.
FileOutputStream fos = new FileOutputStream("pk101.ser");
ObjectOutputStream outStream = new ObjectOutputStream(fos);
outStream.writeObject(pk_1);
outStream.flush();
outStream.close();
pk_1 = null;

// Deserialize the primary key for cabin 101.
FileInputStream fis = new FileInputStream("pk101.ser");
ObjectInputStream inStream = new ObjectInputStream(fis);
Integer pk_2 = (Integer)inStream.readObject();
inStream.close();

// Reobtain a remote reference to cabin 101 and read its name.
CabinRemote cabin_2 = home.findByPrimaryKey(pk_2);
System.out.println(cabin_2.getName());
```

Comparing beans for identity

The EJBObject.isIdentical() method compares two EJB object remote references. It's worth considering why Object.equals() isn't sufficient for comparing EJB objects. An EJB object is a distributed object stub and therefore contains a lot of networking and other state. As a result, references to two EJB objects may be unequal, even if they both represent the same unique bean. The EJBObject.isIdentical() method returns true if two EJB object references represent the same bean, even if the EJB object stubs are different object instances.

The following code shows how this works. It starts by creating two remote references to the TravelAgent EJB. These remote EJB objects both refer to the same type of enterprise bean; comparing them with isIdentical() returns true. The two TravelAgent EJBs were created separately, but because they are stateless they are considered to be equivalent. If TravelAgent EJB had been a stateful bean (which it becomes in Chapter 12) the outcome would have been different. Comparing two stateful beans in this manner will result in false because stateful beans have conversational state, which makes them unique. When we use CabinHomeRemote.findByPrimaryKey()

to locate two EJB objects that refer to the same Cabin entity bean, we know the entity beans are identical, because we used the same primary key. In this case, isIdentical() also returns true because both remote EJB object references point to the same entity. Here's the code:

```
Context ctx  = getInitialContext();

Object ref = ctx.lookup("TravelAgentHomeRemote");
TravelAgentHomeRemote agentHome =(TravelAgentHomeRemote)
    PortableRemoteObject.narrow(ref, TravelAgentHomeRemote.class);

TravelAgentRemote agent_1 = agentHome.create();
TravelAgentRemote agent_2 = agentHome.create();
boolean x = agent_1.isIdentical(agent_2);
// x will equal true; the two EJB objects are equal.

ref = ctx.lookup("CabinHomeRemote");
CabinHomeRemote c_home = (CabinHomeRemote)
    PortableRemoteObject.narrow(ref, CabinHomeRemote.class);

Integer pk_1 = new Integer(101);
Integer pk_2 = new Integer(101);
CabinRemote cabin_1 = c_home.findByPrimaryKey(pk_1);
CabinRemote cabin_2 = c_home.findByPrimaryKey(pk_2);
x = cabin_1.isIdentical(cabin_2);
// x will equal true; the two EJB objects are equal.
```

The Integer primary key used in the Cabin bean is simple. More complex, custom-defined primary keys require us to override Object.equals() and Object.hashCode() for the EJBObject.isIdentical() method to work. Chapter 11 discusses the development of more complex custom primary keys, which are called *compound primary keys*.

Removing beans

The EJBObject.remove() method is used to remove session and entity beans. The impact of this method is the same as the EJBHome.remove() method discussed previously. For session beans, remove() causes the session to be released and the remote EJB object reference to become invalid. For entity beans, the actual entity data is deleted from the database and the remote reference becomes invalid. The following code shows the EJBObject.remove() method in use:

```
Context jndiContext = getInitialContext();

Object ref = jndiContext.lookup("CabinHomeRemote");
CabinHomeRemote c_home = (CabinHomeRemote)
    PortableRemoteObject.narrow(ref,CabinHomeRemote.class);

Integer pk = new Integer(101);
CabinRemote cabin = c_home.findByPrimaryKey(pk);
cabin.remove();
```

The remove() method throws a RemoveException if for some reason the reference can't be deleted.

The enterprise bean Handle

The EJBObject.getHandle() method returns a javax.ejb.Handle object. The Handle is a serializable reference to the remote EJB object. This means that the client can save the Handle object using Java serialization and then deserialize it to reobtain a reference to the same remote EJB object. This is similar to serializing and reusing the primary key. The Handle allows us to recreate a remote EJB object reference that points to the same type of session bean or the same unique entity bean from which the Handle originated.

Here is the interface definition of the Handle:

```
public interface javax.ejb.Handle {
    public abstract EJBObject getEJBObject()
        throws RemoteException;
}
```

The Handle interface specifies only one method, getEJBObject(). Calling this method returns the remote EJB object from which the Handle was created. Once you've gotten the object back, you can narrow it to the appropriate remote interface type. The following code shows how to serialize and deserialize the EJB Handle on a client:

```
// Obtain cabin 100.
Context jndiContext = getInitialContext();

Object ref = jndiContext.lookup("CabinHomeRemote");
CabinHomeRemote home = (CabinHomeRemote)
    PortableRemoteObject.narrow(ref,CabinHomeRemote.class);

Integer pk_1 = new Integer(101);
CabinRemote cabin_1 = home.findByPrimaryKey(pk_1);

// Serialize the Handle for cabin 100 to a file.
Handle handle = cabin_1.getHandle();
FileOutputStream fos = new FileOutputStream("handle100.ser");
ObjectOutputStream outStream = new ObjectOutputStream(fos);
outStream.writeObject(handle);
outStream.flush();
fos.close();
handle = null;

// Deserialize the Handle for cabin 100.
FileInputStream fis = new FileInputStream("handle100.ser");
ObjectInputStream inStream = new ObjectInputStream(fis);
handle = (Handle)inStream.readObject();
fis.close();

// Reobtain a remote reference to cabin 100 and read its name.
```

```
ref = handle.getEJBObject();
CabinRemote cabin_2 = (CabinRemote)
    PortableRemoteObject.narrow(ref, CabinRemote.class);

if(cabin_1.isIdentical(cabin_2))
    // This will always be true.
```

At first glance, the `Handle` and the primary key appear to do the same thing, but in truth they are very different. Using the primary key requires you to have the correct remote EJB home—if you no longer have a reference to the EJB remote home, you must look up the container using JNDI and get a new home. Only then can you call `findByPrimaryKey()` to locate the actual enterprise bean. The following code shows how this might work:

```
// Obtain the primary key from an input stream.
Integer primaryKey = (Integer)inStream.readObject();

// The JNDI API is used to get a root directory or initial context.
javax.naming.Context ctx = new javax.naming.InitialContext();

// Using the initial context, obtain the EJBHome for the Cabin bean.

Object ref = ctx.lookup("CabinHomeRemote");
CabinHomeRemote home = (CabinHomeRemote)
    PortableRemoteObject.narrow(ref,CabinHomeRemote.class);

// Obtain a reference to an EJB object that represents the entity instance.
CabinRemote cabin_2 = home.findByPrimaryKey(primaryKey);
```

The `Handle` object is easier to use because it encapsulates the details of doing a JNDI lookup on the container. With a `Handle`, the correct EJB object can be obtained in one method call, `Handle.getEJBObject()`, rather than the three method calls required to look up the context, get the home, and find the actual bean.

Furthermore, while the primary key can obtain remote references to unique entity beans, it is not available for session beans; `Handle`, on the other hand, can be used with either type of enterprise bean. This makes using a `Handle` more consistent across bean types. Consistency is, of course, good in its own right, but it isn't the whole story. Normally, we think of session beans as not having identifiable instances because they exist for only the life of the client session, but this is not exactly true. We have mentioned (but not yet shown) stateful session beans, which retain state information between method invocations. With stateful session beans, two instances are not equivalent. A `Handle` allows you to work with a stateful session bean, deactivate the bean, and then reactivate it at a later time using the `Handle`.

A client could, for example, be using a stateful session bean to process an order when the process is interrupted for some reason. Instead of losing all the work performed in the session, a `Handle` can be obtained from the EJB object and the client application can be closed down. When the user is ready to continue the order, the `Handle` can be used to obtain a reference to the stateful session EJB object. Note that this process is not as fault tolerant as using the Handle or primary key of an entity object. If the EJB server goes down or crashes, the stateful session bean will be lost and the Handle will be useless. It's also possible for the session bean to time out, which would cause the container to remove it from service so that it is no longer available to the client.

Changes to the container technology can invalidate both Handles and primary keys. If you think your container technology might change, be careful to take this limitation into account. Primary keys obtain EJB objects by providing unique identification of instances in persistent data stores. A change in the persistence mechanism, however, can impact the integrity of the key.

HomeHandle

The javax.ejb.HomeHandle is similar in purpose to javax.ejb.Handle. Just as the Handle is used to store and retrieve references to remote EJB objects, the HomeHandle is used to store and retrieve references to remote EJB homes. In other words, the HomeHandle can be stored and later used to access an EJB home's remote reference the same way that a Handle can be serialized and later used to access an EJB object's remote reference. The following code shows how the HomeHandle can be obtained, serialized, and used:

```
// Obtain cabin 100.
Context jndiContext = getInitialContext();

Object ref = jndiContext.lookup("CabinHomeRemote");
CabinHomeRemote home = (CabinHomeRemote)
    PortableRemoteObject.narrow(ref,CabinHomeRemote.class);

// Serialize the HomeHandle for the Cabin bean.
HomeHandle homeHandle = home.getHomeHandle();
FileOutputStream fos = new FileOutputStream("handle.ser");
ObjectOutputStream outStream = new ObjectOutputStream(fos);
outStream.writeObject(homeHandle);
outStream.flush();
fos.close();
homeHandle = null;

// Deserialize the HomeHandle for the Cabin bean.
FileInputStream fis = new FileInputStream("handle.ser");
ObjectInputStream inStream = new ObjectInputStream(fis);
homeHandle = (HomeHandle)inStream.readObject();
fis.close();

EJBHome homeRef = homeHandle.getEJBHome();
CabinHomeRemote home2 = (CabinHomeRemote)
    PortableRemoteObject.narrow(homeRef,CabinHomeRemote.class);
```

Inside the Handle

Different vendors define their concrete implementations of the EJB Handle objects differently. However, thinking about hypothetical implementations of Handles will give you a better understanding of how they work. In this example, we define the implementation of a Handle for an entity bean. Our implementation encapsulates the JNDI lookup and the use of the home's findByPrimaryKey() method so that any change that invalidates the key invalidates preserved Handle objects that depend on that key. Here's the code for our hypothetical implementation:

```
package com.titan.cabin;

import javax.naming.InitialContext;
import javax.naming.Context;
import javax.naming.NamingException;
import javax.ejb.EJBObject;
import javax.ejb.Handle;
import java.rmi.RemoteException;
import java.util.Properties;
import javax.rmi.PortableRemoteObject;

public class VendorX_CabinHandle
    implements javax.ejb.Handle, java.io.Serializable {

    private Integer primary_key;
    private String home_name;
    private Properties jndi_properties;

    public VendorX_CabinHandle(Integer pk, String hn, Properties p) {
        primary_key = pk;
        home_name = hn;
        jndi_properties = p;
    }

    public EJBObject getEJBObject() throws RemoteException {
        try {
            Context ctx = new InitialContext(jndi_properties);

            Object ref = ctx.lookup(home_name);
            CabinHomeRemote home =(CabinHomeRemote)
                PortableRemoteObject.narrow(ref,CabinHomeRemote.class);

            return home.findByPrimaryKey(primary_key);
        } catch (javax.ejb.FinderException fe) {
            throw new RemoteException("Cannot locate EJB object",fe);
        } catch (javax.naming.NamingException ne) {
            throw new RemoteException("Cannot locate EJB object",ne);
        }
    }
}
```

The Handle is less stable than the primary key because it relies on the networking configuration and naming—the IP address of the EJB server and the JNDI name of the bean's home—to remain stable. If the EJB server's network address changes or the name used to identify the home changes, the Handle becomes useless.

In addition, some vendors choose to implement a security mechanism in the Handle that prevents its use outside the scope of the client application that originally requested it. How this mechanism would work is unclear, but the security limitation it implies should be considered before attempting to use a Handle outside the client's scope.

📖 Workbook Exercise 5.2, The EJBObject, Handle, and Primary Key

EJB 2.0: The Local Client API

EJB 2.0 introduces the concept of local component interfaces, which are intended to provide different semantics and a different execution context for enterprise beans that work together within the same EJB container system.

When two or more enterprise beans interact, they are usually *co-located*; that is, they are deployed in the same EJB container system and execute within the same Java Virtual Machine. Co-located beans do not need to use the network to communicate. Since they are in the same JVM, they can communicate more directly by avoiding the overhead of Java RMI-IIOP. However, the EJB 1.1 specification required that even co-located beans utilize Java RMI-IIOP semantics for communication. This specification did not require that a network protocol be used, but it did require that Java RMI-IIOP types be used and that all objects be copied, rather then referenced, when passed as arguments to methods.

EJB 1.1 vendors, determined to squeeze every ounce of performance out of their servers, optimized co-located beans. The optimizations required that the EJB container interpose on invocations from one EJB to another but allowed vendors to avoid the overhead of the network; arguments and returned values were processed within the JVM by the container and not serialized over the network. However, arguments still had to be copied, rather then passed by reference, which slowed invocations down slightly. Many, if not most, vendors offered a proprietary switch that allowed deployers to turn off the copy semantics of co-located beans, so that objects passed from one enterprise bean to another in the same container system could be passed by reference rather then copied, which improved performance.

Optimizations of co-located beans that included switches for toggling argument copying eventually became so pervasive across vendors that Sun Microsystems decided to make this option part of the specification. This is why local component interfaces, which make up the Local Client API, were introduced.

Session and entity beans can choose to implement either remote or local component interfaces, or both. Any type of enterprise bean (entity, session, or message-driven) can become a co-located client of a session or entity bean: for example, a message-driven bean can call methods on co-located entity beans using its local component interfaces. The Local Client API is similar in many respects to the Remote Client API, but it is less complicated. The Local Client API is composed of two interfaces, the local and local home interfaces, which are similar to the remote and remote home interfaces discussed earlier in this chapter.

While explaining the local and local home interfaces and how they are used, we will create these interfaces for the Cabin EJB we developed in Chapter 4.

The Local Interface

The local interface, like the remote interface, defines the enterprise bean's business methods that can be invoked by other co-located beans (co-located clients). These business methods must match the signatures of business methods defined in the bean class. For example, the `CabinLocal` interface is the local interface defined for the Cabin EJB:

```
package com.titan.cabin;

import javax.ejb.EJBException;

public interface CabinLocal extends javax.ejb.EJBLocalObject {
    public String getName() throws EJBException;
    public void setName(String str) throws EJBException;
    public int getDeckLevel() throws EJBException;
    ·public void setDeckLevel(int level) throws EJBException;
    public int getShipId() throws EJBException;
    public void setShipId(int sp) throws EJBException;
    public int getBedCount() throws EJBException;
    public void setBedCount(int bc) throws EJBException;
}
```

The `CabinLocal` interface is basically the same as the `CabinRemote` interface we developed in Chapter 4, with a couple of key differences. Most importantly, the `CabinLocal` interface extends the `javax.ejb.EJBLocalObject` interface and its methods do not throw the `java.rmi.RemoteException`.

Local interfaces must extend the `javax.ejb.EJBLocalObject` interface, while remote interfaces must extend the `javax.ejb.EJBObject` interface:

```
package javax.ejb;

import javax.ejb.EJBException;
import javax.ejb.RemoteException;

public interface EJBLocalObject {
    public EJBLocalHome getEJBLocalHome() throws EJBException;
    public Object getPrimaryKey() throws EJBException;
    public boolean isIdentical(EJBLocalObject obj) throws EJBException;
    public void remove() throws RemoveException, throws EJBException;
}
```

The `EJBLocalObject` interface defines several methods that should be familiar to you from the previous sections. The `getEJBLocalHome()` method returns a local home object; the getPrimaryKey() method returns the primary key (entity beans only); the isIdentical() method compares two local EJB objects; and the remove() method removes the enterprise bean. These methods work just like their corresponding methods in the javax.ejb.EJBObject interface. It is also important to point out that the EJBLocalObject, unlike the EJBObject, does not extend the java.rmi.Remote interface, because it is not a remote object.

You may have noticed that the EJBLocalObject, unlike the EJBObject, does not define a getHandle() method. EJB local interfaces do not define a getHandle() method because a javax.ejb.Handle is not relevant when the client and enterprise beans are located in the same EJB container system. The Handle is a serializable reference that makes it easier for a remote client to obtain a reference to an enterprise bean on a remote node on a network. Since co-located beans are located in the same container system, not across a network, the Handle object is not necessary.

The EJBLocalObject and the local interfaces that extend it do not throw a java.rmi.RemoteException. These interfaces are used for co-located beans in the same JVM, not for accessing remote enterprise beans, so the RemoteException—which is used to report network or partial failures of a remote system—is not relevant. Instead, the local interfaces and EJBLocalObject throw the EJBException. The EJBException is thrown from local interface methods automatically by the container when some kind of container system error occurs or when a transaction errors occurs that causes the bean instance to be discarded.

The EJBException is a subtype of the java.lang.RuntimeException and is therefore an unchecked exception. Unchecked exceptions do not have to be declared in the throws clause of the local component interfaces and do not require the client to explicitly handle them using try/catch blocks. However, we choose to declare the EJBException in the methods signatures of the CabinLocal interface to better communicate to the client application that this type of exception is possible.

The Local Home Interface

The local home interface, like the remote home interface, defines the enterprise bean's life-cycle methods that can be invoked by other co-located beans (co-located clients). The life-cycle methods of the local home interface include find, create, and remove methods similar to those of the remote home interface. The CabinHomeLocal, the local home interface of the Cabin EJB, is shown in the following listing:

```
package com.titan.cabin;

import javax.ejb.EJBException;
import javax.ejb.CreateException;
import javax.ejb.FinderException;

public interface CabinHomeLocal extends javax.ejb.EJBLocalHome {
```

```
    public CabinLocal create(Integer id)
        throws CreateException, EJBException;

    public CabinLocal findByPrimaryKey(Integer pk)
        throws FinderException, EJBException;
}
```

The CabinHomeLocal interface is very similar to its counterpart, CabinHomeRemote, which we developed in Chapter 4. However, the CabinHomeLocal extends the javax. ejb.EJBLocalHome and does not throw the RemoteException from its create and find methods. You may also have noticed that the type returned from the create() and findByPrimaryKey() methods is the CabinLocal interface, not the remote interface of the Cabin EJB. The create and find methods of local home interfaces will always return EJB objects that implement the local interface of that enterprise bean.

Local interfaces must always extend the EJBLocalHome interface, which is much simpler than its remote counterpart, EJBHome:

```
    package javax.ejb;

    import javax.ejb.RemoveException;
    import javax.ejb.EJBException;

    public interface EJBLocalHome {
        public void remove(Object primaryKey)
            throws RemoveException, EJBException;
    }
```

Unlike the EJBHome, the EJBLocalHome does not provide EJBMetaData and HomeHandle accessors. The EJBMetaData, which is primarily used by visual development tools, is not needed for co-located beans. In addition, the HomeHandle is not relevant to co-located client beans any more than the Handle was, because co-located beans do not need special network references. The EJBLocalHome does define a remove() method that takes the primary key as its argument; this method works the same as its corresponding method in the remote EJBObject interface.

Deployment Descriptor

When an enterprise bean uses local component interfaces, they must be declared in the XML deployment descriptor. This is a trivial matter. The changes are highlighted below:

```
    <!DOCTYPE ejb-jar PUBLIC "-//Sun Microsystems, Inc.//DTD Enterprise
    JavaBeans 2.0//EN" "http://java.sun.com/dtd/ejb-jar_2_0.dtd">

    <ejb-jar>
        <enterprise-beans>
            <entity>
                <ejb-name>CabinEJB</ejb-name>
                <home>com.titan.cabin.CabinHomeRemote</home>
                <remote>com.titan.cabin.CabinRemote</remote>
```

```
<local-home>com.titan.cabin.CabinHomeLocal</local-home>
<local>com.titan.cabin.CabinLocal</local>
<ejb-class>com.titan.cabin.CabinBean</ejb-class>
```

In addition to adding the `<local-home>` and `<local>` elements, the `<ejb-ref>` element is changed to an `<ejb-local-ref>` element, indicating that a local EJB object is being used instead of a remote one:

```
<ejb-local-ref>
    <ejb-ref-name>ejb/CabinHomeLocal</ejb-ref-name>
    <ejb-ref-type>Entity</ejb-ref-type>
    <local-home>com.titan.cabin.CabinHomeLocal</local-home>
    <local>com.titan.cabin.CabinLocal</local>
</ejb-local-ref>
```

Using the Local Client API

We can easily redesign the TravelAgent EJB developed in Chapter 4 so that it uses the Cabin EJB's local component interfaces instead of the remote component interfaces:

```java
public String [] listCabins(int shipID, int bedCount) {

    try {
        javax.naming.Context jndiContext = new InitialContext();
        CabinHomeLocal home = (CabinHomeLocal)
            jndiContext.lookup("java:comp/env/ejb/CabinHomeLocal");

        Vector vect = new Vector();
        for (int i = 1; ; i++) {
            Integer pk = new Integer(i);
            CabinLocal cabin;
            try {
                cabin = home.findByPrimaryKey(pk);
            } catch(javax.ejb.FinderException fe) {
                break;
            }
            // Check to see if the bed count and ship ID match.
            if (cabin.getShipId() == shipID &&
                cabin.getBedCount() == bedCount) {
                String details =
                i+","+cabin.getName()+","+cabin.getDeckLevel();
                vect.addElement(details);
            }
        }

        String [] list = new String[vect.size()];
        vect.copyInto(list);
        return list;

    } catch(NamingException ne) {
        throw new EJBException(ne);
    }
}
```

The bold code text shows the three small changes that were needed. The most important change is using local component interfaces for the Cabin EJB instead of remote interfaces. In addition, we do not need to use the PortableRemoteObject.narrow() method when obtaining the Cabin EJB's home object from the JNDI ENC. This is because we are not accessing the home across the network; we are accessing it from within the same JVM, so we know that the client is a Java client and that no network protocol is in use. The elimination of this method makes the code much easier to look at. We also changed the try/catch block so that it will catch the javax.naming.NamingException and not the EJBException thrown by any of the local component interface methods. In this case it is easier to allow those exception to propagate directly to the container, where they can be handled better. Chapter 14 covers exception handling in detail.

📖 Workbook Exercise 5.3, The Local Component Interfaces

When to Use Local Component Interfaces

Entity and session beans can use either local or remote component interfaces, or they may use both so that the bean is accessible from remote and local clients. Any time you are going to have enterprise beans accessing each other from within the same container system you should seriously consider using local component interfaces, as their performance is likely to be better than that of remote component interfaces. With the Local Client API, no network infrastructure is involved and there is no argument copying.

Because local clients are in the same JVM, there is no need for network comminations. When a co-located client bean invokes a method on a local EJB object, the container intervenes to apply transaction and security management, but then delegates the invocation directly to the target bean instance. No network. Very little overhead. The complete absence of a network can increase the speed of an RMI loop by a full magnitude, so it is very desirable. However, relying on the Local Client API eliminates the location transparency of enterprise bean references. In other words, you cannot move the bean to a different server on the network, because it must be co-located. With the Remote Client API, you can move enterprise beans from one server to another without impacting the bean code. In other words, the Remote Client API provides better location transparency: you are not dependent on the location of the enterprise bean in order to invoke its methods.

The Local Client API also passes object arguments by reference from one bean to another, as illustrated in Figure 5-5. This means that an object passed from enterprise bean A to enterprise bean B is referenced by both beans, so if B changes its values A will see those changes.

With the Remote Client API, objects' arguments (parameters or return values) are always copied, so changes made to one copy are not reflected in the other (see Figure 5-1).

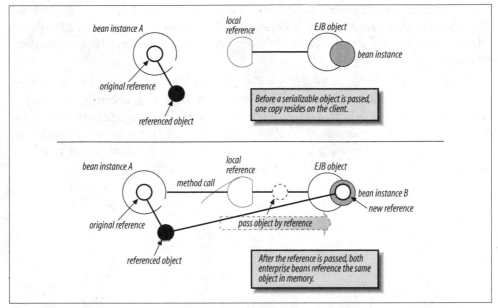

Figure 5-5. Passing by reference with the Local Client API

Passing by reference can create some pretty dangerous situations if the enterprise beans that share the object reference are not coded carefully. In most cases, it is best to pass immutable objects without copying them first. Chapter 16 discusses using immutable dependent objects, which are also good candidates for passing by reference. However, if you are going to pass an object that is not immutable, the object should be copied before it is passed. That's the rule of thumb, unless the passed objects are not modified by any beans other than the enterprise beans from which they came.

Are Local Component Interfaces Necessary?

Some vendors have argued that local component interfaces were never needed in the first place and only added more complexity and no real functionality to the EJB platform. This is a reasonable argument, considering that most EJB 1.1 vendors were already optimizing the Remote Client API for co-located beans. As we discussed earlier, these vendors did not use the network for co-located bean invocations and provided argument-copy switches.

So why was the Local Client API needed at all? An alternative would have been to amend the specification of the Remote Client API to account for co-located container optimizations, making those optimizations standard configurable attributes in the deployment descriptor. The only problem with that solution is semantics. The remote interfaces extend java.rmi.Remote, which is specifically intended for remote objects. In addition, all subtypes of the java.rmi.Remote interface are required to throw java.rmi.RemoteException types from methods. It may have been difficult for developers to distinguish between a co-located EJB object and a remote EJB object, which is important if one is passing objects by reference while the other passes them by copy.

However, it is also going to be difficult for EJB developers to get used to local component interfaces and to use them effectively. With local component interfaces, you are locked into a single JVM, and you cannot move beans from one container to the next at will. The arguments for and against the local component interfaces both have their merits. Whether you agree with the need for the Local Client API or not, local interfaces are here to stay, and you should learn to use them appropriately.

CHAPTER 6

EJB 2.0 CMP: Basic Persistence

Overview

In Chapter 4, we started developing some simple enterprise beans, skipping over a lot of the details about developing enterprise beans. In this chapter, we'll take a thorough look at the process of developing entity beans. Entity beans model business concepts that can be expressed as nouns. This is a rule of thumb rather than a requirement, but it helps in determining when a business concept is a candidate for implementation as an entity bean. In grammar school, you learned that nouns are words that describe a person, place, or thing. The concepts of "person" and "place" are fairly obvious: a person EJB might represent a customer or passenger, and a place EJB might represent a city or port-of-call. Similarly, entity beans often represent "things": real-world objects like ships, credit cards, and so on. An entity bean can even represent a fairly abstract thing, such as a reservation. Entity beans describe both the state and behavior of real-world objects and allow developers to encapsulate the data and business rules associated with specific concepts; a Customer EJB encapsulates the data and business rules associated with a customer, for example. This makes it possible for data associated with a concept to be manipulated consistently and safely.

In Titan's cruise ship business, we can identify hundreds of business concepts that are nouns and, therefore, could conceivably be modeled by entity beans. We've already seen a simple Cabin EJB in Chapter 4, and we'll develop Customer and Address EJBs in this chapter. Titan could clearly make use of a Cruise EJB, a Reservation EJB, and many others. Each of these business concepts represents data that needs to be tracked and possibly manipulated.

Entities represent data in the database, so changes to an entity bean result in changes to the database. There are many advantages to using entity beans instead of accessing the database directly. Utilizing entity beans to objectify data provides programmers with a simpler mechanism for accessing and changing data. It is much easier, for example, to change a customer's name by calling `Customer.setName()` than by executing an SQL command against the database. In addition, objectifying the data using entity beans provides for more software reuse. Once an entity bean has been defined, its definition can be used throughout Titan's system in a consistent manner. The concept of a customer, for example, is used in many areas of Titan's business, including booking, scheduling, and marketing. A Customer EJB provides Titan with one complete way of accessing customer information, and thus it ensures that access to the information is consistent and simple. Representing data as entity beans can make development easier and more cost-effective.

When a new EJB is created, a new record must be inserted into the database and a bean instance must be associated with that data. As the EJB is used and its state changes, these changes must be synchronized with the data in the database: entries must be inserted, updated, and removed. The process of coordinating the data represented by a bean instance with the database is called *persistence*.

There are two basic types of entity beans, distinguished by how they manage persistence: container-managed persistence beans and bean-managed persistence beans. For *container-managed persistence* beans, the container knows how a bean instance's persistence and relationship fields map to the database and automatically takes care of inserting, updating, and deleting the data associated with entities in the database. Entity beans using *bean-managed persistence* do all this work manually: the bean developer must write the code to manipulate the database. The EJB container tells the bean instance when it is safe to insert, update, and delete its data from the database, but it provides no other help. The bean instance does all the persistence work itself. Bean-managed persistence is covered in Chapter 10.

In EJB 2.0, container-managed persistence has undergone a change so dramatic that it is not backward compatible with EJB 1.1. For this reason, EJB 2.0 vendors must support both EJB 2.0's and EJB 1.1's container-managed persistence models. The EJB 1.1 model is supported so that application developers can migrate their existing applications to the new EJB 2.0 platform as painlessly as possible. It's expected that all new entity beans and new applications will use the EJB 2.0 container-managed persistence and not the EJB 1.1 version. Although EJB 1.1 container-managed persistence is covered in this book, it should be avoided unless you maintain a legacy EJB 1.1 system. EJB 1.1 container-managed persistence is covered in Chapter 9.

This chapter and the two that follow focus on developing entity beans that use EJB 2.0 container-managed persistence. In EJB 2.0, the data associated with an entity bean can be much more complex than was possible in EJB 1.1. In EJB 2.0, container-managed persistence entity beans can have relationships with other entity beans, which was not well supported in the older version—as a result, vendors sometimes offered proprietary solutions that were not portable. In addition, container-managed persistence entity beans, in EJB 2.0, can be finer in granularity so that they can easily model things such as the address, line item, or cabin.

This chapter develops two very simple entity beans—the Customer and Address EJBs—which will be used to explain how Enterprise JavaBeans 2.0 container-managed persistence entity beans are defined and operate at runtime. The Customer EJB has relationships with several other entities, including the Address, Phone, Credit-Card, Cruise, Ship, Cabin, and Reservation EJBs. In the next few chapters, you'll learn how to leverage EJB 2.0's powerful support for entity bean-to-bean relationships and will also come to understand their limitations. In addition, in Chapter 8 you will learn about the Enterprise JavaBeans Query Language (EJB QL), which is used to define how the find methods and the new select methods should behave at runtime.

It is common to refer to EJB 2.0 container-managed persistence as *CMP 2.0*. In the chapters that follow, we will use this abbreviation to distinguish between CMP 2.0 and CMP 1.1 (EJB 1.1 container-managed persistence).

The Abstract Programming Model

In CMP 2.0, entity beans have their state managed automatically by the container. The container takes care of enrolling the entity bean in transactions and persisting its state to the database. The enterprise bean developer describes the attributes and relationships of an entity bean using *virtual* persistence fields and relationship fields. They are called virtual fields because the bean developer does not declare these fields explicitly; instead, abstract accessor (get and set) methods are declared in the entity bean class. The implementations of these methods are generated at deployment time by the EJB vendor's container tools. It's important to remember that the terms *relationship field* and *persistence field* are referring to the abstract accessor methods and not to actual fields declared in the classes. This use of terminology is a convention in EJB 2.0 with which you should become comfortable.

In Figure 6-1, the Customer EJB has six accessor methods. The first four read and update the last and first names of the customer. These are examples of *persistence* fields: simple direct attributes of the entity bean. The last two accessor methods obtain and set references to the Address EJB through its local interface, Address-Local. This is an example of a relationship field called the homeAddress field.

Abstract Persistence Schema

The CMP 2.0 entity bean classes are defined using abstract accessor methods that represent virtual persistence and relationship fields. As already mentioned, the actual fields themselves are not declared in the entity classes. Instead, the characteristics of these fields are described in detail in the XML deployment descriptor used by the entity bean. The abstract persistence schema is the set of XML elements in the deployment descriptor that describes the relationship fields and the persistence fields. Together with the abstract programming model (the abstract accessor methods) and some help from the deployer, the container tool will have enough information to map the entity and its relationships with other entity beans to the database.

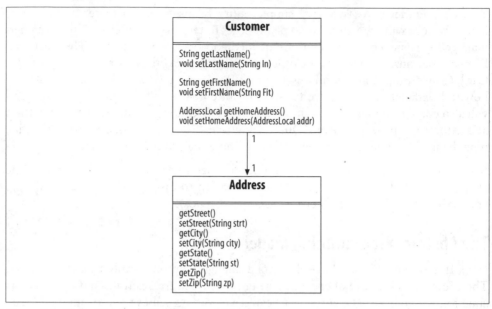

Figure 6-1. Class diagram of Customer and Address EJBs

Container Tools and Persistence

One of the responsibilities of the vendor's container-deployment tool is generating concrete implementations of the abstract entity beans. The concrete classes generated by the container tool are called *persistence classes*. Instances of the persistence classes are responsible for working with the container to read and write data between the entity bean and the database at runtime. Once the persistence classes are generated, they can be deployed into the EJB container. The container informs the *persistence instances* (instances of persistence classes) when it's a good time to read and write data to the database. The persistence instances perform the reading and writing in a way that is optimized for the database being used.

The persistence classes will include database access logic tailored to a particular database. For example, an EJB product might provide a container that can map an entity bean to a specific database, such as the Oracle relational database or the POET object database. This specificity allows the persistence classes to employ native database optimizations particular to a brand or kind of database, schema, and configuration. Persistence classes may also employ optimizations such as lazy loading and optimistic locking to further improve performance.

The container tool generates all the database access logic at deployment time and embeds it in the persistence classes. This means that the bean developers do not have to write the database access logic themselves, which saves them a lot of work; it can also result in better-performing entity beans, because the implementations are optimized. As an entity bean developer, you will never have to deal with database access code when working with CMP 2.0 entities. In fact, you probably won't have access to the persistence classes that contain that logic, because they are generated by the container tool automatically. In most cases, the source code is not available to the bean developer.

Figures 6-2 and 6-3 show different container tools, both of which are being used to map the Customer entity bean to a relational database.

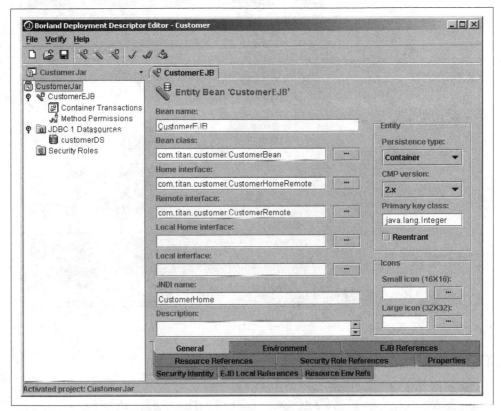

Figure 6-2. Borland AppServer deployment tool

The Customer EJB

In the following example we will develop a simple CMP 2.0 entity bean—the Customer EJB. The Customer EJB models the concept of a cruise customer or passenger, but its design and use are applicable across many commercial domains.

As the chapter progresses, the Customer EJB will be expanded and its complexity will increase to illustrate concepts discussed in each section. This section serves only to introduce you to the entity bean and some basic concepts regarding its development, packaging, and deployment. To simplify things, we will skim over some concepts that are discussed in detail later in the chapter.

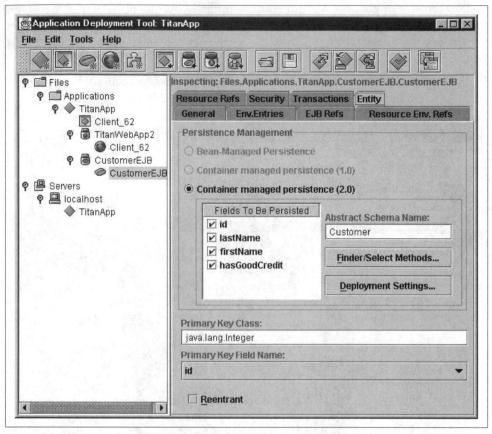

Figure 6-3. J2EE 1.3 SDK deployment tool

The Customer Table

Although CMP 2.0 is database independent, the examples throughout this book assume that you are using a relational database. This means that we will need a CUSTOMER table from which to get our customer data. The relational database table definition in SQL is as follows:

```
CREATE TABLE CUSTOMER
(
    ID INT PRIMARY KEY NOT NULL,
    LAST_NAME CHAR(20),
    FIRST_NAME CHAR(20)
)
```

The CustomerBean

The CustomerBean class is an abstract class that will be used by the container tool for generating a concrete implementation, the persistence entity class, which will run in the EJB container. The mechanism used by the container tool for generating a persistence entity class varies, but most vendors generate a subclass of the abstract class provided by the bean developer (see Figure 6-4).

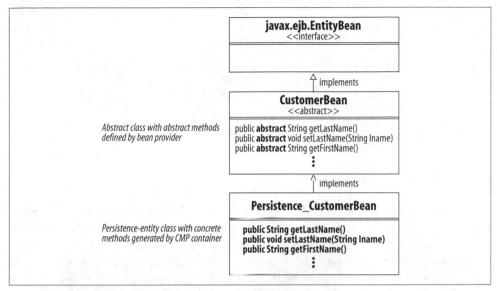

Figure 6-4. The container tool typically extends the bean class

The bean class must declare accessor (set and get) methods for each persistence and relationship field defined in the abstract persistence schema of the deployment descriptor. The container tool needs both the abstract accessor methods (defined in the entity bean class) and the XML elements of the deployment descriptor to fully describe the bean's persistence schema. In this book, the entity bean class is always defined before the XML elements, because it's a more natural approach to developing entity beans.

Here is a very simple definition of the CustomerBean class that is developed and packaged for deployment by the bean developer:

```
package com.titan.customer;

import javax.ejb.EntityContext;

public abstract class CustomerBean implements javax.ejb.EntityBean {

    public Integer ejbCreate(Integer id){
        setId(id);
        return null;
    }
    public void ejbPostCreate(Integer id){
    }

    // abstract accessor methods
```

```
    public abstract Integer getId();
    public abstract void setId(Integer id);

    public abstract String getLastName();
    public abstract void setLastName(String lname);

    public abstract String getFirstName();
    public abstract void setFirstName(String fname);

    // standard callback methods

    public void setEntityContext(EntityContext ec){}
    public void unsetEntityContext(){}
    public void ejbLoad(){}
    public void ejbStore(){}
    public void ejbActivate(){}
    public void ejbPassivate(){}
    public void ejbRemove(){}
}
```

The CustomerBean class is defined as an abstract class. This is required by CMP 2.0 to reinforce the idea that the CustomerBean is not deployed directly into the container system. Since abstract classes cannot be instantiated, in order to be deployed the bean class must be subclassed by a persistence class generated by the deployment tool. Also, the accessor methods are themselves declared as abstract, which necessitates that the container tool implement them.

The CustomerBean extends the javax.ejb.EntityBean interface, which defines several callback methods, including setEntityContext(), unsetEntityContext(), ejbLoad(), ejbStore(), ejbActivate(), ejbPassivate(), and ejbRemove(). These methods are important for notifying the bean instance about events in its life cycle, but we do not need to worry about them yet. We will discuss these methods in detail in Chapter 11.

The first method in the entity bean class is ejbCreate(), which takes a reference to an Integer object as its only argument. The ejbCreate() method is called when the remote client invokes the create() method on the entity bean's home interface. This concept should be familiar, since it's the same way ejbCreate() worked in the Cabin bean developed in Chapter 4. The ejbCreate() method is responsible for initializing any persistence fields before the entity bean is created. In this first example, the ejbCreate() method is used to initialize the id persistence field, which is represented by the setId()/getId() accessor methods.

The return type of the ejbCreate() method is an Integer, which is the *primary key* of the entity bean. The primary key is a unique identifier that can take a variety of forms, including that of a wrapper for primitive types and custom-defined classes. In this case, the primary key (the Integer) is mapped to the ID field in the CUSTOMER table. This will become evident when we define the XML deployment descriptor. Although the return type of the ejbCreate() method is the primary key, the value actually returned by the ejbCreate() method is null. The EJB container and persistence class will extract the primary key from the bean when it is needed. See the sidebar "Why ejbCreate() Returns Null" for an explanation of ejbCreate()'s return type.

Why ejbCreate( ) Returns Null

In EJB 1.0, the first release of EJB, the ejbCreate() method in container-managed persistence was declared as returning void, while the ejbCreate() method in bean-managed persistence returns the primary key type. However, in EJB 1.1 it was changed to the primary key type, with an actual return value of null.

EJB 1.1 changed the return value of ejbCreate() from void to the primary key type to facilitate subclassing; i.e., to make it easier for a bean-managed entity bean to extend a container-managed entity bean. In EJB 1.0, this was not possible because Java doesn't allow you to overload methods with different return values. By changing this definition so that a bean-managed entity bean can extend a container-managed entity bean, EJB 1.1 allowed vendors to support container-managed persistence by extending the container-managed bean with a generated bean-managed bean—a fairly simple solution to a difficult problem.

With the introduction of CMP 2.0, this little trick has become less useful to EJB vendors than it once was. The abstract persistence schema of EJB CMP 2.0 beans is, in many cases, too complex for a simple BMP container. However, it remains a part of the programming model for backward compatibility and to facilitate bean-managed persistence subclassing if needed.

The ejbPostCreate() method is used to perform initialization after the entity bean is created but before it services any requests from the client. This method usually is used to perform work on the entity bean's relationship fields, which can occur only after the bean's ejbCreate() method is invoked and it's added to the database. For each ejbCreate() method there must be a matching ejbPostCreate() method that has the same method name and arguments but returns void. This pairing of ejbCreate() and ejbPostCreate() ensures that the container calls the correct methods together. We'll explore the use of the ejbPostCreate() in more detail later; for now it's not needed, so its implementation is left empty.

The abstract accessor methods (setLastName(), getLastName(), setFirstName(), getFirstName()) represent the persistence fields in the CustomerBean class. These methods are defined as abstract without method bodies. As was already mentioned, when the bean is processed by a container tool, these methods will be implemented by a persistence class based on the abstract persistence schema (XML deployment descriptor elements), the particular EJB container, and the database used. Basically, these methods fetch and update values in the database and are not implemented by the bean developer.

The Remote Interface

We will need a `CustomerRemote` interface for the Customer EJB, because the bean will be accessed by clients outside the container system. The remote interface defines the business methods clients will use to interact with the entity bean. The remote interface should define methods that model the public aspects of the business concept being modeled; that is, those behaviors and data that should be exposed to client applications. Here is the remote interface for `CustomerRemote`:

```
package com.titan.customer;
import java.rmi.RemoteException;

public interface CustomerRemote extends javax.ejb.EJBObject {

    public String getLastName() throws RemoteException;
    public void setLastName(String lname) throws RemoteException;

    public String getFirstName() throws RemoteException;
    public void setFirstName(String fname) throws RemoteException;
}
```

Any methods defined in the remote interface must match the signatures of methods defined in the bean class. In this case, the accessor methods in the `CustomerRemote` interface match persistence field accessor methods in the `CustomerBean` class. When the remote interface methods match the persistence field methods, the client has direct access to the entity bean's persistence fields.

You are not required to match abstract accessor methods in the bean class with methods in the remote interface. In fact, it's recommended that the remote interface be as independent of the abstract programming model as possible.

While remote methods can match persistence fields in the bean class, the specification prohibits the remote methods from matching relationship fields, which access other entity beans. In addition, remote methods may not modify any container-managed persistence fields that are part of the primary key of an entity bean. Notice that the remote interface does not define a `setId()` method, which would allow it to modify the primary key.

The Remote Home Interface

The remote home interface of any entity bean is used to create, locate, and remove entities from the EJB container. Each entity bean type may have its own remote home interface, local home interface, or both. As you learned in Chapter 5, the remote and local home interfaces perform essentially the same function. The home interfaces define three basic kinds of methods: home business methods, zero or more create methods, and one or more find methods.[*] The create() methods act like

---

[*] Chapter 15 explains when you should not define any create methods in the home interface.

remote constructors and define how new entity beans are created. In our remote home interface, we provide only a single create() method, which matches the corresponding ejbCreate() method in the bean class. The find method is used to locate a specific Customer EJB using the primary key as a unique identifier.

The following code contains the complete definition of the CustomerHomeRemote interface:

```
package com.titan.customer;

import java.rmi.RemoteException;
import javax.ejb.CreateException;
import javax.ejb.FinderException;

public interface CustomerHomeRemote extends javax.ejb.EJBHome {

    public CustomerRemote create(Integer id)
        throws CreateException, RemoteException;

    public CustomerRemote findByPrimaryKey(Integer id)
        throws FinderException, RemoteException;

}
```

A create() method may be suffixed with a name in order to further qualify it when overloading method arguments. This is useful if you have two different create() methods that take arguments of the same type. For example, we could declare two create() methods for Customer that both declare an Integer and a String argument. The String argument might be a social security number (SSN) in one case and a tax identification number (TIN) in another—individuals have social security numbers while corporations have tax identification numbers:

```
public interface CustomerHomeRemote extends javax.ejb.EJBHome {

    public CustomerRemote createWithSSN(Integer id, String socialSecurityNumber)
        throws CreateException, RemoteException;

    public CustomerRemote createWithTIN(Integer id, String taxIdentificationNumber)
        throws CreateException, RemoteException;

    public CustomerRemote findByPrimaryKey(Integer id)
        throws FinderException, RemoteException;
}
```

Suffixes are useful when you need create() methods to be more descriptive or need to further qualify them for method overloading. Each create<*SUFFIX*>() method must have a corresponding ejbCreate<*SUFFIX*>() in the bean class. For example, the CustomerBean class needs to define ejbCreateWithSSN() and ejbCreateWithTIN() methods as well as matching ejbPostCreateWithSSN() and ejbPostCreateWithTIN() methods. We are keeping this example simple, so we need only one create() method and, therefore, no suffix.

Enterprise JavaBeans specifies that create() methods in the remote home interface must throw the javax.ejb.CreateException. In the case of container-managed persistence, the container needs a common exception for communicating problems experienced during the create process.

Entity remote home interfaces must define a findByPrimaryKey() method that takes the entity bean's primary key type as its only argument, but no matching method needs to be defined in the entity bean class. The implementation of findByPrimaryKey() is generated automatically by the deployment tool. At runtime, the findByPrimaryKey() method will automatically locate and return a remote reference to the entity bean with the matching primary key.

The bean developer can also declare other find methods. For example, the CustomerHomeRemote interface could define a findByLastName(String lname) method that locates all the Customer entities with the specified last name. These types of finder methods are automatically implemented by the deployment tool based on the method signature and an EJB QL statement, which is similar to SQL but is specific to EJB. Custom finder methods and EJB QL are discussed in detail in Chapter 8.

The XML Deployment Descriptor

CMP 2.0 entity beans must be packaged for deployment with an XML deployment descriptor that describes the bean and its abstract persistence schema. In most cases, the bean developer is not directly exposed to the XML deployment descriptor but rather will use the container's visual deployment tools to package the beans. In this book, however, I will describe the declarations of the deployment descriptor in detail so you have a full understanding of their content and organization.

The XML deployment descriptor, for our simple Customer EJB, contains many elements that should be familiar to you from Chapter 4. The elements specific to entity beans and persistence are most important to us in this chapter. The following is the complete XML deployment descriptor for the Customer EJB:

```
<!DOCTYPE ejb-jar PUBLIC "-//Sun Microsystems, Inc.//DTD Enterprise
JavaBeans 2.0//EN" "http://java.sun.com/dtd/ejb-jar_2_0.dtd">

<ejb-jar>
    <enterprise-beans>
        <entity>
            <ejb-name>CustomerEJB</ejb-name>
            <home>com.titan.customer.CustomerHomeRemote</home>
            <remote>com.titan.customer.CustomerRemote</remote>
            <ejb-class>com.titan.customer.CustomerBean</ejb-class>
            <persistence-type>Container</persistence-type>
            <prim-key-class>java.lang.Integer</prim-key-class>
            <reentrant>False</reentrant>
            <cmp-version>2.x</cmp-version>
            <abstract-schema-name>Customer</abstract-schema-name>
```

```
        <cmp-field><field-name>id</field-name></cmp-field>
        <cmp-field><field-name>lastName</field-name></cmp-field>
        <cmp-field><field-name>firstName</field-name></cmp-field>
        <primkey-field>id</primkey-field>
        <security-identity><use-caller-identity/></security-identity>
    </entity>
</enterprise-beans>
<assembly-descriptor>
    <security-role>
        <role-name>Employees</role-name>
    </security-role>
    <method-permission>
        <role-name>Employees</role-name>
        <method>
            <ejb-name>CustomerEJB</ejb-name>
            <method-name>*</method-name>
        </method>
    </method-permission>
    <container-transaction>
        <method>
            <ejb-name>CustomerEJB</ejb-name>
            <method-name>*</method-name>
        </method>
        <trans-attribute>Required</trans-attribute>
    <container-transaction>
</assembly-descriptor>
</ejb-jar>
```

The first few elements, which declare the Customer EJB name, (CustomerEJB) as well as its home, remote, and bean class, should already be familiar to you from Chapter 4. The <security-identity> element was covered in Chapter 3.

The <assembly-descriptor> elements, which declare the security and transaction attributes of the bean, were also covered briefly in Chapter 4. In this case, they state that all employees can access any CustomerEJB method and that all methods use the Required transaction attribute.

Container-managed persistence entities also need to declare their persistence type, version, and whether they are reentrant. These elements are declared under the <entity> element.

The <persistence-type> element tells the container system whether the bean will be a container-managed persistence entity or a bean-managed persistence entity. In this case it's container-managed, so we use Container. Had it been bean-managed, the value would have been Bean.

The <cmp-version> element tells the container system which version of container-managed persistence is being used. EJB 2.0 containers must support the new container-managed persistence model as well as the old one defined in EJB 1.1. The value of the <cmp-version> element can be either 2.x or 1.x, for the EJB 2.0 and 1.1 versions, respectively. The <cmp-version> element is optional. If it is not declared, the default value is 2.x. It's not really needed here, but it's specified as an aid to other developers who might read the deployment descriptor.

The <reentrant> element indicates whether reentrant behavior is allowed. In this case the value is False, which indicates that the CustomerEJB is not reentrant (i.e., loopbacks are not allowed). A value of True would indicate that the CustomerEJB is reentrant and that loopbacks are permitted. Reentrant behavior was covered in Chapter 3.

The entity bean must also declare its container-managed persistence fields and its primary key:

```
<entity>
    <ejb-name>CustomerEJB</ejb-name>
    <home>com.titan.customer.CustomerHomeRemote</home>
    <remote>com.titan.customer.CustomerRemote</remote>
    <ejb-class>com.titan.customer.CustomerBean</ejb-class>
    <persistence-type>Container</persistence-type>
    <prim-key-class>java.lang.Integer</prim-key-class>
    <reentrant>False</reentrant>
    <cmp-version>2.x</cmp-version>
    <cmp-field><field-name>id</field-name></cmp-field>
    <cmp-field><field-name>lastName</field-name></cmp-field>
    <cmp-field><field-name>firstName</field-name></cmp-field>
    <primkey-field>id</primkey-field>
</entity>
```

The container-managed persistence fields are the id, lastName, and firstName, as indicated by the <cmp-field> elements. The <cmp-field> elements must have matching accessor methods in the CustomerBean class. As you can see in Table 6-1, the values declared in the <field-name> element match the names of abstract accessor methods we declared in the CustomerBean class—the get and set parts of the method names are ignored when matching methods to <field-name> declarations.

Table 6-1. Field names for abstract accessor methods

CMP field	Abstract accessor method
id	public abstract Integer getId() public abstract void setId(Integer id)
lastName	public abstract String getLastName() public abstract void setLastName(String lname)
firstName	public abstract String getFirstName() public abstract void setFirstName(String lname)

CMP 2.0 requires that the <field-name> values start with a lowercase letter while their matching accessor methods take the form get<field-name value>(), set<field-name value>(), with the first letter of the <field-name> capitalized. The return type of the get method and the parameter of the set method determine the type of the <cmp-field>. It's the convention of this book, but not a requirement of CMP 2.0, that field

names with multiple words are declared using "camel case," where each new word starts with a capital letter (e.g., lastName).

Finally, we declare the primary key using two fields, <prim-key-class> and <primkey-field>. <prim-key-class> indicates the type of the primary key, and <primkey-field> indicates which of the <cmp-field> elements designates the primary key. The Customer EJB uses a *single-field* primary key, in which only one field of the entity bean's container-managed fields describes a unique identifier for the bean. The <primkey-field> must be declared if the entity bean uses a single-field primary key. *Compound* primary keys, which use more than one of the persistence fields as a key, are often used instead. In this case, the bean developer creates a custom primary key. The <prim-key-class> element is always required, whether it's a single-field, compound, or unknown primary key. Unknown keys use a field that may not be declared in the bean at all. The different types of primary keys are covered in more detail in Chapter 11.

The EJB JAR File

Now that you have created the interfaces, bean class, and deployment descriptor, you're ready to package the bean for deployment. As you learned in Chapter 4, the JAR file provides a way to "shrink-wrap" a component so it can be sold and/or deployed in an EJB container. The examples available from *http://www.oreilly.com/ catalog/entjbeans3/* contain a properly prepared JAR file that includes the Customer EJB's interfaces, bean class, and deployment descriptor. You may use these files or develop them yourself. The command for creating a new EJB JAR file is:

```
\dev % jar cf customer.jar com/titan/customer/*.class
com/titan/customer/META-INF/ejb-jar.xml

F:\..\dev>jar cf cabin.jar com\titan\customer\*.class com\titan\customer
\META-INF\ejb-jar.xml
```

Most EJB servers provide graphical or command-line tools that create the XML deployment descriptor and package the enterprise bean into a JAR file automatically. Some of these tools even create the home and remote interfaces automatically, based on input from the developer. If you prefer to use these tools, the workbooks will step you through the process of deploying an entity bean using specific vendors' container-deployment tools.

Deployment

Once the CustomerEJB is packaged in a JAR file, it's ready to be processed by the deployment tools. For most vendors, these tools are combined into one graphical user interface used at deployment time. The point is to map the container-managed persistence fields of the bean to fields or data objects in the database. (Earlier in this chapter, Figures 6-2 and 6-3 showed two visual tools used to map the Customer EJB's persistence fields.)

In addition, the security roles need to be mapped to the subjects in the security realm of the target environment and the bean needs to be added to the naming service and given a JNDI lookup name (name binding). These tasks are also accomplished using the deployment tools provided by your vendor. The workbooks provide step-by-step instructions for deploying the CustomerEJB in specific vendor environments.

The Client Application

The Client application is a remote client to the CustomerEJB that will create several customers, find them, and then remove them. Here is the complete definition of the Client application:

```java
import javax.naming.InitialContext;
import javax.naming.Context;
import javax.naming.NamingException;
import java.util.Properties;

public class Client {
    public static void main(String [] args)) throws Exception {
        //obtain CustomerHome
        Context jndiContext = getInitialContext();
        Object obj=jndiContext.lookup("CustomerHomeRemote");
        CustomerHomeRemote home = (CustomerHomeRemote)
            javax.rmi.PortableRemoteObject.narrow(obj,CustomerHomeRemote.class);
        //create Customers
        for(int i =0;i <args.length;i++){
            Integer primaryKey =new Integer(args [ i ]);
            String firstName = args [ i ];
            String lastName = args [ i ];
            CustomerRemote customer = home.create(primaryKey);
            customer.setFirstName(firstName);
            customer.setLastName(lastName);
        }
        //find and remove Customers
        for(int i =0;i <args.length;i++){
            Integer primaryKey = new Integer(args [i ]);
            CustomerRemote customer = home.findByPrimaryKey(primaryKey);
            String lastName = customer.getLastName();
            String firstName = customer.getFirstName();
            System.out.print(primaryKey+"=");
            System.out.println(firstName+""+lastName);
            //remove Customer
            customer.remove();
        }
    }
    public static Context getInitialContext(
        throws javax.naming.NamingException {
        Properties p =new Properties();
        //...Specify the JNDI properties specific to the vendor.
        return new javax.naming.InitialContext(p);
    }
}
```

The Client application creates several Customer EJBs, sets their first and last names, prints out the persistence field values, and then removes the entities from the container system and, effectively, the database.

📖 Workbook Exercise 6.1, Basic Persistence in CMP 2.0

Persistence Fields

Container-managed persistence (CMP) fields are virtual fields whose values map directly to the database. Persistence fields can be Java serializable types and Java primitive types.

Java serializable types can be any class that implements the java.io.Serializable interface. Most deployment tools handle java.lang.String, java.util.Date, and the primitive wrappers (Byte, Boolean, Short, Integer, Long, Double, and Float) easily, because these types of objects are part of the Java core and map naturally to fields in relational and other databases.

The CustomerEJB declares three serializable fields, id, lastName, and firstName, which map naturally to the INT and CHAR fields of the CUSTOMER table in the database.

You can also define your own serializable types, called *dependent value classes*, and declare them as CMP fields. However, I recommend that you do not use custom serializable objects as persistence field types unless it is absolutely necessary—they are usually recommended for unstructured types, such as multimedia data (images, blobs, etc.). Arbitrary dependent value classes usually will not map naturally to database types, so they must be stored in their serializable forms in some type of binary database field.

Serializable objects are always returned as copies and not references, so modifying a serializable object will not impact its database value. The entire value must be updated using the abstract set<field-name> method.

The primitive types (byte, short, int, long, double, float, and boolean) are also allowed to be CMP fields. These types are easily mapped to the database and are supported by all deployment tools. As an example, the CustomerEJB might declare a boolean that represents a customer's credit worthiness:

```
public abstract class CustomerBean implements javax.ejb.EntityBean {

    public Integer ejbCreate(Integer id){
        setId(id);
        return null;
    }

    // abstract accessor methods

    public abstract boolean getHasGoodCredit();
    public abstract void setHasGoodCredit(boolean creditRating);
```

Dependent Value Classes

As discussed in the previous section, dependent value classes are custom serializable objects that can be used as persistence fields—(although this use is not recommended). Dependent value classes are useful for packaging data and moving it between an entity bean and its remote clients. They separate the client's view of the entity bean from its abstract persistence model, which makes it easier for the entity bean class to change without impacting existing clients.

The remote interface methods of an entity bean should be defined independently of the anticipated abstract persistence schema. In other words, you should design the remote interfaces to model the business concepts, not the underlying persistence programming model. Dependent value classes can help separate a remote client's view from the persistence model by providing objects that fill the gaps in these perspectives. Dependent value classes are used a lot in remote interfaces where packaging data together can reduce network traffic, but are less useful in local interfaces.

For example, the CustomerEJB could be modified so that its lastName and firstName fields are not exposed directly to remote clients through their accessor methods. This is a reasonable design approach, since most clients access the entire name of the customer at once. In this case, the remote interface might be modified to look as follows:

```
import java.rmi.RemoteException;

public interface CustomerRemote extends javax.ejb.EJBObject {

    public Name getName() throws RemoteException;
    public void setName(Name name) throws RemoteException;

}
```

The remote interface here is simpler than the one we saw earlier. It allows the remote client to get all the name information in one method call instead of two—this reduces network traffic and improves performance for remote clients. The use of the Name dependent value is also semantically more consistent with how the client interacts with the Customer EJB.

To implement this interface, the CustomerBean class adds a business method that matches the remote interface methods. The setName() method updates the lastName and firstName fields, while the getName() method constructs a Name object from these fields:

```
import javax.ejb.EntityContext;

public abstract class CustomerBean implements javax.ejb.EntityBean {

    public Integer ejbCreate(Integer id){
        setId(id);
        return null;
    }
```

```
    public void ejbPostCreate(Integer id) {
    }
    // business methods
    public Name getName() {
        Name name = new Name(getLastName(),getFirstName());
        return name;
    }
    public void setName(Name name) {
        setLastName(name.getLastName());
        setFirstName(name.getFirstName());
    }

    // abstract accessor methods

    public abstract String getLastName();
    public abstract void setLastName(String lname);

    public abstract String getFirstName();
    public abstract void setFirstName(String fname);
```

This is a good example of how dependent value classes can be used to separate the client's view from the abstract persistence schema.

The getName() and setName() methods are not abstract persistence methods, they are business methods. Entity beans can have as many business methods as needed. Business methods introduce business logic to the Customer EJB; otherwise, the bean would be only a data wrapper. For example, validation logic could be added to the setName() method to ensure that the data is correct before applying the update. In addition, the entity bean class can use other methods that help with processing data—these are just instance methods and may not be exposed as business methods in the remote interface.

How dependent value classes are defined is important to understanding how they should be used. The Name dependent value class is defined as follows:

```
public class Name implements java.io.Serializable {
    private String lastName;
    private String firstName;

    public Name(String lname, String fname){
        lastName = lname;
        firstName = fname;
    }
    public String getLastName() {
        return lastName;
    }
    public String getFirstName() {
        return firstName;
    }
}
```

You'll notice that the Name dependent value class has get accessor methods but not set methods. It's immutable. This is a design strategy used in this book, not a requirement of the specification; CMP 2.0 does not specify how dependent value classes are defined. We make dependent values immutable so that "remote clients cannot change the Name object's fields. The reason is simple: the Name object is a copy, not a remote reference. Changes to Name objects are not reflected in the database. Making the Name immutable helps to ensure that clients do not mistake this dependent value for a remote object reference, thinking that a change to the Name object is automatically reflected in the database. To change the customer's name, the client is required to create a new Name object and use the setName() method to update the Customer EJB.

The following code listing illustrates how a client would modify the name of a customer using the Name dependent value class:

```
// find Customer
customer = home.findByPrimaryKey(primaryKey);
name = customer.getName();
System.out.print(primaryKey+" = ");
System.out.println(name.getFirstName()+" "+name.getLastName());

// change Customer's name
name = new Name("Monson-Haefel", "Richard");
customer.setName(name);
name = customer.getName();
System.out.print(primaryKey+" = ");
System.out.println(name.getFirstName()+" "+name.getLastName());
```

The output will look like this:

```
1 = Richard Monson
1 = Richard Monson-Haefel
```

Defining the bean's interfaces according to the business concept and not the underlying data is not always reasonable, but you should try to employ this strategy when the underlying data model doesn't clearly map to the business purpose or concept being modeled by the entity bean. The bean's interfaces may be used by developers who know the business but not the abstract programming model. It is important to them that the entity beans reflect the business concept. In addition, defining the interfaces independently of the persistence model enables the component interfaces and persistence model to evolve separately. This allows the abstract persistence programming model to change over time and allows for new behavior to be added to the entity bean as needed.

While the dependent value classes serve a purpose, they should not be used indiscriminately. Generally speaking, it is foolish to use dependent value classes when a CMP field will do just fine. For example, checking a client's credit worthiness before processing an order can be accomplished easily using the getHasGoodCredit() method directly. In this case, a dependent value class would serve no purpose.

📖 Workbook Exercise 6.2, Dependent Value Classes in CMP 2.0

Relationship Fields

Entity beans can form relationships with other entity beans. In Figure 6-1, at the beginning of this chapter, the Customer EJB is shown to have a one-to-one relationship with the Address EJB. The Address EJB is a fine-grained business object that should always be accessed in the context of another entity bean, which means it should have only local interfaces and not remote interfaces. An entity bean can have relationships with many different entity beans at the same time. For example, we could easy add relationship fields for Phone, CreditCard, and other entity beans to the Customer EJB. At this point, however, we're choosing to keep the Customer EJB simple.

Following Figure 6-1 (earlier in the chapter) as a guide, we define the Address EJB as follows:

```
package com.titan.address;

import javax.ejb.EntityContext;

public abstract class AddressBean implements javax.ejb.EntityBean {

    public Integer ejbCreateAddress(String street, String city,
        String state, String zip)
    {
        setStreet(street);
        setCity(city);
        setState(state);
        setZip(zip);
        return null;
    }
    public void ejbPostCreateAddress(String street, String city,
        String state, String zip) {
    }

    // persistence fields

    public abstract Integer getId();
    public abstract void setId(Integer id);
    public abstract String getStreet();
    public abstract void setStreet(String street);
    public abstract String getCity();
    public abstract void setCity(String city);
    public abstract String getState();
    public abstract void setState(String state);
    public abstract String getZip();
    public abstract void setZip(String zip);

    // standard callback methods

    public void setEntityContext(EntityContext ec){}
    public void unsetEntityContext(){}
```

```
    public void ejbLoad(){}
    public void ejbStore(){}
    public void ejbActivate(){}
    public void ejbPassivate(){}
    public void ejbRemove(){}

}
```

The AddressBean class defines an ejbCreateAddress() method, which is called when a new Address EJB is created, as well as several persistence fields (street, city, state, and zip). The persistence fields are represented by the abstract accessor methods, which is the idiom required for persistence fields in all entity bean classes. These abstract accessor methods are matched with their own set of XML deployment descriptor elements, which define the abstract persistence schema of the Address EJB. At deployment time, the container's deployment tool will map the Customer EJB's and Address EJB's persistence fields to the database. This means that there must be a table in our relational database that contains columns that match the persistence fields in the Address EJB. In this example, we will use a separate ADDRESS table for storing address information, but the data could just as easily have been declared in the other table:

```
CREATE TABLE ADDRESS
(
    ID INT PRIMARY KEY NOT NULL,
    STREET CHAR(40),
    CITY CHAR(20),
    STATE CHAR(2),
    ZIP CHAR(10)
)
```

Entity beans do not have to define all the columns from corresponding tables as persistence fields. In fact, an entity bean may not even have a single corresponding table; it may be persisted to several tables. The bottom line is that the container's deployment tool allows the abstract persistence schema of an entity bean to be mapped to a database in a variety of ways, allowing a clean separation between the persistence classes and the database. The ID column is an auto-increment field, created automatically by the database or container system. It is the primary key of the Address EJB.

Once the bean is created the primary key must never again be modified. When primary keys are autogenerated values, such as the ID column in the ADDRESS table, the EJB container will obtain the primary key value from the database.

In addition to the bean class, we will define the local interface for the Address EJB, which allows it to be accessed by other entity beans (namely, the Customer EJB) within the same address space or process:

```
// Address EJB's local interface
public interface AddressLocal extends javax.ejb.EJBLocalObject {
    public String getStreet();
```

```
        public void setStreet(String street);
        public String getCity();
        public void setCity(String city);
        public String getState();
        public void setState(String state);
        public String getZip();
        public void setZip(String zip);
    }

    // Address EJB's local home interface
    public interface AddressHomeLocal extends javax.ejb.EJBLocalHome {
        public AddressLocal createAddress(String street,String city,
            String state,String zip) throws javax.ejb.CreateException;
        public AddressLocal findByPrimaryKey(Integer primaryKey)
            throws javax.ejb.FinderException;


    }
```

You may have noticed that the ejbCreate() method of the AddressBean class and the findByPrimaryKey() method of the home interface both define the primary key type as java.lang.Integer. As I mentioned earlier, the primary key is autogenerated. Most EJB 2.0 vendors will allow entity beans' primary keys to be mapped to autogenerated fields. If your vendor does not support autogenerated primary keys, you will need to set the primary key value in the ejbCreate() method. This is usually true of single-value primary keys, but not necessarily of compound primary keys.

The relationship field for the Address EJB is defined in the CustomerBean class using an abstract accessor method, the same way that persistence fields are declared. In the following code, the CustomerBean has been modified to include the Address EJB as a relationship field:

```
    import javax.ejb.EntityContext;
    import javax.ejb.CreateException;

    public abstract class CustomerBean implements javax.ejb.EntityBean {
        ...

        // persistence relationships
        public abstract AddressLocal getHomeAddress();
        public abstract void setHomeAddress(AddressLocal address);

        // persistence fields
        public abstract boolean getHasGoodCredit();
        public abstract void setHasGoodCredit(boolean creditRating);
        ...
```

The getHomeAddress() and setHomeAddress() accessor methods are self-explanatory; they allow the bean to access and modify its homeAddress relationship. These accessor methods represent a *relationship field*, which is a virtual field that references another entity bean. The name of the accessor method is determined by the name of the relationship field, as declared in the XML deployment descriptor. In this case we have named the customer's address homeAddress, so the corresponding accessor method names will be getHomeAddress() and setHomeAddress().

To accommodate the relationship between the Customer EJB and the home address, a foreign key, ADDRESS_ID, will be added to the CUSTOMER table. The foreign key will point to the ADDRESS record. In practice, this schema is actually the reverse of what is usually done, where the ADDRESS table contains a foreign key to the CUSTOMER table. However, the schema used here is useful in demonstrating alternative database mappings and is utilized again in Chapter 7:

```
CREATE TABLE CUSTOMER
(
    ID INT PRIMARY KEY NOT NULL,
    LAST_NAME CHAR(20),
    FIRST_NAME CHAR(20),
    ADDRESS_ID INT
)
```

When a new Address EJB is created and set as the Customer EJB's homeAddress relationship, the Address EJB's primary key will be placed in the ADDRESS_ID column of the CUSTOMER table, creating a relationship in the database:

```
// get local reference
AddressLocal address = ...

// establish the relationship
customer.setHomeAddress(address);
```

To give the Customer a home address, we need to deliver the address information to the Customer. This appears to be a simple matter of declaring matching setHomeAddress()/getHomeAddress() accessors in the remote interface, but it's not! While it's valid to make persistence fields directly available to remote clients, persistence relationships are more complicated than that.

The remote interface of a bean is not allowed to expose its relationship fields. In the case of the homeAddress field, we have declared the type to be AddressLocal, which is a local interface, so the setHomeAddress()/getHomeAddress() accessors cannot be declared in the remote interface of the Customer EJB. The reason for this restriction on remote interfaces is fairly simple: the EJBLocalObject, which implements the local interface, is optimized for use within the same address space or process as the bean instance and is not capable of being used across the network. In other words, references that implement the local interface of a bean cannot be passed across the network, so a local interface cannot declared as a return type of a parameter of a remote interface.

We take advantage of the EJBLocalObject optimization for better performance, but that same advantage limits location transparency; we must use it only within the same address space.

Local interfaces (interfaces that extend javax.ejb.EJBLocalObject), on the other hand, can expose any kind of relationship field. With local interfaces, the caller and the enterprise bean being called are located in the same address space, so they can pass around local references without a problem. For example, if we had defined a local interface for the Customer EJB, it could include a method that allows local clients to access its Address relationship directly:

```
public interface CustomerLocal extends javax.ejb.EJBLocalObject {
    public AddressLocal getHomeAddress();
    public void setHomeAddress(AddressLocal address);
}
```

When it comes to the Address EJB, it's better to define a local interface only because it's such a fine-grained bean. To get around remote-interface restrictions, the business methods in the bean class exchange address data instead of Address references. For example, we can declare a method that allows the client to send address information to create a home address for the Customer:

```
public abstract class CustomerBean implements javax.ejb.EntityBean {

    public Integer ejbCreate(Integer id) {
        setId(id);
        return null;
    }
    public void ejbPostCreate(Integer id) {
    }
    // business method
    public void setAddress(String street,String city,String state,String zip) {
        try {

            AddressLocal addr = this.getHomeAddress();
            if(addr == null) {
                // Customer doesn't have an address yet. Create a new one.
                InitialContext cntx = new InitialContext();
                AddressHomeLocal addrHome =
                    (AddressHomeLocal)cntx.lookup("AddressHomeLocal");
                addr = addrHome.createAddress(street,city,state,zip);
                this.setHomeAddress(addr);
            } else {
                // Customer already has an address. Change its fields.
                addr.setStreet(street);
                addr.setCity(city);
                addr.setState(state);
                addr.setZip(zip);
            }

        } catch(Exception e) {
            throw new EJBException(e);
        }
    }

    ...
```

The setAddress() business method in the CustomerBean class is also declared in the remote interface of the Customer EJB, so it can be called by remote clients:

```
public interface Customer extends javax.ejb.EJBObject {

  public void setAddress(String street,String city,String state,String zip);

    public Name getName() throws RemoteException;
    public void setName(Name name) throws RemoteException;

    public boolean getHasGoodCredit() throws RemoteException;
    public void setHasGoodCredit(boolean creditRating) throws RemoteException;

}
```

When the CustomerRemote.setAddress() business method is invoked on the CustomerBean, the method's arguments are used to create a new Address EJB and set it as the homeAddress relationship field, if one doesn't already exist. If the Customer EJB already has a homeAddress relationship, that Address EJB is modified to reflect the new address information.

When creating a new Address EJB, the home object is obtained from the JNDI ENC (environment naming context) and its createAddress() method is called. This results in the creation of a new Address EJB and the insertion of a corresponding ADDRESS record into the database. After the Address EJB is created, it's used in the setHomeAddress() method. The CustomerBean class must explicitly call the setHomeAddress() method, or the new address will not be assigned to the customer. In fact, simply creating an Address EJB without assigning it to the customer with the setHomeAddress() method will result in a *disconnected* Address EJB. More precisely, it will result in an ADDRESS record in the database that is not referenced by any CUSTOMER records. Disconnected entity beans are fairly normal and even desirable in many cases. In this case, however, we want the new Address EJB to be assigned to the homeAddress relationship field of the Customer EJB.

 The viability of disconnected entities depends, in part, on the referential integrity of the database. For example, if the referential integrity allows only non-null values for the foreign key column, creating a disconnected entity may result in a database error.

When the setHomeAddress() method is invoked, the container links the ADDRESS record to the CUSTOMER record automatically. In this case, it places the ADDRESS primary key in the CUSTOMER record's ADDRESS_ID field and creates a reference from the CUSTOMER record to the ADDRESS record.

If the Customer EJB already has a homeAddress, we want to change its values instead of creating a new Address EJB. We don't need to use setHomeAddress() if we are simply updating the values of an existing Address EJB, because the Address EJB we modified already has a relationship with the entity bean.

We also want to provide clients with a business method for obtaining a Customer EJB's home address information. Since we are prohibited from sending an instance of the Address EJB directly to the client (because it's a local interface), we must package the address data in some other form and send that to the client. There are two solutions to this problem: acquire the remote interface of the Address EJB and return that; or return the data as a dependent value object.

We can obtain the remote interface for the Address EJB only if one was defined. Entity beans can have a set of either local interfaces or remote interfaces, or both. In the situation with which we're dealing the Address EJB is too fine-grained to justify creating a remote interface, but in many other circumstances a bean may indeed want to have a remote interface. If, for example, the Customer EJB referenced a SalesPerson EJB, the CustomerBean could convert the local reference into a remote reference. This would be done by accessing the local EJB object, getting its primary key (EJBLocalObject.getPrimaryKey()), obtaining the SalesPerson EJB's remote home from the JNDI ENC, and then using the primary key and remote home reference to find a remote interface reference:

```
public SalesRemote getSalesRep(){
    SalesLocal local = getSalesPerson();
    Integer primKey = local.getPrimaryKey();

    Object ref = jndiEnc.lookup("SalesHomeRemote");
    SalesHomeRemote home = (SalesHomeRemote)
        PortableRemoteObject.narrow(ref, SalesHomeRemote.class);

    SalesRemote remote = home.findByPrimaryKey( primKey );
    return remote;
}
```

The other option is to use a dependent value to pass the Address EJB's data between remote clients and the Customer EJB. This is the approach recommended for fine-grained beans like the Address EJB—in general, we don't want to expose these beans directly to remote clients.

The following code shows how the AddressDO dependent value class is used in conjunction with the local component interfaces of the Address EJB (the DO in AddressDO is a convention used in this book—it's a qualifier that stands for "dependent object"):

```
public abstract class CustomerBean implements javax.ejb.EntityBean {

    public Integer ejbCreate(Integer id) {
        setId(id);
        return null;
    }
    public void ejbPostCreate(Integer id) {
    }
    // business method
    public AddressDO getAddress() {
        AddressLocal addrLocal = getHomeAddress();
        if(addrLocal == null) return null;
```

```java
        String street = addrLocal.getStreet();
        String city = addrLocal.getCity();
        String state = addrLocal.getState();
        String zip = addrLocal.getZip();
        AddressDO addrValue = new AddressDO(street,city,state,zip);
        return addrValue;
    }
    public void setAddress(AddressDO addrValue)
        throws EJBException {

        String street = addrValue.getStreet();
        String city = addrValue.getCity();
        String state = addrValue.getState();
        String zip = addrValue.getZip();

        AddressLocal addr = getHomeAddress();

        try {

        if(addr == null) {
            // Customer doesn't have an address yet. Create a new one.
            InitialContext cntx = new InitialContext();
            AddressHomeLocal addrHome = (AddressHomeLocal)cntx.lookup
                ("AddressHomeLocal");
            addr = addrHome.createAddress(street, city, state, zip);
            this.setHomeAddress(addr);
        } else {
            // Customer already has an address. Change its fields.
            addr.setStreet(street);
            addr.setCity(city);
            addr.setState(state);
            addr.setZip(zip);
        }

        } catch(NamingException ne) {
            throw new EJBException(ne);
        } catch(CreateException ce) {
            throw new EJBException(ce);
        }

    }
    ...
```

Here is the definition for an AddressDO dependent value class, which is used by the enterprise bean to send address information to the client:

```java
public class AddressDO implements java.io.Serializable {
    private String street;
    private String city;
    private String state;
    private String zip;

    public AddressDO(String street, String city, String state, String zip ) {
        this.street = street;
```

```
            this.city = city;
            this.state = state;
            this.zip = zip;
        }
        public String getStreet() {
            return street;
        }
        public String getCity() {
            return city;
        }
        public String getState() {
            return state;
        }
        public String getZip() {
            return zip;
        }
    }
```

The `AddressDO` dependent value follows the conventions laid out in this book. It's immutable, which means it cannot be altered once it is created. As stated earlier, immutability helps to reinforce the fact that the dependent value class is a copy, not a remote reference.

You can now use a client application to test the Customer EJB's relationship with the Address EJB. Here is the client code that creates a new Customer, gives it an address, then changes the address using the method defined earlier:

```
import javax.naming.InitialContext;
import javax.rmi.PortableRemoteObject;
import javax.naming.Context;
import javax.naming.NamingException;
import java.util.Properties;

public class Client {
    public static void main(String [] args) throws Exception {
        // obtain CustomerHome
        Context jndiContext = getInitialContext();
        Object obj=jndiContext.lookup("CustomerHomeRemote");
        CustomerHome home = (CustomerHomeRemote)
            javax.rmi.PortableRemoteObject.narrow(obj,
            CustomerHomeRemote.class);

        // create a Customer
        Integer primaryKey = new Integer(1);
        Customer customer = home.create(primaryKey);

        // create an address
        AddressDO address = new AddressDO("1010 Colorado",
            "Austin", "TX", "78701");
        // set address
        customer.setAddress(address);

        address = customer.getAddress();
```

```
                System.out.print(primaryKey+" = ");
                System.out.println(address.getStreet());
                System.out.println(address.getCity()+","+
                                address.getState()+" "+
                                address.getZip());

            // create a new address
            address = new AddressDO("1600 Pennsylvania Avenue NW",
                "DC", "WA", "20500");

            // change Customer's address
            customer.setAddress(address);

            address = customer.getAddress();

                System.out.print(primaryKey+" = ");
                System.out.println(address.getStreet());
                System.out.println(address.getCity()+","+
                                address.getState()+" "+
                                address.getZip());

            // remove Customer
            customer.remove();
        }

    public static Context getInitialContext()
        throws javax.naming.NamingException {
        Properties p = new Properties();
        // ... Specify the JNDI properties specific to the vendor.
        //return new javax.naming.InitialContext(p);
        return null;
        }
    }
}
```

The following listing shows the deployment descriptor for the Customer and Address
EJBs. You don't need to worry about the details of the deployment descriptor yet; it
will be covered in depth in Chapter 7.

```
<!DOCTYPE ejb-jar PUBLIC "-//Sun Microsystems, Inc.//DTD Enterprise
JavaBeans 2.0//EN" "http://java.sun.com/dtd/ejb-jar_2_0.dtd">

<ejb-jar>
    <enterprise-beans>
        <entity>
            <ejb-name>CustomerEJB</ejb-name>
            <home>com.titan.customer.CustomerHomeRemote</home>
            <remote>com.titan.customer.CustomerRemote</remote>
            <ejb-class>com.titan.customer.CustomerBean</ejb-class>
            <persistence-type>Container</persistence-type>
            <prim-key-class>java.lang.Integer</prim-key-class>
            <reentrant>False</reentrant>
            <cmp-version>2.x</cmp-version>
            <abstract-schema-name>Customer</abstract-schema-name>
            <cmp-field><field-name>id</field-name></cmp-field>
```

```xml
            <cmp-field><field-name>lastName</field-name></cmp-field>
            <cmp-field><field-name>firstName</field-name></cmp-field>
            <primkey-field>id</primkey-field>
            <security-identity><use-caller-identity/></security-identity>
        </entity>
        <entity>
            <ejb-name>AddressEJB</ejb-name>
            <local-home>com.titan.address.AddressHomeLocal</local-home>
            <local>com.titan.address.AddressLocal</local>
            <ejb-class>com.titan.address.AddressBean</ejb-class>
            <persistence-type>Container</persistence-type>
            <prim-key-class>java.lang.Integer</prim-key-class>
            <reentrant>False</reentrant>
            <cmp-version>2.x</cmp-version>
            <abstract-schema-name>Address</abstract-schema-name>
            <cmp-field><field-name>id</field-name></cmp-field>
            <cmp-field><field-name>street</field-name></cmp-field>
            <cmp-field><field-name>city</field-name></cmp-field>
            <cmp-field><field-name>state</field-name></cmp-field>
            <cmp-field><field-name>zip</field-name></cmp-field>
            <primkey-field>id</primkey-field>
            <security-identity><use-caller-identity/></security-identity>
        </entity>
    </enterprise-beans>
    <relationships>
        <ejb-relation>
            <ejb-relation-name>Customer-Address</ejb-relation-name>
            <ejb-relationship-role>
                <ejb-relationship-role-name>
                    Customer-has-an-Address
                </ejb-relationship-role-name>
                <multiplicity>One</multiplicity>
                <relationship-role-source>
                    <ejb-name>CustomerEJB</ejb-name>
                </relationship-role-source>
                <cmr-field>
                    <cmr-field-name>homeAddress</cmr-field-name>
                </cmr-field>
            </ejb-relationship-role>
            <ejb-relationship-role>
                <ejb-relationship-role-name>
                    Address-belongs-to-Customer
                </ejb-relationship-role-name>
                <multiplicity>One</multiplicity>
                <relationship-role-source>
                    <ejb-name>AddressEJB</ejb-name>
                </relationship-role-source>
            </ejb-relationship-role>
        </ejb-relation>
    </relationships>
    <assembly-descriptor>
        <security-role>
            <role-name>Employees</role-name>
        </security-role>
```

```
        <method-permission>
            <role-name>Employees</role-name>
            <method>
                <ejb-name>CustomerEJB</ejb-name>
                <method-name>*</method-name>
            </method>
            <method>
                <ejb-name>AddressEJB</ejb-name>
                <method-name>*</method-name>
            </method>
        </method-permission>
        <container-transaction>
            <method>
                <ejb-name>AddressEJB</ejb-name>
                <method-name>*</method-name>
            </method>
            <method>
                <ejb-name>CustomerEJB</ejb-name>
                <method-name>*</method-name>
            </method>
            <trans-attribute>Required</trans-attribute>
        </container-transaction>
    </assembly-descriptor>
</ejb-jar>
```

📖 Workbook Exercise 6.3, A Simple Relationship in CMP 2.0

CHAPTER 7

EJB 2.0 CMP: Entity Relationships

In Chapter 6, you learned about basic EJB 2.0 container-managed persistence. This material included coverage of container-managed persistence fields and an introduction to a basic container-managed relationship field. In this chapter, we will continue to develop the Customer EJB and discuss in detail each of the seven possible relationships that entity beans can have with each other.

For entity beans to model real-world business concepts, they must be capable of forming complex relationships with each other. This was difficult to accomplish in EJB 1.1 container-managed persistence because of the simplicity of the programming model. In EJB 1.1, entity beans could have persistence fields but not relationship fields.

In EJB 2.0, relationship fields can model complex relationships between entity beans. In Chapter 6, we demonstrated a one-to-one relationship between the Customer and Address EJBs. This relationship was unidirectional; the Customer had a reference to the Address, but the Address did not have a reference back to the Customer. This is a perfectly legitimate relationship, but other relationships are also possible. For example, each Address could also reference its Customer. This is an example of a bidirectional one-to-one relationship, in which both participants maintain references to one another. In addition to one-to-one relationships, entity beans can have one-to-many, many-to-one, and many-to-many relationships. For example, the Customer EJB can have many phone numbers, but each phone number belongs to only one Customer (a one-to-many relationship). A Customer may also have been on many Cruises in the past, and each Cruise will have had many Customers (a many-to-many relationship).

The Seven Relationship Types

Seven types of relationships can exist between EJBs. This chapter examines those relationships and how the beans' code and deployment descriptors work together to define the relationships. First, let's look at the different types of relationships that are possible. There are four types of cardinality: one-to-one, one-to-many, many-to-one, and many-to-many. On top of that, each relationship can be either unidirectional or bidirectional. That yields eight possibilities, but if you think about it, you'll realize that one-to-many and many-to-one bidirectional relationships are actually the same thing. Thus, there are only seven distinct relationship types. To understand the relationships, it helps to think about some simple examples. We'll expand on the following examples in the course of the chapter:

One-to-one, unidirectional

The relationship between a customer and an address. You clearly want to be able to look up a customer's address, but you probably don't care about looking up an address's customer.

One-to-one, bidirectional

The relationship between a customer and a credit card number. Given a customer, you obviously want to be able to look up his credit card number. Given a credit card number, it is also conceivable that you would want to look up the customer who owns the credit card.

One-to-many, unidirectional

The relationship between a customer and a phone number. A customer can have many phone numbers (business, home, cell, etc.). You might need to look up a customer's phone number, but you probably wouldn't use one of those numbers to look up the customer.

One-to-many, bidirectional

The relationship between a cruise and a reservation. Given a reservation, you want to be able to look up the cruise for which the reservation was made. And given a cruise, you want to be able to look up all the reservations for that cruise. Note that a many-to-one bidirectional relationship is just another perspective on the same concept.

Many-to-one, unidirectional

The relationship between a cruise and a ship. You want to be able to look up the ship that will be used for a particular cruise, and many cruises share the same ship, though at different times. It's less useful to look up the ship to see which cruises are associated it, though if you want this capability, you can implement a many-to-one bidirectional relationship.

Many-to-many, unidirectional

The relationship between a reservation and a cabin. It's possible to make a reservation for multiple cabins, and you clearly want to be able to look up the cabin assigned to a reservation. However, you're not likely to want to look up the reservation associated with a particular cabin. (If you think you need to do so, you'd implement it as a bidirectional relationship.)

Many-to-many, bidirectional

The relationship between a cruise and a customer. A customer can make reservations on many cruises, and each cruise has many customers. You clearly want to be able to look up both the cruises on which a customer has a booking, and the customers that will be going on any given cruise.

Abstract Persistence Schema

In Chapter 6, you learned how to form a basic relationship between the Customer and Address entity beans using the abstract programming model. In reality, the abstract programming model is only half the equation. In addition to declaring abstract accessor methods, a bean developer must describe the cardinality and direction of the entity-to-entity relationships in the bean's deployment descriptor. This is handled in the <relationships> section of the XML deployment descriptor. As we discuss each type of relationship in the following sections, we will examine both the abstract programming model and the XML elements. The purpose of this section is to introduce you to the basic elements used in the XML deployment descriptor, to better prepare you for subsequent sections on specific relationship types.

In this book we always refer to the Java programming idioms used to describe relationships—specifically, the abstract accessor methods—as the *abstract programming model*. When referring to the XML deployment descriptor elements, we use the term *abstract persistence schema*. In the EJB 2.0 specification the term abstract persistence schema actually refers to both the Java idioms and the XML elements, but this book separate these concepts so we can discuss them more easily.

An entity bean's abstract persistence schema is defined in the <relationships> section of the XML deployment descriptor for that bean. The <relationships> section falls between the <enterprise-beans> section and the <assembly-descriptor> section. Within the <relationships> element, each entity-to-entity relationship is defined in a separate <ejb-relation> element:

```
<ejb-jar>
    <enterprise-beans>
    ...
    </enterprise-beans>
    <relationships>
        <ejb-relation>
        ...
        </ejb-relation>
        <ejb-relation>
        ...
        </ejb-relation>
    </relationships>
    <assembly-descriptor>
    ...
    </assembly-descriptor>
</ejb-jar>
```

Defining relationship fields requires that an <ejb-relation> element be added to the XML deployment descriptor for each entity-to-entity relationship. These <ejb-relation> elements complement the abstract programming model. For each pair of abstract accessor methods that define a relationship field, there is an <ejb-relation> element in the deployment descriptor. EJB 2.0 requires that the entity beans that participate in a relationship be defined in the same XML deployment descriptor.

Here is a partial listing of the deployment descriptor for the Customer and Address EJBs, with the emphasis on the elements that define the relationship:

```
<ejb-jar>
    ...
    <enterprise-beans>
        <entity>
            <ejb-name>CustomerEJB</ejb-name>
            <local-home>com.titan.customer.CusomterHomeLocal</local-home>
            <local>com.titan.customer.CustomerLocal</local>
            ...
        </entity>
        <entity>
            <ejb-name>AddressEJB</ejb-name>
            <local-home>com.titan.address.AddressHomeLocal</local-home>
            <local>com.titan.address.AddressLocal</local>
            ...
        </entity>
        ...
    </enterprise-beans>

    <relationships>
        <ejb-relation>
            <ejb-relation-name>Customer-Address</ejb-relation-name>
            <ejb-relationship-role>
                <ejb-relationship-role-name>
                    Customer-has-an-Address
                </ejb-relationship-role-name>
                <multiplicity>One</multiplicity>
                <relationship-role-source>
                    <ejb-name>CustomerEJB</ejb-name>
                </relationship-role-source>
                <cmr-field>
                    <cmr-field-name>homeAddress</cmr-field-name>
                </cmr-field>
            </ejb-relationship-role>
            <ejb-relationship-role>
                <ejb-relationship-role-name>
                    Address-belongs-to-Customer
                </ejb-relationship-role-name>
                <multiplicity>One</multiplicity>
                <relationship-role-source>
                    <ejb-name>AddressEJB</ejb-name>
                </relationship-role-source>
            </ejb-relationship-role>
        </ejb-relation>
    </relationships>
</ejb-jar>
```

All relationships between the Customer EJB and other entity beans, such as Credit-Card, Address, and Phone, require that we define an <ejb-relation> element to complement the abstract accessor methods.

Every relationship may have a relationship name, which is declared in the <ejb-relation-name> element. This serves to identify the relationship for individuals reading the deployment descriptor or for deployment tools, but it's not required.

Every <ejb-relation> element has exactly two <ejb-relationship-role> elements, one for each participant in the relationship. In the previous example, the first <ejb-relationship-role> declares the Customer EJB's role in the relationship. We know this because the <relationship-role-source> element specifies the <ejb-name> as CustomerEJB. CustomerEJB is the <ejb-name> used in the Customer EJB's original declaration in the <enterprise-beans> section. The <relationship-role-source> element's <ejb-name> must always match an <ejb-name> element in the <enterprise-beans> section.

The <ejb-relationship-role> element also declares the cardinality, or *multiplicity*, of the role. The <multiplicity> element can either be One or Many. In this case, the Customer EJB's <multiplicity> element has a value of One, which means that every Address EJB has a relationship with exactly *one* Customer EJB. The Address EJB's <multiplicity> element also specifies One, which means that every Customer EJB has a relationship with exactly one Address EJB. If the Customer EJB had a relationship with many Address EJBs, the Address EBJ's <multiplicity> element would be set to Many.

In Chapter 6, we defined the Customer EJB as having abstract accessor methods for getting and setting the Address EJB in the homeAddress field, but the Address EJB did not have abstract accessor methods for the Customer EJB. In this case, the Customer EJB maintains a reference to the Address EJB, but the Address EJB doesn't maintain a reference back to the Customer EJB. This is a unidirectional relationship, which means that only one of the entity beans in the relationship maintains a container-managed relationship field.

If the bean described by the <ejb-relationship-role> element maintains a reference to the other bean in the relationship, that reference must be declared as a *container-managed relationship field* in the <cmr-field> element. The <cmr-field> element is declared under the <ejb-relationship-role> element:

```
<ejb-relationship-role>
    <ejb-relationship-role-name>
        Customer-has-an-Address
    </ejb-relationship-role-name>
    <multiplicity>One</multiplicity>
    <relationship-role-source>
        <ejb-name>CustomerEJB</ejb-name>
    </relationship-role-source>
    <cmr-field>
        <cmr-field-name>homeAddress</cmr-field-name>
    </cmr-field>
</ejb-relationship-role>
```

EJB 2.0 requires that the <cmr-field-name> begin with a lowercase letter. For every relationship field defined by a <cmr-field> element, there must be a pair of matching abstract accessor methods in the bean class. One method in this pair must be defined with the method name set<cmr-field-name>(), with the first letter of the <cmr-field-name> value changed to uppercase. The other method is defined as get<cmr-field-name>(), also with the first letter of the <cmr-field-name> value in uppercase. In the previous example, the <cmr-field-name> is homeAddress, which corresponds to the getHomeAddress() and setHomeAddress() abstract accessor methods defined in the CustomerBean class:

```
// bean class code
public abstract void setHomeAddress(AddressLocal address);
public abstract AddressLocal getHomeAddress();

// XML deployment descriptor declaration
<cmr-field>
    <cmr-field-name>homeAddress</cmr-field-name>
</cmr-field>
```

The return type of the get<cmr-field-name>() method and the parameter type of the set<cmr-field-name>() must be the same. The type must be the local interface of the entity bean that is referenced or one of two java.util.Collection types. In the case of the homeAddress relationship field, we are using the Address EJB's local interface, AddressLocal. Collection types are discussed in more detail in one-to-many, many-to-one, and many-to-many relationships later in this chapter.

Now that we have established a basic understanding of how elements are declared in the abstract persistence schema, we are ready to discuss each of the seven types of relationships in more detail. In the process, we will introduce additional entity beans that have relationships with the Customer EJB, including the CreditCard, Phone, Ship, and Reservation EJBs.

It's important to understand that although entity beans may have both local and remote interfaces, a container-managed relationship field can use only the entity bean's local interface when persisting a relationship. So, for example, it is illegal to define an abstract accessor method that has an argument type of javax.ejb.EJBObject (a remote interface type). All container-managed relationships are based on javax.ejb.EJBLocalObject (local interface) types.

Database Modeling

This chapter discusses several different database table schemas. These schemas are intended only to demonstrate possible relationships between entities in the database; they are not prescriptive. For example, the Address-Customer relationship is manifested by having the CUSTOMER table maintain a foreign key to the ADDRESS table. This is not how most databases will be organized—instead, they will probably use a link table or have the ADDRESS table maintain a foreign key to the CUSTOMER. However, this schema shows how EJB 2.0's container-managed persistence can support different database organizations.

Throughout this chapter, we assume that the database tables are created before the EJB application—in other words, that the EJB application is mapped to a legacy database. Some vendors offer tools that generate tables automatically according to the relationships defined between the entity beans. These tools may create schemas that are very different from the ones explored here. In other cases, vendors that support established database schemas may not have the flexibility to support the schemas illustrated in this chapter. As an EJB developer, you must be flexible enough to adapt to the facilities provided by your EJB vendor.

One-to-One Unidirectional Relationship

An example of a one-to-one unidirectional relationship is the relationship between the Customer EJB and the Address EJB defined in Chapter 6. In this case, each Customer has exactly one Address and each Address has exactly one Customer. Which bean references which determines the direction of navigation. While the Customer has a reference to the Address, the Address doesn't reference the Customer. This is a unidirectional relationship because you can go only from the Customer to the Address, and not the other way around. In other words, an Address EJB has no idea who owns it. Figure 7-1 shows this relationship.

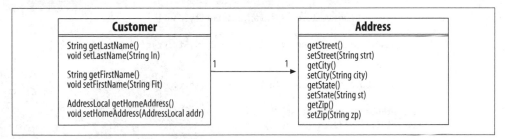

Figure 7-1. One-to-one unidirectional relationship

Relational database schema

As shown in Figure 7-2, one-to-one unidirectional relationships normally use a fairly typical relational database schema in which one table contains a foreign key (pointer) to another table. In this case, the CUSTOMER table contains a foreign key to the ADDRESS table, but the ADDRESS table doesn't contain a foreign key to the CUSTOMER table. This allows records in the ADDRESS table to be shared by other tables, a scenario explored in the section "Many-to-Many Unidirectional Relationship." The fact that the database schema is not the same as the abstract persistence schema illustrates that they are somewhat independent.

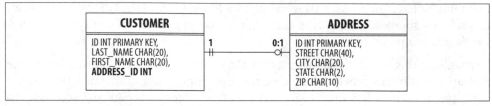

Figure 7-2. One-to-one unidirectional relationship in RDBMS

Abstract programming model

As you learned in Chapter 6, abstract accessor methods are used to define relationship fields in the bean class. When an entity bean maintains a reference to another bean, it defines a pair of abstract accessor methods to model that reference. In unidirectional relationships, which can be navigated only one way, only one of the enterprise beans defines these abstract accessor methods. Thus, inside the CustomerBean class you can call the getHomeAddress()/setHomeAddress() methods to access the Address EJBs, but there are no methods inside the AddressBean class to access the Customer EJB.

The Address EJB can be shared between relationship fields of the same enterprise bean, but it cannot be shared between Customer EJBs. If, for example, the Customer EJB defines two relationship fields, billingAddress and homeAddress, as one-to-one unidirectional relationships with the Address EJB, these two fields can reference the same Address EJB:

```
public class CustomerBean implements javax.ejb.EntityBean {
    ...
    public void setAddress(String street,String city,String state,String zip) {
        ...

        address = addressHome.createAddress(street, city, state, zip);

        this.setHomeAddress(address);
        this.setBillingAddress(address);

        AddressLocal billAddr = this.getBillingAddress();
        AddressLocal homeAddr = this.getHomeAddress();

        if(billAddr.isIdentical(homeAddr))
        // always true

        ...
    }
    ...
}
```

If at any time you want to make the billingAddress different from the homeAddress, you can simply set it equal to a different Address EJB. Sharing a reference to another bean between two relationship fields in the same entity is sometimes very convenient, though. In order to support this type of relationship, a new billing address field might be added to the CUSTOMER table:

```
CREATE TABLE CUSTOMER
(
    ID INT PRIMARY KEY,
    LAST_NAME CHAR(20),
    FIRST_NAME CHAR(20),
    ADDRESS_ID INT,
    BILLING_ADDRESS_ID INT
}
```

As the earlier example shows, it is possible for two fields in a bean (in this case, the homeAddress and billingAddress fields in the Customer EJB) to reference the same relationship (i.e., a single Address EJB) if the relationship type is the same. However, it is not possible to share a single Address EJB between two different Customer EJBs. If, for example, the home Address of Customer A were assigned as the home Address of Customer B, the Address would be moved, not shared, so that Customer A wouldn't have a home Address any longer. As you can see in Figure 7-3, Address 2 is initially assigned to Customer B, but becomes disconnected when Address 1 is reassigned to Customer B.

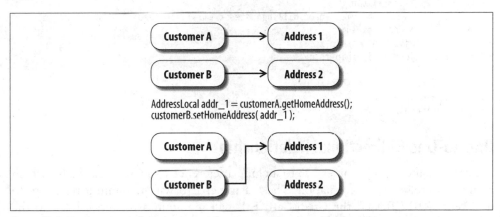

Figure 7-3. Exchanging references in a one-to-one unidirectional relationship

This seemingly strange side effect is simply a natural result of how the relationship is defined. The Customer-to-Address EJB relationship was defined as one-to-one, so the Address EJB can be referenced by only one Customer EJB.

If the Customer EJB does not have an Address EJB associated with its AddressHome field, the getHomeAddress() method will return null. This is true of all container-managed relationship fields that reference a single entity bean.

Abstract persistence schema

We defined the XML elements for the Customer-Address relationship earlier in this chapter, so we won't go over them again. The <ejb-relation> element used in that section declared a one-to-one unidirectional relationship. If, however, the Customer EJB did maintain two relationship fields with the Address EJB—homeAddress and billingAddress—each of these relationships would have to be described in its own <ejb-relation> element:

```
<relationships>
    <ejb-relation>
        <ejb-relation-name>Customer-HomeAddress</ejb-relation-name>
        <ejb-relationship-role>
            ...
            <cmr-field>
                <cmr-field-name>homeAddress</cmr-field-name>
            </cmr-field>
        </ejb-relationship-role>
        <ejb-relationship-role>
            ...
        </ejb-relationship-role>
    </ejb-relation>
    <ejb-relation>
        <ejb-relation-name>Customer-BillingAddress</ejb-relation-name>
        <ejb-relationship-role>
            ...
            <cmr-field>
                <cmr-field-name>billingAddress</cmr-field-name>
            </cmr-field>
        </ejb-relationship-role>
        <ejb-relationship-role>
            ...
        </ejb-relationship-role>
    </ejb-relation>
</relationships>
```

One-to-One Bidirectional Relationship

We can expand our Customer EJB to include a reference to a CreditCard EJB, which maintains credit card information. The Customer EJB will maintain a reference to its CreditCard EJB and the CreditCard EJB will maintain a reference back to the Customer—this makes good sense, since a CreditCard should be aware of who owns it. Since each CreditCard has a reference back to one Customer and each Customer references one CreditCard, we have a one-to-one bidirectional relationship.

Relational database schema

The CreditCard EJB has a corresponding CREDIT_CARD table, so we need to add a CREDIT_CARD foreign key to the CUSTOMER table:

```
CREATE TABLE CREDIT_CARD
(
    ID INT PRIMARY KEY NOT NULL,
    EXP_DATE DATE,
    NUMBER CHAR(20),
```

```
    NAME CHAR(40),
    ORGANIZATION CHAR(20),
    CUSTOMER_ID INT
}

CREATE TABLE CUSTOMER
(
    ID INT PRIMARY KEY,
    LAST_NAME CHAR(20),
    FIRST_NAME CHAR(20),
    HOME_ADDRESS_ID INT,
    ADDRESS_ID INT,
    CREDIT_CARD_ID INT
)
```

One-to-one bidirectional relationships may model relational database schemas in which the two tables hold foreign keys for one another (specifically, two rows in different tables point to each other). Figure 7-4 illustrates how this schema would be implemented for rows in the CUSTOMER and CREDIT_CARD tables.

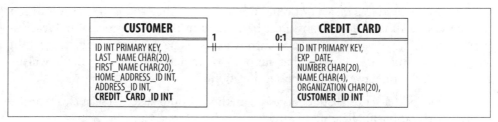

Figure 7-4. One-to-one bidirectional relationship in RDBMS

It is also possible for a one-to-one bidirectional relationship to be established through a linking table, in which each foreign key column must be unique. This is convenient when you do not want to impose relationships on the original tables. We will use linking tables in one-to-many and many-to-many relationships later in this chapter, but it is important to remember that the database schema used in these examples is purely illustrative. The abstract persistence schema of an entity bean may map to a variety of database schemas; the database schema used in these examples are only one possibility.

Abstract programming model

To model the relationship between the Customer and CreditCard EJBs, we'll need to declare a relationship field named customer in the CreditCardBean class:

```
public abstract class CreditCardBean extends javax.ejb.EntityBean {

    ...

    // relationship fields
    public abstract CustomerLocal getCustomer();
    public abstract void setCustomer(CustomerLocal local);
```

```
    // persistence fields
    public abstract Integer getId();
    public abstract void setId(Integer id);
    public abstract Date getExpirationDate();
    public abstract void setExpirationDate(Date date);
    public abstract String getNumber();
    public abstract void setNumber(String number);
    public abstract String getNameOnCard();
    public abstract void setNameOnCard(String name);
    public abstract String getCreditOrganization();
    public abstract void setCreditOrganization(String org);

    // standard callback methods
    ...

}
```

In this case, we use the Customer EJB's local interface (assume one has been created) because relationship fields require local interface types. All the relationships explored in the rest of this chapter assume local interfaces. Of course, the limitation of using local interfaces instead of remote interfaces is that you don't have location transparency. All the entity beans must be located in the same process or Java Virtual Machine (JVM). Although relationship fields using remote interfaces are not supported in EJB 2.0, it's likely that support for remote relationship fields will be added in a subsequent version of the specification.

We can also add a set of abstract accessor methods in the CustomerBean class for the creditCard relationship field:

```
    public class CustomerBean implements javax.ejb.EntityBean {
        ...
        public abstract void setCreditCard(CreditCardLocal card);
        public abstract CreditCardLocal getCreditCard();
        ...
    }
```

Although a setCustomer() method is available in the CreditCardBean, we do not have to set the Customer reference on the CreditCard EJB explicitly. When a CreditCard EJB reference is passed into the setCreditCard() method on the CustomerBean class, the EJB container will automatically establish the customer relationship on the Address EJB to point back to the Customer EJB:

```
    public class CustomerBean implements javax.ejb.EntityBean {
        ...
        public void setCreditCard(Date exp, String numb, String name, String org)
            throws CreateException {
            ...

            card = creditCardHome.create(exp,numb,name,org);

            // the CreditCard EJB's customer field will be set automatically
            this.setCreditCard(card);
```

```
            Customer customer = card.getCustomer();

            if(customer.isIdentical(ejbContext.getEJBLocalObject())
            // always true

            ...
        }
        ...
    }
```

The rules for sharing a single bean in a one-to-one bidirectional relationship are the same as those for one-to-one unidirectional relationships. While the CreditCard EJB may be shared between relationship fields of the same Customer EJB, it can't be shared between different Customer EJBs. As Figure 7-5 shows, assigning Customer A's CreditCard to Customer B disassociates that CreditCard from Customer A and moves it to Customer B.

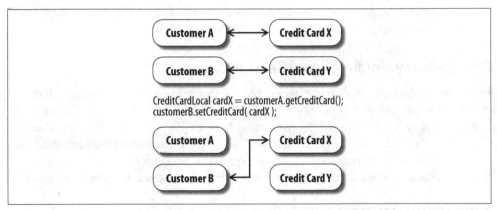

Figure 7-5. Exchanging references in a one-to-one bidirectional relationship

Abstract persistence schema

The <ejb-relation> element that defines the Customer-to-CreditCard relationship is similar to the one used for the Customer-to-Address relationship, with one important difference—both <ejb-relationship-role> elements have a <cmr-field>:

```
<relationships>
    <ejb-relation>
        <ejb-relation-name>Customer-CreditCard</ejb-relation-name>
        <ejb-relationship-role>
            <ejb-relationship-role-name>
                Customer-has-a-CreditCard
            </ejb-relationship-role-name>
            <multiplicity>One</multiplicity>
            <relationship-role-source>
                <ejb-name>CustomerEJB</ejb-name>
            </relationship-role-source>
            <cmr-field>
```

```
                <cmr-field-name>creditCard</cmr-field-name>
            </cmr-field>
        </ejb-relationship-role>
        <ejb-relationship-role>
            <ejb-relationship-role-name>
                CreditCard-belongs-to-Customer
            </ejb-relationship-role-name>
            <multiplicity>One</multiplicity>
            <relationship-role-source>
                <ejb-name>CreditCardEJB</ejb-name>
            </relationship-role-source>
            <cmr-field>
                <cmr-field-name>customer</cmr-field-name>
            </cmr-field>
        </ejb-relationship-role>
    </ejb-relation>
</relationships>
```

The fact that both participants in the relationship define `<cmr-field>` elements (relationship fields) tells us that the relationship is bidirectional.

One-to-Many Unidirectional Relationship

Entity beans can also maintain relationships with multiplicity. This means that one entity bean can aggregate or contain many other entity beans. For example, the Customer EJB may have relationships with many Phone EJBs, each of which represents a phone number. This is very different from the simple one-to-one relationships. One-to-many and many-to-many relationships require the developer to work with a collection of references when accessing the relationship field, instead of a single reference.

Relational database schema

To illustrate a one-to-many unidirectional relationship, we will use a new entity bean, the Phone EJB, for which we must define a table, the PHONE table:

```
CREATE TABLE PHONE
(
    ID INT PRIMARY KEY NOT NULL,
    NUMBER CHAR(20),
    TYPE INT,
    CUSTOMER_ID INT
}
```

One-to-many unidirectional relationships between the CUSTOMER and PHONE tables could be manifested in a relational database in a variety of ways. For this example, we chose to have the PHONE table include a foreign key to the CUSTOMER table.

The table of aggregated data can maintain a column of nonunique foreign keys to the aggregating table. In the case of the Customer and Phone EJBs, the PHONE table maintains a foreign key to the CUSTOMER table, and one or more PHONE records may contain foreign keys to the same CUSTOMER record. In other words, in the database the PHONE records point to the CUSTOMER records. In the abstract programming model, however, it is the Customer EJB that points to the Phone EJBs—two schemas are reversed. How does this work? The container system hides the reverse pointer so that it appears as if the Customer is aware of the Phone EJB and not the other way around. When you ask the container to return a Collection of Phone EJBs (invoking the getPhoneNumbers() method), it will query the PHONE table for all the records with a foreign key matching the Customer EJB's primary key. The use of reverse pointers in this type of relationship is illustrated in Figure 7-6.

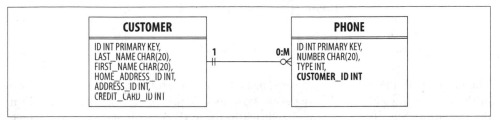

Figure 7-6. One-to-many unidirectional relationship in RDBMS using reverse pointers

This database schema illustrates that the structure and relationships of the actual database can differ from the relationships as defined in the abstract programming model. In this case the tables are set up in reverse, but the EJB container system will manage the beans to meet the specification of the bean developer. This isn't always possible; sometimes the database schema is incompatible with a desired relationship field. however, when you are dealing with legacy databases (i.e., databases that were established before the EJB application) reverse-pointer scenarios like the one illustrated here are common, so supporting this kind of relationship mapping is important.

A simpler implementation of the Customer-Phone relationship could use a link table that maintains two columns with foreign keys pointing to both the CUSTOMER and PHONE records. We could then place a unique constraint on the PHONE foreign key column in the link table to ensure that it contains only unique entries (i.e., that every phone has only one customer), while allowing the CUSTOMER foreign key column to contain duplicates. The advantage of the link table is that it doesn't impose the relationship between the CUSTOMER and PHONE records onto either of the tables.

Abstract programming model

In the abstract programming model, we represent multiplicity by defining a relationship field that can point to many entity beans. To do this, we employ the same abstract accessor methods we used for one-to-one relationships, but this time we set the field type to either java.util.Collection or java.util.Set. The Collection maintains a homogeneous group of local EJB object references, which means it contains many references to one kind of entity bean. The Collection type may contain duplicate references to the same entity bean, while the Set type may not.

For example, a Customer EJB may have relationships with several phone numbers (e.g., a home phone, work phone, cell phone, fax, etc.), each represented by a Phone EJB. Instead of having a different relationship field for each of these Phone EJBs, the Customer EJB keeps all the Phone EJBs in a collection-based relationship field, which can be accessed through abstract accessor methods:

```
public abstract class CustomerBean implements javax.ejb.EntityBean {
    ...
    // relationship fields
    public java.util.Collection getPhoneNumbers();
    public void setPhoneNumbers(java.util.Collection phones);

    public AddressLocal getHomeAddress();()
    public void setHomeAddress(AddressLocal local);
    ...
```

The Phone EJB, like other entity beans, has a bean class and local interface, as shown in the next listing. Notice that the PhoneBean doesn't provide a relationship field for the Customer EJB. It's a unidirectional relationship; the Customer maintains a relationship with many Phone EJBs, but the Phone EJBs do not maintain a relationship field back to the Customer. Only the Customer EJB is aware of the relationship:

```
// the local interface for the Phone EJB
public interface PhoneLocal extends javax.ejb.EJBLocalObject {
    public String getNumber();
    public void setNumber(String number);
    public byte getType();
    public void setType(byte type);
}

// the bean class for the Phone EJB
public class PhoneBean implements javax.ejb.EntityBean {

    public Integer ejbCreate(String number, byte type) {
        setNumber(number);
        setType(type);
        return null;
    }
    public void ejbPostCreate(String number,byte type) {
    }

    // persistence fields
    public abstract Integer getId();
    public abstract void setId(Integer id);
    public abstract String getNumber();
    public abstract void setNumber(String number);
    public abstract byte getType();
    public abstract void setType(byte type);

    // standard callback methods
    ...
}
```

To illustrate how an entity bean uses a collection-based relationship field, we will define a method in the CustomerBean class that allows remote clients to add new phone numbers. The method, addPhoneNumber(), uses the phone number arguments to create a new Phone EJB and then add that Phone EJB to a collection-based relationship field named phoneNumbers:

```
public abstract class CustomerBean implements javax.ejb.EntityBean {

    // business methods
    public void addPhoneNumber(String number, String type) {

        InitialContext jndiEnc = new InitialContext();
        PhoneHomeLocal phoneHome = jndiEnc.lookup("PhoneHomeLocal");
        PhoneLocal phone = phoneHome.create(number,type);

        Collection phoneNumbers = this.getPhoneNumbers();
        phoneNumbers.add(phone);

    }
    ...
    // relationship fields
    public java.util.Collection getPhoneNumbers();
    public void setPhoneNumbers(java.util.Collection phones);

    ...
```

Note that we created the Phone EJB first, then added it to the phoneNumbers collection-based relationship. We obtained the phoneNumbers Collection object from the getPhoneNumbers() accessor method, then added the new Phone EJB to the Collection just as we would add any object to a Collection. Adding the Phone EJB to the Collection causes the EJB container to set the foreign key on the new PHONE record so that it points back to the Customer EJB's CUSTOMER record. If we had used a link table, a new link record would have been created. From this point forward, the new Phone EJB will be available from the phoneNumbers collection-based relationship.

You can also update or remove references in a collection-based relationship field from the relationship using the relationship field accessor method. For example, the following code defines two methods in the CustomerBean class that allow clients to remove or update phone numbers in the bean's phoneNumbers relationship field:

```
public abstract class CustomerBean implements javax.ejb.EntityBean {

    // business methods
    public void removePhoneNumber(byte typeToRemove) {

        Collection phoneNumbers = this.getPhoneNumbers();
        Iterator iterator = phoneNumbers.iterator();
        while(iterator.hasNext()) {
            PhoneLocal phone = (PhoneLocal)iterator.next();
            if(phone.getType() = typeToRemove) {
                iterator.remove(phone);
```

```
                break;
            }
        }
    }
    public void updatePhoneNumber(String number,byte typeToUpdate) {
        Collection phoneNumbers = this.getPhoneNumbers();
        Iterator iterator = phoneNumbers.iterator();
        while(iterator.hasNext()) {
            PhoneLocal phone = (PhoneLocal)iterator.next();
            if(phone.getType() = typeToUpdate) {
                phone.setNumber(number);
                break;
            }
        }
    }
    ...
    // relationship fields
    public java.util.Collection getPhoneNumbers();
    public void setPhoneNumbers(java.util.Collection phones);
```

In the removePhoneNumber() business method, a Phone EJB with the matching type
was found and then removed from the collection-based relationship. The phone
number is not deleted from the database, it's just disassociated from the Customer
EJB (i.e., it is no longer referenced by a Customer). Figure 7-7 shows what happens
when a Phone EJB reference is removed from the collection-based relationship.

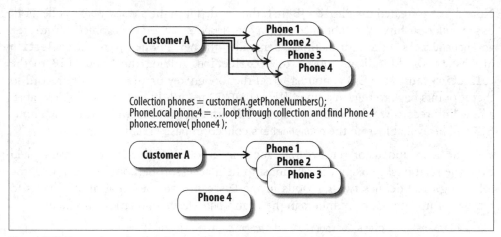

Figure 7-7. Removing a bean reference from a relationship-field collection

The updatePhoneNumber() method actually modifies an existing Phone EJB, changing
its state in the database. The Phone EJB is still referenced by the collection-based
relationship, but its data has changed.

The removePhoneNumber() and updatePhoneNumber() methods illustrate that a collection-based relationship can be accessed and updated just like any other Collection
object. In addition, a java.util.Iterator can be obtained from the Collection object

---

for looping operations. However, you should exercise caution when using an iterator over a collection-based relationship. You must not add elements to or remove elements from the Collection object while you are using its Iterator. The only exception to this rule is that the Iterator.remove() method may be called to remove an entry. Although the Collection.add() and Collection.remove() methods can be used in other circumstances, calling these methods while an iterator is in use will result in a java.util.IllegalStateException exception.

If no beans have been added to the phoneNumbers relationship field, the getPhoneNumbers() method will return an empty Collection object. <multiplicity> relationship fields never return null. The Collection object used with the relationship field is implemented by the container system, proprietary to the vendor, and tightly coupled with the inner workings of the container. This allows the EJB container to implement performance enhancements such as lazy loading or optimistic concurrency seamlessly, without exposing those proprietary mechanisms to the bean developer.* Application-defined Collection objects may be used with container-manager relationship fields only if the elements are of the proper type. For example, it is legal to create a new Collection object and then add that Collection object to the Customer EJB using the setPhoneNumbers() method:

```
public void addPhoneNumber(String number, String type) {

    ...
    PhoneLocal phone = phoneHome.create(number,type);

    Collection phoneNumbers = java.util.Vector();
    phoneNumbers.add(phone);

    // This is allowed
    this.setPhoneNumbers(phoneNumbers);

}

// relationship fields
public java.util.Collection getPhoneNumbers();

public void setPhoneNumbers(java.util.Collection phones);
```

We have used the getPhoneNumbers() method extensively but have not yet used the setPhoneNumbers() method. In most cases this method will not be used, because it updates an entire collection of phone numbers. However, it can be useful for exchanging like relationships between entity beans.

If two Customer EJBs want to exchange phone numbers, they can do so in a variety of ways. The most important thing to keep in mind is that a Phone EJB, as the subject of a one-to-many unidirectional relationship, may reference only one Customer EJB. It

---

* A Collection from a collection-based relationship that is materialized in a transaction cannot be modified outside the scope of that transaction. See Chapter 14 for more details.

can be copied, so that both Customers have Phone EJBs with similar data, but the Phone EJB itself cannot be shared.

Imagine, for example, that Customer A wants to transfer all of its phone numbers to Customer B. It can accomplish this by using Customer B's setPhoneNumbers() method, as shown in the following listing (we assume the Customer EJBs are interacting through their local interfaces):

```
CustomerLocal customerA = ... get Customer A
CustomerLocal customerB = ... get Customer B

Collection phonesA = customerA.getPhoneNumbers();
customerB.setPhoneNumbers( phonesA );

if( customerA.getPhoneNumbers().isEmpty())
    // this will be true
if( phonesA.isEmpty()) )
    // this will be true
```

As Figure 7-8 illustrates, passing one collection-based relationship to another actually disassociates those relationships from the first bean and associates them with the second. In addition, if the second bean already has a Collection of Phone EJBs in its phoneNumbers relationship field, those beans are bumped out of the relationship and disassociated from the bean.

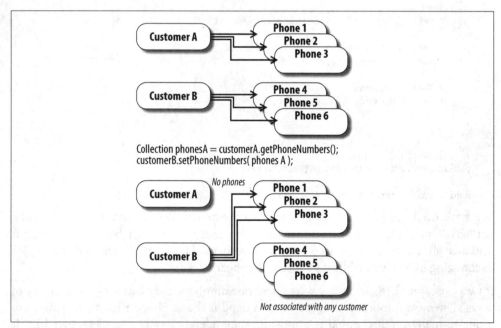

Figure 7-8. Exchanging a relationship collection in a one-to-many unidirectional relationship

The result of this exchange may be counterintuitive, but it is necessary to uphold the multiplicity of the relationship, which says that the Phone EJB may have only one

Customer EJB. This explains why Phone EJBs 1, 2, and 3 don't reference both Customers A and B, but it doesn't explain why Phone EJBs 4, 5, and 6 are disassociated from Customer B. Why isn't Customer B associated with all the Phone EJBs? The reason is purely a matter of semantics, since the relational database schema wouldn't technically prevent this from occurring. The act of replacing one Collection with another by calling setPhoneNumbers(Collection collection) implies that Customer B's initial Collection object is no longer referenced.

In addition to moving whole collection-based relationships between beans, it is possible to move individual Phone EJBs between Customers. These cannot be shared either. For example, if a Phone EJB aggregated by Customer A is added to the relationship collection of Customer B, that Phone EJB changes so that it's now referenced by Customer B instead of Customer A, as Figure 7-9 illustrates.

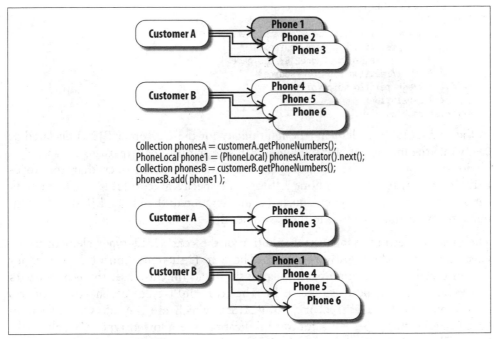

Figure 7-9. Exchanging a bean in a one-to-many unidirectional relationship

One again, it's the multiplicity of the relationship that prevents Phone 1 from referencing both Customer A and Customer B.

Abstract persistence schema

The abstract persistence schema for one-to-many unidirectional relationships has a few significant differences from the <ejb-relation> elements seen so far:

```
<relationships>
    <ejb-relation>
```

```
            <ejb-relation-name>Customer-Phones</ejb-relation-name>
            <ejb-relationship-role>
                <ejb-relationship-role-name>
                    Customer-has-many-Phone-numbers
                </ejb-relationship-role-name>
                <multiplicity>One</multiplicity>
                <relationship-role-source>
                    <ejb-name>CustomerEJB</ejb-name>
                </relationship-role-source>
                <cmr-field>
                    <cmr-field-name>phoneNumbers</cmr-field-name>
                    <cmr-field-type>java.util.Collection</cmr-field-type>
                </cmr-field>
            </ejb-relationship-role>
            <ejb-relationship-role>
                <ejb-relationship-role-name>
                    Phone-belongs-to-Customer
                </ejb-relationship-role-name>
                <multiplicity>Many</multiplicity>
                <relationship-role-source>
                    <ejb-name>PhoneEJB</ejb-name>
                </relationship-role-source>
            </ejb-relationship-role>
        </ejb-relation>
    </relationships>
```

In the <ejb-relation> element, the multiplicity for the Customer EJB is declared as One, while the multiplicity for the Phone EJB's <ejb-relationship-role> is Many. This obviously establishes the relationship as one-to-many. The fact that the <ejb-relationship-role> for the Phone EJB doesn't specify a <cmr-field> element indicates that the one-to-many relationship is unidirectional; the Phone EJB doesn't contain a reciprocating reference to the Customer EJB.

The most interesting change is the addition of the <cmr-field-type> element in the Customer EJB's <cmr-field> declaration. The <cmr-field-type> must be specified for a bean that has a collection-based relationship field (in this case, the phoneNumbers field maintained by the Customer EJB). The <cmr-field-type> can have one of two values, java.util.Collection or java.util.Set, which are the allowed collection-based relationship types. In a future specification, the allowed types for collection-based relationships may be expanded to include java.util.List and java.util.Map, but these are not yet supported.

📖 Workbook Exercise 7.1, Entity Relationships in CMP 2.0: Part 1

The Cruise, Ship, and Reservation EJBs

To make things more interesting, we are going to introduce some more entity beans so that we can model the remaining four relationships: many-to-one unidirectional, one-to-many bidirectional, many-to-many bidirectional, and many-to-many unidirectional.

In Titan's reservation system, every customer (a.k.a. passenger) can be booked on one or more cruises. Each booking requires a reservation. A reservation may be for one or more (usually two) passengers. Each cruise requires exactly one ship, but each ship may be used for many cruises throughout the year. Figure 7-10 illustrates these relationships.

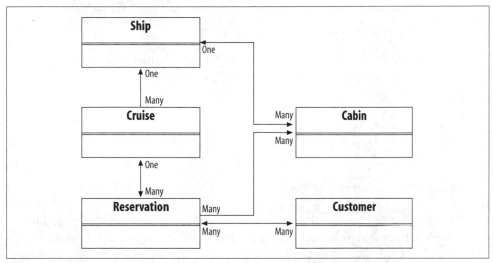

Figure 7-10. Cruise, Ship, Reservation, Cabin, and Customer class diagram

The relationships investigated in the next four sections will each refer back to the above diagram.

Many-to-One Unidirectional Relationship

Many-to-one unidirectional relationships result when many entity beans reference a single entity bean, but the referenced entity bean is unaware of the relationship. In the Titan Cruise business, for example, the concept of a cruise can be captured by a Cruise EJB. As shown in Figure 7-10, each Cruise has a many-to-one relationship with a Ship. This relationship is unidirectional; the Cruise EJB maintains a relationship with the Ship EJB, but the Ship EJB does not keep track of the Cruises for which it is used.

Relational database schema

The relational database schema for the Cruise-to-Ship relationship is fairly simple; it requires that the CRUISE table maintain a foreign key column for the SHIP table, with each row in the CRUISE table pointing to a row in the SHIP table. The CRUISE and SHIP tables are defined below; Figure 7-11 shows the relationship between these tables in the database.

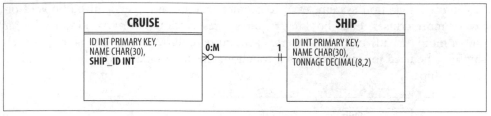

Figure 7-11. Many-to-one unidirectional relationship in RDBMS

An enormous amount of data would be required to adequately describe an ocean liner, but we'll use a simple definition of the SHIP table here:

```
CREATE TABLE SHIP
(
    ID INT PRIMARY KEY NOT NULL,
    NAME CHAR(30),
    TONNAGE DECIMAL (8,2)
}
```

The CRUISE table maintains data on each cruise's name, ship, and other information that is not germane to this discussion. (Other tables, such as RESERVATIONS, SCHEDULES, and CREW, would have relationships with the CRUISE table through linking tables.) We'll keep it simple and focus on a definition that is useful for the examples in this book:

```
CREATE TABLE CRUISE
(
    ID INT PRIMARY KEY NOT NULL,
    NAME CHAR(30),
    SHIP_ID INT
}
```

Abstract programming model

In the abstract programming model, the relationship field is of type ShipLocal and is maintained by the Cruise EJB. The abstract accessor methods are similar to those defined in the previous examples:

```
public abstract class CruiseBean implements javax.ejb.EntityBean {
    public Integer ejbCreate(String name, ShipLocal ship) {
        setName(name);
        return null;
    }
    public void ejbPostCreate(String name, ShipLocal ship) {
        setShip(ship);
    }
    public abstract Integer getId();
    public abstract void setId(Integer id);
    public abstract void setName(String name);
    public abstract String getName();
    public abstract void setShip(ShipLocal ship);
    public abstract ShipLocal getShip();
```

```
// EJB callback methods
...
}
```

Notice that the Cruise EJB requires that a `ShipLocal` reference be passed as an argument when the Cruise is created; this is perfectly natural, since a cruise cannot exist without a ship. According to the EJB 2.0 specification, relationship fields cannot be modified or set in the `ejbCreate()` method. They must be modified in the `ejbPostCreate()`, a constraint that is followed in the `CruiseBean` class.

The reasons relationships are set in `ejbPostCreate()` and not `ejbCreate()` are simple: the primary key for the entity bean may not be available until after `ejbCreate()` executes. The primary key is needed if the mapping for the relationship uses the key as a foreign key, so assignment of relationships is postponed until the `ejbPostCreate()` method completes and the primary key becomes available. This is also true with autogenerated primary keys, which usually require that the insert be done before a primary key can be generated. In addition, referential integrity may specify non-null foreign keys in referencing tables, so the insert must take place first. In reality, the transaction does not complete until both the `ejbCreate()` and `ejbPostCreate()` methods have executed, so the vendors are free to choose the best time for database inserts and linking of relationships.

The relationship between the Cruise and Ship EJBs is unidirectional, so the Ship EJB doesn't define any relationship fields, just persistence fields:

```
public abstract class ShipBean implements javax.ejb.EntityBean {

    public Integer ejbCreate(Integer primaryKey,String name,double tonnage) {
        setId(primaryKey);
        setName(name);
        setTonnage(tonnage);
        return null;
    }
    public void ejbPostCreate(Integer primaryKey,String name,double tonnage) {
    }
    public abstract void setId(Integer id);
    public abstract Integer getId();
    public abstract void setName(String name);
    public abstract String getName();
    public abstract void setTonnage(double tonnage);
    public abstract double getTonnage();

    // EJB callback methods
    ...
}
```

This should all be fairly mundane for you now. The impact of exchanging Ship references between Cruise EJBs should be equally obvious. As shown previously in Figure 7-10, each Cruise may reference only a single Ship, but each Ship may reference many Cruise EJBs. If you take Ship A, which is referenced by Cruise 1, and pass it to Cruise 4, both Cruise 1 and 4 will reference Ship A, as shown in Figure 7-12.

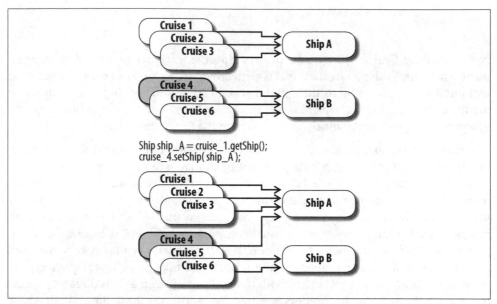

Figure 7-12. Sharing a bean reference in a many-to-one unidirectional relationship

Abstract persistence schema

The abstract persistence schema is simple in a many-to-one unidirectional relationship. It uses everything you have already learned, and shouldn't contain any surprises:

```
<ejb-jar>
...
<enterprise-beans>
    <entity>
        <ejb-name>CruiseEJB</ejb-name>
        <local-home>com.titan.cruise.CruiseHomeLocal</local-home>
        <local>com.titan.cruise.CruiseLocal</local>
        ...
    </entity>
    <entity>
        <ejb-name>ShipEJB</ejb-name>
        <local-home>com.titan.ship.ShipHomeLocal</local-home>
        <local>com.titan.ship.ShipLocal</local>
        ...
    </entity>
    ...
</enterprise-beans>

<relationships>
    <ejb-relation>
        <ejb-relation-name>Cruise-Ship</ejb-relation-name>
        <ejb-relationship-role>
            <ejb-relationship-role-name>
                Cruise-has-a-Ship
            </ejb-relationship-role-name>
```

```
            <multiplicity>Many</multiplicity>
            <relationship-role-source>
                <ejb-name>CruiseEJB</ejb-name>
            </relationship-role-source>
            <cmr-field>
                <cmr-field-name>ship</cmr-field-name>
            </cmr-field>
        </ejb-relationship-role>
        <ejb-relationship-role>
            <ejb-relationship-role-name>
                Ship-has-many-Cruises
            </ejb-relationship-role-name>
            <multiplicity>One</multiplicity>
            <relationship-role-source>
                <ejb-name>ShipEJB</ejb-name>
            </relationship-role-source>
        </ejb-relationship-role>
    </ejb-relation>
</relationships>
```

The <ejb-relationship-role> of the Cruise EJB defines its multiplicity as Many and declares ship as its relationship field. The <ejb-relationship-role> of the Ship EJB defines its multiplicity as One and contains no <cmr-field> declaration, because it's a unidirectional relationship.

One-to-Many Bidirectional Relationship

One-to-many and many-to-one bidirectional relationships are the same thing, so they are both covered in this section. A one-to-many bidirectional relationship occurs when one entity bean maintains a collection-based relationship field with another entity bean, and each entity bean referenced in the collection maintains a single reference back to its aggregating bean. For example, in the Titan Cruise system, each Cruise EJB maintains a collection of references to all the passenger reservations made for that Cruise, and each Reservation EJB maintains a single reference to its Cruise. The relationship is a one-to-many bidirectional relationship from the perspective of the Cruise EJB, and a many-to-one bidirectional relationship from the perspective of the Reservation EJB.

Relational database schema

The first table we need is the RESERVATION table, which is defined in the following listing. Notice that the RESERVATION table contains, among other things, a column that serves as a foreign key to the CRUISE table:

```
CREATE TABLE RESERVATION
(
    ID INT PRIMARY KEY NOT NULL,
    AMOUNT_PAID DECIMAL (8,2),
    DATE_RESERVED DATE,
    CRUISE_ID INT
}
```

While the RESERVATION table contains a foreign key to the CRUISE table, the CRUISE table doesn't maintain a foreign key back to the RESERVATION table. The EJB container system can determine the relationship between the Cruise and Reservations EJBs by querying the RESERVATION table, so explicit pointers from the CRUISE table to the RESERVATION table are not required. This illustrates once again the separation between the entity bean's view of its persistence relationships and the database's actual implementation of those relationships.

The relationship between the RESERVATION and CRUISE tables is shown in Figure 7-13.

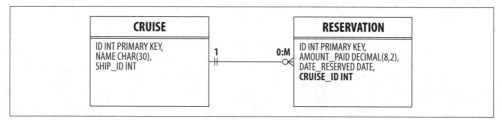

Figure 7-13. One-to-many/many-to-one bidirectional relationship in RDBMS

As an alternative, we could have used a link table that would declare foreign keys to both the CRUISE and RESERVATION tables. This link table would probably impose a unique constraint on the RESERVATION foreign key to ensure that each RESERVATION record had only one corresponding CRUISE record.

Abstract programming model

To model the relationship between Cruises and Reservations, we'll first define the Reservation EJB, which maintains a relationship field to the Cruise EJB:

```
public abstract class ReservationBean implements javax.ejb.EntityBean {

    public Integer ejbCreate(CruiseLocal cruise) {
        return null;
    }
    public void ejbPostCreate(CruiseLocal cruise) {
        setCruise(cruise);
    }

    public abstract void setCruise(CruiseLocal cruise);
    public abstract CruiseLocal getCruise();
    public abstract Integer getId();
    public abstract void setId(Integer id);
    public abstract void setAmountPaid(float amount);
    public abstract float getAmountPaid();
    public abstract void setDate(Date date);
    public abstract Date getDate();

    // EJB callback methods
    ...
}
```

When a Reservation EJB is created, a reference to the Cruise for which it is created must be passed to the create() method. Notice that the CruiseLocal reference is set in the ejbPostCreate() method and not the ejbCreate() method. As stated previously, the ejbCreate() method is not allowed to update relationship fields; that is the job of the ejbPostCreate() method.

We need to add a collection-based relationship field to the Cruise EJB so that it can reference all the Reservation EJBs that were created for it:

```
public abstract class CruiseBean implements javax.ejb.EntityBean {
    ...

    public abstract void setReservations(Collection res);
    public abstract Collection getReservations();
    public abstract Integer getId();
    public abstract void setId(Integer id);
    public abstract void setName(String name);
    public abstract String getName();
    public abstract void setShip(ShipLocal ship);
    public abstract ShipLocal getShip();

    // EJB callback methods
    ...
}
```

The interdependency between the Cruise and Reservation EJBs produces some interesting results when you create a relationship between these beans. For example, the act of creating a Reservation EJB automatically adds that entity bean to the collection-based relationship of the Cruise EJB:

```
CruiseLocal cruise = ... get CruiseLocal reference

ReservationLocal reservation = reservationHomeLocal.create( cruise );

Collection collection = cruise.getReservations();

if(collection.contains(reservation))
    // always returns true
```

This is a side effect of the bidirectional relationship. Any Cruise referenced by a specific Reservation has a reciprocal reference back to that Reservation. If Reservation X references Cruise A, Cruise A must have a reference to Reservation X. When you create a new Reservation EJB and set the Cruise reference on that bean, the Reservation is automatically added to the Cruise EJB's reservation field.[*]

Sharing references between beans has some of the ugly consequences we learned about earlier. For example, passing a collection of Reservations referenced by Cruise

---

[*] This actually depends in large part on the sequence of operations, the transaction context, and even the isolation levels used in the database. Chapter 14 provides more information on these topics.

A to Cruise B actually moves those relationships to Cruise B, so Cruise A has no more Reservations (see Figure 7-14).

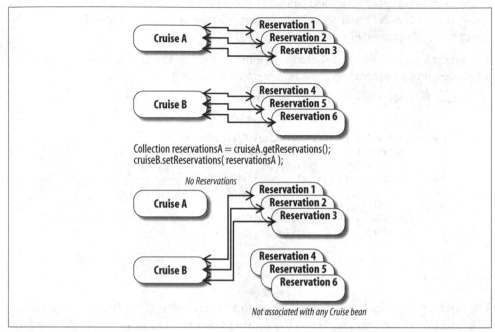

Figure 7-14. Sharing an entire collection in a one-to-many bidirectional relationship

As was the case with the Customer and Phone EJBs (see Figure 7-8), this effect is usually undesirable and should be avoided, as it displaces the set of Reservation EJBs formerly associated with Cruise B.

You can move an entire collection from one bean to another and combine it with the second bean's collection by using the Collection.addAll() method, as shown in Figure 7-15.[*] If you move Cruise A's collection of references to Cruise B, Cruise A will no longer reference any Reservation EJBs, while Cruise B will reference those it referenced before the exchange as well as those it acquired from Cruise A.

The impact of moving an individual Reservation EJB from one Cruise to another is similar to what we have seen with other one-to-many relationships: the result is the same as was shown in Figure 7-9, when a Phone was moved from one Customer to another. It's interesting to note that the net effect of using Collection.addAll() in this scenario is the same as using Collection.add() on the target collection for every element in the source collection. In both cases, you move every element from the source collection to the target collection.

---

[*] The addAll() method must be supported by collection-based relationship fields in EJB 2.0.

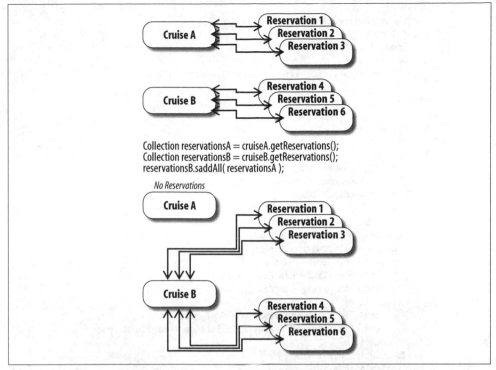

```
Collection reservationsA = cruiseA.getReservations();
Collection reservationsB = cruiseB.getReservations();
reservationsB.saddAll( reservationsA );
```

Figure 7-15. Using Collection.addAll() in a one-to-many bidirectional relationship

Once again, container-managed relationship fields, collection-based or otherwise, must always use the javax.ejb.EJBLocalObject (local) interface of a bean and never the javax.ejb.EJBObject (remote) interface. It would be illegal, for example, to try to add the remote interface of the Reservation EJB (if it has one) to the Cruise EJB's Reservation Collection. Any attempt to add a remote interface type to a collection-based relationship field will result in a java.lang.IllegalArgumentException.

Abstract persistence schema

The abstract persistence schema for the Cruise-Reservation relationship doesn't introduce any new concepts. The Cruise and Reservation <ejb-relationship-role> elements both have <cmr-field> elements. The Cruise specifies One as its multiplicity, while Reservation specifies Many. Here's the code:

```
<ejb-jar>
...
<enterprise-beans>
    <entity>
        <ejb-name>CruiseEJB</ejb-name>
        <local-home>com.titan.cruise.CruiseHomeLocal</local-home>
        <local>com.titan.cruise.CruiseLocal</local>
        ...
    </entity>
```

```
        <entity>
            <ejb-name>ReservationEJB</ejb-name>
            <local-home>
                com.titan.reservations.ReservationHomeLocal
            </local-home>
            <local>com.titan.reservation.ReservationLocal</local>
            ...
        </entity>
        ...
    </enterprise-beans>
    <relationships>
        <ejb-relation>
            <ejb-relation-name>Cruise-Reservation
            </ejb-relation-name>
            <ejb-relationship-role>
                <ejb-relationship-role-name>
                    Cruise-has-many-Reservations
                </ejb-relationship-role-name>
                <multiplicity>One</multiplicity>
                <relationship-role-source>
                    <ejb-name>CruiseEJB</ejb-name>
                </relationship-role-source>
                <cmr-field>
                    <cmr-field-name>reservations</cmr-field-name>
                    <cmr-field-type> java.util.Collection</cmr-field-type>
                </cmr-field>
            </ejb-relationship-role>
            <ejb-relationship-role>
                <ejb-relationship-role-name>
                    Reservation-has-a-Cruise
                </ejb-relationship-role-name>
                <multiplicity>Many</multiplicity>
                <relationship-role-source>
                    <ejb-name>ReservationEJB</ejb-name>
                </relationship-role-source>
                <cmr-field>
                    <cmr-field-name>cruise</cmr-field-name>
                </cmr-field>
            </ejb-relationship-role>
        </ejb-relation>
    </relationships>
```

Many-to-Many Bidirectional Relationship

Many-to-many bidirectional relationships occur when many beans maintain a collection-based relationship field with another bean, and each bean referenced in the Collection maintains a collection-based relationship field back to the aggregating beans. For example, in Titan Cruises every Reservation EJB may reference many Customers (a family can make a single reservation) and each Customer can have many reservations (a person may make more than one reservation in a year). This is an example of a many-to-many bidirectional relationship; the customer keeps track of all of its reservations, and each reservation may be for many customers.

Relational database schema

The RESERVATION and CUSTOMER tables have already been established. In order to establish a many-to-many bidirectional relationship, the RESERVATION_CUSTOMER_LINK table is created. This table maintains two foreign key columns: one for the RESERVATION table and another for the CUSTOMER table:

```
CREATE TABLE RESERVATION_CUSTOMER_LINK
(
    RESERVATION_ID INT,
    CUSTOMER_ID INT
}
```

The relationship between the CUSTOMER, RESERVATION, and CUSTOMER_RESERVATION_LINK tables is illustrated in Figure 7-16.

Figure 7-16. Many-to-many bidirectional relationship in RDBMS

Many-to-many bidirectional relationships always require a link in a normalized relational database.

Abstract programming model

To model the many-to-many bidirectional relationship between the Customer and Reservation EJBs, we need to modify both bean classes to include collection-based relationship fields:

```
public abstract class ReservationBean implements javax.ejb.EntityBean {

    public Integer ejbCreate(CruiseLocal cruise,Collection customers) {
        return null;
    }
    public void ejbPostCreate(CruiseLocal cruise,Collection customers) {
        setCruise(cruise);
        Collection myCustomers = this.getCustomers();
        myCustomers.addAll(customers);
    }

    public abstract void setCustomers(Set customers);
```

```
        public abstract Set getCustomers();
        ...
    }
```

The abstract accessor methods defined for the customers relationship field declare the Collection type as java.util.Set. The Set type should contain only unique Customer EJBs and no duplicates. Duplicate Customers would introduce some interesting but undesirable side effects in Titan's reservation system. To maintain a valid passenger count, and to avoid overcharging customers, Titan requires that a Customer be booked only once in the same Reservation. The Set collection type expresses this restriction. The effectiveness of the Set collection type depends largely on referential-integrity constraints established in the underlying database.

In addition to adding the getCustomers()/setCustomers() abstract accessors, we have modified the ejbCreate()/ejbPostCreate() methods to take a Collection of Customer EJBs. When a Reservation EJB is created, it must be provided with a list of Customer EJBs that it will add to its own Customer EJB collection. As is always the case, container-managed relationship fields cannot be modified in the ejbCreate() method. It's the ejbPostCreate() method's job to modify container-managed relationships fields when a bean is created.

We have also modified the Customer EJB to allow it to maintain a collection-based relationship with all of its Reservations. While the idea of a Customer having multiple Reservations may seem odd, it's possible for someone to book more than one cruise in advance. To allow for this possibility, we have enhanced the Customer EJB to include a reservations relationship field:

```
    public abstract class CustomerBean implements javax.ejb.EntityBean {
        ...
        // relationship fields
        public abstract void setReservations(Collection reservations);

        public abstract Collection getReservations();
        ...
```

When a Reservation EJB is created, it is passed references to its Cruise and to a collection of Customers. Because the relationship is defined as bidirectional, the EJB container will automatically add the Reservation EJB to the reservations relationship field of the Customer EJB. The following code fragment illustrates this:

```
    Collection customers = ... get local Customer EJBs
    CruiseLocal cruise = ... get a local Cruise EJB
    ReservationHomeLocal = ... get local Reservation home

    ReservationLocal myReservation = resHome.create(cruise, customers);

    Iterator iterator = customers.iterator();
    while(iterator.hasNext()) {
        CustomerLocal customer = (CustomerLocal)iterator.next();
        Collection reservations = customer.getReservations();
```

```
    if( reservations.contains( myReservation ))
        // this will always be true
}
```

Exchanging bean references in many-to-many bidirectional relationships results in true sharing, where each relationship maintains a reference to the transferred collection. This type of relationship is illustrated in Figure 7-17.

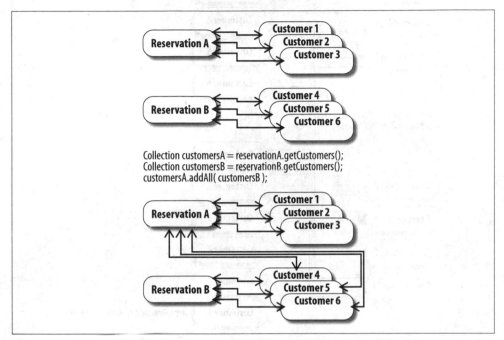

Figure 7-17. Using Collection.addAll() in a many-to-many bidirectional relationship

Of course, using the setCustomers() or setReservations() method will end up changing the references between the entity bean and the elements in the original collection, but the other relationships held by those elements are unaffected. Figure 7-18 illustrates what happens when an entire collection is shared in a many-to-many bidirectional relationship.

After the setCustomers() method is invoked on Reservation D, Reservation D's Customers change to Customers 1, 2, and 3. Customers 1, 2, and 3 were also referenced by Reservation A before the sharing operation and remain referenced by Reservation A after it's complete. In fact, only the relationships between Reservation D and Customers 4, 5, and 6 are impacted. The relationship between Customers 4, 5, and 6 and other Reservation EJBs are not affected by the sharing operation. This is a unique property of many-to-many relationships (both bidirectional and unidirectional); operations on the relationship fields affect only those specific relationships, they do not impact either party's relationships with other beans of the same relationship type.

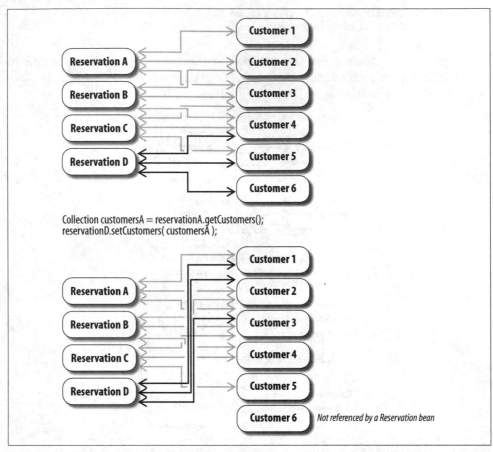

Collection customersA = reservationA.getCustomers();
reservationD.setCustomers(customersA);

Customer 6 — *Not referenced by a Reservation bean*

Figure 7-18. Sharing an entire collection in a many-to-many bidirectional relationship

Abstract persistence schema

The abstract persistence schema of a many-to-many bidirectional relationship introduces nothing new and should contain no surprises. Each <ejb-relationship-role> specifies Many as its multiplicity and declares a <cmr-field> of a specific Collection type:

```
<ejb-jar>
...
<enterprise-beans>
    <entity>
        <ejb-name>CustomerEJB</ejb-name>
        <local-home>com.titan.customer.CustomerHomeLocal</local-home>
        <local>com.titan.customer.CustomerLocal</local>
        ...
    </entity>
    <entity>
        <ejb-name>ReservationEJB</ejb-name>
```

```
            <local-home> com.titan.reservation.ReservationHomeLocal</local-home>
            <local>com.titan.reservation.ReservationLocal</local>
            ...
        </entity>
        ...
    </enterprise-beans>

    <relationships>
        <ejb-relation>
            <ejb-relation-name>Customer-Reservation</ejb-relation-name>
            <ejb-relationship-role>
                <ejb-relationship-role-name>
                    Customer-has-many-Reservations
                </ejb-relationship-role-name>
                <multiplicity>Many</multiplicity>
                <relationship-role-source>
                    <ejb-name>CustomerEJB</ejb-name>
                </relationship-role-source>
                <cmr-field>
                    <cmr-field-name>reservations</cmr-field-name>
                    <cmr-field-type>java.util.Collection</cmr-field-type>
                </cmr-field>
            </ejb-relationship-role>
            <ejb-relationship-role>
                <ejb-relationship-role-name>
                    Reservation-has-many-Customers
                </ejb-relationship-role-name>
                <multiplicity>Many</multiplicity>
                <relationship-role-source>
                    <ejb-name>ReservationEJB</ejb-name>
                </relationship-role-source>
                <cmr-field>
                    <cmr-field-name>customers</cmr-field-name>
                    <cmr-field-type>java.util.Set</cmr-field-type>
                </cmr-field>
            </ejb-relationship-role>
        </ejb-relation>
    </relationships>
```

Many-to-Many Unidirectional Relationship

Many-to-many unidirectional relationships occur when many beans maintain a collection-based relationship with another bean, but the bean referenced in the Collection does not maintain a collection-based relationship back to the aggregating beans. In Titan's reservation system, every Reservation is assigned a Cabin on the Ship. This allows a Customer to reserve a specific Cabin (e.g., a deluxe suite or a cabin with sentimental significance) on the Ship. In this case, each Reservation may be for more than one Cabin, since each Reservation can be for more than one Customer. An example is a family that makes a Reservation for five people for two adjacent Cabins (one for the kids and the other for the parents).

While the Reservation must keep track of the Cabins it reserves, it's not necessary for the Cabins to track all the Reservations made by all the Cruises. The Reservation EJBs reference a collection of Cabin beans, but the Cabin beans do not maintain references back to the Reservations.

Relational database schema

Our first order of business is to declare a CABIN table:

```
CREATE TABLE CABIN
(
    ID INT PRIMARY KEY NOT NULL,
    SHIP_ID INT,
    NAME CHAR(10),
    DECK_LEVEL INT,
    BED_COUNT INT
}
```

Notice that the CABIN table maintains a foreign key to the SHIP table. While this relationship is important, we won't explore it here because we've already covered the one-to-many bidirectional relationship in this chapter. The Cabin-Ship relationship is included in Figure 7-10, however, for completeness. To accommodate the many-to-many unidirectional relationship between the RESERVATION and CABIN table, we will need a RESERVATION_CABIN_LINK table:

```
CREATE TABLE RESERVATION_CABIN_LINK
(
    RESERVATION_ID INT,
    CABIN_ID INT
}
```

The relationship between the CABIN records and the RESERVATION records through the RESERVATION_CABIN_LINK table is illustrated in Figure 7-19.

Figure 7-19. Many-to-many unidirectional relationship in RDBMS

Abstract programming model

To model this relationship, we need to add a collection-based relationship field for Cabin beans to the Reservation EJB:

```
public abstract class ReservationBean implements javax.ejb.EntityBean {
    ...
    public abstract void setCabins(Set cabins);
```

```
        public abstract Set getCabins();
        ...
    }
```

In addition, we need to define a Cabin bean. Notice that the Cabin bean doesn't maintain a relationship back to the Reservation EJB. The lack of a container-managed relationship field for the Reservation EJB tells us the relationship is unidirectional:

```
public abstract class CabinBean implements javax.ejb.EntityBean {

    public Integer ejbCreate(ShipLocal ship, String name) {
        this.setName(name);
        return null;
    }
    public void ejbPostCreate(ShipLocal ship, String name) {
        this.setShip(ship);
    }
    public abstract void setShip(ShipLocal ship);
    public abstract ShipLocal getShip();
    public abstract Integer getId();
    public abstract void setId(Integer id);
    public abstract void setName(String name);
    public abstract String getName();
    public abstract void setBedCount(int count);
    public abstract int getBedCount();
    public abstract void setDeckLevel(int level);
    public abstract int getDeckLevel();

    // EJB callback methods
}
```

Although the Cabin bean doesn't define a relationship field for the Reservation EJB, it does define a one-to-many bidirectional relationship for the Ship EJB.

The effect of exchanging relationship fields in a many-to-many unidirectional relationship is basically the same as that in a many-to-many bidirectional relationship. Use of the Collection.addAll() operation to share entire collections has the same net effect we noted in the previous section on many-to-many bidirectional relationships. The only difference is that the arrows point only one way, instead of both ways.

If a Reservation removes a Cabin bean from its collection-based relationship field, the operation doesn't affect other Reservation EJBs that reference that Cabin bean. This is illustrated in Figure 7-20.

Abstract persistence schema

The abstract persistence schema for the Reservation-Cabin relationship holds no surprises. The multiplicity of both <ejb-relationship-role> elements is Many, but only the Reservation EJB's <ejb-relationship-role> defines a <cmr-field>:

```
<ejb-jar>
...
<enterprise-beans>
```

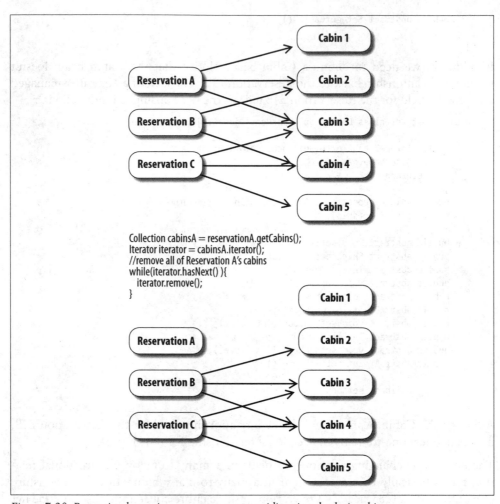

Figure 7-20. Removing beans in a many-to-many unidirectional relationship

```
    <entity>
        <ejb-name>CabinEJB</ejb-name>
        <local-home>com.titan.cabin.CabinHomeLocal</local-home>
        <local>com.titan.cabin.CabinLocal</local>
        ...
    </entity>
    <entity>
        <ejb-name>ReservationEJB</ejb-name>
        <local-home> com.titan.reservation.ReservationHomeLocal</local-home>
        <local>com.titan.reservation.ReservationLocal</local>
        ...
    </entity>
    ...
</enterprise-beans>
```

```
<relationships>
    <ejb-relation>
        <ejb-relation-name>Cabin-Reservation</ejb-relation-name>
        <ejb-relationship-role>
            <ejb-relationship-role-name>
                Cabin-has-many-Reservations
            </ejb-relationship-role-name>
            <multiplicity>Many</multiplicity>
            <relationship-role-source>
                <ejb-name>CabinEJB</ejb-name>
            </relationship-role-source>
        </ejb-relationship-role>
        <ejb-relationship-role>
            <ejb-relationship-role-name>
                Reservation-has-many-Customers
            </ejb-relationship-role-name>
            <multiplicity>Many</multiplicity>
            <relationship-role-source>
                <ejb-name>ReservationEJB</ejb-name>
            </relationship-role-source>
            <cmr-field>
                <cmr-field-name>cabins</cmr-field-name>
                <cmr-field-type>java.util.Set</cmr-field-type>
            </cmr-field>
        </ejb-relationship-role>
    </ejb-relation>
</relationships>
```

📖 Workbook Exercise 7.2, Entity Relationships in CMP 2.0: Part 2

Co-location and the Deployment Descriptor

Only entity beans that are deployed together with the same deployment descriptor can have relationships with each other. When deployed together, the entity beans are seen as a single deployment unit or application, in which all the entities are using the same database and are co-located in the same JVM. This restriction makes it possible for the EJB container system to use lazy loading, optimistic concurrency, and other performance optimizations. While it would technically be possible to support relationships across deployments or even across container systems, the difficulty of doing so, combined with the expected degradation in performance, was reason enough to limit the relationship fields to those entity beans that are deployed together. In the future, entity relationships may be expanded to include remote references to entities deployed in other containers or other JAR files in the same container, but remote references are not allowed as relationship types in EJB 2.0.

Cascade Delete and Remove

As you learned in Chapter 5, invoking the remove() operation on the EJB home or EJB object of an entity bean deletes that entity bean's data from the database. Deleting the bean's data, of course, has an impact on the relationships that entity bean has with other entity beans.

When an entity bean is deleted, the EJB container first removes it from any relationships it maintains with other entity beans. Consider, for example, the relationship between the entity beans we have created in this chapter (shown in Figure 7-21).

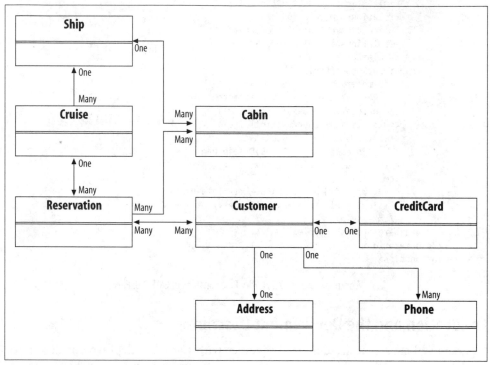

Figure 7-21. Titan Cruises class diagram

If an EJB application invokes remove() on a CreditCard EJB, the Customer EJB that referenced that bean would now have a value of null for its creditCard relationship field, as the following code fragment illustrates:

```
CustomerLocal customer = ... get Customer EJB
CreditCardLocal creditCard = customer.getCreditCard();
creditCard.remove();
if(customer.getCreditCard() == null)
    // this will always be true
```

The moment the remove() operation is invoked on the CreditCard EJB's local reference, the bean is disassociated from the Customer bean and deleted. The impact of removing a bean is even more interesting when that bean participates in several relationships. For example, invoking remove() on a Customer EJB will impact the relationship fields of the Reservation, Address, Phone, and CreditCard EJBs. With single EJB object relationship fields, such as the CreditCard EJB's reference to the

Customer EJB, the field will be set to null for the entity bean that was removed. With collection-based relationship fields, the entity that was deleted will be removed from the collection. In some cases, you want the removal of an entity bean to cause a cascade of deletions. For example, if a Customer EJB is removed, we would want the Address EJBs referenced in its billingAddress and homeAddress relationship field to be deleted. This would avoid the problem of disconnected Address EJBs in the database. The <cascade-delete> element requests cascade delete; it can be used with one-to-one or one-to-many relationships. It does not make sense in many-to-many and many-to-one relationships, because of the nature of those relationships. For example, in the many-to-one relationship between the Reservation and Cruise EJBs, cancellation of a reservation by one passenger should not cancel the cruise itself! In other words, we would not want the deletion of a Reservation EJB to cause the deletion of its Cruise EJB.

Here's how to modify the relationship declaration for the Customer and Address EJBs to obtain a cascade delete:

```
<relationships>
    <ejb-relation>
        <ejb-relationship-role>
            <multiplicity>One</multiplicity>
            <relationship-role-source>
                <ejb-name>CustomerEJB</ejb-name>
            </relationship-role-source>
            <cmr-field>
                <cmr-field-name>homeAddress</cmr-field-name>
            </cmr-field>
        </ejb-relationship-role>
        <ejb-relationship-role>
            <multiplicity>One</multiplicity>
            <cascade-delete/>
            <relationship-role-source>
                <ejb-name>AddressEJB</ejb-name>
            </relationship-role-source>
        </ejb-relationship-role>
    </ejb-relation>
</relationships>
```

If you do not specify a cascade delete, the ADDRESS record associated with the Address EJB will not be removed when the CUSTOMER record is deleted. This can result in a disconnected dependent object value, which means that the data is not linked to anything. In some cases, we want to specify a cascading delete to ensure that no detached entities remain after a bean is removed. In other cases, however, we do not want to use a cascading delete. If, for example, the ADDRESS record associated with an entity bean is shared by other CUSTOMER records (i.e., if two different customers reside at the same residence), we probably do not want it to be deleted when the CUSTOMER record is deleted. A cascade delete can be specified only on an entity bean that has a single reference to the entity being deleted. For example, you can specify a cascade delete in the <ejb-relationship-role> for the Phone EJB in the

Customer-Phone relationship if the Customer is deleted, because each Phone EJB is referenced by only one Customer. However, you cannot specify a cascade delete for the Customer EJB in this relationship, because a Customer maybe referenced by many Phone EJBs. The entity bean that causes the cascade delete must have a multiplicity of One in the relationship.

A cascade delete affects only the relationship for which it is specified. So, for example, if you specify a cascade delete for the Customer-Phone relationship but not the Customer-HomeAddress relationship, deleting a Customer will cause all the Phone EJBs to be deleted, but not the Address EJBs. You must also specify a cascade delete for the Address EJBs if you want them to be deleted.

Cascade delete can propagate through relationships in a chain reaction. For example, if the Ship-Cruise relationship specifies a cascade delete on the Cruise relationship field and the Cruise-Reservation relationship specifies a cascade delete on the Reservation relationship field, when a Ship is removed all of its Cruises and the Reservations for those Cruises will be removed.

Cascade delete is a powerful tool, but it's also dangerous and should be handled with care. The effectiveness of a cascade delete depends in large part on the referential integrity of the database. For example, if the database is set up so that a foreign key must point to an existing record, deleting an entity's data could violate that restriction and cause a transaction rollback.

📖 Workbook Exercise 7.3, Cascade Deletes in CMP 2.0

CHAPTER 8

EJB 2.0 CMP: EJB QL

Find methods have been a part of the Enterprise JavaBeans specification since EJB 1.0. These methods are defined on the entity bean's local and remote home interfaces and are used for locating entity beans. All entity beans must have a `findByPrimaryKey()` method, which takes the primary key of the entity bean as an argument and returns a reference to an entity bean. For example, the Cruise EJB defines the standard primary key find method in its home interface as follows:

```
public CruiseHomeLocal extends javax.ejb.EJBLocalHome
{
    public Integer create(String name,ShipLocal ship);

    public CruiseLocal findByPrimaryKey(Integer key);

}
```

In addition to the mandatory `findByPrimaryKey()` method, entity bean developers may define as many custom find methods as they like. For example, the Cruise EJB might define a method, such as `findByName()`, for locating a Cruise with a specific name:

```
public CruiseHomeLocal extends javax.ejb.EJBLocalHome
{
    public Integer create(String name,ShipLocal ship)
        throws CreateException;

    public CruiseLocal findByPrimaryKey(Integer key)
        throws FinderException;

    public CruiseLocal findByName(String cruiseName)
        throws FinderException;
}
```

The option of defining custom find methods is nothing new, but until EJB 2.0 there was no standard way of defining how the find methods should work. The behavior of the `findByPrimaryKey()` method is obvious: find the entity bean with the same primary key. However, the behavior of custom find methods is not always obvious, so additional information is needed to tell the container how these methods should behave. EJB 1.1 didn't provide any standard mechanism for declaring the behavior of custom find methods, so vendors came up with their own query languages and methods. Consequently, the custom methods generally were not portable, and guesswork was required on the part of the deployer to determine how to properly execute queries against them. EJB 2.0 introduced the Enterprise JavaBeans Query Language (EJB QL)—a standard query language for declaring the behavior of custom find methods—and the new select methods. Select methods are similar to find methods, but they are more flexible and are visible to the bean class only. Find and select methods are collectively referred to as *query* methods in EJB 2.0.

EJB QL is a declarative query language that is similar to the Structured Query Language (SQL) used in relational databases, but it is tailored to work with the abstract persistence schema of entity beans in EJB 2.0.

EJB QL queries are defined in terms of the abstract persistence schema of entity beans and not the underlying data store, so they are portable across databases and data schemas. When an entity bean's abstract bean class is deployed by the container, the EJB QL statements are typically examined and translated into data access code optimized for that container's data store. At runtime, query methods defined in EJB QL usually execute in the native language of the underlying data store. For example, a container that uses a relational database for persistence might translate EJB QL statements into standard SQL 92, while an object-database container might translate the same EJB QL statements into an object query language.

EJB QL makes it possible for bean developers to describe the behavior of query methods in an abstract fashion, making queries portable across databases and EJB vendors. The EJB QL language is easy for developers to learn, yet precise enough to be interpreted into native database code. It is a fairly rich and flexible query language that empowers developers at development time, while executing in fast native code at runtime. However, EJB QL is not a silver bullet and is not without its problems, as we'll see later in this chapter.

Declaring EJB QL

EJB QL statements are declared in <query> elements in an entity bean's deployment descriptor. In the following listing, you can see that the findByName() method defined in the Cruise bean's local home interface has its own query element and EJB QL statement:

```
<ejb-jar>
    <enterprise-beans>
        <entity>
            <ejb-name>CruiseEJB</ejb-name>
            ...
            <reentrant>False</reentrant>
            <abstract-schema-name>Cruise</abstract-schema-name>
            <cmp-version>2.x</cmp-version>
```

```
<cmp-field>
        <field-name>name</field-name>
</cmp-field>
<primkey-field>id</primkey-field>
<query>
    <query-method>
        <method-name>findByName</method-name>
        <method-params>
            <method-param>java.lang.String</method-param>
        </method-params>
    </query-method>
    <ejb-ql>
        SELECT OBJECT(c) FROM Cruise c WHERE c.name = ?1
    </ejb-ql>
</query>
            </entity>
        </enterprise-beans>
    </ejb-jar>
```

The <query> element contains two primary elements. The <query-method> element identifies the find method of the remote and/or local home interfaces, and the <ejb-ql> element declares the EJB QL statement. The <query> element binds the EJB QL statement to the proper find method. Don't worry too much about the EJB QL statement just yet; we'll cover that in detail starting in the next section.

Every entity bean that will be referenced in an EJB QL statement must have a special designator called an *abstract schema name*, which is declared by the <abstract-schema-name> element. The <abstract-schema-name> elements must have unique names; no two entity beans may have the same abstract schema name. In the entity element that describes the Cruise EJB, the abstract schema name is declared as Cruise. The <ejb-ql> element contains an EJB QL statement that uses this identifier in its FROM clause.

In Chapter 7, you learned that the abstract persistence schema of an entity bean is defined by its <cmp-field> and <cmr-field> elements. The abstract schema name is also an important part of the abstract persistence schema. EJB QL statements are always expressed in terms of the abstract persistence schemas of entity beans. EJB QL uses the abstract schema names to identify entity bean types, the container-managed persistence (CMP) fields to identify specific entity bean data, and the container-managed relationship (CMR) fields to create paths for navigating between entity beans.

The Query Methods

There are two main types of query methods: find methods and select methods. These are discussed in the following sections.

Find Methods

Find methods are invoked by EJB clients (applications or beans) in order to locate and obtain the remote or local EJB object references to specific entity beans. For example, you might call the `findByPrimaryKey()` method on the Customer EJB's home interface to obtain a reference to a specific Customer bean.

Find methods are always declared in the local and remote home interfaces of an entity bean. As you have already learned, every home interface must define a `findByPrimaryKey()` method; this is a type of single-entity find method. Specifying a single remote or local return type for a find method indicates that the method locates only one bean. `findByPrimaryKey()` obviously returns only one remote reference, because there is a one-to-one relationship between a primary key's value and an entity. Other single-entity find methods can also be declared. For example, in the following code segment the Customer EJB declares several single-entity find methods, each of which supports a different query:

```
public interface CustomerHomeRemote extends javax.ejb.EJBHome {
    public CustomerRemote findByPrimaryKey(Integer primaryKey)
        throws javax.ejb.FinderException, java.rmi.RemoteException;

    public CustomerRemote findByName(String lastName, String firstName)
        throws javax.ejb.FinderException, java.rmi.RemoteException;

    public CustomerRemote findBySSN(String socialSecurityNumber)
        throws javax.ejb.FinderException, java.rmi.RemoteException;
}
```

Bean developers can also define multi-entity find methods, which return a collection of EJB objects. The following listing shows a couple of multi-entity find methods:

```
public interface CustomerHomeLocal extends javax.ejb.EJBLocalHome {
    public CustomerLocal findByPrimaryKey(Integer primaryKey)
        throws javax.ejb.FinderException;

    public Collection findByCity(String city,String state)
        throws javax.ejb.FinderException;

    public Collection findByGoodCredit()
        throws javax.ejb.FinderException;
}
```

To return several references from a find method, you must use a `java.util.Collection` type.* A find method that uses this return type may have duplicates. To avoid duplicates, you can use the keyword DISTINCT in the EJB QL statement associated with the find method. This technique is explained in more detail in the "Using DISTINCT" section later in this chapter. Multi-entity finds return an empty Collection if no matching beans are found.

Enterprise JavaBeans specifies that all query methods (find or select) must be declared as throwing the `javax.ejb.FinderException`. Find methods that return a single remote reference throw a `FinderException` if an application error occurs and a `javax.ejb.`

---

* In CMP 2.0, java.util.Collection is the only collection type supported for multi-entity find methods. EJB 1.1 CMP and EJB 2.0 BMP also support java.util.Enumeration.

`ObjectNotFoundException` if a matching bean cannot be found. The `ObjectNotFoundException` is a subtype of `FinderException` and is thrown only by single-entity find methods.

Every find method declared in the local or remote home interface of a CMP 2.0 entity bean must have a matching query declaration in the bean's deployment descriptor. The following snippet from the Customer EJB's deployment descriptor shows declarations of two find methods, `findByName()` and `findByGoodCredit()`, from the earlier examples:

```
<query>
    <query-method>
        <method-name>findByName</method-name>
        <method-params>
            <method-param>java.lang.String</method-param>
            <method-param>java.lang.String</method-param>
        </method-params>
    </query-method>
    <ejb-ql>
        SELECT OBJECT(c) FROM Customer c
        WHERE c.lastName = ?1 AND c.firstName = ?2
    </ejb-ql>
</query>
<query>
    <query-method>
        <method-name>findByGoodCredit</method-name>
        <method-params/>
    </query-method>
    <ejb-ql>
        SELECT OBJECT(c) FROM Customer c
        WHERE c.hasGoodCredit = TRUE
    </ejb-ql>
</query>
```

The query elements in the deployment descriptor allow the bean developer to associate EJB QL statements with specific find methods. When the bean is deployed, the container attempts to match the find method declared in each of the query elements with find methods in the entity bean's home interfaces. This is done by matching the values of the `<method-name>` and `<method-params>` elements with method names and parameter types (ordering is important) in the home interfaces.

When two find methods in the local and remote home interfaces have the same method name and parameters, the query declaration will apply to both of the methods. The container will return the proper type for each query method: the remote home will return one or more remote EJB objects, and the local home will return one or more local EJB objects. This allows you to define the behavior of both the local and remote home find methods using a single `<query>` element, which is convenient if you want local clients to have access to the same find methods as remote clients.

The `<ejb-ql>` element specifies the EJB QL statement for a specific find method. You may have noticed that EJB QL statements can use input parameters (e.g., ?1, ?2, …

?n), which are mapped to the <method-param> of the find method, as well as literals (e.g., TRUE). The use of input parameters and literals will be discussed in more detail throughout this chapter.

With the exception of findByPrimaryKey() methods, all single-entity and multi-entity find methods must be declared in <query> elements in the deployment descriptor. Query declarations for findByPrimaryKey() methods are not necessary and, in fact, are forbidden. It's obvious what this method should do, and you may not try to change its behavior.

Select Methods

Select methods are similar to find methods, but they are more versatile and can be used only internally, by the bean class. In other words, select methods are private query methods; they are not exposed to an entity bean's clients through the home interfaces.

Another difference between the select and find methods is the transaction context under which they execute. The select method executes in the transaction context of the business or callback method that is using it, while the find methods execute according to their own transaction attributes, as specified by the bean provider.

Select methods are declared as abstract methods using the naming convention ejbSelect<*METHOD-NAME*>. The following code shows four select methods declared in the AddressBean class:

```
public class AddressBean implements javax.ejb.EntityBean {
    ...
    public abstract String ejbSelectMostPopularCity()
        throws FinderException;

    public abstract Set ejbSelectZipCodes(String state)
        throws FinderException;

    public abstract Collection ejbSelectAll()
        throws FinderException;

    public abstract CustomerLocal ejbSelectCustomer(AddressLocal addr)
        throws FinderException;
    ...
```

Select methods can return the values of CMP fields. The ejbSelectMostPopularCity() method, for example, returns a single String value, the name of the city referenced by the most Address EJBs.

To return several references from a select method, you must declare the return type to be either a java.util.Collection or java.util.Set.* A select method that uses a

---

* Other collection types, such as java.util.List and java.util.Map, may be added in future versions.

Set return type will not have duplicate values, while a Collection return type may have duplicates. Multi-entity selects return an empty Collection or Set if no matching beans are found. The ejbSelectZipCodes() method returns a java.util.Set of String values: a unique collection of all the Zip Codes declared for the Address EJBs for a specific state.

Like find methods, select methods can declare zero or more arguments, which are used to limit the scope of the query. The ejbSelectZipCodes() and ejbSelect-Customer() methods both declare arguments used to limit the scope of the results. These arguments are used as input parameters in the EJB QL statements assigned to the select methods.

Select methods can return local or remote EJB objects. For single-entity select methods, the type is determined by the return type of the ejbSelect() method. The ejbSelectCustomer() method, for example, returns a local EJB object, the CustomerLocal. This method could easily have been defined to return a remote EJB object by changing the return type to the Customer bean's remote interface (CustomerRemote). Multi-entity select methods, which return a collection of EJB objects, return local EJB objects by default. However, the bean provider can override this default behavior using a special element, the <result-type-mapping> element, in the select method's <query> element.

The following portion of an XML deployment descriptor declares two of the select methods from the above example. Notice that they are exactly the same as the find method declarations. Find and select methods are declared in the same part of the deployment descriptor, within a <query> element inside an <entity> element:

```
<query>
    <query-method>
        <method-name>ejbSelectZipCodes</method-name>
        <method-params>
            <method-param>java.lang.String</method-param>
        </method-params>
    </query-method>
    <ejb-ql>
        SELECT a.homeAddress.zip FROM Address AS a
        WHERE a.homeAddress.state = ?1
    </ejb-ql>
</query>
<query>
    <query-method>
        <method-name>ejbSelectAll</method-name>
        <method-params/>
    </query-method>
    <result-type-mapping>Remote</result-type-mapping>
    <ejb-ql>
        SELECT OBJECT(a) FROM Address AS a
    </ejb-ql>
</query>
```

The name given in each <method-name> element must match one of the ejbSelect<*METHOD-NAME*>() methods defined in the bean class. This is different from find methods of CMP 2.0 beans, which do not have a corresponding ejbFind method in the bean class. For find methods, we use the method name in the local or remote home interface. Select methods, on the other hand, are not declared in the local or remote home interface, so we use the ejbSelect() method name in the bean class.

Select methods can return local or remote EJB objects. The default is to return local EJB object types for both single-entity and multi-entity select methods. However, the bean provider can override this default behavior using a special element, <result-type-mapping>, in the select method's <query> element. The value of <result-type-mapping> can be either Remote or Local. A value of Local indicates that the select method should return local EJB objects; Remote indicates remote EJB objects. If the <result-type-mapping> element is not declared, the default is Local. For single-entity select, the actual return type of the ejbSelect() method must match the <result-type-mapping>. For example, if a single-entity ejbSelect() method returns an EJBObject type, the <result-type-mapping> must be Remote. In the previous example, the <result-type-mapping> in the <query> element for the ejbSelectAll() method is declared as Remote, which means the query should return remote EJB object types (i.e., remote references to the Address EJB).[*]

Select methods are not limited to the context of any specific entity bean. They can be used to query across all the entity beans declared in the same deployment descriptor. Select methods may be used by the bean class from its ejbHome() methods, from any business methods, or from the ejbLoad() and ejbStore() methods. In most cases, select methods will be called from ejbHome() or from business methods in the bean class. The ejbHome(), ejbLoad(), and ejbStore() methods are covered in more detail in Chapter 11.

The most important thing to remember about select methods is that while they can do anything find methods can and more, they can be used only by the entity bean class that declares them, not by the entity bean's clients.

EJB QL Examples

EJB QL is expressed in terms of the abstract persistence schema of an entity bean: its abstract schema name, CMP fields, and CMR fields. EJB QL uses the abstract schema names to identify beans, the CMP fields to specify values, and the CMR fields to navigate across relationships.

To discuss EJB QL, we will make use of the relationships among the Customer, Address, CreditCard, Cruise, Ship, Reservation, and Cabin EJBs defined in Chapter 7.

---

[*] This is illustrative. As a developer, it is unlikely (although possible) that you would define a remote interface for the Address EJB, because it is too fine-grained for use by remote clients.

Figure 8-1 is a class diagram that shows the direction and cardinality (multiplicity) of the relationships among these beans.

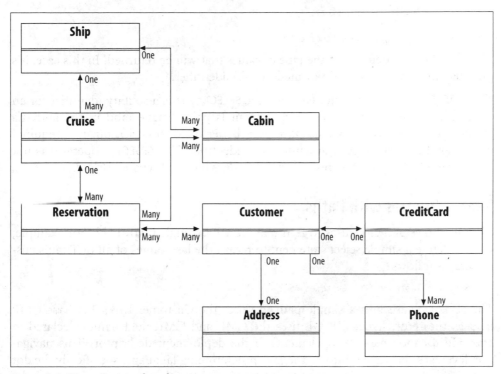

Figure 8-1. Titan Cruises class diagram

Simple Queries

The simplest EJB QL statement has no WHERE clause and only one abstract schema type. For example, you could define a query method to select all Customer beans:

```
SELECT OBJECT( c ) FROM Customer AS c
```

The FROM clause determines which entity bean types will be included in the select statement (i.e., provides the *scope* of the select). In this case, the FROM clause declares the type to be Customer, which is the abstract schema name of the Customer EJB. The AS c part of the clause assigns c as the identifier of the Customer EJB. This is similar to SQL, which allows an identifier to be associated with a table. Identifiers can be any length and follow the same rules that are applied to field names in the Java programming language. However, identifiers cannot be the same as existing <ejb-name> or <abstract-schema-name> values. In addition, identification variable names are *not* case-sensitive, so an identifier of customer would be in conflict with an abstract schema name of Customer. For example, the following statement is illegal because Customer is the abstract schema name of the Customer EJB:

```
SELECT OBJECT( customer ) FROM Customer AS customer
```

The AS operator is optional, but it is used in this book to help make the EJB QL statements more clear. The following two statements are equivalent:

```
SELECT OBJECT(c) FROM Customer AS c
```

```
SELECT OBJECT(c) FROM Customer c
```

The SELECT clause determines the type of values that will be returned. In this case, it's the Customer entity bean, as indicated by the c identifier.

The OBJECT() operator is required when the SELECT type is a solitary identifier for an entity bean. The reason for this requirement is pretty vague (and in the author's opinion, the specification would have been better off without it), but it is required whenever the SELECT type is an entity bean identifier. The OBJECT() operator is not used if the SELECT type is expressed using a *path*, which is discussed below.

Simple Queries with Paths

EJB QL allows SELECT clauses to return any CMP or single CMR field. For example, we can define a simple select statement to return the last names of all of Titan's customers, as follows:

```
SELECT c.lastName FROM Customer AS c
```

The SELECT clause uses a simple path to select the Customer EJB's lastName CMP field as the return type. EJB QL uses the CMP and CMR field names declared in <cmp-field> and <cmr-field> elements of the deployment descriptor. This navigation leverages the same syntax as the Java programming language, specifically the dot (.) navigation operator. For example, the previous EJB QL statement is based on the Customer EJB's deployment descriptor:

```
<ejb-jar>
    <enterprise-beans>
        <entity>
            <ejb-name>CustomerEJB</ejb-name>
            <home>com.titan.customer.CustomerHomeRemote</home>
            <remote>com.titan.customer.CustomerRemote</remote>
            <ejb-class>com.titan.customer.CustomerBean</ejb-class>
            <persistence-type>Container</persistence-type>
            <prim-key-class>java.lang.Integer</prim-key-class>
            <reentrant>False</reentrant>
            <abstract-schema-name>Customer</abstract-schema-name>
            <cmp-version>2.x</cmp-version>
            <cmp-field><field-name>id</field-name></cmp-field>
            <cmp-field><field-name>lastName</field-name></cmp-field>
            <cmp-field><field-name>firstName</field-name></cmp-field>
```

You can also use CMR field types in simple select statements. For example, the following EJB QL statement selects all the CreditCard EJBs from all the Customer EJBs:

```
SELECT c.creditCard FROM Customer c
```

In this case, the EJB QL statement uses a path to navigate from the Customer EJBs to their `creditCard` relationship fields. The `creditCard` identifier is obtained from the `<cmr-field>` name used in the relationship element that describes the Customer-CreditCard relationship:

```
<enterprise-beans>
    <entity>
        <ejb-name>CustomerEJB</ejb-name>
        ...
        <abstract-schema-name>Customer</abstract-schema-name>
    </entity>
</enterprise-beans>
...
<relationships>
    <ejb-relation>
        <ejb-relation-name>Customer-CreditCard</ejb-relation-name>

        <ejb-relationship-role>
            <ejb-relationship-role-name>
                Customer-has-a-CreditCard
            </ejb-relationship-role-name>
            <multiplicity>One</multiplicity>
            <relationship-role-source>
                <ejb-name>CustomerEJB</ejb-name>
            </relationship-role-source>
            <cmr-field>
                <cmr-field-name>creditCard</cmr-field-name>
            </cmr-field>
        </ejb-relationship-role>
        <ejb-relationship-role>
        ...
```

Paths can be as long as required. It's common to use paths that navigate over one or more CMR fields to end at either a CMR or CMP field. For example, the following EJB QL statement selects all the city CMP fields of all the Address EJBs in each Customer EJB:

```
SELECT c.homeAddress.city FROM Customer c
```

In this case, the path uses the abstract schema name of the Customer EJB, the Customer EJB's `homeAddress` CMR field, and the Address EJB's `city` CMP field. Using paths in EJB QL is similar to navigating through object references in the Java language.

To illustrate more complex paths, we'll need to expand the class diagram. Figure 8-2 shows that the CreditCard EJB is related to a CreditCompany EJB that has its own Address EJB.

Using these relationships, we can specify a more complex path that navigates from the Customer EJB to the CreditCompany EJB to the Address EJB. The following EJB QL statement selects all the addresses of all the credit card companies:

```
SELECT c.creditCard.creditCompany.address FROM Customer AS c
```

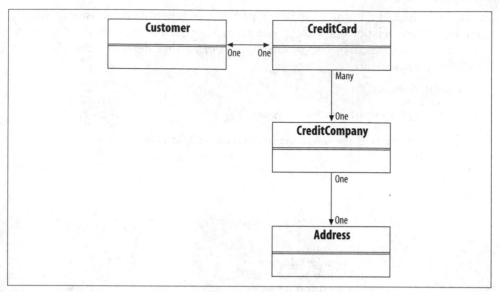

Figure 8-2. Expanded class diagram for CreditCard EJB

The EJB QL statement could also navigate all the way to the Address bean's CMP fields. For example, the following statement selects all the cities in which the credit card companies that distribute credit cards used by Titan's customers are based:

```
SELECT c.creditCard.creditCompany.address.city FROM Customer AS c
```

Note that these EJB QL statements return address CMR fields or city CMP fields only for those credit card companies responsible for cards owned by Titan's customers. The address information of any credit card companies whose cards are not currently used by Titan's customers won't be included in the results.

Paths cannot navigate beyond CMP fields. For example, imagine that the Address EJB uses a ZipCode class as its zip CMP field:

```
public class ZipCode implements java.io.Serializable {
    public int mainCode;
    public int codeSuffix;
    ...
}
```

It would be illegal to attempt to navigate to one of the ZipCode class's instance fields:

```
// this is illegal
SELECT c.homeAddress.zip.mainCode FROM Customer AS c
```

CMP fields cannot be further decomposed and navigated by paths. All CMP fields are considered opaque.

The paths used in SELECT clauses of EJB QL statements must always end with a single type. They may not end with a collection-based relationship field. For example, the following is not legal because the CMR field reservations is a collection-based relationship field:

```
// this is illegal
SELECT c.reservations FROM Customer AS c
```

In fact, it's illegal to navigate across a collection-based relationship field. The following EJB QL statement is also illegal, even though the path ends in a single-type relationship field:

```
SELECT c.reservations.cruise FROM Customer AS c
```

If you think about it, this limitation makes sense. You cannot use a navigation operator (.) in Java to access elements of a java.util.Collection object either. For example, you cannot do the following (assume getReservations() returns a java.util. Collection type):

```
// this is illegal in the Java programming language
customer.getReservations().getCruise();
```

Referencing the elements of a collection-based relationship field is possible in EJB QL, but it requires the use of an IN operator and an identification assignment in the FROM clause, which are discussed next.

The IN Operator

Many relationships between entity beans are collection-based, and being able to access and select from these relationships is important. We've seen that it is illegal to select elements directly from a collection-based relationship. To overcome this limitation, EJB QL introduces the IN operator, which allows an identifier to represent individual elements in a collection-based relationship field.

The following query uses the IN operator to select the elements from a collection-based relationship. It returns all the reservations of all the customers:

```
SELECT OBJECT( r )
FROM Customer AS c,  IN( c.reservations ) AS r
```

The IN operator assigns the individual elements in the reservations CMR field to the identifier r. Once we have an identifier to represent the individual elements of the collection, we can reference them directly and even select them in the EJB QL statement. We can also use the element identifier in path expressions. For example, the following EJB QL statement will select every cruise for which Titan's customers have made reservations:

```
SELECT r.cruise
FROM Customer AS c, IN( c.reservations ) AS r
```

The identifiers assigned in the FROM clause are evaluated from left to right. Once you declare an identifier, you can use it in subsequent declarations in the FROM clause.

Notice that the identifier c, which was declared first, was subsequently used in the IN operator to define the identifier r.

 The OBJECT() operator is used for single identifiers in the select statement and not for path expressions. While this convention makes little sense, it is nonetheless required by the EJB 2.0 specification. As a rule of thumb, if the select type is a solitary identifier of an entity bean, it must be wrapped in an OBJECT() operator. If the select type is a path expression, this is not necessary.

Identification chains, in which subsequent identifications depend on previous identifications, can become very long. The following EJB QL statement uses two IN operators to navigate two collection-based relationships and a single CMR relationship. While not necessarily useful, this statement demonstrates how a query can use IN operators across many relationships:

```
SELECT cbn.ship
FROM Customer AS c, IN ( c.reservations ) AS r,
IN( r.cabins ) AS cbn
```

📖 Workbook Exercise 8.1, Simple EJB QL Statements

Using DISTINCT

The DISTINCT keyword ensures that the query does not return duplicates. This is especially valuable when applied to EJB QL statements used by find methods. Find methods in CMP 2.0 have only one return type, java.util.Collection, which may return duplicates. However, if the keyword DISTINCT is used, the query results of the find method will not contain duplicates.

For example, the following find method and its associated query will return duplicates:

```
// the find method declared in the remote or local home interface
public java.util.Collection findAllCustomersWithReservations()

// the EJB QL statement associated with the find method
SELECT OBJECT( cust ) FROM Reservation res, IN (res.customers) cust
```

The previous find method and associated EJB QL statement will return all Customer EJBs with reservations, but if a Customer EJB has more than one reservation, there will be duplicate references to that Customer EJB in the result Collection. Using the DISTINCT keyword will ensure that each Customer EJB is represented only once in the result Collection:

```
SELECT DISTINCT OBJECT( cust ) FROM Reservation res,
IN (res.customers) cust
```

The DISTINCT keyword can also be used with select methods. It works the same way for select methods that have a return type of Collection. If the select method's return type is `java.util.Set`, the distinct (no duplicates) result will be returned whether the `DISTINCT` keyword is used or not.

The `Set` type is explicitly defined as having no duplicates. Using the `Set` return type in combination with the `DISTINCT` keyword is redundant, but it is not illegal.

The WHERE Clause and Literals

You can also use literal values in EJB QL to narrow the scope of the elements selected. This is accomplished through the `WHERE` clause, which behaves in much the same way as the `WHERE` clause in SQL.

For example, you could define an EJB QL statement to select all the Customer EJBs that use a specific brand of credit card. The literal in this case is a `String` literal. Literal strings are enclosed by single quotes. Literal values that include a single quote, like the restaurant name "Wendy's," use two single quotes to escape the quote: `'Wendy''s'`. The following statement returns customers that use the American Express credit card:

```
SELECT OBJECT( c ) FROM Customer AS c
WHERE c.creditCard.organization = 'American Express'
```

Path expressions are always used in the `WHERE` clause in the same way they're used in the `SELECT` clause. When making comparisons with a literal, the path expression must evaluate to a CMP field; you can't compare a CMR field with a literal.

In addition to literal strings, literals can be exact numeric values (`long` types) and approximate numeric values (`double` types). Exact numeric literal values are expressed using the Java integer literal syntax (321, -8932, +22). Approximate numeric literal values are expressed using Java floating point literal syntax in scientific (5E3, -8.932E5) or decimal (5.234, 38282.2) notation.

For example, the following EJB QL statement selects all the ships that weigh 100,000.00 metric tons:

```
SELECT OBJECT( s )
FROM Ship AS s
WHERE s.tonnage = 100000.00
```

Boolean literal values use `TRUE` and `FALSE`. Here's an EJB QL statement that selects all the customers who have good credit:

```
SELECT OBJECT( c ) FROM Customer AS c
WHERE c.hasGoodCredit = TRUE
```

The WHERE Clause and Input Parameters

Query methods (find and select methods) that use EJB QL statements may specify method arguments. *Input parameters* allow those method arguments to be mapped to EJB QL statements and are used to narrow the scope of the query. For example, the ejbSelectByCity() method is designed to select all the customers that reside in a particular city and state:

```
public abstract class CustomerBean implements javax.ejb.EntityBean {
    ...
    public abstract Collection ejbSelectByCity(String city,String state)
        throws FinderException;
    ...
}
```

The EJB QL statement for this method would use the city and state arguments as input parameters:

```
SELECT OBJECT( c ) FROM Customer AS c
WHERE c.homeAddress.state = ?2
AND c.homeAddress.city = ?1
```

Input parameters use a ? prefix followed by the argument's position, in order of the query method's parameters. In this case, city is the first argument listed in the ejbSelectByCity() method and state is the second. When a query method declares one or more arguments, the associated EJB QL statement may use some or all of the arguments as input parameters.

Input parameters are not limited to simple CMP field types; they can also be EJB object references. For example, the following find method, findByShip(), is declared in the Cruise bean's local interface:

```
public interface CruiseLocal extends javax.ejb.EJBLocalObject {
    public Collection findByShip( ShipLocal ship )
        throws FinderException;
}
```

The EJB QL statement associated with this method would use the ship argument to locate all the cruises scheduled for the specified Ship bean:

```
SELECT OBJECT( crs ) FROM Cruise AS crs
WHERE crs.ship = ?1
```

When an EJB object is used as an input parameter, the container bases the comparison on the primary key of the EJB object. In this case, it searches through all the Cruise EJBs looking for references to a Ship EJB with the same primary key value as the one the Ship EJB passed to the query method.

The WHERE Clause and Operator Precedence

The WHERE clause is composed of conditional expressions that reduce the scope of the query and limit the number of items selected. Several conditional and logical operators can be used in expressions; they are listed below in order of precedence. The operators at the top of the list have the highest precedence and are evaluated first:

1. Navigation operator (.)

2. Arithmetic operators:

   +, −   unary
   *, /   multiplication and division
   +, −   addition and subtraction

3. Comparison operators:

   =, >, >=, <, <=, <> (not equal)
   LIKE, BETWEEN, IN, IS NULL, IS EMPTY, MEMBER OF

4. Logical operators:

   NOT, AND, OR

The WHERE Clause and CDATA Sections

EJB QL statements are declared in XML deployment descriptors. XML uses the greater than (>) and less than (<) characters as delimiters for tags, so using these symbols in the EJB QL statements will cause parsing errors unless CDATA sections are used. For example, the following EJB QL statement causes a parsing error, because the XML parser interprets the > symbol as an incorrectly placed XML tag delimiter:

```
<query>
    <query-method>
        <method-name>findWithPaymentGreaterThan</method-name>
        <method-params>
            <method-param>java.lang.Double</method-param>
        </method-params>
    </query-method>
    <ejb-ql>
        SELECT OBJECT( r ) FROM Reservation r
        WHERE r.amountPaid  > ?1
    </ejb-ql>
</query>
```

To avoid this problem, you must place the EJB QL statement in a CDATA section:

```
<query>
    <query-method>
        <method-name>findWithPaymentGreaterThan</method-name>
        <method-params>
            <method-param>java.lang.Double</method-param>
        </method-params>
    </query-method>
    <ejb-ql>
        <![CDATA[
        SELECT OBJECT( r ) FROM Reservation r
        WHERE r.amountPaid  > 300.00
        ]]>
    </ejb-ql>
</query>
```

The CDATA section takes the form `<![CDATA[ literal-text ]]>`. When an XML processor encounters a CDATA section, it doesn't attempt to parse the contents enclosed by the CDATA section; instead, the parser treats the contents as literal text.[*]

The WHERE Clause and Arithmetic Operators

The arithmetic operators allow a query to perform arithmetic in the process of doing a comparison. In EJB QL, arithmetic operators can be used only in the WHERE clause, not in the SELECT clause.

The following EJB QL statement returns references to all the Reservation EJBs that will be charged a port tax of more than $300.00:

```
SELECT OBJECT( r ) FROM Reservation r
WHERE (r.amountPaid * .01)  > 300.00
```

The rules applied to arithmetic operations are the same as those used in the Java programming language, where numbers are *widened* or *promoted* in the process of performing a calculation. For example, multiplying a double and an int value requires that the int first be promoted to a double value. (The result will always be that of the widest type used in the calculation, so multiplying an int and a double results in a double value.)

String, boolean, and EJB object types cannot be used in arithmetic operations. For example, using the addition operator with two String values is considered an illegal operation. There is a special function for concatenating String values, which is covered in the later section "The WHERE Clause and Functional Expressions."

The WHERE Clause and Logical Operators

Logical operators such as AND, OR, and NOT operate the same way in EJB QL as their corresponding logical operators in SQL.

Logical operators evaluate only Boolean expressions, so each operand (i.e., each side of the expression) must evaluate to true or false. Logical operators have the lowest precedence so that all the expressions can be evaluated before they are applied.

The AND and OR operators may not, however, behave like their Java language counterparts && and ||. EJB QL does not specify whether the righthand operands are evaluated conditionally. For example, the && operator in Java evaluates its righthand operand *only* if the lefthand operand is true. Similarly, the || logical operator evaluates the righthand operand *only* if the lefthand operand is false. We can't make the same assumption for the AND and OR operators in EJB QL. Whether these operators evaluate righthand operands depends on the native query language into which the

---

[*] To learn more about XML and the use of CDATA sections, see *XML in a Nutshell* by Elliotte Rusty Harold and W. Scott Means (O'Reilly).

statements are translated. It's best to assume that both operands are evaluated on all logical operators.

NOT simply reverses the Boolean result of its operand; expressions that evaluate to the Boolean value of true become false, and vice versa.

The WHERE Clause and Comparison Symbols

Comparison operators, which use the symbols =, >, >=, <, <=, and <>, should be familiar to you. The following statement selects all the Ship EJBs whose tonnage CMP field is greater than or equal to 80,000 tons but less than or equal to 130,000 tons:

```
SELECT OBJECT( s ) FROM Ship s
WHERE s.tonnage >= 80000.00 AND s.tonnage <= 130000.00
```

Only the = and <> (not equal) operators may be used on String, boolean, and EJB object references. The greater-than and less than symbols (>, >=, <, <=) can be used only on numeric values. It would be illegal, for example, to use the greater-than or less-than symbols to compare two Strings. There is no mechanism to compare Strings in this way in EJB QL.

The WHERE Clause and Equality Semantics

While it's legal to compare an exact numeric value (short, int, long) to an approximate numeric value (double, float), all other equality comparisons must compare the same types. You cannot, for example, compare a String value of 123 to the Integer literal 123. However, you can compare two String types for equality.

You can also compare EJB objects for equality, but these too must be of the same type. To be more specific, they must both be EJB object references to beans from the same deployment. As an example, the following method finds all the Reservation EJBs made by a specific Customer EJB:

```
public interface ReservationHomeLocal extends EJBLocalObject {
    public Collection findByCustomer(CustomerLocal customer)
        throws FinderException;
    ...
}
```

The matching EJB QL statement uses the customer argument as an input parameter:

```
SELECT OBJECT( r )
FROM Reservation r, IN ( r.customers ) cust
WHERE  cust = ?1
```

It's not enough for the EJB object used in the comparison to implement the CustomerLocal interface; it must be of the same bean type as the Customer EJB used in the Reservation's customers CMR field. In other words, they must be from the same deployment. Once it's determined that the bean is the correct type, the actual comparison is performed on the beans' primary keys. If they have the same primary key, they are considered equal.

You cannot use java.util.Date objects in equality comparisons. To compare dates you must use the long millisecond value of the date, which means that the date must be persisted in a long CMP field and not a java.util.Date CMP field. The input value or literal must also be a long value.

The WHERE Clause and BETWEEN

The BETWEEN clause is an inclusive operator specifying a range of values. In this example, we use it to select all ships weighing between 80,000 and 130,000 tons:

```
SELECT OBJECT( s ) FROM Ship s
WHERE s.tonnage BETWEEN 80000.00 AND 130000.00
```

The BETWEEN clause may be used only on numeric primitives (byte, short, int, long, double, float) and their corresponding java.lang.Number types (Byte, Short, Integer, etc.). It cannot be used on String, boolean, or EJB object references.

Using the NOT logical operator in conjunction with BETWEEN excludes the range specified. For example, the following EJB QL statement selects all the ships that weigh less than 80,000 tons or greater than 130,000 tons but excludes everything in between:

```
SELECT OBJECT( s ) FROM Ship s
WHERE s.tonnage NOT BETWEEN 80000.00 AND 130000.00
```

The net effect of this query is the same as if it had been executed with comparative symbols, like this:

```
SELECT OBJECT( s ) FROM Ship s
WHERE s.tonnage < 80000.00 OR s.tonnage > 130000.00
```

The WHERE Clause and IN

The IN conditional operator used in the WHERE clause is not the same as the IN operator used in the FROM clause. In the WHERE clause, IN tests for membership in a list of literal string values and can be used only with operands that evaluate to string values. For example, the following EJB QL statement uses the IN operator to select all the customers who reside in a specific set of states:

```
SELECT OBJECT( c ) FROM Customer c
WHERE c.homeAddress.state IN ('FL', 'TX', 'MI', 'WI', 'MN')
```

Applying the NOT operator to this expression reverses the selection, excluding all customers who reside in the list of states:

```
SELECT OBJECT( c ) FROM Customer c
WHERE c.homeAddress.city NOT IN ('FL', 'TX', 'MI', 'WI', 'MN')
```

If the field tested is null, the value of the expression is "unknown", which means it cannot be predicted.

The WHERE Clause and IS NULL

The IS NULL comparison operator allows you to test whether a path expression is null. For example, the following EJB QL statement selects all the customers who do not have home addresses:

```
SELECT OBJECT( c ) FROM Customer c
WHERE c.homeAddress IS NULL
```

Using the NOT logical operator, we can reverse the results of this query, selecting all the customers who do have home addresses:

```
SELECT OBJECT( c ) FROM Customer c
WHERE c.homeAddress IS NOT NULL
```

When null fields appear in comparison operations such as IN and BETWEEN, they can have side effects. In most cases, evaluating a null field in a comparison operation (other than IS NULL) produces in an UNKNOWN result. Unknown evaluations throw the entire EJB QL result set into question; since we cannot predict the outcome of the EJB QL statement, it is unreliable. One way to avoid this situation is to require that fields used in the expressions have values. This requires careful programming. To ensure that an entity bean field is never null, you must initialize the field when the entity is created. For primitive values, this not a problem; they have default values, so they cannot be null. Other fields, such as single CMR fields and object-based CMP fields such as String, must be initialized in the ejbCreate() and ejbPostCreate() methods.

The WHERE Clause and IS EMPTY

The IS EMPTY operator allows the query to test if a collection-based relationship is empty. Remember from Chapter 7 that a collection-based relationship will never be null. If a collection-based relationship field has no elements, it will return an empty Collection or Set.

Testing whether a collection-based relationship is empty has the same purpose as testing whether a single CMR field or CMP field is null: it can be used to limit the scope of the query and items selected. For example, the following query selects all the cruises that have not booked any reservations:

```
SELECT OBJECT( crs ) FROM Cruise crs
WHERE crs.reservations IS EMPTY
```

The NOT operator reverses the result of IS EMPTY. The following query selects all the cruises that have at least one reservation:

```
SELECT OBJECT( crs ) FROM Cruise crs
WHERE crs.reservations IS NOT EMPTY
```

It is illegal to use IS EMPTY against collection-based relationships that have been assigned an identifier in the FROM clause:

```
// illegal query
SELECT OBJECT( r )
```

```
FROM Reservation r, IN( r.customers ) c
WHERE
r.customers IS NOT EMPTY AND
c.address.city = 'Boston'
```

While this query appears to be good insurance against UNKNOWN results, it's not. In fact, it's an illegal EJB QL statement, because the IS EMPTY operator cannot be used on a collection-based relationship identified in an IN operator in the FROM clause. Because the relationship is specified in the IN clause, only those Reservation EJBs that have a nonempty customers field will be included in the query; any Reservation EJB that has an empty CMR field will be excluded because its customers elements cannot be assigned the c identifier.

The WHERE Clause and MEMBER OF

The MEMBER OF operator is a powerful tool for determining whether an EJB object is a member of a specific collection-based relationship. The following query determines whether a particular Customer (specified by the input parameter) is a member of any of the Reservation-Customer relationships:

```
SELECT OBJECT( crs )
FROM Cruise crs, IN (crs.reservations) res, Customer cust
WHERE
cust = ?1
  AND
cust MEMBER OF res.customers
```

Applying the NOT operator to MEMBER OF has the reverse effect, selecting all the cruises on which the specified customer does not have a reservation:

```
SELECT OBJECT( crs )
FROM Cruise crs, IN (crs.reservations) res, Customer cust
WHERE
cust = ?1
  AND
cust NOT MEMBER OF res.customers
```

Checking whether an EJB object is a member of an empty collection always returns false.

The WHERE Clause and LIKE

The LIKE comparison operator allows the query to select String type CMP fields that match a specified pattern. For example, the following EJB QL statement selects all the customers with hyphenated names, like "Monson-Haefel" and "Berners-Lee":

```
SELECT OBJECT( c ) FROM Customer c
WHERE c.lastName LIKE '%-%'
```

You can use two special characters when establishing a comparison pattern: % (percent) stands for any sequence of characters, and _ (underscore) stands for any single character. You can use % and _ characters at any location within a string pattern. If a % or _ actually occurs in the string, you can escape it with the \ character. The NOT logical operator reverses the evaluation so that matching patterns are excluded.

The following examples show how the LIKE clause would evaluate String type CMP fields:

- phone.number LIKE '617%'

    True for "617-322-4151"
    False for "415-222-3523"

- cabin.name LIKE 'Suite _100'

    True for "Suite A100"
    False for "Suite A233"

- phone.number NOT LIKE '608%'

    True for "415 222-3523"
    False for "608-233-8484"

- someField.underscored LIKE '_%'

    True for "_xyz"
    False for "abc"

- someField.percentage LIKE '\%%'

    True for "% XYZ"
    False for "ABC"

The LIKE operator *cannot* be used with input parameters. This is an important point that is confusing to many new EJB developers. The LIKE operator compares a String type CMP field to a String literal. As it is currently defined, it cannot be used in a comparison with an input parameter, because an input parameter is, by definition, unknown until the method is invoked. Only the input parameter's type is known at deployment time. How would you compare a CMP field, whose value varies, with an arbitrary input parameter using a comparison pattern? It's just not possible. The comparison pattern is composed of special comparison characters (% and _) as well as regular characters. The comparison pattern must be known at deployment time in order to match it against the variable CMP fields at runtime.

The WHERE Clause and Functional Expressions

EJB QL has six functional expressions that allow for simple String manipulation and two basic numeric operations. The String functions are:

CONCAT(String1, String2)
    Returns the String that results from concatenating String1 and String2.

LENGTH(String)
    Returns an int indicating the length of the string.

LOCATE(String1, String2 [, start])
> Returns an int indicating the position at which String1 is found within String2. If it's present, start indicates the character position in String2 at which the search should start.

SUBSTRING(String1, start, length)
> Returns the String consisting of length characters taken from String1, starting at the position given by start.

The start and length parameters indicate positions in a String as integer values. You can use these expressions in the WHERE clause to help refine the scope of the items selected. Here is an example of how the LOCATE and LENGTH functions might be used:

```
SELECT OBJECT( c )
FROM Customer c
WHERE
LENGTH(c.lastName) > 6
   AND
LOCATE( c.lastName, 'Monson') > -1
```

This EJB QL statement selects all the customers with Monson somewhere in their last name, but specifies that the name must be longer than 6 characters. Therefore, "Monson-Haefel" and "Monson-Ares" evaluate to true, but "Monson" returns false because it has only 6 characters.

The arithmetic functions in EJB QL are:

ABS(number)
> Returns the absolute value of a number (int, float, or double)

SQRT(double)
> Returns the square root of a double

     📖 Workbook Exercise 8.2, Complex EJB QL Statements

Problems with EJB QL

EJB QL is a powerful new tool that promises to improve performance, flexibility, and portability of entity beans in container-managed persistence, but it has some design flaws and omissions.

The OBJECT( ) Operator

The use of the OBJECT() operator is unnecessary and cumbersome and provides little or no value to the bean developer. It's trivial for EJB vendors to determine when an abstract schema type is the return value, so the OBJECT() operator provides little real value during query translation. In addition, the OBJECT() operator is applied haphazardly. It's required when the return type is an abstract schema identifier, but not when a path expression of the SELECT clause ends in a CMR field. Both return an EJB object reference, so the use of OBJECT() in one scenario and not the other is illogical and confusing.

When questioned about this, Sun replied that several vendors had requested the use of the OBJECT() operator because it will be included in the next major release of the SQL programming language. EJB QL was designed to be similar to SQL because SQL is the query language that is most familiar to developers, but this doesn't mean it should include functions and operations that have no real meaning in Enterprise JavaBeans.

The Missing ORDER BY Clause

Soon after you begin using EJB QL, you will probably realize that it's missing a major component, the ORDER BY clause. Requesting ordered lists is extremely important in any query language, and most major query languages, including SQL and object query languages, support this function. The ORDER BY clause has a couple of big advantages:

- It provides a clear mechanism for the bean developer to communicate her intentions to the EJB QL interpreter. The ORDER BY clause is unambiguous; it states exactly how a collection should be ordered (by which attributes, ascending or descending, etc.). Given that EJB QL's purpose is to clearly describe the behavior of the find and select operations in a portable fashion, ORDER BY is clearly a significant omission.

- In most cases, it would allow EJB QL interpreters used by EJB vendors to choose an ordering mechanism that is optimized for a particular database. Allowing the resource to perform the ordering is more efficient than having the container do it after the data is retrieved.* However, even if the application server vendor chooses to have the container do the ordering, the ORDER BY clause still provides the EJB vendor with a clear indication of how to order the collection. It's up to the vendor to choose how to support the ORDER BY clause. For databases and other resources that support it, ordering can be delegated to the resource. For those resources that don't support ordering, it can be performed by container. Without an ORDER BY clause, the deployer has to manipulate collections manually or force the container's collection implementations to do the ordering. These two options are untenable in real-world applications in which performance is critical.

According to Sun, the ORDER BY clause was not included in this version of the specification because of problems dealing with the mismatch in ordering behavior between the Java language and databases. The example they gave had to do with string values. The semantics of ordering strings in a database may be different than those of the Java language. For example, Java orders String types according to character sequence and case (uppercase vs. lowercase). Different databases may or may not consider case

---

* It was suggested that EJB vendors could provide ordering mechanically, by having the collection sorted after it's obtained. This is a rather ridiculous expectation, since it would require collections to be fully manifested after the query completes, eliminating the advantages of lazy loading.

while ordering, or they may not consider leading or trailing whitespace. In light of these possible differences, it seems as though Sun has a reasonable argument, but only for limiting the portability of ORDER BY, not for eliminating its use all together. EJB developers can live with less than perfect portability of the ORDER BY clause, but they cannot live without the ORDER BY clause altogether.

Another argument against using the ORDER BY clause is that it necessitates the use of java.util.List as a return type. Although the List type is supposed to be used for ordered lists, it also allows developers to place items in a specific location in the list, which in EJB would mean a specific location in the database. This is nearly impossible to support, and so appears to be a reasonable argument against using the ORDER BY clause. However, this reasoning is flawed, because there is nothing preventing EJB from using the simple Collection type for ordered queries. The understanding would be that the items are ordered, but only as long as the collection is not modified (i.e., elements are not added or removed after it is obtained). Another option is to require that EJB QL statements that use the ORDER BY clause return a java.util.Enumeration type. This seems perfectly reasonable, since the Collection received by a select or find operation shouldn't be manipulated anyway.

While Sun has not defined EJB QL as supporting the ORDER BY clause, some EJB servers (such as BEA's WebLogic) are expected to support it anyway using nonstandard extensions. This support is both welcome and problematic, because nonstandard extensions to EJB QL can result in nonportable enterprise beans.

Lack of Support for Date

EJB QL doesn't provide native support for the java.util.Date class. This is not acceptable. The java.util.Date class should be supported as a natural type in EJB QL. It should be possible, for example, to do comparisons with Date CMP fields and literal and input parameters using comparison operators (=, >, >=, <, <=, <>). It should also be possible to introduce common date functions so that comparisons can be done at different levels, such as comparing the day of the week (DOW()) or month (MONTH()), etc. Of course, including the Date as a supported type in EJB QL is not trivial and problems with interpretation of dates and locales would need to be considered, but the failure to address Date as a supported type is a significant omission.

Limited Functional Expressions

While the functional expressions provided by EJB QL will be valuable to developers, many other functions should also have been included. For example, COUNT() is used often in real-world applications, but it is not currently supported in EJB QL. Other functions that would be useful include (but are not limited to) CAST() (useful for comparing different types), MAX() and MIN(), SUM(), and UPPER(). In addition, if support for java.util.Date was included in EJB QL, other date functions, such as DOW(), MONTH(), etc., could be added.

CHAPTER 9

EJB 1.1 CMP

A Note for EJB 2.0 Readers

Container-managed persistence has undergone a dramatic change in EJB 2.0, which is not backward compatible with EJB 1.1. For that reason, EJB 2.0 vendors must support both EJB 2.0's container-managed persistence model and EJB 1.1's container-managed persistence model. The EJB 1.1 model is supported purely for backward compatibility, so that application developers can migrate their existing applications to the new EJB 2.0 platform as painlessly as possible. It's expected that all new entity beans and new applications will use EJB 2.0 container-managed persistence, not the EJB 1.1 version. Although EJB 1.1 container-managed persistence is covered in this book, avoid it unless you maintain a legacy EJB 1.1 system. EJB 2.0 container-managed persistence is covered in Chapters 6 through 8.

EJB 1.1 container-managed persistence is limited in several ways. For example, EJB 1.1 CMP beans can have only remote component interfaces; they are not allowed to have local or local home interfaces. Most importantly, EJB 1.1 container-managed entity beans do not support relationships. Other subtle differences also make EJB 1.1 CMP more limiting than EJB 2.0 CMP. For example, the ejbCreate() and ejbPostCreate() methods in EJB 1.1 do not support the <METHOD-NAME> suffix allowed in EJB 2.0, which makes method overloading more difficult. EJB 2.0 CMP is a major improvement over CMP 1.1 and should be used if at all possible.

Overview for EJB 1.1 Readers

The following overview of EJB 1.1 container-managed persistence is pretty much duplicated in Chapter 6, but for EJB 1.1 readers who have not read Chapter 6, the overview is important to understanding the context of entity beans and container-managed persistence.

In Chapter 4, we started developing some simple enterprise beans, skipping over a lot of the details about developing enterprise beans. In this chapter, we'll take a thorough look at the process of developing entity beans.

Entity beans model business concepts that can be expressed as nouns. This is a rule of thumb rather than a requirement, but it helps in determining when a business concept is a candidate for implementation as an entity bean. In grammar school you learned that nouns are words that describe a person, place, or thing. The concepts of person and place are fairly obvious: a person EJB might represent a customer or passenger, and a place EJB might represent a city or port-of-call. Similarly, entity beans often represent things: real-world objects like ships, customers, and so on. An entity bean can even represent a fairly abstract thing, such as a reservation. Entity beans describe both the state and behavior of real-world objects and allow developers to encapsulate the data and business rules associated with specific concepts; a Ship EJB encapsulates the data and business rules associated with a ship, and so on. This makes it possible for data associated with a concept to be manipulated consistently and safely.

In Titan's cruise ship business, we can identify hundreds of business concepts that are nouns and therefore could conceivably be modeled by entity beans. We've already seen a simple Cabin EJB in Chapter 4, and we'll develop a Ship EJB in this chapter. Titan could clearly make use of a Customer EJB, a Cruise EJB, a Reservation EJB, and many others. Each of these business concepts represents data that needs to be tracked and possibly manipulated.

Entities really represent data in the database, so changes to an entity bean result in changes to the database. There are many advantages to using entity beans instead of accessing the database directly. Utilizing entity beans to objectify data provides programmers with a simpler mechanism for accessing and changing data. It is much easier, for example, to change a ship's name by calling `ShipRemote.setName()` than by executing an SQL command against the database. In addition, objectifying the data using entity beans provides for more software reuse. Once an entity bean has been defined, its definition can be used throughout Titan's system in a consistent manner. The concept of a ship, for example, is used in many areas of Titan's business, including booking, scheduling, and marketing. A Ship EJB provides Titan with one complete way of accessing ship information, and thus it ensures that access to the information is consistent and simple. Representing data as entity beans makes development easier and more cost-effective.

When a new EJB is created, a new record must be inserted into the database and a bean instance must be associated with that data. As the EJB is used and its state changes, these changes must be synchronized with the data in the database: entries must be inserted, updated, and removed. The process of coordinating the data represented by a bean instance with the database is called *persistence*.

There are two basic types of entity beans, and they are distinguished by how they manage persistence. *Container-managed persistence* beans have their persistence automatically managed by the EJB container. The container knows how a bean instance's persistence fields and relationships map to the database and automatically takes care of inserting, updating, and deleting the data associated with entities in the database. Entity beans using *bean-managed persistence* do all this work manually: the bean developer must write the code to manipulate the database. The EJB container tells the bean instance when it is safe to insert, update, and delete its data from the database, but it provides no other help. The bean instance does all the persistence work itself. Bean-managed persistence is covered in Chapter 10.

Container-Managed Persistence

When you deploy an EJB 1.1 CMP entity bean, you must identify which fields in the entity will be managed by the container and how they map to the database. The container then automatically generates the logic necessary to save the bean instance's state.

Fields that are mapped to the database are called container-managed fields—EJB 1.1 doesn't support relationship fields, as EJB 2.0 does. Container-managed fields can be any Java primitive type or serializable object. Most beans use Java primitive types when persisting to a relational database, since it's easier to map Java primitives to relational data types.

EJB 1.1 also allows references to other beans to be container-managed fields. For this to work, the EJB vendor must support converting bean references (remote or home interface types) from remote references to something that can be persisted in the database and converted back to a remote reference automatically. Vendors will normally convert remote references to primary keys, Handle or HomeHandle objects, or some other proprietary pointer type that can be used to preserve the bean reference in the database. The container will manage this conversion from remote reference to a persistent pointer and back automatically. This feature was abandoned in EJB 2.0 CMP in favor of container-managed relationship fields.

The advantage of container-managed persistence is that the bean can be defined independently of the database used to store its state. Container-managed beans can take advantage of both relational and object-oriented databases. The bean state is defined independently, which makes the bean reusable and more flexible.

The disadvantage of container-managed beans is that they require sophisticated mapping tools to define how the beans' fields map to the database. In some cases, this is a simple matter of mapping each field in the bean instance to a column in the database or of serializing the bean to a file. In other cases, it is more difficult. The state of some beans, for example, may be defined in terms of a complex relational database join or mapped to some kind of legacy system such as CICS or IMS.

In this chapter we will create a new container-managed entity bean, the Ship EJB, which we will examine in detail. A Ship EJB is also used in both Chapter 7, when discussing complex relationships in EJB 2.0, and Chapter 10, when discussing bean-managed persistence. When you are done with this chapter you may want compare the Ship EJB developed here with the ones created in Chapters 7 and 10.

Let's start by thinking about what we're trying to do. An enormous amount of data would go into a complete description of a ship, but for our purposes we will limit the scope of the data to a small set of information. For now, we can say that a ship has the following characteristics or attributes: its name, passenger capacity, and tonnage (i.e., size). The Ship EJB will encapsulate this data, and we'll need to create a SHIP table in our database to hold the data.

Here is the definition for the SHIP table expressed in standard SQL:

```
CREATE TABLE SHIP (ID INT PRIMARY KEY NOT NULL, NAME CHAR(30), CAPACITY INT,
TONNAGE DECIMAL(8,2))
```

When defining any bean, we start by coding the remote interfaces. This focuses our attention on the most important aspect of the bean: its business purpose. Once we have defined the interfaces, we can start working on the actual bean definition.

The Remote Interface

We will need a remote interface for the Ship EJB. This interface defines the business methods clients will use to interact with the bean. When defining the remote interface, we will take into account all the different areas in Titan's system that may want to use the ship concept. Here is the remote interface, ShipRemote, for the Ship EJB:

```
package com.titan.ship;

import javax.ejb.EJBObject;
import java.rmi.RemoteException;

public interface ShipRemote extends javax.ejb.EJBObject {
    public String getName() throws RemoteException;
    public void setName(String name) throws RemoteException;
    public void setCapacity(int cap) throws RemoteException;
    public int getCapacity() throws RemoteException;
    public double getTonnage() throws RemoteException;
    public void setTonnage(double tons) throws RemoteException;
}
```

The Remote Home Interface

The remote home interface of any entity bean is used to create, locate, and remove objects from EJB systems. Each entity bean type has its own home interface. The home interface defines two basic kinds of methods: zero or more create methods and one or more find methods.[*] The create methods act like remote constructors and define how new Ship EJBs are created. (In our home interface, we provide only a single create method.) The find method is used to locate a specific Ship or Ships.

The following code contains the complete definition of the ShipHomeRemote interface.

---

[*] Chapter 15 explains when you should not define any create methods in the home interface.

```
package com.titan.ship;

import javax.ejb.EJBHome;
import javax.ejb.CreateException;
import javax.ejb.FinderException;
import java.rmi.RemoteException;
import java.util.Enumeration;

public interface ShipHomeRemote extends javax.ejb.EJBHome {

    public ShipRemote create(Integer id, String name,
        int capacity, double tonnage)
        throws RemoteException,CreateException;
    public ShipRemote create(Integer id, String name)
        throws RemoteException,CreateException;
    public ShipRemote findByPrimaryKey(Integer primaryKey)
        throws FinderException, RemoteException;
    public Enumeration findByCapacity(int capacity)
        throws FinderException, RemoteException;
}
```

Enterprise JavaBeans specifies that create methods in the home interface must throw the javax.ejb.CreateException. In the case of container-managed persistence, the container needs a common exception for communicating problems experienced during the create process.

The find methods

EJB 1.1 CMP supports only find methods, not EJB 2.0's select methods. In addition, only the remote home interface supports find methods; EJB 1.1 entity beans do not support local component interfaces.

With EJB 1.1 container-managed persistence, implementations of the find methods are generated automatically at deployment time. Different EJB-container vendors employ different strategies for defining how the find methods work. Regardless of the implementation, when you deploy the bean, you'll need to do some work to define the rules of the find method. findByPrimaryKey() is a standard method that all home interfaces for entity beans must support. This method locates beans based on the attributes of the primary key. In the case of the Ship EJB, the primary key is the Integer class, which maps to the id field of the ShipBean. With relational databases, the primary key attributes usually map to a primary key in a table. In the ShipBean class, for example, the id attribute maps to the ID primary key column in the SHIP table. In an object-oriented database, the primary key's attributes might point to some other unique identifier.

EJB 1.1 allows you to specify other find methods in the home interface, in addition to findByPrimaryKey(). All find methods must have names that match the pattern find<SUFFIX>(). So, for example, if we were to include a find method based on the Ship EJB's capacity, it might be called findByCapacity(int capacity). In container-managed persistence, any find method included in the home interface must be explained to the container. In other words, the deployer needs to define how the find method should work in terms the container understands. This is done at deployment time, using the vendor's deployment tools and syntax specific to the vendor.

Find methods return either the remote interface type appropriate for that bean, or an instance of the java.util.Enumeration or java.util.Collection type. Unlike EJB 2.0 CMP, EJB 1.1 CMP doesn't support java.util.Set as a return type for find methods.

Specifying a remote interface type indicates that the method locates only one bean. The findByPrimaryKey() method obviously returns a single remote reference because there is a one-to-one relationship between a primary key's value and an entity. The findByCapacity(int capacity) method, however, could return several remote references, one for every ship that has a capacity equal to the parameter capacity. To be able to return more than one remote reference, the find method must return either the Enumeration or Collection type. Enterprise JavaBeans specifies that any find method used in a home interface must throw the javax.ejb.FinderException. Find methods that return a single remote reference throw a FinderException if an application error occurs and a javax.ejb.ObjectNotFoundException if a matching bean cannot be found. The ObjectNotFoundException is a subtype of FinderException and is thrown *only* by find methods that return single remote references. Find methods that return an Enumeration or Collection type (multi-entity finders) return an empty collection (not a null reference) if no matching beans can be found and throw a FinderException if an application error occurs.

How find methods are mapped to the database for container-managed persistence is not defined in the EJB 1.1 specification—it is vendor specific. Consult the documentation provided by your EJB vendor to determine how find methods are defined at deployment time. Unlike EJB 2.0 CMP, there is no standard query language for expressing the behavior of find methods at runtime.

The Primary Key

A primary key is an object that uniquely identifies an entity bean according to the bean type, home interface, and container context from which it is used. In container-managed persistence, a primary key can be a serializable object defined specifically for the bean by the bean developer, or its definition can be deferred until deployment. The primary key defines attributes that can be used to locate a specific bean in the database. In this case we need only one attribute, id, but it is possible for a primary key to have several attributes, all of which uniquely identify a bean's data. We will examine primary keys in detail in Chapter 11; for now, we'll specify that the Ship EJB use a simple single-value primary key of type java.lang.Integer.

The ShipBean Class

No bean is complete without its implementation class. Now that we have defined the Ship EJB's remote interfaces and primary key, we are ready to define the ShipBean itself. The ShipBean will reside on the EJB server. When a client application or bean invokes a business method on the Ship EJB's remote interface, that method invocation will be received by the EJB object, which will then delegate it to the ShipBean instance.

When developing any bean, we have to use the bean's remote interfaces as a guide. Business methods defined in the remote interface must be duplicated in the bean class. In container-managed beans, the create methods of the home interface must also have matching methods in the bean class, according to the EJB 1.1 specification. Finally, callback methods defined by the javax.ejb.EntityBean interface must be implemented. Here is the code for the ShipBean class:

```
package com.titan.ship;

import javax.ejb.EntityContext;

public class ShipBean implements javax.ejb.EntityBean {
    public Integer id;
    public String name;
    public int capacity;
    public double tonnage;

    public EntityContext context;

    public Integer ejbCreate(Integer id, String name, int capacity, double tonnage) {
        this.id = id;
        this.name = name;
        this.capacity = capacity;
        this.tonnage = tonnage;
        return null;
    }

    public Integer ejbCreate(Integer id, String name) {
        this.id = id;
        this.name = name;
        capacity = 0;
        tonnage = 0;
        return null;
    }

    public void ejbPostCreate(Integer id, String name, int capacity,
        double tonnage) {
        Integer pk = (Integer)context.getPrimaryKey();
        // Do something useful with the primary key.
    }

    public void ejbPostCreate(int id, String name) {
        ShipRemote myself = (ShipRemote)context.getEJBObject();
        // Do something useful with the EJBObject reference.
    }
    public void setEntityContext(EntityContext ctx) {
        context = ctx;
    }
```

```
    public void unsetEntityContext() {
        context = null;
    }
    public void ejbActivate() {}
    public void ejbPassivate() {}
    public void ejbLoad() {}
    public void ejbStore() {}
    public void ejbRemove() {}

    public String getName() {
        return name;
    }
    public void setName(String n) {
        name = n;
    }
    public void setCapacity(int cap) {
        capacity = cap;
    }
    public int getCapacity() {
        return capacity;
    }
    public double getTonnage() {
        return tonnage;
    }
    public void setTonnage(double tons) {
        tonnage = tons;
    }
}
```

The Ship EJB defines four persistence fields: id, name, capacity, and tonnage. These fields represent the persistence state of the Ship EJB; they are the state that defines a unique Ship entity in the database. The Ship EJB also defines another field, context, which holds the bean's EntityContext. We'll have more to say about this field later.

The set and get methods are the business methods we defined for the Ship EJB; both the remote interface and the bean class must support them. This means that the signatures of these methods must be exactly the same, except for the javax.ejb. RemoteException. The bean class's business methods aren't required to throw the RemoteException. This makes sense because these methods aren't actually invoked remotely—they're invoked by the EJB object. If a communication problem occurs, the container will throw the RemoteException for the bean automatically.

Implementing the javax.ejb.EntityBean Interface

Because it is an entity bean, the Ship EJB must implement the javax.ejb.EntityBean interface. The EntityBean interface contains a number of callback methods that the container uses to alert the bean instance of various runtime events:

```
public interface javax.ejb.EntityBean extends javax.ejb.EnterpriseBean {
    public abstract void ejbActivate() throws RemoteException;
    public abstract void ejbPassivate() throws RemoteException;
```

```
        public abstract void ejbLoad() throws RemoteException;
        public abstract void ejbStore() throws RemoteException;
        public abstract void ejbRemove() throws RemoteException;
        public abstract void setEntityContext(EntityContext ctx)
            throws RemoteException;
        public abstract void unsetEntityContext() throws RemoteException;
    }
```

Each callback method is called at a specific time during the life cycle of a `ShipBean` instance. In many cases, container-managed beans (like the Ship EJB) don't need to do anything when a callback method is invoked. The persistence of container-managed beans is managed automatically; much of the resources and logic that might be managed by these methods is already handled by the container.

This version of the Ship EJB has empty implementations for its callback methods. It is important to note, however, that even a container-managed bean can take advantage of these callback methods if needed; we just don't need them in our `ShipBean` class at this time. The callback methods are examined in detail in Chapter 11. You should read that chapter to learn more about the callback methods and when they are invoked.

The Create Methods

When a `create()` method is invoked on the home interface, the EJB home delegates it to the bean instance in the same way that business methods on the remote interface are handled. This means we need an `ejbCreate()` method in the bean class that corresponds to each `create()` method in the home interface.

The `ejbCreate()` method returns a `null` value of type `Integer` for the bean's primary key. The return value of the `ejbCreate()` method for a container-managed bean is actually ignored by the container.

 EJB 1.1 changed the `ejbCreate()` method's return value from void, which was the return type in EJB 1.0, to the primary key type to facilitate subclassing—this makes it easier for a bean-managed bean to extend a container-managed bean. In EJB 1.0, because the return type was void, this was not possible: Java won't allow you to overload methods with different return values. By changing this definition so that a bean-managed bean can extend a container-managed bean, the EJB 1.1 specification allows vendors to support container-managed persistence by extending the container-managed bean with a generated bean-managed bean—a fairly simple solution to a difficult problem. Bean developers can also take advantage of inheritance to change an existing CMP bean into a BMP bean, which may be necessary to overcome difficult persistence problems.

For every `create()` method defined in the entity bean's home interface, there must be a corresponding `ejbPostCreate()` method in the bean instance class. In other words, the ejbCreate() and ejbPostCreate() methods occur in pairs with matching signatures; there must be one pair for each create() method defined in the home interface.

ejbCreate( ) and ejbPostCreate( )

In a container-managed bean, the ejbCreate() method is called just prior to writing the bean's container-managed fields to the database. Values passed in to the ejbCreate() method should be used to initialize the fields of the bean instance. Once the ejbCreate() method completes, a new record, based on the container-managed fields, is written to the database.

The bean developer must ensure that the ejbCreate() method sets the persistence fields that correspond to the fields of the primary key. When a compound primary key is defined for a container-managed bean, it must define fields that match one or more of the container-managed (persistence) fields in the bean class. The fields must match exactly with regard to type and name. At runtime, the container will assume that fields in the primary key match some or all of the fields in the bean class. When a new bean is created, the container will use the container-managed fields in the bean class to instantiate and populate a primary key for the bean automatically.

Once the bean's state has been populated and its EntityContext has been established, an ejbPostCreate() method is invoked. This method gives the bean an opportunity to perform any postprocessing prior to servicing client requests. The bean identity isn't available to the bean during the call to ejbCreate(), but it is available in the ejbPostCreate() method. This means that the bean can access its own primary key and EJB object, which can be useful for initializing the bean instance prior to servicing business-method invocations. You can use the ejbPostCreate() method to perform any additional initialization. Each ejbPostCreate() method must have the same parameters as its corresponding ejbCreate() method. The ejbPostCreate() method returns void.

For more information about the ejbCreate() and ejbPostCreate() methods and how they relate to the life cycle of entity beans, see Chapter 11.

Using ejbLoad( ) and ejbStore( ) in container-managed beans

The process of ensuring that the database record and the entity bean instance are equivalent is called *synchronization*. In container-managed persistence, the bean's container-managed fields are automatically synchronized with the database. In most cases we will not need the ejbLoad() and ejbStore() methods, because persistence in container-managed beans is uncomplicated. These methods are covered in more detail in Chapter 11.

Deployment Descriptor

With a complete definition of the Ship EJB, including the remote interface and the home interface, we are ready to create a deployment descriptor. The following code shows the bean's XML deployment descriptor. The `<cmp-field>` element is particularly important. These elements list the fields that are managed by the container; they have the same meaning as they do in EJB 2.0 container-managed persistence:

```xml
<!DOCTYPE ejb-jar PUBLIC "-//Sun Microsystems, Inc.//DTD Enterprise
JavaBeans 1.1//EN" "http://java.sun.com/j2ee/dtds/ejb-jar_1_1.dtd">

<ejb-jar>
    <enterprise-beans>
        <entity>
            <description>
                This bean represents a cruise ship.
            </description>
            <ejb-name>ShipEJB</ejb-name>
            <home>com.titan.ship.ShipHomeRemote</home>
            <remote>com.titan.ship.ShipRemote</remote>
            <ejb-class>com.titan.ship.ShipBean</ejb-class>
            <persistence-type>Container</persistence-type>
            <prim-key-class>java.lang.Integer</prim-key-class>
            <reentrant>False</reentrant>
            <cmp-field><field-name>id</field-name></cmp-field>
            <cmp-field><field-name>name</field-name></cmp-field>
            <cmp-field><field-name>capacity</field-name></cmp-field>
            <cmp-field><field-name>tonnage</field-name></cmp-field>
            <primkey-field>id</primkey-field>
        </entity>
    </enterprise-beans>

    <assembly-descriptor>
        <security-role>
            <description>
                This role represents everyone who is allowed full access
                to the Ship EJB.
            </description>
            <role-name>everyone</role-name>
        </security-role>

        <method-permission>
            <role-name>everyone</role-name>
            <method>
                <ejb-name>ShipEJB</ejb-name>
                <method-name>*</method-name>
            </method>
        </method-permission>

        <container-transaction>
            <method>
                <ejb-name>ShipEJB</ejb-name>
                <method-name>*</method-name>
            </method>
            <trans-attribute>Required</trans-attribute>
        </container-transaction>
    </assembly-descriptor>
</ejb-jar>
```

The <cmp-field> elements list all the container-managed fields in the entity bean class. These are the fields that will be persisted in the database and are managed by the container at runtime.

📖 Workbook Exercise 9.1, A CMP 1.1 Entity Bean

CHAPTER 10

Bean-Managed Persistence

From the developer's point of view, bean-managed persistence (BMP) requires more effort than container-managed persistence, because you must explicitly write the persistence logic into the bean class. In order to write the persistence-handling code into the bean class, you must know what type of database is being used and the how the bean class's fields map to that database.

Given that container-managed persistence saves a lot of work, why would anyone bother with bean-managed persistence? The main advantage of BMP is that it gives you more flexibility in how state is managed between the bean instance and the database. Entity beans that use data from a combination of different databases or other resources such as legacy systems can benefit from BMP. Essentially, bean-managed persistence is the alternative to container-managed persistence when the container tools are inadequate for mapping the bean instance's state to the backend databases or resources.

The primary disadvantage of BMP is obvious: more work is required to define the bean. You have to understand the structure of the database or resource and the APIs that access them, and you must develop the logic to create, update, and remove data associated with entities. This requires diligence in using the EJB callback methods (e.g., ejbLoad() and ejbStore()) appropriately. In addition, you must explicitly develop the find methods defined in the bean's home interfaces.

The select methods used in EJB 2.0 container-managed persistence are not supported in bean-managed persistence.

Another disadvantage of BMP is that it ties the bean to a specific database type and structure. Any changes in the database or in the structure of data require changes to the bean instance's definition, and these changes may not be trivial. A bean-managed entity is not as database independent as a container-managed entity, but it can better accommodate a complex or unusual set of data.

To help you understand how BMP works, we will create a new Ship EJB that is similar to the one used in Chapters 7 and 9. For BMP, we need to implement the ejbCreate(), ejbLoad(), ejbStore(), and ejbRemove() methods to handle synchronizing the bean's state with the database.

 EJB 1.1 readers will notice that some of the information in this chapter is repeated from Chapter 9, which covers CMP 1.1. However, for EJB 2.0 readers, who will probably skip Chapter 9, most of this material will be new. EJB 1.1 readers are encouraged to skim familiar material as it is encountered.

The Remote Interface

We will need a remote interface for the Ship EJB. This interface is basically the same as any other remote or local interface. It defines the business methods used by clients to interact with the bean:

```
package com.titan.ship;

import javax.ejb.EJBObject;
import java.rmi.RemoteException;

public interface ShipRemote extends javax.ejb.EJBObject {
    public String getName() throws RemoteException;
    public void setName(String name) throws RemoteException;
    public void setCapacity(int cap) throws RemoteException;
    public int getCapacity() throws RemoteException;
    public double getTonnage() throws RemoteException;
    public void setTonnage(double tons) throws RemoteException;
}
```

We will not develop a local interface for the bean-managed Ship bean in this chapter; however, in EJB 2.0, bean-managed entity beans can have either local or remote component interfaces, just like container-managed entity beans.

Set and Get Methods

The ShipRemote definition uses a series of accessor methods whose names begin with "set" and "get." This is not a required signature pattern, but it is the naming convention used by most Java developers when obtaining and changing the values of object attributes or fields. These methods are often referred to as *setters* and *getters* (a.k.a. *mutators* and *accessors*), and the attributes they manipulate are called *properties*.* Properties should be defined independently of the anticipated storage structure of the data. In other words, you should design the remote interface to model the business

---

* Although EJB is different from its GUI counterpart, JavaBeans, the concepts of accessors and properties are similar. You can learn about this idiom by reading *Developing Java Beans™* by Rob Englander (O'Reilly).

concepts, not the underlying data. Just because there's a capacity property doesn't mean that there has to be a capacity field in the bean or the database; the getCapacity() method could conceivably compute the capacity from a list of cabins by looking up the ship's model and configuration, or with some other algorithm.

Defining entity properties according to the business concept and not the underlying data is not always possible, but you should try to employ this strategy whenever you can. The reason is twofold. First, the underlying data doesn't always clearly define the business purpose or concept being modeled by the entity bean. Remote interfaces are often used by developers who know the business but not the database configuration. It is important to them that the entity bean reflect the business concept. Second, defining the properties of the entity bean independently of the data allows the bean and data to evolve separately. This is important because it allows a database implementation to change over time; it also allows for new behavior to be added to the entity bean as needed. If the bean's definition is independent of the data source, the impact of these developments is limited.

The Remote Home Interface

Entity beans' home interfaces (local and remote) are used to create, locate, and remove objects from EJB systems. Each entity bean has its own remote or local home interface. The home interface defines two basic kinds of methods: zero or more create methods, and one or more find methods.[*] In this example, the create methods act like remote constructors and define how new Ship EJBs are created. (In our home interface, we provide only a single create method.) The find method is used to locate a specific Ship or Ships. The following code contains the complete definition of the ShipHomeRemote interface:

```
package com.titan.ship;

import javax.ejb.EJBHome;
import javax.ejb.CreateException;
import javax.ejb.FinderException;
import java.rmi.RemoteException;
import java.util.Collection;

public interface ShipHomeRemote extends javax.ejb.EJBHome {

    public ShipRemote create(Integer id, String name, int capacity, double tonnage)
        throws RemoteException,CreateException;
    public ShipRemote create(Integer id, String name)
        throws RemoteException,CreateException;
    public ShipRemote findByPrimaryKey(Integer primaryKey)
        throws FinderException, RemoteException;
```

[*] Chapter 15 explains when you should not define any create methods in the home interface.

```
    public Collection findByCapacity(int capacity)
        throws FinderException, RemoteException;
}
```

Enterprise JavaBeans specifies that create methods in the home interface must throw the javax.ejb.CreateException. This provides the EJB container with a common exception for communicating problems experienced during the create process.

The RemoteException is thrown by all remote interfaces and is used to report network problems that occurred while processing invocations between a remote client and the EJB container system.

The Primary Key

In bean-managed persistence, a primary key can be a serializable object defined specifically for the bean by the bean developer. The primary key defines attributes we can use to locate a specific bean in the database. For the ShipBean we need only one attribute, id, but in other cases a primary key may have several attributes, which together uniquely identify a bean's data.

We will examine primary keys in detail in Chapter 11; for now, we specify that the Ship EJB uses a simple single-value primary key of type java.lang.Integer. The actual persistence field in the bean class is an Integer named id.

The ShipBean

The ShipBean defined for this chapter uses JDBC to synchronize the bean's state to the database. In reality, an entity bean this simple could easily be deployed as a CMP bean. The purpose of this chapter, however, is to illustrate exactly where the resource-access code goes for BMP and how to implement it. When learning about bean-managed persistence, you should focus on when and where the resource is accessed in order to synchronize the bean with the database. The fact that we are using JDBC and synchronizing the bean state against a relational database is not important. The bean could just as easily be persisted to some legacy system, to an ERP application, or to some other resource that is not supported by your vendor's version of CMP, such as LDAP or a hierarchical database.

Here is the complete definition of the ShipBean:

```
package com.titan.ship;

import javax.naming.Context;
import javax.naming.InitialContext;
import javax.naming.NamingException;
import javax.ejb.EntityContext;
import java.rmi.RemoteException;
import java.sql.SQLException;
import java.sql.Connection;
```

```java
import java.sql.PreparedStatement;
import java.sql.DriverManager;
import java.sql.ResultSet;
import javax.sql.DataSource;
import javax.ejb.CreateException;
import javax.ejb.EJBException;
import javax.ejb.FinderException;
import javax.ejb.ObjectNotFoundException;
import java.util.Collection;
import java.util.Properties;
import java.util.Vector;
import java.util.Collection;

public class ShipBean implements javax.ejb.EntityBean {
    public Integer id;
    public String name;
    public int capacity;
    public double tonnage;

    public EntityContext context;

    public Integer ejbCreate(Integer id, String name, int capacity, double tonnage)
        throws CreateException {
        if ((id.intValue() < 1) || (name == null))
            throw new CreateException("Invalid Parameters");
        this.id = id;
        this.name = name;
        this.capacity = capacity;
        this.tonnage = tonnage;

        Connection con = null;
        PreparedStatement ps = null;
        try {
            con = this.getConnection();
            ps = con.prepareStatement(
                "insert into Ship (id, name, capacity, tonnage) " +
                "values (?,?,?,?)");
            ps.setInt(1, id.intValue());
            ps.setString(2, name);
            ps.setInt(3, capacity);
            ps.setDouble(4, tonnage);
            if (ps.executeUpdate() != 1) {
                throw new CreateException ("Failed to add Ship to database");
            }
            return id;
        }
        catch (SQLException se) {
            throw new EJBException (se);
        }
        finally {
            try {
                if (ps != null) ps.close();
                if (con!= null) con.close();
```

```java
            } catch(SQLException se) {
                se.printStackTrace();
            }
        }
    }
    public void ejbPostCreate(Integer id, String name, int capacity,
        double tonnage) {
        // Do something useful with the primary key.
    }
    public Integer ejbCreate(Integer id, String name) throws CreateException {
        return ejbCreate(id,name,0,0);
    }
    public void ejbPostCreate(Integer id, String name) {
        // Do something useful with the EJBObject reference.
    }
    public Integer ejbFindByPrimaryKey(Integer primaryKey) throws FinderException {
        Connection con = null;
        PreparedStatement ps = null;
        ResultSet result = null;
        try {
            con = this.getConnection();
            ps = con.prepareStatement("select id from Ship where id = ?");
            ps.setInt(1, primaryKey.intValue());
            result = ps.executeQuery();
            // Does the ship ID exist in the database?
            if (!result.next()) {
                throw new ObjectNotFoundException("Cannot find Ship with id = "+id);
            }
        } catch (SQLException se) {
            throw new EJBException(se);
        }
        finally {
            try {
                if (result != null) result.close();
                if (ps != null) ps.close();
                if (con!= null) con.close();
            } catch(SQLException se){
                se.printStackTrace();
            }
        }
        return primaryKey;
    }
    public Collection ejbFindByCapacity(int capacity) throws FinderException {
        Connection con = null;
        PreparedStatement ps = null;
        ResultSet result = null;
        try {
            con = this.getConnection();
            ps = con.prepareStatement("select id from Ship where capacity = ?");
            ps.setInt(1,capacity);
            result = ps.executeQuery();
            Vector keys = new Vector();
            while(result.next()) {
```

```java
                keys.addElement(result.getObject("id"));
            }
            return keys;


        }
        catch (SQLException se) {
            throw new EJBException (se);
        }
        finally {
            try {
                if (result != null) result.close();
                if (ps != null) ps.close();
                if (con!= null) con.close();
            } catch(SQLException se) {
                se.printStackTrace();
            }
        }
    }
    public void setEntityContext(EntityContext ctx) {
        context = ctx;
    }
    public void unsetEntityContext() {
        context = null;
    }
    public void ejbActivate() {}
    public void ejbPassivate() {}
    public void ejbLoad() {

        Integer primaryKey = (Integer)context.getPrimaryKey();
        Connection con = null;
        PreparedStatement ps = null;
        ResultSet result = null;
        try {
            con = this.getConnection();
            ps = con.prepareStatement("select name, capacity,
                tonnage from Ship where id = ?");
            ps.setInt(1, primaryKey.intValue());
            result = ps.executeQuery();
            if (result.next()){
                id =primaryKey;
                name = result.getString("name");
                capacity = result.getInt("capacity");
                tonnage = result.getDouble("tonnage");
            } else {
                throw new EJBException();
            }
        } catch (SQLException se) {
            throw new EJBException(se);
        }
        finally {
            try {
                if (result != null) result.close();
                if (ps != null) ps.close();
```

```
                if (con!= null) con.close();
            } catch(SQLException se) {
                se.printStackTrace();
            }
        }
    }
    public void ejbStore() {
        Connection con = null;
        PreparedStatement ps = null;
        try {
            con = this.getConnection();
            ps = con.prepareStatement(
                "update Ship set name = ?, capacity = ?, " +
                "tonnage = ? where id = ?");
            ps.setString(1,name);
            ps.setInt(2,capacity);
            ps.setDouble(3,tonnage);
            ps.setInt(4,id.intValue());
            if (ps.executeUpdate() != 1) {
                throw new EJBException("ejbStore");
            }
        }
        catch (SQLException se) {
            throw new EJBException (se);
        }
        finally {
            try {
                if (ps != null) ps.close();
                if (con!= null) con.close();
            } catch(SQLException se) {
                se.printStackTrace();
            }
        }
    }
    public void ejbRemove() {
        Connection con = null;
        PreparedStatement ps = null;
        try {
            con = this.getConnection();
            ps = con.prepareStatement("delete from Ship where id = ?");
            ps.setInt(1, id.intValue());
            if (ps.executeUpdate() != 1) {
                throw new EJBException("ejbRemove");
            }
        }
        catch (SQLException se) {
            throw new EJBException (se);
        }
        finally {
            try {
                if (ps != null) ps.close();
                if (con!= null) con.close();
            } catch(SQLException se) {
```

```
                se.printStackTrace();
            }
        }
    }
    public String getName() {
        return name;
    }
    public void setName(String n) {
        name = n;
    }
    public void setCapacity(int cap) {
        capacity = cap;
    }
    public int getCapacity() {
        return capacity;
    }
    public double getTonnage() {
        return tonnage;
    }
    public void setTonnage(double tons) {
        tonnage = tons;
    }
    private Connection getConnection() throws SQLException {
        // Implementations shown below.
    }
}
```

Obtaining a Resource Connection

In order for a BMP entity bean to work, it must have access to the database or
resource to which it will persist itself. To get access to the database, the bean usually
obtains a resource factory from the JNDI ENC. The JNDI ENC is covered in detail in
Chapter 12, but an overview here will be helpful since this is the first time it is actually used in this book. The first step in accessing the database is to request a connection from a DataSource, which we obtain from the JNDI environment naming
context:

```
private Connection getConnection() throws SQLException {
    try {
        Context jndiCntx = new InitialContext();
        DataSource ds = (DataSource)jndiCntx.lookup("java:comp/env/jdbc/titanDB");
        return ds.getConnection();
    }
    catch (NamingException ne) {
        throw new EJBException(ne);
    }
}
```

In EJB, every enterprise bean has access to its JNDI environment naming context
(ENC), which is part of the bean-container contract. The bean's deployment descriptor maps resources such as the JDBC DataSource, JavaMail, and Java Message Service

to a context (name) in the ENC. This provides a portable model for accessing these types of resources. Here's the relevant portion of the deployment descriptor that describes the JDBC resource:

```
<enterprise-beans>
    <entity>
        <ejb-name>ShipEJB</ejb-name>
        ...
        <resource-ref>
            <description>DataSource for the Titan database</description>
            <res-ref-name>jdbc/titanDB</res-ref-name>
            <res-type>javax.sql.DataSource</res-type>
            <res-auth>Container</res-auth>
        </resource-ref>
        ...
    </entity>
    ...
</enterprise-beans>
```

The `<resource-ref>` tag is used for any resource (e.g., JDBC, JMS, JavaMail) that is accessed from the ENC. It describes the JNDI name of the resource (`<res-ref-name>`), the factory type (`<res-type>`), and whether authentication is performed explicitly by the bean or automatically by the container (`<res-auth>`). In this example, we are declaring that the JNDI name jdbc/titanDB refers to a javax.sql.DataSource resource manager and that authentication to the database is handled automatically by the container. The JNDI name specified in the `<res-ref-name>` tag is always relative to the standard JNDI ENC context name, java:comp/env.

When the bean is deployed, the deployer maps the information in the `<resource-ref>` tag to a live database. This is done in a vendor-specific manner, but the end result is the same. When a database connection is requested using the JNDI name java:comp/jdbc/titanDB, a DataSource for the Titan database is returned. Consult your vendor's documentation for details on how to map the DataSource to the database at deployment time.

The getConnection() method provides us with a simple and consistent mechanism for obtaining a database connection for our ShipBean class. Now that we have a mechanism for obtaining a database connection, we can use it to insert, update, delete, and find Ship EJBs in the database.

Exception Handling

Exception handling is particularly relevant to this discussion because, unlike in container-managed persistence, in bean-managed persistence the bean developer is responsible for throwing the correct exceptions at the right moments. For this reason, we'll take a moment to discuss the different types of exceptions in BMP. This discussion will be useful when we get into the details of database access and implementing the callback methods.

Bean-managed beans throw three types of exceptions:

Application exceptions

Application exceptions include standard EJB application exceptions and custom application exceptions. The standard EJB application exceptions are `Create-Exception`, `FinderException`, `ObjectNotFoundException`, `DuplicateKeyException`, and `RemoveException`. These exceptions are thrown from the appropriate methods to indicate that a business logic error has occurred. Custom exceptions are exceptions developed for specific business problems. We cover developing custom exceptions in Chapter 12.

Runtime exceptions

Runtime exceptions are thrown from the virtual machine itself and indicate that a fairly serious programming error has occurred. Examples include the `NullPointerException` and `IndexOutOfBoundsException`. These exceptions are handled by the container automatically and should not be handled inside a bean method.

You will notice that all the callback methods (`ejbLoad()`, `ejbStore()`, `ejbActivate()`, `ejbPassivate()`, and `ejbRemove()`) throw an `EJBException` when a serious problem occurs. All EJB callback methods declare the `EJBException` and `RemoteException` in their throws clauses. Any exception thrown from one of the callback methods must be an `EJBException` or a subclass. The `RemoteException` type is included in the method signature to support backward compatibility with EJB 1.0 beans. Its use has been deprecated since EJB 1.1. `RemoteExceptions` should never be thrown by callback methods of EJB 1.1 or EJB 2.0 beans.

Subsystem exceptions

Checked exceptions thrown by other subsystems should be wrapped in an `EJBException` or application exception and rethrown from the method. Several examples of this can be found in the previous example, in which an `SQLException` that was thrown from JDBC was caught and rethrown as an `EJBException`. Checked exceptions from other subsystems, such as those thrown from JNDI, JavaMail, and JMS, should be handled in the same fashion. The `EJBException` is a subtype of the `RuntimeException`, so it doesn't need to be declared in the method's throws clause. If the exception thrown by the subsystem is not serious, you can opt to throw an application exception, but this is not recommended unless you are sure of the cause and the effects of the exception on the subsystem. In most cases, throwing an `EJBException` is preferred.

Exceptions have an impact on transactions and are fundamental to transaction processing. They are examined in greater detail in Chapter 14.

The ejbCreate( ) Method

`ejbCreate()` methods are called by the container when a client invokes the corresponding `create()` method on the bean's home. With bean-managed persistence, the ejbCreate() methods are responsible for adding new entities to the database. This means that the BMP version of ejbCreate() will be much more complicated than the equivalent methods in container-managed entities; with container-managed beans, ejbCreate() doesn't have to do much more than initialize a few fields. Another difference between bean-managed and container-managed persistence is that the EJB specification states that ejbCreate() methods in bean-managed persistence must return the primary key of the newly created entity. By contrast, in container-managed beans ejbCreate() is required to return null.

The following code contains the ejbCreate() method of the ShipBean. Its return type is the Ship EJB's primary key, Integer. The method uses the JDBC API to insert a new record into the database based on the information passed as parameters:

```java
public Integer ejbCreate(Integer id, String name, int capacity, double tonnage)
    throws CreateException {
    if ((id.intValue() < 1) || (name == null))
        throw new CreateException("Invalid Parameters");
    this.id = id;
    this.name = name;
    this.capacity = capacity;
    this.tonnage = tonnage;

    Connection con = null;
    PreparedStatement ps = null;
    try {
        con = this.getConnection();
        ps = con.prepareStatement(
            "insert into Ship (id, name, capacity, tonnage) " +
            "values (?,?,?,?)");
        ps.setInt(1, id.intValue());
        ps.setString(2, name);
        ps.setInt(3, capacity);
        ps.setDouble(4, tonnage);
        if (ps.executeUpdate() != 1) {
            throw new CreateException ("Failed to add Ship to database");
        }
        return id;
    }
    catch (SQLException se) {
        throw new EJBException (se);
    }
    finally {
        try {
            if (ps != null) ps.close();
            if (con!= null) con.close();
        } catch(SQLException se) {
            se.printStackTrace();
        }
    }
}
```

At the beginning of the method, we verify that the parameters are correct and throw a CreateException if the id is less than 1 or the name is null. This shows how you would typically use a CreateException to report an application-logic error.

The ShipBean instance fields are initialized using the parameters passed to ejbCreate() by setting the instance fields of the ShipBean. We will use these values to manually insert the data into the SHIP table in our database.

To perform the database insert, we use a JDBC PreparedStatement for SQL requests, which makes it easier to see the parameters being used (we could also have used a stored procedure through a JDBC CallableStatement or a simple JDBC Statement object). We insert the new bean into the database using a SQL INSERT statement and the values passed into ejbCreate() parameters. If the insert is successful (i.e., no exceptions are thrown), we create a primary key and return it to the container.

If the insert operation is unsuccessful we throw a new CreateException, which illustrates this exception's use in a more ambiguous situation. Failure to insert the record could be construed as an application error or a system failure. In this situation, the JDBC subsystem hasn't thrown an exception, so we shouldn't interpret the inability to insert a record as a failure of the subsystem. Therefore, we throw a CreateException instead of an EJBException. Throwing a CreateException allows the application to recover from the error, a transactional concept that is covered in more detail in Chapter 14.

When the insert operation is successful, the primary key is returned to the EJB container from the ejbCreate() method. In this case we simply return the same Integer object passed into the method, but in many cases a new key might be derived from the method arguments. This is especially true when using compound primary keys, which are discussed in Chapter 11. Behind the scenes, the container uses the primary key and the ShipBean instance that returned it to provide the client with a reference to the new Ship entity. Conceptually, this means that the ShipBean instance and primary key are assigned to a newly constructed EJB object, and the EJB object stub is returned to the client.

Our home interface requires us to provide a second ejbCreate() method with different parameters. We can save work and write more bulletproof code by making the second method call the first:

```
public Integer ejbCreate(Integer id, String name) throws CreateException {
    return ejbCreate(id,name,0,0);
}
```

The ejbLoad( ) and ejbStore( ) Methods

Throughout the life of an entity, its data will be changed by client applications. In the ShipBean, we provide accessor methods to change the name, capacity, and tonnage of the Ship EJB after it has been created. Invoking any of these accessor methods changes the state of the ShipBean instance, and these changes must be reflected in the database.

In container-managed persistence, synchronization between the entity bean and the database takes place automatically; the container handles it for you. With bean-managed persistence, you are responsible for synchronization: the entity bean must read from and write to the database directly. The container works closely with the BMP entities by advising them when to synchronize their state through the use of two callback methods: ejbStore() and ejbLoad().

The ejbStore() method is called when the container decides that it is a good time to write the entity bean's data to the database. The container makes these decisions based on all the activities it is managing, including transactions, concurrency, and resource management. Vendor implementations may differ slightly as to when the ejbStore() method is called, but this is not the bean developer's concern. In most cases, the ejbStore() method will be called after one or more business methods have been invoked or at the end of a transaction.

Here is the ejbStore() method for the ShipBean:

```
public void ejbStore() {
    Connection con = null;
    PreparedStatement ps = null;
    try {
        con = this.getConnection();
        ps = con.prepareStatement(
            "update Ship set name = ?, capacity = ?, " +
            "tonnage = ? where id = ?");
        ps.setString(1,name);
        ps.setInt(2,capacity);
        ps.setDouble(3,tonnage);
        ps.setInt(4,id.intValue());
        if (ps.executeUpdate() != 1) {
            throw new EJBException("ejbStore");
        }
    }
    catch (SQLException se) {
        throw new EJBException (se);
    }
    finally {
        try {
            if (ps != null) ps.close();
            if (con!= null) con.close();
        } catch(SQLException se) {
            se.printStackTrace();
        }
    }
}
```

Except for the fact that we are doing an update instead of an insert, this method is similar to the ejbCreate() method we examined earlier. We use a JDBC

PreparedStatement to execute the SQL UPDATE command, and we use the entity bean's persistence fields as parameters to the request. This method synchronizes the database with the state of the bean.

EJB also provides an ejbLoad() method that synchronizes the state of the entity with the database. This method is usually called at the start of a new transaction or business-method invocation. The idea is to make sure that the bean always represents the most current data in the database, which could be changed by other beans or other non-EJB applications.

Here is the ejbLoad() method for a bean-managed ShipBean class:

```java
public void ejbLoad() {

    Integer primaryKey = (Integer)context.getPrimaryKey();
    Connection con = null;
    PreparedStatement ps = null;
    ResultSet result = null;
    try {
        con = this.getConnection();
        ps = con.prepareStatement(
            "select name, capacity, tonnage from Ship where id = ?");
        ps.setInt(1, primaryKey.intValue());
        result = ps.executeQuery();
        if (result.next()){
            id = primaryKey;
            name = result.getString("name");
            capacity = result.getInt("capacity");
            tonnage = result.getDouble("tonnage");
        } else {
            throw new EJBException();
        }
    } catch (SQLException se) {
        throw new EJBException(se);
    }
    finally {
        try {
            if (result != null) result.close();
            if (ps != null) ps.close();
            if (con!= null) con.close();
        } catch(SQLException se) {
            se.printStackTrace();
        }
    }
}
```

To execute the ejbLoad() method, we need a primary key. To get the primary key, we query the bean's EntityContext. Note that we don't get the primary key directly from the ShipBean's id field, because we cannot guarantee that this field is always valid—the ejbLoad() method might be populating the bean instance's state for the first time, in which case the fields would all be set to their default values. This situation would occur following bean activation. We can guarantee that the EntityContext for the

ShipBean is valid because the EJB specification requires that the bean instance's EntityContext reference be valid before the ejbLoad() method can be invoked.

At this point you may want to jump to Chapter 11 and read the section titled "Entity-Context" to get a better understanding of the EntityContext's purpose and usefulness in entity beans.

The ejbRemove( ) Method

In addition to handling their own inserts and updates, bean-managed entities must handle their own deletions. When a client application invokes the remove method on the EJB home or EJB object, that method invocation is delegated to the bean-managed entity by calling ejbRemove(). It is the bean developer's responsibility to implement an ejbRemove() method that deletes the entity's data from the database. Here's the ejbRemove() method for our bean-managed ShipBean:

```
public void ejbRemove() {
    Connection con = null;
    PreparedStatement ps = null;
    try {
        con = this.getConnection();
        ps = con.prepareStatement("delete from Ship where id = ?");
        ps.setInt(1, id.intValue());
        if (ps.executeUpdate() != 1) {
            throw new EJBException("ejbRemove");
        }
    }
    catch (SQLException se) {
        throw new EJBException (se);
    }
    finally {
        try {
            if (ps != null) ps.close();
            if (con!= null) con.close();
        } catch(SQLException se) {
            se.printStackTrace();
        }
    }
}
```

The ejbFind( ) Methods

In bean-managed persistence, the find methods in the remote or local home interface must match the ejbFind() methods in the actual bean class. In other words, for each method named find<SUFFIX>() in a home interface, there must be a corresponding ejbFind<SUFFIX>() method in the entity bean class with the same arguments and exceptions. When a find method is invoked on an EJB home, the container delegates the find() method to a corresponding ejbFind() method on the bean instance. The bean-managed entity is responsible for locating records that match the find requests. There are two find methods in ShipHomeRemote:

```
public interface ShipHomeRemote extends javax.ejb.EJBHome {

    public ShipRemote findByPrimaryKey(Integer primaryKey)
        throws FinderException, RemoteException;
    public Collection findByCapacity(int capacity)
        throws FinderException, RemoteException;
}
```

Here are the signatures of the corresponding ejbFind() methods in the ShipBean:

```
public class ShipBean extends javax.ejb.EntityBean {

    public Integer ejbFindByPrimaryKey(Integer primaryKey)
        throws FinderException {}
    public Collection ejbFindByCapacity(int capacity)
        throws FinderException {}
}
```

Aside from the names, there's a significant difference between these two groups of methods. The find methods in the home interface returns either an EJB object implementing the bean's remote interface—in this case, ShipRemote—or a collection of EJB objects in the form of a java.util.Enumeration or java.util.Collection. The ejbFind() methods in the bean class, on the other hand, return either a primary key for the appropriate bean—in this case, Integer—or a collection of primary keys. The methods that return a single value (whether a remote/local interface or a primary key) are used whenever you need to look up a single reference to a bean. If you are looking up a group of references (for example, all ships with a certain capacity), you have to use the method that returns either the Collection or Enumeration type. In either case, the container intercepts the primary keys and converts them into remote references for the client.

The EJB 2.0 specification recommends that EJB 2.0 bean-managed persistence beans use the Collection type instead of the Enumeration type. This recommendation is made so that BMP beans are more consistent with EJB 2.0 CMP beans, which use only the Collection type.

It shouldn't come as a surprise that the type returned—whether it's a primary key or a remote (or local, in EJB 2.0) interface—must be appropriate for the type of bean you're defining. For example, you shouldn't put find methods in a Ship EJB to look up and return Cabin EJB objects. If you need to return collections of a different bean type, use a business method in the remote interface, not a find method from one of the home interfaces.

In EJB 2.0, the EJB container takes care of returning the proper (local or remote) interface to the client. For example, the Ship EJB may define a local and a remote home interface, both of which have a findByPrimaryKey() method. When findByPrimary() is invoked on the local or remote interface, it will be delegated to the ejbFindByPrimary() key method. After the ejbFindByPrimaryKey() method executes and returns the primary key, the EJB container takes care of returning a ShipRemote or ShipLocal reference to the client, depending on which home interface (local or remote) was used. The EJB container also handles this for multi-entity find methods, returning a collection of remote references for remote home interfaces or local references for local home interfaces.

Both find methods defined in the ShipBean class throw an EJBException if a failure in the request occurs when an SQL exception condition is encountered. findByPrimaryKey() throws an ObjectNotFoundException if no records in the database match the id argument. This is exception should always be thrown by single-entity find methods if no entity is found.

The findByCapacity() method returns an empty collection if no SHIP records with a matching capacity are found; multi-entity find methods do *not* throw ObjectNotFoundExceptions if no entities are found.

It is mandatory for all entity remote and local home interfaces to include the findByPrimaryKey() method. This method returns the remote interface type (in this case, Ship). It declares one parameter, the primary key for that bean type. With local home interfaces, the return type of any single-entity finder method is always the bean's local interface. With remote home interfaces, the return type of any single-entity find method is the remote interface. You cannot deploy an entity bean that doesn't include a findByPrimaryKey() method in its home interfaces.

Following the rules outlined earlier, we can define two ejbFind() methods in ShipBean that match the two find() methods defined in the ShipHome:

```
public Integer ejbFindByPrimaryKey(Integer primaryKey) throws FinderException, {
    Connection con = null;
    PreparedStatement ps = null;
    ResultSet result = null;
    try {
        con = this.getConnection();
        ps = con.prepareStatement("select id from Ship where id = ?");
        ps.setInt(1, primaryKey.intValue());
        result = ps.executeQuery();
        // Does the ship ID exist in the database?
        if (!result.next()) {
            throw new ObjectNotFoundException("Cannot find Ship with id = "+id);
        }
    } catch (SQLException se) {
        throw new EJBException(se);
    }
    finally {
        try {
            if (result != null) result.close();
            if (ps != null) ps.close();
            if (con!= null) con.close();
```

```
        } catch(SQLException se) {
            se.printStackTrace();
        }
    }
    return primaryKey;
}
public Collection ejbFindByCapacity(int capacity) throws FinderException {
    Connection con = null;
    PreparedStatement ps = null;
    ResultSet result = null;
    try {
        con = this.getConnection();
        ps = con.prepareStatement("select id from Ship where capacity = ?");
        ps.setInt(1,capacity);
        result = ps.executeQuery();
        Vector keys = new Vector();
        while(result.next()) {
            keys.addElement(result.getObject("id"));
        }
        return keys;
    }
    catch (SQLException se) {
        throw new EJBException (se);
    }
    finally {
        try {
            if (result != null) result.close();
            if (ps != null) ps.close();
            if (con!= null) con.close();
        } catch(SQLException se) {
            se.printStackTrace();
        }
    }
}
```

The mandatory findByPrimaryKey() method uses the primary key to locate the corresponding database record. Once it has verified that the record exists, it simply returns the primary key to the container, which then uses the key to activate a new instance and associate it with that primary key at the appropriate time. If no record is associated with the primary key, the method throws an ObjectNotFoundException.

The ejbFindByCapacity() method returns a collection of primary keys that match the criteria passed into the method. Again, we construct a prepared statement that we use to execute our SQL query. This time, however, we expect multiple results, so we use the java.sql.ResultSet to iterate through the results, creating a vector of primary keys for each SHIP_ID returned.

Find methods are not executed on bean instances that are currently supporting a client application. Only bean instances that are not currently assigned to an EJB object (i.e., instances in the instance pool) are supposed to service find requests, which means that the ejbFind() methods in the bean instance have somewhat limited use of the EntityContext. The EntityContext methods getPrimaryKey() and getEJBObject() will throw exceptions because the bean instance is in the pool and is not associated with a primary key or EJB object when the ejbFind() method is called.

Where do the objects returned by find methods originate? This seems like a simple enough question, but the answer is surprisingly complex. Remember that find methods aren't executed by bean instances that are actually supporting the client; rather, the container selects an idle bean instance from the instance pool to execute the method. The container is responsible for creating the EJB objects and local or remote references for the primary keys returned by the ejbFind() method in the bean class. As the client accesses these remote references, bean instances are swapped into the appropriate EJB objects, loaded with data, and made ready to service the client's requests.

The Deployment Descriptor

With a complete definition of the Ship EJB, including the remote interface, home interface, and primary key, we are ready to create a deployment descriptor. XML deployment descriptors for bean-managed entity beans are a little different from the descriptors we created for the container-managed entity beans in Chapters 6, 7, and 9. In this deployment descriptor, the <persistence-type> is Bean and there are no <container-managed> or <relationship-field> declarations. We also must declare the DataSource resource factory that we use to query and update the database.

Here is the deployment descriptor for EJB 2.0:

```
<!DOCTYPE ejb-jar PUBLIC "-//Sun Microsystems, Inc.//DTD Enterprise
JavaBeans 2.0//EN" "http://java.sun.com/dtd/ejb-jar_2_0.dtd">

<ejb-jar>
    <enterprise-beans>
        <entity>
            <description>
                This bean represents a cruise ship.
            </description>
            <ejb-name>ShipEJB</ejb-name>
            <home>com.titan.ship.ShipHomeRemote</home>
            <remote>com.titan.ship.ShipRemote</remote>
            <ejb-class>com.titan.ship.ShipBean</ejb-class>
            <persistence-type>Bean</persistence-type>
            <prim-key-class>java.lang.Integer</prim-key-class>
            <reentrant>False</reentrant>
            <security-identity><use-caller-identity/></security-identity>
            <resource-ref>
                <description>DataSource for the Titan database</description>
                <res-ref-name>jdbc/titanDB</res-ref-name>
                <res-type>javax.sql.DataSource</res-type>
                <res-auth>Container</res-auth>
            </resource-ref>
        </entity>
    </enterprise-beans>
```

```
        <assembly-descriptor>
            <security-role>
                <description>
                    This role represents everyone who is allowed full access
                    to the Ship EJB.
                </description>
                <role-name>everyone</role-name>
            </security-role>

            <method-permission>
                <role-name>everyone</role-name>
                <method>
                    <ejb-name>ShipEJB</ejb-name>
                    <method-name>*</method-name>
                </method>
            </method-permission>

            <container-transaction>
                <method>
                    <ejb name>ShipEJB</ejb-name>
                    <method-name>*</method-name>
                </method>
                <trans-attribute>Required</trans-attribute>
            </container-transaction>
        </assembly-descriptor>
    </ejb-jar>
```

The EJB 1.1 deployment descriptor is exactly the same except for two things. First, the `<!DOCTYPE>` element references EJB 1.1 instead of 2.0:

```
<!DOCTYPE ejb-jar PUBLIC "-//Sun Microsystems, Inc.//DTD Enterprise
JavaBeans 1.1//EN" "http://java.sun.com/j2ee/dtds/ejb-jar_1_1.dtd">
```

Second, the `<security-identity>` element:

```
<security-identity><use-caller-identity/></security-identity>
```

is specific to EJB 2.0 and is not found in the EJB 1.1 deployment descriptor.

📖 Workbook Exercise 10.1, A BMP Entity Bean

CHAPTER 11

The Entity-Container Contract

Although each of the three entity type components (EJB 2.0 CMP, EJB 1.1 CMP, and BMP) are programmed differently, their relationships to the container system at runtime are very similar. This chapter covers the relationship between EJBs and their containers. It includes discussions of primary keys, callback methods, and the entity bean life cycle. When differences between the bean types are important, they will be noted.

The Primary Key

A primary key is an object that uniquely identifies an entity bean. A primary key can be any serializable type, including primitive wrappers (Integer, Double, Long, etc.) or custom classes defined by the bean developer. In the Ship EJB discussed in Chapters 7, 9, and 10, we used the Integer type as a primary key. Primary keys can be declared by the bean developer, or the primary key type can be deferred until deployment. We will talk about deferred primary keys later.

Because the primary key may be used in remote invocations, it must adhere to the restrictions imposed by Java RMI-IIOP; that is, it must be a valid Java RMI-IIOP value type. These restrictions are discussed in Chapter 5, but for most cases, you just need to make the primary key serializable. In addition, the primary key must implement equals() and hashCode() appropriately.

EJB allows two types of primary keys: single-field and compound. *Single-field* primary keys map to a single persistence field defined in the bean class. The Customer and Ship EJBs, for example, use a java.lang.Integer primary key that maps to the container-managed persistence field named id. A *compound* primary key is a custom-defined object that contains several instance variables that map to more than one persistence field in the bean class.

Single-Field Primary Keys

The String class and the standard wrapper classes for the primitive data types (java.lang.Integer, java.lang.Double, etc.) can be used as primary keys. These are referred to as single-field primary keys because they are atomic; they map to one of the bean's persistence fields. Compound primary keys map to two or more persistence fields.

In the Ship EJB, we specified an `Integer` type as the primary key:

```
public interface ShipHomeRemote extends javax.ejb.EJBHome {

    public Ship findByPrimaryKey(java.lang.Integer primarykey)
        throws FinderException, RemoteException;
    ...
}
```

In this case, there must be a single persistence field in the bean class with the same type as the primary key. For the `ShipBean`, the `id` CMP field is of type `java.lang.Integer`, so it maps well to the `Integer` primary key type.

In EJB 2.0 container-managed persistence, the primary key type must map to one of the bean's CMP fields. The abstract accessor methods for the `id` field in the `ShipBean` class fit this description:

```
public class ShipBean implements javax.ejb.EntityBean {
    public abstract Integer getId();
    public abstract void setId(Integer id);
    ...
}
```

The single-field primary key must also map to a CMP field in bean-managed persistence (covered in Chapter 10) and EJB 1.1 container-managed persistence (discussed in Chapter 9). For the `ShipBean` defined in Chapters 9 and 10, the `Integer` primary key maps to the `id` instance field:

```
public class ShipBean implements javax.ejb.EntityBean {
    public Integer id;
    public String name;
    ...
}
```

With single-field types, you identify the matching persistence field in the bean class by using the `<primkey-field>` element in the deployment descriptor to specify one of the bean's CMP fields as the primary key. The `<prim-key-class>` element specifies the type of object used for the primary key class. The Ship EJB uses both of these elements when defining the `id` persistence field as the primary key:

```
<entity>
    <ejb-name>ShipEJB</ejb-name>
    <home>com.titan.ShipHomeRemote</home>
    <remote>com.titan.ShipRemote</remote>
    <ejb-class>com.titan.ShipBean</ejb-class>
    <persistence-type>Container</persistence-type>
    <prim-key-class>java.lang.Integer</prim-key-class>
    <reentrant>False</reentrant>
    <cmp-field><field-name>id</field-name></cmp-field>
    <cmp-field><field-name>name</field-name></cmp-field>
```

```
<cmp-field><field-name>tonnage</field-name></cmp-field>
    <primkey-field>id</primkey-field>
</entity>
```

Although primary keys can be primitive wrappers (Integer, Double, Long, etc.), they cannot be primitive types (int, double, long, etc.) because some of the semantics of EJB interfaces prohibit the use of primitives. For example, the EJBObject. getPrimaryKey() method returns an Object type, thus forcing primary keys to be Objects. Primitives also cannot be primary keys because primary keys must be managed by Collection objects, which work only with Object types. Primitives are not Object types and do not have equals() or hashcode() methods.

Compound Primary Keys

A compound primary key is a class that implements java.io.Serializable and contains one or more public fields whose names and types match a subset of persistence fields in the bean class. They are defined by bean developers for specific entity beans.

For example, if a Ship EJB didn't have an id field, we might uniquely identify ships by their names and registration numbers. (We are adding the registration CMP field to the Ship EJB for this example.) In this case, the name and registration CMP fields would become our primary key fields, which match corresponding fields (NAME and REGISTRATION) in the SHIP database table. To accommodate multiple fields as a primary key, we need to define a primary key class.

The convention in this book is to define all compound primary keys as serializable classes with names that match the pattern BeanNamePK. In this case we can construct a new class called ShipPK, which serves as the compound primary key for our Ship EJB:

```
public class ShipPK implements java.io.Serializable {
    public String name;
    public String registration;

    public ShipPK(){
    }
    public ShipPK(String name, String registration) {
        this.name = name;
        this.registration = registration;
    }
    public String getName() {
        return name;
    }
    public String getRegistration() {
        return registration;
    }
    public boolean equals(Object obj) {
        if (obj == null || !(obj instanceof ShipPK))
            return false;

        ShipPK other = (ShipPK)obj;
```

```
            if(this.name.equals(other.name) and
                this.registration.equals(other.registration))
                return true;
            else
                return false;

    }
    public int hashCode() {
        return name.hashCode()^registration.hashCode();
    }

    public String toString() {
        return name+" "+registration;
    }

}
```

To make the ShipPK class work as a compound primary key, we must make its fields public. This allows the container system to use reflection when synchronizing the values in the primary key class with the persistence fields in the bean class. We must also define equals() and hashCode() methods to allow the primary key to be easily manipulated within collections by container systems and application developers.

It's important to make sure that the variables declared in the primary key have corresponding CMP fields in the entity bean with matching identifiers (names) and data types. This is required so that the container, using reflection, can match the variables declared in the compound key to the correct CMP fields in the bean class. In this case, the name and registration instance variables declared in the ShipPK class correspond to name and registration CMP fields in the Ship EJB, so it's a good match.

We have also overridden the toString() method to return a meaningful value. The default implementation defined in Object returns the class name of the object appended to the object identity for that name space.

The ShipPK class defines two constructors: a *no-argument* constructor and an *overloaded* constructor that sets the name and registration variables. The overloaded constructor is a convenience method for developers that reduces the number of steps required to create a primary key. The no-argument constructor is *required* for container-managed persistence. When a new bean is created, the container automatically instantiates the primary key using the Class.newInstance() method and populates it from the bean's container-managed fields. A no-argument constructor must exist in order for this process to work.

To accommodate the ShipPK, we change the ejbCreate()/ejbPostCreate() methods so that they have name and registration arguments to set the primary key fields in the bean. Here is how the ShipPK primary key class would be used in the ShipBean class we developed for EJB 2.0 in Chapter 7:

```
import javax.ejb.EntityContext;
import javax.ejb.CreateException;
```

```
public abstract class ShipBean implements javax.ejb.EntityBean {

    public ShipPK ejbCreate(String name, String registration) {
        setName(name);
        setRegistration(registration);
        return null;
    }
    public void ejbPostCreate(String name, String registration) {
    }
    ...
```

In EJB 1.1 container-managed persistence, the container-managed fields are set directly. Here is an example of how this would be done with the Ship EJB in CMP 1.1:

```
public class ShipBean implements javax.ejb.EntityBean {
    public String name;
    public String registration;

    public ShipPK ejbCreate(String name, String registration) {
        this.name = name;
        this.registration = registration;
        return null;
    }
}
```

In bean-managed persistence, the Ship EJB sets its instance fields, instantiates the primary key, and returns it to the container:

```
public class ShipBean implements javax.ejb.EntityBean {
    public String name;
    public String registration;

    public ShipPK ejbCreate(String name, String registration){
        this.name = name;
        this.registration = registration;
        ...
        // database insert logic goes here
        ...
        return new ShipPK(name, registration);
    }
}
```

The ejbCreate() method now returns the ShipPK as the primary key type. The return type of the ejbCreate() method must match the primary key type if the primary key is defined or the java.lang.Object type if it is undefined.

In EJB 2.0 container-managed persistence, if the primary key fields are defined—i.e., if they are accessible through abstract accessor methods—they *must* be set in the ejbCreate() method. While the return type of the ejbCreate() method is always the primary key type, the value returned must always be null. The EJB container itself takes care of extracting the proper primary key directly. In bean-managed persistence, the bean class is responsible for constructing the primary key and returning it to the container.

The ShipHomeRemote interface must be modified so that it uses the name and registration arguments in the create() method and the ShipPK in the findByPrimaryKey() method (EJB requires that we use the primary key type in that method):

```
import java.rmi.RemoteException;
import javax.ejb.CreateException;
import javax.ejb.FinderException;

public interface ShipHomeRemote extends javax.ejb.EJBHome {

    public ShipRemote create(String name, String registration)
        throws CreateException, RemoteException;

    public ShipRemote findByPrimaryKey(ShipPK primaryKey)
        throws FinderException, RemoteException;

}
```

setName() and setRegistration(), which modify the name and registration fields of the Ship EJB, should not be declared in the bean's remote or local interfaces. As explained in the next paragraph, the primary key of an entity bean must *not* be changed once the bean is created. However, methods that simply read the primary key fields (e.g., getName() and getRegistration()) may be exposed because they don't change the key's values.

EJB 2.0 specifies that the primary key may be set only once, either in the ejbCreate() method or, if it's undefined, automatically by the container when the bean is created. Once the bean is created, the primary key fields *must never* be modified by the bean or any of its clients. This is a reasonable requirement that should also be applied to EJB 1.1 CMP and bean-managed persistence beans, because the primary key is the unique identifier of the bean. Changing it could violate referential integrity in the database, possibly resulting in two beans being mapped to the same identifier or breaking any relationships with other beans that are based on the value of the primary key.

Undefined Primary Keys

Undefined primary keys for container-managed persistence were introduced in EJB 1.1. Basically, undefined primary keys allow the bean developer to defer declaring the primary key to the deployer, which makes it possible to create more portable entity beans.

One problem with container-managed persistence in EJB 1.0 was that the entity bean developer had to define the primary key before the entity bean was deployed. This requirement forced the developer to make assumptions about the environment in which the entity bean would be used, which limited the entity bean's portability across databases. For example, a relational database uses a set of columns in a table as the primary key, to which an entity bean's fields map nicely. An object database, however, uses a completely different mechanism for indexing objects, to which a primary key may not map well. The same is true for legacy systems and Enterprise Resource Planning (ERP) systems.

An undefined primary key allows the deployer to choose a system-specific key at deployment time. An object database may generate an object ID, while an ERP system may generate some other primary key. These keys may be automatically generated by the database or backend system. The CMP bean may need to be altered or extended by the deployment tool to support the key, but this is immaterial to the bean developer; she concentrates on the business logic of the bean and leaves the indexing to the container.

To facilitate the use of undefined primary keys, the bean class and its interfaces use the Object type to identify the primary key. The Ship EJB developed in Chapters 7 and 9 could use an undefined primary key. As the following code shows, the Ship EJB's ejbCreate() method returns an Object type:

```
public abstract class ShipBean extends javax.ejb.EntityBean {

    public Object ejbCreate(String name, int capacity, double tonnage) {
        ...
        return null;
    }
}
```

The findByPrimaryKey() method defined in the local and remote home interfaces must also use an Object type:

```
public interface ShipHomeRemote extends javax.ejb.EJBHome {

    public ShipRemote findByPrimaryKey(Object primaryKey)
        throws javax.ejb.FinderException;

}
```

The Ship EJB's deployment descriptor defines its primary key type as java.lang. Object and does not define any <prim-key-field> elements:

```
<ejb-jar>
    <enterprise-beans>
        <entity>
            <ejb-name>ShipEJB</ejb-name>
            ...
            <ejb-class>com.titan.ship.ShipBean</ejb-class>
            <persistence-type>Container</persistence-type>
            <prim-key-class>java.lang.Object</prim-key-class>
            <reentrant>False</reentrant>
            <cmp-field><field-name>name</field-name></cmp-field>
            <cmp-field><field-name>capacity</field-name></cmp-field>
            <cmp-field><field-name>tonnage</field-name></cmp-field>
        </entity>
```

One drawback of using an undefined primary key is that it requires the bean developer and application developer (client code) to work with a java.lang.Object type and not a specific primary key type, which can be limiting. For example, it's not possible to construct an undefined primary key to use in a find method if you don't know its type. This limitation can be quite daunting if you need to locate an entity bean by its primary key. However, entity beans with undefined primary keys can be located easily using other query methods that do not depend on the primary key value, so this limitation is not a serious handicap.

In bean-managed persistence, you can declare an undefined primary key simply by making the primary key type java.lang.Object. However, this is pure semantics; the primary key value will not be auto-generated by the container because the bean developer has total control over persistence. In this case the bean developer would still need to use a valid primary key, but its type would be hidden from the bean clients. This method can be useful if the primary key type is expected to change over time.

The Callback Methods

All entity beans (container- and bean-managed) must implement the javax.ejb. EntityBean interface. The EntityBean interface contains a number of callback methods that the container uses to alert the bean instance of various runtime events:

```
public interface javax.ejb.EntityBean extends javax.ejb.EnterpriseBean {
    public abstract void ejbActivate() throws EJBException, RemoteException;
    public abstract void ejbPassivate() throws EJBException, RemoteException;
    public abstract void ejbLoad() throws EJBException, RemoteException;
    public abstract void ejbStore() throws EJBException, RemoteException;
    public abstract void ejbRemove() throws EJBException, RemoteException;
    public abstract void setEntityContext(EntityContext ctx) throws EJBException,
        RemoteException;
    public abstract void unsetEntityContext() throws EJBException,
        RemoteException;
}
```

Each callback method is invoked on an entity bean instance at a specific time during its life cycle.

As described in Chapter 10, BMP beans must implement most of these callback methods to synchronize the bean's state with the database. The ejbLoad() method tells the BMP bean when to read its state from the database; ejbStore() tells it when to write to the database; and ejbRemove() tells the bean when to delete itself from the database.

While BMP beans take full advantage of callback methods, CMP entity beans may not need to use all of them. The persistence of CMP entity beans is managed automatically, so in most cases the resources and logic that might be managed by these methods is already handled by the container. However, a CMP entity bean can take advantage of these callback methods if it needs to perform actions that are not automatically supported by the container.

You may have noticed that each method in the EntityBean interface throws both a javax.ejb.EJBException and a java.rmi.RemoteException. EJB 1.0 required that a

RemoteException be thrown if a system exception occurred while a bean was executing a callback method. However, since EJB 1.1 the use of RemoteException in these methods has been deprecated in favor of the javax.ejb.EJBException. EJB 1.1 and EJB 2.0 suggest that the EJBException be thrown if the bean encounters a system error, such as a SQLException, while executing a method. The EJBException is a subclass of RuntimeException, so you don't have to declare it in the method signature. Since the use of the RemoteException is deprecated, you also don't have to declare it when implementing the callback methods; in fact, it's recommended that you don't.

setEntityContext( ) and unsetEntityContext( )

The first method called after a bean instance is instantiated is setEntityContext(). As the method signature indicates, this method passes the bean instance a reference to a javax.ejb.EntityContext, which is the bean instance's interface to the container. The purpose and functionality of the EntityContext is covered in detail later in this chapter.

The setEntityContext() method is called prior to the bean instance's entry into the instance pool. In Chapter 3, we discussed the instance pool that EJB containers maintain, where instances of entity and stateless session beans are kept ready to use. EntityBean instances in the instance pool are not associated with any data in the database; their state is not unique. When a client requests a specific entity, an instance from the pool is chosen, populated with data from the database, and assigned to service the client. Any nonmanaged resources needed for the life of the instance should be obtained when this method is called. This ensures that such resources are obtained only once in the life of a bean instance. A nonmanaged resource is one that is not automatically managed by the container (e.g., references to CORBA objects). Only resources that are not specific to the entity bean's identity should be obtained in the setEntityContext() method. Other managed resources (e.g., Java Message Service factories) and entity bean references are obtained as needed from the JNDI ENC. Bean references and managed resources obtained through the JNDI ENC are not available from setEntityContext(). The JNDI ENC is discussed later in this chapter.

At the end of the entity bean instance's life, after it is removed permanently from the instance pool and before it is garbage collected, the unsetEntityContext() method is called, indicating that the bean instance is about to be evicted from memory by the container. This is a good time to free up any resources obtained in the setEntityContext() method.

ejbCreate( )

In a CMP bean, the ejbCreate() method is called before the bean's state is written to the database. Values passed in to the ejbCreate() method should be used to initialize the CMP fields of the bean instance. Once the ejbCreate() method completes, a new record, based on the persistence fields, is written to the database.

In bean-managed persistence, the ejbCreate() method is called when it's time for the bean to add itself to the database. Inside the ejbCreate() method, a BMP bean must use some kind of API to insert its data into the database.

Each ejbCreate() method must have parameters that match a create() method in the home interface. If you look at the ShipBean class definition and compare it to the Ship EJB's home interface (see Chapters 7, 9, and 10), you can see how the parameters for the create methods match exactly in type and sequence. This enables the container to delegate each create() method on the home interface to the proper ejbCreate() method in the bean instance.

In EJB 2.0, the ejbCreate() method can take the form ejbCreate<*SUFFIX*>(), which allows for easier method overloading when parameters are the same but the methods act differently. For example, ejbCreateByName(String name) and ejbCreateByRegistration(String registration) would have corresponding create() methods defined in the local or home interface, in the form createByName(String name) and createByRegistration(String registration). EJB 1.1 CMP does not allow the use of suffixes on ejbCreate() names. The ejbCreate() and create() methods may differ only by the number and type of parameters defined.

The EntityContext maintained by the bean instance does not provide an entity bean with the proper identity until ejbCreate() has completed. This means that while the ejbCreate() method is executing, the bean instance doesn't have access to its primary key or EJB object. The EntityContext does, however, provide the bean with information about the caller's identity and access to its EJB home object (local and remote) and properties. The bean can also use the JNDI naming context to access other beans and resource managers such as javax.sql.DataSource.

However, the CMP entity bean developer must ensure that ejbCreate() sets the persistence fields that correspond to the fields of the primary key. When a new CMP entity bean is created, the container will use the CMP fields in the bean class to instantiate and populate a primary key automatically. If the primary key is undefined, the container and database will work together to generate the primary key for the entity bean.

Once the bean's state has been populated and its EntityContext has been established, the ejbPostCreate() method is invoked. This method gives the bean an opportunity to perform any postprocessing prior to servicing client requests. In EJB 2.0 CMP entity beans, ejbPostCreate() is used to manipulate container-managed relationship fields. These CMR fields must not be modified by ejbCreate(). The reason for this restriction has to do with referential integrity. The primary key for the entity bean may not be available until after ejbCreate() executes. The primary key is needed if the mapping for the relationship uses it as a foreign key, so assignment of relationships is postponed until ejbPostCreate() completes and the primary key becomes available. This is also true with autogenerated primary keys, which usually require that the insert be done before a primary key can be generated. In addition, referential integrity may specify non-null foreign keys in referencing tables, so the insert must take place first. In reality, the transaction does not complete until both ejbCreate() and ejbPostCreate() have executed, so the vendors are free to choose the best time for database inserts and linking of relationships.

The bean identity is not available during the call to ejbCreate(), but it is available in ejbPostCreate(). This means that the bean can access its own primary key and EJB object (local or remote) inside of ejbPostCreate(). This can be useful for performing postprocessing prior to servicing business-method invocations; in CMP 2.0 ejbPostCreate() can be used for initializing CMR fields of the entity bean.

Each ejbPostCreate() method must have the same parameters as the corresponding ejbCreate() method, as well as the same method name. For example, if the ShipBean class defines an ejbCreateByName(String name) method, it must also define a matching ejbPostCreateByName(String name) method. The ejbPostCreate() method returns void. In EJB 1.1 CMP, suffixes are not allowed on create methods.

Matching the name and parameter lists of ejbCreate() and ejbPostCreate() methods is important for two reasons. First, it indicates which ejbPostCreate() method is associated with which ejbCreate() method. This ensures that the container calls the correct ejbPostCreate() method after ejbCreate() is done. Second, it is possible that one of the parameters passed is not assigned to a persistence field. In this case, you would need to duplicate the parameters of the ejbCreate() method to have that information available in the ejbPostCreate() method. Relationship fields are the primary reason for utilizing the ejbPostCreate() method in EJB 2.0 CMP, because of referential integrity.

ejbCreate( ) and ejbPostCreate( ) Sequence of Events

To understand how an entity bean instance gets up and running, we have to think of a entity bean in the context of its life cycle. Figure 11-1 shows the sequence of events during a portion of a CMP bean's life cycle, as defined by the EJB specification. Every EJB vendor must support this sequence of events.

The process begins when the client invokes one of the create() methods on the bean's EJB home. A create() method is invoked on the EJB home stub (step 1), which communicates the method to the EJB home across the network (step 2). The EJB home plucks a ShipBean instance from the pool and invokes its corresponding ejbCreate() method (step 3).

The create() and ejbCreate() methods are responsible for initializing the bean instance so that the container can insert a record into the database. In the case of the ShipBean, the minimal information required to add a new customer to the system is the customer's unique id. This CMP field is initialized during the ejbCreate() method invocation (step 4).

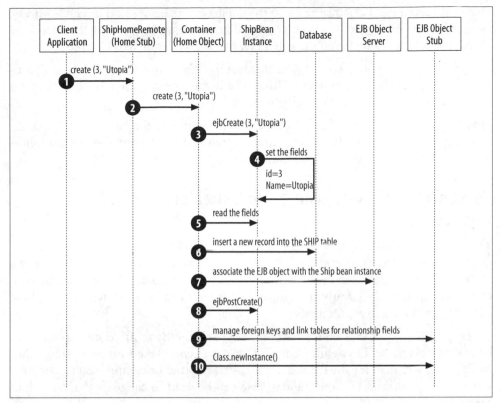

Figure 11-1. Event sequence for bean-instance creation

In container-managed persistence (EJB 2.0 and 1.1), the container uses the bean's CMP fields (id, name, tonnage), which it reads from the bean, to insert a record into the database (step 5). Only the fields described as CMP fields in the deployment descriptor are accessed. Once the container has read the CMP fields from the bean instance, it will automatically insert a new record into the database using those fields (step 6).* How the data is written to the database is defined when the bean's fields are mapped at deployment time. In our example, a new record is inserted into the CUSTOMER table.

 In bean-managed persistence, the bean class itself reads the fields and performs a database insert to add the bean's data to the database. This would take place in steps 5 and 6.

---

* The specification does not actually require that the record be inserted into the database immediately after the ejbCreate() method is called (step 6). As an alternative, the record insert may be deferred until after the ejbPostCreate() method executes or even until the end of the transaction.

Once the record has been inserted into the database, the bean instance is ready to be assigned to an EJB object (step 7). Once the bean is assigned to an EJB object, the bean's identity is available. This is when ejbPostCreate() is invoked (step 8).

In EJB 2.0 CMP entity beans, ejbPostCreate() is used to manage the beans' container-managed relationship fields. This might involve setting the Cruise in the Ship EJB's cruise CMR field or some other relationship (step 9).

Finally, when the ejbPostCreate() processing is complete, the bean is ready to service client requests. The EJB object stub is created and returned to the client application, which will use it to invoke business methods on the bean (step 10).

Using ejbLoad( ) and ejbStore( ) in Container-Managed Persistence

The process of ensuring that the database record and the entity bean instance are equivalent is called *synchronization*. In container-managed persistence, the bean's CMP fields are automatically synchronized with the database. Persistence in container-managed beans is fairly straightforward, so in most cases we will not need the ejbLoad() and ejbStore() methods.

Leveraging the ejbLoad() and ejbStore() callback methods in container-managed beans, however, can be useful if custom logic is needed when synchronizing CMP fields. Data intended for the database can be reformatted or compressed to conserve space; data just retrieved from the database can be used to calculate derived values for nonpersistent fields.

Imagine a hypothetical bean class that includes some binary value you want to store in the database. The binary value may be very large (an image, for example), so you may need to compress it before storing it away. Using the ejbLoad() and ejbStore() methods in a container-managed bean allows the bean instance to reformat the data as appropriate for the state of the bean and the structure of the database. Here's how this might work:

```
import java.util.zip.Inflater;
import java.util.zip.Deflater;

public abstract class HypotheticalBean implements javax.ejb.EntityBean {
    // Instance variable
    public byte [] inflatedImage;

    // CMP field methods
    public abstract void setImage(byte [] image);
    public abstract byte [] getImage();

    // Business methods. Used by client.
    public byte [] getImageFile() {
        if(inflatedImage == null) {
```

```
            Inflater unzipper = new Inflater();
            byte [] temp = getImage();
            unzipper.setInput(temp);
            unzipper.inflate(inflatedImage);
        }
        return inflatedImage;
    }
    public void setImageFile(byte [] image) {
        inflatedImage = image;
    }

    // callback methods
    public void ejbLoad() {
        inflatedImage = null;
    }
    public void ejbStore() {
        if(inflatedImage != null) {
            Deflater zipper = new Deflater();
            zipper.setInput(inflatedImage);
            byte [] temp = new byte[inflatedImage.length];
            int size = zipper.deflate(temp);
            byte [] temp2 = new byte[size];
            System.arraycopy(temp, 0, temp2, 0, size);
            setImage(temp2);
        }
    }
}
```

Just before the container synchronizes the state of entity bean with the database, it calls the ejbStore() method. This method uses the java.util.zip package to compress the image file, if it has been modified, before writing it to the database.

Just after the container updates the fields of the HypotheticalBean with fresh data from the database, it calls ejbLoad(), which reinitializes the inflatedImage instance variable to null. Decompression is preformed lazily, so it's done only when it is needed. Compression is performed by ejbStore() only if the image was accessed; otherwise, the image field is not modified.

Using ejbLoad( ) and ejbStore( ) in Bean-Managed Persistence

In bean-managed persistence, the ejbLoad() and ejbStore() methods are called by the container when it's time to read from or write to the database. The ejbLoad() method is invoked after the start of a transaction, but before the entity bean can service a method call. The ejbStore() method is usually called after the business method is called, but it must be called before the end of the transaction.

While the entity bean is responsible for reading and writing its state from and to the database, the container is responsible for managing the scope of the transaction. This means that the entity bean developer need not worry about committing operations on database-access APIs, provided the resource is managed by the container. The container will take care of committing the transaction and persisting the changes at the appropriate times.

If a BMP entity bean uses a resource that is not managed by the container system, the entity bean must manage the scope of the transaction manually, using operations specific to the API. Examples of how to use the ejbLoad() and ejbStore() methods in BMP are shown in detail in Chapter 10.

ejbPassivate( ) and ejbActivate( )

The ejbPassivate() method notifies the bean developer that the entity bean instance is about to be pooled or otherwise disassociated from the entity bean identity. This gives the entity bean developer an opportunity to do some last-minute cleanup before the bean is placed in the pool, where it will be reused by some other EJB object. In real-world implementations, the ejbPassivate() method is rarely used, because most resources are obtained from the JNDI ENC and are managed automatically by the container.

The ejbActivate() method notifies the bean developer that the entity bean instance has just returned from the pool and is now associated with an EJB object and has been assigned an identity. This gives the entity bean developer an opportunity to prepare the entity bean for service, for example by obtaining some kind of resource connection.

As with the ejbPassivate() method, it's difficult to see why this method would be used in practice. It is best to secure resources lazily (i.e., as needed). The ejbActivate() method suggests that some kind of eager preparation can be accomplished, but this is rarely actually done.

 Even in EJB containers that do not pool entity bean instances, the value of ejbActivate() and ejbPassivate() is questionable. It's possible that an EJB container may choose to evict instances from memory between client invocations and create a new instance for each new transaction. While this may appear to hurt performance, it's a reasonable design, provided that the container system's Java Virtual Machine has an extremely efficient garbage collection and memory allocation strategy. Hotspot is an example of a JVM that has made some important advances in this area. Even in this case, however, ejbActivate() and ejbPassivate() provide little value because the setEntityContext() and unsetEntityContext() methods can accomplish the same thing.

One of the few practical reasons for using ejbActivate() is to reinitialize nonpersistent instance fields of the bean class that may have become "dirty" while the instance serviced another client.

Regardless of their general usefulness, these callback methods are at your disposal if you need them. In most cases, you are better off using setEntityContext() and unsetEntityContext(), since these methods will execute only once in the life cycle of a bean instance.

ejbRemove( )

The component interfaces (remote, local, remote home, and local home) define remove methods that can be used to delete an entity from the system. When a client invokes one of the remove methods, as shown in the following code, the container must delete the entity's data from the database:

```
CustomerHomeRemote customerHome;
CustomerRemote customer;

customer.remove();
// or
customerHome.remove(customer.getPrimaryKey());
```

The data deleted from the database includes all the CMP fields. So, for example, when you invoke a remove method on a Customer EJB, the corresponding record in the CUSTOMER table is deleted.

In CMP 2.0, the remove method also removes the link between the CUSTOMER record and the ADDRESS record. However, the ADDRESS record associated with the CUSTOMER record will not be automatically deleted. The address data will be deleted along with the customer data only if a cascade delete is specified. A cascade delete must be declared explicitly in the XML deployment descriptor, as explained in Chapter 7.

The ejbRemove() method in container-managed persistence notifies the entity bean that it's about to be removed and its data is about to be deleted. This notification occurs after the client invokes one of the remove methods defined in a component interface but before the container actually deletes the data. It gives the bean developer a chance to do some last-minute cleanup before the entity is removed. Any cleanup operations that might ordinarily be done in the ejbPassivate() method should also be done in the ejbRemove() method, because the bean will be pooled after the ejbRemove() method completes without having its ejbPassivate() method invoked.

In bean-managed persistence, the bean developer is responsible for implementing the logic that removes the entity bean's data from the database.

EJB 2.0: ejbHome( )

In EJB 2.0, CMP and BMP entity beans can declare *home methods* that perform operations related to the EJB component but that are not specific to an entity bean instance. A home method must have a matching implementation in the bean class with the signature ejbHome<METHOD-NAME>().

For example, the Cruise EJB might define a home method that calculates the total revenue in bookings for a specific Cruise:

```
public interface CruiseHomeLocal extends javax.ejb.EJBLocalHome {

    public CruiseLocal create(String name, ShipLocal ship);
    public void setName(String name);
    public String getName();
    public void setShip(ShipLocal ship);
    public ShipLocal getShip();

    public double totalReservationRevenue(CruiseLocal cruise);

}
```

Every method in the home interfaces must have a corresponding ejbHome<*METHOD-NAME*>() in the bean class. For example, the CruiseBean class would have an ejbHomeTotalReservationRevenue() method, as shown in the following code:

```
public abstract class CruiseBean implements javax.ejb.EntityBean {
    public Integer ejbCreate(String name, ShipLocal ship) {
        setName(name);
    }
    ...
    public double ejbHomeTotalReservationRevenue(CruiseLocal cruise) {

        Set reservations = ejbSelectReservations(cruise);
        Iterator enum = set.iterator();
        double total = 0;
        while(enum.hasNext()) {
            ReservationLocal res = (ReservationLocal)enum.next();
            Total += res.getAmount();
        }
        return total;

    }

    public abstract ejbSelectReservations(CruiseLocal cruise);
    ...
}
```

The ejbHome() methods execute without an identity within the instance pool. This is why ejbHomeTotalReservationRevenue() required that a CruiseLocal EJB object reference be passed in to the method. This makes sense once you realize that the caller is invoking the home method on the entity bean's EJB home object and not an entity bean reference directly. The EJB home (local or remote) is not specific to any one entity instance.

The bean developer may implement home methods in both EJB 2.0 bean-managed and container-managed persistence implementations typically rely on select methods, while BMP implementations frequently use direct database access and find methods to query data and apply changes.

EntityContext

The first method called by the container after a bean instance is created is `setEntityContext()`. This method passes the bean instance a reference to its `javax.ejb.EntityContext`, which is really the instance's interface to the container.

The `setEntityContext()` method should be implemented by the entity bean developer so that it places the `EntityContext` reference in an instance field of the bean where it will be kept for the life of the instance. The definition of `EntityContext` in EJB 2.0 is as follows:

```
public interface javax.ejb.EntityContext extends javax.ejb.EJBContext {
    public EJBLocalObject getEJBLocalObject() throws IllegalStateException
    public abstract EJBObject getEJBObject() throws IllegalStateException;
    public abstract Object getPrimaryKey() throws IllegalStateException;
}
```

`EJBLocalObject` is new to EJB 2.0 and is not supported by EJB 1.1. The definition of the `EntityContext` in EJB 1.1 is as follows:

```
public interface javax.ejb.EntityContext extends javax.ejb.EJBContext {
    public abstract EJBObject getEJBObject() throws IllegalStateException;
    public abstract Object getPrimaryKey() throws IllegalStateException;
}
```

As the bean instance is swapped from one EJB object to the next, the information obtainable from the `EntityContext` changes to reflect the EJB object to which the instance is assigned. This change is possible because the `EntityContext` is an interface, not a static class definition, and it means that the container can implement the `EntityContext` with a concrete class that it controls. As the entity bean instance is swapped from one EJB object to another, some of the information made available through the `EntityContext` will also change.

The `getEJBObject()` method returns a remote reference to the bean instance's EJB object. The `getEJBLocalObject()` method (EJB 2.0), on the other hand, returns a local reference to the bean instance's EJB object.

 Session beans also define the getEJBObject() and getEJBLocalObject() (EJB 2.0) methods in the `SessionContext` interface; their behavior is exactly the same.

The EJB objects obtained from the `EntityContext` are the same kinds of references that might be used by an application client, in the case of a remote reference, or another co-located bean, in the case of a local reference. These methods allow the bean instance to get its own EJB object reference, which it can then pass to other beans. Here is an example:

```
public class A_Bean extends EntityBean {
    public EntityContext context;
    public void someMethod() {
```

```
    B_Bean  b = ... // Get a remote reference to B_Bean.
    EJBObject obj = context.getEJBObject();
    A_Bean mySelf = (A_Bean)PortableRemoteObject.narrow(obj,A_Bean.class);
    b.aMethod( mySelf );
  }
  ...
}
```

 It is illegal for a bean instance to pass a this reference to another bean; instead, it passes its remote or local EJB object reference, which the bean instance gets from its EntityContext.

In EJB 2.0, the ability of a bean to obtain an EJB object reference to itself is also useful when establishing relationships with other beans in container-managed persistence. For example, the Customer EJB might implement a business method that allows it to assign itself a Reservation:

```
public abstract class CustomerBean implements javax.ejb.EntityBean {
    public EntityContext context;

    public void assignToReservation(ReservationLocal reservation) {
        EJBLocalObject localRef = context.getEJBLocalObject();
        Collection customers = reservation.getCustomers();
        customers.add(localRef);
    }
    ...
}
```

The getPrimaryKey() method allows a bean instance to get a copy of the primary key to which it is currently assigned. Use of this method outside of the ejbLoad() and ejbStore() methods of BMP entity beans is probably rare, but the EntityContext makes the primary key available for those unusual circumstances when it is needed.

As the context in which the bean instance operates changes, some of the information made available through the EntityContext reference will be changed by the container. This is why the methods in the EntityContext throw the java.lang. IllegalStateException. The EntityContext is always available to the bean instance, but the instance is not always assigned to an EJB object. When the bean is between EJB objects (i.e., when it's in the pool), it has no EJB object or primary key to return. If the getEJBObject(), getEJBLocalObject(), or getPrimaryKey() methods are invoked when the bean is in the pool, they will throw an IllegalStateException. Appendix B provides tables of allowed operations for each bean type describing which EJBContext methods can be invoked at what times.

EJBContext

The EntityContext extends the javax.ejb.EJBContext class, which is also the base class for the SessionContext session beans use. EJBContext defines several methods that provide useful information to a bean at runtime.

Here is the definition of the EJBContext interface:

```
package javax.ejb;
public interface EJBContext {

    // EJB home methods
    public EJBHome getEJBHome();
    // EJB 2.0 only
    public EJBLocalHome getEJBLocalHome();

    // security methods
    public java.security.Principal getCallerPrincipal();
    public boolean isCallerInRole(java.lang.String roleName);

    // transaction methods
    public javax.transaction.UserTransaction getUserTransaction()
        throws java.lang.IllegalStateException;
    public boolean getRollbackOnly()
        throws java.lang.IllegalStateException;
    public void setRollbackOnly()
        throws java.lang.IllegalStateException;

    // deprecated methods
    public java.security.Identity getCallerIdentity();
    public boolean isCallerInRole(java.security.Identity role);
    public java.util.Properties getEnvironment();

}
```

The getEJBHome() and getEJBLocalHome() (EJB 2.0) methods return a reference to the bean's EJB home. This is useful if the bean needs to create or find entity beans of its own type. Access to the EJB home proves more useful in bean-managed entity beans and CMP 1.1 entity beans than in CMP 2.0 entity beans, which have select methods and CMR fields.

As an example, if all of the employees in Titan's system (including managers) are represented by CMP 1.1 Employee beans, a manager who needs access to subordinate employees can use the getEJBHome() method to get beans representing the appropriate employees:

```
public class EmployeeBean implements EntityBean {
    int id;
    String firstName;
    ...
    public Enumeration getSubordinates() {
        Object ref = ejbContext.getEJBHome();
        EmployeeHome home = (EmployeeHome)
            PortableRemoteObject.narrow(ref, EmployeeHome.class);
        Integer primKey = (Integer)context.getPrimaryKey();
        Enumeration subordinates = home.findByManagerID(primKey);
        return subordinates;
    }
    ...
}
```

The getCallerPrincipal() method is used to obtain the Principal object representing the client that is currently accessing the bean. The Principal object can, for example, be used by the Ship bean to track the identities of clients making updates:

```
public class ShipBean implements EntityBean {
    String lastModifiedBy;
    EntityContext context;
    ...
    public void setTonnage(double tons) {
        tonnage = tons;
        Principal principal = context.getCallerPrincipal();
        String modifiedBy = principal.getName();
    }
    ...
}
```

The isCallerInRole() method tells you whether the client accessing the bean is a member of a specific role, identified by a role name. This method is useful when more access control is needed than simple method-based access control can provide. In a banking system, for example, you might allow the Teller role to make most withdrawals but only the Manager role to make withdrawals of over $10,000. This kind of fine-grained access control cannot be addressed through EJB's security attributes because it involves a business logic problem. Therefore, we can use the isCallerInRole() method to augment the automatic access control provided by EJB. First, let's assume that all managers are also tellers. The business logic in the withdraw() method uses isCallerInRole() to make sure that only the Manager role can withdraw sums over $10,000.00:

```
public class AccountBean implements EntityBean {
    int id;
    double balance;
    EntityContext context;

    public void withdraw(Double withdraw) throws AccessDeniedException {

        if (withdraw.doubleValue() > 10000) {
            boolean isManager = context.isCallerInRole("Manager");
            if (!isManager) {
                // Only Managers can withdraw more than 10k.
                throw new AccessDeniedException();
            }
        }
        balance = balance - withdraw.doubleValue();

    }
    ...
}
```

The EJBContext contains some methods that were used in EJB 1.0 but were deprecated in EJB 1.1 and have been abandoned in EJB 2.0. Support for these deprecated methods is optional for EJB 1.1 containers, which can host EJB 1.0 beans. EJB containers that do not support the deprecated security methods will throw a

`RuntimeException`. The deprecated security methods are based on EJB 1.0's use of the `Identity` object instead of the `Principal` object. The semantics of the deprecated methods are basically the same but, because `Identity` is an abstract class, it has proven to be too difficult to use.

The `getEnvironment()` method has been replaced by the JNDI environment naming context, which is discussed later in this book. Support for the deprecated `getEnvironment()` method in EJB 1.1 is discussed in detail in Chapter 12. The transactional methods—`getUserTransaction()`, `setRollbackOnly()`, and `getRollbackOnly()`—are described in detail in Chapter 14.

The material on the `EJBContext` covered in this section applies equally well to session and message-driven beans. There are some exceptions, however, and these differences are covered in Chapters 12 and 13.

JNDI ENC

Starting with EJB 1.1, the bean-container contract for entity and stateful beans was expanded beyond the `EJBContext` using the Java Naming and Directory Interface (JNDI). A special JNDI name space, which is referred to as the *environment naming context* (ENC), was added to allow any enterprise bean to access environment entries, other beans, and resources (such as JDBC `DataSource` objects) specific to that enterprise bean.

The JNDI ENC continues to be an extremely important part of the bean-container contract in EJB 2.0. Although we used the JNDI ENC to access JDBC in the bean-managed persistence chapter (Chapter 10), it's not specific to entity beans. The JNDI ENC is used by session, entity, and message-driven beans alike. To avoid unnecessary duplication, a detailed discussion of this important facility is left for Chapter 12. What you learn about using the JNDI ENC in Chapter 12 applies equally well to session, entity, and message-driven beans.

The Life Cycle of an Entity Bean

To understand how to best develop entity beans, it is important to understand how the container manages them. The EJB specification defines just about every major event in an entity bean's life, from the time it is instantiated to the time it is garbage collected. This is called the *life cycle*, and it provides the bean developer and EJB vendors with all the information they need to develop beans and EJB servers that adhere to a consistent protocol. To understand the life cycle, we will follow an entity instance through several life-cycle events and describe how the container interacts with the entity bean during these events. Figure 11-2 illustrates the life cycle of an entity instance.

This section identifies the points at which the container calls each of the methods described in the `EntityBean` interface as well as the find methods and, in EJB 2.0, the

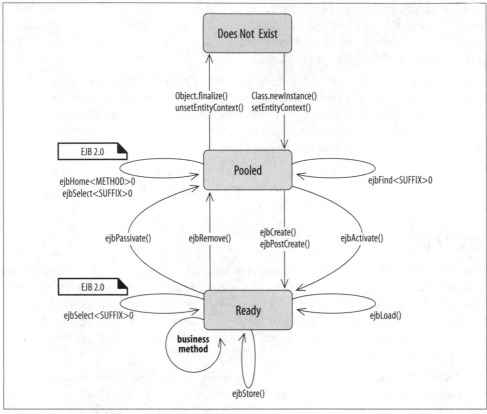

Figure 11-2. Entity bean life cycle

select and home methods. Bean instances must implement the `EntityBean` interface, which means that invocations of the callback methods are invocations on the bean instance itself.

At each stage of the entity bean's life cycle, the bean container provides varying levels of access. For example, the `EntityContext.getPrimary()` method will not work if it is invoked in the `ejbCreate()` method, but it does work when called in the `ejbPostCreate()` method. Other `EJBContext` methods have similar restrictions, as does the JNDI ENC. While this section touches on the accessibility of these methods, a table called "Allowed operations" that details what is available in each bean class method (`ejbCreate()`, `ejbActivate()`, `ejbLoad()`, etc.) can be found in Appendix B.

Does Not Exist

The entity bean begins life as a collection of files. Included in that collection are the bean's deployment descriptor, component interfaces, and all the supporting classes generated at deployment time. At this stage, no instance of the bean exists.

The Pooled State

When the EJB server is started, it reads the EJB's files and instantiates several instances of the entity bean's bean class, which it places in a pool. The instances are created by calling the `Class.newInstance()` method on the bean class. The `newInstance()` method creates an instance using the default constructor, which has no arguments.[*] This means that the persistence fields of the bean instances are set at their default values; the instances themselves do not represent any data in the database.

Immediately following the creation of an instance, and just before it is placed in the pool, the container assigns the instance its `EntityContext`. The `EntityContext` is assigned by calling the `setEntityContext()` method of the `EntityBean` interface, which is implemented by the bean class. After the instance has been assigned its context, it is entered into the instance pool.

In the instance pool, the bean instance is available to the container as a candidate for servicing client requests. Until it is requested, however, the bean instance remains inactive unless it is used to service a query method (i.e., find or select method) or `ejbHome()` request. Bean instances in the Pooled state typically are used to service query and `ejbHome()` requests, which makes perfectly good sense because they aren't busy and these methods don't rely on the bean instance's state. All instances in the Pooled state are equivalent. None of the instances are assigned to an EJB object, and none of them has meaningful state.

The Ready State

When a bean instance is in the Ready state, it can accept client requests. A bean instance moves to the Ready state when the container assigns it to an EJB object. This occurs under two circumstances: when a new entity bean is being created, or when the container is activating an entity.

Transitioning from the Pooled state to the Ready state via creation

When a client application invokes a `create()` method on an EJB home, several operations must take place before the EJB container can return a remote or local reference (EJB object) to the client. First, an EJB object must be created on the EJB server.[†] Once the EJB object is created, a entity bean instance is taken from the instance pool and assigned to the EJB object. Next, the `create()` method, invoked by the client, is

---

[*] Constructors should never be defined in the bean class. The default no-argument constructor must be available to the container.

[†] This is only a conceptual model. In reality, an EJB container and the EJB object may be the same thing, or a single EJB object may provide a multiplexing service for all entities of the same type. The implementation details are not as important as understanding the life-cycle protocol.

delegated to its corresponding ejbCreate() method on the bean instance. After the ejbCreate() method completes, a primary key is created.

When the ejbCreate() method is done, the ejbPostCreate() method on the entity bean instance is called. Finally, after the successful completion of the ejbPostCreate() method, the home is allowed to return a remote or local reference—an EJB object—to the client. The bean instance and EJB object are now ready to service method requests from the client. This is one way that the bean instance can move from the Pooled state to the Ready state.

Transitioning from the Pooled state to the Ready state via a query method

When a query method is executed, each EJB object that is found as a result of the query will be realized by transitioning an instance from the Pooled state to the Ready state. When an entity bean is found, it is assigned to an EJB object and its EJB object reference is returned to the client. A found bean follows the same protocol as a passivated bean; it is activated when the client invokes a business method, and will move into the Ready state through activation, as described in the next section.

In many cases (depending on the EJB vendor), found entity beans don't actually migrate into the Ready state until they are accessed by the client. So, for example, if a find method returns a collection of entity beans, the entity beans may not be activated until they are obtained from the collection or accessed directly by the client. Resources are saved by activating entity beans lazily (as needed).

Transitioning from the Pooled state to the Ready state via activation

The activation process can also move an entity bean instance from the Pooled state to the Ready state. Activation facilitates resource management by allowing a few bean instances to service many EJB objects. Activation was explained in Chapter 3, but we will revisit the process here as it relates to the entity bean instance's life cycle. Activation presumes that the entity bean has previously been *passivated*. More is said about this state transition later; for now, suffice it to say that when a bean instance is passivated, it frees any resources that it does not need and leaves the EJB object for the instance pool. When the bean instance returns to the pool, the EJB object is left without an instance to which to delegate client requests. The EJB object maintains its stub connection on the client, so as far as the client is concerned, the entity bean hasn't changed. When the client invokes a business method on the EJB object, the EJB object must obtain a new bean instance. This is accomplished by activating a bean instance.

When a bean instance is activated, it leaves the instance pool (the Pooled state) to be assigned to an EJB object. Once assigned to the proper EJB object, the ejbActivate() method is called—the instance's EntityContext can now provide information specific to the EJB object, but it cannot provide security or transactional information. The ejbActivate() callback method can be used in the bean instance to reobtain resources or perform any other necessary work before servicing the client.

When an entity bean instance is activated, nonpersistent instance fields of the bean instance may contain arbitrary (dirty) values and so must be reinitialized in the ejbActivate() method.

In container-managed persistence, container-managed fields are automatically synchronized with the database after ejbActivate() is invoked and before a business method can be serviced by the bean instance. The order in which these things happen in CMP entity beans is:

1. ejbActivate() is invoked on the bean instance.
2. Persistence fields are synchronized automatically.
3. ejbLoad() notifies the bean that its persistence fields have been synchronized.
4. Business methods are invoked as needed.

In bean-managed persistence, persistence fields are synchronized by the ejbLoad() method after ejbActivate() has been called and before a business method can be invoked. Here is the order of operations in bean-managed persistence:

1. ejbActivate() is invoked on the bean instance.
2. ejbLoad() is called to let the bean synchronize its persistence fields.
3. Business methods are invoked as needed.

Transitioning from the Ready state to the Pooled state via passivation

A bean can move from the Ready state to the Pooled state via passivation, which is the process of disassociating a bean instance from an EJB object when it is not busy. After a bean instance has been assigned to an EJB object, the EJB container can passivate the instance at any time, provided that the instance is not currently executing a method. As part of the passivation process, the ejbPassivate() method is invoked on the bean instance. This callback method can be used by the instance to release any resources or perform other processing prior to leaving the EJB object. When ejbPassivate() has completed, the bean instance is disassociated from the EJB object server and returned to the instance pool. The bean instance is now back in the Pooled state.

A bean-managed entity instance should not try to save its state to the database in the ejbPassivate() method; this activity is reserved for the ejbStore() method. The container will invoke ejbStore() to synchronize the bean instance's state with the database prior to passivating the bean.

The most fundamental thing to remember is that, for entity beans, passivation is simply a notification that the instance is about to be disassociated from the EJB object. Unlike stateful session beans, an entity bean instance's fields are not serialized and held with the EJB object when the bean is passivated. Whatever values were held in the instance's nonpersistent fields when the entity bean was assigned to the EJB object will be carried with it to its next assignment.

Transitioning from the Ready state to the Pooled state via removal

A bean instance also moves from the Ready state to the Pooled state when it is removed. This occurs when the client application invokes one of the remove methods on the bean's EJB object or EJB home. With entity beans, invoking a remove method deletes the entity's data from the database. Once the entity's data has been deleted from the database, it is no longer a valid entity.

Once the ejbRemove() method has finished, the bean instance is moved back to the instance pool and out of the Ready state. It is important that the ejbRemove() method release any resources that would normally be released by ejbPassivate(), which is not called when a bean is removed. This can be done, if need be, by invoking the ejbPassivate() method within the ejbRemove() method body.

In bean-managed persistence, the ejbRemove() method is implemented by the entity bean developer and includes code to delete the entity bean's data from the database. The EJB container will invoke the ejbRemove() method in response to a client's invocation of the remove() method on one of the component interfaces.

In container-managed persistence, the ejbRemove() method notifies the entity bean instance that its data is about to be removed from the database. Immediately following the ejbRemove() call, the container deletes the entity bean's data.

In EJB 2.0 CMP the container also cleans up the entity bean's relationships with other entity beans in the database. If a cascade delete is specified, it removes each entity bean in the cascade delete relationships. This involves activating each entity bean and calling its ejbActivate() methods, loading each entity bean's state by calling its ejbLoad() method, calling the ejbRemove() on all of the entity beans in the cascade-delete relationship, and then deleting their data. This process can continue in a chain until all the cascade-delete operations of all the relationships have completed.

Life in the Ready State

A bean is in the Ready state when it is associated with an EJB object and is ready to service requests from the client. When the client invokes a business method, like Ship.getName(), on the bean's remote or local reference (EJB object), the method invocation is received by the EJB server and delegated to the bean instance. The instance performs the method and returns the results. As long as the bean instance is in the Ready state, it can service all the business methods invoked by the client. Business methods can be called zero or more times, in any order.

In addition to servicing business methods, an entity bean in the Ready state can execute select methods, which are called by the bean instance while servicing a business method.

The ejbLoad() and ejbStore() methods, which synchronize the bean instance's state with the database, can be called only when the bean is in the Ready state. These methods can be called in any order, depending on the vendor's implementation. Some vendors call ejbLoad() before every method invocation and ejbStore() after every method invocation, depending on the transactional context. Other vendors call these methods less frequently.

In bean-managed persistence, the ejbLoad() method should always use the Entity-Context.getPrimaryKey() method to obtain data from the database and should not trust any primary key or other data that the bean has stored in its fields. (This is how we implemented it in the bean-managed version of the Ship bean in Chapter 10.) It should be assumed, however, that the state of the bean is valid when calling the ejbStore() method.

In container-managed persistence, the ejbLoad() method is always called immediately following the synchronization of the bean's container-managed fields with the database—in other words, right after the container updates the state of the bean instance with data from the database. This provides an opportunity to perform any calculations or reformat data before the instance can service business-method invocations from the client. The ejbStore() method is called just before the database is synchronized with the state of the bean instance—just before the container writes the container-managed fields to the database. This provides the CMP entity bean instance with an opportunity to change the data in the container-managed fields prior to their persistence to the database.

In bean-managed persistence, the ejbLoad() and ejbStore() methods are called when the container deems it appropriate to synchronize the bean's state with the database. These are the only callback methods that should be used to synchronize the bean's state with the database. Do not use ejbActivate(), ejbPassivate(), setEntity-Context(), or unsetEntityContext() to access the database for the purpose of synchronization. You should use the ejbCreate() and ejbRemove() methods, however, to insert and delete (respectively) the entity's data into and from the database.

End of the Life Cycle

A bean instance's life cycle ends when the container decides to remove it from the pool and allow it to be garbage collected. This happens under a few different circumstances. If the container decides to reduce the number of instances in the pool—usually to conserve resources—it releases one or more bean instances and allows them to be garbage collected. The ability to adjust the size of the instance pool allows the EJB server to manage its resources (the number of threads, available memory, etc.) so that it can achieve the highest possible performance.

When an EJB server is shut down, most containers release all the bean instances so that they can be safely garbage collected. Some containers may also decide to release any instances that are behaving unfavorably or that have suffered from some kind of unrecoverable error that makes them unstable. For example, any time an entity bean instance throws a type of RuntimeException from any of its methods, the EJB container will evict that instance from memory and replace it with a stable instance from the instance pool.

When an entity bean instance leaves the instance pool to be garbage collected, the unsetEntityContext() method is invoked by the container to alert the bean instance that it is about be destroyed. This callback method lets the bean instance release any resources it maintains before being garbage collected. Once the bean's unsetEntityContext() method has been called, it is garbage collected.

The bean instance's finalize() method may or may not be invoked following the unsetEntityContext() method. A bean should not rely on its finalize() method, since each vendor handles evicting instances differently.

CHAPTER 12

Session Beans

As Chapters 6–11 demonstrated, entity beans provide an object-oriented interface that makes it easier for developers to create, modify, and delete data from the database. Entity beans allow developers to be more productive by encouraging reuse and reducing development costs. You can reuse a concept like a Ship throughout a business system without having to redefine, recode, or retest the business logic and data access.

However, entity beans are not the entire story. We have also seen another kind of enterprise bean: the session bean. Session beans fill the gaps left by entity beans. They are useful for describing interactions between other beans (workflow) and for implementing particular tasks. Unlike entity beans, session beans do not represent shared data in the database, but they can access shared data. This means that we can use session beans to read, update, and insert data. For example, we might use a session bean to provide lists of information, such as a list of all available cabins. Sometimes we might generate the list by interacting with entity beans, like the cabin list we developed in the TravelAgent EJB in Chapter 4. More frequently, session beans will generate lists by accessing the database directly.

So when do you use an entity bean and when do you use a session bean to directly access data? Good question! As a rule of thumb, an entity bean is developed to provide a safe and consistent interface to a set of shared data that defines a concept. This data may be updated frequently. Session beans access data that spans concepts, is not shared, and is usually read-only.

In addition to accessing data directly, session beans can represent *workflow*. Workflow describes all the steps required to accomplish a particular task, such as booking passage on a ship or renting a video. Session beans are part of the same business API as entity beans, but as workflow components, they serve a different purpose. Session beans can manage the interactions between entity beans, describing how they work together to accomplish a specific task. The relationship between session beans and entity beans is like the relationship between a script for a play and the actors that perform the play. Where entity beans are the actors, the session bean is the script. Actors without a script can each serve a function individually, but only in the context of a script can they tell a story. In terms of our example, it makes no sense to have a database full of cabins, ships, customers, and other entities if we can't create interactions between them, such as booking a customer for a cruise.

Session beans are divided into two basic types: stateless and stateful. A *stateless* session bean is a collection of related services, each represented by a method; the bean maintains no state from one method invocation to the next. When you invoke a method on a stateless session bean, it executes the method and returns the result without knowing or caring what other requests have gone before or might follow. Think of a stateless session bean as a set of procedures or batch programs that execute a request based on some parameters and return a result. Stateless session beans tend to be general-purpose or reusable, such as a software service.

A *stateful* session bean is an extension of the client application. It performs tasks on behalf of the client and maintains state related to that client. This state is called *conversational state* because it represents a continuing conversation between the stateful session bean and the client. Methods invoked on a stateful session bean can write and read data to and from this conversational state, which is shared among all methods in the bean. Stateful session beans tend to be specific to one scenario. They represent logic that might have been captured in the client application of a two-tier system. Session beans, whether they are stateful or stateless, are not persistent like entity beans. In other words, session beans are not saved to the database.

Depending on the vendor, stateful session beans may have a timeout period. If the client fails to use the stateful bean before it times out, the bean instance is destroyed and the EJB object reference is invalidated. This prevents the stateful session bean from lingering long after a client has shut down or otherwise finished using it. A client can also explicitly remove a stateful session bean by calling one of its remove methods.

Stateless session beans have longer lives because they do not retain any conversational state and are not dedicated to one client, but they still are not saved in a database because they do not represent any data. Once a stateless session bean has finished a method invocation for a client, it can be reassigned to any other EJB object to service a new client. A client can maintain a connection to a stateless session bean's EJB object, but the bean instance itself is free to service requests from any client. Because it does not contain any state information, a stateless session bean does not distinguish between clients. Stateless session beans may also have a timeout period and can be removed by the client, but the impact of these events is different than with a stateful session bean. With a stateless session bean, a timeout or remove operation simply invalidates the EJB object reference for that client; the bean instance is not destroyed and is free to service other client requests.

The Stateless Session Bean

A stateless session bean is very efficient and relatively easy to develop. Stateless session beans require few server resources because they are neither persistent nor dedicated to one client. Because they are not dedicated to one client, many EJB objects can share a few instances of a stateless bean. A stateless session bean does not maintain conversational state relative to the client it is servicing, so it can be swapped freely between EJB objects. As soon as a stateless instance finishes servicing a method invocation, it can be swapped to another EJB object. Because it does not maintain conversational state, a stateless session bean does not require passivation or activation, further reducing the overhead of swapping. In short, stateless session beans are lightweight and fast.

Stateless session beans often perform services that are fairly generic and reusable. The services may be related, but they are not interdependent. This means that everything a method needs to know has to be passed via the method's parameters. This provides an interesting limitation. Stateless session beans can't remember anything from one method invocation to the next, which means that they have to take care of the entire task in one method invocation. The only exception to this rule is information obtainable from the `SessionContext` and the JNDI ENC.

Stateless session beans are EJB's version of the traditional transaction-processing applications, which are executed using a procedure call. The procedure executes from beginning to end and then returns the result. Once the procedure is done, nothing about the data that was manipulated or the details of the request are remembered. There is no state.

These restrictions don't mean that a stateless session bean can't have instance variables or maintain any kind of internal state. Nothing prevents you from keeping a variable that tracks the number of times a bean has been called or that saves data for debugging. An instance variable can even hold a reference to a live resource, such as a URL connection for logging, verifying credit cards, or anything else that might be useful—the resource should be obtained from the JNDI ENC. However, it is important to remember that this state can never be visible to a client. A client can't assume that the same bean instance will service it every time. If these instance variables have different values in different bean instances, their values will appear to change randomly as stateless session beans are swapped from one client to another. Therefore, any resources you reference in instance variables should be generic. For example, each bean instance might reasonably record debugging messages—that might be the only way to figure out what is happening on a large server with many bean instances. The client doesn't know or care where debugging output is going. However, it would clearly be inappropriate for a stateless bean to remember that it was in the process of making a reservation for Madame X—the next time it is called, it may be servicing another client entirely.

Stateless session beans can be used for report generation, batch processing, or some stateless services such as validating credit cards. Another good application would be a StockQuote EJB that returns a stock's current price. Any activity that can be accomplished in one method call is a good candidate for the high-performance stateless session bean.

The ProcessPayment EJB

Chapters 2 and 3 discussed the TravelAgent EJB, which has a business method called `bookPassage()` that uses the ProcessPayment EJB. The next section develops a complete definition of the TravelAgent EJB, including the logic of the `bookPassage()` method. At this point, however, we are primarily interested in the ProcessPayment EJB, which is a stateless bean the TravelAgent EJB uses to charge the customer for the price of the cruise.

Charging customers is a common activity in Titan's business systems. Not only does the reservation system need to charge customers, but so do Titan's gift shops, boutiques, and other related businesses. The process of charging a customer for services is common to many systems, so it has been encapsulated in its own bean.

Payments are recorded in a special database table called PAYMENT. The PAYMENT data is batch processed for accounting purposes and is not normally used outside of accounting. In other words, the data is only inserted by Titan's system; it is not read, updated, or deleted. Because the process of making a charge can be completed in one method, and because the data is not updated frequently or shared, we will use a stateless session bean for processing payments. Several different forms of payment can be used: credit card, check, or cash. We will model these payment forms in our stateless ProcessPayment EJB.

PAYMENT: The database table

The ProcessPayment EJB accesses an existing table in Titan's system called the PAYMENT table. Create a table in your database called PAYMENT with this definition:

```
CREATE TABLE PAYMENT
(
    customer_id     INTEGER,
    amount          DECIMAL(8,2),
    type            CHAR(10),
    check_bar_code  CHAR(50),
    check_number    INTEGER,
    credit_number   CHAR(20),
    credit_exp_date DATE
)
```

ProcessPaymentRemote: The remote interface

A stateless session bean, like any other bean, needs a component interface. While EJB 1.1 uses only remote interfaces, in EJB 2.0 session beans may have either a local or remote interface.

For the remote interface, we obviously need a `byCredit()` method because the TravelAgent EJB uses it. We can also identify two other methods that we'll need: `byCash()` for customers paying cash and `byCheck()` for customers paying with a personal check.

Here is a complete definition of the remote interface for the ProcessPayment EJB:

```
package com.titan.processpayment;

import java.rmi.RemoteException;
import java.util.Date;
import com.titan.customer.CustomerRemote;

public interface ProcessPaymentRemote extends javax.ejb.EJBObject {

    public boolean byCheck(CustomerRemote customer, CheckDO check, double amount)
        throws RemoteException,PaymentException;

    public boolean byCash(CustomerRemote customer, double amount)
        throws RemoteException,PaymentException;

    public boolean byCredit(CustomerRemote customer, CreditCardDO card,
        double amount) throws RemoteException,PaymentException;
}
```

Remote interfaces in session beans follow the same rules as in entity beans. Here we have defined the three business methods, byCheck(), byCash(), and byCredit(), which take information relevant to the form of payment used and return a boolean value that indicates the success of the payment. In addition to the required RemoteException, these methods can throw an application-specific exception, the PaymentException. The PaymentException is thrown if any problems occur while processing the payment, such as a low check number or an expired credit card. Notice, however, that nothing about the ProcessPaymentRemote interface is specific to the reservation system. It could be used just about anywhere in Titan's system. In addition, each method defined in the remote interface is completely independent of the others. All the data that is required to process a payment is obtained through the method's arguments.

As an extension of the javax.ejb.EJBObject interface, the remote interface of a session bean inherits the same functionality as the remote interface of an entity bean. However, the getPrimaryKey() method throws a RemoteException, since session beans do not have a primary key to return:

```
public interface javax.ejb.EJBObject extends java.rmi.Remote {
    public abstract EJBHome getEJBHome() throws RemoteException;
    public abstract Handle getHandle() throws RemoteException;
    public abstract Object getPrimaryKey() throws RemoteException;
    public abstract boolean isIdentical(EJBObject obj) throws RemoteException;
    public abstract void remove() throws RemoteException, RemoveException;
}
```

The getHandle() method returns a serializable Handle object, just like the getHandle() method in the entity bean. For stateless session beans, this Handle can be serialized and reused any time, as long as the stateless bean type is still available in the container that generated the Handle.

Unlike stateless session beans, stateful session beans are available through the Handle for only as long as that specific bean instance is kept alive on the EJB server. If the client explicitly destroys the stateful session bean using one of the remove() methods, or if the bean times out, the instance is destroyed and the Handle becomes invalid. As soon as the server removes a stateful session bean, its Handle is no longer valid and will throw a RemoteException when its getEJBObject() is invoked.

You can obtain a remote reference to the bean from the Handle by invoking its getEJBObject() method:

```
public interface javax.ejb.Handle {
    public abstract EJBObject getEJBObject() throws RemoteException;
}
```

The ProcessPayment EJB has its own package, which means it has its own directory in our development tree, *dev/com/titan/processpayment*. That's where we'll store all the code and compile class files for this bean.

Dependent objects: The CreditCardDO and CheckDO classes

The ProcessPayment EJB's remote interface uses two classes in its definition that are particularly interesting: CreditCardDO and CheckDO. The definitions for these classes are as follows:

```
/* CreditCardDO.java */
package com.titan.processpayment;

import java.util.Date;

public class CreditCardDO implements java.io.Serializable {
    final static public String MASTER_CARD = "MASTER_CARD";
    final static public String VISA = "VISA";
    final static public String AMERICAN_EXPRESS = "AMERICAN_EXPRESS";
    final static public String DISCOVER = "DISCOVER";
    final static public String DINERS_CARD = "DINERS_CARD";

    public String number;
    public Date expiration;
    public String type;

    public CreditCardDO(String nmbr, Date exp, String typ) {
        number = nmbr;
        expiration = exp;
        type = typ;
    }
}

/* CheckDO.java */
package com.titan.processpayment;
```

```
public class CheckDO implements java.io.Serializable {
    public String checkBarCode;
    public int checkNumber;

    public CheckDO(String barCode, int number) {
        checkBarCode = barCode;
        checkNumber = number;
    }
}
```

CreditCardDO and CheckDO are dependent objects a concept we explored with the Address EJB in Chapter 6. If you examine the class definitions of the CreditCardDO and CheckDO classes, you will see that they are not enterprise beans; they are simply serializable Java classes. These classes provide a convenient mechanism for transporting and binding together related data. CreditCardDO, for example, binds all the credit card data together in one class, making it easier to pass the information across the network as well as making our interfaces a little cleaner.

PaymentException: An application exception

Any remote or local interface, whether it's for an entity bean or a session bean, can throw application exceptions. Application exceptions are created by the bean developer and should describe a business logic problem—in this case, a problem making a payment. Application exceptions should be meaningful to the client, providing a brief and relevant identification of the error.

It is important to understand what exceptions to use and when to use them. The RemoteException indicates subsystem-level problems and is used by the RMI facility. Likewise, exceptions such as javax.naming.NamingException and java.sql. SQLException are thrown by other Java subsystems; usually these should not be thrown explicitly by your beans. The Java Compiler requires that you use try/catch blocks to capture checked exceptions like these.

In EJB 2.0, the EJBException can express problems the container has with processing local interface invocations. The EJBException is an unchecked exception, so you won't get a compile error if you don't write code to handle it. However, under certain circumstances it is a good idea to catch EJBException, and in other circumstances it should be propagated.

When a checked exception from a subsystem (JDBC, JNDI, JMS, etc.) is caught by a bean method, it should be rethrown as an EJBException or an application exception. You would rethrow a checked exception as an EJBException if it represented a system-level problem; checked exceptions are rethrown as application exceptions when they result from business logic problems. Your beans incorporate your business logic; if a problem occurs in the business logic, that problem should be represented by an application exception. When the enterprise bean throws an EJBException or some other type of RuntimeException, the exception is first processed by the container, which discards the bean instance and replaces it with another. After the container processes the exception, it propagates an exception to the client. For remote clients, the container throws a RemoteException; for local clients (co-located enterprise beans), the container rethrows the original EJBException or RuntimeException thrown by the bean instance.

The PaymentException describes a specific business problem, so it is an application exception. Application exceptions extend java.lang.Exception. Any instance variables you include in these exceptions should be serializable.

Here is the definition of the PaymentException application exception:

```java
package com.titan.processpayment;

public class PaymentException extends java.lang.Exception {
    public PaymentException() {
        super();
    }
    public PaymentException(String msg) {
        super(msg);
    }
}
```

ProcessPaymentHomeRemote: The home interface

The home interface of a stateless session bean must declare a single create() method with no arguments. This is a requirement of the EJB specification. It is illegal to define create() methods with arguments, because stateless session beans do not maintain conversational state that needs to be initialized. There are no find methods in session beans, because session beans do not have primary keys and do not represent data in the database.

Although EJB 2.0 defines create<*SUFFIX*>() methods for stateful session beans and entity beans, stateless session beans may define only a single create() method, with no suffix and no arguments. This is also the case in EJB 1.1. The reason for this restriction has to do with the life cycle of stateless session beans, which is explained later in this chapter.

Here is the definition of the remote home interface for the ProcessPayment EJB:

```java
package com.titan.processpayment;

import java.rmi.RemoteException;
import javax.ejb.CreateException;

public interface ProcessPaymentHomeRemote extends javax.ejb.EJBHome {
    public ProcessPaymentRemote create() throws RemoteException, CreateException;
}
```

The CreateException is mandatory, as is the RemoteException. The CreateException can be thrown by the bean itself to indicate an application error in creating the bean. A RemoteException is thrown when other system errors occur; for example, when there is a problem with network communication or when an unchecked exception is thrown from the bean class.

The ProcessPaymentHomeRemote interface, as an extension of the javax.ejb.EJBHome, offers the same EJBHome methods as entity beans. The only difference is that remove(Object primaryKey) does not work, because session beans do not have primary keys. If EJBHome.remove(Object primaryKey) is invoked on a session bean (stateless or stateful), a RemoteException is thrown. Logically, this method should never be invoked on the remote home interface of a session bean. Here are the definitions of the javax.ejb.EJBHome interface for EJB 1.1 and 2.0:

```
public interface javax.ejb.EJBHome extends java.rmi.Remote {
    public abstract HomeHandle getHomeHandle() throws RemoteException;
    public abstract EJBMetaData getEJBMetaData() throws RemoteException;
    public abstract void remove(Handle handle) throws RemoteException,
        RemoveException;
    public abstract void remove(Object primaryKey) throws RemoteException,
        RemoveException;
}
```

The home interface of a session bean can return the EJBMetaData for the bean, just like an entity bean. EJBMetaData is a serializable object that provides information about the bean's interfaces. The only difference between the EJBMetaData for a session bean and an entity bean is that the getPrimaryKeyClass() on the session bean's EJBMetaData throws a java.lang.RuntimeException when invoked:

```
public interface javax.ejb.EJBMetaData {
    public abstract EJBHome getEJBHome();
    public abstract Class getHomeInterfaceClass();
    public abstract Class getPrimaryKeyClass();
    public abstract Class getRemoteInterfaceClass();
    public abstract boolean isSession();
    public abstract boolean isStateless();  // EJB 1.0 only
}
```

ProcessPaymentBean: The bean class

As stated earlier, the ProcessPayment EJB accesses data that is not generally shared by systems, so it is an excellent candidate for a stateless session bean. This bean really represents a set of independent operations—another indication that it is a good candidate for a stateless session bean.

Here is the definition of the ProcessPaymentBean class, which supports the remote interface functionality:

```
package com.titan.processpayment;
import com.titan.customer.*;

import java.sql.*;
import java.rmi.RemoteException;
import javax.ejb.SessionContext;
```

```
import javax.naming.InitialContext;
import javax.sql.DataSource;
import javax.ejb.EJBException;
import javax.naming.NamingException;

public class ProcessPaymentBean implements javax.ejb.SessionBean {

    final public static String CASH = "CASH";
    final public static String CREDIT = "CREDIT";
    final public static String CHECK = "CHECK";

    public SessionContext context;

    public void ejbCreate() {
    }

    public boolean byCash(CustomerRemote customer, double amount)
        throws PaymentException{
        return process(getCustomerID(customer), amount, CASH, null, -1, null, null);
    }

    public boolean byCheck(CustomerRemote customer, CheckDO check, double amount)
        throws PaymentException{
        int minCheckNumber = getMinCheckNumber();
        if (check.checkNumber > minCheckNumber) {
            return process(getCustomerID(customer), amount, CHECK,
                check.checkBarCode, check.checkNumber, null, null);
        }
        else {
            throw new PaymentException("Check number is too low.
                Must be at least "+minCheckNumber);
        }
    }
    public boolean byCredit(CustomerRemote customer, CreditCardDO card,
        double amount) throws PaymentException {
        if (card.expiration.before(new java.util.Date())) {
            throw new PaymentException("Expiration date has"+ " passed");
        }
        else {
            return process(getCustomerID(customer), amount, CREDIT, null,
            -1, card.number, new java.sql.Date(card.expiration.getTime()));
        }
    }
    private boolean process(Integer customerID, double amount, String type,
        String checkBarCode, int checkNumber, String creditNumber,
        java.sql.Date creditExpDate) throws PaymentException {

        Connection con = null;

        PreparedStatement ps = null;

        try {
            con = getConnection();
```

```
                ps = con.prepareStatement
                    ("INSERT INTO payment (customer_id, amount, type,"+
                    "check_bar_code,check_number,credit_number,"+
                    "credit_exp_date) VALUES (?,?,?,?,?,?,?)");
                ps.setInt(1,customerID.intValue());
                ps.setDouble(2,amount);
                ps.setString(3,type);
                ps.setString(4,checkBarCode);
                ps.setInt(5,checkNumber);
                ps.setString(6,creditNumber);
                ps.setDate(7,creditExpDate);
                int retVal = ps.executeUpdate();
                if (retVal!=1) {
                    throw new EJBException("Payment insert failed");
                }
                return true;
            } catch(SQLException sql) {
                throw new EJBException(sql);
            } finally {
                try {
                    if (ps != null) ps.close();
                    if (con!= null) con.close();
                } catch(SQLException se) {
                    se.printStackTrace();
                }
            }
        }
        public void ejbActivate() {}
        public void ejbPassivate() {}
        public void ejbRemove() {}
        public void setSessionContext(SessionContext ctx) {
            context = ctx;
        }
        private Integer getCustomerID(CustomerRemote customer) {
            try {
                return (Integer)customer.getPrimaryKey();
            } catch(RemoteException re) {
                throw new EJBException(re);
            }
        }
        private Connection getConnection() throws SQLException {
            // Implementations shown below
        }
        private int getMinCheckNumber() {
            // Implementations shown below
        }
    }
```

The three payment methods all use the private helper method process(), which does the work of adding the payment to the database. This strategy reduces the possibility of programmer error and makes the bean easier to maintain. The process() method simply inserts the payment information into the PAYMENT table. The use of JDBC in this method should be familiar to you from your work on the bean-managed Ship EJB in Chapter 10. The JDBC connection is obtained from the getConnection() method, as shown in the following code:

```
private Connection getConnection() throws SQLException {
    try {
        InitialContext jndiCntx = new InitialContext();
        DataSource ds = (DataSource)
            jndiCntx.lookup("java:comp/env/jdbc/titanDB");
        return ds.getConnection();
    } catch(NamingException ne) {
        throw new EJBException(ne);
    }
}
```

The byCheck() and byCredit() methods contain some logic to validate the data before processing it. The byCredit() method verifies that the credit card's expiration date does not precede the current date. If it does, a PaymentException is thrown.

The byCheck() method verifies that the serial number of the check is above a certain minimum, which is determined by a property that is defined when the bean is deployed. If the check number is below this value, a PaymentException is thrown. The property is obtained from the getMinCheckNumber() method. We can use the JNDI ENC to read the value of the minCheckNumber property:

```
private int getMinCheckNumber() {
    try {
        InitialContext jndiCntx = new InitialContext();
        Integer value = (Integer)
            jndiCntx.lookup("java:comp/env/minCheckNumber");
        return value.intValue();
    } catch(NamingException ne) {
        throw new EJBException(ne);
    }
}
```

Here we are using an environment property set in the deployment descriptor to change the business behavior of the bean. It is a good idea to capture thresholds and other limits in the environment properties of the bean rather than hardcoding them. This gives you greater flexibility. If, for example, Titan decided to raise the minimum check number, you would need to change the bean's deployment descriptor only, not the class definition. (You could also obtain this type of information directly from the database.)

JNDI ENC: Accessing environment properties

In EJB, the bean container contract includes the JNDI environment naming context (JNDI ENC). The JNDI ENC is a JNDI name space that is specific to each bean type. This name space can be referenced from within any bean, not just entity beans, using the name "java:comp/env". The enterprise naming context provides a flexible, yet standard, mechanism for accessing properties, other beans, and resources from the container.

We've already seen the JNDI ENC several times. In Chapter 10, we used it to access a resource factory, the DataSource. The ProcessPaymentBean also uses the JNDI ENC to access a DataSource in the getConnection() method. Furthermore, it uses the JNDI ENC to access an environment property in the getMinCheckNumber() method. This section examines the use of the JNDI ENC to access environment properties.

Named properties can be declared in a bean's deployment descriptor. The bean accesses these properties at runtime by using the JNDI ENC. Properties can be of type String or one of several primitive wrapper types including Integer, Long, Double, Float, Byte, Boolean, and Short. By modifying the deployment descriptor, the bean deployer can change the bean's behavior without changing its code. As we've seen in the ProcessPayment EJB, we could change the minimum check number that we're willing to accept by modifying the minCheckNumber property at deployment. Two ProcessPayment EJBs deployed in different containers could easily have different minimum check numbers. Here's how to declare a named property:

```
<ejb-jar>
    <enterprise-beans>
        <session>
            <env-entry>
                <env-entry-name>minCheckNumber</env-entry-name>
                <env-entry-type>java.lang.Integer</env-entry-type>
                <env-entry-value>2000</env-entry-value>
            </env-entry>
            ...
        </session>
        ...
    </enterprise-beans>
    ...
</ejb-jar>
```

EJBContext

The EJBContext.getEnvironment() method is optional in EJB 2.0 and 1.1, which means that it may or may not be supported. If it is not functional, the method will throw a RuntimeException. If it is functional, it returns only those values declared in the deployment descriptor as follows (where minCheckNumber is the property name):

```
<ejb-jar>
    <enterprise-beans>
        <session>
            <env-entry>
                <env-entry-name>ejb10-properties/minCheckNumber</env-entry-name>
                <env-entry-type>java.lang.String</env-entry-type>
                <env-entry-value>20000</env-entry-value>
            </env-entry>
            ...
        </session>
        ...
    </enterprise-beans>
    ...
</ejb-jar>
```

The ejb10-properties subcontext specifies that the minCheckNumber property is available from both the JNDI ENC "java:comp/env/ejb10-properties/minCheckNumber" (as a String value) and the getEnvironment() method.

Only those properties declared under the ejb10-properties subcontext are available via the EJBContext. Furthermore, such properties are available through the EJBContext only in containers that choose to support the EJB 1.0 getEnvironment() method; all other containers will throw a RuntimeException. It is expected that most EJB 2.0 vendors will have dropped support for this feature, and developers are encouraged to use the JNDI ENC instead of the EJBContext.getEnvironment() method to obtain property values.

The ProcessPayment EJB's deployment descriptor

Deploying the ProcessPayment EJB presents no significant problems. It is essentially the same as deploying entity beans, except that the ProcessPayment EJB has no primary key or persistence fields. Here is the XML deployment descriptor for the Process-Payment EJB:

```
<!DOCTYPE ejb-jar PUBLIC "-//Sun Microsystems, Inc.//DTD Enterprise
JavaBeans 2.0//EN" "http://java.sun.com/dtd/ejb-jar_2_0.dtd">

<ejb-jar>
    <enterprise-beans>
        <session>
            <description>
                A service that handles monetary payments.
            </description>
            <ejb-name>ProcessPaymentEJB</ejb-name>
            <home>
                com.titan.processpayment.ProcessPaymentHomeRemote
            </home>
            <remote>
                com.titan.processpayment.ProcessPaymentRemote
            </remote>
            <ejb-class>
                com.titan.processpayment.ProcessPaymentBean
            </ejb-class>
            <session-type>Stateless</session-type>
            <transaction-type>Container</transaction-type>
            <env-entry>
                <env-entry-name>minCheckNumber</env-entry-name>
                <env-entry-type>java.lang.Integer</env-entry-type>
                <env-entry-value>2000</env-entry-value>
            </env-entry>
            <resource-ref>
                <description>DataSource for the Titan database</description>
                <res-ref-name>jdbc/titanDB</res-ref-name>
                <res-type>javax.sql.DataSource</res-type>
                <res-auth>Container</res-auth>
            </resource-ref>
```

```
        </session>
    </enterprise-beans>

    <assembly-descriptor>
        <security-role>
            <description>
                This role represents everyone who is allowed full access
                to the ProcessPayment EJB.
            </description>
            <role-name>everyone</role-name>
        </security-role>

        <method-permission>
            <role-name>everyone</role-name>
            <method>
                <ejb-name>ProcessPaymentEJB</ejb-name>
                <method-name>*</method-name>
            </method>
        </method-permission>

        <container-transaction>
            <method>
                <ejb-name>ProcessPaymentEJB</ejb-name>
                <method-name>*</method-name>
            </method>
            <trans-attribute>Required</trans-attribute>
        </container-transaction>
    </assembly-descriptor>
</ejb-jar>
```

The deployment descriptor for EJB 1.1 is exactly the same, except its header specifies the EJB 1.1 specification and deployment descriptor:

```
<!DOCTYPE ejb-jar PUBLIC "-//Sun Microsystems, Inc.//DTD Enterprise
JavaBeans 1.1//EN" "http://java.sun.com/j2ee/dtds/ejb-jar_1_1.dtd">
```

   📖 Workbook Exercise 12.1, A Stateless Session Bean

EJB 2.0: Local component interfaces

Like entity beans, stateless session beans can define local component interfaces. This allows the local interfaces of a stateless session bean to be used by other co-located enterprise beans, including other stateless and stateful session beans and even entity beans. Obviously, it is more efficient to use local component interfaces between two beans in the same container system than to use the remote interfaces.

The process of defining local interfaces for a stateless or stateful session bean is the same as that for entity beans. The local interfaces extend javax.ejb.EJBLocalObject (for business methods) and javax.ejb.EJBLocalHome (for the home interfaces). These interfaces are then defined in the XML deployment descriptor in the <local> and <local-home> elements.

For the sake of brevity, we will not define local interfaces for either the stateless ProcessPayment EJB or the stateful TravelAgent EJB developed later in this chapter. Your experience creating local interfaces for entity beans in Chapters 5, 6, and 7 can be applied easily to any kind of session bean.

The Life Cycle of a Stateless Session Bean

Just as the entity bean has a well-defined life cycle, so does the stateless session bean. The stateless session bean's life cycle has two states: *Does Not Exist* and *Method-Ready Pool*. The Method-Ready Pool is similar to the instance pool used for entity beans. This is one of the significant life-cycle differences between stateless and stateful session beans; stateless beans define instance pooling in their life cycle and stateful beans do not.[*] Figure 12-1 illustrates the states and transitions a stateless session bean instance goes through in its lifetime.

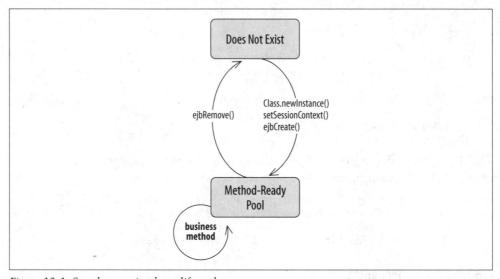

Figure 12-1. Stateless session bean life cycle

Does Not Exist

When a bean is in the Does Not Exist state, it is not an instance in the memory of the system. In other words, it has not been instantiated yet.

---

[*] Some vendors do *not* pool stateless instances, but may instead create and destroy instances with each method invocation. This is an implementation-specific decision that shouldn't impact the specified life cycle of the stateless bean instance.

The Method-Ready Pool

Stateless bean instances enter the Method-Ready Pool as the container needs them. When the EJB server is first started, it may create a number of stateless bean instances and enter them into the Method-Ready Pool. (The actual behavior of the server depends on the implementation.) When the number of stateless instances servicing client requests is insufficient, more can be created and added to the pool.

Transitioning to the Method-Ready Pool

When an instance transitions from the Does Not Exist state to the Method-Ready Pool, three operations are performed on it. First, the bean instance is instantiated by invoking the Class.newInstance() method on the stateless bean class.

Second, the SessionBean.setSessionContext(SessionContext context) method is invoked on the bean instance. This is when the instance receives its reference to the EJBContext for its lifetime. The SessionContext reference may be stored in a nontransient instance field of the stateless session bean.

Finally, the no-argument ejbCreate() method is invoked on the bean instance. Remember that a stateless session bean has only one ejbCreate() method, which takes no arguments. The ejbCreate() method is invoked only once in the life cycle of the stateless session bean; when the client invokes the create() method on the EJB home, it is not delegated to the bean instance.

 Entity, session, and message-driven beans must never define constructors. Take care of initialization needs within ejbCreate() and other callback methods. The container instantiates instances of the bean class using Class.newInstance(), which requires a no-argument constructor.

Stateless session beans are not subject to activation, so they can maintain open connections to resources for their entire life cycles.* The ejbRemove() method should close any open resources before the stateless session bean is evicted from memory at the end of its life cycle. You'll read more about ejbRemove() later in this section.

Life in the Method-Ready Pool

Once an instance is in the Method-Ready Pool, it is ready to service client requests. When a client invokes a business method on an EJB object, the method call is delegated to any available instance in the Method-Ready Pool. While the instance is executing the request, it is unavailable for use by other EJB objects. Once the instance

---

* The duration of a stateless bean instance's life is assumed to be very long. However, some EJB servers may actually destroy and create instances with every method invocation, making this strategy less attractive. Consult your vendor's documentation for details on how your EJB server handles stateless instances.

has finished, it is immediately available to any EJB object that needs it. This is slightly different from the instance pool for entity beans described in Chapter 11. In the entity instance pool, a bean instance might be swapped in to service an EJB object for several method invocations. Stateless session instances, however, are typically dedicated to an EJB object only for the duration of a single method call.

Although vendors can choose different strategies to support stateless session beans, it is likely that they will use an instance-swapping strategy similar to that used for entity beans (see Chapter 11). However, the swap is very brief, lasting only as long as the business method needs to execute. When an instance is swapped in, its SessionContext changes to reflect the context of its EJB object and the client invoking the method. The bean instance may be included in the transactional scope of the client's request and it may access SessionContext information specific to the client request: for example, the security and transactional methods. Once the instance has finished servicing the client, it is disassociated from the EJB object and returned to the Method-Ready Pool.

Stateless session beans are not subject to activation and never have their ejb-Activate() or ejbPassivate() callback methods invoked. The reason is simple: stateless instances have no conversational state to be preserved. (*Stateful* session beans do depend on activation, as we'll see later.)

Clients that need a remote or local reference to a stateless session bean begin by invoking the create() method on the bean's EJB home:

```
Object ref = jndiConnection.lookup("ProcessPaymentHomeRemote");
ProcessPaymentHomeRemote home = (ProcessPaymentHomeRemote)
    PortableRemoteObject.narrow(ref,ProcessPaymentHomeRemote.class);

ProcessPaymentRemote pp = home.create();
```

Unlike the entity bean and stateful session bean, invoking the create() method does not result in a call to the bean's ejbCreate() method. In stateless session beans, calling the EJB home's create() method results in the creation of an EJB óbject for the client, but that is all.

A stateless session bean's ejbCreate() method is invoked only once in the life cycle of an instance—when it is transitioning from the Does Not Exist state to the Method-Ready Pool. It is not reinvoked every time a client requests a remote reference to the bean. Stateless session beans are limited to a single no-argument create() method because there is no way for the container to anticipate which create() method the client will invoke.

Transitioning out of the Method-Ready Pool: The death of a stateless bean instance

Bean instances leave the Method-Ready Pool for the Does Not Exist state when the server no longer needs them; that is, when the server decides to reduce the total size of the Method-Ready Pool by evicting one or more instances from memory. The process begins by invoking the ejbRemove() method on the instance. At this time, the bean instance should perform any cleanup operations, such as closing open resources. The ejbRemove() method is invoked only once in the life cycle of a stateless session bean's instance—when it is about to transition to the Does Not Exist state. When a client invokes one of the remove methods on a stateless session bean's remote or home interface, the method is not delegated to the bean instance. The client's invocation of the method simply invalidates the stub and releases the EJB object: it notifies the container that the client no longer needs the bean. The container itself invokes the ejbRemove() method on the stateless instance, but only at the end of the instance's life cycle. Again, this is different from both stateful session beans and entity beans, which suffer more destructive consequences when the client invokes a remove method. During the ejbRemove() method, the SessionContext and access to the JNDI ENC are still available to the bean instance. Following the execution of the ejbRemove() method, the bean is dereferenced and eventually garbage collected.

The Stateful Session Bean

Each stateful session bean is dedicated to one client for the life of the bean instance; it acts on behalf of that client as its agent. Stateful session beans are not swapped among EJB objects or kept in an instance pool like entity and stateless session bean instances. Once a stateful session bean is instantiated and assigned to an EJB object, it is dedicated to that EJB object for its entire life cycle.*

Stateful session beans maintain conversational state, which means that the instance variables of the bean class can cache data relative to the client between method invocations. This makes it possible for methods to be interdependent, so that changes made to the bean's state in one method call can affect the results of subsequent method invocations. In contrast, the stateless session beans we have been talking about do not maintain conversational state. Although stateless beans may have instance variables, these fields are not specific to one client. A stateless instance is swapped among many EJB objects, so you cannot predict which instance will service a method call. With stateful session beans, every method call from a client is serviced by the same instance (at least conceptually), so the bean instance's state can be predicted from one method invocation to the next.

Although stateful session beans maintain conversational state, they are not themselves persistent like entity beans. Entity beans represent data in the database; their persistence fields are written directly to the database. Stateful session beans, like stateless beans, can access the database but do not represent data in the database. In

---

* This is a conceptual model. Some EJB containers may actually use instance swapping with stateful session beans but make it appear as if the same instance is servicing all requests. Conceptually, however, the same stateful session bean instance services all requests.

addition, stateful beans are not used concurrently like entity beans. If you have an entity EJB object that wraps an instance of the ship called *Paradise*, for example, all client requests for that ship will be coordinated through the same EJB object.* With stateful session beans, the EJB object is dedicated to one client—stateful session beans are not used concurrently.

Stateful session beans are often thought of as extensions of the client. This makes sense if you think of a client as being made up of operations and state. Each task may rely on some information gathered or changed by a previous operation. A GUI client is a perfect example: when you fill in the fields on a GUI client you are creating conversational state. Pressing a button executes an operation that might fill in more fields, based on the information you entered previously. The information in the fields is conversational state.

Stateful session beans allow you to encapsulate some of the business logic and conversational state of a client and move it to the server. Moving this logic to the server thins the client application and makes the system as a whole easier to manage. The stateful session bean acts as an agent for the client, managing processes or *workflow* to accomplish a set of tasks; it manages the interactions of other beans in addition to direct data access over several operations to accomplish a complex set of tasks. By encapsulating and managing workflow on behalf of the client, stateful beans present a simplified interface that hides the details of many interdependent operations on the database and other beans from the client.

EJB 2.0: Getting Set Up for the TravelAgent EJB

The TravelAgent EJB will make use of the Cabin, Cruise, Reservation, and Customer beans developed in Chapters 6 and 7. It will coordinate the interaction of these entity beans to book a passenger on a cruise.

The Reservation EJB that was used in Chapter 7 will be modified slightly so that it can be created with all its relationships identified right away. To accommodate this, we overload its ejbCreate() method:

```
public abstract class ReservationBean implements javax.ejb.EntityBean {

    public Integer ejbCreate(CustomerRemote customer, CruiseLocal cruise,
        CabinLocal cabin, double price, Date dateBooked) {

        setAmountPaid(price);
        setDate(dateBooked);
        return null;
    }
```

* This is also a conceptual model. Some EJB containers may use separate EJB objects for concurrent access to the same entity, relying on the database to control concurrency. Conceptually, however, the end result is the same.

```
public void ejbPostCreate(CustomerRemote customer, CruiseLocal cruise,
    CabinLocal cabin, double price, Date dateBooked)
    throws javax.ejb.CreateException {

    setCruise(cruise);

    // add Cabin to collection-based CMR field
    Set cabins = new HashSet();
    cabins.add(cabin);
    this.setCabins(cabins);

    try {
        Integer primKey = (Integer)customer.getPrimaryKey();
        javax.naming.Context jndiContext = new InitialContext();
        CustomerHomeLocal home = (CustomerHomeLocal)
            jndiContext.lookup("java:comp/env/ejb/CustomerHomeLocal");
        CustomerLocal custL = home.findByPrimaryKey(primKey);

        // add Customer to collection-based CMR field
        Set customers = new HashSet();
        customers.add(custL);
        this.setCustomers(customers);

    } catch (RemoteException re) {
        throw new CreateException("Invalid Customer");
    } catch (FinderException fe) {
        throw new CreateException("Invalid Customer");
    } catch (NamingException ne) {
        throw new CreateException("Invalid Customer");
    }
}
```

Relationship fields use local EJB object references, so we must convert the CustomerRemote reference to a CustomerLocal reference in order to set the Reservation EJB's customer relationship field. To do this, you can either use the JNDI ENC to locate the local home interface and then executing the findByPrimaryKey() method or implement an ejbSelect() method in the Reservation EJB to locate the CustomerLocal reference.

EJB 1.1: Getting Set Up for the TravelAgent EJB

Both the TravelAgent EJB and the ProcessPayment EJB, which we develop in this chapter, depend on other entity beans, some of which we developed earlier in this book and several of which you can download from O'Reilly's web site. We developed the Cabin EJB in Chapter 4, but we still need several other beans for this example: namely, the Cruise, Customer, and Reservation EJBs. The source code for these beans is available with the rest of the examples for this book at the O'Reilly download site. Instructions for downloading code are available in the Preface of this book and in the workbooks.

Before you can use these beans, you need to create some new tables in your database. Here are the table definitions the new entity beans will need. The Cruise EJB maps to the CRUISE table:

```
CREATE TABLE CRUISE
(
    ID          INT PRIMARY KEY,
    NAME        CHAR(30),
    SHIP_ID     INT
)
```

The Customer EJB maps to the CUSTOMER table:

```
CREATE TABLE CUSTOMER
(
    ID           INT PRIMARY KEY,
    FIRST_NAME   CHAR(30),
    LAST_NAME    CHAR(30),
    MIDDLE_NAME  CHAR(30)
)
```

The Reservation EJB maps to the RESERVATION table:

```
CREATE TABLE RESERVATION
(
    CUSTOMER_ID   INT,
    CABIN_ID      INT,
    CRUISE_ID     INT,
    AMOUNT_PAID DECIMAL (8,2),
    DATE_RESERVED DATE
)
```

Once you have created the tables, deploy these beans as container-managed entities in your EJB server and test them to ensure that they are working properly.

The TravelAgent EJB

The TravelAgent EJB, which we have already seen, is a stateful session bean that encapsulates the process of making a reservation on a cruise. We will develop this bean further in this chapter to demonstrate how stateful session beans can be used as workflow objects.

Although EJB 2.0 readers will use the local interfaces of other beans than the Travel-Agent EJB, we will not develop a local interface for the TravelAgent EJB. The rules for developing local interfaces for stateful session beans are the same as those for stateless session and entity beans. The TravelAgent EJB is designed to be used only by remote clients and therefore does not require a set of local component interfaces.

TravelAgent: The remote interface

In Chapter 4, we developed an early version of the TravelAgentRemote interface that contained a single business method, listCabins(). We are now going to remove the listCabins() method and redefine the TravelAgent EJB so that it behaves like a workflow object. Later in this chapter, we will add a modified listing method for obtaining a more specific list of cabins for the user.

As a stateful session bean that models workflow, the TravelAgent EJB manages the interactions of several other beans while maintaining conversational state. The following code contains the modified TravelAgentRemote interface:

```
package com.titan.travelagent;

import java.rmi.RemoteException;
import javax.ejb.FinderException;
import com.titan.processpayment.CreditCardDO;

public interface TravelAgentRemote extends javax.ejb.EJBObject {

    public void setCruiseID(Integer cruise)
        throws RemoteException, FinderException;

    public void setCabinID(Integer cabin)
        throws RemoteException, FinderException;

    public TicketDO bookPassage(CreditCardDO card, double price)
        throws RemoteException,IncompleteConversationalState;
}
```

The purpose of the TravelAgent EJB is to make cruise reservations. To accomplish this task, the bean needs to know which cruise, cabin, and customer make up the reservation. Therefore, the client using the TravelAgent EJB needs to gather this kind of information before making the booking. The TravelAgentRemote interface provides methods for setting the IDs of the cruise and cabin that the customer wants to book. We can assume that the cabin ID comes from a list and that the cruise ID comes from some other source. The customer is set in the create() method of the home interface—more about this later.

Once the customer, cruise, and cabin are chosen, the TravelAgent EJB is ready to process the reservation. This operation is performed by the bookPassage() method, which needs the customer's credit card information and the price of the cruise. bookPassage() is responsible for charging the customer's account, reserving the chosen cabin in the right ship on the right cruise, and generating a ticket for the customer. How this is accomplished is not important to us at this point; when we are developing the remote interface, we are concerned only with the business definition of the bean. We will discuss the implementation when we talk about the bean class.

Note that the bookPassage() method throws an application-specific exception, IncompleteConversationalState. This exception is used to communicate business problems encountered while booking a customer on a cruise. The Incomplete-ConversationalState exception indicates that the TravelAgent EJB did not have enough information to process the booking. The IncompleteConversationalState application exception class is defined as follows:

```
package com.titan.travelagent;

public class IncompleteConversationalState extends java.lang.Exception {
    public IncompleteConversationalState(){super();}
    public IncompleteConversationalState(String msg){super(msg);}
}
```

Dependent object: TicketDO

Like the CreditCardDO and CheckDO classes used in the ProcessPayment EJB, the TicketDO class bookPassage() returns is defined as a pass-by-value object. One could argue that a ticket should be an entity bean since it is not dependent and may be accessed outside the context of the TravelAgent EJB. However, determining how a business object is used can also dictate whether it should be a bean or simply a class. The TicketDO object, for example, could be digitally signed and emailed to the client as proof of purchase. This would not be feasible if the TicketDO object were an entity bean. Enterprise beans are referenced only through their component interfaces and are not passed by value, as are serializable objects such as TicketDO, CreditCardDO, and CheckDO. As an exercise in passing by value, we will define TicketDO as a simple serializable object instead of a bean.

EJB 2.0 utilizes the local interfaces of the Cruise and Cabin EJBs and the remote interface of the Customer EJB when creating a new TicketDO object:

```
package com.titan.travelagent;

import com.titan.cruise.CruiseLocal;
import com.titan.cabin.CabinLocal;
import com.titan.customer.CustomerRemote;

public class TicketDO implements java.io.Serializable {
    public Integer customerID;
    public Integer cruiseID;
    public Integer cabinID;
    public double price;
    public String description;

    public TicketDO(CustomerRemote customer, CruiseLocal cruise,
        CabinLocal cabin, double price) throws javax.ejb.FinderException,
        RemoteException, javax.naming.NamingException {

            description = customer.getFirstName()+
                " " + customer.getLastName() +
                " has been booked for the "
                + cruise.getName() +
                " cruise on ship " +
                cruise.getShip().getName() + ".\n" +
                " Your accommodations include " +
                cabin.getName() +
```

```
                    " a " + cabin.getBedCount() +
                    " bed cabin on deck level " + cabin.getDeckLevel() +
                    ".\n Total charge = " + price;
              customerID = (Integer)customer.getPrimaryKey();
              cruiseID = (Integer)cruise.getPrimaryKey();
              cabinID = (Integer)cabin.getPrimaryKey();
              this.price = price;
          }

      public String toString() {
          return description;
      }
  }
```

EJB 1.1 also utilizes the remote interfaces of the Customer, Cruise, and Cabin EJBs when creating a new `TicketDO` object:

```
package com.titan.travelagent;

import com.titan.cruise.CruiseRemote;
import com.titan.cabin.CabinRemote;
import com.titan.customer.CustomerRemote;
import java.rmi.RemoteException;

public class TicketDO implements java.io.Serializable {
    public Integer customerID;
    public Integer cruiseID;
    public Integer cabinID;
    public double price;
    public String description;

    public TicketDO(CustomerRemote customer, CruiseRemote cruise,
        CabinRemote cabin, double price) throws javax.ejb.FinderException,
        RemoteException, javax.naming.NamingException {

            description = customer.getFirstName()+
                " " + customer.getLastName() +
                " has been booked for the "
                + cruise.getName() +
                " cruise on ship " + cruise.getShipID() + ".\n" +
                " Your accommodations include " +
                  cabin.getName() +
                " a " + cabin.getBedCount() +
                " bed cabin on deck level " + cabin.getDeckLevel() +
                ".\n Total charge = " + price;
            customerID = (Integer)customer.getPrimaryKey();
            cruiseID = (Integer)cruise.getPrimaryKey();
            cabinID = (Integer)cabin.getPrimaryKey();
            this.price = price;

        }
    public String toString() {
        return description;
    }
}
```

TravelAgentHomeRemote: The home interface

Starting with the `TravelAgentHomeRemote` interface we developed in Chapter 4, we can modify the `create()` method to take a remote reference to the customer who is making the reservation:

```
package com.titan.travelagent;

import java.rmi.RemoteException;
import javax.ejb.CreateException;
import com.titan.customer.CustomerRemote;

public interface TravelAgentHomeRemote extends javax.ejb.EJBHome {
    public TravelAgentRemote create(CustomerRemote cust)
        throws RemoteException, CreateException;
}
```

The `create()` method in this home interface requires that a remote reference to a Customer EJB be used to create the TravelAgent EJB. Because there are no other `create()` methods, you cannot create a TravelAgent EJB if you do not know who the customer is. The Customer EJB reference provides the TravelAgent EJB with some of the conversational state it will need to process the `bookPassage()` method.

Taking a peek at the client view

Before settling on definitions for your component interfaces, it is a good idea to figure out how the bean will be used by clients. Imagine that the TravelAgent EJB is used by a Java application with GUI fields. The GUI fields capture the customer's preference for the type of cruise and cabin. We start by examining the code used at the beginning of the reservation process:

```
Context jndiContext = getInitialContext();
Object ref = jndiContext.lookup("CustomerHomeRemote");
CustomerHomeRemote customerHome =(CustomerHomeRemote)
    PortableRemoteObject.narrow(ref, CustomerHomeRemote.class);

String ln = tfLastName.getText();
String fn = tfFirstName.getText();
String mn = tfMiddleName.getText();
CustomerRemote customer = customerHome.create(nextID, ln, fn, mn);

ref = jndiContext.lookup("TravelAgentHomeRemote");
TravelAgentHomeRemote home = (TravelAgentHomeRemote)
    PortableRemoteObject.narrow(ref, TravelAgentHomeRemote.class);

TravelAgentRemote agent = home.create(customer);
```

This snippet of code creates a new Customer EJB based on information the travel agent gathered over the phone. The `CustomerRemote` reference is then used to create a TravelAgent EJB. Next, we gather the cruise and cabin choices from another part of the applet:

```
Integer cruise_id = new Integer(textField_cruiseNumber.getText());

Integer cabin_id = new Integer( textField_cabinNumber.getText());

agent.setCruiseID(cruise_id);
agent.setCabinID(cabin_id);
```

The travel agent chooses the cruise and cabin the customer wishes to reserve. These IDs are set in the TravelAgent EJB, which maintains the conversational state for the whole process.

At the end of the process, the travel agent completes the reservation by processing the booking and generating a ticket. Because the TravelAgent EJB has maintained the conversational state, caching the customer, cabin, and cruise information, only the credit card and price are needed to complete the transaction:

```
String cardNumber = textField_cardNumber.getText();
Date date = dateFormatter.parse(textField_cardExpiration.getText());
String cardBrand = textField_cardBrand.getText();
CreditCardDO card = new CreditCardDO(cardNumber,date,cardBrand);
double price = double.valueOf(textField_cruisePrice.getText()).doubleValue();
TicketDO ticket = agent.bookPassage(card,price);
PrintingService.print(ticket);
```

We can now move ahead with development. This summary of how the client will use the TravelAgent EJB confirms that our remote interface and home interface definitions are workable.

TravelAgentBean: The bean class

We can now implement all of the behavior expressed in the new remote interface and home interface for the TravelAgent EJB.[*]

Here is a partial definition of the new TravelAgentBean class for EJB 2.0:

```
import com.titan.reservation.*;

import java.sql.*;
import javax.sql.DataSource;
import java.util.Vector;
import java.rmi.RemoteException;
import javax.naming.NamingException;
import javax.ejb.EJBException;
import com.titan.processpayment.*;
import com.titan.cruise.*;
import com.titan.customer.*;
import com.titan.cabin.*;
```

---

[*] If you are modifying the bean developed in Chapter 4, remember to delete the listCabin() method. We will add a new implementation of that method later in this chapter.

```java
public class TravelAgentBean implements javax.ejb.SessionBean {

    public CustomerRemote customer;
    public CruiseLocal cruise;
    public CabinLocal cabin;

    public javax.ejb.SessionContext ejbContext;

    public javax.naming.Context jndiContext;

    public void ejbCreate(CustomerRemote cust) {
        customer = cust;
    }
    public void setCabinID(Integer cabinID) throws javax.ejb.FinderException {
        try {
            CabinHomeLocal home = (CabinHomeLocal)
                jndiContext.lookup("java:comp/env/ejb/CabinHomeLocal");

            cabin = home.findByPrimaryKey(cabinID);
        } catch(RemoteException re) {
            throw new EJBException(re);
        }
    }
    public void setCruiseID(Integer cruiseID) throws javax.ejb.FinderException {
        try {
            CruiseHomeLocal home = (CruiseHomeLocal)
                jndiContext.lookup("java:comp/env/ejb/CruiseHomeLocal");

            cruise = home.findByPrimaryKey(cruiseID);
        } catch(RemoteException re) {
            throw new EJBException(re);
        }

    }
    public TicketDO bookPassage(CreditCardDO card, double price)
        throws IncompleteConversationalState {

        if (customer == null || cruise == null || cabin == null)
        {
            throw new IncompleteConversationalState();
        }
        try {
            ReservationHomeLocal resHome = (ReservationHomeLocal)
                jndiContext.lookup("java:comp/env/ejb/ReservationHomeLocal");

            ReservationLocal reservation =
                resHome.create(customer, cruise, cabin, price, new Date());

            Object ref = jndiContext.lookup("java:comp/env/ejb/
                ProcessPaymentHomeRemote");

            ProcessPaymentHomeRemote ppHome = (ProcessPaymentHomeRemote)
                PortableRemoteObject.narrow (ref, ProcessPaymentHomeRemote.class);
```

```
                    ProcessPaymentRemote process = ppHome.create();
                    process.byCredit(customer, card, price);

                    TicketDO ticket = new TicketDO(customer, cruise, cabin, price);
                    return ticket;
                } catch(Exception e) {
                    throw new EJBException(e);
                }
            }
            public void ejbRemove() {}
            public void ejbActivate() {}
            public void ejbPassivate() {}

            public void setSessionContext(javax.ejb.SessionContext cntx)
            {

                ejbContext = cntx;
                try {
                    jndiContext = new javax.naming.InitialContext();
                } catch(NamingException ne) {
                    throw new EJBException(ne);
                }
            }
        }
```

In EJB 1.1, the TravelAgentBean class definition looks like this:

```
    import com.titan.reservation.*;

    import java.sql.*;
    import javax.sql.DataSource;
    import java.util.Vector;
    import java.rmi.RemoteException;
    import javax.naming.NamingException;
    import javax.ejb.EJBException;
    import com.titan.processpayment.*;
    import com.titan.cruise.*;
    import com.titan.customer.*;
    import com.titan.cabin.*;

    public class TravelAgentBean implements javax.ejb.SessionBean {

        public CustomerRemote customer;
        public CruiseRemote cruise;
        public CabinRemote cabin;

        public javax.ejb.SessionContext ejbContext;

        public javax.naming.Context jndiContext;

        public void ejbCreate(CustomerRemote cust) {
            customer = cust;
        }
        public void setCabinID(Integer cabinID) throws javax.ejb.FinderException {
```

```
        try {
            CabinHomeRemote home = (CabinHomeRemote)
                getHome("CabinHomeRemote", CabinHomeRemote.class);
            cabin = home.findByPrimaryKey(cabinID);
        } catch(Exception re) {
            throw new EJBException(re);
        }
    }
    public void setCruiseID(Integer cruiseID) throws javax.ejb.FinderException {
        try {
            CruiseHomeRemote home = (CruiseHomeRemote)
                getHome("CruiseHomeRemote", CruiseHomeRemote. class);
            cruise = home.findByPrimaryKey(cruiseID);
        } catch(Exception re) {
            throw new EJBException(re);
        }


    }
    public TicketDO bookPassage(CreditCardDO card, double price)
        throws IncompleteConversationalState {

        if (customer == null || cruise == null || cabin == null){
            throw new IncompleteConversationalState();
        }
        try {
            ReservationHomeRemote resHome = (ReservationHomeRemote)
                getHome("ReservationHomeRemote", ReservationHomeRemote.class);
            ReservationRemote reservation =
                resHome.create(customer, cruise, cabin, price, new Date());
            ProcessPaymentHomeRemote ppHome = (ProcessPaymentHomeRemote)
                getHome("ProcessPaymentHomeRemote", ProcessPaymentHomeRemote.class);
            ProcessPaymentRemote process = ppHome.create();
            process.byCredit(customer, card, price);

            TicketDO ticket = new TicketDO(customer,cruise,cabin,price);
            return ticket;
        } catch(Exception e) {
            throw new EJBException(e);
        }
    }
    public void ejbRemove() {}
    public void ejbActivate() {}
    public void ejbPassivate() {}

    public void setSessionContext(javax.ejb.SessionContext cntx)
    {

        ejbContext = cntx;
        try {
            jndiContext = new javax.naming.InitialContext();
        } catch(NamingException ne) {
            throw new EJBException(ne);
        }
    }
```

```
        protected Object getHome(String name,Class type) {
            try {
                Object ref = jndiContext.lookup("java:comp/env/ejb/"+name);
                return PortableRemoteObject.narrow(ref, type);
            } catch(NamingException ne) {
                throw new EJBException(ne);
            }
        }
    }
}
```

There is a lot of code to digest in the TravelAgentBean class definition, so we will approach it in small pieces. First, let's examine the ejbCreate() method:

```
public class TravelAgentBean implements javax.ejb.SessionBean {

    public CustomerRemote customer;
        ...

    public javax.ejb.SessionContext ejbContext;
    public javax.naming.Context jndiContext;

    public void ejbCreate(CustomerRemote cust) {
        customer = cust;
    }
```

When the bean is created, the remote reference to the Customer EJB is passed to the bean instance and maintained in the customer field. The customer field is part of the bean's conversational state. We could have obtained the customer's identity as an integer ID and constructed the remote reference to the Customer EJB in the ejbCreate() method. However, we passed the reference directly to demonstrate that remote references to beans can be passed from a client application to a bean. They can also be returned from the bean to the client and passed between beans on the same EJB server or between EJB servers.

References to the SessionContext and JNDI context are held in fields called ejbContext and jndiContext. The "ejb" and "jndi" prefixes help to avoid confusion between the different content types.

When a bean is passivated, the JNDI ENC must be maintained as part of the bean's conversational state. This means that the JNDI context should not be transient. Once a field is set to reference the JNDI ENC, the reference remains valid for the life of the bean. In the TravelAgentBean, we set the jndiContext field to reference the JNDI ENC when the SessionContext is set at the beginning of the bean's life cycle:

```
public void setSessionContext(javax.ejb.SessionContext cntx) {
    ejbContext = cntx;
    try {
        jndiContext = new InitialContext();
    } catch(NamingException ne) {
        throw new EJBException(ne);
    }
}
```

The EJB container makes special accommodations for references to SessionContext, the JNDI ENC, references to other beans (remote and home interface types), and the JTA UserTransaction type, which is discussed in detail in Chapter 14. The container must maintain any instance fields that reference objects of these types as part of the conversational state, even if they are not serializable. All other fields must be serializable or null when the bean is passivated.

The TravelAgent EJB has methods for setting the desired cruise and cabin. These methods take Integer IDs as arguments and retrieve references to the appropriate Cruise or Cabin EJB from the appropriate home interface. These references are also part of the TravelAgent EJB's conversational state.

Here's how setCabinID( ) and getCabinID( ) are used in EJB 2.0:

```
public void setCabinID(Integer cabinID)
    throws javax.ejb.FinderException {
    try {
        CabinHomeLocal home = (CabinHomeLocal)
            jndiContext.lookup("java:comp/env/ejb/CabinHomeLocal");

        cabin = home.findByPrimaryKey(cabinID);
    } catch(RemoteException re) {
        throw new EJBException(re);
    }
}
public void setCruiseID(Integer cruiseID)
    throws javax.ejb.FinderException {
    try {
        CruiseHomeLocal home = (CruiseHomeLocal)
            jndiContext.lookup("java:comp/env/ejb/CruiseHomeLocal");

        cruise = home.findByPrimaryKey(cruiseID);
    } catch(RemoteException re) {
        throw new EJBException(re);
    }
}
```

Here's how setCabinID( ) and getCabinID( ) are used in EJB 1.1:

```
public void setCabinID(Integer cabinID)
    throws javax.ejb.FinderException {
    try {
        CabinHomeRemote home = (CabinHome)
            getHome("CabinHomeRemote", CabinHome.class);
        cabin = home.findByPrimaryKey(cabinID);
    } catch(RemoteException re) {
        throw new EJBException(re);
    }
}
public void setCruiseID(Integer cruiseID)
    throws javax.ejb.FinderException {
    try {
        CruiseHome home = (CruiseHome)
```

```
            getHome("CruiseHomeRemote", CruiseHome.class);
        cruise = home.findByPrimaryKey(cruiseID);
    } catch(RemoteException re) {
        throw new EJBException(re);
    }
}
```

It may seem strange that we set these values using the Integer IDs, but we keep them in the conversational state as entity bean references. Using the Integer IDs for these objects is simpler for the client, which does not work with their entity bean references. In the client code, we get the cabin and cruise IDs from text fields. Why make the client obtain a bean reference to the Cruise and Cabin EJBs when an ID is simpler? In addition, using the IDs is cheaper than passing a remote reference in terms of network traffic. We need the EJB object references to these bean types in the bookPassage() method, so we use their IDs to obtain actual entity bean references. We could have waited until the bookPassage() method was invoked before reconstructing the remote references, but this way we keep the bookPassage() method simple.

JNDI ENC and EJB references

You can use the JNDI ENC to obtain a reference to the home interfaces of other beans. Using the ENC lets you avoid hardcoding vendor-specific JNDI properties into the bean. In other words, the JNDI ENC allows EJB references to be network and vendor independent.

In the EJB 2.0 listing for the TravelAgentBean, we used the JNDI ENC to access both the remote home interface of the ProcessPayment EJB and the local home interfaces of the Cruise and Cabin EJBs. This illustrates the flexibility of the JNDI ENC, which can provide directories for both local and remote enterprise beans.

In the EJB 1.1 listing for the TravelAgentBean class, getHome() is a convenience method that hides the details of obtaining remote references to EJB home objects. The getHome() method uses the jndiContext reference to obtain references to the Cabin, Ship, ProcessPayment, and Cruise EJB home objects.

The EJB specification recommends that all EJB references be bound to the "java:comp/env/ejb" context, which is the convention followed here. In the TravelAgent EJB, we pass in the name of the home object we want and append it to the "java:comp/env/ejb" context to do the lookup.

Remote EJB references in the JNDI ENC. The deployment descriptor provides a special set of tags for declaring remote EJB references. Here's how the <ejb-ref> tag and its subelements are used:

```
<ejb-ref>
    <ejb-ref-name>ejb/ProcessPaymentHomeRemote</ejb-ref-name>
    <ejb-ref-type>Session</ejb-ref-type>
```

```
<home>
    com.titan.processpayment.ProcessPaymentHomeRemote
</home>
<remote>
    com.titan.processpayment.ProcessPaymentRemote
</remote>
</ejb-ref>
```

These elements should be self-explanatory: they define a name for the bean within the ENC, declare the bean's type, and give the names of its remote and home interfaces. When a bean is deployed, the deployer maps the <ejb-ref> elements to actual beans in a way specific to the vendor. The <ejb-ref> elements can also be linked by the application assembler to beans in the same deployment (a subject covered in detail in Chapter 16). EJB 2.0 developers should try to use local component interfaces for beans located in the same deployment and container.

At deployment time, the EJB container's tools map the remote references declared in the <ejb-ref> elements to enterprise beans, which might located on the same machine or at a different node on the network.

EJB 2.0: Local EJB references in the JNDI ENC. The deployment descriptor also provides a special set of tags, the <ejb-local-ref> elements, to declare local EJB references: enterprise beans that are co-located in the same container and deployed in the same EJB JAR file. The <ejb-local-ref> elements are declared immediately after the <ejb-ref> elements:

```
<ejb-local-ref>
    <ejb-ref-name>ejb/CruiseHomeLocal</ejb-ref-name>
    <ejb-ref-type>Entity</ejb-ref-type>
    <local-home>
        com.titan.cruise.CruiseHomeLocal
    </local-home>
    <local>
        com.titan.cruise.CruiseLocal
    </local>
    <ejb-link>CruiseEJB</ejb-link>
</ejb-local-ref>
<ejb-local-ref>
    <ejb-ref-name>ejb/CabinHomeLocal</ejb-ref-name>
    <ejb-ref-type>Entity</ejb-ref-type>
    <local-home>
        com.titan.cabin.CabinHomeLocal
    </local-home>
    <local>
        com.titan.cabin.CabinLocal
    </local>
    <ejb-link>CabinEJB</ejb-link>
</ejb-local-ref>
```

The <ejb-local-ref> element defines a name for the bean within the ENC, declares the bean's type, and gives the names of its local component interfaces. These elements should be linked explicitly to other co-located beans using the <ejb-link> element, although linking them is not strictly required at this stage—the application assembler or deployer can do it later. The value of the <ejb-link> element within the <ejb-local-ref> must equal the <ejb-name> of the appropriate bean in the same JAR file.

At deployment time the EJB container's tools map the local references declared in the <ejb-local-ref> elements to entity beans that are co-located in the same container system.

The bookPassage( ) method

The last point of interest in our bean definition is the bookPassage() method. This method leverages the conversational state accumulated by the ejbCreate(), setCabinID(), and setCruiseID() methods to process a reservation for a customer.

Here's how the bookPassage() method is used in EJB 2.0:

```
public TicketDO bookPassage(CreditCardDO card, double price)
    throws IncompleteConversationalState {

    if (customer == null || cruise == null || cabin == null) {
        throw new IncompleteConversationalState();
    }
    try {
        ReservationHomeLocal resHome = (ReservationHomeLocal)
            jndiContext.lookup("java:comp/env/ejb/ReservationHomeLocal");

        ReservationLocal reservation =
            resHome.create(customer, cruise, cabin, price, new Date());

        Object ref = jndiContext.lookup("java:comp/env/ejb/
            ProcessPaymentHomeRemote");

        ProcessPaymentHomeRemote ppHome = (ProcessPaymentHomeRemote)
            PortableRemoteObject.narrow(ref, ProcessPaymentHomeRemote.class);

        ProcessPaymentRemote process = ppHome.create();
        process.byCredit(customer, card, price);

        TicketDO ticket = new TicketDO(customer,cruise,cabin,price);
        return ticket;
    } catch(Exception e) {
        throw new EJBException(e);
    }
}
```

Here's how the bookPassage() method is used in EJB 1.1:

```
public TicketDO bookPassage(CreditCardDO card, double price)
    throws IncompleteConversationalState {

    if (customer == null || cruise == null || cabin == null) {
        throw new IncompleteConversationalState();
    }
```

```
        try {
            ReservationHomeRemote resHome = (ReservationHomeRemote)
            getHome("ReservationHomeRemote", ReservationHomeRemote.class);
            ReservationRemote reservation =
                resHome.create(customer, cruise, cabin, price, new Date());
            ProcessPaymentHomeRemote ppHome = (ProcessPaymentHomeRemote)
                getHome("ProcessPaymentHomeRemote", ProcessPaymentHomeRemote.class);
            ProcessPaymentRemote process = ppHome.create();
            process.byCredit(customer, card, price);

            TicketDO ticket = new TicketDO(customer,cruise,cabin,price);
            return ticket;
        } catch(Exception e) {
            // EJB 1.0: throw new RemoteException("",e);
            throw new EJBException(e);
        }
    }
```

This method exemplifies the workflow concept. It uses several beans, including the
Reservation, ProcessPayment, Customer, Cabin, and Cruise EJBs, to accomplish one
task: booking a customer on a cruise. Deceptively simple, this method encapsulates
several interactions that ordinarily might have been performed on the client. For the
price of one bookPassage() call from the client, the TravelAgent EJB performs many
operations:

1. Looks up and obtains a reference to the Reservation EJB's home.

2. Creates a new Reservation EJB.

3. Looks up and obtains a remote reference to the ProcessPayment EJB's home.

4. Creates a new ProcessPayment EJB.

5. Charges the customer's credit card using the ProcessPayment EJB.

6. Generates a new TicketDO with all the pertinent information describing the customer's purchase.

From a design standpoint, encapsulating the workflow in a stateful session bean
means a less complex interface for the client and more flexibility for implementing
changes. We could, for example, easily change the bookPassage() method to check
for overlapped booking (when a customer books passage on two different cruises
that overlap). This type of enhancement would not change the remote interface, so
the client application would not need modification. Encapsulating workflow in stateful session beans allows the system to evolve over time without impacting clients.

In addition, the type of clients used can change. One of the biggest problems with
two-tier architectures—besides scalability and transactional control—is that the
business logic is intertwined with the client logic. This makes it difficult to reuse the
business logic in a different kind of client. With stateful session beans this is not a
problem, because stateful session beans are an extension of the client but are not
bound to the client's presentation. Let's say that our first implementation of the reservation system used a Java applet with GUI widgets. The TravelAgent EJB would

manage conversational state and perform all the business logic while the applet focused on the GUI presentation. If, at a later date, we decide to go to a thin client (HTML generated by a Java servlet, for example), we would simply reuse the Travel-Agent EJB in the servlet. Because all the business logic is in the stateful session bean, the presentation (Java applet or servlet or something else) can change easily.

The TravelAgent EJB also provides transactional integrity for processing the customer's reservation. If any one of the operations within the body of the bookPassage() method fails, all the operations are rolled back so that none of the changes are accepted. If the credit card cannot be charged by the ProcessPayment EJB, the newly created Reservation EJB and its associated record are not created. The transactional aspects of the TravelAgent EJB are explained in detail in Chapter 14.

> In EJB 2.0, remote and local EJB references can be used within the same workflow. For example, the bookPassage() method uses local references when accessing the Cruise and Cabin beans, but remote references when accessing the ProcessPayment and Customer EJBs. This usage is totally appropriate. The EJB container ensures that the transaction is atomic, i.e., that failures in either the remote or local EJB reference will impact the entire transaction.

Why use a Reservation entity bean?

If we have a Reservation EJB, why do we need a TravelAgent EJB? Good question! The TravelAgent EJB uses the Reservation EJB to create a reservation, but it also has to charge the customer and generate a ticket. These activities are not specific to the Reservation EJB, so they need to be captured in a stateful session bean that can manage workflow and transactional scope. In addition, the TravelAgent EJB provides listing behavior, which spans concepts in Titan's system. It would have been inappropriate to include any of these other behaviors in the Reservation entity bean. (For EJB 2.0 readers, the Reservation EJB was developed in Chapter 7. For EJB 1.1 readers, the code for this bean is available at *http://www.oreilly.com/catalog/entjbeans3/*.)

listAvailableCabins( ): Listing behavior

As promised, we are going to bring back the cabin-listing behavior we played around with in Chapter 4. This time, however, we are not going to use the Cabin EJB to get the list; instead, we will access the database directly. Accessing the database directly is a double-edged sword. On one hand, we don't want to access the database directly if entity beans exist that can access the same information. Entity beans provide a safe and consistent interface for a particular set of data. Once an entity bean has been tested and proven, it can be reused throughout the system, substantially reducing data-integrity problems. The Reservation EJB is an example of that kind of usage. Entity beans can also pull together disjointed data and apply additional business logic such as validation, limits, and security to ensure that data access follows the business rules.

But entity beans cannot define every possible data access needed, and they shouldn't. One of the biggest problems with entity beans is that they tend to become bloated over time. Huge entity beans containing dozens of methods are a sure sign of poor design. Entity beans should be focused on providing data access to a very limited, but conceptually bound, set of data. You should be able to update, read, and insert records or data. Data access that spans concepts, like listing behavior, should not be encapsulated in one entity bean.

Systems always need listing behavior to present clients with choices. In the reservation system, for example, customers need to choose a cabin from a list of available cabins. The word *available* is key to the definition of this behavior. The Cabin EJB can provide us with a list of cabins, but it does not know whether any given cabin is available. As you may recall, the Cabin-Reservation relationship we defined for EJB 2.0 in Chapter 7 was *unidirectional*: the Reservation was aware of its Cabin relationships, but the reverse was not true.

The question of whether a cabin is available is relevant to the process using it—in this case, the TravelAgent EJB—but may not be relevant to the cabin itself. As an analogy, an automobile entity would not care what road it is on; it is concerned only with characteristics that describe its state and behavior. An automobile-tracking system, on the other hand, would be concerned with the locations of individual automobiles.

To get availability information, we need to compare the list of cabins on our ship to the list of cabins that have already been reserved. The listAvailableCabins() method does exactly that. It uses a complex SQL query to produce a list of cabins that have not yet been reserved for the cruise chosen by the client:

```
public String [] listAvailableCabins(int bedCount)
    throws IncompleteConversationalState {
    if (cruise == null)
        throw new IncompleteConversationalState();

    Connection con = null;
    PreparedStatement ps = null;;
    ResultSet result = null;
    try {
        Integer cruiseID = (Integer)cruise.getPrimaryKey();
        Integer shipID = (Integer)cruise.getShip().getPrimaryKey();
        con = getConnection();
        ps = con.prepareStatement(
            "select ID, NAME, DECK_LEVEL  from CABIN "+
            "where SHIP_ID = ? and BED_COUNT = ? and ID NOT IN "+
            "(SELECT CABIN_ID FROM RESERVATION "+" WHERE CRUISE_ID = ?)");

        ps.setInt(1,shipID.intValue());
        ps.setInt(2, bedCount);
        ps.setInt(3,cruiseID.intValue());
        result = ps.executeQuery();
        Vector vect = new Vector();
        while(result.next()) {
```

```
                StringBuffer buf = new StringBuffer();
                buf.append(result.getString(1));
                buf.append(',');
                buf.append(result.getString(2));
                buf.append(',');
                buf.append(result.getString(3));
                vect.addElement(buf.toString());
            }
            String [] returnArray = new String[vect.size()];
            vect.copyInto(returnArray);
            return returnArray;
        } catch (Exception e) {
            throw new EJBException(e);
        }
        finally {
            try {
                if (result != null) result.close();
                if (ps != null) ps.close();
                if (con!- null) con.close();
            } catch(SQLException se){se.printStackTrace();}
        }
    }
```

EJB 1.1 readers use almost exactly the same code for listAvailableCabins(), but obtain the Ship EJB's ID differently. EJB 1.1 readers should replace the line:

```
Integer shipID = (Integer)cruise.getShip().getPrimaryKey();
```

With the line:

```
Integer shipID = cruise.getShipID();
```

This change is necessary because EJB 1.1 does not support relationship fields.

As you can see, the SQL query is complex. It could have been defined using a method like Cabin.findAvailableCabins(Cruise cruise) in the Cabin EJB. However, this method would be difficult to implement because the Cabin EJB would need to access the Reservation EJB's data. Another reason for accessing the database directly in this example is to demonstrate that this kind of behavior is both normal and, in some cases, preferred. Sometimes the query is fairly specific to the scenario and is not reusable. To avoid adding find methods for every possible query, you can instead simply use direct database access as shown in the listAvailableCabins() method. Direct database access generally has less impact on performance because the container does not have to manifest EJB object references, but it is also less reusable. These things must be considered when deciding if a query for information should be done using direct database access or if a new find method should be defined.

The listAvailableCabins() method returns an array of String objects to the remote client. We could have opted to return an collection of remote Cabin references, but we didn't. The reason is simple: we want to keep the client application as lightweight as possible. A list of String objects is much more lightweight than the alternative, a collection of remote references. In addition, using a collection of remote would require the client to work with many stubs, each with its own connection to EJB objects on the server. By returning a lightweight String array we reduce the number of stubs on the client, which keeps the client simple and conserves resources on the server.

To make this method work, you need to create a getConnection() method for obtaining a database connection and add it to the TravelAgentBean:

```
private Connection getConnection() throws SQLException {
    try {
        DataSource ds = (DataSource)jndiContext.lookup(
            "java:comp/env/jdbc/titanDB");
        return ds.getConnection();
    } catch(NamingException ne) {
        throw new EJBException(ne);
    }
}
```

Change the remote interface for TravelAgent EJB to include the listAvailableCabins() method:

```
package com.titan.travelagent;

import java.rmi.RemoteException;
import javax.ejb.FinderException;
import com.titan.processpayment.CreditCard;

public interface TravelAgentRemote extends javax.ejb.EJBObject {

    public void setCruiseID(Integer cruise) throws RemoteException, FinderException;

    public void setCabinID(Integer cabin) throws RemoteException, FinderException;

    public TicketDO bookPassage(CreditCardDO card, double price)
        throws RemoteException,IncompleteConversationalState;

    public String [] listAvailableCabins(int bedCount)
        throws RemoteException, IncompleteConversationalState;
}
```

EJB 2.0: The TravelAgent deployment descriptor

The following listing is an abbreviated version of the XML deployment descriptor used for the TravelAgent EJB. It defines not only the TravelAgent EJB, but also the Customer, Cruise, Cabin, and Reservation EJBs. The ProcessPayment EJB is not defined in this deployment descriptor because it is assumed to be deployed in a separate JAR file, or possibly even an EJB server on a different network node:

```
<!DOCTYPE ejb-jar PUBLIC "-//Sun Microsystems, Inc.//DTD Enterprise
JavaBeans 2.0//EN" "http://java.sun.com/dtd/ejb-jar_2_0.dtd">

<ejb-jar>
    <enterprise-beans>
```

```
<session>
    <ejb-name>TravelAgentEJB</ejb-name>
    <home>com.titan.travelagent.TravelAgentHomeRemote</home>
    <remote>com.titan.travelagent.TravelAgentRemote</remote>
    <ejb-class>com.titan.travelagent.TravelAgentBean</ejb-class>
    <session-type>Stateful</session-type>
    <transaction-type>Container</transaction-type>

    <ejb-ref>
        <ejb-ref-name>ejb/ProcessPaymentHomeRemote</ejb-ref-name>
        <ejb-ref-type>Session</ejb-ref-type>
        <home>com.titan.processpayment.ProcessPaymentHomeRemote</home>
        <remote>com.titan.processpayment.ProcessPaymentRemote</remote>
    </ejb-ref>
    <ejb-local-ref>
        <ejb-ref-name>ejb/CabinHomeLocal</ejb-ref-name>
        <ejb-ref-type>Entity</ejb-ref-type>
        <local-home>com.titan.cabin.CabinHomeLocal</local-home>
        <local>com.titan.cabin.CabinLocal</local>
    </ejb-local-ref>
    <ejb-local-ref>
        <ejb-ref-name>ejb/CruiseHomeLocal</ejb-ref-name>
        <ejb-ref-type>Entity</ejb-ref-type>
        <local-home>com.titan.cruise.CruiseHomeLocal</local-home>
        <local>com.titan.cruise.CruiseLocal</local>
    </ejb-local-ref>
    <ejb-local-ref>
        <ejb-ref-name>ejb/ReservationHomeLocal</ejb-ref-name>
        <ejb-ref-type>Entity</ejb-ref-type>
        <local-home>com.titan.reservation.ReservationHomeLocal</local-home>
        <local>com.titan.reservation.ReservationLocal</local>
    </ejb-local-ref>

    <resource-ref>
        <description>DataSource for the Titan database</description>
        <res-ref-name>jdbc/titanDB</res-ref-name>
        <res-type>javax.sql.DataSource</res-type>
        <res-auth>Container</res-auth>
    </resource-ref>
</session>
<entity>
    <ejb-name>CabinEJB</ejb-name>
    <local-home>com.titan.cabin.CabinHomeLocal</local-home>
    <local>com.titan.cabin.CabinLocal</local>
    ...
</entity>
<entity>
    <ejb-name>CruiseEJB</ejb-name>
    <local-home>com.titan.cruise.CruiseHomeLocal</local-home>
    <local>com.titan.cruise.CruiseLocal</local>
    ...
</entity>
<entity>
    <ejb-name>ReservationEJB</ejb-name>
```

```
            <local-home>com.titan.reservation.ReservationHomeLocal</local-home>
            <local>com.titan.reservation.ReservationLocal</local>
            ...
        </entity>
    </enterprise-beans>

    <assembly-descriptor>
        <security-role>
            <description>This role represents everyone</description>
            <role-name>everyone</role-name>
        </security-role>

        <method-permission>
            <role-name>everyone</role-name>
            <method>
                <ejb-name>TravelAgentEJB</ejb-name>
                <method-name>*</method-name>
            </method>
        </method-permission>

        <container-transaction>
            <method>
                <ejb-name>TravelAgentEJB</ejb-name>
                <method-name>*</method-name>
            </method>
            <trans-attribute>Required</trans-attribute>
        </container-transaction>
    </assembly-descriptor>
</ejb-jar>
```

EJB 1.1: The TravelAgent deployment descriptor

Use the following XML deployment descriptor when deploying the TravelAgent EJB in EJB 1.1. The most important differences between this descriptor and the deployment descriptor used for the ProcessPayment EJB are the <session-type> tag, which states that this bean is stateful, and the use of the <ejb-ref> elements to describe beans that are referenced through the ENC:

```
<!DOCTYPE ejb-jar PUBLIC "-//Sun Microsystems, Inc.//DTD Enterprise
JavaBeans 1.1//EN" "http://java.sun.com/j2ee/dtds/ejb-jar_1_1.dtd">

<ejb-jar>
    <enterprise-beans>
        <session>
            <description>
                Acts as a travel agent for booking passage on a ship.
            </description>
            <ejb-name>TravelAgentEJB</ejb-name>
            <home>com.titan.travelagent.TravelAgentHomeRemote</home>
            <remote>com.titan.travelagent.TravelAgentRemote</remote>
            <ejb-class>com.titan.travelagent.TravelAgentBean</ejb-class>
            <session-type>Stateful</session-type>
            <transaction-type>Container</transaction-type>
```

```xml
<ejb-ref>
    <ejb-ref-name>ejb/ProcessPaymentHomeRemote</ejb-ref-name>
    <ejb-ref-type>Session</ejb-ref-type>
    <home>com.titan.processpayment.ProcessPaymentHome</home>
    <remote>com.titan.processpayment.ProcessPayment</remote>
</ejb-ref>
<ejb-ref>
    <ejb-ref-name>ejb/CabinHomeRemote</ejb-ref-name>
    <ejb-ref-type>Entity</ejb-ref-type>
    <home>com.titan.cabin.CabinHome</home>
    <remote>com.titan.cabin.Cabin</remote>
</ejb-ref>
<ejb-ref>
    <ejb-ref-name>ejb/CruiseHomeRemote</ejb-ref-name>
    <ejb-ref-type>Entity</ejb-ref-type>
    <home>com.titan.cruise.CruiseHome</home>
    <remote>com.titan.cruise.Cruise</remote>
</ejb-ref>
<ejb-ref>
    <ejb-ref-name>ejb/CustomerHomeRemote</ejb-ref-name>
    <ejb-ref-type>Entity</ejb-ref-type>
    <home>com.titan.customer.CustomerHome</home>
    <remote>com.titan.customer.Customer</remote>
</ejb-ref>
<ejb-ref>
    <ejb-ref-name>ejb/ReservationHomeRemote</ejb-ref-name>
    <ejb-ref-type>Entity</ejb-ref-type>
    <home>com.titan.reservation.ReservationHome</home>
    <remote>com.titan.reservation.Reservation</remote>
</ejb-ref>

<resource-ref>
    <description>DataSource for the Titan database</description>
    <res-ref-name>jdbc/titanDB</res-ref-name>
    <res-type>javax.sql.DataSource</res-type>
    <res-auth>Container</res-auth>
</resource-ref>
    </session>
</enterprise-beans>

<assembly-descriptor>
    <security-role>
        <description>This role represents everyone</description>
        <role-name>everyone</role-name>
    </security-role>

    <method-permission>
        <role-name>everyone</role-name>
        <method>
            <ejb-name>TravelAgentEJB</ejb-name>
            <method-name>*</method-name>
        </method>
    </method-permission>
```

```
        <container-transaction>
            <method>
                <ejb-name>TravelAgentEJB</ejb-name>
                <method-name>*</method-name>
            </method>
            <trans-attribute>Required</trans-attribute>
        </container-transaction>
    </assembly-descriptor>
</ejb-jar>
```

Once you have generated the deployment descriptor, *jar* the TravelAgent EJB and deploy it in your EJB server. You will also need to deploy the Reservation, Cruise, and Customer EJBs you downloaded earlier. Based on the business methods in the remote interface of the TravelAgent EJB and your past experiences with the Cabin, Ship, and ProcessPayment EJBs, you should be able to create your own client application to test this code.

📖 Workbook Exercise 12.2, A Stateful Session Bean

The Life Cycle of a Stateful Session Bean

The biggest difference between the stateful session bean and the other bean types is that stateful session beans do not use instance pooling. Stateful session beans are dedicated to one client for their entire lives, so there is no swapping or pooling of instances.* Instead of being pooled, stateful session bean instances are simply evicted from memory to conserve resources. The EJB object remains connected to the client, but the bean instance is dereferenced and garbage collected during inactive periods. This means that each stateful bean must be passivated before it is evicted to preserve the conversational state of the instance, and it must be activated to restore the state when the EJB object becomes active again.

The bean's perception of its life cycle depends on whether or not it implements a special interface called javax.ejb.SessionSynchronization. This interface defines an additional set of callback methods that notify the bean of its participation in transactions. A bean that implements SessionSynchronization can cache database data across several method calls before making an update. We have not discussed transactions in detail yet, so we will not consider this part of the bean's life cycle until Chapter 14. This section describes the life cycle of stateful session beans that do not implement the SessionSynchronization interface.

The life cycle of a stateful session bean has three states: Does Not Exist, Method-Ready, and Passivated. This sounds a lot like a stateless session bean, but the

---

* Some vendors use pooling with stateful session beans, but that is a proprietary implementation and should not impact the specified life cycle of the stateful session bean.

Method-Ready state is significantly different from the Method-Ready Pool of stateless beans. Figure 12-2 shows the state diagram for stateful session beans.

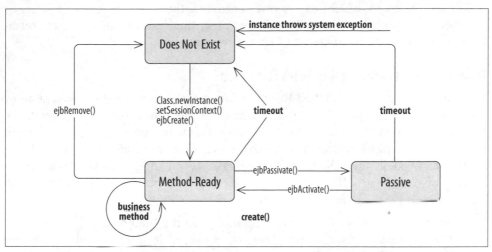

Figure 12-2. Stateful session bean life cycle

Does Not Exist State

When a stateful bean instance is in the Does Not Exist state, it is not an instance in the memory of the system. In other words, it has not been instantiated yet.

Method-Ready State

The Method-Ready state is the state in which the bean instance can service requests from its clients. This section explore the instance's transition into and out of the Method-Ready state.

Transitioning to the Method-Ready state

When a client invokes the create() method on an EJB home of a stateful session bean, the bean's life cycle begins. When the create() method is received by the container, the container invokes newInstance() on the bean class, creating a new instance of the bean. Next, the container invokes setSessionContext() on the instance, handing it its reference to the SessionContext, which it must maintain for life. At this point, the bean instance is assigned to its EJB object. Finally, the container invokes the ejbCreate() method on the instance that matches the create() method invoked by the client. Once ejbCreate() has completed, the container returns the EJB object's reference to the client. The instance is now in the Method-Ready state and is ready to service business methods invoked by the client on the bean's remote reference.

Life in the Method-Ready state

While in the Method-Ready state, the bean instance is free to receive method invocations from the client, which may involve controlling the workflow of other beans or accessing the database directly. During this time, the bean can maintain conversational state and open resources in its instance variables.

Transitioning out of the Method-Ready state

Bean instances leave the Method-Ready state to enter either the Passivated state or the Does Not Exist state. Depending on how the client uses the stateful bean, the EJB container's load, and the passivation algorithm used by the vendor, a bean instance may be passivated (and activated) several times in its life or not at all. If the bean is removed, it enters the Does Not Exist state. A client application can remove a bean by invoking one of the remove() methods on the client API, or the container can choose to remove the bean.

The container can also move the bean instance from the Method-Ready state to the Does Not Exist state if the bean times out. Timeouts are declared at deployment time in a vendor-specific manner. When a timeout occurs in the Method-Ready state, the container may, but is not required to, call the ejbRemove() method. A stateful bean cannot time out while a transaction is in progress.

Passivated State

During the lifetime of a stateful session bean, there may be periods of inactivity when the bean instance is not servicing methods from the client. To conserve resources, the container can passivate the bean instance while it is inactive by preserving its conversational state and evicting the bean instance from memory.

When a stateful bean is passivated, the instance fields are read and then written to the secondary storage associated with the EJB object. When the stateful session bean has been successfully passivated, the instance is evicted from memory; it is destroyed.

When a bean is about to be passivated, its ejbPassivate() method is invoked, alerting the bean instance that it is about to enter the Passivated state. At this time, the bean instance should close any open resources and set all nontransient, nonserializable fields to null. This will prevent problems from occurring when the bean is serialized. Transient fields will simply be ignored.

A bean's conversational state may consist of only primitive values, objects that are serializable, and the following special types:

- EJB 2.0 and 1.1

    ```
    javax.ejb.SessionContext
    javax.ejb.EJBHome (remote home interface types)
    javax.ejb.EJBObject (remote interface types)
    ```

javax.jta.UserTransaction (bean transaction interface)
javax.naming.Context (only when it references the JNDI ENC)

- EJB 2.0 only

    javax.ejb.EJBLocalHome (local home interface types)
    javax.ejb.EJBLocalObject (local interface types)
    References to managed resource factories (e.g., javax.sql.DataSource)

The types in this list (and their subtypes) are handled specially by the passivation mechanism. They do not need to be serializable; they will be maintained through passivation and restored automatically to the bean instance when it is activated.

A bean instance's conversational state is written to secondary storage to preserve it when the instance is passivated and destroyed. Containers can use standard Java serialization to preserve the bean instance, or some other mechanism that achieves the same result. Some vendors, for example, simply read the values of the fields and store them in a cache. The container is required to preserve remote references to other beans with the conversational state. When the bean is activated, the container must restore any bean references automatically. The container must also restore any references to the special types listed earlier.

Fields declared transient will not be preserved when the bean is passivated. Except for the special types listed earlier, all fields that are nontransient and nonserializable must be set to null before the instance is passivated or else the container will destroy the bean instance, making it unavailable for continued use by the client. References to special types must automatically be preserved with the serialized bean instance by the container so that they can be reconstructed when the bean is activated.

When the client makes a request on an EJB object whose bean is passivated, the container activates the instance. This involves deserializing the bean instance and reconstructing the SessionContext reference, bean references, and managed resource factories (EJB 2.0 only) held by the instance before it was passivated. When a bean's conversational state has been successfully restored, the ejbActivate() method is invoked. The bean instance should open any resources that cannot be passivated and initialize the values of any transient fields within the ejbActivate() method. Once ejbActivate() is complete, the bean is back in the Method-Ready state and available to service client requests delegated by the EJB object.

 In EJB 1.1, open resources such as sockets or JDBC connections must be closed whenever the bean is passivated. In stateful session beans, open resources will not be maintained for the life of the bean instance. When a stateful session bean is passivated, any open resource can cause problems with the activation mechanism.

The activation of a bean instance follows the rules of Java serialization. The exception to this is transient fields. In Java serialization, transient fields are set to their default values when an object is deserialized; primitive numbers become zero, Boolean fields false, and object references null. In EJB, transient fields do not have to be set to their initial values; therefore, they can contain arbitrary values when the bean is activated. The values held by transient fields following activation are unpredictable across vendor implementations, so do not depend on them to be initialized. Instead, use ejbActivate() to reset their values.

The container can also move the bean instance from the Passivated state to the Does Not Exist state if the bean times out. When a timeout occurs in the Passivated state, the ejbRemove() method is not invoked.

System exceptions

Whenever a system exception is thrown by a bean method, the container invalidates the EJB object and destroys the bean instance. The bean instance moves directly to the Does Not Exist state and the ejbRemove() method is *not* invoked.

A system exception is any unchecked exception, including EJBException. Checked exceptions thrown from subsystems are usually wrapped in an EJBException and rethrown as system exceptions. A checked exception thrown by a subsystem does not need to be handled this way if the bean can safely recover from the exception. In most cases, however, the subsystem exception should be rethrown as an EJBException.

In EJB 1.1, the java.rmi.RemoteException is also considered a system exception for backward compatibly with EJB 1.0. However, throwing the RemoteException from a bean class method has been deprecated and is discouraged.

CHAPTER 13

Message-Driven Beans

This chapter is divided into two subsections: "JMS as a Resource" and "Message-Driven Beans." The first section describes the Java Message Service (JMS) and its role as a resource that is available to any enterprise bean (session, entity, or message-driven). Readers unfamiliar with JMS should read the first section before proceeding to the second section.

If you're already familiar with JMS, you can skip directly to the second section, which provides an overview of the new enterprise bean type—the message-driven bean. A message-driven bean is an asynchronous bean activated by message delivery. In EJB 2.0, vendors are required to support JMS-based message-driven bean, that receive JMS messages from specific topics or queues and process those messages as they are delivered.

All EJB 2.0 vendors must, by default, support a JMS provider. Most EJB 2.0 vendors have a JMS provider built in, but some may also support other JMS providers. Regardless of how the EJB 2.0 vendor provides the JMS service, having one is a requirement if the vendor expects to support message-driven beans. The advantage of this forced adoption of JMS is that EJB developers can expect to have a working JMS provider on which messages can be both sent and received.

JMS as a Resource

JMS is a standard vendor-neutral API that is part of the J2EE platform and can be used to access enterprise messaging systems. Enterprise messaging systems (a.k.a. message-oriented middleware) facilitate the exchange of messages among software applications over a network. JMS is analogous to JDBC: whereas JDBC is an API that can be used to access many different relational databases, JMS provides the same vendor-independent access to enterprise messaging systems. Many enterprise messaging products currently support JMS, including IBM's MQSeries, BEA's WebLogic JMS service, Sun Microsystems' iPlanet Message Queue, and Progress' SonicMQ, to name a few. Software applications that use the JMS API for sending or receiving messages are portable across brands of JMS vendors.

Java applications that use JMS are called *JMS clients*, and the messaging system that handles routing and delivery of messages is called the *JMS provider*. A *JMS application* is a business system composed of many JMS clients and, generally, one JMS provider.

A JMS client that sends a message is called a *producer*, while a JMS client that receives a message is called a *consumer*. A single JMS client can be both a producer and a consumer. When we use the terms consumer and producer, we mean a JMS client that receives messages or sends messages, respectively.

In EJB, enterprise beans of all types can use JMS to send messages to various destinations. Those messages are consumed by other Java applications or message-driven beans. JMS facilitates sending messages from enterprise beans by using a messaging service, sometimes called a message broker or router. Message brokers have been around for a couple of decades—the oldest and most established being IBM's MQSeries—but JMS is fairly new and is specifically designed to deliver a variety of message types from one Java application to another.

Reimplementing the TravelAgent EJB with JMS

We can modify the TravelAgent EJB developed in Chapter 12 so that it uses JMS to alert some other Java application that a reservation has been made. The following code shows how to modify the bookPassage() method so that the TravelAgent EJB will send a simple text message based on the description information from the TicketDO object:

```
public TicketDO bookPassage(CreditCardDO card, double price)
    throws IncompleteConversationalState {

    if (customer == null || cruise == null || cabin == null) {
        throw new IncompleteConversationalState();
    }
    try {
        ReservationHomeLocal resHome = (ReservationHomeLocal)
            jndiContext.lookup("java:comp/env/ejb/ReservationHomeLocal");

        ReservationLocal reservation =
            resHome.create(customer, cruise, cabin, price, new Date());

        Object ref = jndiContext.lookup
            ("java:comp/env/ejb/ProcessPaymentHomeRemote");

        ProcessPaymentHomeRemote ppHome = (ProcessPaymentHomeRemote)
            PortableRemoteObject.narrow(ref, ProcessPaymentHomeRemote.class);

        ProcessPaymentRemote process = ppHome.create();
        process.byCredit(customer, card, price);

        TicketDO ticket = new TicketDO(customer,cruise,cabin,price);
```

```
        String ticketDescription = ticket.toString();

        TopicConnectionFactory factory = (TopicConnectionFactory)
            jndiContext.lookup("java:comp/env/jms/TopicFactory");

        Topic topic = (Topic)
            jndiContext.lookup("java:comp/env/jms/TicketTopic");

        TopicConnection connect = factory.createTopicConnection();

        TopicSession session = connect.createTopicSession(true,0);

        TopicPublisher publisher = session.createPublisher(topic);

        TextMessage textMsg = session.createTextMessage();
        textMsg.setText(ticketDescription);
        publisher.publish(textMsg);
        connect.close();

        return ticket;
    } catch(Exception e) {
        throw new EJBException(e);
    }
}
```

We needed to add a lot of new code to send a message. However, while it may look a little overwhelming at first, the basics of JMS are not all that complicated.

TopicConnectionFactory and Topic

In order to send a JMS message we need a connection to the JMS provider and a destination address for the message. The connection to the JMS provider is made possible by a JMS connection factory; the destination address of the message is identified by a Topic object. Both the connection factory and the Topic object are obtained from the TravelAgent EJB's JNDI ENC:

```
TopicConnectionFactory factory = (TopicConnectionFactory)
    jndiContext.lookup("java:comp/env/jms/TopicFactory");

Topic topic = (Topic)
    jndiContext.lookup("java:comp/env/jms/TicketTopic");
```

The TopicConnectionFactory in JMS is similar in function to the DataSource in JDBC. Just as the DataSource provides a JDBC connection to a database, the Topic-ConnectionFactory provides a JMS connection to a message router.[*]

The Topic object itself represents a network-independent destination to which the message will be addressed. In JMS, messages are sent to destinations—either topics or

---

[*] This analogy is not perfect. One might also say that the TopicSession is analogous to the DataSource, since both represent transaction-resources connections.

queues—instead of directly to other applications. A topic is analogous to an email list or newsgroup; any application with the proper credentials can receive messages from and send messages to a topic. When a JMS client receives messages from a topic, the client is said to *subscribe* to that topic. JMS decouples applications by allowing them to send messages to each other through a destination, which serves as virtual channel.

JMS also supports another destination type, called a Queue. The difference between topics and queues is explained in more detail later.

TopicConnection and TopicSession

The TopicConnectionFactory is used to create a TopicConnection, which is an actual connection to the JMS provider:

```
TopicConnection connect = factory.createTopicConnection();

TopicSession session = connect.createTopicSession(true,0);
```

Once a TopicConnection is obtained, it can be used to create a TopicSession. A TopicSession allows the Java developer to group the actions of sending and receiving messages. In this case you will need only a single TopicSession. However, having more than one TopicSession object is frequently helpful: if you wish to produce and consume messages using multithreading, a different Session needs to be created by each thread accessing that thread. This is because JMS Session objects use a single-threaded model, which prohibits concurrent accessing of a single Session from multiple threads. The thread that creates a TopicSession is usually the thread that uses that Session's producers and consumers (i.e., TopicPublisher and TopicSubscriber objects). If you wish to produce and consume messages using multithreading, a different Session should be created and used by each thread.

The createTopicSession() method has two parameters:

```
createTopicSession(boolean transacted, int acknowledgeMode)
```

According to the EJB 2.0 specification, these arguments are ignored at runtime because the EJB container manages the transaction and acknowledgment mode of any JMS resource obtained from the JNDI ENC. The specification recommends that developers use the arguments true for transacted and 0 for acknowlegeMode, but since they are supposed to be ignored, it should not matter what you use. Unfortunately, not all vendors adhere to this part of the specification. Some vendors ignore these parameters while some do not. Consult your vendor's documentation to determine the proper values for these parameters in both container-managed and bean-managed transactions.

It's good programming practice to close a TopicConnection after its been used, in order to conserve resources:

```
TopicConnection connect = factory.createTopicConnection();
...

connect.close();
```

TopicPublisher

The TopicSession is used to create a TopicPublisher, which sends messages from the TravelAgent EJB to the destination specified by the Topic object. Any JMS clients that subscribe to that topic will receive a copy of the message:

```
TopicPublisher publisher = session.createPublisher(topic);

TextMessage textMsg = session.createTextMessage();
textMsg.setText(ticketDescription);
publisher.publish(textMsg);
```

Message types

In JMS, a message is a Java object with two parts: a header and a message body. The header is composed of delivery information and metadata, while the message body carries the application data, which can take several forms: text, serializable objects, byte streams, etc. The JMS API defines several message types (TextMessage, MapMessage, ObjectMessage, and others) and provides methods for delivering messages to and receiving messages from other applications.

For example, we can change the TravelAgent EJB so that it sends a MapMessage instead of a TextMessage:

```
TicketDO ticket = new TicketDO(customer,cruise,cabin,price);
...
TopicPublisher publisher = session.createPublisher(topic);

MapMessage mapMsg = session.createTextMessage();
mapMsg.setInt("CustomerID", ticket.customerID.intValue());
mapMsg.setInt("CruiseID", ticket.cruiseID.intValue());
mapMsg.setInt("CabinID", ticket.cabinID.intValue());
mapMsg.setDouble("Price", ticket.price);

publisher.publish(mapMsg);
```

The attributes of the MapMessage (CustomerID, CruiseID, CabinID, and Price) can be accessed by name from those JMS clients that receive it.

As an alternative, the TravelAgent EJB could be modified to use the ObjectMessage type, which would allow us to send the entire TicketDO object as the message using Java serialization:

```
TicketDO ticket = new TicketDO(customer,cruise,cabin,price);
...
TopicPublisher publisher = session.createPublisher(topic);

ObjectMessage objectMsg = session.createObjectMessage();
ObjectMsg.setObject(ticket);

publisher.publish(objectMsg);
```

In addition to the TextMessage, MapMessage, and ObjectMessage, JMS provides two other message types: StreamMessage and BytesMessage. StreamMessage can take the contents of an I/O stream as its payload. BytesMessage can take any array of bytes, which it treats as opaque data.

XML deployment descriptor

When a JMS resource is used, it must be declared in the bean's XML deployment descriptor, in a manner similar to the JDBC resource used by the Ship EJB in Chapter 10:

```
<enterprise-beans>
    <session>
        <ejb-name>TravelAgentBean</ejb-name>
        ...
        <resource-ref>
            <res-ref-name>jms/TopicFactory</res-ref-name>
            <res-type>javax.jms.TopicConnectionFactory</res-type>
            <res-auth>Container</res-auth>
        </resource-ref>
        <resource-ref>
            <res-ref-name>jdbc/titanDB</res-ref-name>
            <res-type>javax.sql.DataSource</res-type>
            <res-auth>Container</res-auth>
        </resource-ref>
        <resource-env-ref>
            <resource-env-ref-name>jms/TicketTopic</resource-env-ref-name>
            <resource-env-ref-type>javax.jms.Topic</resource-env-ref-type>
        </resource-env-ref>
        ...
    </session>
```

The <resource-ref> for the JMS TopicConnectionFactory is similar to the <resource-ref> declaration for the JDBC DataSource: it declares the JNDI ENC name, interface type, and authorization protocol. In addition to the <resource-ref>, the TravelAgent EJB must also declare the <resource-env-ref>, which lists any "administered objects" associated with a <resource-ref> entry. In this case, we declare the Topic used for sending a ticket message. At deployment time the deployer will map the JMS TopicConnectionFactory and Topic declared by the <resource-ref> and <resource-env-ref> elements to a JMS factory and topic.

JMS application client

To get a better idea of how JMS is used, we can create a Java application whose sole purpose is receiving and processing reservation messages. We will develop a very simple JMS client that simply prints a description of each ticket as it receives the messages. We'll assume that the TravelAgent EJB is using the TextMessage to send a description of the ticket to the JMS clients. The following code shows how the JMS application client might look:

```
import javax.jms.Message;
import javax.jms.TextMessage;
import javax.jms.TopicConnectionFactory;
```

```java
import javax.jms.TopicConnection;
import javax.jms.TopicSession;
import javax.jms.Topic;
import javax.jms.Session;
import javax.jms.TopicSubscriber;
import javax.jms.JMSException;
import javax.naming.InitialContext;


public class JmsClient_1 implements javax.jms.MessageListener {

    public static void main(String [] args) throws Exception {

        if(args.length != 2)
            throw new Exception("Wrong number of arguments");

        new JmsClient_1(args[0], args[1]);

        while(true){Thread.sleep(10000);}

    }

    public JmsClient_1(String factoryName, String topicName) throws Exception {

        InitialContext jndiContext = getInitialContext();

        TopicConnectionFactory factory = (TopicConnectionFactory)
            jndiContext.lookup("TopicFactoryNameGoesHere");

        Topic topic = (Topic)jndiContext.lookup("TopicNameGoesHere");

        TopicConnection connect = factory.createTopicConnection();

        TopicSession session =
            connect.createTopicSession(false,Session.AUTO_ACKNOWLEDGE);

        TopicSubscriber subscriber = session.createSubscriber(topic);

        subscriber.setMessageListener(this);

        connect.start();
    }

    public void onMessage(Message message) {
        try {

            TextMessage textMsg = (TextMessage)message;
            String text = textMsg.getText();
            System.out.println("\n RESERVATION RECIEVED:\n"+text);

        } catch(JMSException jmsE) {
            jmsE.printStackTrace();
        }
    }
```

```
        public static InitialContext getInitialContext() {
            // create vendor-specific JNDI context here
        }
    }
```

The constructor of JmsClient_1 obtains the TopicConnectionFactory and Topic from the JNDI InitialContext. This context is created with vendor-specific properties so that the client can connect to the same JMS provider as the one used by the Travel-Agent EJB. For example, the getInitialContext() method for the WebLogic application server would be coded as follows:[*]

```
    public static InitialContext getInitialContext() {
        Properties env = new Properties();
        env.put(Context.SECURITY_PRINCIPAL, "guest");
        env.put(Context.SECURITY_CREDENTIALS, "guest");
        env.put(Context.INITIAL_CONTEXT_FACTORY,
            "weblogic.jndi.WLInitialContextFactory");
        env.put(Context.PROVIDER_URL, "t3://localhost:7001");
        return new InitialContext(env);
    }
```

Once the client has the TopicConnectionFactory and Topic, it creates a Topic-Connection and a TopicSession in the same way as the TravelAgent EJB. The main difference is that the TopicSession object is used to create a TopicSubscriber instead of a TopicPublisher. The TopicSubscriber is designed specifically to process incoming messages that are published to its specified Topic:

```
    TopicSession session =
        connect.createTopicSession(false,Session.AUTO_ACKNOWLEDGE);

    TopicSubscriber subscriber = session.createSubscriber(topic);

    subscriber.setMessageListener(this);

    connect.start();
```

The TopicSubscriber can receive messages directly, or it can delegate the processing of the messages to a javax.jms.MessageListener. We chose to have JmsClient_1 implement the MessageListener interface so that it can process the messages itself. MessageListener objects implement a single method, onMessage(), which is invoked every time a new message is sent to the subscriber's topic. In this case, every time the TravelAgent EJB sends a reservation message to the topic, the JMS client will have its onMessage() method invoked so that it can receive a copy of the message and process it:

```
    public void onMessage(Message message) {
        try {
```

---

[*] JNDI also allows the properties to be set in a *jndi.properties* file, which contains the property values for the InitialContext and can be discovered dynamically at runtime. In this book, I chose to set the properties explicitly.

```
        TextMessage textMsg = (TextMessage)message;
        String text = textMsg.getText();
        System.out.println("\n RESERVATION RECIEVED:\n"+text);

    } catch(JMSException jmsE) {
        jmsE.printStackTrace();
    }
}
```

📖 Workbook Exercise 13.1, JMS as a Resource

JMS Is Asynchronous

One of the principal advantages of JMS messaging is that it's *asynchronous*. In other words, a JMS client can send a message without having to wait for a reply. Contrast this flexibility with the synchronous messaging of Java RMI. RMI is an excellent choice for assembling transactional components, but is too restrictive for some uses. Each time a client invokes a bean's method it blocks the current thread until the method completes execution. This lock-step processing makes the client dependent on the availability of the EJB server, resulting in a tight coupling between the client and enterprise bean.

In JMS, a client sends messages asynchronously to a destination (topic or queue), from which other JMS clients can also receive messages. When a JMS client sends a message, it doesn't wait for a reply; it sends the message to a router, which is responsible for forwarding it to other clients. Clients sending messages are decoupled from the clients receiving them; senders are not dependent on the availability of receivers.

The limitations of RMI make JMS an attractive alternative for communicating with other applications. Using the standard JNDI environment naming context, an enterprise bean can obtain a JMS connection to a JMS provider and use it to deliver asynchronous messages to other Java applications. For example, a TravelAgent session bean can use JMS to notify other applications that a reservation has been processed, as shown in Figure 13-1.

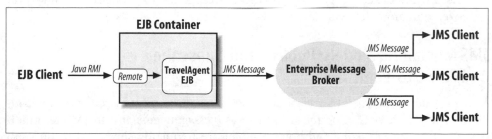

Figure 13-1. Using JMS with the TravelAgent EJB

In this case, the applications receiving JMS messages from the TravelAgent EJB may be message-driven beans, other Java applications in the enterprise, or applications in other organizations that benefit from being notified that a reservation has been processed. Examples might include business partners who share customer information or an internal marketing application that adds customers to a catalog mailing list.

JMS enables the enterprise bean to send messages without blocking. The enterprise bean doesn't know who will receive the message, because it delivers the message to a virtual channel (destination) and not directly to another application. Applications can choose to receive messages from that virtual channel and receive notification of new reservations.

One interesting aspect of enterprise messaging is that the decoupled asynchronous nature of the technology means that the transactions and security contexts of the sender are not propagated to the receiver of the message. For example, when the TravelAgent EJB sends the ticket message, it may be authenticated by the JMS provider but its security context won't be propagated to the JMS client that received the message. When a JMS client receives the message from the TravelAgent EJB, it will have no idea about the security context under which the message was sent. This is how it should be, because the sender and receiver often operate in different environments with different security domains.

Similarly, transactions are never propagated from the sender to the receiver. For one thing, the sender has no idea who the receivers of the message will be. If the message is sent to a topic there could be one receiver or thousands; managing a distributed transaction under such ambiguous circumstances is not tenable. In addition, the clients receiving the message may not get it for a long time after it is sent because they are temporarily down or otherwise unable to receive messages. One key strength of JMS is that it allows senders and receivers to be temporally decoupled. Transactions are designed to be executed quickly because they lock up resources; the possibility of a long transaction with an unpredictable end is also not tenable.

A JMS client can, however, have a distributed transaction with the JMS provider so that it manages the send or receive operation in the context of a transaction. For example, if the TravelAgent EJB's transaction fails for any reason, the JMS provider will discard the ticket message sent by the TravelAgent EJB. Transactions and JMS are covered in more detail in Chapter 14.

JMS Messaging Models: Publish-and-Subscribe and Point-to-Point

JMS provides two types of messaging models: *publish-and-subscribe* and *point-to-point*. The JMS specification refers to these as *messaging domains*. In JMS terminology, publish-and-subscribe and point-to-point are frequently shortened to pub/sub and p2p (or PTP), respectively. This chapter uses both the long and short forms throughout.

In the simplest sense, publish-and-subscribe is intended for a one-to-many broadcast of messages, while point-to-point is intended for one-to-one delivery of messages (see Figure 13-2).

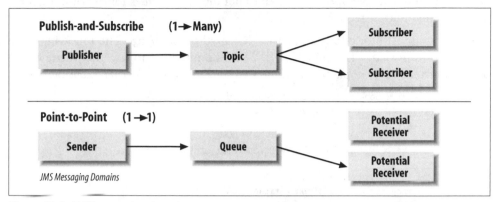

Figure 13-2. JMS messaging domains

Publish-and-subscribe

In publish-and-subscribe messaging, one producer can send a message to many consumers through a virtual channel called a *topic*. Consumers can choose to *subscribe* to a topic. Any messages addressed to a topic are delivered to all the topic's consumers. Every consumer receives a copy of each message. The pub/sub messaging model is by and large a push-based model, where messages are automatically broadcast to consumers without them having to request or poll the topic for new messages.

In the pub/sub messaging model, the producer sending the message is not dependent on the consumers receiving the message. Optionally, JMS clients that use pub/sub can establish durable subscriptions that allow consumers to disconnect and later reconnect and collect messages that were published while they were disconnected.

The TravelAgent EJB in this chapter uses the pub/sub programming model with a Topic object as a destination.

Point-to-point

The point-to-point messaging model allows JMS clients to send and receive messages both synchronously and asynchronously via virtual channels known as *queues*. The p2p messaging model has traditionally been a pull- or polling-based model, where messages are requested from the queue instead of being pushed to the client automatically.*

---

* The JMS specification does not specifically state how the p2p and pub/sub models must be implemented. Either one may use push or pull, but at least conceptually pub/sub is push and p2p is pull.

A queue may have multiple receivers, but only one receiver may receive each message. As shown earlier in Figure 13-2, the JMS provider will take care of doling out the messages among JMS clients, ensuring that each message is consumed by only one JMS client. The JMS specification does not dictate the rules for distributing messages among multiple receivers.

The messaging API for p2p is similar to that used for pub/sub. The following code listing shows how the TravelAgent EJB could be modified to use the queue-based p2p API instead of the topic-based pub/sub model used in the earlier example:

```
public TicketDO bookPassage(CreditCardDO card, double price)
    throws IncompleteConversationalState {
    ...

        TicketDO ticket = new TicketDO(customer,cruise,cabin,price);


        String ticketDescription = ticket.toString();

        QueueConnectionFactory factory = (QueueConnectionFactory)
            jndiContext.lookup("java:comp/env/jms/QueueFactory");

        Queue queue = (Queue)
            jndiContext.lookup("java:comp/env/jms/TicketQueue");

        QueueConnection connect = factory.createQueueConneciton();

        QueueSession session = connect.createQueueSession(true,0);

        QueueSender sender = session.createSender(queue);

        TextMessage textMsg = session.createTextMessage();
        textMsg.setText(ticketDescription);
        sender.send(textMsg);
        connect.close();

        return ticket;
    } catch(Exception e) {
        throw new EJBException(e);
    }
}
```

Which messaging model should you use?

The rationale behind the two models lies in the origin of the JMS specification. JMS started out as a way of providing a common API for accessing existing messaging systems. At the time of its conception, some messaging vendors had a p2p model and some had a pub/sub model. Hence JMS needed to provide an API for both models to gain wide industry support. The JMS 1.0.2 specification does not require a JMS provider to support both models. EJB 2.0 vendors, however, are required to support both messaging models.

Almost anything that can be done with the pub/sub model can be done with point-to-point, and vice versa. An analogy can be drawn to developers' programming language preferences. In theory, any application that can be written with Pascal can also be written with C. Anything that can be written in C++ can also be written in Java. In some cases it comes down to a matter of preference, or which model you are already familiar with.

In most cases, the decision about which model to use depends on the distinct merits of each model. With pub/sub, any number of subscribers can be listening on a topic, and they will all receive copies of the same message. The publisher may not care if everybody is listening, or even if nobody is listening. For example, consider a publisher that broadcasts stock quotes. If any particular subscriber is not currently connected and misses out on a great quote, the publisher is not concerned. In contrast, a point-to-point session is likely to be intended for a one-on-one conversation with a specific application at the other end. In this scenario, every message really matters.

The range and variety of the data the messages represent can be a factor as well. Using pub/sub, messages are dispatched to the consumers based on filtering that is provided through the use of specific topics. Even when messaging is being used to establish a one-on-one conversation with another known application, it can be advantageous to use pub/sub with multiple topics to segregate different kinds of messages. Each kind of message can be dealt with separately through its own unique consumer and onMessage() listener.

Point-to-point is more convenient when you want only a particular receiver to process a given message once. This is perhaps the most critical difference between the two models: p2p guarantees that only one consumer processes each message. This is extremely important when messages need to be processed separately but in tandem.

Entity and Session Beans Should Not Receive Messages

JmsClient_1 was designed to consume messages produced by the TravelAgent EJB. Can another entity or session bean receive those messages also? The answer is yes, but it's a really bad idea.

Entity and session beans respond to Java RMI calls from EJB clients and cannot be programmed to respond to JMS messages as do message-driven beans. That means it's impossible to write a session or entity bean that will be driven by incoming messages. The inability to make EJBs respond to JMS messages was why message-driven beans were introduced in EJB 2.0. Message-driven beans are designed to consume messages from topics and queues. They fill an important niche; we'll learn more about how to program them in the next section.

It is possible to develop an entity or session bean that can consume a JMS message from a business method, but the method must be called by an EJB client first. For example, when the business method on the Hypothetical EJB is called, it sets up a JMS session and then attempts to read a message from a queue:

```
public class HypotheticalBean implements javax.ejb.SessionBean {
    InitialContext jndiContext;

    public String businessMethod() {

        try{

            QueueConnectionFactory factory = (QueueConnectionFactory)
                jndiContext.lookup("java:comp/env/jms/QueueFactory");

            Queue topic = (Queue)
                jndiContext.lookup("java:comp/env/jms/Queue");

            QueueConnection connect = factory.createQueueConneciton();
            QueueSession session = connect.createQueueSession(true,0);
            QueueReceiver receiver = session.createReceiver(queue);

            TextMessage textMsg = (TextMessage)receiver.receive();

            connect.close();

            return textMsg.getText();

        } catch(Exception e) {
            throws new EJBException(e);
        }


    }
    ...
}
```

The QueueReceiver, which is a message consumer, is used to proactively fetch a message from the queue. While this has been programmed correctly, it is a dangerous operation because a call to the QueueReceiver.receive() method blocks the thread until a message becomes available. If a message is never delivered to the receiver's queue, the thread will be blocked indefinitely! In other words, if no one ever sends a message to the queue, the QueueReceiver will just sit there waiting forever.

To be fair, there are other receive() methods that are less dangerous. For example, receive(long timeout) allows you to specify a time after which the QueueReceiver should stop blocking the thread and give up waiting for a message. There is also receiveNoWait(), which checks for a message and returns null if there are none waiting, thus avoiding a prolonged thread block.

While the alternative receive() methods are much safer, this is still a dangerous operation to perform. There is no guarantee that the less risky receive() methods will perform as expected, and the risk of programmer error (e.g., using the wrong receive() method) is too great. Besides, the message-driven bean provides you with a powerful and simple enterprise bean that is specially designed to consume JMS messages. This book recommends that you do not attempt to consume messages from entity or session beans.

Learning More About JMS

JMS (and enterprise messaging in general) represents a powerful paradigm in distributed computing. In my opinion, the Java Message Service is as important as Enterprise JavaBeans itself and should be well understood before it is used in development.

While this chapter has provided a brief overview of JMS, it has presented you only with enough material to prepare you for the discussion of message-driven beans in the next section. JMS has a cornucopia of features and details that are simply too extensive to cover in this book. To understand JMS and how it is used, you will need to study it independently.[*] Taking the time to learn JMS is well worth the effort.

Message-Driven Beans

Message-driven beans (MDBs) are stateless, server-side, transaction-aware components for processing asynchronous JMS messages. Newly introduced in EJB 2.0, message-driven beans process messages delivered via the Java Message Service.

Message-driven beans can receive JMS messages and process them. While a message-driven bean is responsible for processing messages, its container takes care of automatically managing the component's entire environment, including transactions, security, resources, concurrency, and message acknowledgment.

One of the most important aspects of message-driven beans is that they can consume and process messages concurrently. This capability provides a significant advantage over traditional JMS clients, which must be custom-built to manage resources, transactions, and security in a multithreaded environment. The message-driven bean containers provided by EJB manage concurrency automatically, so the bean developer can focus on the business logic of processing the messages. The MDB can receive hundreds of JMS messages from various applications and process them all at the same time, because numerous instances of the MDB can execute concurrently in the container.

A message-driven bean is a complete enterprise bean, just like a session or entity bean, but there are some important differences. While a message-driven bean has a bean class and XML deployment descriptor, it does not have component interfaces. The component interfaces are absent because the message-driven bean is not accessible via the Java RMI API; it responds only to asynchronous messages.

---

[*] For a detailed treatment of JMS, see *Java Message Service* by Richard Monson-Haefel and David Chappell (O'Reilly).

The ReservationProcessor EJB

The ReservationProcessor EJB is a message-driven bean that receives JMS messages notifying it of new reservations. The ReservationProcessor EJB is an automated version of the TravelAgent EJB that processes reservations sent via JMS by other travel organizations. It requires no human intervention; it is completely automated.

The JMS messages that notify the ReservationProcessor EJB of new reservations might come from another application in the enterprise or an application in some other organization. When the ReservationProcessor EJB receives a message, it creates a new Reservation EJB (adding it to the database), processes the payment using the ProcessPayment EJB, and sends out a ticket. This process is illustrated in Figure 13-3.

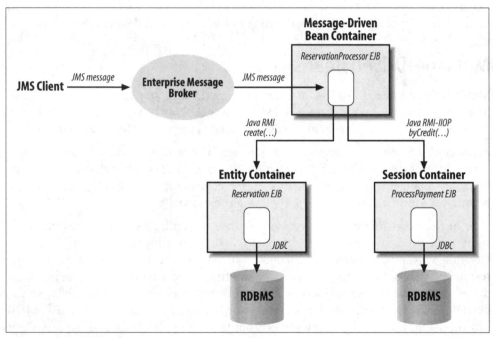

Figure 13-3. The ReservationProcessor EJB processing reservations

The ReservationProcessorBean Class

Here is a partial definition of the ReservationProcessorBean class. Some methods are left empty; they will be filled in later. Notice that the onMessage() method contains the business logic of the bean class; it is similar to the business logic developed in the bookPassage() method of the TravelAgent EJB in Chapter 12. Here's the code:

```
package com.titan.reservationprocessor;

import javax.jms.Message;
```

```java
import javax.jms.MapMessage;
import com.titan.customer.*;
import com.titan.cruise.*;
import com.titan.cabin.*;
import com.titan.reservation.*;
import com.titan.processpayment.*;
import com.titan.travelagent.*;
import java.util.Date;

public class ReservationProcessorBean implements javax.ejb.MessageDrivenBean,
    javax.jms.MessageListener {

    MessageDrivenContext ejbContext;
    Context jndiContext;

    public void setMessageDrivenContext(MessageDrivenContext mdc) {
        ejbContext = mdc;
        try {
            jndiContext = new InitialContext();
        } catch(NamingException ne) {
            throw new EJBException(ne);
        }
    }

    public void ejbCreate() {}

    public void onMessage(Message message) {
        try {
            MapMessage reservationMsg = (MapMessage)message;

            Integer customerPk = (Integer)reservationMsg.getObject("CustomerID");
            Integer cruisePk = (Integer)reservationMsg.getObject("CruiseID");
            Integer cabinPk = (Integer)reservationMsg.getObject("CabinID");

            double price = reservationMsg.getDouble("Price");

            // get the credit card
            Date expirationDate =
                new Date(reservationMsg.getLong("CreditCardExpDate"));
            String cardNumber = reservationMsg.getString("CreditCardNum");
            String cardType = reservationMsg.getString("CreditCardType");
            CreditCardDO card = new CreditCardDO(cardNumber,
                expirationDate, cardType);

            CustomerRemote customer = getCustomer(customerPk);
            CruiseLocal cruise = getCruise(cruisePk);
            CabinLocal cabin = getCabin(cabinPk);

            ReservationHomeLocal resHome = (ReservationHomeLocal)
                jndiContext.lookup("java:comp/env/ejb/ReservationHomeLocal");

            ReservationLocal reservation =
                resHome.create(customer, cruise, cabin, price, new Date());
```

```
                    Object ref = jndiContext.lookup
                        ("java:comp/env/ejb/ProcessPaymentHomeRemote");

                    ProcessPaymentHomeRemote ppHome = (ProcessPaymentHomeRemote)
                        PortableRemoteObject.narrow(ref, ProcessPaymentHomeRemote.class);

                    ProcessPaymentRemote process = ppHome.create();
                    process.byCredit(customer, card, price);

                    TicketDO ticket = new TicketDO(customer,cruise,cabin,price);

                    deliverTicket(reservationMsg, ticket);

                } catch(Exception e) {
                    throw new EJBException(e);
                }
            }

            public void deliverTicket(MapMessage reservationMsg, TicketDO ticket) {

                // send it to the proper destination
            }
            public CustomerRemote getCustomer(Integer key)
                throws NamingException, RemoteException, FinderException {
                // get a remote reference to the Customer EJB
            }
            public CruiseLocal getCruise(Integer key)
                throws NamingException, FinderException {
                // get a local reference to the Cruise EJB
            }
            public CabinLocal getCabin(Integer key)
                throws NamingException, FinderException {
                // get a local reference to the Cabin EJB
            }

            public void ejbRemove() {
                try {
                    jndiContext.close();
                    ejbContext = null;
                } catch(NamingException ne) { /* do nothing */ }
            }
        }
```

MessageDrivenBean interface

The message-driven bean class is required to implement the javax.ejb.
MessageDrivenBean interface, which defines callback methods similar to those in
entity and session beans. Here is the definition of the MessageDrivenBean interface:

```
package javax.ejb;

public interface MessageDrivenBean extends javax.ejb.EnterpriseBean {
```

```
        public void setMessageDrivenContext(MessageDrivenContext context)
            throws EJBException;
        public void ejbRemove() throws EJBException;
    }
```

The setMessageDrivenContext() method is called at the beginning of the MDB's life cycle and provides the MDB instance with a reference to its MessageDrivenContext:

```
MessageDrivenContext ejbContext;
Context jndiContext;

public void setMessageDrivenContext(MessageDrivenContext mdc) {
    ejbContext = mdc;
    try {
        jndiContext = new InitialContext();
    } catch(NamingException ne) {
        throw new EJBException(ne);
    }
}
```

The setMessageDrivenContext() method in the ReservationProcessorBean class sets the ejbContext instance field to the MessageDrivenContext, which was passed into the method. It also obtains a reference to the JNDI ENC, which it stores in the jndiContext. MDBs may have instance fields that are similar to a stateless session bean's instance fields. These instance fields are carried with the MDB instance for its lifetime and may be reused every time it processes a new message. Unlike stateful session beans, MDBs do not have conversational state and are not specific to a single JMS client. MDB instances are used to processes messages from many different JMS clients and are tied to a specific topic or queue from which they receive messages, not to a specific JMS client. They are stateless in the same way that stateless session beans are stateless.

ejbRemove() provides the MDB instance with an opportunity to clean up any resources it stores in its instance fields. In this case, we use it to close the JNDI context and set the ejbContext field to null. These operations are not absolutely necessary, but they illustrate the kind of operation that an ejbRemove() method might do. Note that ejbRemove() is called at the end of the MDB's life cycle, before it is garbage collected. It may not be called if the EJB server hosting the MDB fails or if an EJBException is thrown by the MDB instance in one of its other methods. When an EJBException (or any RuntimeException type) is thrown by any method in the MDB instance, the instance is immediately removed from memory and the transaction is rolled back.

MessageDrivenContext

The MessageDrivenContext simply extends the EJBContext; it does not add any new methods. The EJBContext is defined as:

```
package javax.ejb;
public interface EJBContext {
```

```
        // transaction methods
        public javax.transaction.UserTransaction getUserTransaction()
            throws java.lang.IllegalStateException;
        public boolean getRollbackOnly() throws java.lang.IllegalStateException;
        public void setRollbackOnly() throws java.lang.IllegalStateException;

        // EJB home methods
        public EJBHome getEJBHome();
        public EJBLocalHome getEJBLocalHome();

        // security methods
        public java.security.Principal getCallerPrincipal();
        public boolean isCallerInRole(java.lang.String roleName);

        // deprecated methods
        public java.security.Identity getCallerIdentity();
        public boolean isCallerInRole(java.security.Identity role);
        public java.util.Properties getEnvironment();

    }
```

Only the transactional methods the `MessageDrivenContext` inherits from `EJBContext` are available to message-driven beans. The home methods—`getEJBHome()` and `getEJBLocalHome()`—throw a `RuntimeException` if invoked, because MDBs do not have home interfaces or EJB home objects. The security methods— `getCallerPrincipal()` and `isCallerInRole()`—also throw a `RuntimeException` if invoked on a `MessageDrivenContext`. When an MDB services a JMS message there is no "caller," so there is no security context to be obtained from the caller. Remember that JMS is asynchronous and doesn't propagate the sender's security context to the receiver—that wouldn't make sense, since senders and receivers tend to operate in different environments.

MDBs usually execute in a container-initiated or bean-initiated transaction, so the transaction methods allow the MDB to manage its context. The transaction context is not propagated from the JMS sender, but rather is either initiated by the container or by the bean explicitly using `javax.jta.UserTransaction`. The transaction methods in the `EJBContext` are explained in more detail in Chapter 14.

Message-driven beans also have access to their own JNDI environment naming contexts (ENCs), which provide the MDB instances access to environment entries, other enterprise beans, and resources. For example, the ReservationProcessor EJB takes advantage of the JNDI ENC to obtain references to the Customer, Cruise, Cabin, Reservation, and ProcessPayment EJBs as well as a JMS `QueueConnectionFactory` and Queue for sending out tickets.

MessageListener interface

In addition to the `MessageDrivenBean` interface, MDBs implement the `javax.jms.MessageListener` interface, which defines the `onMessage()` method; bean developers implement this method to process JMS messages received by a bean. It's in the onMessage() method that the bean processes the JMS message:

```
package javax.jms;
public interface MessageListener {
    public void onMessage(Message message);
}
```

It's interesting to consider why the MDB implements the MessageListener interface separately from the MessageDrivenBean interface. Why not just put the onMessage() method, MessageListener's only method, in the MessageDrivenBean interface so that there is only one interface for the MDB class to implement? This was the solution taken by an early proposed version of EJB 2.0. However, it was quickly realized that message-driven beans could, in the future, process messages from other types of systems, not just JMS. To make the MDB open to other messaging systems, it was decided that it should implement the javax.jms.MessageListener interface separately, thus separating the concept of the message-driven bean from the types of messages it can process. In a future version of the specification, other types of MDB might be available for technologies such as SMTP (email) or JAXM (Java API for XML Messaging) for ebXML. These technologies will use methods other than onMessage(), which is specific to JMS.

The onMessage( ) method: Workflow and integration for B2B

The onMessage() method is where all the business logic goes. As messages arrive, they are passed to the MDB by the container via the onMessage() method. When the method returns, the MDB is ready to process a new message.

In the ReservationProcessor EJB, the onMessage() method extracts information about a reservation from a MapMessage and uses that information to create a reservation in the system:

```
public void onMessage(Message message) {
    try {
        MapMessage reservationMsg = (MapMessage)message;

        Integer customerPk = (Integer)reservationMsg.getObject("CustomerID");
        Integer cruisePk = (Integer)reservationMsg.getObject("CruiseID");
        Integer cabinPk = (Integer)reservationMsg.getObject("CabinID");

        double price = reservationMsg.getDouble("Price");

        // get the credit card

        Date expirationDate =
            new Date(reservationMsg.getLong("CreditCardExpDate"));
        String cardNumber = reservationMsg.getString("CreditCardNum");
        String cardType = reservationMsg.setString("CreditCardType");
        CreditCardDO card = new CreditCardDO(cardNumber,
            expirationDate, cardType);
```

JMS is frequently used as an integration point for business-to-business applications, so it's easy to imagine the reservation message coming from one of Titan's business partners (perhaps a third-party processor or branch travel agency).

The ReservationProcessor EJB needs to access the Customer, Cruise, and Cabin EJBs in order to process the reservation. The MapMessage contains the primary keys for these entities; the ReservationProcessor EJB uses helper methods (getCustomer(), getCruise(), and getCabin()) to look up the entity beans and obtain EJB object references to them:

```
public void onMessage(Message message) {
    ...
    CustomerRemote customer = getCustomer(customerPk);
    CruiseLocal cruise = getCruise(cruisePk);
    CabinLocal cabin = getCabin(cabinPk);
    ...
}

public CustomerRemote getCustomer(Integer key)
    throws NamingException, RemoteException, FinderException {

    Object ref = jndiContext.lookup("java:comp/env/ejb/CustomerHomeRemote");
    CustomerHomeRemote home = (CustomerHomeRemote)
        PortableRemoteObject.narrow(ref, CustomerHomeRemote.class);
    CustomerRemote customer = home.findByPrimaryKey(key);
    return customer;
}
public CruiseLocal getCruise(Integer key)
    throws NamingException, FinderException {

    CruiseHomeLocal home = (CruiseHomeLocal)
        jndiContext.lookup("java:comp/env/ejb/CruiseHomeLocal");
    CruiseLocal cruise = home.findByPrimaryKey(key);
    return cruise;
}
public CabinLocal getCabin(Integer key)
    throws NamingException, FinderException{

    CabinHomeLocal home = (CabinHomeLocal)
        jndiContext.lookup("java:comp/env/ejb/CabinHomeLocal");
    CabinLocal cabin = home.findByPrimaryKey(key);
    return cabin;
}
```

Once the information is extracted from the MapMessage, it is used to create a reservation and process the payment. This is basically the same workflow that was used by the TravelAgent EJB in Chapter 12. A Reservation EJB is created that represents the reservation itself, and a ProcessPayment EJB is created to process the credit card payment:

```
ReservationHomeLocal resHome = (ReservationHomeLocal)
    jndiContext.lookup("java:comp/env/ejb/ReservationHomeLocal");
```

```
ReservationLocal reservation =
    resHome.create(customer, cruise, cabin, price, new Date());

Object ref = jndiContext.lookup("java:comp/env/ejb/ProcessPaymentHomeRemote");

ProcessPaymentHomeRemote ppHome = (ProcessPaymentHomeRemote)
    PortableRemoteObject.narrow (ref, ProcessPaymentHomeRemote.class);

ProcessPaymentRemote process = ppHome.create();
process.byCredit(customer, card, price);

TicketDO ticket = new TicketDO(customer,cruise,cabin,price);

deliverTicket(reservationMsg, ticket);
```

This illustrates that, like a session bean, the MDB can access any other entity or session bean and use that bean to complete a task. In this way, the MDB fulfills its role as an integration point in B2B application scenarios. MDB can manage a process and interact with other beans as well as resources. For example, it is commonplace for an MDB to use JDBC to access a database based on the contents of the message it is processing.

Sending messages from a message-driven bean

MDB can also send messages using JMS. The deliverTicket() method sends the ticket information to a destination defined by the sending JMS client:

```
public void deliverTicket(MapMessage reservationMsg, TicketDO ticket)
    throws NamingException, JMSException{

    Queue queue = (Queue)reservationMsg.getJMSReplyTo();

    QueueConnectionFactory factory = (QueueConnectionFactory)
        jndiContext.lookup("java:comp/env/jms/QueueFactory");

    QueueConnection connect = factory.createQueueConneciton();

    QueueSession session = connect.createQueueSession(true,0);

    QueueSender sender = session.createSender(queue);

    ObjectMessage message = session.createObjectMessage();
    message.setObject(ticket);

    sender.send(message);

    connect.close();

}
```

As stated earlier, every message type has two parts: a message header and a message body (a.k.a. payload). The message header contains routing information and may also have properties for message filtering and other attributes, including a JMS-ReplyTo attribute. When a JMS client sends a message, it may set the JMSReplyTo attribute to be any destination accessible to its JMS provider.* In the case of the reservation message, the sender set the JMSReplyTo attribute to the queue to which the resulting ticket should be sent. Another application can access this queue to read tickets and distribute them to customers or store the information in the sender's database.

You can also use the JMSReplyTo address to report business errors that occur while processing the message. For example, if the Cabin is already reserved, the ReservationProcessor EJB might send an error message to the JMSReplyTo queue explaining that the reservation could not be processed. Including this type of error handling is left as an exercise for the reader.

XML deployment descriptor

MDBs have XML deployment descriptors, just like entity and session beans. They can be deployed alone or, more often than not, together with other enterprise beans. For example, the ReservationProcessor EJB would have to be deployed in the same JAR using the same XML deployment descriptor as the Customer, Cruise, and Cabin beans if it's going to use their local interfaces.

Here's the XML deployment descriptor that defines the ReservationProcessor EJB. This deployment descriptor also defines the Customer, Cruise, Cabin, and other beans, but these are left out here for brevity:

```
<enterprise-beans>
    ...
    <message-driven>
        <ejb-name>ReservationProcessorEJB</ejb-name>
        <ejb-class>
            com.titan.reservationprocessor.ReservationProcessorBean
        </ejb-class>
        <transaction-type>Container</transaction-type>
        <message-selector>MessageFormat = 'Version 3.4'</message-selector>
        <acknowledge-mode>Auto-acknowledge</acknowledge-mode>
        <message-driven-destination>
            <destination-type>javax.jms.Queue</destination-type>
        </message-driven-destination>
        <ejb-ref>
            <ejb-ref-name>ejb/ProcessPaymentHomeRemote</ejb-ref-name>
            <ejb-ref-type>Session</ejb-ref-type>
            <home>com.titan.processpayment.ProcessPaymentHomeRemote</home>
            <remote>com.titan.processpayment.ProcessPaymentRemote</remote>
        </ejb-ref>
```

---

* Obviously, if the destination identified by the JMSReplyTo attribute is of type Queue, the point-to-point (queue-based) messaging model must be used. If the destination type identified by the JMSReplyTo attribute is Topic, the publish-and-subscribe (topic-based) messaging model must be used.

```
<ejb-ref>
    <ejb-ref-name>ejb/CustomerHomeRemote</ejb-ref-name>
    <ejb-ref-type>Entity</ejb-ref-type>
    <home>com.titan.customer.CustomerHomeRemote</home>
    <remote>com.titan.customer.CustomerRemote</remote>
</ejb-ref>
<ejb-local-ref>
    <ejb-ref-name>ejb/CruiseHomeLocal</ejb-ref-name>
    <ejb-ref-type>Entity</ejb-ref-type>
    <local-home>com.titan.cruise.CruiseHomeLocal</local-home>
    <local>com.titan.cruise.CruiseLocal</local>
</ejb-local-ref>
<ejb-local-ref>
    <ejb-ref-name>ejb/CabinHomeLocal</ejb-ref-name>
    <ejb-ref-type>Entity</ejb-ref-type>
    <local-home>com.titan.cabin.CabinHomeLocal</local-home>
    <local>com.titan.cabin.CabinLocal</local>
</ejb-local-ref>
<ejb-local-ref>
    <ejb-ref-name>ejb/ReservationHomeLocal</ejb-ref-name>
    <ejb-ref-type>Entity</ejb-ref-type>
    <local-home>com.titan.reservation.ReservationHomeLocal</local-home>
    <local>com.titan.reservation.ReservationLocal</local>
</ejb-local-ref>
<security-identity>
    <run-as>
        <role-name>everyone</role-name>
    </run-as>
</security-identity>
<resource-ref>
    <res-ref-name>jms/QueueFactory</res-ref-name>
    <res-type>javax.jms.QueueConnectionFactory</res-type>
    <res-auth>Container</res-auth>
</resource-ref>
</message-driven>
...
</enterprise-beans>
```

An MDB is declared in a <message-driven> element within the <enterprise-beans> element, alongside <session> and <entity> beans. Similar to <session> bean types, it defines an <ejb-name>, <ejb-class>, and <transaction-type>, but it does not define component interfaces (local or remote). MDBs do not have component interfaces, so these definitions aren't needed.

<message-selector>

An MDB can also declare a <message-selector> element, which is unique to message-driven beans:

```
<message-selector>MessageFormat = 'Version 3.4'</message-selector>
```

Message selectors allow an MDB to be more selective about the messages it receives from a particular topic or queue. Message selectors use Message properties as criteria in conditional expressions.* These conditional expressions use Boolean logic to declare which messages should be delivered to a client.

Message properties, upon which message selectors are based, are additional headers that can be assigned to a message. They give the application developer or JMS vendor the ability to attach more information to a message. The Message interface provides several accessor and mutator methods for reading and writing properties. Properties can have a String value or one of several primitive values (boolean, byte, short, int, long, float, double). The naming of properties, together with their values and conversion rules, is strictly defined by JMS.

The ReservationProcessor EJB uses a message selector filter to select messages of a specific format. In this case the format is "Version 3.4"; this is a string Titan uses to identify messages of type MapMessage that contain the name values CustomerID, CruiseID, CabinID, CreditCard, and Price. In other words, by specifying a MessageFormat on every reservation message, we can write MDBs that are designed to process different kinds of reservation messages. If a new business partner needs to use a different type of Message object, Titan would use a new message version and an MDB to process it.

This is how a JMS producer would go about setting a MessageFormat property on a Message:

```
Message message = session.createMapMessage();
message.setStringPropery("MessageFormat","Version 3.4");

// set the reservation named values

sender.send(message);
```

The message selectors are based on a subset of the SQL-92 conditional expression syntax that is used in the WHERE clauses of SQL statements. They can become fairly complex, including the use of literal values, Boolean expressions, unary operators, and so on.

Message selector examples

Here are three complex selectors used in hypothetical environments. Although you will have to use your imagination a little, the purpose of these examples is to convey the power of the message selectors. When a selector is declared, the identifier always refers to a property name or JMS header name. For example, the selector UserName !='William' assumes that there is a property in the message named UserName, which can be compared to the value 'William'.

Managing claims in an HMO. Due to some fraudulent claims, an automatic process is implemented using MDBs that will audit all claims submitted by patients who are

---

* Message selectors are also based on message headers, which are outside the scope of this chapter.

employees of the ACME manufacturing company for visits to chiropractors, psychologists, and dermatologists:

```
<message-selector>
<![CDATA[
    PhysicianType IN ('Chiropractic','Psychologists','Dermatologist')
    AND PatientGroupID LIKE 'ACME%'
]]>
</message-selector>
```

 MDB <message-selector> statements are declared in XML deployment descriptors. XML assigns special meaning to a variety of characters, such as the greater than (>) and less than (<) symbols, so using these symbols in the <message-selector> statements will cause parsing errors unless CDATA sections are used. This is the same reason CDATA sections were needed in EJB QL <ejb-ql> statements, as explained in Chapter 8.

Notification of certain bids on inventory. A supplier wants notification of requests for bids on specific inventory items at specific quantities:

```
<message-selector>
<![CDATA[
    InventoryID ='S93740283-02' AND Quantity BETWEEN 1000 AND 13000
]]>
</message-selector>
```

Selecting recipients for a catalog mailing. An online retailer wants to deliver a special catalog to any customer that orders more than $500.00 worth of merchandise where the average price per item ordered is greater than $75.00 and the customer resides in one several states. The retailer creates an MBD that subscribes to the order-processing topic and processes catalog deliveries for only those customers that meet the defined criteria:

```
<message-selector>
<![CDATA[
    TotalCharge >500.00 AND ((TotalCharge /ItemCount)>=75.00)
    AND State IN ('MN','WI','MI','OH')
]]>
</message-selector>
```

<acknowledge-mode>

JMS has the concept of acknowledgment, which means that the JMS client notifies the JMS provider (message router) when a message is received. In EJB, it's the MDB container's responsibility to send an acknowledgment to the JMS provider when it receives a message. Acknowledging a message tells the JMS provider that MDB container has received the message and processed it using an MDB instance. Without an acknowledgment, the JMS provider will not know whether the MDB container has received the message, so it will try to redeliver it. This can cause problems. For example, once we have processed a reservation message using the ReservationProcessor EJB, we don't want to receive the same message again.

When transactions are involved, the acknowledgment mode set by the bean provider is ignored. In this case, the acknowledgment is performed within the context of the transaction. If the transaction succeeds, the message is acknowledged. If the transaction fails, the message is not acknowledged. If the MDB is using container-managed transactions, as it will in most cases, the acknowledgment mode is ignored by the MDB container. When using container-managed transactions with a Required transaction attribute, the <acknowledge-mode> is usually not specified; however, we included it in the deployment descriptor for the sake of discussion:

```
<acknowledge-mode>Auto-acknowledge</acknowledge-mode>
```

When the MDB executes with bean-managed transactions, or with the container-managed transaction attribute NotSupported (see Chapter 14), the value of <acknowledge-mode> becomes important.

Two values can be specified for <acknowledge-mode>: Auto-acknowledge and Dups-ok-acknowledge. Auto-acknowledge tells the container that it should send an acknowledgment to the JMS provider soon after the message is given to an MDB instance to process. Dups-ok-acknowledge tells the container that it doesn't have to send the acknowledgment immediately; any time after the message is given to the MDB instance will be fine. With Dups-ok-acknowledge, it's possible for the MDB container to delay acknowledgment so long that the JMS provider assumes that the message was not received and sends a "duplicate" message. Obviously, with Dups-ok-acknowledge, your MDBs must be able to handle duplicate messages correctly.

Auto-acknowledge avoids duplicate messages because the acknowledgment is sent immediately. Therefore, the JMS provider won't send a duplicate. Most MDBs use Auto-acknowledge, to avoid processing the same message twice. Dups-ok-acknowledge exists because it may allow a JMS provider to optimize its use of the network. In practice, though, the overhead of an acknowledgment is so small, and the frequency of communication between the MDB container and JMS provider is so high, that Dups-ok-acknowledge doesn't have a big impact on performance.

<message-driven-destination>

The <message-driven-destination> element designates the type of destination from which the MDB receives messages. The allowed values for this element are javax.jms.Queue and javax.jms.Topic. In the ReservationProcessor EJB this value is set to javax.jms.Queue, indicating that the MDB is getting its messages via the p2p messaging model from a queue:

```
<message-driven-destination>
    <destination-type>javax.jms.Queue</destination-type>
</message-driven-destination>
```

When the MDB is deployed, the deployer will map the MDB so that it listens to a real queue on the network.

When the `<destination-type>` is a `javax.jms.Topic`, the `<subscription-durability>` element must be declared with either `Durable` or `NonDurable` as its value:

```
<message-driven-destination>
    <destination-type>javax.jms.Topic</destination-type>
    <subscription-durability>Durable</subscription-durability>
</message-driven-destination>
```

The `<subscription-durability>` element determines whether or not the MDB's sub-scription to the topic is `Durable`. A `Durable` subscription outlasts an MDB container's connection to the JMS provider, so if the EJB server suffers a partial failure, is shut down, or is otherwise disconnected from the JMS provider, the messages that it would have received will not be lost. While a `Durable` MDB container is discon-nected from the JMS provider, it is the responsibility of the JMS provider to store any messages the subscriber misses. When the `Durable` MDB container reconnects to the JMS provider, the JMS provider sends it all the unexpired messages that accumu-lated while it was down. This behavior is commonly referred to as *store-and-forward messaging*. `Durable` MDBs are tolerant of disconnections, whether they are inten-tional or the result of a partial failure.

If `<subscription-durability>` is `NonDurable`, any messages the bean would have received while it was disconnected will be lost. Developers use `NonDurable` subscrip-tions when it is not critical that all messages be processed. Using a `NonDurable` sub-scription improves the performance of the JMS provider but significantly reduces the reliability of the MDBs.

When `<destination-type>` is `javax.jms.Queue`, as is the case in the Reservation-Processor EJB, durability is not a factor because of the nature of p2p or queue-based messaging systems. With a queue, messages may be consumed only once and remain in the queue until they are distributed to one of the queue's listeners.

The rest of the elements in the deployment descriptor should already be familiar. The `<ejb-ref>` element provides JNDI ENC bindings for a remote EJB home object while the `<ejb-local-ref>` elements provide JNDI ENC bindings for local EJB home objects. Note that the `<resource-ref>` element that defined the JMS `Queue-ConnectionFactory` used by the ReservationProcessor EJB to send ticket messages is not accompanied by a `<resource-env-ref>` element. The queue to which the tickets are sent is obtained from the `JMSReplyTo` header of the `MapMessage` itself, and not from the JNDI ENC.

The ReservationProcessor clients

In order to test the ReservationProcessor EJB, we need to develop two new client applications: one to send reservation messages and the other to consume ticket mes-sages produced by the ReservationProcessor EJB.

The reservation message producer. The JmsClient_ReservationProducer is designed to send 100 reservation requests very quickly. The speed with which it sends these messages will force many MDB containers to use multiple instances to process the reservation messages. The code for JmsClient_ReservationProducer looks like this:

```
import javax.jms.Message;
import javax.jms.MapMessage;
import javax.jms.QueueConnectionFactory;
import javax.jms.QueueConnection;
import javax.jms.QueueSession;
import javax.jms.Session;
import javax.jms.Queue;
import javax.jms.QueueSender;
import javax.jms.JMSException;
import javax.naming.InitalContext;
import java.util.Date;

import com.titan.processpayment.CreditCardDO;

public class JmsClient_ReservationProducer {

    public static void main(String [] args) throws Exception {

        InitialContext jndiContext = getInitialContext();

        QueueConnectionFactory factory = (QueueConnectionFactory)
            jndiContext.lookup("QueueFactoryNameGoesHere");

        Queue reservationQueue = (Queue)
            jndiContext.lookup("QueueNameGoesHere");

        QueueConnection connect = factory.createQueueConneciton();

        QueueSession session =
            connect.createQueueSession(false,Session.AUTO_ACKNOWLEDGE);

        QueueSender sender = session.createSender(reservationQueue);

        Integer cruiseID = new Integer(1);

        for(int i = 0; i < 100; i++){
            MapMessage message = session.createMapMessage();
            message.setStringProperty("MessageFormat","Version 3.4");

            message.setInt("CruiseID",1);
            message.setInt("CustomerID",i%10);
            message.setInt("CabinID",i);
            message.setDouble("Price", (double)1000+i);

            // the card expires in about 30 days
            Date expirationDate = new Date(System.currentTimeMillis()+43200000);
            message.setString("CreditCardNum", "923830283029");
            message.setLong("CreditCardExpDate", expirationDate.getTime());
```

```
        message.setString("CreditCardType", CreditCardDO.MASTER_CARD);

        sender.send(message);

    }

    connect.close();
}

public static InitialContext getInitialContext()
    throws JMSException {
    // create vendor-specific JNDI context here
}
}
```

You may have noticed that the JmsClient_ReservationProducer sets the CustomerID, CruiseID, and CabinID as primitive int values, but the ReservationProcessorBean reads these values as java.lang.Integer types. This is not a mistake. The MapMessage automatically converts any primitive to its proper wrapper if that primitive is read using MapMessage.getObject(). So, for example, a named value that is loaded into a MapMessage using setInt() can be read as an Integer using getObject(). For example, the following code sets a value as a primitive int and then accesses it as a java. long.Integer object:

```
MapMessage mapMsg = session.createMapMessage();

mapMsg.setInt("TheValue",3);

Integer myInteger = (Integer)mapMsg.getObject("TheValue");

if(myInteger.intValue() == 3 )
    // this will always be true
```

The ticket message consumer. The JmsClient_TicketConsumer is designed to consume all the ticket messages delivered by ReservationProcessor EJB instances to the queue. It consumes the messages and prints out the descriptions:

```
import javax.jms.Message;
import javax.jms.ObjectMessage;
import javax.jms.QueueConnectionFactory;
import javax.jms.QueueConnection;
import javax.jms.QueueSession;
import javax.jms.Session;
import javax.jms.Queue;
import javax.jms.QueueReceiver;
import javax.jms.JMSException;
import javax.naming.InitalContext;

import com.titan.travelagent.TicketDO;

public class JmsClient_TicketConsumer
    implements javax.jms.MessageListener {
```

```
        public static void main(String [] args) throws Exception {

            new JmsClient_TicketConsumer();

            while(true){Thread.sleep(10000);}

        }

        public JmsClient_TicketConsumer() throws Exception {

            InitialContext jndiContext = getInitialContext();

            QueueConnectionFactory factory = (QueueConnectionFactory)
                jndiContext.lookup("QueueFactoryNameGoesHere");

            Queue ticketQueue = (Queue)jndiContext.lookup("QueueNameGoesHere");

            QueueConnection connect = factory.createQueueConneciton();

            QueueSession session =
                connect.createQueueSession(false,Session.AUTO_ACKNOWLEDGE);

            QueueReceiver receiver = session.createReceiver(ticketQueue);

            receiver.setMessageListener(this);

            connect.start();
        }

        public void onMessage(Message message) {
            try {

                ObjectMessage objMsg = (ObjectMessage)message;
                TicketDO ticket = (TicketDO)objMsg.getObject();
                System.out.println("*******************************");
                System.out.println(ticket);
                System.out.println("*******************************");

            } catch(JMSException jmsE) {
                jmsE.printStackTrace();
            }
        }
        public static InitialContext getInitialContext() throws JMSException {
            // create vendor-specific JNDI context here
        }
    }
```

To make the ReservationProcessor EJB work with the two client applications, JmsClient_ReservationProducer and JmsClient_TicketConsumer, you must configure your EJB container's JMS provider so that it has two queues: one for reservation messages and another for ticket messages.

    📖 Workbook Exercise 13.2, The Message-Driven Bean

The Life Cycle of a Message-Driven Bean

Just as the entity and session beans have well-defined life cycles, so does the MDB bean. The MDB instance's life cycle has two states: *Does Not Exist* and *Method-Ready Pool*. The Method-Ready Pool is similar to the instance pool used for stateless session beans. Like stateless beans, MDBs define instance pooling in their life cycles.[*]

Figure 13-4 illustrates the states and transitions that an MDB instance goes through in its lifetime.

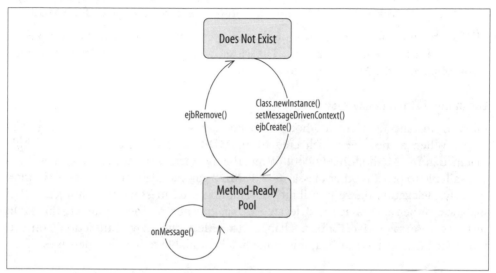

Figure 13-4. MDB life cycle

Does Not Exist

When an MDB instance is in the Does Not Exist state, it is not an instance in the memory of the system. In other words, it has not been instantiated yet.

The Method-Ready Pool

MDB instances enter the Method-Ready Pool as the container needs them. When the EJB server is first started, it may create a number of MDB instances and enter them into the Method-Ready Pool. (The actual behavior of the server depends on the implementation.) When the number of MDB instances handling incoming messages is insufficient, more can be created and added to the pool.

---

[*] Some vendors may *not* pool MDB instances, but may instead create and destroy instances with each new message. This is an implementation-specific decision that should not impact the specified life cycle of the stateless bean instance.

Transitioning to the Method-Ready Pool

When an instance transitions from the Does Not Exist state to the Method-Ready Pool, three operations are performed on it. First, the bean instance is instantiated when the container invokes the `Class.newInstance()` method on the MDB class. Second, the `setMessageDrivenContext()` method is invoked by the container providing the MDB instance with a reference to its `EJBContext`. The `MessageDrivenContext` reference may be stored in an instance field of the MDB.

Finally, the no-argument `ejbCreate()` method is invoked by the container on the bean instance. The MDB has only one `ejbCreate()` method, which takes no arguments. The `ejbCreate()` method is invoked only once in the life cycle of the MDB.

MDBs are not subject to activation, so they can maintain open connections to resources for their entire life cycles.[*] The `ejbRemove()` method should close any open resources before the MDB is evicted from memory at the end of its life cycle.

Life in the Method-Ready Pool

Once an instance is in the Method-Ready Pool, it is ready to handle incoming messages. When a message is delivered to an MDB, it is delegated to any available instance in the Method-Ready Pool. While the instance is executing the request, it is unavailable to process other messages. The MDB can handle many messages simultaneously, delegating the responsibility of handling each message to a different MDB instance. When a message is delegated to an instance by the container, the MDB instance's `MessageDrivenContext` changes to reflect the new transaction context. Once the instance has finished, it is immediately available to handle a new message.

Transitioning out of the Method-Ready Pool: The death of an MDB instance

Bean instances leave the Method-Ready Pool for the Does Not Exist state when the server no longer needs them. This occurs when the server decides to reduce the total size of the Method-Ready Pool by evicting one or more instances from memory. The process begins by invoking the `ejbRemove()` method on the instance. At this time, the bean instance should perform any cleanup operations, such as closing open resources. The `ejbRemove()` method is invoked only once in the life cycle of an MDB instance—when it is about to transition to the Does Not Exist state. During the `ejbRemove()` method, the `MessageDrivenContext` and access to the JNDI ENC are still available to the bean instance. Following the execution of the `ejbRemove()` method, the bean is dereferenced and eventually garbage collected.

---

[*] The duration of an MDB instance's life is assumed to be very long. However, some EJB servers may actually destroy and create instances with every new message, making this strategy less attractive. Consult your vendor's documentation for details on how your EJB server handles stateless instances.

CHAPTER 14

Transactions

ACID Transactions

To understand how transactions work, we will revisit the TravelAgent EJB, a stateful session bean that encapsulates the process of making a cruise reservation for a customer.

In EJB 2.0, the TravelAgent EJB's bookPassage() method looks like this:

```
public TicketDO bookPassage(CreditCardDO card, double price)
    throws IncompleteConversationalState {

    if (customer == null || cruise == null || cabin == null) {
        throw new IncompleteConversationalState();
    }
    try {
        ReservationHomeLocal resHome = (ReservationHomeLocal)
            jndiContext.lookup("java:comp/env/ejb/ReservationHomeLocal");
        ReservationLocal reservation =
            resHome.create(customer, cruise, cabin, price);
        Object ref = jndiContext.lookup
            ("java:comp/env/ejb/ProcessPaymentHomeRemote");
        ProcessPaymentHomeRemote ppHome = (ProcessPaymentHomeRemote)
            PortableRemoteObject.narrow(ref, ProcessPaymentHomeRemote.class);
        ProcessPaymentRemote process = ppHome.create();
        process.byCredit(customer, card, price);

        TicketDO ticket = new TicketDO(customer,cruise,cabin,price);

        return ticket;
    } catch(Exception e) {
        throw new EJBException(e);
    }
}
```

In EJB 1.1, the bookPassage() method looks like this:

```
public TicketDO bookPassage(CreditCardDO card, double price)
    throws IncompleteConversationalState {
```

```
if (customer == null || cruise == null || cabin == null) {
    throw new IncompleteConversationalState();
}
try {
    ReservationHomeRemote resHome = (ReservationHomeRemote)
        getHome("ReservationHomeRemote", ReservationHomeRemote.class);
    ReservationRemote reservation =
        resHome.create(customer, cruise, cabin, price);
    ProcessPaymentHomeRemote ppHome = (ProcessPaymentHomeRemote)
        getHome("ProcessPaymentHomeRemote", ProcessPaymentHomeRemote.class);
    ProcessPaymentRemote process = ppHome.create();
    process.byCredit(customer, card, price);

    TicketDO ticket = new TicketDO(customer,cruise,cabin,price);

    return ticket;
} catch(Exception e) {
    throw new EJBException(e);
}
}
```

The TravelAgent EJB is a fairly simple session bean, and its use of other EJBs is a typical example of business-object design and workflow. Unfortunately, good business-object design is not enough to make these EJBs useful in an industrial-strength application. The problem is not with the definition of the EJBs or the workflow; the problem is that a good design does not, in and of itself, guarantee that the TravelAgent EJB's bookPassage() method represents a good *transaction*. To understand why, we will take a closer look at what a transaction is and what criteria a transaction must meet to be considered reliable.

In business, a transaction usually involves an exchange between two parties. When you purchase an ice cream cone, you exchange money for food; when you work for a company, you exchange skill and time for money (which you use to buy more ice cream). When you are involved in these exchanges, you monitor the outcome to ensure that you don't get "ripped off." If you give the ice cream vendor a $20 bill, you don't want him to drive off without giving you your change; likewise, you want to make sure that your paycheck reflects all the hours you worked. By monitoring these commercial exchanges, you are attempting to ensure the reliability of the transactions; you are making sure that each transaction meets everyone's expectations.

In business software, a transaction embodies the concept of a commercial exchange. A business system transaction (transaction for short) is the execution of a *unit-of-work* that accesses one or more shared resources, usually databases. A unit-of-work is a set of activities that relate to each other and must be completed together. The reservation process is a unit-of-work made up of several activities: recording a reservation, debiting a credit card, and generating a ticket together make up a unit-of-work.

Transactions are part of many different types of systems. In each transaction, the objective is the same: to execute a unit-of-work that results in a reliable exchange.

Here are some examples of other types of business systems that employ transactions:

ATM

The ATM (automatic teller machine) you use to deposit, withdraw, and transfer funds executes these units-of-work as transactions. In an ATM withdrawal, for example, the ATM checks to make sure you don't overdraw and then debits your account and spits out some money.

Online book order

You've probably purchased many of your Java books—maybe even this book—from an online bookseller. This type of purchase is also a unit-of-work that takes place as a transaction. In an online book purchase, you submit your credit card number, it is validated, and a charge is made for price of the book. Then an order to ship you the book is sent to the bookseller's warehouse.

Medical system

In a medical system, important data—some of it critical—is recorded about patients every day, including information about clinical visits, medical procedures, prescriptions, and drug allergies. The doctor prescribes the drug, then the system checks for allergies, contraindications, and appropriate dosages. If all tests pass, the drug can be administered. The tasks just described make up a unit-of-work in a medical system. A unit-of-work in a medical system may not be financial, but it's just as important. A failure to identify a drug allergy in a patient could be fatal.

As you can see, transactions are often complex and usually involve the manipulation of a lot of data. Mistakes in data can cost money, or even a life. Transactions must therefore preserve data integrity, which means that the transaction must work perfectly every time or not be executed at all. This is a pretty tall order, especially for complex systems. As difficult as this requirement is, however, when it comes to commerce there is no room for error. Units-of-work involving money or anything of value always require the utmost reliability, because errors impact the revenues and the well-being of the parties involved.

To give you an idea of the accuracy required by transactions, think about what would happen if a transactional system suffered from seemingly infrequent errors. ATMs provide customers with convenient access to their bank accounts and represent a significant percentage of the total transactions in personal banking. The transactions handled by ATMs are simple but numerous, providing us with a great example of why transactions must be error-proof. Let's say that a bank has 100 ATMs in a metropolitan area, and each ATM processes 300 transactions (deposits, withdrawals, or transfers) a day, for a total of 30,000 transactions per day. If each transaction, on average, involves the deposit, withdrawal, or transfer of about $100, about three million dollars will move through the ATM system per day. In the course of a year, that's a little over a billion dollars:

365 days × 100 ATMs × 300 transactions × $100.00 = $1,095,000,000.00

How well do the ATMs have to perform to be considered reliable? For the sake of argument, let's say that ATMs execute transactions correctly 99.99% of the time. This seems to be more than adequate: after all, only one out of every ten thousand transactions executes incorrectly. But over the course of a year, if you do the math, that could result in over $100,000 in errors!

$1,095,000,000.00 \times .01\% = \$109,500.00$

Obviously, this is an oversimplification of the problem, but it illustrates that even a small percentage of errors is unacceptable in high-volume or mission-critical systems. For this reason, experts in the field of transaction services have identified four characteristics of a transaction that must be met for a system to be considered safe. Transactions must be *atomic, consistent, isolated,* and *durable* (ACID)—the four horsemen of transaction services. Here's what each term means:

Atomic

To be atomic, a transaction must execute completely or not at all. This means that every task within a unit-of-work must execute without error. If any of the tasks fails, the entire unit-of-work or transaction is aborted, meaning that any changes to the data are undone. If all the tasks execute successfully, the transaction is committed, which means that the changes to the data are made permanent or durable.

Consistent

Consistency is a transactional characteristic that must be enforced by both the transactional system and the application developer. Consistency refers to the integrity of the underlying data store. The transactional system fulfills its obligation for consistency by ensuring that a transaction is atomic, isolated, and durable. The application developer must ensure that the database has appropriate constraints (primary keys, referential integrity, and so forth) and that the unit-of-work, the business logic, doesn't result in inconsistent data (i.e., data that is not in harmony with the real world it represents). In an account transfer, for example, a debit to one account must equal the credit to another account.

Isolated

A transaction must be allowed to execute without interference from other processes or transactions. In other words, the data that a transaction accesses cannot be affected by any other part of the system until the transaction or unit-of-work is completed.

Durable

Durability means that all the data changes made during the course of a transaction must be written to some type of physical storage before the transaction is successfully completed. This ensures that the changes are not lost if the system crashes.

To get a better idea of what these principles mean, we will examine the TravelAgent EJB in terms of the four ACID properties.

Is the TravelAgent EJB Atomic?

Our first measure of the TravelAgent EJB's reliability is its atomicity: does it ensure that the transaction executes completely or not at all? What we are really concerned with are the critical tasks that change or create information. In the bookPassage() method, a Reservation EJB is created, the ProcessPayment EJB debits a credit card, and a TicketDO object is created. All of these tasks must be successful for the entire transaction to be successful.

To understand the importance of the atomic characteristic, you have to imagine what would happen if even one of the subtasks failed to execute. If, for example, the creation of a Reservation EJB failed but all other tasks succeeded, your customer would probably end up getting bumped from the cruise or sharing the cabin with a stranger. As far as the travel agent is concerned, the bookPassage() method executed successfully because a TicketDO was generated. If a ticket is generated without the creation of a reservation, the state of the business system becomes inconsistent with reality, because the customer paid for a ticket but the reservation was not recorded. Likewise, if the ProcessPayment EJB fails to charge the customer's credit card, the customer gets a free cruise. He may be happy, but management won't be. Finally, if the TicketDO is never created, the customer will have no record of the transaction and probably will not be allowed onto the ship.

So the only way bookPassage() can be completed is if all the critical tasks execute successfully. If something goes wrong, the entire process must be aborted. Aborting a transaction requires more than simply not finishing the tasks; in addition, all the tasks that did execute within the transaction must be undone. If, for example, the creation of the Reservation EJB and ProcessPayment.byCredit() method succeeded but the creation of the TicketDO failed, throwing an exception from the constructor, the reservation record and payment records must not be added to the database.

Is the TravelAgent EJB Consistent?

In order for a transaction to be consistent, the business system must make sense after the transaction has completed. In other words, the *state* of the business system must be consistent with the reality of the business. This requires that the transaction enforce the atomic, isolated, and durable characteristics of the transaction, and it also requires diligent enforcement of integrity constraints by the application developer. If, for example, the application developer fails to include the credit card charge operation in the bookPassage() method, the customer will be issued a ticket but will never be charged. The data will be inconsistent with the expectation of the business—a customer should be charged for passage.

In addition, the database must be set up to enforce integrity constraints. For example, it should not be possible for a record to be added to the RESERVATION table unless the CABIN_ID, CRUISE_ID, and CUSTOMER_ID foreign keys map to corresponding records in the CABIN, CRUISE, and CUSTOMER tables, respectively. If a CUSTOMER_ID that does not map to a CUSTOMER record is used, referential integrity should cause the database to throw an error message.

Is the TravelAgent EJB Isolated?

If you are familiar with the concept of thread synchronization in Java or row-locking schemes in relational databases, isolation will be a familiar concept. To be isolated, a transaction must protect the data it is accessing from other transactions. This is necessary to prevent other transactions from interacting with data that is in transition. In the TravelAgent EJB, the transaction is isolated to prevent other transactions from modifying the EJBs that are being updated. Imagine the problems that would arise if separate transactions were allowed to change any entity bean at any time—transactions would walk all over each other. You could easily have several customers book the same cabin because their travel agents happened to make their reservations at the same time.

The isolation of data accessed by EJBs does not mean that the entire application shuts down during a transaction. Only those entity beans and data directly affected by the transaction are isolated. In the TravelAgent EJB, for example, the transaction isolates only the Reservation EJB created. There can be many Reservation EJBs in existence; there's no reason these other EJBs can't be accessed by other transactions.

Is the TravelAgent EJB Durable?

To be durable, the bookPassage() method must write all changes and new data to a permanent data store before it can be considered successful. While this may seem like a no-brainer, often it is not what happens in real life. In the name of efficiency, changes are often maintained in memory for long periods of time before being saved on a disk drive. The idea is to reduce disk accesses—which slow systems down—and only periodically write the cumulative effect of data changes. While this approach is great for performance, it is also dangerous because data can be lost when the system goes down and memory is wiped out. Durability requires the system to save all updates made within a transaction as the transaction successfully completes, thus protecting the integrity of the data.

In the TravelAgent EJB, this means that the new RESERVATION and PAYMENT records inserted are made persistent before the transaction can complete successfully. Only when the data is made durable are those specific records accessible through their respective EJBs from other transactions. Hence, durability also plays a role in isolation. A transaction is not finished until the data is successfully recorded.

Ensuring that transactions adhere to the ACID principles requires careful design. The system has to monitor the progress of a transaction to ensure that it does all its work, that the data is changed correctly, that transactions do not interfere with each other, and that the changes can survive a system crash. Engineering all this functionality into a system is a lot of work, and not something you would want to reinvent for every business system on which you work. Fortunately, EJB is designed to support transactions automatically, making the development of transactional systems easier. The rest of this chapter examines how EJB supports transactions implicitly (through declarative transaction attributes) and explicitly (through the Java Transaction API).

Declarative Transaction Management

One of the primary advantages of Enterprise JavaBeans is that it allows for declarative transaction management. Without this feature, transactions must be controlled using explicit transaction demarcation. This involves the use of fairly complex APIs like the OMG's Object Transaction Service (OTS) or its Java implementation, the Java Transaction Service (JTS). Explicit demarcation is difficult for developers to use at best, particularly if you are new to transactional systems. In addition, explicit transaction demarcation requires that the transactional code be written within the business logic, which reduces the clarity of the code and, more importantly, creates inflexible distributed objects. Once transaction demarcation is hardcoded into the business object, changes in transaction behavior require changes to the business logic itself. We talk more about explicit transaction management and EJB later in this chapter.

With declarative transaction management, the transactional behavior of EJBs can be controlled using the deployment descriptor, which sets transaction attributes for individual enterprise bean methods. This means that the transactional behavior of an EJB can be changed without changing the EJB's business logic. In addition, an EJB deployed in one application can be defined with different transactional behavior than the same EJB deployed in a different application. Declarative transaction management reduces the complexity of transactions for EJB developers and application developers and makes it easier to create robust transactional applications.

Transaction Scope

Transaction scope is a crucial concept for understanding transactions. In this context, transaction scope means those EJBs—both session and entity—that are participating in a particular transaction.

In the bookPassage() method of the TravelAgent EJB, all the EJBs involved are part of the same transaction scope. The scope of the transaction starts when a client invokes the TravelAgent EJB's bookPassage() method. Once the transaction scope has started, it is *propagated* to both the newly created Reservation EJB and the Process-Payment EJB.

As you know, a transaction is a unit-of-work made up of one or more tasks. In a transaction, all the tasks that make up the unit-of-work must succeed for the entire transaction to succeed; the transaction must be atomic. If any task fails, the updates made by all the other tasks in the transaction will be rolled back or undone. In EJB, tasks are expressed as enterprise bean methods, and a unit-of-work consists of every enterprise bean method invoked in a transaction. The scope of a transaction includes every EJB that participates in the unit-of-work.

It is easy to trace the scope of a transaction by following the thread of execution. If the invocation of the bookPassage() method begins a transaction, then logically, the transaction ends when the method completes. The scope of the bookPassage() transaction would include the TravelAgent, Reservation, and ProcessPayment EJBs—every EJB touched by the bookPassage() method. A transaction is propagated to an EJB when that EJB's method is invoked and included in the scope of that transaction.

A transaction can end if an exception is thrown while the bookPassage() method is executing. The exception can be thrown from one of the other EJBs or from the bookPassage() method itself. An exception may or may not cause a rollback, depending on its type. We'll discuss exceptions and transactions in more detail later.

The thread of execution is not the only factor that determines whether an EJB is included in the scope of a transaction; the EJB's transaction attributes also play a role. Determining whether an EJB participates in the transaction scope of any unit-of-work is accomplished either implicitly using the EJB's transaction attributes or explicitly using the Java Transaction API (JTA).

Transaction Attributes

As an application developer, you do not normally need to control transactions explicitly when using an EJB server. EJB servers can manage transactions implicitly, based on the transaction attributes established for EJBs at deployment time. The ability to specify how business objects participate in transactions through attribute-based programming is a common characteristic of CTMs, and one of the most important features of the EJB component model.

When an EJB is deployed, you can set its runtime transaction attribute in the deployment descriptor to one of several values. The following list shows the XML attribute values used to specify these transaction attributes:

- NotSupported
- Supports
- Required
- RequiresNew
- Mandatory
- Never

Using transaction attributes simplifies building transactional applications by reducing the risks associated with improper use of transactional protocols such as JTA (discussed later in this chapter). It's more efficient and easier to use transaction attributes than to control transactions explicitly.

You can set a transaction attribute for the entire EJB (in which case it applies to all methods) or to set different transaction attributes for individual methods. The former method is much simpler and less error prone, but setting attributes at the method level offers more flexibility. The code fragments in the following sections show how to set the default transaction attribute of an EJB in the EJB's deployment descriptor.

Setting a transaction attribute

In the XML deployment descriptor, a <container-transaction> element specifies the transaction attributes for the EJBs described in the deployment descriptor:

```
<ejb-jar>
    ...
    <assembly-descriptor>
        ...
        <container-transaction>
            <method>
                <ejb-name>TravelAgentEJB</ejb-name>
                <method-name> * </method-name>
            </method>
            <trans-attribute>Required</trans-attribute>
        </container-transaction>
        <container-transaction>
            <method>
                <ejb-name>TravelAgentEJB</ejb-name>
                <method-name>listAvailableCabins</method-name>
            </method>
            <trans-attribute>Supports</trans-attribute>
        </container-transaction>
        ...
    </assembly-descriptor>
    ...
</ejb-jar>
```

This deployment descriptor specifies the transaction attributes for the TravelAgent EJB. Each <container-transaction> element specifies a method and the transaction attribute that should be applied to that method. The first <container-transaction> element specifies that all methods by default have a transaction attribute of Required; the * is a wildcard that indicates all the methods of the TravelAgent EJB. The second <container-transaction> element overrides the default setting to specify that the listAvailableCabins() method will have a Supports transaction attribute. Note that we have to specify which EJB we are referring to with the <ejb-name> element; an XML deployment descriptor can cover many EJBs.

Transaction attributes defined

Here are the definitions of the transaction attributes listed earlier. In a few of the definitions, we say that the client transaction is *suspended*. This means that the transaction is not propagated to the enterprise bean method being invoked; propagation of the transaction is temporarily halted until the enterprise bean method returns. To make things easier, we will talk about attribute types as if they were bean types: for example, we'll say a "Required EJB" as shorthand for "an enterprise bean with the Required transaction attribute." The attributes are:

NotSupported

> Invoking a method on an EJB with this transaction attribute suspends the transaction until the method is completed. This means that the transaction scope is not propagated to the NotSupported EJB or any of the EJBs it calls. Once the method on the NotSupported EJB is done, the original transaction resumes its execution.
>
> Figure 14-1 shows that a NotSupported EJB does not propagate the client transaction when one of its methods is invoked.

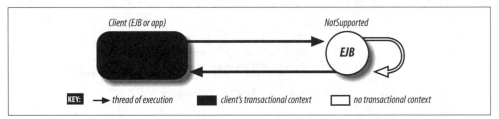

Figure 14-1. NotSupported attribute

Supports

> This attribute means that the enterprise bean method will be included in the transaction scope if it is invoked within a transaction. In other words, if the EJB or client that invokes the Supports EJB is part of a transaction scope, the Supports EJB and all EJBs accessed by it become part of the original transaction. However, the Supports EJB doesn't have to be part of a transaction and can interact with clients and other EJBs that are not included in a transaction scope.
>
> Figure 14-2(a) shows the Supports EJB being invoked by a transactional client and propagating the transaction. Figure 14-2(b) shows the Supports EJB being invoked by a nontransactional client.

Required

> This attribute means that the enterprise bean method must be invoked within the scope of a transaction. If the calling client or EJB is part of a transaction, the Required EJB is automatically included in its transaction scope. If, however, the calling client or EJB is not involved in a transaction, the Required EJB starts its own new transaction. The new transaction's scope covers only the Required EJB and all other EJBs accessed by it. Once the method invoked on the Required EJB is done, the new transaction's scope ends.

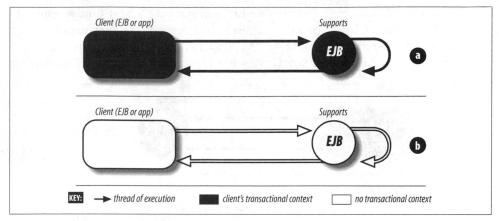

Figure 14-2. Supports attribute

Figure 14-3(a) shows the Required EJB being invoked by a transactional client and propagating the transaction.

Figure 14-3(b) shows the Required EJB being invoked by a nontransactional client, which causes it to start its own transaction.

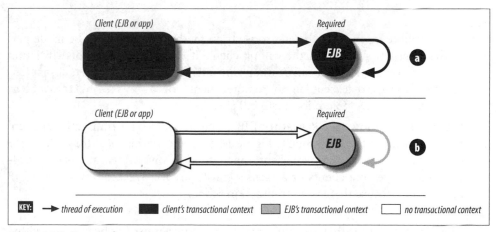

Figure 14-3. Required attribute

RequiresNew

This attribute means that a new transaction is always started. Regardless of whether the calling client or EJB is part of a transaction, a method with the RequiresNew attribute begins a new transaction when invoked. If the calling client is already involved in a transaction, that transaction is suspended until the RequiresNew EJB's method call returns. The new transaction's scope covers only the RequiresNew EJB and all the EJBs accessed by it. Once the method invoked on the RequiresNew EJB is done, the new transaction's scope ends and the original transaction resumes.

Figure 14-4(a) shows the RequiresNew EJB being invoked by a transactional client. The client's transaction is suspended while the EJB executes under its own transaction. Figure 14-4(b) shows the RequiresNew EJB being invoked by a nontransactional client; the RequiresNew EJB executes under its own transaction.

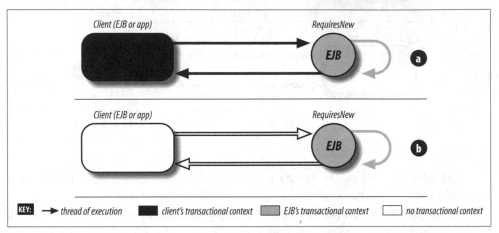

Figure 14-4. RequiresNew attribute

Mandatory

> This attribute means that the enterprise bean method must always be made part of the transaction scope of the calling client. If the calling client or EJB is not part of a transaction, the invocation will fail, throwing a javax.transaction. TransactionRequiredException to remote clients or a javax.ejb.Transaction-RequiredLocalException to local EJB 2.0 clients.

> Figure 14-5(a) shows the Mandatory EJB being invoked by a transactional client and propagating the transaction. Figure 14-5(b) shows the Mandatory EJB being invoked by a nontransactional client; the method throws a TransactionRequired-Exception to remote clients or a TransactionRequredLocalException to local EJB 2.0 clients, because there is no transaction scope.

Never

> This attribute means that the enterprise bean method must not be invoked within the scope of a transaction. If the calling client or EJB is part of a transaction, the Never EJB will throw a RemoteException to remote clients or an EJBException to local EJB 2.0 clients. However, if the calling client or EJB is not involved in a transaction the Never EJB will execute normally without a transaction.

> Figure 14-6(a) shows the Never EJB being invoked by a nontransactional client. Figure 14-6(b) shows the Never EJB being invoked by transactional client; the method throws a RemoteException to remote clients or an EJBException to local EJB 2.0 clients, because the method can never be invoked by a client or EJB that is included in a transaction.

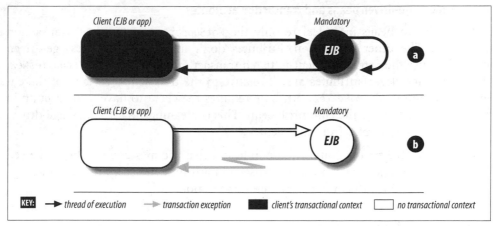

Figure 14-5. Mandatory attribute

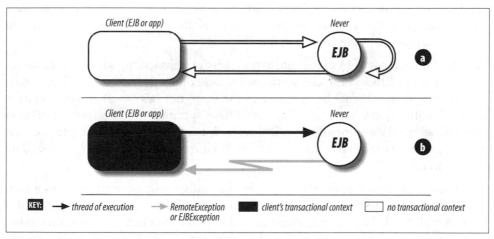

Figure 14-6. Never attribute

EJB 2.0: Container-managed persistence and transaction attributes

The EJB 2.0 specification strongly advises that CMP 2.0 entity beans use only the
Required, RequiresNew, and Mandatory transaction attributes. This restriction ensures
that all database access occurs in the context of a transaction, which is important
when the container is automatically managing persistence. While the specification
requires that these three transaction attributes be supported for CMP 2.0, support
for the Never, Supports, and NotSupported transaction attributes is optional. If a vendor wishes to support these attributes (which allow the bean to execute without a
transaction) they may do so, but it's not recommended. Consult your vendor's documentation to determine if they support the optional transaction attributes. This book
recommends that you use only Required, RequiresNew, or Mandatory with EJB 2.0
container-managed persistence entity beans.

EJB 2.0: Message-driven beans and transaction attributes

Message-driven beans may declare only the `NotSupported` or `Required` transaction attributes. The other transaction attributes don't make sense in message-driven beans because they apply to client-initiated transactions. The `Supports`, `RequiresNew`, `Mandatory`, and `Never` attributes are all relative to the transaction context of the client. For example, the `Mandatory` attribute requires the client to have a transaction in progress before calling the enterprise bean. This is meaningless for a message-driven bean, which is decoupled from the client.

The `NotSupported` transaction attribute indicates that the message will be processed without a transaction. The `Required` transaction attribute indicates that the message will be processed with a container-initiated transaction.

Transaction Propagation

To illustrate the impact of transaction attributes on enterprise bean methods, we'll look once again at the `bookPassage()` method of the TravelAgent EJB created in Chapter 12 (see the listings earlier in this chapter).

In order for `bookPassage()` to execute as a successful transaction, both the creation of the Reservation EJB and the charge to the customer must be successful. This means that both operations must be included in the same transaction. If either operation fails, the entire transaction fails. We could have specified the `Required` transaction attribute as the default for all the EJBs involved, because that attribute enforces our desired policy that all EJBs must execute within a transaction and thus ensures data consistency.

As a transaction monitor, an EJB server watches each method call in the transaction. If any of the updates fail, all the updates to all the EJBs will be reversed or *rolled back*. A rollback is like an *undo* command. If you have worked with relational databases, the concept of a rollback should be familiar to you. Once an update is executed, you can either commit the update or roll it back. A commit makes the changes requested by the update permanent; a rollback aborts the update and leaves the database in its original state. Making EJBs transactional provides the same kind of rollback/commit control. For example, if the Reservation EJB cannot be created, the charge made by the ProcessPayment EJB is rolled back. Transactions make updates an all-or-nothing proposition. This ensures that the unit-of-work, like the `bookPassage()` method, executes as intended, and it prevents inconsistent data from being written to databases.

In cases in which the container implicitly manages the transaction, the commit and rollback decisions are handled automatically. When transactions are managed explicitly within an enterprise bean or by the client, the responsibility falls on the enterprise bean or application developer to commit or roll back a transaction. Explicit demarcation of transactions is covered in detail later in this chapter.

Let's assume that the TravelAgent EJB is created and used on a client as follows:

```
TravelAgent agent = agentHome.create(customer);
agent.setCabinID(cabin_id);
agent.setCruiseID(cruise_id);
try {
    agent.bookPassage(card,price);
} catch(Exception e) {
    System.out.println("Transaction failed!");
}
```

Furthermore, let's assume that the bookPassage() method has been given the transaction attribute RequiresNew. In this case, the client that invokes the bookPassage() method is not itself part of a transaction. When bookPassage() is invoked on the TravelAgent EJB, a new transaction is created, as dictated by the RequiresNew attribute. This means that the TravelAgent EJB registers itself with the EJB server's transaction manager, which will manage the transaction automatically. The transaction manager coordinates transactions, propagating the transaction scope from one EJB to the next to ensure that all EJBs touched by a transaction are included in the transaction's unit-of-work. That way, the transaction manager can monitor the updates made by each enterprise bean and decide, based on the success of those updates, whether to commit all changes made by all enterprise beans to the database or roll them all back. If a *system exception* is thrown by the bookPassage() method, the transaction is automatically rolled back. We will talk more about exceptions later in this chapter.

When the byCredit() method is invoked within the bookPassage() method, the ProcessPayment EJB registers with the transaction manager under the transactional context that was created for the TravelAgent EJB; the transactional context is propagated to the ProcessPayment EJB. When the new Reservation EJB is created, it is also registered with the transaction manager under the same transaction. When all the EJBs are registered and their updates are made, the transaction manager checks to ensure that their updates will work. If all the updates will work, the transaction manager allows the changes to become permanent. If one of the EJBs reports an error or fails, any changes made by either the ProcessPayment or Reservation EJB are rolled back by the transaction manager. Figure 14-7 illustrates the propagation and management of the TravelAgent EJB's transactional context.

In addition to managing transactions in its own environment, an EJB server can coordinate with other transactional systems. If, for example, the ProcessPayment EJB actually came from a different EJB server than the TravelAgent EJB, the two EJB servers would cooperate to manage the transaction as one unit-of-work. This is called a *distributed transaction*.*

---

* Not all EJB servers support distributed transactions.

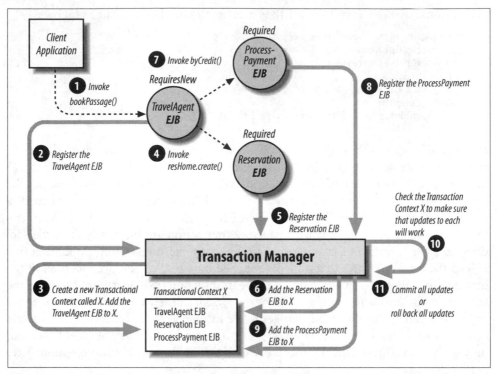

Figure 14-7. Managing the TravelAgent EJB's transactional context

A distributed transaction is a great deal more complicated, requiring what is called a *two-phase commit* (2-PC or TPC). 2-PC is a mechanism that allows transactions to be managed across different servers and resources (e.g., databases and JMS providers). The details of a 2-PC are beyond the scope of this book, but a system that supports it will not require any extra operations by an EJB or application developer. If distributed transactions are supported, the protocol for propagating transactions, as discussed earlier, will be supported. In other words, as an application or EJB developer, you should not notice a difference between local and distributed transactions.

EJB 2.0: Collection-Based Relationships and Transactions

In EJB 2.0 container-managed persistence, collection-based relationships may only be accessed within a single transaction. In other words, it's illegal to obtain a Collection object from a collection-based relationship field in one transaction and then use it in another.

For example, if an enterprise bean accesses another's collection-based relationship field through its local interface, the Collection returned from the accessor method can be used only within the same transaction:

```
public class HypotheticalBean implements javax.ejb.EntityBean {

    public void methodX(CustomerLocal customer) {

        Collection reservations = customer.getReservations();
        Iterator iterator = reservations.iterator;
        while(iterator.hasNext()){
            ...
        ...
    }
    ...
}
```

If the Customer EJB's getReservations() method was declared with a transaction attribute of RequiresNew, attempting to invoke any methods on the Collection, including the iterator() method, will result in a java.lang.IllegalStateException. This exception is thrown because the Collection object was created within the scope of the getReservations() transaction, not in the scope of methodX()'s transaction. The transaction context of methodX() is different from the transaction context of the getReservations() method.

The Collection from an entity bean can be used by another co-located bean only if it is obtained and accessed in the same transaction context. As long as the Customer EJB's getReservations() method propagates the transaction context of methodX(), the Collection can be used without any problems. This can be accomplished by changing the getReservations() method so that it declares its transaction attribute as Required or Mandatory.

Isolation and Database Locking

Transaction isolation (the "I" in ACID) is a critical part of any transactional system. This section explains isolation conditions, database locking, and transaction isolation levels. These concepts are important when deploying any transactional system.

Dirty, Repeatable, and Phantom Reads

Transaction isolation is defined in terms of isolation conditions called *dirty reads*, *repeatable reads*, and *phantom reads*. These conditions describe what can happen when two or more transactions operate on the same data.[*]

To illustrate these conditions, let's think about two separate client applications using their own instances of the TravelAgent EJB to access the same data—specifically, a cabin record with the primary key of 99. These examples revolve around the

---

[*] Isolation conditions are covered in detail by the ANSI SQL-92 Specification, Document Number: ANSI X3. 135-1992 (R1998).

RESERVATION table, which is accessed by both the bookPassage() method (through the Reservation EJB) and the listAvailableCabins() method (through JDBC). It might be a good idea to go back to Chapter 12 and review how the RESERVATION table is accessed through these methods. This will help you to understand how two transactions executed by two different clients can impact each other. Assume that both methods have a transaction attribute of Required.

Dirty reads

A dirty read occurs when the first transaction reads uncommitted changes made by a second transaction. If the second transaction is rolled back, the data read by the first transaction becomes invalid because the rollback undoes the changes. The first transaction will not be aware that the data it has read has become invalid. Here's a scenario showing how a dirty read can occur (illustrated in Figure 14-8):

1. Time 10:00:00: Client 1 executes the TravelAgent.bookPassage() method. Along with the Customer and Cruise EJBs, Client 1 had previously chosen Cabin 99 to be included in the reservation.

2. Time 10:00:01: Client 1's TravelAgent EJB creates a Reservation EJB within the bookPassage() method. The Reservation EJB's create() method inserts a record into the RESERVATION table, which reserves Cabin 99.

3. Time 10:00:02: Client 2 executes TravelAgent.listAvailableCabins(). Cabin 99 has been reserved by Client 1, so it is not in the list of available cabins that is returned from this method.

4. Time 10:00:03: Client 1's TravelAgent EJB executes the ProcessPayment. byCredit() method within the bookPassage() method. The byCredit() method throws an exception because the expiration date on the credit card has passed.

5. Time 10:00:04: The exception thrown by the ProcessPayment EJB causes the entire bookPassage() transaction to be rolled back. As a result, the record inserted into the RESERVATION table when the Reservation EJB was created is not made durable (i.e., it is removed). Cabin 99 is now available.

Client 2 is now using an invalid list of available cabins because Cabin 99 is available but is not included in the list. This omission would be serious if Cabin 99 was the last available cabin, because Client 2 would inaccurately report that the cruise was booked. The customer would presumably try to book a cruise on a competing cruise line.

Repeatable reads

A repeatable read is when the data read is guaranteed to look the same if read again during the same transaction. Repeatable reads are guaranteed in one of two ways: either the data read is locked against changes or the data read is a snapshot that doesn't reflect changes. If the data is locked, it cannot be changed by any other transaction until the current transaction ends. If the data is a snapshot, other transactions

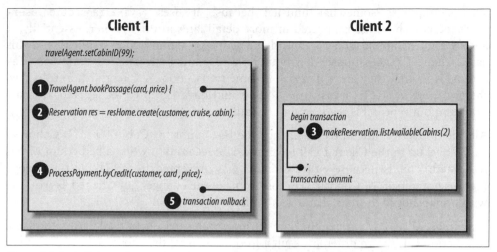

Figure 14-8. A dirty read

can change the data, but these changes will not be seen by this transaction if the read is repeated. Here's an example of a repeatable read (illustrated in Figure 14-9):

1. Time 10:00:00: Client 1 begins an explicit `javax.transaction.UserTransaction`.

2. Time 10:00:01: Client 1 executes `TravelAgent.listAvailableCabins(2)`, asking for a list of available cabins that have two beds. Cabin 99 is in the list of available cabins.

3. Time 10:00:02: Client 2 is working with an interface that manages Cabin EJBs. Client 2 attempts to change the bed count on Cabin 99 from 2 to 3.

4. Time 10:00:03: Client 1 re-executes `TravelAgent.listAvailableCabins(2)`. Cabin 99 is still in the list of available cabins.

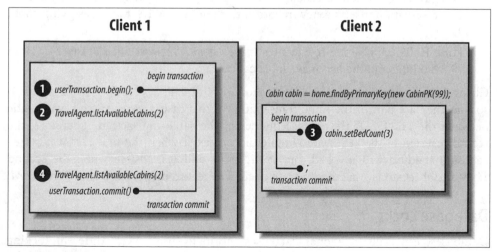

Figure 14-9. Repeatable read

This example is somewhat unusual because it uses javax.transaction.User-Transaction. This class is covered in more detail later in this chapter; essentially, it allows a client application to control the scope of a transaction explicitly. In this case, Client 1 places transaction boundaries around both calls to listAvailable-Cabins(), so that they are a part of the same transaction. If Client 1 didn't do this, the two listAvailableCabins() methods would have executed as separate transactions and our repeatable read condition would not have occurred.

Although Client 2 attempted to change the bed count for Cabin 99 to 3, Cabin 99 still shows up in the Client 1 call to listAvailableCabins() when a bed count of 2 is requested. This is because either Client 2 was prevented from making the change (because of a lock) or Client 2 was able to make the change, but Client 1 is working with a snapshot of the data that doesn't reflect that change.

A *nonrepeatable read* is when the data retrieved in a subsequent read within the same transaction can return different results. In other words, the subsequent read can see the changes made by other transactions.

Phantom reads

Phantom reads occur when new records added to the database are detectable by transactions that started prior to the insert. Queries will include records added by other transactions after their transaction has started. Here's a scenario that includes a phantom read (illustrated in Figure 14-10):

1. Time 10:00:00: Client 1 begins an explicit javax.transaction.UserTransaction.
2. Time 10:00:01: Client 1 executes TravelAgent.listAvailableCabins(2), asking for a list of available cabins that have two beds. Cabin 99 is in the list of available cabins.
3. Time 10:00:02: Client 2 executes bookPassage() and creates a Reservation EJB. The reservation inserts a new record into the RESERVATION table, reserving cabin 99.
4. Time 10:00:03: Client 1 re-executes TravelAgent.listAvailableCabins(2). Cabin 99 is no longer in the list of available cabins.

Client 1 places transaction boundaries around both calls to listAvailableCabins(), so that they are part of the same transaction. In this case, the reservation was made between the listAvailableCabins() queries in the same transaction. Therefore, the record inserted in the RESERVATION table did not exist when the first listAvailable-Cabins() method was invoked, but it did exist and was visible when the second listAvailableCabins() method was invoked. The record inserted is a *phantom record*.

Database Locks

Databases, especially relational databases, normally use several different locking techniques. The most common are *read locks*, *write locks*, and *exclusive write locks*.

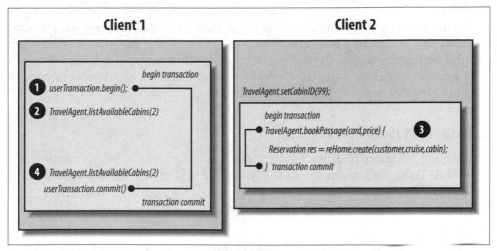

Figure 14-10. Phantom read

(I've taken the liberty of adding "snapshots," although this isn't a formal term.) These locking mechanisms control how transactions access data concurrently. Locking mechanisms impact the read conditions I just described. These types of locks are simple concepts that are not directly addressed in the EJB specification. Database vendors implement these locks differently, so you should understand how your database addresses these locking mechanisms to best predict how the isolation levels described in this section will work.

The four types of lock are:

Read locks

> Read locks prevent other transactions from changing data read during a transaction until the transaction ends, thus preventing nonrepeatable reads. Other transactions can read the data but not write to it. The current transaction is also prohibited from making changes. Whether a read lock locks only the records read, a block of records, or a whole table depends on the database being used.

Write locks

> Write locks are used for updates. A write lock prevents other transactions from changing the data until the current transaction is complete but allows dirty reads by other transactions and by the current transaction itself. In other words, the transaction can read its own uncommitted changes.

Exclusive write locks

> Exclusive write locks are used for updates. An exclusive write lock prevents other transactions from reading or changing the data until the current transaction is complete. An exclusive write lock prevents dirty reads by other transactions. Other transactions are not allowed to read the data while it is exclusively locked. Some databases do not allow transactions to read their own data while it is exclusively locked.

Snapshots

Some databases get around locking by providing every transaction with its own snapshot of the data. A snapshot is a frozen view of the data that is taken when the transaction begins. Snapshots can prevent dirty reads, nonrepeatable reads, and phantom reads. They can be problematic because the data is not real-time; it is old the instant the snapshot is taken.

Transaction Isolation Levels

Transaction isolation is defined in terms of the isolation conditions (dirty reads, repeatable reads, and phantom reads). Isolation levels are commonly used in database systems to describe how locking is applied to data within a transaction.[*] The following terms are usually used to discuss isolation levels:

Read Uncommitted

The transaction can read uncommitted data (i.e., data changed by a different transaction that is still in progress).

Dirty reads, nonrepeatable reads, and phantom reads can occur. Bean methods with this isolation level can read uncommitted changes.

Read Committed

The transaction cannot read uncommitted data; data that is being changed by a different transaction cannot be read.

Dirty reads are prevented; nonrepeatable reads and phantom reads can occur. Bean methods with this isolation level cannot read uncommitted data.

Repeatable Read

The transaction cannot change data that is being read by a different transaction.

Dirty reads and nonrepeatable reads are prevented; phantom reads can occur. Bean methods with this isolation level have the same restrictions as Read Committed and can execute only repeatable reads.

Serializable

The transaction has exclusive read and update privileges to data; different transactions can neither read nor write to the same data.

Dirty reads, nonrepeatable reads, and phantom reads are prevented. This isolation level is the most restrictive.

These isolation levels are the same as those defined for JDBC. Specifically, they map to the static final variables in the java.sql.Connection class. The behavior modeled by the isolation levels in the connection class is the same as the behavior described here.

---

[*] Isolation conditions are covered in detail by ANSI SQL-92 Specification, Document Number: ANSI X3.135-1992 (R1998).

The exact behavior of these isolation levels depends largely on the locking mechanism used by the underlying database or resource. How the isolation levels work depends in large part on how your database supports them.

In EJB, the deployer sets transaction isolation levels in a vendor-specific way if the container manages the transaction. The EJB developer sets the transaction isolation level if the enterprise bean manages its own transactions. Up to this point we have discussed only container-managed transactions; we will discuss bean-managed transactions later in this chapter.

Balancing Performance Against Consistency

Generally speaking, as the isolation levels become more restrictive, the performance of the system decreases because more restrictive isolation levels prevent transactions from accessing the same data. If isolation levels are very restrictive, like Serializable, then all transactions, even simple reads, must wait in line to execute. This can result in a system that is very slow. EJB systems that process a large number of concurrent transactions and need to be very fast will therefore avoid the Serializable isolation level where it is not necessary, since it will be prohibitively slow.

Isolation levels, however, also enforce consistency of data. More restrictive isolation levels help ensure that invalid data is not used for performing updates. The old adage "garbage in, garbage out" applies here. The Serializable isolation level ensures that data is never accessed concurrently by transactions, thus ensuring that the data is always consistent.

Choosing the correct isolation level requires some research about the database you are using and how it handles locking. You must also balance the performance needs of your system against consistency. This is not a cut-and-dried process, because different applications use data differently.

Although there are only three ships in Titan's system, the entity beans that represent them are included in most of Titan's transactions. This means that many, possibly hundreds, of transactions will be accessing these Ship EJBs at the same time. Access to Ship EJBs needs to be fast or it becomes a bottleneck, so we do not want to use a restrictive isolation level. At the same time, the ship data also needs to be consistent; otherwise, hundreds of transactions will be using invalid data. Therefore, we need to use a strong isolation level when making changes to ship information. To accommodate these conflicting requirements, we can apply different isolation levels to different methods.

Most transactions use the Ship EJB's get methods to obtain information. This is *read-only* behavior, so the isolation level for the get methods can be very low, such as Read Uncommitted. The set methods of the Ship EJB are almost never used; the name of the ship probably will not change for years. However, the data changed by the set methods must be isolated to prevent dirty reads by other transactions, so we will use the most restrictive isolation level, Serializable, on the ship's set methods. By using different isolation levels on different business methods, we can balance consistency against performance.

Controlling isolation levels

Different EJB servers allow different levels of granularity for setting isolation levels; some servers defer this responsibility to the database. Most EJB servers control the isolation level through the resource access API (e.g., JDBC and JMS) and may allow different resources to have different isolation levels, but will generally require that access to the same resource within a single transaction use a consistent isolation level. You will need to consult your vendor's documentation to find out the level of control your server offers.

Bean-managed transactions in session beans (stateful and stateless) and message-driven beans (EJB 2.0), however, allow the EJB developer to specify the transaction isolation level using the API of the resource providing persistent storage. The JDBC API, for example, provides a mechanism for specifying the isolation level of the database connection. The following code shows how this is done. Bean-managed transactions are covered in more detail later in this chapter.

```
...
DataSource source = (javax.sql.DataSource)
    jndiCntxt.lookup("java:comp/env/jdbc/titanDB");

Connection con = source.getConnection();
con.setTransactionIsolation(Connection.TRANSACTION_SERIALIZABLE);
...
```

You can set the isolation level to be different for different resources within the same transaction, but all enterprise beans that use the same resource in a transaction should use the same isolation level.

Nontransactional Beans

Beans that reside outside a transaction scope normally provide some kind of stateless service that does not directly manipulate data in a data store. While these types of enterprise beans may be necessary as utilities during a transaction, they do not need to meet the stringent ACID requirements of a transaction.

Consider a nontransactional stateless session bean, the Quote EJB, that provides live stock quotes. This EJB may respond to a request from a transactional EJB involved in a stock purchase transaction. The success or failure of the stock purchase, as a transaction, will not impact the state or operations of the Quote EJB, so it does not need to be part of the transaction. Beans that are involved in transactions are subjected to the isolated ACID property, which means that their services *cannot* be shared during the life of the transaction. Making an enterprise bean transactional can be an expensive runtime activity. Declaring an EJB to be nontransactional (i.e., NotSupported) leaves it out of the transaction scope, which may improve the performance and availability of that service.

Explicit Transaction Management

 Although this section covers JTA, it is strongly recommended that you do not attempt to manage transactions explicitly. Through transaction attributes, Enterprise JavaBeans provides a comprehensive and simple mechanism for delimiting transactions at the method level and propagating transactions automatically. Only developers with a thorough understanding of transactional systems should attempt to use JTA with EJB.

In EJB, implicit transaction management is provided on the enterprise bean method level so that we can define transactions that are delimited by the scope of the method being executed. This is one of the primary advantages of EJB over cruder distributed object implementations: it reduces complexity and therefore programmer error. In addition, declarative transaction demarcation, as used in EJB, separates the transactional behavior from the business logic; a change to transactional behavior does not require changes to the business logic. In rare situations, however, it may be necessary to take control of transactions explicitly. To do this, it is necessary to have a much more complete understanding of transactions.

Explicit management of transactions is complex and is normally accomplished using the OMG's Object Transaction Service (OTS) or the Java implementation of OTS, the Java Transaction Service (JTS). OTS and JTS provide APIs that allow developers to work with transaction managers and resources (e.g., databases and JMS providers) directly. While the JTS implementation of OTS is robust and complete, it is not the easiest API to work with; it requires clean and intentional control over the bounds of enrollment in transactions.

Enterprise JavaBeans supports a much simpler API, the Java Transaction API (JTA), for working with transactions. This API is implemented by the javax.transaction package. JTA actually consists of two components: a high-level transactional client interface and a low-level X/Open XA interface. We are concerned with the high-level client interface, since that is the one accessible to the enterprise beans and is the recommended transactional interface for client applications. The low-level XA interface is used by the EJB server and container to automatically coordinate transactions with resources such as databases.

As an application and EJB developer, your use of explicit transaction management will probably focus on one very simple interface: javax.transaction.UserTransaction. UserTransaction provides an interface to the transaction manager that allows the application developer to manage the scope of a transaction explicitly. Here is an example of how explicit demarcation might be used in an EJB or client application:

```
Object ref = getInitialContext().lookup("TravelAgentHomeRemote");
TravelAgentHome home = (TravelAgentHome)
    PortableRemoteObject.narrow(ref, TravelAgentHome.class);

TravelAgent tr1 = home.create(customer);
tr1.setCruiseID(cruiseID);
tr1.setCabinID(cabin_1);
TravelAgent tr2 = home.create(customer);
tr2.setCruiseID(cruiseID);
tr2.setCabinID(cabin_2);

javax.transaction.UserTransaction tran = ...; // Get the UserTransaction.
tran.begin();
tr1.bookPassage(visaCard,price);
tr2.bookPassage(visaCard,price);
tran.commit();
```

The client application needs to book two cabins for the same customer—in this case, the customer is purchasing a cabin for himself and his children. The customer does not want to book either cabin unless he can get both, so the client application is designed to include both bookings in the same transaction. Explicitly marking the transaction's boundaries through the use of the javax.transaction.UserTransaction object does this. Each enterprise bean method invoked by the current thread between the UserTransaction.begin() and UserTransaction.commit() methods is included in the same transaction scope, according to the transaction attributes of the enterprise bean methods invoked.

Obviously this example is contrived, but the point it makes is clear. Transactions can be controlled directly, instead of depending on method scope to delimit them. The advantage of using explicit transaction demarcation is that it gives the client control over the bounds of a transaction. The client, in this case, may be a client application or another enterprise bean.[*] In either case, the same javax.transaction. UserTransaction is used, but it is obtained from different sources depending on whether it is needed on the client or in an enterprise bean.

Java 2 Enterprise Edition (J2EE) specifies how a client application can obtain a UserTransaction object using JNDI. Here's how a client obtains a UserTransaction object if the EJB container is part of a J2EE system (J2EE and its relationship with EJB is covered in more detail in Chapter 17):

```
...
Context jndiCntx = new InitialContext();
UserTransaction tran = (UserTransaction)
    jndiCntx.lookup("java:comp/UserTransaction");
```

---

[*] Only beans declared as managing their own transactions (bean-managed transaction beans) can use the UserTransaction interface.

```
    utx.begin();
    ...
    utx.commit();
    ...
```

Enterprise beans can also manage transactions explicitly. Only session beans and message-driven beans with the <transaction-type> value of Bean can manage their own transactions. Enterprise beans that manage their own transactions are frequently referred to as bean-managed transaction (BMT) beans. Entity beans can never be BMT beans. BMT beans do not declare transaction attributes for their methods. Here's how a session bean declares that it will manage transactions explicitly:

```
<ejb-jar>
    <enterprise-beans>
    ...
        <session>
        ...
        <transaction-type>Bean</transaction-type>
        ...
```

To manage its own transaction, an enterprise bean needs to obtain a UserTransaction object. An enterprise bean obtains a reference to the UserTransaction from the EJBContext, as shown here:

```
public class HypotheticalBean extends SessionBean {
    SessionContext ejbContext;

    public void someMethod() {
        try {
            UserTransaction ut = ejbContext.getUserTransaction();
            ut.begin();

            // Do some work.

            ut.commit();
        } catch(IllegalStateException ise) {...}
            catch(SystemException se) {...}
            catch(TransactionRolledbackException tre) {...}
            catch(HeuristicRollbackException hre) {...}
            catch(HeuristicMixedException hme) {...}
```

An enterprise bean can also access the UserTransaction from the JNDI ENC, as shown in the following example. Both methods are legal and proper. The enterprise bean performs the lookup using the "java:comp/env/UserTransaction" context:

```
InitialContext jndiCntx = new InitialContext();
UserTransaction tran = (UserTransaction)
    jndiCntx.lookup("java:comp/env/UserTransaction");
```

Transaction Propagation in Bean-Managed Transactions

With stateless session beans, transactions that are managed using the UserTransaction must be started and completed within the same method. In other words, `UserTransaction` transactions cannot be started in one method and ended in another. This makes sense because stateless session bean instances are shared across many clients; so while one stateless instance may service a client's first request, a completely different instance may service a subsequent request by the same client. With stateful session beans, however, a transaction can begin in one method and be committed in another because a stateful session bean is used by only one client. This allows a stateful session bean to associate itself with a transaction across several different client-invoked methods. As an example, imagine the TravelAgent EJB as a BMT bean. In the following code, the transaction is started in the `setCruiseID()` method and completed in the `bookPassage()` method. This allows the TravelAgent EJB's methods to be associated with the same transaction.

EJB 2.0: TravelAgentBean

The definition of the `TravelAgentBean` class looks like this in EJB 2.0:

```
import com.titan.reservation.*;

import java.sql.*;
import javax.sql.DataSource;
import java.util.Vector;
import java.rmi.RemoteException;
import javax.naming.NamingException;
import javax.ejb.EJBException;

public class TravelAgentBean implements javax.ejb.SessionBean {
    ...
    public void setCruiseID(Integer cruiseID)
        throws javax.ejb.FinderException {
        try {
            ejbContext.getUserTransaction().begin();
            CruiseHomeLocal home = (CruiseHomeLocal)
                jndiContext.lookup("java:comp/env/ejb/CruiseHome");

            cruise = home.findByPrimaryKey(cruiseID);
        } catch(RemoteException re) {
            throw new EJBException(re);
        }

    }
    public TicketDO bookPassage(CreditCardDO card, double price)
        throws IncompleteConversationalState {

        try {
            if (ejbContext.getUserTransaction().getStatus() !=
                javax.transaction.Status.STATUS_ACTIVE) {

                throw new EJBException("Transaction is not active");
            }
        } catch(javax.transaction.SystemException se) {
            throw new EJBException(se);
        }
```

```
        if (customer == null || cruise == null || cabin == null)
        {
            throw new IncompleteConversationalState();
        }
        try {
            ReservationHomeLocal resHome = (ReservationHomeLocal)
                jndiContext.lookup("java:comp/env/ejb/ReservationHomeLocal");

            ReservationLocal reservation =
                resHome.create(customer, cruise, cabin, price);

            Object ref =
                jndiContext.lookup("java:comp/env/ejb/ProcessPaymentHomeRemote");

            ProcessPaymentHomeRemote ppHome = (ProcessPaymentHomeRemote)
                PortableRemoteObject.narrow(ref, ProcessPaymentHomeRemote.class);

            ProcessPaymentRemote process = ppHome.create();
            process.byCredit(customer, card, price);

            TicketDO ticket = new TicketDO(customer,cruise,cabin,price);

            ejbContext.getUserTransaction().commit();

            return ticket;
        } catch(Exception e) {
            throw new EJBException(e);
        }
    }
    ...
}
```

EJB 1.1: TravelAgentBean

In EJB 1.1, the TravelAgentBean class definition looks like this:

```
public class TravelAgentBean implements javax.ejb.SessionBean {
    ...
    public void setCruiseID(Integer cruiseID) throws javax.ejb.FinderException {
        try {
            ejbContext.getUserTransaction().begin();
            CruiseHomeRemote home = (CruiseHomeRemote)
                getHome("CruiseHome", CruiseHomeRemote. class);
            cruise = home.findByPrimaryKey(cruiseID);
        } catch(RemoteException re) {
            throw new EJBException(re);
        }

    }
    public TicketDO bookPassage(CreditCardDO card, double price)
        throws IncompleteConversationalState {

        try {
            if (ejbContext.getUserTransaction().getStatus() !=
                javax.transaction.Status.STATUS_ACTIVE) {
```

```
            throw new EJBException("Transaction is not active");
        }
    } catch(javax.transaction.SystemException se) {
        throw new EJBException(se);
    }

    if (customer == null || cruise == null || cabin == null) {
        throw new IncompleteConversationalState();
    }
    try {
        ReservationHomeRemote resHome = (ReservationHomeRemote)
            getHome("ReservationHomeRemote", ReservationHomeRemote.class);
        ReservationRemote reservation =
            resHome.create(customer, cruise, cabin, price);
        ProcessPaymentHomeRemote ppHome = (ProcessPaymentHomeRemote)
            getHome("ProcessPaymentHomeRemote", ProcessPaymentHomeRemote.class);
        ProcessPaymentRemote process = ppHome.create();
        process.byCredit(customer, card, price);

        TicketDO ticket = new TicketDO(customer,cruise,cabin,price);

        ejbContext.getUserTransaction().commit();

        return ticket;
    } catch(Exception e) {
        throw new EJBException(e);
    }
}
...
}
```

Repeated calls to the EJBContext.getUserTransaction() method return a reference to the same UserTransaction object. The container is required to retain the association between the transaction and the stateful bean instance across multiple client calls until the transaction terminates.

In the bookPassage() method, we can check the status of the transaction to ensure that it is still active. If the transaction is no longer active, we throw an exception. The use of the getStatus() method is covered in more detail later in this chapter.

When a bean-managed transaction method is invoked by a client that is already involved in a transaction, the client's transaction is suspended until the method returns. This suspension occurs regardless of whether the BMT bean explicitly started its own transaction within the method or the transaction was started in a previous method invocation. The client transaction is always suspended until the BMT method returns.

Transaction control across methods is strongly discouraged because it can result in improperly managed transactions and long-lived transactions that lock up resources.

EJB 2.0: Message-driven beans and bean-managed transactions

Message-driven beans also have the option of managing their own transactions. In the case of MDBs, the scope of the transaction must begin and end within the onMessage() method—it is not possible for a bean-managed transaction to span onMessage() calls.

You can transform the ReservationProcessor EJB into a BMT bean simply by changing its <transaction-type> value to Bean:

```
<ejb-jar>
    <enterprise-beans>
    ...
        <message-driven>
        ...
        <transaction-type>Bean</transaction-type>
        ...
```

In this case, the ReservationProcessorBean class would be modified to use the javax.transaction.UserTransaction to mark the beginning and end of the transaction in onMessage():

```
public class ReservationProcessorBean implements javax.ejb.MessageDrivenBean,
    javax.jms.MessageListener {

    MessageDrivenContext ejbContext;
    Context jndiContext;

    public void onMessage(Message message) {
        try {

            ejbContext.getUserTransaction().begin();

            MapMessage reservationMsg = (MapMessage)message;

            Integer customerPk = (Integer)reservationMsg.getObject("CustomerID");
            Integer cruisePk = (Integer)reservationMsg.getObject("CruiseID");
            Integer cabinPk = (Integer)reservationMsg.getObject("CabinID");
            double price = reservationMsg.getDouble("Price");

            //get the credit card
            Date expirationDate =
                new Date(reservationMsg.getLong("CreditCardExpDate"));
            String cardNumber = reservationMsg.getString("CreditCardNum");
            String cardType = reservationMsg.getString("CreditCardType");

            CreditCardDO card = new CreditCardDO(cardNumber,expirationDate,cardType);
            CustomerRemote customer = getCustomer(customerPk);
            CruiseLocal cruise = getCruise(cruisePk);
            CabinLocal cabin = getCabin(cabinPk);

            ReservationHomeLocal resHome = (ReservationHomeLocal)
                jndiContext.lookup("java:comp/env/ejb/ReservationHomeLocal");
```

```
    ReservationLocal reservation =
        resHome.create(customer,cruise,cabin,price,new Date());

    Object ref =
        jndiContext.lookup("java:comp/env/ejb/ProcessPaymentHomeRemote");
    ProcessPaymentHomeRemote ppHome = (ProcessPaymentHomeRemote)
        PortableRemoteObject.narrow(ref,ProcessPaymentHomeRemote.class);
    ProcessPaymentRemote process = ppHome.create();

    process.byCredit(customer,card,price);
    TicketDO ticket = new TicketDO(customer,cruise,cabin,price);
    deliverTicket(reservationMsg,ticket);

    ejbContext.getUserTransaction.commit();

  } catch(Exception e) {
      throw new EJBException(e);
  }
}
...
```

It is important to understand that in BMT, the message consumed by the MDB is not part of the transaction. When an MDB uses container-managed transactions, the message it is handling is a part of the transaction, so if the transaction is rolled back, the consumption of the message is also rolled back, forcing the JMS provider to redeliver the message. But with bean-managed transactions, the message is not part of the transaction, so if the BMT transaction is rolled back, the JMS provider will not be aware of the transaction's failure. However, all is not lost, because the JMS provider can still rely on message acknowledgment to determine if the message was successfully delivered.

The EJB container will acknowledge the message if the onMessage() method returns successfully. If, however, a RuntimeException is thrown by the onMessage() method, the container will not acknowledge the message and the JMS provider will suspect a problem and will probably attempt to redeliver the message. If redelivery of a message is important when a transaction fails in BMT, your best course of action is to ensure that the onMessage() method throws an EJBException, so that the container will *not* acknowledge the message received from the JMS provider.

 Vendors use proprietary (declarative) mechanisms to specify the number of times to redeliver messages to BMT/NotSupported MDBs that "fail" to acknowledge receipt. The JMS provider may provide a "dead message" area into which such messages will be placed if they cannot be successfully processed according to the retry count. The dead message area can be monitored by administrators, and delivered messages can be detected and handled manually.

Although the message is not part of the transaction, everything else between the UserTransaction.begin() and UserTransaction.commit() methods is part of the same transaction. This includes creating a new Reservation EJB and processing the credit card using the ProcessPayment EJB. If a transaction failure occurs, these operations will be rolled back. The transaction also includes the use of the JMS API in the deliverTicket() method to send the ticket message. If a transaction failure occurs, the ticket message will not be sent.

Heuristic Decisions

Transactions are normally controlled by a *transaction manager* (often the EJB server) that manages the ACID characteristics across several enterprise beans, databases, and servers. This transaction manager uses a two-phase commit (2-PC) to manage transactions. 2-PC is a protocol for managing transactions that commits updates in two stages. 2-PC is complex, but basically it requires that servers and databases cooperate through an intermediary, the transaction manager, to ensure that all the data is made durable together. Some EJB servers support 2-PC while others do not, and the value of this transaction mechanism is a source of some debate. The important point to remember is that a transaction manager controls the transaction; based on the results of a poll against the resources (databases, JMS providers, and other resources), it decides whether all the updates should be committed or rolled back. A *heuristic decision* is when one of the resources makes a unilateral decision to commit or roll back without permission from the transaction manager. Once a heuristic decision has been made, the atomicity of the transaction is lost and data-integrity errors can occur.

UserTransaction, discussed in the next section, throws a few different exceptions related to heuristic decisions; these are included in the following discussion.

UserTransaction

UserTransaction is a Java interface defined in the following code. EJB servers are not required to support the rest of JTA, nor are they required to use JTS for their transaction service. The UserTransaction is defined as follows:

```
public interface javax.transaction.UserTransaction {

    public abstract void begin() throws IllegalStateException, SystemException;
    public abstract void commit() throws IllegalStateException, SystemException,
        TransactionRolledbackException, HeuristicRollbackException,
        HeuristicMixedException;
    public abstract int getStatus();
    public abstract void rollback() throws IllegalStateException, SecurityException,
        SystemException;
    public abstract void setRollbackOnly() throws IllegalStateException,
        SystemException;
    public abstract void setTransactionTimeout(int seconds) throws SystemException;

}
```

Here's what the methods defined in this interface do:

begin()

Invoking the begin() method creates a new transaction. The thread that executes the begin() method is immediately associated with the new transaction, which is then propagated to any EJB that supports existing transactions. The begin() method can throw one of two checked exceptions. An IllegalStateException is thrown when begin() is called by a thread that is already associated with a transaction. You must complete any transactions associated with that thread before beginning a new transaction. A SystemException is thrown if the transaction manager (i.e., the EJB server) encounters an unexpected error condition.

commit()

The commit() method completes the transaction that is associated with the current thread. When commit() is executed, the current thread is no longer associated with a transaction. This method can throw several checked exceptions. An IllegalStateException is thrown if the current thread is not associated with a transaction. A SystemException is thrown if the transaction manager (the EJB server) encounters an unexpected error condition. A TransactionRolledback-Exception is thrown when the entire transaction is rolled back instead of committed; this can happen if one of the resources was unable to perform an update or if the UserTransaction.rollBackOnly() method was called. A HeuristicRollbackException indicates that heuristic decisions were made by one or more resources to roll back the transaction. A HeuristicMixedException indicates that heuristic decisions were made by resources to both roll back and commit the transaction; that is, some resources decided to roll back while others decided to commit.

rollback()

The rollback() method is invoked to roll back the transaction and undo updates. The rollback() method can throw one of three different checked exceptions. A SecurityException is thrown if the thread using the UserTransaction object is not allowed to roll back the transaction. An IllegalStateException is thrown if the current thread is not associated with a transaction. A SystemException is thrown if the transaction manager (the EJB server) encounters an unexpected error condition.

setRollbackOnly()

The setRollbackOnly() method is invoked to mark the transaction for rollback. This means that, whether or not the updates executed within the transaction succeed, the transaction must be rolled back when completed. This method can be invoked by any TX_BEAN_MANAGED EJB participating in the transaction or by the client application. The setRollBackOnly() method can throw one of two checked exceptions. An IllegalStateException is thrown if the current thread is not associated with a transaction. A SystemException is thrown if the transaction manager (the EJB server) encounters an unexpected error condition.

setTransactionTimeout(int seconds)

> The setTransactionTimeout(int seconds) method sets the life span of a transaction; i.e., how long it will live before timing out. The transaction must complete before the transaction timeout is reached. If this method is not called, the transaction manager (EJB server) automatically sets the timeout. If this method is invoked with a value of 0 seconds, the default timeout of the transaction manager will be used. This method must be invoked after the begin() method. A SystemException is thrown if the transaction manager (EJB server) encounters an unexpected error condition.

getStatus()

> The getStatus() method returns an integer that can be compared to constants defined in the javax.transaction.Status interface. This method can be used by a sophisticated programmer to determine the status of a transaction associated with a UserTransaction object. A SystemException is thrown if the transaction manager (EJB server) encounters an unexpected error condition.

Status

Status is a simple interface that contains no methods, only constants. Its sole purpose is to provide a set of constants that describe the current status of a transactional object—in this case, the UserTransaction:

```
interface javax.transaction.Status
{
    public final static int STATUS_ACTIVE;
    public final static int STATUS_COMMITTED;
    public final static int STATUS_COMMITTING;
    public final static int STATUS_MARKED_ROLLBACK;
    public final static int STATUS_NO_TRANSACTION;
    public final static int STATUS_PREPARED;
    public final static int STATUS_PREPARING;
    public final static int STATUS_ROLLEDBACK;
    public final static int STATUS_ROLLING_BACK;
    public final static int STATUS_UNKNOWN;
}
```

The value returned by getStatus() tells the client using the UserTransaction the status of a transaction. Here's what the constants mean:

STATUS_ACTIVE

> An active transaction is associated with the UserTransaction object. This status is returned after a transaction has been started and prior to a transaction manager beginning a two-phase commit. (Transactions that have been suspended are still considered active.)

STATUS_COMMITTED

> A transaction is associated with the UserTransaction object; the transaction has been committed. It is likely that heuristic decisions have been made; otherwise,

the transaction would have been destroyed and the STATUS_NO_TRANSACTION constant would have been returned instead.

STATUS_COMMITTING

A transaction is associated with the UserTransaction object; the transaction is in the process of committing. The UserTransaction object returns this status if the transaction manager has decided to commit but has not yet completed the process.

STATUS_MARKED_ROLLBACK

A transaction is associated with the UserTransaction object; the transaction has been marked for rollback, perhaps as a result of a UserTransaction.set-RollbackOnly() operation invoked somewhere else in the application.

STATUS_NO_TRANSACTION

No transaction is currently associated with the UserTransaction object. This occurs after a transaction has completed or if no transaction has been created. This value is returned rather than throwing an IllegalStateException.

STATUS_PREPARED

A transaction is associated with the UserTransaction object. The transaction has been prepared, which means that the first phase of the two-phase commit process has completed.

STATUS_PREPARING

A transaction is associated with the UserTransaction object; the transaction is in the process of preparing, which means that the transaction manager is in the middle of executing the first phase of the two-phase commit.

STATUS_ROLLEDBACK

A transaction is associated with the UserTransaction object; the outcome of the transaction has been identified as a rollback. It is likely that heuristic decisions have been made; otherwise, the transaction would have been destroyed and the STATUS_NO_TRANSACTION constant would have been returned.

STATUS_ROLLING_BACK

A transaction is associated with the UserTransaction object; the transaction is in the process of rolling back.

STATUS_UNKNOWN

A transaction is associated with the UserTransaction object; its current status cannot be determined. This is a transient condition and subsequent invocations will ultimately return a different status.

EJBContext Rollback Methods

Only BMT beans have access to the UserTransaction from the EJBContext and JNDI ENC. Container-managed transaction (CMT) beans cannot use the UserTransaction.

CMT beans use the `setRollbackOnly()` and `getRollbackOnly()` methods of the `EJBContext` to interact with the current transaction instead.

The `setRollbackOnly()` method gives an enterprise bean the power to veto a transaction. This power can be used if the enterprise bean detects a condition that would cause inconsistent data to be committed when the transaction completes. Once an enterprise bean invokes the `setRollbackOnly()` method, the current transaction is marked for rollback and cannot be committed by any other participant in the transaction—including the container.

The `getRollbackOnly()` method returns `true` if the current transaction has been marked for rollback. This can be used to avoid executing work that would not be committed anyway. If, for example, an exception is thrown and captured within an enterprise bean method, `getRollbackOnly()` can be used to determine whether the exception caused the current transaction to be rolled back. If it did, there is no sense in continuing the processing. If it did not, the EJB has an opportunity to correct the problem and retry the task that failed. Only expert EJB developers should attempt to retry tasks within a transaction. Alternatively, if the exception did not cause a rollback (`getRollbackOnly()` returns `false`), a rollback can be forced using the `setRollbackOnly()` method.

BMT beans must *not* use the `setRollbackOnly()` and `getRollbackOnly()` methods of the `EJBContext`. BMT beans should use the `getStatus()` and `rollback()` methods on the `UserTransaction` object to check for rollback and force a rollback, respectively.

Exceptions and Transactions

Exceptions have a large impact on the outcome of transactions and must be discussed in detail so that bean developers understand the relationship between them.

Application Exceptions Versus System Exceptions

An application exception is any exception that does *not* extend `java.lang.RuntimeException` or `java.rmi.RemoteException`. System exceptions are `java.lang.RuntimeException` and its subtypes, including `EJBException`.

 An application exception must never extend either the `RuntimeException`, the `RemoteException`, or one of their subtypes.

Transactions are *automatically* rolled back if a system exception is thrown from an enterprise bean method. Transactions are *not* automatically rolled back if an application exception is thrown. If you remember these two rules, you will be well prepared to deal with exceptions and transactions in EJB.

The bookPassage() method is a good illustration of an application exception and how it is used. The following sections show the code for the bookPassage() method.

EJB 2.0: bookPassage() method

```java
public TicketDO bookPassage(CreditCardDO card, double price)
    throws IncompleteConversationalState {

    if (customer == null || cruise == null || cabin == null) {
        throw new IncompleteConversationalState();
    }
    try {
        ReservationHomeLocal resHome = (ReservationHomeLocal)
            jndiContext.lookup("java:comp/env/ejb/ReservationHomeLocal");

        ReservationLocal reservation =
            resHome.create(customer, cruise, cabin, price);

        Object ref =
            jndiContext.lookup("java:comp/env/ejb/ProcessPaymentHomeRemote");

        ProcessPaymentHomeRemote ppHome = (ProcessPaymentHomeRemote)
            PortableRemoteObject.narrow(ref, ProcessPaymentHomeRemote.class);

        ProcessPaymentRemote process = ppHome.create();
        process.byCredit(customer, card, price);

        TicketDO ticket = new TicketDO(customer,cruise,cabin,price);

        return ticket;
    } catch(Exception e) {
        throw new EJBException(e);
    }
}
```

EJB 1.1: bookPassage() method

```java
public TicketDO bookPassage(CreditCardDO card, double price)
    throws IncompleteConversationalState {

    if (customer == null || cruise == null || cabin == null) {
        throw new IncompleteConversationalState();
    }
    try {
        ReservationHomeRemote resHome = (ReservationHomeRemote)
            getHome("ReservationHomeRemote", ReservationHomeRemote.class);
        ReservationRemote reservation =
            resHome.create(customer, cruise, cabin, price);
        ProcessPaymentHomeRemote ppHome = (ProcessPaymentHomeRemote)
            getHome("ProcessPaymentHomeRemote", ProcessPaymentHomeRemote.class);
        ProcessPaymentRemote process = ppHome.create();
        process.byCredit(customer, card, price);
```

```
        TicketDO ticket = new TicketDO(customer,cruise,cabin,price);

        return ticket;
    } catch(Exception e) {
        throw new EJBException(e);
    }
}
```

System exceptions

System exceptions are the RuntimeException and its subclasses. The EJBException is a subclass of the RuntimeException, so it is considered a system exception.

System exceptions always cause a transaction to roll back when they are thrown from an enterprise bean method. Any RuntimeException (EJBException, NullPointer-Exception, IndexOutOfBoundsException, etc.) thrown within the bookPassage() method is handled by the container automatically and results in a transaction roll-back. In Java, RuntimeException types do not need to be declared in the throws clause of the method signature or handled using try/catch blocks; they are automatically thrown from the method.

RuntimeException types thrown from within enterprise beans always cause the current transaction to roll back. If the method in which the exception occurs started the transaction, the transaction is rolled back. If the transaction started from a client that invoked the method, the client's transaction is marked for rollback and cannot be committed.

System exceptions are handled automatically by the container, which will always:

- Roll back the transaction.
- Log the exception to alert the system administrator.
- Discard the EJB instance.

RuntimeExceptions thrown from the callback methods (ejbLoad(), ejbActivate(), etc.) are treated the same as exceptions thrown from business methods.

While EJB requires that system exceptions be logged, it does not specify how exceptions should be logged or the format of the log file. The exact mechanism for recording exceptions and reporting them to the system administrator is left to the vendor.

When a system exception occurs, the EJB instance is discarded, which means that it is dereferenced and garbage collected. The container assumes that the EJB instance may have corrupt variables or otherwise be unstable and is therefore unsafe to use.

The impact of discarding an EJB instance depends on the enterprise bean's type. In the case of stateless session beans and entity beans, the client does not notice that the instance was discarded. These instance types are not dedicated to a particular client; they are swapped in and out of an instance pool, so any instance can service a new request. With stateful session beans, however, the impact on the client is severe. Stateful session beans are dedicated to a single client and maintain conversational state. Discarding a stateful bean instance destroys the instance's conversational state and invalidates the client's reference to the EJB. When stateful session instances are discarded, subsequent invocations of the EJB's methods by the client result in a NoSuchObjectException, a subclass of the RemoteException.[*]

With message-driven beans, a system exception thrown by the onMessage() method or one of the callback methods (ejbCreate() or ejbRemove()) will cause the bean instance to be discarded. If the MDB was BMT bean, the message it was handling may or may not be redelivered, depending on when the EJB container acknowledges delivery. In the case of container-managed transactions, the container will roll back the transaction, so the message will not be acknowledged and may be redelivered.

In session and entity beans, when a system exception occurs and the instance is discarded, a RemoteException is always thrown to remote clients; that is, clients using the beans' remote component interfaces. If the client started the transaction, which was then propagated to the EJB, a system exception (thrown by the enterprise bean method) will be caught by the container and rethrown as a javax.transaction. TransactionRolledbackException. The TransactionRolledbackException is a subtype of the RemoteException; it is a more explicit indication to the client that a rollback occurred.

In EJB 2.0 session and entity beans, when a system exception occurs and the instance is discarded, an EJBException is always thrown to any local enterprise bean clients (i.e., clients using the enterprise bean's local component interfaces). If the client started the transaction and it was then propagated to the EJB, a system exception (thrown by the enterprise bean method) will be caught by the container and rethrown as a javax.ejb. TransactionRolledbackLocalException. The TransactionRolledbackLocalException is a subtype of the EJBException; it is a more explicit indication to the client that a rollback occurred. In all other cases, whether the EJB is container-managed or bean-managed, a RuntimeException thrown from within the enterprise bean method will be caught by the container and rethrown as an EJBException.

An EJBException should generally be thrown when a subsystem throws an exception, such as JDBC throwing a SQLException or JMS throwing a JMSException. In some cases, however, the bean developer may attempt to handle the exception and retry an operation rather then throw an EJBException. This should be done only when the exceptions thrown by the subsystem and their repercussions on the transaction are well understood. As a rule of thumb, rethrow subsystem exceptions as EJBExceptions and allow the EJB container to roll back the transaction and discard the bean instance.

---

[*] Although the instance is always discarded with a RuntimeException, the impact on the remote reference may vary depending on the vendor.

The callback methods defined in the javax.ejb.EntityBean and javax.ejb.SessionBean interfaces declare the java.rmi.RemoteException in their throws clauses. This is left over from EJB 1.0 and has been deprecated since EJB 1.1. You should never throw RemoteExceptions from callback methods or any other bean class methods.

Application exceptions

An application exception is normally thrown in response to a business-logic error, as opposed to a system error. Application exceptions are always delivered directly to the client, without being repackaged as RemoteException or EJBException (EJB 2.0) types. They do not typically cause transactions to roll back; the client usually has an opportunity to recover after an application exception is thrown. For example, the bookPassage() method throws an application exception called Incomplete-ConversationalState; this is an application exception because it does not extend RuntimeException or RemoteException. The IncompleteConversationalState exception is thrown if one of the arguments passed into the bookPassage() method is null. (Application errors are frequently used to report validation errors like this.) In this case, the exception is thrown before tasks are started and is clearly not the result of a subsystem (e.g., JDBC, JMS, Java RMI, JNDI) failure.

Because it is an application exception, throwing an IncompleteConversationalState exception does not result in a transaction rollback. The exception is thrown before any work is done, avoiding unnecessary processing by the bookPassage() method and providing the client (the enterprise bean or application that invoked the bookPassage() method) with an opportunity to recover and possibly retry the method call with valid arguments.

Business methods defined in the remote and local interfaces can throw any kind of application exception. These application exceptions must be declared in the method signatures of the remote and local interfaces and in the corresponding methods in the enterprise EJB classes.

The EJB create, find, and remove methods can also throw several exceptions defined in the javax.ejb package: CreateException, DuplicateKeyException, FinderException, ObjectNotFoundException, and RemoveException. These exceptions are considered application exceptions: they are delivered to the client as-is, without being repackaged as RemoteExceptions. Furthermore, these exceptions don't necessarily cause a transaction to roll back, giving the client the opportunity to retry the operation. These exceptions may be thrown by the EJBs themselves; in the case of container-managed persistence, the container can also throw any of these exceptions while handling the EJB's create, find, or remove methods (ejbCreate(), ejbFind(), and ejbRemove()). The container might, for example, throw a CreateException if it encounters a bad argument while attempting to insert a record for a container-managed EJB. You can always choose to throw a standard application exception from the appropriate method regardless of how persistence is managed.

Here is a detailed explanation of the five standard application exceptions and the situations in which they are thrown:

CreateException

The CreateException is thrown by the create() method in the remote interface. This exception can be thrown by the container if the container is managing persistence, or it can be thrown explicitly by the EJB developer in the ejbCreate() or ejbPostCreate() methods. It indicates that an application error (invalid arguments, etc.) occurred while the EJB was being created. If the container throws this exception, it may or may not roll back the transaction. Explicit transaction methods must be used to determine the outcome. Bean developers should roll back the transaction before throwing this exception only if data integrity is a concern.

DuplicateKeyException

The DuplicateKeyException is a subtype of the CreateException; it is thrown by the create() method in the remote interface. This exception can be thrown by the container if the container is managing persistence, or it can be thrown explicitly by the EJB developer in the ejbCreate() method. It indicates that an EJB with the same primary key already exists in the database. The transaction is typically not rolled back by the EJB provider or container before throwing this exception.

FinderException

The FinderException is thrown by the find methods in the home interface. This exception can be thrown by the container if the container is managing persistence, or it can be thrown explicitly by the EJB developer in the ejbFind() methods. It indicates that an application error (invalid arguments, etc.) occurred while the container was attempting to find the EJBs. Do not use this method to indicate that entities were not found. Multi-entity find methods return an empty collection if no entities were found; single-entity find methods throw an ObjectNotFoundException to indicate that no object was found. The transaction is typically not rolled back by the EJB provider or container before throwing this exception.

ObjectNotFoundException

The ObjectNotFoundException is thrown from a single-entity find method to indicate that the container could not find the requested entity. This exception can be thrown either by the container (if the container is managing persistence) or explicitly by the EJB developer in the ejbFind() methods. It should not be thrown to indicate a business-logic error (invalid arguments, etc.). Use the FinderException to indicate business-logic errors in single-entity find methods. The ObjectNotFoundException is thrown by single-entity find methods only to indicate that the entity requested was not found. Find methods that return multiple entities should return an empty collection if nothing is found. The transaction is typically not rolled back by the EJB provider or container before throwing this exception.

RemoveException

> The `RemoveException` is thrown from the `remove()` methods in the remote and home interfaces. This exception can be thrown by the container if the container is managing persistence, or it can be thrown explicitly by the EJB developer in the `ejbRemove()` method. It indicates that an application error has occurred while the EJB was being removed. The transaction may or may not have been rolled back by the container before throwing this exception. Explicit transaction methods must be used to determine the outcome. Bean developers should roll back the transaction before throwing the exception only if data integrity is a concern.

Table 14-1 summarizes the interactions between different types of exceptions and transactions in session and entity beans.

Table 14-1. Exception summary for session and entity beans

Transaction scope	Transaction type attributes	Exception thrown	Container's action	Client's view
Client-initiated transaction. The transaction is started by the client (application or EJB) and is propagated to the enterprise bean method.	transaction-type = Container transaction-attribute = Required| Mandatory| Supports	Application exception	If the EJB invoked `setRollbackOnly()`, mark the client's transaction for rollback. Rethrow the application exception.	Receives the application exception. The client's transaction may or may not have been marked for rollback.
		System exception	Mark the client's transaction for rollback. Log the error. Discard the instance. Rethrow the JTA `TransactionRolledbackException` to remote clients or the `javax.ejb.TransactionRolledbackLocalException` to EJB 2.0 local clients.	Remote clients receive the JTA `TransactionRolledbackException`; local clients receive the `javax.ejb.TransactionRolledbackLocalException`. The client's transaction has been rolled back.
Container-initiated transaction. The transaction started when the EJB's method was invoked and will end when the method completes.	transaction-type = Container transaction-attribute = Required| RequiresNew	Application exception	If the EJB invoked `setRollbackOnly()`, roll back the transaction and rethrow the application exception. If the EJB did not explicitly roll back the transaction, attempt to commit the transaction and rethrow the application exception.	Receives the application exception. The EJB's transaction may or may not have been rolled back. The client's transaction is not affected.

Table 14-1. Exception summary for session and entity beans (continued)

Transaction scope	Transaction type attributes	Exception thrown	Container's action	Client's view
		System exception	Roll back the transaction. Log the error. Discard the instance. Rethrow the RemoteException to remote clients or the EJBException to EJB 2.0 local clients.	Remote clients receive the RemoteException; local EJB 2.0 clients receive the EJBException. The EJB's transaction was rolled back. The client's transaction may or may not be marked for rollback, depending on the vendor.
The bean is not part of a transaction. The EJB was invoked but does not propagate the client's transaction and does not start its own transaction.	transaction-type = Container transaction-attribute = Never | NotSupported | Supports |	Application exception	Rethrow the application exception.	Receives the application exception. The client's transaction is not affected.
		System exception	Log the error. Discard the instance. Rethrow the RemoteException to remote clients or the EJBException to EJB 2.0 local clients.	Remote clients receive the RemoteException; local EJB 2.0 clients receive the EJBException. The client's transaction may or may not be marked for rollback, depending on the vendor.
Bean-managed transaction. The stateful or stateless session EJB uses the EJBContext to explicitly manage its own transaction.	transaction-type = Bean transaction-attribute = Bean-managed transaction EJBs do not use transaction attributes.	Application exception	Rethrow the application exception.	Receives the application exception. The client's transaction is not affected.
		System exception	Roll back the transaction. Log the error. Discard the instance. Rethrow the RemoteException to remote clients or the EJBException to EJB 2.0 local clients.	Remote clients receive the RemoteException; local EJB 2.0 clients receive the EJBException. The client's transaction is not affected.

Table 14-2 summarizes the interactions between different types of exceptions and transactions in message-driven beans.

Table 14-2. Exception summary for message-driven beans

Transaction scope	Transaction type attributes	Exception thrown	Container's action
Container-initiated transaction. The transaction started before the onMessage() method was invoked and will end when the method completes.	transaction-type = Container transaction-attribute = `Required`	System exception	Roll back the transaction. Log the error. Discard the instance.
Container-initiated transaction. No transaction was started.	transaction-type = Container transaction-attribute = `NotSupported`	System exception	Log the error. Discard the instance.
Bean-managed transaction. The message-driven bean uses the EJBContext to explicitly manage its own transaction.	transaction-type = Bean transaction-attribute = Bean-managed transaction EJBs do not use transaction attributes.	System exception	Roll back the transaction. Log the error. Discard the instance.

Transactional Stateful Session Beans

As you saw in Chapter 12, session beans can interact directly with the database as easily as they can manage the workflow of other enterprise beans. The ProcessPayment EJB, for example, makes inserts into the PAYMENT table when the byCredit() method is invoked, and the TravelAgent EJB queries the database directly when the listAvailableCabins() method is invoked. Stateless session beans such as the ProcessPayment EJB have no conversational state, so each method invocation must make changes to the database immediately. With stateful session beans, however, we may not want to make changes to the database until the transaction is complete. Remember, a stateful session bean can be just one participant out of many in a transaction, so it may be advisable to postpone database updates until the entire transaction is committed or to avoid updates if it is rolled back.

There are several different scenarios in which a stateful session bean would want to cache changes before applying them to the database. For example, think of a shopping cart implemented by a stateful session bean that accumulates several items for purchase. If the stateful bean implements SessionSynchronization, it can cache the items and write them to the database only when the transaction is complete.

The javax.ejb.SessionSynchronization interface allows a session bean to receive additional notification of the session's involvement in transactions. The addition of these transaction callback methods by the SessionSynchronization interface expands the EJB's awareness of its life cycle to include a new state, the *Transactional Method-Ready state*. This third state, although not discussed in Chapter 12, is always a part of the life cycle of a transactional stateful session bean. Implementing the SessionSynchronization interface simply makes it visible to the EJB. Figure 14-11 shows the stateful session bean with the additional state.

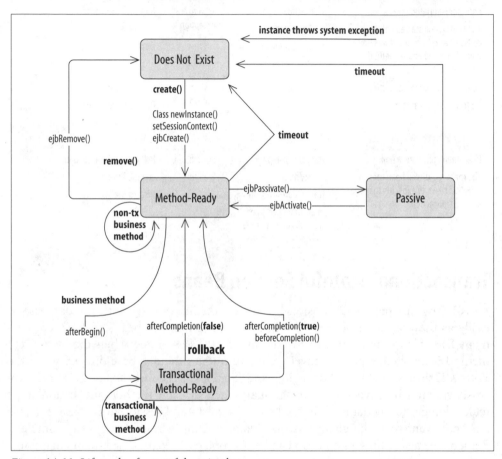

Figure 14-11. Life cycle of a stateful session bean

The SessionSynchronization interface is defined as follows:

```
package javax.ejb;

public interface javax.ejb.SessionSynchronization {
    public abstract void afterBegin() throws RemoteException;
    public abstract void beforeCompletion() throws RemoteException;
    public abstract void afterCompletion(boolean committed) throws RemoteException;
}
```

When a method of the SessionSynchronization bean is invoked outside of a transaction scope, the method executes in the Method-Ready state, as discussed in Chapter 12. However, when a method is invoked within a transaction scope (or creates a new transaction), the EJB moves into the Transactional Method-Ready state.

The Transactional Method-Ready State

The SessionSynchronization methods are called in the Transactional Method-Ready state.

Transitioning into the Transactional Method-Ready state

When a transactional method is invoked on a SessionSynchronization bean, the stateful bean becomes part of the transaction. This causes the afterBegin() callback method defined in the SessionSynchronization interface to be invoked. This method should take care of reading any data from the database and storing the data in the bean's instance fields. The afterBegin() method is called before the EJB object delegates the business-method invocation to the EJB instance.

Life in the Transactional Method-Ready state

When the afterBegin() callback method completes, the business method originally invoked by the client is executed on the EJB instance. Any subsequent business methods invoked within the same transaction will be delegated directly to the EJB instance.

Once a stateful session bean is a part of a transaction—whether it implements SessionSynchronization or not—it cannot be accessed by any other transactional context. This is true regardless of whether the client tries to access the EJB with a different context or the EJB's own method creates a new context. If, for example, a method with a transaction attribute of RequiresNew is invoked, the new transactional context causes an error to be thrown. Since the NotSupported and Never attributes specify a different transactional context (no context), invoking a method with these attributes also causes an error. A stateful session bean cannot be removed while it is involved in a transaction. This means that invoking ejbRemove() while the Session-Synchronization bean is in the middle of a transaction will cause an error to be thrown.

At some point, the transaction in which the SessionSynchronization bean has been enrolled will come to an end. If the transaction is committed, the SessionSynchronization bean will be notified through its beforeCompletion() method. At this time, the EJB should write its cached data to the database. If the transaction is rolled back, the beforeCompletion() method will not be invoked, avoiding the pointless effort of writing changes that won't be committed to the database.

The afterCompletion() method is always invoked, whether the transaction ended successfully with a commit or unsuccessfully with a rollback. If the transaction was a success—which means that beforeCompletion() was invoked—the committed parameter of the afterCompletion() method will be true. If the transaction was unsuccessful, committed will be false.

It may be desirable to reset the stateful session bean's instance variables to some initial state if the afterCompletion() method indicates that the transaction was rolled back.

CHAPTER 15

Design Strategies

The previous 14 chapters have presented the core EJB technology. What's left is a grab bag of miscellaneous issues: how to solve particular design problems, how to work with particular kinds of databases, and topics of that nature.

Hash Codes in Compound Primary Keys

Chapter 11 discusses the necessity of overriding the Object.hashCode() and Object.equals() methods in the primary key class of an entity bean. With complex primary keys that have several fields, overriding Object.equals() is fairly trivial. However, overriding Object.hashCode() is more complicated, because an integer value that can serve as a suitable hash code must be created from several fields.

One solution is to concatenate all the values into a String and use the String object's hashCode() method to create a hash code value for the whole primary key. The String class has a decent hash code algorithm that generates a fairly well-distributed and repeatable hash code value from any set of characters.

The following code shows how to create such a hash code for a hypothetical primary key:

```java
public class HypotheticalPrimaryKey implements java.io.Serializable {
    public int primary_id;
    public short secondary_id;
    public java.util.Date date;
    public String desc;

    public int hashCode() {

        StringBuffer strBuff = new StringBuffer();
        strBuff.append(primary_id);
        strBuff.append(secondary_id);
        strBuff.append(date);
        strBuff.append(desc);
        String str = strBuff.toString();
```

```
          int hashCode = str.hashCode();
          return hashCode;
     }
     // the constructor, equals, and toString methods follow
}
```

A `StringBuffer` cuts down on the number of objects created, since `String` concatenation is expensive. The code could be improved by saving the hash code in a private variable and returning that value in subsequent method calls; this way, the hash code is calculated only once in the life of the instance.

Well-Distributed Versus Unique Hash Codes

A `Hashtable` is designed to provide fast lookups by binding an object to a key. Given any object's key, looking up the object in a hash table is a quick operation. For the lookup, the key is converted to an integer value using the key's `hashCode()` method.

Hash codes do not need to be unique, only well distributed. By "well distributed" we mean that, given any two keys, the chances are very good that the hash codes for the keys will be different. A well-distributed hash code algorithm reduces, but does not eliminate, the possibility that different keys evaluate to the same hash code. When keys evaluate to the same hash code, they are stored together and uniquely identified by their `equals()` methods. If you look up an object using a key that evaluates to a hash code that is shared by several other keys, the `Hashtable` locates the group of objects that have been stored with the same hash code; then it uses the key's `equals()` method to determine which key (and hence, which object) you want. (That's why you have to override the `equals()` method in primary keys as well as the `hashCode()` method.) Therefore, the emphasis in designing a good hash code algorithm is on producing codes that are well distributed rather than unique. This strategy allows you to design an index for associating keys with objects that is easy to compute and therefore fast.

Passing Objects by Value

Passing objects by value is tricky with Enterprise JavaBeans. Two simple rules will keep you out of most problem areas: objects that are passed by value should be fine-grained dependent objects or wrappers used in bulk accessors, and dependent objects should be immutable.

EJB 1.1: Dependent Objects

The concept of dependent objects was addressed in Chapter 6, which describes the use of dependent objects in EJB 2.0. But for EJB 1.1, dependent objects are a new concept. EJB 2.0 and EJB 1.1 use dependent objects differently, because EJB 2.0 can accommodate much more fine-grained entity beans than EJB 1.1.

Dependent objects are objects that have meaning only within the context of another business object. They typically represent fairly fine-grained business concepts, such as an address, phone number, or order item. For example, an address has little meaning when it is not associated with a business object such as Person or Organization. It depends on the context of the business object to give it meaning. Such an object can be thought of as a wrapper for related data. The fields that make up an address (street, city, state, and zip) should be packaged together in a single object called AddressDO. In turn, the AddressDO object is usually an attribute or property of another business object; in EJB, we would typically see a dependent object such as AddressDO as a property of an entity bean.

Here's a typical implementation of an AddressDO object:

```
public class AddressDO implements java.io.Serializable {

    private String street;
    private String city;
    private String state;
    private String zip;

    public Address(String str, String cty, String st, String zp) {
        street = str;
        city = cty;
        state = st;
        zip = zp;
    }
    public String getStreet() {return street;}
    public String getCity() {return city;}
    public String getState() {return state;}
    public String getZip() {return zip;}
}
```

We want to make sure that clients do not change an AddressDO object's fields. The reason is quite simple: the AddressDO object is a copy, not a remote reference. Changes to an AddressDO object are not reflected in the entity from which it originated. If a client changes the AddressDO object, those changes will not be reflected in the database. Making the AddressDO object immutable helps to ensure that clients do not mistake this fine-grained object for a remote reference, thinking that a change to an address property will be reflected on the server.

To change an address, the client is required to remove the AddressDO object and add a new one with the changes. Again, this is because the dependent object is not a remote object and changes to its state are not reflected on the server. Here is the remote interface to a hypothetical Employee bean that aggregates address information:

```
public interface Employee extends javax.ejb.EJBObject {
    public AddressDO [] getAddresses() throws RemoteException;
    public void removeAddress(AddressDO adrs) throws RemoteException;
    public void addAddress(AddressDO adrs) throws RemoteException;
    // ... Other business methods follow.
}
```

In this interface, the Employee can have many addresses, which are obtained as a collection of pass-by-value AddressDO objects. To remove an address, the target AddressDO object is passed back to the bean in the removeAddress() method. The bean class then removes the matching AddressDO object from its persistence fields. To add an address, an AddressDO object is passed to the bean by value.

Dependent objects may be persistence fields or they may be properties that are created as needed. The following code demonstrates both strategies using the AddressDO object. In the first listing, the AddressDO object is a persistence field, while in the second the AddressDO object is a property that does not correspond to any single field; we create the AddressDO object as needed but do not save it as part of the bean. Instead, the AddressDO object corresponds to four persistence fields: street, city, state, and zip.

```
// Address as a persistence field
public class Person extends javax.ejb.EntityBean {
    public AddressDO address;
    public AddressDO getAddress() {
        return address;
    }
    public void setAddress(AddressDO addr) {
        address = addr;
    }
    ...
}

// Address as a property
public class Person extends javax.ejb.EntityBean {
    public String street;
    public String city;
    public String state;
    public String zip;

    public AddressDO getAddress() {
        return new AddressDO(street, city, state, zip);
    }
    public void setAddress(AddressDO addr) {
        street = addr.street;
        city = addr.city;
        state = addr.state;
        zip = addr.zip;
    }
    ...
}
```

When a dependent object is used as a property, it can be synchronized with the persistence fields in the accessor methods themselves or in the ejbLoad() and ejbStore() methods. Both strategies are acceptable.

This discussion of dependent objects has been full of generalizations and thus may not be applicable to all situations. That said, it is recommended that only very fine-grained, dependent, immutable objects should be passed by value. All other business concepts should be represented as entity or session beans. A very fine-grained object is one that has very little behavior, consisting mostly of get and set methods. A dependent object is one that has little meaning outside the context of its aggregator. An immutable object is one that provides only get methods and thus cannot be modified once created.

Validation Rules in Dependent Objects

Dependent objects make excellent homes for format-validation rules. Format validation ensures that a simple data construct adheres to a predetermined structure or form. As an example, a Zip Code always has a certain format. It must be composed of digits; it must be five or nine digits in length; and if it has nine digits, it must use a hyphen as a separator between the fifth and sixth digits. Checking to see that a Zip Code follows these rules is format validation.

One problem that all developers face is deciding where to put validation code. Should data be validated at the user interface (UI), or should it be done by the bean that uses the data? Validating the data at the UI has the advantage of conserving network resources and improving performance. However, validating data in the bean, on the middle tier, ensures that the logic is reusable across user interfaces. Dependent objects provide a logical compromise that allows data to be validated on the client but remain independent of the UI. Since the validation logic is located in the constructor of the dependent object, the object automatically validates the data when it is created. When data is entered at the UI (e.g., GUI, servlet, or JSP), the UI can validate it using its corresponding dependent object. If the data is valid, the dependent object is created; if the data is invalid, the constructor throws an exception.

The following code shows a dependent object that represents a Zip Code. It adheres to the rules for a dependent object as I have defined them and also includes format-validation rules in the constructor:

```
public class ZipCodeDO implements java.io.Serializable {

    private String code;
    private String boxNumber;

    public ZipCode(String zipcode) throws ValidationException {
        if (zipcode == null)
            throw new ValidationException("Zip Code cannot be null");
        else if (zipcode.length()==5 && ! isDigits(zipcode))
            throw new ValidationException("Zip Code must be all digits");
        else if (zipcode.length()==10 ) {
            if (zipcode.charAt(5) == '-' ) {
                code = zipcode.substring(0,5);
                if (isDigits( code )){
                    boxNumber = zipcode.substring(6);
```

```
                    if (isDigits( boxNumber ))
                        return;
                }
            }
            throw new ValidationException("Zip Code must be of form #####-####");
        }
    }
    private boolean isDigits(String str) {
        for (int i = 0; i < str.length(); i++) {
            char chr = str.charAt(i);
            if ( ! Character.isDigit(chr)) {
                return false;
            }
        }
        return true;
    }
    public String getCode() { return code; }

    public String getBoxNumber() { return boxNumber; }

    public String toString() {
        return code+'-'+boxNumber;
    }
}
```

This simple example illustrates that format validation can be performed by dependent objects when the object is constructed at the user interface or client. Any format-validation errors are reported immediately, without any interaction with the middle tier of the application. In addition, any business object that uses `ZipCodeDO` automatically gains the benefit of the validation code, making the validation rules reusable (and consistent) across beans. Placing format validation in the dependent object is also a good coding practice because it makes the dependent object responsible for its own validation; responsibility is a key concept in object-oriented programming. Of course, dependent objects are useful for validation only if the Enterprise JavaBeans implementation supports pass-by-value.

As an alternative to using dependent objects, format validation can be performed by the accessors of enterprise beans. If, for example, a customer bean has accessors for setting and obtaining the Zip Code, those accessors could incorporate the validation code. While this strategy is more efficient from a network perspective—passing a `String` value is more efficient than passing a dependent object by value—it is less reusable than housing format-validation rules in dependent objects.

Bulk Accessors for Remote Clients

Most entity beans have several persistence fields that are manipulated through accessor methods. Unfortunately, the one-to-one nature of the accessor idiom can result in many invocations when accessing an entity, which translates into a lot of network traffic when using remote references. Every field you want to modify requires a method invocation, which in turn requires you to go out to the network. One way to reduce network traffic when accessing entities from remote clients is to use bulk accessors, which package access to several persistence fields into a single accessor method. Bulk accessors provide get and set methods that work with structures or simple pass-by-value objects. The following code shows how a bulk accessor could be implemented for the Cabin bean:

```java
// CabinData DataObject
public class CabinData {
    public String name;
    public int deckLevel;
    public int bedCount;
    public CabinData() {
    }
    public CabinData(String name, int deckLevel, int bedCount) {
        this.name = name;
        this.deckLevel = deckLevel;
        this.bedCount = bedCount;
    }
}

// CabinBean using bulk accessors
public class CabinBean implements javax.ejb.EntityBean {
    public int id;
    public String name;
    public int deckLevel;
    public int ship;
    public int bedCount;
    // bulk accessors
    public CabinData getData() {
        return new CabinData(name,deckLevel,bedCount);
    }
    public void setData(CabinData data) {
        name = data.name;
        deckLevel = data.deckLevel;
        bedCount = data.bedCount;
    }
    // simple accessors and entity methods
    public String getName() {
        return name;
    }
    public void setName(String str) {
        name = str;
    }
    // more methods follow
}
```

The getData() and setData() methods allow several fields to be packaged into a simple object and passed between the client and bean in one method call. This is much more efficient than requiring three separate calls to set the name, deck level, and bed count.

Rules-of-thumb for bulk accessors

Here are some guidelines for creating bulk accessors:

Data objects are not dependent objects

> Data objects and dependent objects serve clearly different purposes, but they may appear at first to be the same. Where dependent objects represent business concepts, data objects do not; they are simply an efficient way of packaging an entity's fields for access by clients. Data objects may package dependent objects along with more primitive attributes, but they are not dependent objects themselves.

Data objects are simple structures

> Keep the data objects as simple as possible; ideally, they should be similar to a simple struct in C. In other words, the data object should not have any business logic at all; it should only have fields. All the business logic should remain in the entity bean, where it is centralized and can be maintained easily.

> In order to keep the semantics of a C struct, data objects should not have accessor (get and set) methods for reading and writing their fields. The CabinData class does not have accessor methods; it only has fields and a couple of constructors. The lack of accessors reinforces the idea that the data object exists only to bundle fields together, not to "behave" in a particular manner. As a design concept, we want the data object to be a simple structure devoid of behavior; this is a matter of form following function. The exception is the multiargument constructor, which is left as a convenience for the developer.

Bulk accessors bundle related fields

> The bulk accessors can pass a subset of the entity's data. Some fields may have different security or transaction needs, which require that they be accessed separately. In the CabinBean, only a subset of the fields (name, deckLevel, bedCount) is passed in the data object. The id field is not included for several reasons: it does not describe the business concept, it is already found in the primary key, and the client should not edit it. The ship field is not passed because it should be updated only by certain individuals; the identities authorized to change this field are different from the identities allowed to change the other fields. Similarly, access to the ship may fall under a different transaction isolation level than the other fields (e.g., Serializable versus Read Committed).

> In addition, it is more efficient to design bulk accessors that pass logically related fields. In entity beans with many fields, it is possible to group together certain fields that are normally edited at the same time. An Employee bean, for example, might have several fields that are demographic in nature (address, phone, email) and can be logically separated from fields that are specific to benefits (compensation, 401K, health, vacation). A group of logically related fields can have its own bulk accessor. You might even want several bulk accessors in the same bean:

```
public interface Employee extends javax.ejb.EJBObject {

    public EmployeeBenefitsData getBenefitsData()
        throws RemoteException;

    public void setBenefitsData(EmployeeBenefitsData data)
        throws RemoteException;

    public EmployeeDemographicData getDemographicData()
        throws RemoteException;

    public void setDemographicData(EmployeeDemographicData data)
        throws RemoteException;

    // more simple accessors and other business methods follow

}
```

Retain simple accessors

Simple accessors (get and set methods for single fields) should not be abandoned when using bulk accessors. It is still important to allow editing of single fields. It's just as wasteful to use a bulk accessor to change one field as it is to change several fields using simple accessors.

Local references in EJB 2.0 container-managed persistence are very efficient, so the performance benefits of bulk accessors are minimal. If you're using EJB 2.0, use bulk accessors with remote interfaces whenever it makes sense according to the guidelines given here, but use them sparingly with local interfaces.

Entity Objects

The earlier section on passing objects by value gave you some good ground rules for when and how to use pass-by-value in EJB. Business concepts that do not meet the dependent object criteria should be modeled as either session or entity beans. It is easy to mistakenly adopt a strategy of passing business objects that would normally qualify as entity beans (e.g., Customer, Ship, and City) by value to the clients. Overzealous use of bulk accessors that pass data objects loaded with business behavior is bad design. The belief is that passing the entity objects to the client avoids unnecessary network traffic by keeping the set and get methods local. The problem with this approach is object equivalence. Entities are supposed to represent the actual data on the database, which means that they are shared and always reflect the current state of the data. Once an object is resident on the client, it is no longer representative of the data. It is easy for a client to end up with many dirty copies of the same entity, resulting in inconsistent processing and representation of data.

While it is true that the set and get methods of entity objects can introduce a lot of network traffic, implementing pass-by-value objects instead of using entity beans is not the answer. The network problem can be avoided if you stick to the design strategy elaborated throughout this book: remote clients interact primarily with session beans, not entity beans. You can also reduce network traffic significantly by using bulk accessors, provided that these accessors transfer only structures with no business logic. Finally, try to keep the entity beans on the server encapsulated in workflow defined by session beans. This eliminates the network traffic associated with entities, while ensuring that they always represent the correct data.

Improved Performance with Session Beans

In addition to defining the interactions among entity beans and other resources (workflow), session beans have another substantial benefit: they improve performance. The performance gains from using session beans are related to the concept of *granularity*. Granularity describes the scope of a business component, or how much business territory the component covers. The scope of these beans is limited to a single concept and can impact only the data associated with that concept. Session beans represent large, coarse-grained components with a scope that covers several business concepts—all the business concepts or processes the bean needs in order to accomplish a task. In distributed business computing, you rely on fine-grained components like entity beans to ensure simple, uniform, reusable, and safe access to data. Coarse-grained business components like session beans capture the interactions of entities or business processes that span multiple entities so that they can be reused; in doing so, they also improve performance on both the client and the server. As a rule of thumb, client applications should do most of their work with coarse-grained components like session beans, with limited direct interaction with entity beans.

To understand how session beans improve performance, we must address the most common problems cited with distributed component systems: network traffic, latency, and resource consumption.

Network Traffic and Latency with Remote Clients

One of the biggest problems of distributed component systems is that they generate a lot of network traffic. This is especially true of component systems that rely solely on entity-type business components, such as EJB's EntityBean component. Every method call on a remote reference begins a remote method–invocation loop, which sends information from the stub to the server and back to the stub. The loop requires data to be streamed to and from the client, consuming bandwidth. The reservation system for Titan Cruise Lines uses several entity beans (e.g., the Ship, Cabin, Cruise, and Customer EJBs). As we navigate through these fine-grained beans, requesting information, updating their states, and creating new beans, we generate network traffic if we are accessing the beans from remote clients. One client probably does not generate much traffic, but if we multiply that traffic level by thousands of clients, problems start to develop. Eventually, thousands of clients will produce so much network traffic that the system as a whole will suffer.

Another aspect of network communications is *latency*. Latency is the delay between the time at which we execute a command and the time at which it completes. With enterprise beans there is always a bit of latency due to the time it takes to communicate requests via the network. Each method invocation requires an RMI loop that takes time to travel from the client to the server and back to the client. A client that uses many beans will suffer from a time delay with each method invocation. Collectively, the latency delays can result in very slow clients that take several seconds to respond to each user action.

Accessing coarse-grained session beans from the client instead of fine-grained entity beans from remote clients can substantially reduce problems with network bandwidth and latency. In Chapter 12, we developed the bookPassage() method on the TravelAgent bean. The bookPassage() method encapsulates the interactions of entity beans that would otherwise have resided on the client. For the network cost of one method invocation on the client (bookPassage()), several tasks are performed on the EJB server. Using session beans to encapsulate several tasks reduces the number of remote method invocations needed to accomplish a task, which reduces the amount of network traffic and latency encountered while performing these tasks.

In EJB 2.0, a good design is to use remote component interfaces on the session bean that manages the workflow and local component interfaces on the enterprise beans (both entity and session) that it manages. This ensures the best performance.

Striking a Balance with Remote Clients

We don't want to abandon the use of entity business components, because they provide several advantages over traditional two-tier computing. They allow us to encapsulate the business logic and data of a business concept so that it can be used consistently and reused safely across applications. In short, entity business components are better for accessing business state because they simplify data access.

At the same time, we don't want to overuse entity beans on remote clients. Instead, we want the client to interact with coarse-grained session beans that encapsulate the interactions of small-grained entity beans. There are situations in which the client application should interact with entity beans directly. If a remote client application needs to edit a specific entity—change the address of a customer, for example— exposing the client to the entity bean is more practical than using a session bean. If, however, a task needs to be performed that involves the interactions of more than one entity bean—transferring money from one account to another, for example—a session bean should be used.

When a client application needs to perform a specific operation on an entity, such as an update, it makes sense to make the entity available to the client directly. If the client is performing a task that spans business concepts or otherwise involves more than one entity, that task should be modeled in a session bean as a workflow. A good design will emphasize the use of coarse-grained session beans as workflow and will limit the number of activities that require direct client access to entity beans.

In EJB 2.0, entity beans that are accessed by both remote clients and local enterprise beans can accommodate both by implementing both remote and local component interfaces. The methods defined in the remote and local component interfaces do not need to be identical; each should define methods appropriate to the clients that will use them. For example, the remote interfaces might make more use of bulk accessors than the local interface.

Listing Behavior

Make decisions about whether to access data directly or through entity beans with care. Listing behavior that is specific to a workflow can be provided by direct data access from a session bean. Methods like listAvailableCabins() in the TravelAgent bean use direct data access because it is less expensive than creating a find method in the Cabin bean that returns a list of Cabin beans. Every bean that the system has to deal with requires resources; by avoiding the use of components where their benefit is questionable, we can improve the performance of the whole system. A CTM is like a powerful truck, and each business component it manages is like a small weight. A truck is much better at hauling around a bunch of weights than an lightweight vehicle like a bicycle, but piling too many weights on the truck will make it just as ineffective as the bicycle. If neither vehicle can move, which one is better?

Chapter 12 discussed the TravelAgent bean's listAvailableCabins() method as an example of a method that returns a list of tabular data. This section provides several different strategies for implementing listing behavior in your beans.

Tabular data is data that is arranged into rows and columns. Tabular data is often used to let application users select or inspect data in the system. Enterprise JavaBeans lets you use find methods to list entity beans, but this mechanism is not a silver bullet. In many circumstances, find methods that return remote references are a heavyweight solution to a lightweight problem. For example, Table 15-1 shows the schedule for a cruise.

Table 15-1. Hypothetical cruise schedule

Cruise ID	Port-of-call	Arrive	Depart
233	San Juan	June 4, 2002	June 5, 2002
233	Aruba	June 7, 2002	June 8, 2002
233	Cartagena	June 9, 2002	June 10, 2002
233	San Blas Islands	June 11, 2002	June 12, 2002

It would be possible to create a Port-Of-Call entity object that represents every destination and then obtain a list of destinations using a find method, but this would be overkill. Recognizing that the data is not shared and is useful only in this one circumstance, we would rather present the data as a simple tabular listing.

In this case, we will present the data to the bean client as an array of String objects, with the values separated by a character delimiter. Here is the method signature used to obtain the data:.

```
public interface Schedule implements javax.ejb.EJBObject {
    public String [] getSchedule(int ID) throws RemoteException;
}
```

And here is the structure of the String values returned by the getSchedule() method:

```
233; San Juan; June 4, 2002; June 5, 2002
233; Aruba; June 7, 2002; June 8, 2002
233; Cartegena; June 9, 2002; June 10, 2002
233; San Blas Islands; June 11, 2002; June 12, 2002
```

The data could also be returned as a multidimensional array of strings, in which each column represents one field. This would certainly make it easier to reference each data item, but would also complicate navigation.

One disadvantage of using the simple array strategy is that Java is limited to single-type arrays. In other words, all the elements in the array must be of the same type. We use an array of Strings here because it has the most flexibility for representing other data types. We could also have used an array of Objects or even a Vector. The problem with using an Object array or a Vector is that there is no typing information at runtime or development time.

Implementing lists as arrays of structures

Instead of returning a simple array, a method that implements some sort of listing behavior can return an array of structures. For example, the cruise ship schedule data illustrated in Table 15-1 could be returned as an array of schedule structures. The structures are simple Java objects with no behavior (i.e., no methods) that are passed in an array. The definitions of the structure and the bean interface that would be used are:

```
// Definition of the bean that uses the structure
public interface Schedule implements javax.ejb.EJBObject {
    public CruiseScheduleItem [] getSchedule(int ID)
        throws RemoteException;
}

// Definition of the structure
public class CruiseScheduleItem {
    public int cruiseID;
    public String portName;
    public java.util.Date arrival;
    public java.util.Date departure;
}
```

Using structures allows the data elements to be of different types. In addition, the structures are self-describing: it is easy to determine the structure of the data in the tabular set based on its class definition.

Implementing lists as ResultSets

A more sophisticated and flexible way to implement a list is to provide a pass-by-value implementation of the java.sql.ResultSet interface. Although it is defined in the JDBC package (java.sql), the ResultSet interface is semantically independent of relational databases; it can be used to represent any set of tabular data. Since the ResultSet interface is familiar to most enterprise Java developers, it is an excellent construct for use in listing behavior. Using the ResultSet strategy, the signature of the getSchedule() method would be:

```
public interface Schedule implements javax.ejb.EJBObject {
    public ResultSet getSchedule(int cruiseID) throws RemoteException;
}
```

In some cases, the tabular data displayed at the client may be generated using standard SQL through a JDBC driver. If the circumstances permit, you may choose to perform the query in a session bean and return the result set directly to the client through a listing method. However, there are many cases in which you don't want to return a ResultSet that comes directly from JDBC drivers. A ResultSet from a JDBC 1.x driver is normally connected directly to the database, which increases network overhead and exposes your data source to the client. In these cases, you can implement your own ResultSet object that uses arrays or vectors to cache the data. JDBC 2.0 provides a cached javax.sql.RowSet that looks like a ResultSet but is passed by value and provides features such as reverse scrolling. You can use the RowSet, but do not expose behavior that allows the result set to be updated. Data updates should be performed only by bean methods.

Sometimes the tabular data comes from several data sources or nonrelational databases. In these cases, you can query the data using the appropriate mechanisms within the listing bean and then reformat the data into your ResultSet implementation. Regardless of the source of the data, you should still present it as tabular data using a custom implementation of the ResultSet interface.

Using a ResultSet has a number of advantages and disadvantages. First, the advantages:

Consistent interface for developers
> The ResultSet interface provides a consistent interface that developers are familiar with and that is consistent across different listing behaviors. Developers do not need to learn several different constructs for working with tabular data; they use the same ResultSet interface for all listing methods.

Consistent interface for automation
> The ResultSet interface provides a consistent interface that allows software algorithms to operate on data independent of its content. You can create a builder

that constructs an HTML or GUI table based on any set of results that implements the ResultSet.

Metadata operations

The ResultSet interface defines several metadata methods that provide developers with runtime information describing the result set with which they are working.

Flexibility

The ResultSet interface is independent of the data content, which allows tabular sets to change their schemas independently of the interfaces. A change in schema does not require a change to the method signatures of the listing operations.

And now, the disadvantages of using a ResultSet:

Complexity

The ResultSet interface strategy is much more complex than returning a simple array or an array of structures. It normally requires you to develop a custom implementation of the ResultSet interface. If properly designed, the custom implementation can be reused across all your listing methods, but it is still a significant development effort.

Hidden structure at development time

Although the ResultSet can describe itself through metadata at runtime, it cannot describe itself at development time. Unlike a simple array or an array of structures, the ResultSet interface provides no clues at development time about the structure of the underlying data. At runtime, metadata is available, but at development time, good documentation is required to express the structure of the data explicitly.

Bean Adapters

One of the most awkward aspects of the EJB bean interface types is that, in some cases, the callback methods are never used or are not relevant to the bean at all. A simple container-managed entity bean might have empty implementations for its ejbLoad(), ejbStore(), ejbActivate(), ejbPassivate(), or even its setEntityContext() methods. Stateless session beans provide an even better example of unnecessary callback methods: they must implement the ejbActivate() and ejbPassivate() methods even though these methods are never invoked!

To simplify the appearance of the bean class definitions, we can introduce *adapter classes* that hide callback methods that are never used or have only minimal implementations. Here is an adapter for the entity bean that provides empty implementations of all the EntityBean methods:

```
public class EntityAdapter implements javax.ejb.EntityBean {
    public EntityContext ejbContext;

    public void ejbActivate() {}
```

```
    public void ejbPassivate() {}
    public void ejbLoad() {}
    public void ejbStore() {}
    public void ejbRemove() {}

    public void setEntityContext(EntityContext ctx) {
        ejbContext = ctx;
    }
    public void unsetEntityContext() {
        ejbContext = null;
    }
    public EntityContext getEJBContext() {
        return ejbContext;
    }
}
```

We took care of capturing the EntityContext for use by the subclass. We can do this because most entity beans implement the context methods in exactly this way. We simply leverage the adapter class to manage this logic for our subclasses.

If a callback method is deemed necessary, we can just override it with a method in the bean class.

We can create a similar Adapter class for stateless session beans:

```
public class SessionAdapter implements javax.ejb.SessionBean {
    public SessionContext ejbContext;

    public void ejbActivate() {}
    public void ejbPassivate() {}
    public void ejbRemove() {}

    public void setSessionContext(SessionContext ctx) {
        ejbContext = ctx;
    }
    public SessionContext getEJBContext() {
        return ejbContext;
    }
}
```

Do not use these adapter classes when you need to override more than one or two of their methods. If you need to implement several of the callback methods, your code will be clearer if you do not use the adapter class. The adapter class also impacts the inheritance hierarchy of the bean class. If you need to implement a different superclass later, one that captures business logic, you will have to modify the class inheritance.

Implementing a Common Interface

This book discourages implementing the remote interface in the bean class, even though this makes it a little more difficult to enforce consistency between the business

---

methods defined in the remote interface and the corresponding methods on the bean class. There are good reasons for not implementing the remote interface in the bean class, but there is also a need for a common interface to ensure that the bean class and remote interface define the same business methods. This section describes a design alternative that allows you to use a common interface to ensure consistency between the bean class and the remote interface.

Why the Bean Class Should Not Implement the Remote Interface

There should be no difference, other than the missing `java.rmi.RemoteException`, between the business methods defined in the `ShipBean` class and their corresponding business methods defined in the `ShipRemote` interface. EJB requires you to match the method signatures so that the remote interface can accurately represent the bean class on the client. Why not implement the remote interface `com.titan.ShipRemote` in the `ShipBean` class to ensure that these methods are matched correctly?

EJB allows a bean class to implement its remote interface, but this practice is discouraged for a couple of reasons. First, the remote interface is actually an extension of the `javax.ejb.EJBObject` interface, which you learned about in Chapter 5. This interface defines several methods that are implemented by the EJB container when the bean is deployed. Here is the definition of the `javax.ejb.EJBObject` interface:

```
public interface javax.ejb.EJBObject extends java.rmi.Remote {
    public abstract EJBHome getEJBHome();
    public abstract Handle getHandle();
    public abstract Object getPrimaryKey();
    public abstract boolean isIdentical(EJBObject obj);
    public abstract void remove();
}
```

The methods defined here are implemented and supported by the EJB object for use by client software and are not implemented by the `javax.ejb.EntityBean` class. In other words, these methods are intended for the remote interface's implementation, not the bean instance's. The bean instance implements the business methods defined in the remote interface, but it does so indirectly. The EJB object receives all the method invocations made on the remote interface; those that are business methods (like the `getName()` or `setCapacity()` methods in `Ship`) are delegated to the bean instance. The other methods, defined by the `EJBObject`, are handled by the container and are never delegated to the bean instance.

Just for kicks, change the `ShipBean` definition so that it implements the `Ship` interface as shown here:

```
public class ShipBean implements ShipRemote {
```

When you recompile the `ShipBean`, you should have five errors stating that the ShipBean must be declared abstract because it does not implement the methods from the `javax.ejb.EJBObject` interface. EJB allows you to implement the remote interface, but in so doing you clutter the bean class's definition with a bunch of methods that have nothing to do with its functionality. You can hide these methods in an adapter class; however, using an adapter for methods that have empty implementations is one thing, but using an adapter for methods that should not be in the class at all is decidedly bad practice.

Another reason that beans should not implement the remote interface is that a client can be an application on a remote computer or it can be another bean. Beans as clients are very common. When calling a method on an object, the caller sometimes passes itself as one of the parameters.* In normal Java programming, an object passes a reference to itself using the `this` keyword. In EJB, however, clients—even bean clients—are allowed to interact only with the remote interfaces of beans. When one bean calls a method on another bean, it is not allowed to pass the `this` reference; it must obtain its own remote reference from its context and pass that reference instead. The fact that a bean class does not implement its remote interface prevents you from passing the `this` reference and forces you to get a reference to the interface from the context. The bean class will not compile if you attempt to use `this` as a remote reference. For example, assume that the `ShipBean` needs to call `someMethod(ShipRemote ship)`. It cannot simply call `someMethod(this)`, because `ShipBean` does not implement `ShipRemote`. If, however, the bean instance implements the remote interface, you could mistakenly pass the bean instance reference using the `this` keyword to another bean.

Beans should always interact with the remote references of other beans so that method invocations are intercepted by the EJB objects. Remember that the EJB objects apply security, transaction, concurrency, and other system-level constraints to method calls before they are delegated to the bean instance; the EJB object works with the container to manage the bean at runtime.

The proper way to obtain a bean's remote reference, within the bean class, is to use the `EJBContext`. Here is an example of how this works:

```
public class HypotheticalBean extends EntityBean {
    public EntityContext ejbContext;
    public void someMethod() throws RemoteException {

        Hypothetical mySelf = (Hypothetical) ejbContext.getEJBObject();

        // Do something interesting with the remote reference.
    }
    // More methods follow.
}
```

---

* This is frequently done in loopbacks, where the invokee needs information about the invoker. Loopbacks are discouraged in EJB because they require reentrant programming, which should be avoided.

EJB 2.0: Why the Bean Class Should Not Implement the Local Interface

In EJB 2.0, the bean class should not implement the local interface for the exact same reasons that it should not implement the remote interface. Specifically, the bean instance would have to support the methods of the javax.ejb.EJBLocalObject interface, which are not germane to the bean class.

EJB 1.1: The Business Interface Alternative

Although it is undesirable for the bean class to implement its remote interface, we can define an intermediate interface that is used by both the bean class and the remote interface to ensure consistent business-method definitions. We will call this intermediate interface the *business interface*.

The following code contains an example of a business interface defined for the Ship bean, called ShipBusiness. All the business methods formerly defined in the ShipRemote interface are now defined in the ShipBusiness interface. The business interface defines all the business methods, including every exception that will be thrown from the remote interface at runtime:

```
package com.titan.ship;
import java.rmi.RemoteException;

public interface ShipBusiness {
    public String getName() throws RemoteException;
    public void setName(String name) throws RemoteException;
    public void setCapacity(int cap) throws RemoteException;
    public int getCapacity() throws RemoteException;
    public double getTonnage() throws RemoteException;
    public void setTonnage(double tons) throws RemoteException;
}
```

Once the business interface is defined, it can be extended by the remote interface. The remote interface extends both the ShipBusiness and EJBObject interfaces, giving it all the business methods and the EJBObject methods that the container will implement at deployment time:

```
package com.titan.ship;
import javax.ejb.EJBObject;

public interface ShipRemote extends ShipBusiness, javax.ejb.EJBObject {
}
```

Finally, we can implement the business interface in the bean class as we would any other interface:

```
public class ShipBean implements ShipBusiness, javax.ejb.EntityBean {
    public int id;
    public String name;
```

```
        public int capacity;
        public double tonnage;

        public String getName() {
            return name;
        }
        public void setName(String n) {
            name = n;
        }
        public void setCapacity(int cap) {
            capacity = cap;
        }
        public int getCapacity() {
            return capacity;
        }
        public double getTonnage() {
            return tonnage;
        }
        public void setTonnage(double tons) {
            tonnage = tons;
        }

        // More methods follow...
    }
```

In this case, we chose not to throw the RemoteException. Classes that implement interfaces can choose not to throw exceptions defined in the interface. They cannot, however, add exceptions. This is why the business interface must declare that its methods throw the RemoteException and all application exceptions. The remote interface should not modify the business interface definition. The bean class can choose not to throw the RemoteException, but it must throw all the application-specific exceptions.

The business interface is an easily implemented design strategy that will make it easier for you to develop beans. This book recommends that you use the business interface strategy in your own implementations. Remember not to pass the business interface in method calls; always use the bean's remote interface in method parameters and as return types.

Entity Beans Without Create Methods

If an entity bean is never meant to be created by a client, you can simply not implement a create() method on the home interface. This means that the entity in question can be obtained only by using the find() methods on the home interface. Titan might implement this strategy with their Ship beans, so that new Ships must be created by directly inserting records into the database—a privilege that might be reserved for the database administrator (they wouldn't want some crazed travel agent inserting random ships into their cruise line).

EJB 1.1: Object-to-Relational Mapping Tools

Some EJB vendors provide object-to-relational mapping tools that, using wizards, can create object representations of relational databases, generate tables from objects, or map existing objects to existing tables. These tools are outside the scope of this book because they are proprietary in nature and cannot generally be used to produce beans that can be used across EJB servers. In other words, in many cases, once you have begun to rely on a mapping tool to define a bean's persistence, you might not be able to migrate your beans to a different EJB server; the bean definition is bound to that mapping tool.

Mapping tools can make bean developers much more productive, but you should consider the implementation-specific details of your tool before using it. If you will need to migrate your application to a bigger, faster EJB server in the future, make sure the mapping tool you use is supported in other EJB servers.

Some products that perform object-to-relational mapping use JDBC. Object People's TOPLink and Watershed's ROF are examples of this type of product. These products provide more flexibility for mapping objects to relational databases and are not as dependent on the EJB server. However, EJB servers must support these products in order for them to be used, so again let caution guide your decisions about using these products.

Avoid Emulating Entity Beans with Session Beans

Session beans that implement the SessionSynchronization interface (discussed in Chapter 14) can emulate some of the functionality of bean-managed entity beans. This approach provides a couple of advantages. First, these session beans, like entity beans, can represent entity business concepts; second, dependency on vendor-specific object-to-relational mapping tools is avoided.

Unfortunately, session beans were not designed to represent data directly in the database, so using them as a replacement for entity beans is problematic. Entity beans fulfill this duty nicely because they are transactional objects. When the attributes of a bean are changed, the changes are reflected in the database automatically in a transactionally safe manner. This is not possible in stateful session beans because, although they are transactionally aware, they are not transactional objects. The difference is subtle but important. Stateful session beans are not shared like entity beans. There is no concurrency control when two clients attempt to access the same bean at the same time. With stateful session beans each client gets its own instance, so many copies of the same session bean representing the same entity data can be in use concurrently. Database isolation can prevent some problems, but the danger of obtaining and using dirty data is high.

Another problem is that session beans emulating entity beans cannot have find methods in their home interfaces. Entity beans support find methods as a convenient way to locate data. Find methods could be placed in the session bean's remote interface, but this would be inconsistent with the EJB component model. Also, a stateful session bean must use the `SessionSynchronization` interface to be transactionally safe, which requires that it be used only in the scope of the client's transaction. This is because methods such as `ejbCreate()` and `ejbRemove()` are not transactional. In addition, `ejbRemove()` has a significantly different function in session beans than in entity beans. Should `ejbRemove()` end the conversation, delete data, or both?

Weighing all the benefits against the problems and risks of data inconsistency, I recommend that you do not use stateful session beans to emulate entity beans.

Direct Database Access from Session Beans

Perhaps the most straightforward and portable option for using a server that supports only session beans is direct database access. We did some of this with the ProcessPayment bean and the TravelAgent bean in Chapter 12. When entity beans are not an option, we simply take this option a step further. The following code is an example of the TravelAgent bean's bookPassage() method, coded with direct JDBC data access instead of using entity beans:

```
public Ticket bookPassage(CreditCard card, double price)
    throws RemoteException, IncompleteConversationalState {
    if (customerID == 0 || cruiseID == 0 || cabinID == 0) {
        throw new IncompleteConversationalState();
    }
    Connection con = null;
    PreparedStatement ps = null;;
    try {
        con = getConnection();

        // Insert reservation.
        ps = con.prepareStatement("insert into RESERVATION "+
            "(CUSTOMER_ID, CRUISE_ID, CABIN_ID, PRICE) values (?,?,?,?)");
        ps.setInt(1, customerID);
        ps.setInt(2, cruiseID);
        ps.setInt(3, cabinID);
        ps.setDouble(4, price);
        if (ps.executeUpdate() != 1) {
            throw new RemoteException ("Failed to add Reservation to database");
        }

        // Insert payment.
        ps = con.prepareStatement("insert into PAYMENT "+
            "(CUSTOMER_ID, AMOUNT, TYPE, CREDIT_NUMBER, CREDIT_EXP_DATE) "+
            "values(?,?,?,?,?)");
        ps.setInt(1, customerID);
        ps.setDouble(2, price);
        ps.setString(3, card.type);
```

```
            ps.setLong(4, card.number);
            ps.setDate(5, new java.sql.Date(card.experation.getTime()));
            if (ps.executeUpdate() != 1) {
                throw new RemoteException ("Failed to add Reservation to database");
            }
            Ticket ticket = new Ticket(customerID,cruiseID,cabinID,price);
            return ticket;

        } catch (SQLException se) {
            throw new RemoteException (se.getMessage());
        }
        finally {
            try {
                if (ps != null) ps.close();
                if (con!= null) con.close();
            } catch(SQLException se){
                se.printStackTrace();
            }
        }
    }
```

No mystery here: we have simply redefined the TravelAgent bean so that it works directly with the data through JDBC rather than using entity beans. This method is transactionally safe because an exception thrown anywhere within the method will cause all the database inserts to be rolled back. Very clean and simple.

The idea behind this strategy is to continue to model workflow or processes with session beans. The TravelAgent bean models the process of making a reservation. Its conversational state can be changed over the course of a conversation, and safe database changes can be made based on the conversational state.

Object-to-relational mapping provides another mechanism for "direct" access to data in a stateful session bean. The advantage of object-to-relational mapping tools is that data can be encapsulated as an object-like entity bean. So, for example, an object-to-relational mapping approach could end up looking very similar to our entity bean design. The problem with object-to-relational mapping is that most tools are proprietary and may not be reusable across EJB servers. In other words, the object-to-relational tool may bind you to one brand of EJB server. Object-to-relational mapping tools are, however, an expedient, safe, and productive mechanism for obtaining direct database access when entity beans are not available.

Avoid Chaining Stateful Session Beans

In developing session-only systems, you may be tempted to use stateful session beans from inside other stateful session beans. While this appears to be a good modeling approach, it is problematic. Chaining stateful session beans can lead to problems when beans time out or throw exceptions that cause them to become invalid. Figure 15-1 shows a chain of stateful session beans, each of which maintains conversational state on which the other beans depend to complete the operation encapsulated by bean A.

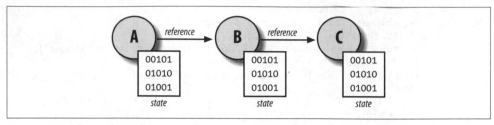

Figure 15-1. Chain of stateful session beans

If any one of the beans in this chain times out—say, bean B—the conversational state trailing that bean is lost. If this conversational state was built up over a long time, considerable work can be lost. The chain of stateful session beans is only as strong as its weakest link. If one bean times out or becomes invalid, the entire conversational state on which bean A depends becomes invalid. Avoid chaining stateful session beans.

Using stateless session beans from within stateful session beans is not a problem, because a stateless session bean does not maintain any conversational state. Use stateless session beans from within stateful session beans as much as you need.

Using a stateful session bean from within a stateless session bean is almost nonsensical because the benefit of the stateful session bean's conversational state cannot be leveraged beyond the scope of the stateless session bean's method.

CHAPTER 16

XML Deployment Descriptors

What Is an XML Deployment Descriptor?

This chapter discusses what goes into an XML deployment descriptor; it teaches you how to write deployment descriptors for your beans. Keep in mind that you may never need to write a deployment descriptor by hand; most vendors of integrated development tools and EJB servers will provide tools for creating the descriptor automatically. Even if you have such a tool available, however, you should be familiar enough with deployment descriptors to be able to read them on your own.

This chapter does not attempt to teach you how to read or write correct XML. There are many books on the subject: a good quick reference is *XML Pocket Reference* by Bob Eckstein (O'Reilly); *XML in a Nutshell*, by Elliotte Rusty Harold and W. Scott Means (O'Reilly), provides a more detailed treatment. Very briefly, XML looks like HTML, but with different tag names and different attributes inside the tags. You won't see <h1> and <p> inside a deployment descriptor; you'll see tags like <ejb-jar>. But otherwise, if you expect an XML document to look like HTML, you're most of the way toward reading it. The tag names and attribute names for an XML document are defined by a special document called a Document Type Definition (DTD). Therefore, for XML deployment descriptors, there is a DTD that defines the tags and attributes that can be used in the document; the DTDs for deployment descriptors in EJB 2.0 and 1.1 are available online at *http://java.sun.com/dtd/ejb-jar_2_0.dtd* and *http://java.sun.com/j2ee/dtds/ejb-jar_1_1.dtd*.

There are a few other important differences between XML and HTML. XML is much more strict; many things that are acceptable in HTML are errors in XML. This should not make a difference if you're just reading a deployment descriptor, but if you're writing one, you have to be careful. Two differences are particularly important. First, XML is case-sensitive. You cannot mix uppercase and lowercase in your tag names. HTML does not care about the difference between <h1> and <H1>, but XML does. All the tags and attributes used in deployment descriptors are lowercase. Second, XML will not forgive you if you fail to supply closing tags. In HTML you can write <p>...<p>, without ever putting in a </p> to end the first paragraph. XML never allows you to be sloppy. Whenever you have an opening tag, there must always be a closing tag.

That's about it. These few paragraphs don't even qualify as a quick introduction to XML, but the basic ideas are very simple, and that's really all you should need to get going.

The Contents of a Deployment Descriptor

We've discussed XML deployment descriptors throughout this book. At this point, you probably know enough to write deployment descriptors on your own. However, it is still worthwhile to take a tour through a complete descriptor. Following are the EJB 2.0 and 1.1 versions of the deployment descriptor for the Cabin EJB, which we created in Chapter 4. The Cabin EJB's deployment descriptor contains most of the tags that are needed to describe entity beans; session and message-driven beans are not much different. The differences between the versions are small but significant. We'll use this deployment descriptor to guide our discussion in the following sections.

Here is the EJB 2.0 deployment descriptor:

```
<?xml version="1.0" encoding="UTF-8"?>

<!DOCTYPE ejb-jar PUBLIC "-//Sun Microsystems, Inc.//DTD Enterprise
JavaBeans 2.0//EN" "http://java.sun.com/dtd/ejb-jar_2_0.dtd">

<ejb-jar>
    <enterprise-beans>
        <entity>
            <description>
                This Cabin enterprise bean entity represents a cabin
                on a cruise ship.
            </description>
            <ejb-name>CabinEJB</ejb-name>
            <home>com.titan.cabin.CabinHomeRemote</home>
            <remote>com.titan.cabin.CabinRemote</remote>
            <local-home>com.titan.cabin.CabinHomeLocal</local-home>
            <local>com.titan.cabin.CabinLocal</local>
            <ejb-class>com.titan.cabin.CabinBean</ejb-class>
            <persistence-type>Container</persistence-type>
            <prim-key-class>com.titan.cabin.CabinPK</prim-key-class>
            <reentrant>False</reentrant>
            <cmp-version>2.x</cmp-version>
            <abstract-schema-name>Cabin</abstract-schema-name>
            <cmp-field><field-name>id</field-name></cmp-field>
            <cmp-field><field-name>name</field-name></cmp-field>
            <cmp-field><field-name>deckLevel</field-name></cmp-field>
            <cmp-field><field-name>shipId</field-name></cmp-field>
            <cmp-field><field-name>bedCount</field-name></cmp-field>
```

```
                    <primkey-field>id</primkey-field>
                </entity>
            </enterprise-beans>

            <assembly-descriptor>
                <security-role>
                    <description>
                        This role represents everyone who is allowed full access
                        to the Cabin EJB.
                    </description>
                    <role-name>everyone</role-name>
                </security-role>

                <method-permission>
                    <role-name>everyone</role-name>
                    <method>
                        <ejb-name>CabinEJB</ejb-name>
                        <method-name>*</method-name>
                    </method>
                </method-permission>

                <container-transaction>
                    <method>
                        <ejb-name>CabinEJB</ejb-name>
                        <method-name>*</method-name>
                    </method>
                    <trans-attribute>Required</trans-attribute>
                </container-transaction>
            </assembly-descriptor>
        </ejb-jar>
```

Here is the EJB 1.1 deployment descriptor:

```
<?xml version="1.0" encoding="UTF-8"?>

<!DOCTYPE ejb-jar PUBLIC "-//Sun Microsystems, Inc.//DTD Enterprise
JavaBeans 1.1//EN" "http://java.sun.com/j2ee/dtds/ejb-jar_1_1.dtd">

<ejb-jar>
    <enterprise-beans>
        <entity>
            <description>
                This Cabin enterprise bean entity represents a cabin
                on a cruise ship.
            </description>
            <ejb-name>CabinEJB</ejb-name>
            <home>com.titan.cabin.CabinHomeRemote</home>
            <remote>com.titan.cabin.CabinRemote</remote>
            <ejb-class>com.titan.cabin.CabinBean</ejb-class>
            <persistence-type>Container</persistence-type>
            <prim-key-class>java.lang.Integer</prim-key-class>
            <reentrant>False</reentrant>
            <cmp-field><field-name>id</field-name></cmp-field>
            <cmp-field><field-name>name</field-name></cmp-field>
            <cmp-field><field-name>deckLevel</field-name></cmp-field>
```

```
                <cmp-field><field-name>shipId</field-name></cmp-field>
                <cmp-field><field-name>bedCount</field-name></cmp-field>
                <primkey-field>id</primkey-field>
            </entity>
        </enterprise-beans>

        <assembly-descriptor>
            <security-role>
                <description>
                    This role represents everyone who is allowed full access
                    to the Cabin EJB.
                </description>
                <role-name>everyone</role-name>
            </security-role>

            <method-permission>
                <role-name>everyone</role-name>
                <method>
                    <ejb-name>CabinEJB</ejb-name>
                    <method-name>*</method-name>
                </method>
            </method-permission>

            <container-transaction>
                <method>
                    <ejb-name>CabinEJB</ejb-name>
                    <method-name>*</method-name>
                </method>
                <trans-attribute>Required</trans-attribute>
            </container-transaction>
        </assembly-descriptor>
    </ejb-jar>
```

The Document Header

An XML document may start with a tag that specifies the version of XML that is in use:

```
<?xml version="1.0" encoding="UTF-8"?>
```

This tag identifies the document as an XML document that adheres to Version 1.0 of the XML specification. The character encoding used (UTF-8) is usually supported by EJB vendors.

The next tag specifies the DTD that defines the document. In EJB 2.0, it looks like this:

```
<!DOCTYPE ejb-jar PUBLIC "-//Sun Microsystems, Inc.//DTD Enterprise
JavaBeans 2.0//EN" "http://java.sun.com/dtd/ejb-jar_2_0.dtd">
```

In EJB 1.1, it looks like this:

```
<!DOCTYPE ejb-jar PUBLIC "-//Sun Microsystems, Inc.//DTD Enterprise
JavaBeans 1.1//EN" "http://java.sun.com/j2ee/dtds/ejb-jar_1_1.dtd">
```

This tag provides the URL from which you (or, more importantly, tools processing the deployment descriptor) can download the document. The DTD can be used to validate the XML document; this means that the EJB server deploying the bean can download the DTD and use it to prove that your deployment descriptor is correct (i.e., that it is organized correctly, it uses the right tag names, and all the tags and attributes have appropriate parameters).

This tag also identifies the name of the document's root element, which is <ejb-jar>. The <ejb-jar> tag marks the beginning of the document proper.

The Descriptor's Body

The body of any XML document begins and ends with the tag for the document's root element, which is defined by the DTD. For a deployment descriptor, the root element is named <ejb-jar>, and looks like this:

```
<ejb-jar>
... other elements ...
</ejb-jar>
```

All other elements must be nested within the <ejb-jar> element. You can place the following kinds of elements within <ejb-jar>:

<description> *(optional)*

> The <description> element can be used to provide a description of the deployment descriptor. This element can be used in many contexts within a deployment descriptor: to describe the descriptor as a whole, to describe particular beans, to describe particular security roles, etc. The Cabin EJB deployment descriptor doesn't use a <description> element for the deployment descriptor as a whole, but it does provide a description for the Cabin EJB itself.

<display-name> *(optional)*

> The <display-name> element is used by tools (such as a deployment wizard) that are working with the deployment descriptor. It provides a convenient visual label for the entire JAR file and individual bean components.

<small-icon> *and* <large-icon> *(optional)*

> These elements point to files within the JAR file that provide icons a deployment wizard or some other tool can use to represent the JAR file. Icons must be image files in either the JPEG or GIF format. Small icons must be 16 × 16 pixels; large icons must be 32 × 32 pixels. These icon elements are also used in the <entity>, <session>, and <message-driven> (EJB 2.0) elements to represent individual enterprise bean components.

<enterprise-beans> *(one required)*

> The <enterprise-beans> element contains descriptions of one or more enterprise beans that are contained in this JAR file. A deployment descriptor may have only

one <enterprise-beans> element. Within this element, <entity>, <session>, and
<message-driven> (EJB 2.0) elements describe the individual beans.

<ejb-client-jar> *(optional)*

The <ejb-client-jar> element provides the path of the client JAR, which normally contains all the classes (including stubs, remote and home interface
classes, etc.) the client will need in order to access the beans defined in the
deployment descriptor. How client JAR files are organized and delivered to the
client is not specified—consult your vendor's documentation.

<assembly-descriptor> *(optional)*

The application assembler or bean developer adds an <assembly-descriptor> element to the deployment descriptor to define how the enterprise beans are used in
an actual application. The <assembly-descriptor> contains a number of elements
that define the security roles used to access the bean, the method permissions
that govern which roles can call different methods, and transaction attributes.

These elements are quite simple, with the exception of the <enterprise-beans> and
<assembly-descriptor> elements. These two elements contain a lot of other material
nested within them. We'll look at the <enterprise-beans> element first.

Describing Enterprise Beans

The enterprise beans contained in a JAR file are described within the deployment
descriptor's <enterprise-beans> element. So far we have talked about deployment
descriptors for only a single enterprise bean, but it is possible to package several
enterprise beans in a JAR file and describe them all within a single deployment
descriptor. We could, for example, have deployed the TravelAgent, ProcessPayment,
Cruise, Customer, and Reservation EJBs in the same JAR file.

In EJB 2.0, we could also add a message-driven bean, such as the ReservationProcessor EJB we developed in Chapter 13. The EJB 2.0 deployment descriptor would look
something like this:

```
<?xml version="1.0" encoding="UTF-8"?>
<!DOCTYPE ejb-jar PUBLIC "-//Sun Microsystems, Inc.//DTD Enterprise
JavaBeans 2.0//EN" "http://java.sun.com/dtd/ejb-jar_2_0.dtd">

<ejb-jar>
    <description>
        This Deployment includes all the beans needed to make a reservation:
        TravelAgent, ProcessPayment, Reservation, Customer, Cruise, and Cabin.
    </description>
    <enterprise-beans>
        <session>
            <ejb-name>TravelAgentEJB</ejb-name>
            <remote>com.titan.travelagent.TravelAgentRemote</remote>
            ...
        </session>
```

```
<entity>
    <ejb-name>CustomerEJB</ejb-name>
    <remote>com.titan.customer.CustomerRemote</remote>
    ...
</entity>
<session>
    <ejb-name>ProcessPaymentEJB</ejb-name>
    <remote>com.titan.processpayment.ProcessPaymentRemote</remote>
    ...
</session>
<message-driven>
    <ejb-name>ReservationProcessorEJB</ejb-name>
    ...
</message-driven>
    ...
</enterprise-beans>
<relationships>
    ...
</relationships>
<assembly-descriptor>
    ...
</assembly-descriptor>
    ...
</ejb-jar>
```

The EJB 1.1 deployment descriptor would look something like this:

```
<?xml version="1.0" encoding="UTF-8"?>
<!DOCTYPE ejb-jar PUBLIC "-//Sun Microsystems, Inc.//DTD Enterprise
JavaBeans 1.1//EN" "http://java.sun.com/j2ee/dtds/ejb-jar_1_1.dtd">

<ejb-jar>
    <description>
        This Deployment includes all the beans needed to make a reservation:
        TravelAgent, ProcessPayment, Reservation, Customer, Cruise, and Cabin.
    </description>
    <enterprise-beans>
        <session>
            <ejb-name>TravelAgentEJB</ejb-name>
            <remote>com.titan.travelagent.TravelAgentRemote</remote>
            ...
        </session>
        <entity>
            <ejb-name>CustomerEJB</ejb-name>
            <remote>com.titan.customer.CustomerRemote</remote>
            ...
        </entity>
        <session>
            <ejb-name>ProcessPaymentEJB</ejb-name>
            <remote>com.titan.processpayment.ProcessPaymentRemote</remote>
            ...
        </session>
        ...
    </enterprise-beans>
```

```
<assembly-descriptor>
    ...
</assembly-descriptor>
    ...
</ejb-jar>
```

In this descriptor, the `<enterprise-beans>` element contains two `<session>` elements, one `<entity>` element, and, for EJB 2.0, a `<message-driven>` element describing the enterprise beans. Other elements within the `<entity>`, `<session>`, and `<message-driven>` elements provide detailed information about the enterprise beans; as you can see, the `<ejb-name>` element defines the enterprise bean's name. We will discuss all the things that can go into a bean's description later.

Multiple-bean deployments have the advantage of being able to share assembly information, which is defined in the `<assembly-descriptor>` element that follows the `<enterprise-beans>` element. In other words, beans can share security and transactional declarations, making it simpler to deploy them consistently. For example, deployment is easier if the same logical security roles control access to all the beans, and it is easiest to guarantee that the roles are defined consistently if they are defined in one place. This strategy also makes it easier to ensure that the transaction attributes are applied consistently to all the beans, because you can declare them all at once.

Session and Entity Beans

The `<session>` and `<entity>` elements, which describe session and entity beans, usually contain many elements nested within them. The lists of allowable subelements are similar so we'll discuss the `<session>` and `<entity>` elements together.

Like the `<ejb-jar>` element, a `<session>` or `<entity>` element can optionally contain `<description>`, `<display-name>`, `<small-icon>`, and `<large-icon>` elements. These are fairly self-explanatory and, in any case, mean the same as they did for the `<ejb-jar>` element. The `<description>` lets you provide a comment that describes the enterprise bean; the `<display-name>` is used by deployment tools to represent the enterprise bean; and the two icon elements are used to represent the enterprise bean in visual environments. The icon elements must point to JPEG or GIF images within the JAR file. The other elements are more interesting:

`<ejb-name>` *(one required)*
> Specifies the name of the enterprise bean component. It is used in the `<methodx>` element to scope method declarations to the correct enterprise bean. Throughout this book, we use a name of the form "NameEJB" as the `<ejb-name>` for an enterprise bean. Other common conventions use names of the form "NameBean" or "TheName."

`<home>` *(EJB 1.1: one required; EJB 2.0: optional)*
> Specifies the fully qualified class name of the enterprise bean's remote home interface.

`<remote>` *(EJB 1.1: one required; EJB 2.0: optional)*
Specifies the fully qualified class name of the enterprise bean's remote interface.

`<local-home>` *(EJB 2.0: optional)*
Specifies the fully qualified class name of the enterprise bean's local home interface.

`<local>` *(EJB 2.0: optional)*
Specifies the fully qualified class name of the enterprise bean's local interface.

`<ejb-class>` *(one required)*
Specifies the fully qualified class name of the bean class.

`<primkey-field>` *(optional; entity beans only)*
Specifies the primary key field for entity beans that use container-managed persistence. This element's value is the name of the field that is used as the primary key. It is not used if the bean has a compound primary key or if the entity bean manages its own persistence. In the Cabin EJB, the `<primkey-field>` is the id CMP field. This element is discussed in more detail in the section "Specifying Primary Keys" later in this chapter.

`<prim-key-class>` *(one required; entity beans only)*
Specifies the class of the primary key for entity beans. This element's value is the fully qualified name of the primary key class; it makes no difference whether you are using a custom compound primary key or a simple `<primkey-field>` such as an Integer, String, Date, etc. If you defer definition of the primary key class to the deployer, specify the type as java.lang.Object in this element.

`<persistence-type>` *(one required; entity beans only)*
Declares that the entity bean uses either container-managed persistence or bean-managed persistence. This element can have one of two values: Container or Bean.

`<reentrant>` *(one required; entity beans only)*
Declares that the bean either allows loopbacks (reentrant invocations) or does not. This element can have one of two values: True or False. True means that the bean allows loopbacks; False means that the bean throws an exception if a loopback occurs.

`<cmp-version>` *(EJB 2.0: optional)*
Describes the version of container-managed persistence for which the entity bean is deployed. EJB containers must support both EJB 2.0 CMP and EJB 1.1 CMP for backward compatibility. This element may have one of two values: 2.x for EJB 2.0 or 1.x for EJB 1.1.

`<abstract-schema-name>` *(EJB 2.0: optional)*
Uniquely identifies entity beans in a JAR file so that they can be referenced by EJB QL statements. This method is described in more detail in the later section "Declaring EJB QL Elements."

`<cmp-field>` *(zero or more; entity beans only)*

> Used in entity beans with container-managed persistence. A `<cmp-field>` element must exist for each container-managed field in the bean class. Each `<cmp-field>` element may include a `<description>` element and must include a `<field-name>` element. The `<description>` is an optional comment describing the field. The `<field-name>` is required and must be the name of one of the bean's CMP fields. In EJB 2.0, it must match the method name of the abstract accessor method (e.g., deckLevel for getDeckLevel()/setDeckLevel()). In EJB 1.1, the `<cmp-field>` must match the field name of one of the bean class's declared instance fields. The container will manage persistence for the given CMP field. The following portion of a descriptor shows several `<cmp-field>` declarations for the Cabin EJB:

```
<cmp-field>
    <description>This is the primary key</description>
    <field-name>id</field-name>
</cmp-field>
<cmp-field>
    <field-name>name</field-name>
</cmp-field>
<cmp-field>
    <field-name>deckLevel</field-name>
</cmp-field>
<cmp-field>
    <field-name>shipId</field-name>
</cmp-field>
<cmp-field>
    <field-name>bedCount</field-name>
</cmp-field>
```

`<env-entry>` *(zero or more)*

> Declares an environment entry that is available through the JNDI ENC. The use of environment entries in a bean and a deployment descriptor is discussed further in the later section "Environment Entries."

`<ejb-ref>` *(zero or more)*

> Declares a remote enterprise bean reference that is available through the JNDI ENC. The mechanism for making bean references available through the ENC is described in more detail later, in the section "References to Other Beans."

`<ejb-local-ref>` *(EJB 2.0: zero or more)*

> Declares a local enterprise bean reference that is available through the JNDI ENC. The mechanism for making bean references available through the ENC is described in more detail later, in the section "References to Other Beans."

`<resource-ref>` *(zero or more)*

> Declares a reference to a connection factory that is available through the JNDI ENC. An example of a resource factory is the javax.sql.DataSource, which is used to obtain a connection to a database. This element is discussed in detail in the section "References to External Resources" later in this chapter.

`<resource-env-ref>` *(EJB 2.0: zero or more)*

> Describes additional "administered objects" required by the resource. The `<resource-env-ref>` element and administered objects are explained in more detail in the section "References to External Resources" later in this chapter.

`<security-role-ref>` *(zero or more)*

> Used to declare security roles in the deployment descriptor and map them into the security roles in effect for the bean's runtime environment. This method is described in more detail in the later section "Security Roles."

`<security-identity>` *(EJB 2.0: optional)*

> Specifies the Principal under which a method will run. This element is described in more detail in the later section "Specifying Security Roles and Method Permissions."

`<session-type>` *(one required; session beans only)*

> Declares that a session bean is either stateful or stateless. This element can have one of two values: Stateful or Stateless.

`<transaction-type>` *(one required; session beans only)*

> Declares either that a session bean manages its own transactions or that its transactions are managed by the container. This element can have one of two values: Bean or Container. A bean that manages its own transactions will not have container-transaction declarations in the `<assembly-descriptor>` section of the deployment descriptor.

`<query>` *(EJB 2.0: zero or more)*

> Contains an EJB QL statement that is bound to a find or select method. The EJB QL statement defines how the find or select method should execute at runtime. This element is described in more detail later, in the section "Declaring EJB QL Elements."

Message-Driven Beans

The `<message-driven>` element describes message-driven bean deployments. `<message-driven>` elements occur after `<entity>` and `<session>` elements within the `<enterprise-bean>` element.

Like the `<entity>` and `<session>` elements, the `<message-driven>` element can optionally have `<description>`, `<display-name>`, `<small-icon>`, and `<large-icon>` elements. These elements are used primarily by visual deployment tools to represent the message-driven bean. The `<message-driven>` element also requires declaration of the `<ejb-name>`, `<ejb-class>`, `<transaction-type>`, and `<security-id-entity>` elements. In addition, it contains the standard JNDI ENC elements `<env-entry>`, `<ejb-ref>`, `<ejb-local-ref>`, `<resource-ref>`, and `<resource-env-ref>`. These are fairly self-explanatory and mean the same as they did in the `<entity>` and `<session>` elements.

The elements that are specific to the message-driven bean are:

`<message-selector>`

Message selectors allow an MDB to be more selective about the messages it receives from a particular topic or queue. Message selectors use `Message` properties as criteria in conditional expressions.* These conditional expressions use Boolean logic to declare which messages should be delivered to a client. The syntax of message selectors can cause problems with XML processing. See the sidebar titled "CDATA Sections."

`<acknowledge-mode>`

This element is considered by the container only if the message-driven bean uses bean-managed transactions; with container-managed transactions, it is ignored. It determines which type of acknowledgment it uses; its value can be either `Auto-acknowledge` or `Dups-ok-acknowledge`. The first acknowledges messages immediately; the second can delay acknowledgment to benefit performance but may result in duplicate or redelivered messages.

`<message-driven-destination>`

This element designates the type of destination to which the MDB subscribes or listens. The allowed values for this element are `javax.jms.Queue` and `javax.jms.Topic`.

Specifying Primary Keys

If there is a single field in the bean that can serve naturally as a unique identifier, you can use that field as the primary key. Optionally, a custom primary key can be used as a compound primary key. In the Cabin EJB, for example, the primary key type could be the `CabinPK`, which is mapped to the bean class fields `id` and `name` as shown here (the `CabinBean` is using bean-managed persistence to better illustrate):

```
public class CabinBean implements javax.ejb.EntityBean {

    public int id;
    public String name;
    public int deckLevel;
    public int ship;
    public int bedCount;

    public CabinPK ejbCreate(int id, String name) {
        this.id = id;
        this.name = name;
        return null;
    }
    ...
}
```

---

* Message selectors are also based on message headers, which are outside the scope of this chapter.

In Chapter 4, instead of using the custom `CabinPK` class, we used the appropriate primitive wrapper, `java.lang.Integer`, and defined the `CabinBean` as:

```
public class CabinBean implements javax.ejb.EntityBean {

    public int id;
    public String name;
    public int deckLevel;
    public int ship;
    public int bedCount;

    public Integer ejbCreate(int id) {
        this.id = id;
        return null;
    }
    ...
}
```

This simplifies things a lot. Instead of taking the time to define a custom primary key like `CabinPK`, we simply use the appropriate wrapper. To do this, we need to add a

`<primkey-field>` element to the Cabin EJB's deployment descriptor, so it knows which field to use as the primary key. We also need to change the `<prim-key-class>` element to state that the `Integer` class is being used to represent the primary key. The following code shows how the Cabin EJB's deployment descriptor would need to change to use `Integer` as the primary key field:

```
<entity>
    <description>
        This Cabin enterprise bean entity represents a cabin on
        a cruise ship.
    </description>
    <ejb-name>CabinEJB</ejb-name>
    <home>com.titan.cabin.CabinHome</home>
    <remote>com.titan.cabin.Cabin</remote>
    <ejb-class>com.titan.cabin.CabinBean</ejb-class>
    <persistence-type>Bean</persistence-type>
    <prim-key-class>java.lang.Integer</prim-key-class>
    <reentrant>False</reentrant>

    <cmp-field><field-name>id</field-name></cmp-field>
    <cmp-field><field-name>name</field-name></cmp-field>
    <cmp-field><field-name>deckLevel</field-name></cmp-field>
    <cmp-field><field-name>ship</field-name></cmp-field>
    <cmp-field><field-name>bedCount</field-name></cmp-field>
    <primkey-field>id</primkey-field>
</entity>
```

Simple primary key fields are not limited to the primitive wrapper classes (`Byte`, `Boolean`, `Integer`, etc.); any container-managed field can be used as a primary key, as long as it is serializable. `String` types are probably the most common, but other types, such as `java.lang.StringBuffer`, `java.util.Date`, or even `java.util.Hashtable` are also valid. Custom types can also be primary keys, provided that they are serializable. Of course, common sense should be used when choosing a primary key: because it is used as an index to the data in the database, it should be lightweight.

Deferring primary key definition

With container-managed persistence, it is also possible for the bean developer to defer defining the primary key, leaving key definition to the bean deployer. This feature might be needed if, for example, the primary key is generated by the database and is not a container-managed field in the bean class. Containers that have a tight integration with database or legacy systems that automatically generate primary keys might use this approach. It is also an attractive approach for vendors that sell shrink-wrapped beans, because it makes the bean more portable. The following code shows how an entity bean using container-managed persistence defers the definition of the primary key to the deployer:

```
// bean class for bean that uses a deferred primary key
public class HypotheticalBean implements javax.ejb.EntityBean {
    ...
```

```
        public java.lang.Object ejbCreate() {
            ...
            return null;
        }
        ...
    }

    // home interface for bean with deferred primary key
    public interface HypotheticalHome extends javax.ejb.EJBHome {
        public Hypothetical create() throws ...;
        public Hypothetical findByPrimaryKey(java.lang.Object key) throws ...;
    }
```

Here's the relevant portion of the deployment descriptor:

```
// primkey-field declaration for the Hypothetical bean
...
<entity>
    <ejb-name>HypotheticalEJB</ejb-name>
    ...
    <persistence-type>Container</persistence-type>
    <prim-key-class>java.lang.Object</prim-key-class>
    <reentrant>False</reentrant>
    <cmp-field><field-name>creationDate</field-name></cmp-field>
    ...
</entity>
```

Because the primary key is of type java.lang.Object, the client application's interaction with the bean's key is limited to the Object type and its methods.

Environment Entries

A deployment descriptor can define environment entries, which are values similar to properties the bean can read when it is running. The bean can use environment entries to customize its behavior, find out about how it is deployed, and so on.

The <env-entry> element is used to define environment entries. This element contains <description> (optional), <env-entry-name> (required), <env-entry-type> (required), and <env-entry-value> (optional) subelements. Here is a typical <env-entry> declaration:

```
<env-entry>
    <env-entry-name>minCheckNumber</env-entry-name>
    <env-entry-type>java.lang.Integer</env-entry-type>
    <env-entry-value>2000</env-entry-value>
</env-entry>
```

The <env-entry-name> is relative to the "java:comp/env" context. For example, the minCheckNumber entry can be accessed using the path "java:comp/env/minCheckNumber" in a JNDI ENC lookup:

```
InitialContext jndiContext = new InitialContext();
Integer miniumValue = (Integer)
    jndiContext.lookup("java:comp/env/minCheckNumber");
```

The <env-entry-type> can be of type String or one of several primitive wrapper types, including Integer, Long, Double, Float, Byte, Boolean, and Short.

The <env-entry-value> is optional. The value can be specified by the bean developer or deferred to the application assembler or deployer.

The subcontext "java:comp/env/ejb10-properties" can be used to make an entry available via the EJBContext.getEnvironment() method. This feature has been deprecated, but it may help you deploy EJB 1.0 beans within an EJB 1.1 server. The <ejb-entry-type> must always be java.lang.String for entries in this subcontext. Here's an example:

```
<env-entry>
    <description>
        This property is available through EJBContext.getEnvironment()
    </description>
    <env-entry-name>ejb10-properties/minCheckNumber</env-entry-name>
    <env-entry-type>java.lang.String</env-entry-name>
    <env-entry-value>20000</env-entry-value>
</env-entry>
```

References to Other Beans

In EJB 2.0, references to other beans can be either local or remote. In EJB 1.1, references to other beans are always remote references.

Remote references

The <env-ref> element is used to define references to other beans within the JNDI ENC. This makes it much easier for beans to reference other beans; they can use JNDI to look up a reference to the home interface for any beans in which they are interested.

The <env-ref> element contains <description> (optional), <ejb-ref-name> (required), <ejb-ref-type> (required), <remote> (required), <home> (required), and <ejb-link> (optional) subelements. Here is a typical <env-ref> declaration:

```
<ejb-ref>
    <ejb-ref-name>ejb/ProcessPaymentHomeRemote</ejb-ref-name>
    <ejb-ref-type>Session</ejb-ref-type>
    <home>com.titan.processpayment.ProcessPaymentHomeRemote</home>
    <remote>com.titan.processpayment.ProcessPaymentHomeRemote</remote>
</ejb-ref>
```

The <ejb-ref-name> is relative to the "java:comp/env" context. It is recommended, but not required, that the name be placed under a subcontext of ejb/. Following this convention, the path used to access the ProcessPayment EJB's home would be "java:comp/env/ejb/ProcessPaymentHomeRemote". The following code shows how a client bean would use this context to look up a reference to the ProcessPayment EJB:

```
InitialContext jndiContext = new InititalContext();
Object ref = jndiContext.lookup("java:comp/env/ejb/ProcessPaymentHomeRemote");
```

```
ProcessPaymentHomeRemote home = (ProcessPaymentHomeRemote)
    PortableRemoteObject.narrow(ref, ProcessPaymentHomeRemote.class);
```

The <ejb-ref-type> can have one of two values, Entity or Session, according to whether the bean is an entity or a session bean.

The <home> element specifies the fully qualified class name of the bean's home interface; the <remote> element specifies the fully qualified class name of the bean's remote interface.

If the bean referenced by the <ejb-ref> element is deployed in the same deployment descriptor (i.e., it is defined under the same <ejb-jar> element), the <ejb-ref> element can be linked to the bean's declaration using the <ejb-link> element. If, for example, the TravelAgent bean uses reference to the ProcessPayment EJB that is declared in the same deployment descriptor, the <ejb-ref> elements for the Travel-Agent bean can use an <ejb-link> element to map its <ejb-ref> elements to the ProcessPayment EJB. The <ejb-link> value must match one of the <ejb-name> values declared in the same deployment descriptor. Here's a portion of a deployment descriptor that uses the <ejb-link> element:

```
<ejb-jar>
    <enterprise-beans>
        <session>
            <ejb-name>TravelAgentEJB</ejb-name>
            <remote>com.titan.travelagent.TravelAgentRemote</remote>
            ...
            <ejb-ref>
                <ejb-ref-name>ejb/ProcessPaymentHome</ejb-ref-name>
                <ejb-ref-type>Session</ejb-ref-type>
                <home>com.titan.processpayment.ProcessPaymentHomeRemote</home>
                <remote>com.titan.processpayment.ProcessPaymentRemote</remote>
                <ejb-link>ProcessPaymentEJB</ejb-link>
            </ejb-ref>
            ...
        </session>

        <session>
            <ejb-name>ProcessPaymentEJB</ejb-name>
            <remote>com.titan.processpayment.ProcessPaymentRemote</remote>
            ...
        </session>
        ...
    </enterprise-beans>
    ...
</ejb-jar>
```

If you are an EJB 2.0 developer, you are probably better off using the <ejb-local-ref> element to obtain references to beans in the same JAR file, unless the referenced enterprise bean does not have a set of local component interfaces. In that case, you should use the <ejb-link> element with the <ejb-ref> element to get a remote reference to the enterprise bean.

EJB 2.0: Local references

The deployment descriptor also provides a special set of tags, the `<ejb-local-ref>` elements, to declare local EJB references; i.e., references to enterprise beans that are co-located in the same container and deployed in the same EJB JAR file. The `<ejb-local-ref>` elements are declared immediately after the `<ejb-ref>` elements:

```
<ejb-local-ref>
    <ejb-ref-name>ejb/CruiseHomeLocal</ejb-ref-name>
    <ejb-ref-type>Entity</ejb-ref-type>
    <local-home>com.titan.cruise.CruiseHomeLocal</local-home>
    <local>com.titan.cruise.CruiseLocal</local>
    <ejb-link>CruiseEJB</ejb-link>
</ejb-local-ref>
<ejb-local-ref>
    <ejb-ref-name>ejb/CabinHomeLocal</ejb-ref-name>
    <ejb-ref-type>Entity</ejb-ref-type>
    <local-home>com.titan.cabin.CabinHomeLocal</local-home>
    <local>com.titan.cabin.CabinLocal</local>
    <ejb-link>CabinEJB</ejb-link>
</ejb-local-ref>
```

The `<ejb-local-ref>` element defines a name for the bean within the ENC, declares the bean's type, and gives the names of its local component interfaces. These elements should be linked explicitly to other co-located beans using the `<ejb-link>` element, but this is not required—the application assembler or deployer can do it later. The value of the `<ejb-link>` element within the `<ejb-local-ref>` must equal the `<ejb-name>` of the appropriate bean in the same JAR file.

At deployment time, the EJB container's tools map the local references declared in the `<ejb-local-ref>` elements to entity beans that are co-located in the same container system.

Enterprise beans declared in the `<ejb-local-ref>` elements are local enterprise beans and so do not require the use of the `PortableRemoteObject.narrow()` method to narrow the reference. Instead, you can use a simple native cast operation:

```
InitialContext jndiContext = new InititalContext();
CabinHome home = (CabinHome)
    jndiContext.lookup("java:comp/env/ejb/CabinHomeLocal");
```

References to External Resources

Enterprise beans also use the JNDI ENC to look up external resources, such as database connections, that they need to access. The mechanism for doing this is similar to the mechanism used for referencing other beans and environment entries: the external resources are mapped into a name within the JNDI ENC name space. For external resources, the mapping is performed by the `<resource-ref>` element.

The `<resource-ref>` element contains `<description>` (optional), `<res-ref-name>` (required), `<res-type>` (required), and `<res-auth>` (required) subelements.

Here is a `<resource-ref>` declaration used for a DataSource connection factory:

```
<resource-ref>
    <description>DataSource for the Titan database</description>
    <res-ref-name>jdbc/titanDB</res-ref-name>
    <res-type>javax.sql.DataSource</res-type>
    <res-auth>Container</res-auth>
</resource-ref>
```

The `<res-ref-name>` is relative to the "java:comp/env" context. Although not a requirement, it is a good idea to place connection factories under a subcontext that describes the resource type. For example:

- jdbc/ for a JDBC DataSource factory
- jms/ for a JMS QueueConnectionFactory or TopicConnectionFactory factory
- mail/ for a JavaMail session factory
- url/ for a javax.net.URL factory

Here is how a bean would use JNDI to look up a resource—in this case, a DataSource:

```
InitialContext jndiContext = new InitialContext();
DataSource source = (DataSource)
    jndiContext.lookup("java:comp/env/jdbc/titanDB");
```

The `<res-type>` element is used to declare the fully qualified class name of the connection factory. In this example, the `<res-type>` is javax.sql.DataSource.

The `<res-auth>` element tells the server who is responsible for authentication. It can have one of two values: Container or Application. If Container is specified, authentication (sign-on or login) to use the resource will be performed automatically by the container as specified at deployment time. If Application is specified, the bean itself must perform the necessary authentication before using the resource. The following code shows how a bean might sign on to a connection factory when Application is specified for `<res-auth>`:

```
InitialContext jndiContext = new InitialContext();
DataSource source = (DataSource)
    jndiContext.lookup("java:comp/env/jdbc/titanDB");

String loginName = ejbContext.getCallerPrincipal().getName();
String password = ...; // get password from somewhere

// use login name and password to obtain a database connection
java.sql.Connection con = source.getConnection(loginName, password);
```

EJB 2.0: Additional administered objects

In addition to the resource factory described in the `<resource-ref>` element, some resources may have other administered objects that need to be obtained from the JNDI ENC. An *administered object* is a resource that is configured at deployment time and managed by the EJB container at runtime. For example, to use JMS, the bean developer must obtain both a JMS factory object and a destination object:

```
TopicConnectionFactory factory = (TopicConnectionFactory)
    jndiContext.lookup("java:comp/env/jms/TopicFactory");

Topic topic = (Topic)
    jndiContext.lookup("java:comp/env/ejb/TicketTopic");
```

Both the JMS factory and destination are administered objects that must be obtained from the JNDI ENC. The <resource-ref> element is used to declare the JMS factory while the <resource-env-ref> element is used to declare the destination:

```
<resource-ref>
    <res-ref-name>jms/TopicFactory</res-ref-name>
    <res-type>javax.jms.TopicConnectionFactory</res-type>
    <res-auth>Container</res-auth>
</resource-ref>
<resource-ref>
    <res-ref-name>jdbc/titanDB</res-ref-name>
    <res-type>javax.sql.DataSource</res-type>
    <res-auth>Container</res-auth>
</resource-ref>
<resource-env-ref>
    <resource-env-ref-name>jms/TicketTopic</resource-env-ref-name>
    <resource-env-ref-type>javax.jms.Topic</resource-env-ref-type>
</resource-env-ref>
```

At deployment time, the deployer maps the JMS TopicConnectionFactory or QueueConnectionFactory and the Topic or Queue declared by the <resource-ref> and <resource-env-ref> elements to a JMS factory and topic.

EJB 2.0: Shareable resources

When several enterprise beans in a unit-of-work or transaction all use the same resource, you will want to configure your EJB server to share that resource. Sharing a resource means that each enterprise bean will use the same connection to access the resource (e.g., database or JMS provider), which is more efficient than using separate resource connections.

For example, in the TravelAgent EJB, the bookPassage() method uses the ProcessPayment EJB and the Reservation EJB to book a passenger on a cruise. If both of these enterprise beans use the same database, they should share their resource connection for efficiency. Enterprise JavaBeans containers share resources by default, but resource sharing can be turned on or off explicitly through the <resource-ref> element:

```
<resource-ref>
    <res-ref-name>jdbc/titanDB</res-ref-name>
    <res-type>javax.sql.DataSource</res-type>
    <res-auth>Container</res-auth>
    <res-sharing-scope>Shareable</res-sharing-scope>
</resource-ref>
```

`<res-sharing-scope>` is an optional element that may be declared as either Shareable, indicating that connections should be shared in local transactions, or Unshareable, indicating that they should not. If it is not specified, the default is Shareable.

Occasionally, advanced developers may run into situations where resource sharing is not desirable—this is relatively rare, but having the option to turn off resource sharing is beneficial in those circumstances. Unless you have a good reason for turning off resource sharing, I recommend that you use Shareable resources.

Security Roles

The `<security-role-ref>` element is used to define the security roles that are used by a bean and to map them into the security roles that are in effect for the runtime environment. It can contain three subelements: an optional `<description>`, a `<role-name>` (required), and an optional `<role-link>`.

Here's how security roles are defined. When a role name is used in the EJBContext. isCallerInRole(String roleName) method, the role name must be statically defined (it cannot be derived at runtime) and it must be declared in the deployment descriptor using the `<security-role-ref>` element:

```
<-- security-role-ref declaration for Account bean -->
<entity>
    <ejb-name>AccountEJB</ejb-name>
    ...
    <security-role-ref>
        <description>
            The caller must be a member of this role in
            order to withdraw over $10,000
        </description>
        <role-name>Manager</role-name>
        <role-link>Administrator</role-link>
    </security-role-ref>
    ...
</entity>
```

The `<role-name>` defined in the deployment descriptor must match the role name used in the EJBContext.isCallerInRole() method. Here is how the role name is used in the bean's code:

```
// Account bean uses the isCallerInRole() method
public class AccountBean implements EntityBean {
    int id;
    double balance;
    EntityContext context;

    public void withdraw(Double withdraw) throws AccessDeniedException {

        if (withdraw.doubleValue() > 10000) {
            boolean isManager = context.isCallerInRole("Manager");
            if (!isManager) {
```

```
                    // only Managers can withdraw more than 10k
                    throw new AccessDeniedException();
                }
            }
            balance = balance - withdraw.doubleValue();

        }
        ...
    }
```

The <role-link> element is optional; it can be used to map the role name used in the bean to a logical role defined in a <security-role> element in the <assembly-descriptor> section of the deployment descriptor. If no <role-link> is specified, the deployer must map the <security-role-ref> to an existing security role in the target environment.

Declaring EJB QL Elements

EJB QL statements are declared in <query> elements in an entity bean's deployment descriptor. In the following listing, you can see that findByName() and ejbSelectShips() methods were declared in the <query> elements of the Cruise EJB deployment descriptor:

```
<ejb-jar>
    <enterprise-beans>
        <entity>
            <ejb-name>ShipEJB</ejb-name>
            ...
            <abstract-schema-name>Ship</abstract-schema-name>
            ...
        </entity>
        <entity>
            <ejb-name>CruiseEJB</ejb-name>
            ...
            <reentrant>False</reentrant>
            <abstract-schema-name>Cruise</abstract-schema-name>
            <cmp-version>2.x</cmp-version>
            <cmp-field>
                <field-name>name</field-name>
            </cmp-field>
            <primkey-field>id</primkey-field>
            <query>
                <query-method>
                    <method-name>findByName</method-name>
                    <method-params>
                        <mehod-param>java.lang.String</method-param>
                    </method-params>
                </query-method>
                <ejb-ql>
                    SELECT OBJECT(c) FROM Cruise c WHERE c.name = ?1
                </ejb-ql>
            </query>
```

```
<query>
    <query-method>
        <method-name>ejbSelectShips</method-name>
        <method-params></method-params>
    </query-method>
    <result-type-mapping>Remote</result-type-mapping>
    <ejb-ql>
        SELECT OBJECT(s) FROM Ship AS s
    </ejb-ql>
</query>
        </entity>
    </enterprise-beans>
</ejb-jar>
```

The <query> element contains two primary elements. The <query-method> element identifies the find method of the remote and/or local home interface, and the <ejb-ql> element declares the EJB QL statement. The <query> element binds the EJB QL statement to the proper find method. The syntax used in EJB QL may cause problems for the XML parser. See the earlier sidebar "CDATA Sections" for more details.

When two find methods in the local and remote home interfaces have the same method name and parameters, the query declaration will apply to both of the methods. The container will return the proper type for each query method: the remote home will return one or more remote EJB objects, and the local home will return one or more local EJB objects. This allows you to define the behavior of both the local and remote home find methods using a single <query> element, which is convenient if you want local clients to have access to the same find methods as remote clients.

The <result-type-mapping> element can be used to declare whether a select method should return local or remote EJB objects. The value Local indicates that a method should return local EJB objects; Remote indicates remote EJB objects. If the <result-type-mapping> element is not declared, the default is Local. In the <query> element for the ejbSelectShips() method, the <result-type-mapping> is declared as Remote, which means the query should return remote EJB object types (i.e., remote references to the Ship EJB).

Every entity bean that will be referenced in an EJB QL statement must have a special designator called an *abstract schema name*, which is declared by the <abstract-schema-name> element. <abstract-schema-name> elements must have unique names; no two entity beans may have the same abstract schema name. In the entity element that describes the Cruise EJB, the abstract schema name is declared as Cruise, while the Ship EJB's abstract schema name is Ship. The <ejb-ql> element contains an EJB QL statement that uses this identifier in its FROM clause.

In Chapter 7 you learned that the abstract persistence schema of an entity bean is defined by its <cmp-field> and <cmr-field> elements. The abstract schema name is also an important part of the abstract persistence schema. EJB QL statements are always expressed in terms of the abstract persistence schemas of entity beans. EJB QL uses the abstract schema names to identify entity bean types, the container-managed persistence (CMP) fields to identify specific entity bean data, and the container-managed relationship (CMR) fields to create paths for navigating from one entity bean to another.

EJB 2.0: Describing Relationships

CMP 2.0 entity bean classes are defined using abstract accessor methods that represent virtual persistence and relationship fields. As you learned in Chapters 6, 7, and 8, the actual fields themselves are not declared in the entity classes. Instead, the characteristics of these fields are described in detail in the XML deployment descriptor used by the entity bean. The *abstract persistence schema* is the set of XML elements in the deployment descriptor that describe the relationship and persistence fields. Together with the abstract programming model (i.e., the abstract accessor methods) and some help from the deployer, the container tool has enough information to map the entity and its relationships with other entity beans.

The relationships between entity beans are described in the <relationships> section of the XML deployment descriptor. The <relationships> section falls between the <enterprise-beans> and <assembly-descriptor> sections. Within the <relationships> element, each entity-to-entity relationship is defined in a separate <ejb-relation> element:

```
<ejb-jar>
    <enterprise-beans>
    ...
    </enterprise-beans>
    <relationships>
        <ejb-relation>
        ...
        </ejb-relation>
        <ejb-relation>
        ...
        </ejb-relation>
    </relationships>
    <assembly-descriptor>
    ...
    </assembly-descriptor>
</ejb-jar>
```

Defining relationship fields requires that an <ejb-relation> element be added to the XML deployment descriptor for each entity-to-entity relationship. These <ejb-relation> elements complement the abstract programming model. For each pair of abstract accessor methods that define a relationship field, there is an <ejb-relation> element in the deployment descriptor. EJB 2.0 requires that the entity beans in a relationship be defined in the same XML deployment descriptor.

Here is a partial listing of the deployment descriptor for the Customer and Address EJBs, emphasizing the elements that define the relationship:

```
<ejb-jar>
    ...
    <enterprise-beans>
        <entity>
            <ejb-name>CustomerEJB</ejb-name>
            <local-home>com.titan.customer.CusomterLocalHome</local-home>
            <local>com.titan.customer.CustomerLocal</local>
            ...
        </entity>
        <entity>
            <ejb-name>AddressEJB</ejb-name>
            <local-home>com.titan.address.AddressLocalHome</local-home>
            <local>com.titan.address.AddressLocal</local>
            ...
        </entity>
        ...
    </enterprise-beans>

    <relationships>
        <ejb-relation>
            <ejb-relation-name>Customer-Address</ejb-relation-name>
            <ejb-relationship-role>
                <ejb-relationship-role-name>
                    Customer-has-an-Address
                </ejb-relationship-role-name>
                <multiplicity>One</multiplicity>
                <relationship-role-source>
                    <ejb-name>CustomerEJB</ejb-name>
                </relationship-role-source>
                <cmr-field>
                    <cmr-field-name>homeAddress</cmr-field-name>
                </cmr-field>
            </ejb-relationship-role>
            <ejb-relationship-role>
                <ejb-relationship-role-name>
                    Address-belongs-to-Customer
                </ejb-relationship-role-name>
                <multiplicity>One</multiplicity>
                <relationship-role-source>
                    <ejb-name>AddressEJB</ejb-name>
                </relationship-role-source>
            </ejb-relationship-role>
        </ejb-relation>
    </relationships>
</ejb-jar>
```

All relationships between the Customer EJB and other entity beans, such as the CreditCard, Address, and Phone EJBs, require that we define an <ejb-relation> element to complement the abstract accessor methods.

Every relationship may have a relationship name, which is declared in the <ejb-relation-name> element. This name identifies the relationship for individuals reading the deployment descriptor or for deployment tools, but it is not required.

Every <ejb-relation> element has exactly two <ejb-relationship-role> elements, one for each participant in the relationship. In the previous example, the first <ejb-relationship-role> declares the Customer EJB's role in the relationship. We know this because the <relationship-role-source> element specifies the <ejb-name> as CustomerEJB. CustomerEJB is the <ejb-name> used in the Customer EJB's original declaration in the <enterprise-beans> section. The <relationship-role-source> element's <ejb-name> must always match an <ejb-name> element in the <enterprise-beans> section.

The <ejb-relationship-role> element also declares the cardinality, or *multiplicity*, of the role. The <multiplicity> element can be either One or Many. In this case, the Customer EJB's <multiplicity> element has a value of One, which means that every Address EJB has a relationship with exactly one Customer EJB. The Address EJB's <multiplicity> element also specifies One, which means that every Customer EJB has a relationship with exactly one Address EJB. If the Customer EJB had a relationship with many Address EJBs, the Address EJB's <multiplicity> element would be set to Many.

If the bean described by the <ejb-relationship-role> element maintains a reference to the other bean in the relationship, that reference must be declared as a container-managed relationship field in the <cmr-field> element. The <cmr-field> element is declared under the <ejb-relationship-role> element:

```
<ejb-relationship-role>
    <ejb-relationship-role-name>
        Customer-has-an-Address
    </ejb-relationship-role-name>
    <multiplicity>One</multiplicity>
    <relationship-role-source>
        <ejb-name>CustomerEJB</ejb-name>
    </relationship-role-source>
    <cmr-field>
        <cmr-field-name>homeAddress</cmr-field-name>
    </cmr-field>
</ejb-relationship-role>
```

EJB 2.0 requires that the <cmr-field-name> begin with a lowercase letter. For every relationship field defined by a <cmr-field> element, the bean class must include a pair of matching abstract accessor methods. One method in this pair must be defined with the method name set<*cmr-field-name*>(), with the first letter of the <cmr-field-name> changed to uppercase. The other method is defined as get<*cmr-field-name*>(), also with the first letter of the <cmr-field-name> in uppercase. In this example, the <cmr-field-name> is homeAddress, which corresponds to the getHomeAddress() and setHomeAddress() methods defined in the CustomerBean class:

```
// bean class code
public abstract void setHomeAddress(AddressLocal address);
public abstract AddressLocal getHomeAddress();
```

```
// XML deployment descriptor declaration
<cmr-field>
    <cmr-field-name>homeAddress</cmr-field-name>
</cmr-field>
```

The <cascade-delete> element requests cascade deletion; it can be used with one-to-one or one-to-many relationships. It is always declared as an empty element: <cascade-delete/>. <cascade-delete> indicates that the lifetime of one entity bean in a particular relationship depends upon the lifetime the other entity bean in the relationship. Here's how to modify the relationship declaration for the Customer and Address EJBs to obtain a cascade delete:

```
<relationships>
    <ejb-relation>
        <ejb-relationship-role>
            <multiplicity>One</multiplicity>
            <role-source>
                <ejb-name>CustomerEJB</ejb-name>
            </role-source>
            <cmr-field>
                <cmr-field-name>homeAddress</cmr-field-name>
            </cmr-field>
        </ejb-relationship-role>
        <ejb-relationship-role>
            <multiplicity>One</multiplicity>
            <cascade-delete/>
            <role-source>
                <dependent-name>Address</dependent-name>
            </role-source>
        </ejb-relationship-role>
    </ejb-relation>
</relationships>
```

With this declaration, the Address EJB will be deleted automatically when the Customer EJB that refers to it is deleted.

Describing Bean Assembly

At this point, we have said just about all that can be said about the bean itself. We have come to the end of the <enterprise-beans> element and are now ready to describe how the beans are assembled into an application. That is, we are ready to talk about the other major element inside the <ejb-jar> element: the <assembly-descriptor> element.

The <assembly-descriptor> element is optional, though it is difficult to imagine a bean being deployed successfully without an <assembly-descriptor>. When we say that the <assembly-descriptor> is optional, we really mean that a developer whose only role is to create enterprise beans (for example, someone who is developing beans for use by another party and who has no role in deploying the beans) can omit this part of the deployment descriptor. The descriptor is valid without it—but someone will almost certainly have to fill in the assembly information before the bean can be deployed.

The <assembly-descriptor> element serves three purposes: it describes the transaction attributes of the bean's methods; it describes the logical security roles that are used in the method permissions; and it specifies the method permissions (i.e., which roles are allowed to call each of the methods). To this end, an <assembly-descriptor> can contain three kinds of elements, each of which is fairly complex in its own right. These are:

<container-transaction> *(zero or more)*
> This element declares which transaction attributes apply to which methods. It contains an optional <description> element, one or more <method> elements, and exactly one <trans-attribute> element. Entity beans must have <container-transaction> declarations for all remote and home interface methods. Session beans that manage their own transactions will not have <container-transaction> declarations. This element is discussed in more detail in the next section.

<security-role> *(zero or more)*
> This element defines the security roles that are used when accessing a bean. These security roles are used in the <method-permission> element. A <security-role> element contains an optional description and one <role-name>. This element and the <method-permission> element are described in more detail in the later section "Specifying Security Roles and Method Permissions."

<method-permission> *(zero or more)*
> This element specifies which security roles are allowed to call one or more of a bean's methods. It contains an optional <description> element, one or more <role-name> elements, and one or more <method> elements. It is discussed in more detail in the section "Specifying Security Roles and Method Permissions," along with the <security-role> element.

The <container-transaction> and <method-permission> elements both rely on the ability to identify particular methods. This can be a complicated affair, given features of the Java language such as method overloading. The <method> element is used within these tags to identify methods; it is described at length in the later section "Identifying Specific Methods."

Specifying a Bean's Transaction Attributes

The <container-transaction> elements are used to declare the transaction attributes for all the beans defined in the deployment descriptor. A <container-transaction> element maps one or more bean methods to a single transaction attribute, so each <container-transaction> specifies one transaction attribute and one or more bean methods.

The <container-transaction> element includes a single <trans-attribute> element, which can have one of six values: NotSupported, Supports, Required, RequiresNew, Mandatory, and Never. These are the transaction attributes we discussed in Chapter 14. In addition to <trans-attribute>, the <container-transaction> element includes one or more <method> elements.

The <method> element itself contains at least two subelements: an <ejb-name> element, which specifies the name of the bean; and a <method-name> element, which specifies a subset of the bean's methods. The value of the <method-name> can be a method name or an asterisk (*), which acts as wildcard for all the bean's methods. A lot more complexity is involved in handling overloading and other special cases, but that's enough for now; we'll discuss the rest later.

Here is an example that shows how the <container-transaction> element is typically used. Let's look again at the Cabin EJB, which we have used as an example throughout. Let's assume that we want to give the transaction attribute Mandatory to the create() method; all other methods use the Required attribute:

```
<container-transaction>
    <method>
        <ejb-name>CabinEJB</ejb-name>
        <method-name>*</method-name>
    </method>
    <trans-attribute>Required</trans-attribute>
</container-transaction>
<container-transaction>
    <method>
        <ejb-name>CabinEJB</ejb-name>
        <method-name>create</method-name>
    </method>
    <trans-attribute>Mandatory</trans-attribute>
</container-transaction>
```

In the first <container-transaction>, we have a single <method> element that uses the wildcard character (*) to refer to all of the Cabin EJB's methods. We set the transaction attribute for these methods to Required. Then, we have a second <container-transaction> element that specifies a single method of the Cabin EJB: create(). We set the transaction attribute for this method to Mandatory. This setting overrides the wildcard setting; in <container-transaction> elements, specific method declarations always override more general declarations.

The following methods must be assigned transaction attributes for each bean declared in the deployment descriptor.

For entity beans:

- All business methods defined in the remote interface (and all superinterfaces)
- Create methods defined in the home interface
- Find methods defined in the home interface

- Home methods defined in the home interface (EJB 2.0)
- Remove methods defined in the `EJBHome` and `EJBObject` interfaces

For session beans:

- All business methods defined in the remote interface (and all superinterfaces)

For session beans, only the business methods have transaction attributes; the create and remove methods in session beans do not have transaction attributes.

In EJB 2.0, `ejbSelect()` methods do not have their own transaction attributes. `ejbSelect()` methods always propagate the transaction of the methods that call them.

Specifying Security Roles and Method Permissions

Two elements are used to define logical security roles and to specify which roles can call particular bean methods. The `<security-role>` element can contain an optional `<description>` element, plus a single `<role-name>` element that provides the name. An `<assembly-descriptor>` element can contain any number of `<security-role>` elements.

It is important to realize that the security role names defined here are not derived from a specific security realm. These security role names are logical; they are simply labels that can be mapped to real security roles in the target environment at deployment time. For example, the following `<security-role>` declarations define two roles—everyone and administrator:

```
<security-role>
    <description>
        This role represents everyone who is allowed read/write access
        to existing Cabin EJBs.
    </description>
    <role-name>everyone</role-name>
</security-role>
<security-role>
    <description>
        This role represents an administrator or manager who is allowed
        to create new Cabin EJBs. This role may also be a member
        of the everyone role.
    </description>
    <role-name>administrator</role-name>
</security-role>
```

These role names might not exist in the environment in which the beans will be deployed. There's nothing inherent about everyone that gives it fewer (or greater) privileges than an administrator. It is up to the deployer to map one or more roles from the target environment to the logical roles in the deployment descriptor. So for example, the deployer may find that the target environment has two roles, DBA (database administrator) and CSR (customer service representative), which map to the administrator and everyone roles defined in the `<security-role>` element.

Assigning roles to methods

Security roles in themselves would not be worth much if you couldn't specify what the roles were allowed to do. That's where the `<method-permission>` element comes in. This element maps the security roles to methods in the remote and home interfaces of the bean. A method permission is a flexible declaration that allows a many-to-many relationship between methods and roles. A `<method-permission>` contains an optional `<description>`, one or more `<method>` elements, and one or more `<role-name>` elements. The names specified in the `<role-name>` elements correspond to the roles that appear in the `<security-role>` elements.

Here's one way to set method permissions for the Cabin EJB:

```
<method-permission>
    <role-name>administrator</role-name>
    <method>
        <ejb-name>CabinEJB</ejb-name>
        <method-name>*</method-name>
    </method>
</method-permission>
<method-permission>
    <role-name>everyone</role-name>
    <method>
        <ejb-name>CabinEJB</ejb-name>
        <method-name>getDeckLevel</method-name>
    </method>
</method-permission>
```

In this example, the administrator role has access to all methods in the Cabin EJB. The everyone role has access only to the getDeckLevel() method—it cannot access any of the other methods of the Cabin EJB. Note that the specific method permissions are combined to form a union. The getDeckLevel() method, for example, is accessible by both the administrator and everyone roles, which is the union of the permissions declared in the descriptor. Once again, it is important to note that we still do not know what administrator and everyone mean. They are defined by the person deploying the bean, who must map these logical security roles to real security roles defined in the target environment.

All the methods defined in the remote or home interface and all superinterfaces, including the methods defined in the EJBObject and EJBHome interfaces, can be assigned security roles in the `<method-permission>` elements. Any method that is excluded will not be accessible by any security role.

EJB 2.0: Unchecked methods

In EJB 2.0, a set of methods can be designated as *unchecked*, which means that the security permissions are not checked before the method is invoked. An unchecked method can be invoked by any client, no matter what role it is using.

To designate a method or methods as unchecked, use the `<method-permission>` element and replace the `<role-name>` element with an empty `<unchecked>` element:

```
<method-permission>
    <unchecked/>
    <method>
        <ejb-name>CabinEJB</ejb-name>
        <method-name>*</method-name>
    </method>
    <method>
        <ejb-name>CustomerEJB</ejb-name>
        <method-name>findByPrimaryKey</method-name>
    </method>
</method-permission>
<method-permission>
    <role-name>administrator</role-name>
    <method>
        <ejb-name>CabinEJB</ejb-name>
        <method-name>*</method-name>
    </method>
</method-permission>
```

This declaration tells us that all the methods of the Cabin EJB, as well as the Customer EJB's `findByPrimaryKey()` method, are unchecked. Although the second `<method-permission>` element gives the administrator permission to access all the Cabin EJB's methods, this declaration is overridden by the unchecked method permission. Unchecked method permissions always override all other method permissions.

EJB 2.0: The runAs security identity

In addition to specifying the `Principals` that have access to an enterprise bean's methods, the deployer can also specify the *runAs* `Principal` for the entire enterprise bean. The runAs security identity was originally specified in EJB 1.0, but was abandoned in EJB 1.1. It has been reintroduced in EJB 2.0 and modified so that it is easier for vendors to implement.

While the `<method-permission>` elements specify which `Principals` have access to the bean's methods, the `<security-identity>` element specifies under which `Principal` the method will run. In other words, the runAs `Principal` is used as the enterprise bean's identity when it tries to invoke methods on other beans—this identity isn't necessarily the same as the identity that's currently accessing the bean.

For example, the following deployment descriptor elements declare that the `create()` method can be accessed only by `JimSmith`, but that the Cabin EJB always runs under the `Administrator` security identity:

```
<enterprise-beans>
...
    <entity>
        <ejb-name>EmployeeService</ejb-name>
        ...
```

```
        <security-identity>
            <run-as>
                <role-name>Administrator</role-name>
            </run-as>
        </security-identity>
        ...
    </entity>
    ...
</enterprise-beans>
<assembly-descriptor>
    <security-role>
        <role-name>Administrator</role-name>
    </security-role>
    <security-role>
        <role-name>JimSmith</role-name>
    </security-role>
    ...
    <method-permission>
        <role-name>JimSmith</role-name>
        <method>
            <ejb-name>CabinEJB</ejb-name>
            <method-name>create</method-name>
        </method>
    </method-permission>
    ...
</assembly-descriptor>
```

To specify that an enterprise bean will execute under the caller's identity, the
<security-identity> role contains a single empty element, <use-caller-identity/>.
For example, the following declarations specify that the Cabin EJB always executes
under the caller's identity, so if Jim Smith invokes the create() method, the bean
will run under the JimSmith security identity:

```
<enterprise-beans>
...
    <entity>
        <ejb-name>EmployeeService</ejb-name>
        ...
        <security-identity>
            <use-caller-identity/>
        </security-identity>
        ...
    </entity>
...
</enterprise-beans>
```

The use of <security-identity> applies equally to entity and stateless session beans.
However, message-driven beans have only a runAs identity; they will never execute
under the caller identity, because there is no "caller." The asynchronous JMS messages that a message-driven bean processes are not considered calls, and the JMS clients that send them are not associated with the messages. With no caller identity to
propagate, message-driven beans must always have a runAs security identity specified.

EJB 2.0: Exclude list

The last element of the <assembly-descriptor> is the optional <exclude-list> element. The <exclude-list> element contains a <description> and a set of <method> elements. Every method listed in the <exclude-list> should be considered uncallable, which means that the deployer needs to set up security permissions for those methods so that all calls, from any client, are rejected. Remote clients should receive a java.rmi.remoteException and local clients should receive a javax.ejb.Access-LocalException:

```
<ejb-jar>
    <enterprise-beans>
        <entity>
            <ejb-name>CabinEJB</ejb-name>
        </entity>
    </enterprise-beans>
    <assembly-descriptor>
        <exclude-list>
            <method>
                <ejb-name>CabinEJB</ejb-name>
                <method-name>getDeckLevel</method-name>
            </method>
            <method>
                ...
            </method>
        </exclude-list>
    </assembly-descriptor>
</ejb-jar>
```

Identifying Specific Methods

The <method> element is used by the <method-permission> and <container-transaction> elements to specify a specific group of methods in a particular bean. The <method> element always contains an <ejb-name> element that specifies the bean's name and a <method-name> element that specifies the method. It may also include a <description> element, <method-params> elements that specify which method parameters will be used to resolve overloaded methods, and a <method-intf> element that specifies whether the method belongs to the bean's home, remote, local home or local interface. This last element takes care of the possibility that the same method name might be used in more than one interface.

Wildcard declarations

The method name in a <method> element can be a simple wildcard (*). A wildcard applies to all methods of the bean's home and remote interfaces. For example:

```
<method>
    <ejb-name>CabinEJB</ejb-name>
    <method-name>*</method-name>
</method>
```

Although it's tempting to combine the wildcard with other characters, don't. The value get*, for example, is illegal. The asterisk (*) character can be used only by itself.

Named method declarations

Named declarations apply to all methods defined in the bean's remote and home interfaces that have the specified name. For example:

```
<method>
    <ejb-name>CabinEJB</ejb-name>
    <method-name>create</method-name>
</method>
<method>
    <ejb-name>CabinEJB</ejb-name>
    <method-name>getDeckLevel</method-name>
</method>
```

These declarations apply to all methods with the given name in both interfaces. They do not distinguish between overloaded methods. For example, if the home interface for the Cabin EJB is modified so that it has three overloaded create() methods, as shown here, the previous <method> declaration would apply to all three methods:

```
public interface CabinHome javax.ejb.EJBHome {
    public Cabin create() throws CreateException, RemoteException;
    public Cabin create(int id) throws CreateException, RemoteException;
    public Cabin create(int id, Ship ship, double [][] matrix)
        throws CreateException, RemoteException;
    ...
}
```

Specific method declarations

Specific method declarations use the <method-params> element to pinpoint a specific method by listing its parameters, allowing you to differentiate between overloaded methods. The <method-params> element contains zero or more <method-param> elements that correspond, in order, to each parameter type (including multidimensional arrays) declared in the method. To specify a method with no arguments, use a <method-params> element with no <method-param> elements nested within it.

For example, let's look again at our Cabin EJB, to which we have added some overloaded create() methods in the home interface. Here are three <method> elements, each of which unambiguously specifies one of the create() methods by listing its parameters:

```
<method>
    <description>Method: public Cabin create(); </description>
    <ejb-name>CabinEJB</ejb-name>
    <method-name>create</method-name>
    <method-params></method-params>
</method>
```

```
<method>
    <description>Method: public Cabin create(int id);</description>
    <ejb-name>CabinEJB</ejb-name>
    <method-name>create</method-name>
    <method-params>
        <method-param>int</method-param>
    </method-params>
</method>
<method>
    <description>
        Method: public Cabin create(int id, Ship ship, double [][] matrix);
    </description>
    <ejb-name>CabinEJB</ejb-name>
    <method-name>create</method-name>
    <method-params>
        <method-param>int</method-param>
        <method-param>com.titan.ship.Ship</method-param>
        <method-param>double [][]</method-param>
    </method-params>
</method>
```

Remote/home/local differentiation

There's one problem left. The same method name can be used in the home interface, the local home interface, the remote interface, and the local interface. To resolve this ambiguity, you can add the <method-intf> element to a method declaration as a modifier. Four values are allowed for a <method-intf> element: Remote, Home, LocalHome, and Local.

In reality, it is unlikely that a good developer would use the same method names in both home and remote interfaces; that would lead to unnecessarily confusing code. However, you would expect to see the same names in the local and remote interfaces or the home and local home interfaces. It is also likely that you will need the <method-intf> element in a wildcarded declaration. For example, the following declaration specifies all the methods in the remote interface of the Cabin EJB:

```
<method>
    <ejb-name>CabinEJB</ejb-name>
    <method-name>*</method-name>
    <method-intf>Remote</method-intf>
</method>
```

All these styles of method declarations can be used in any combination within any element that uses the <method> element. The <method-permission> elements are combined to form a union of role-to-method permissions. For example, in the following listing, the first <method-permission> element declares that the administrator has access to the Cabin EJB's home methods (create and find methods). The second <method-permission> specifies that everyone has access to the findByPrimaryKey() method. This means that both roles (everyone and administrator) have access to the findByPrimaryKey() method:

```
<method-permission>
    <role-name>administrator</role-name>
    <method>
        <ejb-name>CabinEJB</ejb-name>
        <method-name>*</method-name>
        <method-intf>Home</method_intf>
    </method>
</method-permission>
<method-permission>
    <role-name>everyone</role-name>
    <method>
        <ejb-name>CabinEJB</ejb-name>
        <method-name>findByPrimaryKey</method-name>
    </method>
</method-permission>
```

The ejb-jar File

The JAR file format is a platform-independent format for compressing, packaging, and delivering several files together. Based on the ZIP file format and the ZLIB compression standards, the JAR (Java archive) packages and tool were originally developed to make downloads of Java applets more efficient. As a packaging mechanism, however, the JAR file format is a convenient way to "shrink-wrap" components and other software for delivery to third parties. The original JavaBeans component architecture depends on JAR files for packaging, as does Enterprise JavaBeans. The goal in using the JAR file format is to package all the classes and interfaces associated with one or more beans, including the deployment descriptor, into one file.

The JAR file is created using a vendor-specific tool, or using the *jar* utility that is part of the Java 2, Standard Edition development kit. An *ejb-jar* file contains:

- The XML deployment descriptor
- The bean classes
- The remote and home interfaces
- The primary key class
- Dependent classes and interfaces

The XML deployment descriptor must be located in the path *META-INF/ejb-jar.xml* and must contain all the deployment information for all the beans in the *ejb-jar* file. For each bean declared in the XML deployment descriptor, the *ejb-jar* file must contain its bean class, remote and home interfaces, and dependent classes and interfaces. Dependent classes and interfaces are usually things like application-specific exceptions, business interfaces and other supertypes, and dependent objects that are used by the bean. In the *ejb-jar* file for the TravelAgent bean, for example, we would include the IncompleteConversationalState application exception and the Ticket and CreditCard classes, as well as the remote and home interfaces to other beans referenced by the TravelAgent bean, such as the Customer and Process-Payment beans.[*]

You can use the *jar* utility from the command line to package a bean in a JAR file. Here is an example of how the *jar* utility was used to package the Cabin EJB in Chapter 4:

```
\dev % jar cf cabin.jar com/titan/cabin/*.class META-INF/ejb-jar.xml

F:\..\dev>jar cf cabin.jar com\titan\cabin\*.class META-INF\ejb-jar.xml
```

You might have to create the *META-INF* directory first, and copy *ejb-jar.xml* into that directory. The *c* option tells the *jar* utility to create a new JAR file that contains the files indicated in subsequent parameters. It also tells the *jar* utility to stream the resulting JAR file to standard output. The *f* option tells *jar* to redirect the standard output to a new file named in the second parameter (*cabin.jar*). It is important to get the order of the option letters and the command-line parameters to match. You can learn more about the *jar* utility and the java.util.zip package in *Java™ in a Nutshell* by David Flanagan or *Learning Java™* by Pat Niemeyer and Jonathan Knudsen, both published by O'Reilly.

The *jar* utility creates the file *cabin.jar* in the *dev* directory. If you are interested in looking at the contents of the JAR file, you can use any standard ZIP application (WinZip, PKZIP, etc.) or the command *jar tvf cabin.jar*.

The client-jar File

EJB 1.1 also allows for a *client-jar* file, which includes only the interfaces and classes needed by a client application to access a bean. This includes the remote and home interfaces, primary key, and any dependent types to which the client is exposed, such as application exceptions. The specification does not say how this file is delivered to the client, what exactly it contains, or how it is packaged with the *ejb-jar* file. In other words, the *client-jar* file is a fairly vendor-specific concept in EJB.

---

[*] The EJB 1.1 specification also allows remote and home interfaces of referenced beans to be named in the manifest's Class-Path attribute, instead of including them in the JAR file. Use of the Class-Path entry in the JAR's manifest is addressed in more detail in the Java 2, Standard Edition specification.

CHAPTER 17

Java 2, Enterprise Edition

The specification for the Java 2, Enterprise Edition (J2EE) defines a platform for developing web-enabled applications that includes Enterprise JavaBeans, servlets, and JavaServer Pages (JSP). J2EE products are application servers that provide a complete implementation of the EJB, servlet, and JSP technologies. In addition, the J2EE outlines how these technologies work together to provide a complete solution. To help you understand J2EE, we must introduce servlets and JSP and explain the synergy between these technologies and Enterprise JavaBeans.

At the risk of spoiling the story, J2EE provides two kinds of "glue" to make it easier for components to interact. We have already seen both types of glue. First, the JNDI enterprise naming context (ENC) is used to standardize the way components look up resources they need. We have already seen the ENC in the context of enterprise beans; in this chapter, we will look briefly at how servlets, JSPs, and even some clients can use the ENC to find resources. Second, the use of deployment descriptors—in particular, the use of XML to define a language for deployment descriptors—has been extended to servlets and JSP. Java servlets and JSP pages can be packaged with deployment descriptors that define their relationships to their environment. Deployment descriptors are also used to define entire assemblies of many components into applications.

Servlets

The servlet specification defines a server-side component model that can be implemented by web server vendors. Servlets provide a simple but powerful API for generating web pages dynamically. (Although servlets can be used for many different request-response protocols, they are predominantly used to process HTTP requests for web pages.)

Servlets are developed in the same fashion as enterprise beans; they are Java classes that extend a base component class and have a deployment descriptor. Once a servlet is developed and packaged in a JAR file, it can be deployed in a web server. When a servlet is deployed, it is assigned to handle requests for a specific web page or to assist other servlets in handling page requests. The following servlet, for example, might be assigned to handle any request for the *helloworld.html* page on a web server:

```
import javax.servlet.*;
import javax.servlet.http.*;

public class HelloWorld extends HttpServlet {

    protected void doGet(HttpServletRequest req, HttpServletResponse response)
        throws ServletException,java.io.IOException {

    try {
        ServletOutputStream writer = response.getWriter();
        writer.println("<HTML><BODY>");
        writer.println("<h1>Hello World!!</h1>");
        writer.println("</BODY></HTML>");
    } catch(Exception e) {
        // handle exception
    }
    ...
}
```

When a browser sends a request for the page to the web server, the server delegates the request to the appropriate servlet instance by invoking the servlet's doGet() method.* The servlet is provided with information about the request in the HttpServletRequest object and can use the HttpServletResponse object to reply to the request. This simple servlet sends a short HTML document including the text "Hello World" back to the browser, which displays it. Figure 17-1 illustrates how a request is sent by a browser and serviced by a servlet running in a web server.

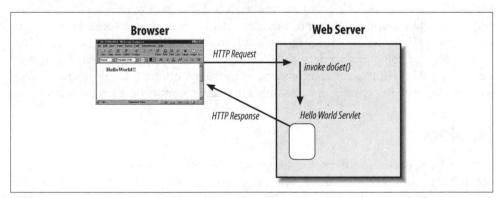

Figure 17-1. Servlet servicing an HTTP request

Servlets are similar to session beans because they both perform a service and can directly access backend resources (e.g., databases) through JDBC, but they do not represent persistent data. Servlets do not, however, have support for container-managed

---

* HttpServlets also have a doPost() method that handles requests for forms.

transactions and are not composed of business methods. Servlets deal with very specific (usually HTTP) requests and respond by writing to an output stream.

The servlet specification is extensive and robust but also simple and elegant. It is a powerful server-side component model. You can learn more about servlets by reading *Java™ Servlet Programming* by Jason Hunter and William Crawford (O'Reilly).

JavaServer Pages

JavaServer Pages is an extension of the servlet component model that simplifies the process of generating HTML dynamically. JSP essentially allows you to incorporate Java directly into an HTML page as a scripting language. In J2EE, the Java code in a JSP page can access the JNDI ENC, just like the code in a servlet. In fact, JSP pages (text documents) are translated and compiled into Java servlets, which are then run in a web server just like any other servlet—some servers do the compilation automatically at runtime. You can also use JSP to generate XML documents dynamically.

You can learn more about JSP by reading *JavaServer Pages™* by Hans Bergsten (O'Reilly).

Web Components and EJB

Together, servlets and JSP provide a powerful platform for generating web pages dynamically. Servlets and JSP, which are collectively called *web components*, can access resources like JDBC and enterprise beans. Because web components can access databases using JDBC, they can provide a powerful platform for e-commerce by allowing an enterprise to expose its business systems to the Web through an HTML interface. HTML has several advantages over more conventional client applications, in Java or any other language. The most important advantages have to do with distribution and firewalls. Conventional clients need to be distributed and installed on client machines, which is their biggest limitation: they require additional work for deployment and maintenance. Applets, which are dynamically downloaded, can be used to eliminate the headache of installation, but applets have other limitations, such as sandbox restrictions and heavyweight downloads. In contrast, HTML is extremely lightweight, does not require prior installation, and does not suffer from security restrictions. In addition, HTML interfaces can be modified and enhanced at their source without having to update the clients.

Firewalls present another significant problem in e-commerce. HTTP, the protocol over which web pages are requested and delivered, can pass through most firewalls without a problem, but other protocols such as IIOP or JRMP cannot. This restriction has proven to be a significant barrier to the success of distributed object systems that must support access from anonymous clients, because it means that distributed object applications generally cannot be created for a client base that may have arbitrary firewall configurations. HTTP does not have this limitation, since practically all firewalls allow HTTP to pass unhindered.

The problems with distribution and firewalls have led the EJB industry to adopt, in large part, an architecture based on the collaborative use of web components (servlets/ JSP) and Enterprise JavaBeans. While web components provide the presentation logic for generating web pages, EJB provides a robust transactional middle tier for business logic. Web components access enterprise beans using the same API as application clients. Each technology is doing what it does best: servlets and JSP are excellent components for generating dynamic HTML, while EJB is an excellent platform for transactional business logic. Figure 17-2 illustrates how this architecture works.

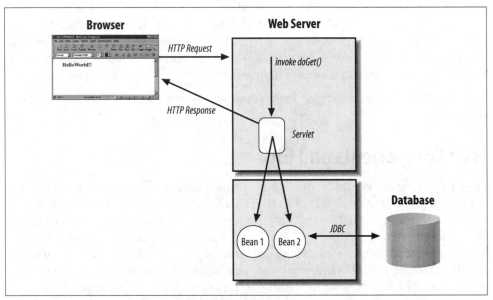

Figure 17-2. Using servlets/JSP and EJB together

This web component–EJB architecture is so widely accepted that it begs the question, "Should there be a united platform?" This is the question the J2EE specification is designed to answer. The J2EE specification defines a single application server platform that focuses on the interaction between servlets, JSP, and EJB. J2EE is important because it provides a specification for the interaction of web components with enterprise beans, making solutions more portable across vendors that support both component models.

J2EE Fills in the Gaps

The J2EE specification attempts to fill the gaps between the web components and Enterprise JavaBeans by defining how these technologies come together to form a complete platform.

One of the ways in which J2EE adds value is by creating a consistent programming model across web components and enterprise beans through the use of the JNDI ENC and XML deployment descriptors. A servlet in J2EE can access JDBC DataSource objects, environment entries, and references to enterprise beans through a JNDI ENC in exactly the same way that enterprise beans use the JNDI ENC. To support the JNDI ENC, web components have their own XML deployment descriptor that declares elements for the JNDI ENC (<ejb-ref>, <resource-ref>, <env-entry>) as well security roles and other elements specific to web components. In J2EE, web components are packaged along with their XML deployment descriptors and deployed in JAR files with the extension .war, which stands for *web ar*chive. The use of the JNDI ENC, deployment descriptors, and JAR files in web components makes them consistent with the EJB programming model and unifies the entire J2EE platform.

Use of the JNDI ENC makes it much simpler for web components to access Enterprise JavaBeans. The web component developer does not need to be concerned with the network location of enterprise beans; the server will map the <ejb-ref> elements listed in the deployment descriptor to the enterprise beans at deployment time.

Optionally, J2EE vendors can allow web components to access the EJB 2.0 local component interfaces of enterprise beans. This makes a lot of sense if the web component and the bean are co-located in the same Java Virtual Machine, because the Java RMI-IIOP semantics can improve performance. It's expected that most J2EE vendors will support this option.

The JNDI ENC also supports access to a javax.jta.UserTransaction object, as is the case in EJB. The UserTransaction object allows the web component to manage transactions explicitly. The transaction context must be propagated to any enterprise beans accessed within the scope of the transaction (according to the transaction attribute of the enterprise bean method). A .war file can contain several servlets and JSP documents, which share an XML deployment descriptor.

J2EE also defines an .ear (enterprise *ar*chive) file, which is a JAR file for packaging EJB JAR files and web component JAR files (.war files) together into one complete deployment called a J2EE application. A J2EE application has its own XML deployment descriptor that points to the EJB and web component JAR files (called modules) as well as other elements such as icons, descriptions, and the like. When a J2EE application is created, interdependencies such as <ejb-ref> and <ejb-local-ref> elements can be resolved and security roles can be edited to provide a unified view of the entire web application. Figure 17-3 illustrates the file structure inside a J2EE archive file.

J2EE Application Client Components

In addition to integrating web and enterprise bean components, J2EE introduces a completely new component model: the application client component. An application client component is a Java application that resides on a client machine and accesses enterprise bean components on the J2EE server. Client components also

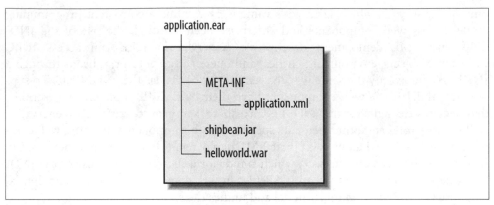

application.ear

META-INF
application.xml

shipbean.jar

helloworld.war

Figure 17-3. Contents of a J2EE EAR file

have access to a JNDI ENC that operates the same way as the JNDI ENC for web and enterprise bean components. The client component includes an XML deployment descriptor that declares the `<env-entry>`, `<ejb-ref>`, and `<resource-ref>` elements of the JNDI ENC in addition to a `<description>`, `<display-name>`, and `<icon>` that can be used to represent the client component in a deployment tool.

A client component is simply a Java program that uses the JNDI ENC to access environment properties, enterprise beans, and resources (JDBC, JavaMail, etc.) made available by the J2EE server. Client components reside on the client machine, not the J2EE server. Here is an extremely simple component:

```
public class MyJ2eeClient {

    public static void main(String [] args) {

        InitialContext jndiCntx = new InitialContext();

        Object ref = jndiCntx.lookup("java:comp/env/ejb/ShipBean");
        ShipHome home = (ShipHome)
            PortableRemoteObject.narrow(ref,ShipHome.class);

        Ship ship = home.findByPrimaryKey(new ShipPK(1));
        String name = ship.getName();
        System.out.println(name);

    }
}
```

`MyJ2eeClient` illustrates how a client component is written. Notice that the client component did not need to use a network-specific JNDI `InitialContext`. In other words, we did not have to specify the service provider in order to connect to the J2EE server. This is the real power of the J2EE application client component: location transparency. The client component does not need to know the exact location of the Ship EJB or choose a specific JNDI service provider; the JNDI ENC takes care of locating the enterprise bean.

When application components are developed, an XML deployment descriptor is created that specifies the JNDI ENC entries. At deployment time, a vendor-specific J2EE tool generates the class files needed to deploy the component on client machines.

A client component is packaged into a JAR file with its XML deployment descriptor and can be included in a J2EE application. Once a client component is included in the J2EE application deployment descriptor, it can be packaged in the EAR file with the other components, as Figure 17-4 illustrates.

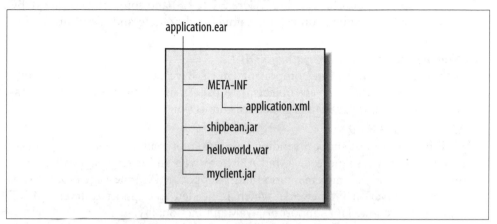

Figure 17-4. Contents of a J2EE EAR file with application component

Guaranteed Services

The J2EE 1.3 specification requires application servers to support a specific set of protocols and Java enterprise extensions. This requirement ensures a consistent platform for deploying J2EE applications. J2EE application servers must provide the following "standard" services:

Enterprise JavaBeans 2.0
> J2EE products must support the complete specification.

Servlets 2.3
> J2EE products must support the complete specification.

JavaServer Pages 1.2
> J2EE products must support the complete specification.

HTTP and HTTPS
> Web components in a J2EE server service both HTTP and HTTPS requests. The J2EE product must be capable of advertising HTTP 1.0 and HTTPS (HTTP 1.0 over SSL 3.0) on ports 80 and 443, respectively.

Java RMI-IIOP
> Support for Java RMI-IIOP is required. However, other protocols may also be used by the vendor, as long as they are compatible with Java RMI-IIOP semantics.

Java RMI-JRMP
> J2EE components can be Java RMI-JRMP clients.

JavaIDL
> Web components and enterprise beans must be able to access CORBA services hosted outside the J2EE environment using JavaIDL, a standard part of the Java 2 platform.

JDBC 2.0
> J2EE requires support for the JDBC Core (JDK 1.3) and some parts of the JDBC 2.0 Extension, including connection naming and pooling and distributed transaction support.

Java Naming and Directory Interface (JNDI) 1.2
> Web and enterprise bean components must have access to the JNDI ENC, which make available `EJBHome` objects, JTA `UserTransaction` objects, JDBC `Data-Source` objects, and Java Message Service connection factory objects.

JavaMail 1.2 and JAF 1.0
> J2EE products must support sending basic Internet mail messages (the protocol is not specified) using the JavaMail API from web and enterprise bean components. The JavaMail implementation must support MIME message types. JAF is the Java Activation Framework, which is needed to support different MIME types and is required for support of JavaMail functionality.

Java Message Service (JMS) 1.0.2
> J2EE products must provide support for both point-to-point (p2p) and publish-and-subscribe (pub/sub) messaging models.

Java API for XML Parsing (JAXP) 1.1
> J2EE products must support JAXP and provide at least one SAX 2 parser, at least one DOM 2 parser, and at least one XSLT transform engine.

J2EE Connector Architecture (JCA) 1.0
> J2EE must support the JCA API from all components and provide full support for resource adapters and transaction capabilities as defined by the JCA.

Java Authentication and Authorization Service (JAAS) 1.0
> J2EE products must support the use of JAAS as described in the JCA specification. In addition, application client containers must support the authentication facilities defined in the JAAS specification.

Java Transaction API 1.0.1
> Web and enterprise bean components must have access to JTA `UserTransaction` objects via the JNDI ENC under the `"java:comp/UserTransaction"` context. The `UserTransaction` interface is used for explicit transaction control.

Fitting the Pieces Together

To illustrate how a J2EE platform would be used, imagine using a J2EE server in Titan's reservation system. To build this system, we would use the TravelAgent,

Cabin, ProcessPayment, Customer, and other enterprise beans we defined in this book, along with web components that would provide an HTML interface.

The web components would access the enterprise beans in the same way that any Java client would, by using the enterprise beans' remote and home interfaces. The web components would generate HTML to represent the reservation system.

Figure 17-5 shows a web page generated by a servlet or JSP page for the Titan reservation system. This web page was generated by web components on the J2EE server. At this point, the person using the reservation system has been guided through a login page, a customer selection page, and a cruise selection page and is about to choose an available cabin for the reservation.

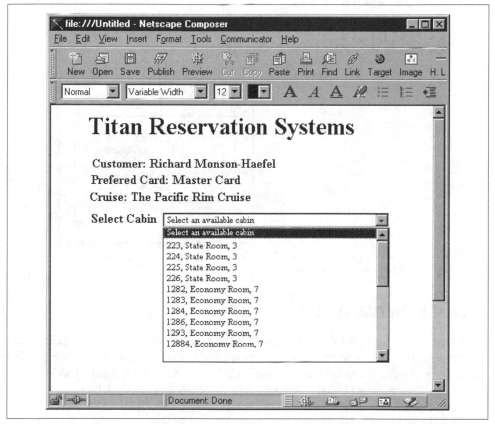

Figure 17-5. HTML interface to the Titan reservation system

The list of available cabins was obtained from the TravelAgent EJB, whose listAvailableCabins() method was invoked by the servlet that generated the web page. The list of cabins was used to create an HTML list box in a web page that was loaded into the user's browser. When the user chooses a cabin and submits the selection, an HTTP request is sent to the J2EE server. The J2EE server receives the request and delegates it to the ReservationServlet, which invokes the TravelAgent. bookPassage() method to do the actual reservation. The ticket information returned by the bookPassage() method is then used to create another web page, which is sent back to the user's browser. Figure 17-6 shows how the different components work together to process this request.

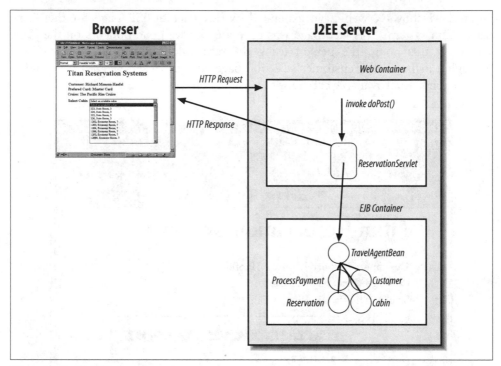

Figure 17-6. J2EE Titan reservation system

Future Enhancements

Several areas are targeted for improvement in the next major release of the J2EE specification. Support for "web services" is expected to be a larger part of the J2EE specification in the future, including support for Java API for XML Messaging (JAXM), Java API for XML Registries (JAXR), and Java API for XML RPC (JAX-RPC). Support for the XML Data Binding API, which considered easier to use than JAXP, may also be required in a future version of the specification.

In addition, J2EE may be expanded to require support for JDBC rowsets, SQLJ, management and deployment APIs, and possibly a J2EE SPI that would build on the advancements made with the JCA specification.

The Enterprise JavaBeans API

This appendix is a quick reference guide to the Enterprise JavaBeans API. Within each package, the classes are organized alphabetically.

Package: javax.ejb

This package contains the heart of the EJB API. It consists mostly of interfaces, many of which are implemented by your EJB vendor. These interfaces essentially define the services provided by the bean's container, the services that must be implemented by the bean itself, and the client interface to an enterprise bean. The javax.ejb package also contains a number of exceptions that are thrown by enterprise beans.

EJB 2.0: AccessLocalException

This standard system exception is thrown by local component interfaces to indicate that the caller (enterprise bean) does not have permission to access the method.

```
public class AccessLocalException extends EJBException
{
    public AccessLocalException();
    public AccessLocalException(String message);
    public AccessLocalException(String message, Exception ex);
}
```

CreateException

This standard application exception must be thrown by all create methods that are defined in the home interface; it indicates that the bean could not be created.

```
public class javax.ejb.CreateException extends java.lang.Exception
{
    public CreateException();
    public CreateException(String message);
}
```

DuplicateKeyException

This standard application exception is thrown by the create methods of the home interface of entity beans; it indicates that a bean with the same primary key already exists.

```
public class javax.ejb.DuplicateKeyException extends javax.ejb.CreateException
{
    public DuplicateKeyException();
    public DuplicateKeyException(String message);
}
```

EJBContext

This is the base class for the EntityContext, SessionContext, and MessageDriven-Context. EJBContext is the bean class's interface to the container system. It provides information about the enterprise bean's security identity and transaction status. It also provides access to environment variables and the bean's EJB home.

```
public interface javax.ejb.EJBContext
{
    public abstract Principal getCallerPrincipal();
    public abstract EJBHome getEJBHome();
    public abstract EJBLocalHome getEJBLocalHome(); // new in 2.0
    public abstract boolean getRollbackOnly();
    public abstract UserTransaction getUserTransaction();

    public abstract Properties getEnvironment(); // deprecated
    public abstract Identity getCallerIdentity(); // deprecated
    public abstract boolean isCallerInRole(Identity role); // deprecated
    public abstract boolean isCallerInRole(String roleName);
    public abstract void setRollbackOnly();
}
```

EJBException

This RuntimeException is thrown by the bean class from its business methods and callback methods to indicate that an unexpected exception has occurred. The exception causes the ongoing transaction to be rolled back and the bean instance to be destroyed.

```
public class javax.ejb.EJBException extends java.lang.RuntimeException
{
    public EJBException();
    public EJBException(String message);
    public EJBException(Exception exception);

    public Exception getCausedByException();
}
```

EJBHome

This interface must be extended by the bean's remote home interface, a developer-provided class that defines the bean's life-cycle methods. The enterprise bean's create, find, and home methods are defined in the remote home interface. This interface is implemented by the bean's EJB home.

```
public interface javax.ejb.EJBHome extends java.rmi.Remote
{
    public abstract HomeHandle getHomeHandle();
    public abstract EJBMetaData getEJBMetaData();
    public abstract void remove(Handle handle);
    public abstract void remove(Object primaryKey);
}
```

EJB 2.0: EJBLocalHome

This interface must be extended by the bean's local home interface, a developer-provided class that defines the bean's life-cycle methods. The enterpise bean's create, find, and home methods are defined in the local home interface. This interface is implemented by the bean's EJB home.

```
public interface EJBLocalHome
{
    public void remove(java.lang.Object primaryKey)
        throws RemoveException,EJBException;
}
```

EJB 2.0: EJBLocalObject

This interface defines the base functionality for access to local enterprise beans; it is implemented by the EJB object. The developer must provide a local interface for the bean that defines the business methods of the bean, and the local interface must extend the EJBLocalObject interface.

```
public interface EJBLocalObject
{
    public EJBLocalHome getEJBLocalHome() throws EJBException;
    public Object getPrimaryKey() throws EJBException;
    public boolean isIdentical(EJBLocalObject obj) throws EJBException;
    public void remove() throws RemoveException, EJBException;
}
```

EJBMetaData

This interface is implemented by the container vendor to provide a serializable class that contains information about the bean.

```
public interface javax.ejb.EJBMetaData
{
```

```
        public abstract EJBHome getEJBHome();
        public abstract Class getHomeInterfaceClass();
        public abstract Class getPrimaryKeyClass();
        public abstract Class getRemoteInterfaceClass();
        public abstract boolean isSession();
        public abstract boolean isStatelessSession();
    }
```

EJBObject

This interface defines the base functionality for access to remote enterprise beans; it is implemented by the EJB object. The developer must provide a remote interface for the bean that defines the business methods of the bean, and the remote interface must extend the EJBObject interface.

```
    public interface javax.ejb.EJBObject extends java.rmi.Remote
    {
        public abstract EJBHome getEJBHome();
        public abstract Handle getHandle();
        public abstract Object getPrimaryKey();
        public abstract boolean isIdentical(EJBObject obj);
        public abstract void remove();
    }
```

EnterpriseBean

This interface is extended by the EntityBean, SessionBean, and MessageDrivenBean interfaces. It serves as a common typing mechanism.

```
    public interface javax.ejb.EnterpriseBean extends java.io.Serializable {}
```

EntityBean

This interface must be implemented by the entity bean class. It provides a set of callback notification methods that alert the bean instance that it is about to experience or has just experienced some change in its life cycle.

```
    public interface javax.ejb.EntityBean extends javax.ejb.EnterpriseBean
    {
        public abstract void ejbActivate();
        public abstract void ejbLoad();
        public abstract void ejbPassivate();
        public abstract void ejbRemove();
        public abstract void ejbStore();
        public abstract void setEntityContext(EntityContext ctx);
        public abstract void unsetEntityContext();
    }
```

EntityContext

This interface is a specialization of the `EJBContext` that provides methods for obtaining an `EntityBean`'s EJB object reference and primary key. The `EntityContext` provides the bean instance with an interface to the container.

```
public interface javax.ejb.EntityContext extends javax.ejb.EJBContext
{
    public abstract EJBObject getEJBObject();
    public abstract Object getPrimaryKey();
    public abstract EJBLocalObject getEJBLocalObject();  //new in EJB 2.0
}
```

FinderException

This standard application exception is thrown by find methods defined in the home interface to indicate that a failure occurred during the execution of the find method.

```
public class javax.ejb.FinderException extends java.lang.Exception
{
    public FinderException();
    public FinderException(String message);
}
```

Handle

This interface provides the client with a serializable object that can be used to obtain a remote reference to a specific bean.

```
public interface javax.ejb.Handle extends java.io.Serializable
{
    public abstract EJBObject getEJBObject();
}
```

HomeHandle

This interface provides the client with a serializable object that can be used to obtain a remote reference to a bean's home.

```
public interface javax.ejb.HomeHandleextends java.io.Serializable
{
    public abstract EJBHome getEJBHome();
}
```

EJB 2.0: MessageDrivenBean

This interface must be implemented by the message-driven bean class. It provides a set of callback notification methods that alert the bean instance that it is about to experience or has just experienced a change in its life cycle.

```
public interface MessageDrivenBean extends EnterpriseBean
{
    public void ejbRemove()throws EJBException;
    public void setMessageDrivenContext(MessageDrivenContext ctx)
        throws EJBException;
}
```

EJB 2.0: MessageDrivenContext

This interface is a subtype of the EJBContext that provides no additional methods; all its methods are defined in the EJBContext. The MessageDrivenContext provides the bean instance with an interface to the container.

```
public interface MessageDrivenContext extends EJBContext {}
```

NoSuchEntityException

This EJBException is typically thrown by the bean class's ejbLoad() and ejbStore() methods to indicate that the entity's data does not exist. For example, this exception will be thrown if an entity bean with bean-managed persistence attempts to read its state—ejbLoad()—from a record that has been deleted from the database.

```
public class javax.ejb.NoSuchEntityException extends javax.ejb.EJBException
{
    public NoSuchEntityException();
    public NoSuchEntityException(String message);
    public NoSuchEntityException(Exception exception);
}
```

ObjectNotFoundException

This standard application exception is thrown by find methods that return a single EJB object. It indicates that no bean matching the specified criteria could be found.

```
public class javax.ejb.ObjectNotFoundException extends javax.ejb.FinderException
{
    public ObjectNotFoundException();
    public ObjectNotFoundException(String message);
}
```

RemoveException

This standard application exception is thrown by remove methods to indicate that a failure occurred while removing the bean.

```
public class javax.ejb.RemoveException extends java.lang.Exception
{
    public RemoveException();
    public RemoveException(String message);
}
```

SessionBean

This interface must be implemented by the session bean class. It provides a set of callback notification methods that alert the bean instance that it has experienced, or is about to experience, some change in its life cycle.

```
public interface javax.ejb.SessionBean extends javax.ejb.EnterpriseBean
{
    public abstract void ejbActivate();
    public abstract void ejbPassivate();
    public abstract void ejbRemove();
    public abstract void setSessionContext(SessionContext ctx);
}
```

SessionContext

This interface is a specialization of the EJBContext that provides methods for obtaining the SessionBean's EJB object reference. The SessionContext provides the bean instance with an interface to the container.

```
public interface javax.ejb.SessionContext extends javax.ejb.EJBContext
{
    public abstract EJBObject getEJBObject();
}
```

SessionSynchronization

This interface provides a stateful bean instance with additional callback notifications. These callback methods notify the bean of its current state with respect to a transaction.

```
public interface javax.ejb.SessionSynchronization
{
    public abstract void afterBegin();
    public abstract void afterCompletion(boolean committed);
    public abstract void beforeCompletion();
}
```

EJB 2.0: TransactionRequiredLocalException

This standard system exception is thrown by local component interfaces to indicate that the call had no transaction context, but the method called requires an active transaction. This situation might occur if the client has no transaction but invokes a method with the Mandatory transaction attribute.

```
public interface TransactionRequiredLocalException extends EJBException
{
    public TransactionRequiredLocalException();
    public TransactionRequiredLocalException(String message);
}
```

EJB 2.0: TransactionRolledbackLocalException

This standard system exception is thrown to indicate that the caller's transaction has been rolled back, or marked to be rolled back, due to some failure that occurred while the method was executing. This exception tells the caller that further work for that transaction would be fruitless.

```
public interface TransactionRolledbackLocalException extends EJBException
{
    public TransactionRolledbackLocalException();
    public TransactionRolledbackLocalException(String message);
    public TransactionRolledbackLocalException(String message,Exception ex);
}
```

EJB 2.0: Package: javax.jms

This package defines the classes and interfaces of the Java Message Service. The MessageListener interface of this package is important to EJB 2.0.

MessageListener

This interface must be implemented by message-driven beans. The onMessage() method is used to deliver JMS Message objects to the message-driven bean at runtime.

```
public interface MessageListener
{
    public void onMessage(Message message);
}
```

EJB 2.0: Package: javax.ejb.spi

This package is used by EJB vendors when implementing EJB container systems. It is not used by enterprise bean developers.

HandleDelegate

When you pass an EJBObject or EJBHome remote reference from one container system to another, the EJB container uses the HandleDelegate object to convert the EJBObject or EJBHome reference from a vendor-specific form to a vendor-neutral form that can be passed between different EJB vendors' servers. HandleDelegate is an interoperability facility that is invisible to the bean developer and is for EJB vendors only. As a bean developer, you should not be concerned with it.

```
public interface HandleDelegate {
    public EJBHome readEJBHome(ObjectInputStream istream)
        throws throws java.io.IOException,java.lang.ClassNotFoundException;
    public EJBObject readEJBObject(ObjectInputStream istream)
        throws throws java.io.IOException,java.lang.ClassNotFoundException;
```

```
        public void writeEJBHome(EJBHome ejbHome, ObjectOutputStream ostream)
            throws throws java.io.IOException;
        public void writeEJBObject(EJBObject ejbObject, ObjectOutputStream ostream)
            throws throws java.io.IOException;
}
```

State and Sequence Diagrams

This appendix contains state and sequence diagrams for all the bean types discussed in this book: container-managed and bean-managed entity beans, stateless and stateful session beans, and message-driven beans. Although standard Unified Modeling Language (UML) is used in these diagrams, some extensions were required to model EJB runtime characteristics. In the state diagrams, for example, callback methods and class instantiation operations are shown as part of the transition event.

In the sequence diagrams, container-provided classes such as the container itself, the EJB object, and the EJB home are shown as separate classes but are also boxed together. Messages sent from classes in the container system box are considered to be sent from the container system as a whole, not necessarily from the specific container-provided class. This generalization is necessary because the container's interaction with the bean is characterized by these classes but differs from one vendor's implementation to the next. The exact source of the message is immaterial, as long as you realize that the container system sent it.

Entity Beans

Life Cycle State Diagram of the Entity Bean

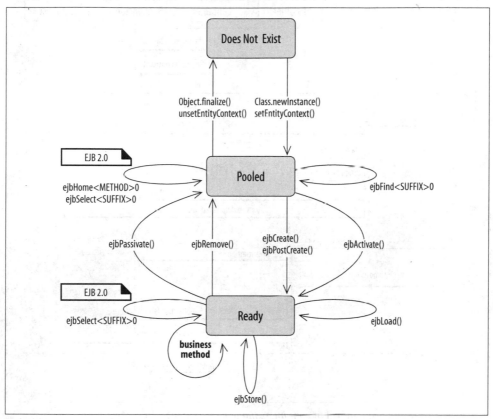

Figure B-1. Life-cycle state diagram of the entity bean

Sequence Diagrams for Container-Managed Persistence

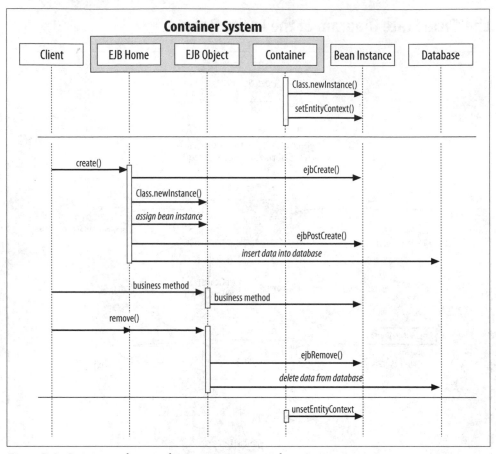

Figure B-2. Creation and removal in container-managed persistence

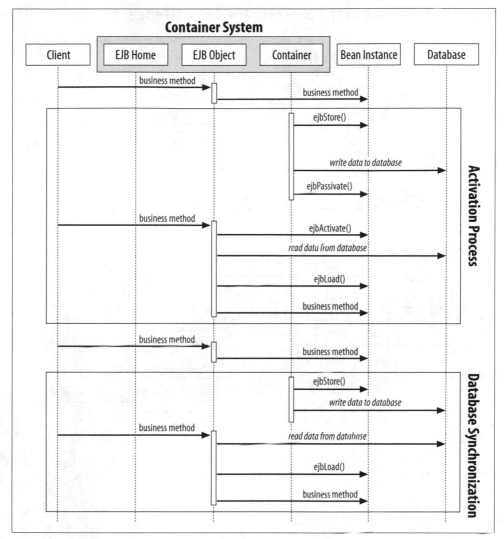

Figure B-3. Activation and synchronization in container-managed persistence

Sequence Diagrams for Bean-Managed Persistence

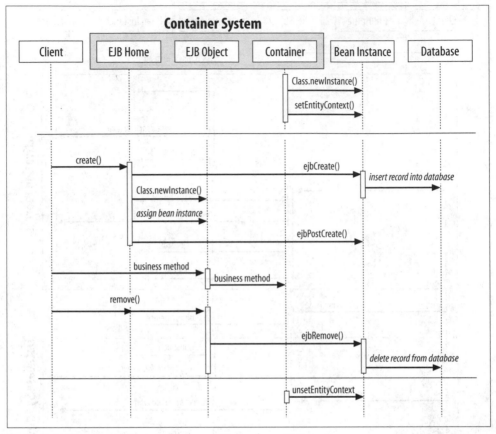

Figure B-4. Creation and removal in bean-managed persistence

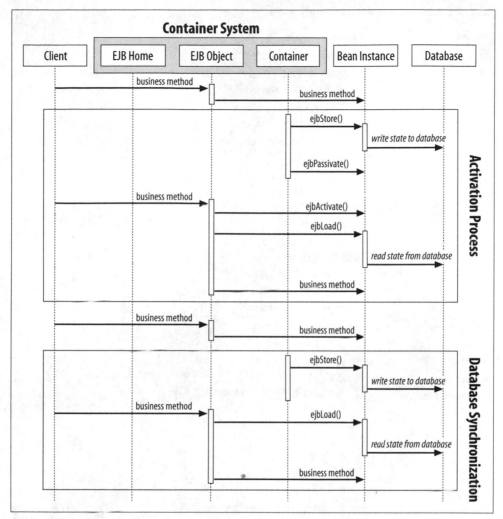

Figure B-5. Activation and synchronization in bean-managed persistence

Table B-1 summarizes the operations an entity bean is allowed to perform in various stages of its life cycle. The allowed operations are the same for EJB 2.0 and 1.1, except for the EntityContext methods getEJBLocalHome() and getEJBLocalObject() and the operations allowed for ejbHome() methods, which are specific to EJB 2.0.

Table B-1. Allowed operations for entity beans

Method	Allowed operations

`setEntityContext()`
`unsetEntityContext()`
	`EntityContext` methods:
	　`getEJBHome()`
	　`getEJBLocalHome()`
	JNDI ENC contexts:
	　Properties: `java:comp/env`

`ejbCreate()`
`ejbFind()`
`ejbHome()`
	`EntityContext` methods:
	　`getEJBHome()`
	　`getEJBLocalHome()`
	　`getCallerPrincipal()`
	　`isCallerInRole()`
	　`getRollbackOnly()`
	　`setRollbackOnly()`
	JNDI ENC contexts:
	　Properties: `java:comp/env`
	　Resource managers: `java:comp/env/jdbc`
	　EJB references: `java:comp/env/ejb`

`ejbPostCreate()`
`ejbLoad()`
`ejbStore()`
`ejbRemove()`
Business methods
	`EntityContext` methods:
	　`getEJBHome()`
	　`getEJBLocalHome()`
	　`getCallerPrincipal()`
	　`isCallerInRole()` `getRollbackOnly()`
	　`setRollbackOnly()`
	　`getEJBObject()`
	　`getEJBLocalObject()`
	　`getPrimaryKey()`
	JNDI ENC contexts:
	　Properties: `java:comp/env`
	　Resource managers: `java:comp/env/jdbc`
	　EJB references: `java:comp/env/ejb`

`ejbActivate()`
`ejbPassivate()`
	`EntityContext` methods:
	　`getEJBHome()`
	　`getEJBLocalHome()`
	　`getEJBObject()`
	　`getEJBLocalObject()`
	　`getPrimaryKey()`
	JNDI ENC contexts:
	　Properties: `java:comp/env`

Note that entity beans can never access the EJBContext.getUserTransaction()
method, because entity beans are not allowed to manage their own transactions.
Only session beans can access this method.

Session Beans

Stateless Session Beans

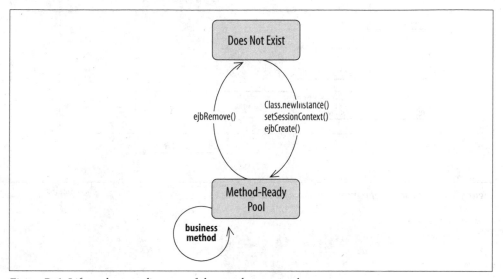

Figure B-6. Life-cycle state diagram of the stateless session bean

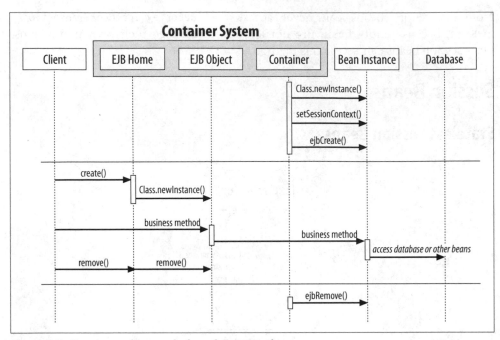

Figure B-7. Creation and removal of stateless session beans

Table B-2 summarizes the operations that are legal for a stateless session bean. The allowed operations are the same for both EJB 2.0 and 1.1, except for the SessionContext methods getEJBLocalHome() and getEJBLocalObject(), which are specific to EJB 2.0.

Table B-2. Allowed operations for stateless session beans

Method	Allowed operations	
	Container-managed transactions	Bean-managed transactions

ejbCreate()
ejbRemove()
	EntityContext methods:
	  getEJBHome()
	  getEJBLocalHome()
	  getEJBObject()
	  getEJBLocalObject()
	JNDI ENC contexts:
	  Properties: java:comp/env
		EntityContext methods:
		  getEJBHome()
		  getEJBLocalHome()
		  getEJBObject()
		  getEJBLocalObject()
		  getUserTransaction()
		JNDI ENC contexts:
		  Properties: java:comp/env

Business methods	EntityContext methods:
	  getEJHome()
	  getEJBLocalHome()
	  getCallerPrincipal()
	  isCallerInRole()
	  getRollbackOnly()
	  setRollbackOnly()
	  getEJBObject()
	  getEJBLocalObject()
	JNDI ENC contexts:
	  Properties: java:comp/env
	  Resource managers: java:comp/env/jdbc
	  EJB references: java:comp/env/ejb
		EntityContext methods:
		  getEJHome()
		  getEJBLocalHome()
		  getCallerPrincipal()
		  isCallerInRole()
		  getEJBObject()
		  getEJBLocalObject()
		  getUserTransaction()
		JNDI ENC contexts:
		  Properties: java:comp/env
		  Resource managers: java:comp/env/jdbc
		  EJB references: java:comp/env/ejb

ejbActivate() ejbPassivate()	Not supported (stateless beans do not use these methods)	Not supported (stateless beans do not use these methods)

Stateful Session Beans

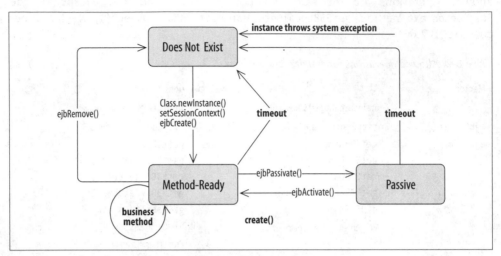

Figure B-8. Life-cycle state diagram of the stateful session bean

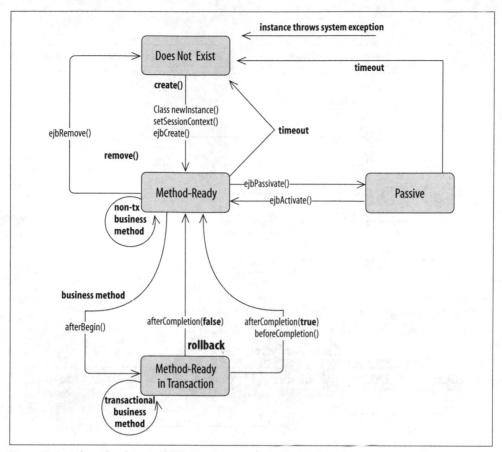

Figure B-9. Life cycle of a stateful session bean with the SessionSynchronization interface

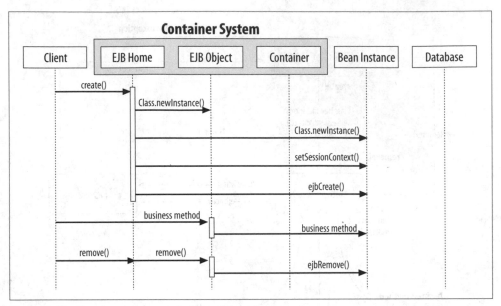

Figure B-10. Creation and removal of stateful session beans

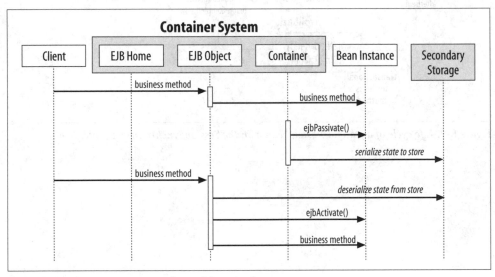

Figure B-11. Activation process of stateful session beans

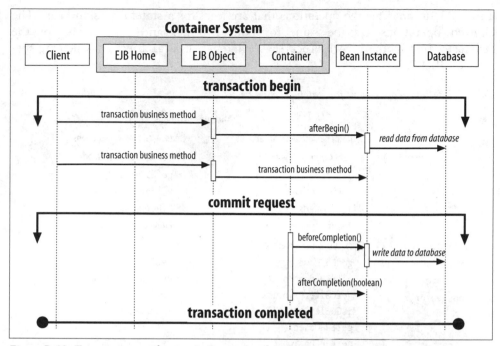

Figure B-12. Transaction notification in SessionSynchronization session beans

Table B-3 summarizes the operations that are legal for a stateful session bean. The allowed operations are the same for both EJB 2.0 and 1.1, except for the SessionContext methods getEJBLocalHome() and getEJBLocalObject(), which are specific to EJB 2.0.

Table B-3. Allowed operations for stateful session beans

Method	Allowed operations	
	Container-managed transactions	Bean-managed transactions

setSessionContext()	EntityContext methods:
	  getEJBHome()
	  getEJBLocalHome()
	JNDI ENC contexts:
	  Properties: java:comp/env
		EntityContext methods:
		  getEJBHome()
		  getEJBLocalHome()
		JNDI ENC contexts:
		  Properties: java:comp/env

ejbCreate()
ejbRemove()
ejbActivate()
ejbPassivate()
	EntityContext methods:
	  getEJBHome()
	  getEJBLocalHome()
	  getCallerPrincipal()
	  isCallerInRole()
	  getEJBObject()
	  getEJBLocalObject()
	JNDI ENC contexts:
	  Properties: java:comp/env
	  Resource managers: java:comp/env/jdbc
	  EJB references: java:comp/env/ejb
		EntityContext methods:
		  getEJBHome()
		  getEJBLocalHome()
		  getCallerPrincipal()
		  isCallerInRole()
		  getEJBObject()
		  getEJBLocalObject()
		  getUserTransaction()
		JNDI ENC contexts:
		  Properties: java:comp/ env
		  Resource managers: java:comp/env/jdbc
		  EJB references: java:comp/env/ejb

Business methods	EntityContext methods:
	  getEJBHome()
	  getEJBLocalHome()
	  getCallerPrincipal()
	  isCallerInRole()
	  getRollbackOnly()
	  setRollbackOnly()
	  getEJBObject()
	  getEJBLocalObject()
	JNDI ENC contexts:
	  Properties: java:comp/env
	  Resource managers: java:comp/env/jdbc
	  EJB references: java:comp/env/ejb
		EntityContext methods:
		  getEJHome()
		  getEJBLocalHome()
		  getCallerPrincipal()
		  isCallerInRole()
		  getEJBObject()
		  getEJBLocalObject()
		  getUserTransaction()
		JNDI ENC contexts:
		  Properties: java:comp/env
		  Resource managers: java:comp/env/jdbc
		  EJB references: java:comp/env/ejb

Table B-3. Allowed operations for stateful session beans (continued)

Method	Allowed operations	
	Container-managed transactions	**Bean-managed transactions**

afterBegin()
beforeCompetion()
	EntityContext methods:
	  getEJBHome()
	  getEJBLocalHome()
	  getCallerPrincipal()
	  isCallerInRole()
	  getRollbackOnly()
	  setRollbackOnly()
	  getEJBObject()
	  getEJBLocalObject()
	JNDI ENC contexts:
	  Properties: java:comp/env
	  Resource managers: java:comp/env/jdbc
	  EJB references: java:comp/env/cjb
		Not supported (bean-managed transaction beans cannot implement the SessionSynchronization interface)

afterCompletion()	EntityContext methods:
	  getEJBHome()
	  getEJBLocalHome()
	  getCallerPrincipal()
	  isCallerInRole()
	  getEJBObject()
	  getEJBLocalObject()
	JNDI ENC contexts:
	  Properties: java:comp/env
		Not supported (bean-managed transaction beans cannot implement the SessionSynchronization interface)

Message-Driven Beans

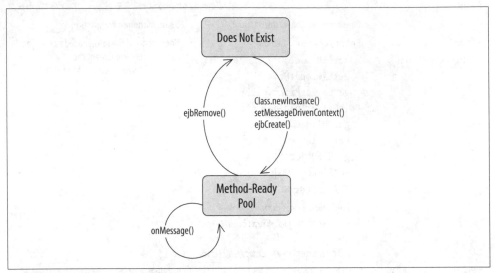

Figure B-13. Message-driven bean life-cycle state diagram

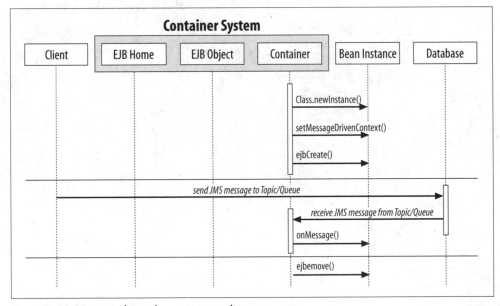

Figure B-14. Message-driven bean sequence diagram

Interactions Between Exceptions and Transactions

Table B-4 summarizes what happens to a transaction if an exception is thrown while the transaction is in process.

Table B-4. Exception summary for session and entity beans

Transaction scope	Transaction type attributes	Exception thrown	Container's action	Client's view
Client-initiated transaction. The transaction is started by the client (application or EJB) and is propagated to the enterprise bean method.	transaction-type = Container transaction-attribute = Required | Mandatory | Supports	Application exception	If the EJB invoked `setRollbackOnly()`, mark the client's transaction for rollback. Rethrow the application exception.	Receives the application exception. The client's transaction may or may not have been marked for rollback.
		System exception	Mark the client's transaction for rollback. Log the error. Discard the instance. Rethrow the JTA `TransactionRolledbackException` to remote clients or the `javax.ejb.TransactionRolledbackLocalException` to EJB 2.0 local clients.	Remote clients receive the JTA `TransactionRolledbackException`; local clients receive the `javax.ejb.TransactionRolledbackLocalException`. The client's transaction has been rolled back.
Container-initiated transaction. The transaction started when the EJB's method was invoked and will end when the method completes.	transaction-type = Container transaction-attribute = Required | RequiresNew	Application exception	If the EJB invoked `setRollbackOnly()`, roll back the transaction and rethrow the application exception. If the EJB did not explicitly roll back the transaction, attempt to commit the transaction and rethrow the application exception.	Receives the application exception. The EJB's transaction may or may not have been rolled back. The client's transaction is not affected.

Table B-4. Exception summary for session and entity beans (continued)

Transaction scope	Transaction type attributes	Exception thrown	Container's action	Client's view
		System exception	Roll back the transaction. Log the error. Discard the instance. Rethrow the `RemoteException` to remote clients or the `EJBException` to EJB 2.0 local clients.	Remote clients receive the `RemoteException`; local EJB 2.0 clients receive the `EJBException`. The EJB's transaction was rolled back. The client's transaction may or may not be marked for rollback, depending on the vendor.
The bean is not part of a transaction. The EJB was invoked but does not propagate the client's transaction and does not start its own transaction.	transaction-type = Container transaction-attribute = `Never` | `NotSupported` | `Supports` |	Application exception	Rethrow the application exception.	Receives the application exception. The client's transaction is not affected.
		System exception	Log the error. Discard the instance. Rethrow the `RemoteException` to remote clients or the `EJBException` to EJB 2.0 local clients.	Remote clients receive the `RemoteException`; local EJB 2.0 clients receive the `EJBException`. The client's transaction may or may not be marked for rollback, depending on the vendor.
Bean-managed transaction. The stateful or stateless session EJB uses the `EJBContext` to explicitly manage its own transaction.	transaction-type = Bean transaction-attribute = Bean-managed transaction EJBs do not use transaction attributes.	Application exception	Rethrow the application exception.	Receives the application exception. The client's transaction is not affected.
		System exception	Roll back the transaction. Log the error. Discard the instance. Rethrow the `RemoteException` to remote clients or the `EJBException` to EJB 2.0 local clients.	Remote clients receive the `RemoteException`; local EJB 2.0 clients receive the `EJBException`. The client's transaction is not affected.

Table B-5 summarizes the interactions between different types of exceptions and transactions in message-driven beans.

Table B-5. Exception summary for message-driven beans

Transaction scope	Transaction type attributes	Exception thrown	Container's action
Container-initiated transaction. The transaction started before the onMessage() method was invoked and will end when the method completes.	transaction-type = Container transaction-attribute = Required	System exception	Roll back the transaction. Log the error. Discard the instance.
Container-initiated transaction. No transaction was started.	transaction-type = Container transaction-attribute = NotSupported	System exception	Log the error. Discard the instance.
Bean-managed transaction. The message-driven bean uses the EJBContext to explicitly manage its own transaction.	transaction-type = Bean transaction-attribute = Bean-managed transaction EJBs do not use transaction attributes.	System exception	Roll back the transaction. Log the error. Discard the instance.

EJB Vendors

This appendix lists vendors of EJB servers. It includes all the vendors of which I am aware, as of publication. However, with the number of vendors that already provide servers and the number that are introducing new products daily, this list is obviously incomplete. Furthermore, I have made no attempt to distinguish EJB 2.0 servers from 1.1 servers; most (if not all) of the EJB 1.1 vendors should migrate to 2.0 by mid-2002.

Commercial Products

Table C-1 lists some of the currently available commercial EJB servers.

Table C-1. Commercial EJB servers

Company name	Company URL	EJB server name
ATG	*http://www.atg.com*	Dynamo Application Server
BEA Systems	*http://www.beasys.com*	BEA WebLogic Server
Blazix	*http://www.blazix.com*	EJB Server
Borland	*http://www.borland.com*	AppServer
BROKAT Infosystems	*http://www.brokat.com*	Twister
		Gemstone/J
Caucho Technology	*http://www.caucho.com*	Resin-CMP
Compaq	*http://nonstop.compaq.com*	NonStop™ Enterprise Application Server
Fujitsu-Seimens	*http://bs2www.fujitsu-siemens.de*	BeanTransactions
Fujitsu Software	*http://www.interstage.com*	Interstage
Hitachi	*http://www.hitachi.co.jp*	Cosminexus
HP Bluestone	*http://www.bluestone.com*	Total-e-Server
IBM	*http://www.software.ibm.com*	WebSphere Application Server
Information Builders	*http://www.ibi.com*	ParlayEJB Application Server
In-Q-My/SAP	*http://www.inqmy.com*	In-Q-My Application Server

Table C-1. Commercial EJB servers (continued)

Company name	Company URL	EJB server name
Iona Technologies	*http://www.iona.com*	iPortal Application Server
ObjectSpace	*http://www.objectspace.com*	Voyager
Oracle	*http://www.oracle.com*	Oracle Application Server Oracle9i
Orion	*http://www.orionserver.com*	Orion Application Server
Persistence Software	*http://www.persistence.com*	PowerTier for J2EE
Pramati	*http://www.pramati.com*	Pramati Application Server
Secant Technologies	*http://www.secant.com*	ModelMethods Enterprise Server
Silverstream	*http://www.silverstream. com*	SilverStream Application Server
Sun Microsystems	*http://java.sun.com/j2ee/*	J2EE 1.3 SDK (Reference Implementation)
Sybase	*http://www.sybase.com*	EAServer
Unify	*http://www.unify.com*	EWave
Versant	*http://www.versant.com*	Versant enJin

Open Source Projects

Several open source EJB servers have become available since the first edition of this book was published. These servers are listed in Table C-2. The author of this book, Richard Monson-Haefel, is the lead architect of ExoLab's OpenEJB server.

Table C-2. Open source EJB servers

Sponsor name	Company URL	EJB server name
Evidian/Objectweb	*http://www.objectweb.org/jonas/*	JOnAS
ExoLab	*http://openejb.exolab.org*	OpenEJB
JBoss	*http://www.jboss.org*	JBoss
Lutris	*http://www.enhydra.com*	Enhydra (EJB server based on JOnAS)

Index

Symbols

<= comparison operator, 245
< comparison operator, 245
<> comparison operator, 245
= comparison operator, 245
>= comparison operator, 245
> comparison operator, 245
\ escape character, 249
> greater than, 243
< less than, 243
% percent, 248
_ underscore, 248
*(see asterisk)

Numbers

2-PC (two-phase commit protocol), 412

A

ABS arithmetic function, 250
abstract persistence schema, 153, 185–188,
        492
    EJB QL and, 234
    terminology conventions and, 185
abstract programming model, 185
abstract schema name, 229, 491
<abstract-schema-name> element, 229, 477,
        491
abstraction, coarse-grained vs.
        fine-grained, 43
access control, 76, 77–80
AccessLocalException, 502

accessor methods (accessors), 153, 190
    <cmr-field> element and, 188
    naming conventions and, 266
    (see also set and get methods)
ACID (atomic, consistent, isolated, and
        durable), 400
ACID transactions, 397–403
<acknowledge-mode> element, 389, 480
activating
    enterprise beans, 59–61
    entity beans, 310
    message-driven beans, 396
    stateful session beans, 358
    stateless session beans, 331
    transient fields, 361
actual types, 120
adapter classes, 459
addPhoneNumber( ), 199
Address EJB (sample entity bean), 171–182
    queries and, 234–250
    relationships and, 189–226
ADDRESS table, creating, 172
AddressBean class, 232
AddressDO dependent value class, 177–179
administered objects, 479, 487
afterBegin( ), 443
AND operator, 244
application client component, 511–513
application developers
    CTMs and, 14
    importance of component models for, 16
application exceptions, 121
    bean-managed persistence and, 275
    DuplicateKeyException and, 518

We'd like to hear your suggestions for improving our indexes. Send email to *index@oreilly.com*.

C

C++ programming language, 3
Cabin EJB (sample entity bean), 28–32
    creating, 87–107
    deploying, 100
    deployment descriptor for, 78, 470–472
    local interface, creating for, 144–146
    many-to-many relationship and, 220–223
    persistence and, 68–70
    queries and, 234–250
    using, 40–48
CABIN table, creating, 99
cabin.jar file, 98
callback methods, 31–33, 293–301
    adapter classes and, 459
    bean class and, 93
    EJBException and, 275
    RemoteException and, 275
cardinality (see multiplicity)
cascade deletes, 223–226
    caution with, 226
    workbook exercise for, 226
casting, programming language support
            for, 124
CCM (CORBA Component Model), 18
CDATA sections, 481
    WHERE clause and, 243
chaining stateful session beans, 467
checked exceptions (see subsystem
            exceptions)
CICS, 13
    CORBA and, 19
classes (see bean class)
Class.newInstance( ), 289
Client API, 119–150
client applications
    container-managed persistence and, 166
    creating
        for entity beans, 100–107
        for session beans, 115
    entity bean relationships, testing
            with, 179–182
    examples of for MDBs, 391–394
    for JMS, 368–371
    stateful session beans and, 334
client view, 117–150
    RMI protocols and, 72
    stateful session beans and, 340
client-jar file, 506
clients, example of (PersonClient), 10
CLR (Common Language Runtime), 17
CMP (see container-managed persistence)

CMP 1.1 vs. CMP 2.0, 153
CMP entity beans, 152
    EJB 1.1 and, 255–264
    primary keys and, 165, 482
    relationships between, 183–226
    sharing, 195, 208, 211, 217
    transaction attributes and, 409
    workbook exercise for, 264
CMP fields (see persistence fields)
<cmp-field> element, 96, 478
    values of, 164
<cmp-version> element, 163, 477
CMR fields, 187, 229, 234, 236–239
<cmr-field> element, 187, 195
<cmr-field-name> element, 188, 494
coarse-grained abstraction, 43
code (see source code)
Collection type, 258
    EJB 2.0 and, 281
Collection.add( ), 201
Collection.addAll( ), 212
collection-based relationships (see
            relationships, collection-based)
Collection.remove( ), 201
co-located enterprise beans, 143–146, 223
COM+, 17
COM (Component Object Model), 17
commit( ), 422, 430
common interface, implementing, 460–464
Common Language Runtime (CLR), 17
Common Object Request Broker
            Architecture (see CORBA)
comparison operators, 243, 245
    unsupported Date class and, 252
    WHERE clause and, 245
component interfaces, 25–29
    differentiating between, 504
    EJB 2.0 and, 38
    implementing a common interface
            and, 460–464
    (see also remote/remote home interfaces;
            local/local home interfaces)
component models, 12
    importance of for application
            developers, 16
    standard model and, 19
Component Object Model (COM), 17
component transaction monitors/servers (see
            CTMs)
compound primary keys, 32, 165, 286,
            288–291
    hash codes in, 445
    specifying, 480–483

E

LIKE comparison operator and, 249
MEMBER OF operator and, 248
notifications, 32
NotSupported transaction attribute, 406,
421
n-tier architectures, 3

O

OBJECT( ) operator, 236, 240, 250
object bindings, 74
Object class, 137
object database persistence, 70
object ID (OID), 135
Object Management Group (see OMG)
Object Request Brokers (see ORBs)
object serialization
    bean instance activation and, 361
    Handles and, 139
object transaction monitors (see CTMs)
Object Transaction Service (OTS), 421
Object type, primary keys and, 292
ObjectMessage, 367
ObjectNotFoundException, 282, 438, 522
    find methods and, 231
object-oriented databases, persistence
        and, 70
object-oriented programming languages, 3
    RMI and, 13
object-to-relational database mapping
        wizards, 69, 465
    direct database access and, 467
object-to-relational persistence, 68
ODBC (Microsoft), 19
OID (object ID), 135
OMG (Object Management Group), 18
    CORBA-compliant ORBs and, 61
one-to-many bidirectional
        relationship, 209–214
one-to-many unidirectional
        relationship, 196–204
one-to-one bidirectional
        relationship, 192–196
one-to-one unidirectional
        relationship, 189–192
online book order transactions, 399
onMessage( ), 49, 370, 378, 382
    business-to-business applications
        and, 383–385
open connections, 331
operator precedence, WHERE clause
        and, 242
OR operator, 244

ORBs (Object Request Brokers), 12, 14
    in application servers, 4
    CTMs and, 15
    services, defining for, 61
ORDER BY clause, 251
OTMs (see CTMs)
OTS (Object Transaction Service), 421
overloaded constructor, 289
overloaded methods, 503

P

parameters, 120
pass-by-value feature, 73
passing objects by value
    dependent objects and, 446–454
    entity objects and, 453
Passivated state, 360–362
passivating enterprise beans, 59–61
paths, simple queries with, 236–239
PAYMENT table, 318
percent (%), 248
performance
    improving with session beans, 45,
        454–459
    of transactions
        across methods, 426
        balancing against consistency, 419
permissions, <method-permission> element
        and, 496, 504
persistence, 67–71, 152
    enterprise beans and, 24
    entity beans and, 152
    stateful session beans and, 333
    workbook exercise for, 167
    (see also bean-managed persistence;
        container-managed persistence)
persistence classes, 154
persistence fields, 93, 153, 167
    manipulating with bulk
        accessors, 450–453
persistence instances, 154
<persistence-type> element, 163, 477
Person (sample business object), 7–12
PersonClient (sample client), 10
PersonServer (sample distributed
        object), 7–12
phantom reads, 413, 416
phantom records, 416
Phone EJB (sample entity bean), 196–204
platform independence, 1
pointers, 189
point-to-point (p2p) messaging model, 373

U

unchecked exceptions, 145
unchecked methods, 80–81, 499
undefined primary keys, 291–293
underscore (_), 248
unit-of-work, 398, 403
unsetEntityContext( ), 294, 314
updatePhoneNumber( ), 200
URLs
    distributed computing technologies, xviii
    EJB, xviii
    JAR files for Customer EJB, 165
    in JNDI, 118
    Sun Microsystems, 87
    this book, xvii
    workbook exercises, xvi, 87
    XML deployment descriptors and, 473
users, 77
UserTransaction interface, 421, 429–431
    definition of, 429
utilities
    container-deployment, 154, 165
    for database tables, 189

V

validation rules, 449
value types, restrictions on, 123
vendors
    of CTMs, 16–20
        fear of lock-in and, 20
    of EJB servers
        list of, 546
        object-to-relational database mapping
            wizards and, 465
    support for JMS, 363
virtual fields, 153
Visual Cafe IDE (WebGain), 87
VisualAge IDE (IBM), 87

W

.war (web archive) files, 511
web components, 509
web servers, in application servers, 4
web-based interfaces, in
        distributed-business-object
        architectures, 2
WebGain's Visual Cafe IDE, 87
WebSphere (IBM), 87
WHERE clause, 241–250
wildcards, asterisk indicating, 497, 502

wizards
    for graphical deployment, 100
    for object-to-relational database
        mapping, 69
workbooks for use with this book, xvi
    deploying Customer EJB and, 166
    exercises in, 86
workflow, modeling with session
        beans, 42–46, 315
    stateful session beans and, 334, 350
wrapper classes for primitive data types, 286
write locks, 417
"write once, run anywhere", 1

X

XML, 469
    version of, specifying in documents, 472
XML deployment descriptors, 34, 469–506
    BMP entity beans and, 284
    for client components, 512
    CMP entity beans and, 162–165
    contents of, 470–472
    document header and, 472
    JMS and, 368
    local interface and, 146
    MDBs and, 386
    <relationships> element and, 185
    roles and, 79
    select methods and, 233
    stateful session beans and, 354–358
    stateless session beans and, 328
    transaction attributes and, 404
XML documents, 472
XML elements, 35
    defining
        for entity beans, 96–98
        for session beans, 113
XML tag delimiters, 243

Z

zipping/unzipping JAR files, 99

About the Author

Richard Monson-Haefel is one of the world's leading experts in Enterprise Java-Beans. He is the architect of OpenEJB (*http://openejb.exolab.org*), an open source EJB container, and has consulted as an architect on Enterprise JavaBeans, CORBA, Java RMI, and other distributed computing projects over the past several years.

Richard is also the coauthor of O'Reilly's *Java Message Service*, the best-selling book on the subject of Sun Microsystems' Java Message Service 1.0.2. In addition, Richard has authored numerous magazine articles and was a contributing author to the book *Special Edition: Using JavaBeans* (MacMillan).

Richard maintains jMiddleware.com, a web site with resources and articles dedicated to the discussion of EJB, JMS, J2EE, and other Java middleware technologies.

Colophon

Our look is the result of reader comments, our own experimentation, and feedback from distribution channels. Distinctive covers complement our distinctive approach to technical topics, breathing personality and life into potentially dry subjects.

The animals on the cover of *Enterprise JavaBeans, Third Edition* are a wallaby and her joey. Wallabies are middle-sized marsupials belonging to the kangaroo family (*Macropodidae*, the second-largest marsupial family). They are grazers and browsers, native to Australia and found in a variety of habitats on that continent. Female wallabies have a well-developed anterior pouch in which they hold their young. When they are born, the tiny, still-blind joeys instinctively crawl up into their mother's pouches and begin to nurse. They stay in the pouch until they are fairly well-grown. A female wallaby can support joeys from up to three litters at once: one in her uterus, one in her pouch, and one that has graduated from the pouch but still returns to nurse.

Like all *Macropodidae*, wallabies have long, narrow hind feet and powerful hind limbs. Their long, heavy tails are used primarily for balance and stability and are not prehensile. Wallabies resemble kangaroos, but are smaller: they can measure anywhere from less than two feet to over five feet long, with the tail accounting for nearly half of their total length. Oddly enough, although they can hop along quite quickly (reaching speeds of up to 50 km/h), it is physically impossible for wallabies to walk backward!

The three main types of wallaby are brush, rock, and nail-tailed. There are 11 species of brush wallaby (genus *Macropus*), including the red-necked and pretty-faced wallabies, and 6 named species of rock wallaby (*Petrogale*). Brush wallabies usually live in brushland or open woods. Rock wallabies, which are notable for their extreme agility, are usually found among rocks and near water. There are only three species of nail-tailed wallaby (*Onychogalea*), which are so named because of the horny growth that appears on the tip of their tails. Two of these species are endangered—

although they were once the most numerous type of wallaby, their numbers have been seriously depleted by foxes and feral cats. Aside from hunting and habitat destruction, predation and competition by introduced species such as these is the primary threat wallabies face today.

Rachel Wheeler was the production editor and copyeditor for *Enterprise JavaBeans, Third Edition*. Nicole Arigo was the proofreader, and Darren Kelly provided quality control. Kimo Carter, Edie Shapiro, and Leanne Soylemez provided production assistance. Brenda Miller wrote the index.

Hanna Dyer designed the cover of this book, based on a series design by Edie Freedman. The cover image is an original engraving from *The Illustrated Natural History: Mammalia*, by J.G. Wood, published in 1865. Emma Colby produced the cover layout with QuarkXPress 4.1 using Adobe's ITC Garamond font.

Melanie Wang designed the interior layout, based on a series design by David Futato. Neil Walls converted the files from Microsoft Word to FrameMaker 5.5.6 using tools created by Mike Sierra. The text font is Linotype Birka; the heading font is Adobe Myriad Condensed; and the code font is LucasFont's TheSans Mono Condensed. The illustrations that appear in the book were produced by Robert Romano and Jessamyn Read using Macromedia FreeHand 9 and Adobe Photoshop 6. The tip and warning icons were drawn by Christopher Bing. This colophon was written by Rachel Wheeler.

Whenever possible, our books use a durable and flexible lay-flat binding. If the page count exceeds this binding's limit, perfect binding is used.

How to stay in touch with O'Reilly

1. Visit Our Award-Winning Web Site

http://www.oreilly.com/

★ "Top 100 Sites on the Web" —*PC Magazine*
★ "Top 5% Web sites" —*Point Communications*
★ "3-Star site" —*The McKinley Group*

Our web site contains a library of comprehensive product
information (including book excerpts and tables of
contents), downloadable software, background articles,
interviews with technology leaders, links to relevant sites,
book cover art, and more. File us in your Bookmarks or
Hotlist!

2. Join Our Email Mailing Lists

New Product Releases

To receive automatic email with brief descriptions of all
new O'Reilly products as they are released, send email to:
ora-news-subscribe@lists.oreilly.com
Put the following information in the first line of your
message (*not* in the Subject field):
subscribe ora-news

O'Reilly Events

If you'd also like us to send information about trade show
events, special promotions, and other O'Reilly events,
send email to:
ora-news-subscribe@lists.oreilly.com
Put the following information in the first line of your
message (*not* in the Subject field):
subscribe ora-events

3. Get Examples from Our Books via FTP

There are two ways to access an archive of example files
from our books:

Regular FTP

- ftp to:
  ftp.oreilly.com
  (login: anonymous
  password: your email address)
- Point your web browser to:
  ftp://ftp.oreilly.com/

FTPMAIL

- Send an email message to:
  ftpmail@online.oreilly.com
  (Write "help" in the message body)

4. Contact Us via Email

order@oreilly.com
To place a book or software order online. Good for
North American and international customers.

subscriptions@oreilly.com
To place an order for any of our newsletters or
periodicals.

books@oreilly.com
General questions about any of our books.

software@oreilly.com
For general questions and product information about
our software. Check out O'Reilly Software Online at
http://software.oreilly.com/ for software and technical
support information. Registered O'Reilly software users
send your questions to: **website-support@oreilly.com**

cs@oreilly.com
For answers to problems regarding your order or our
products.

booktech@oreilly.com
For book content technical questions or corrections.

proposals@oreilly.com
To submit new book or software proposals to our
editors and product managers.

international@oreilly.com
For information about our international distributors
or translation queries. For a list of our distributors
outside of North America check out:
http://www.oreilly.com/distributors.html

5. Work with Us

Check out our website for current employment
opportunites:
http://jobs.oreilly.com/

O'Reilly & Associates, Inc.
101 Morris Street, Sebastopol, CA 95472 USA
TEL   707-829-0515 or 800-998-9938
       (6am to 5pm PST)
FAX   707-829-0104

International Distributors

http://international.oreilly.com/distributors.html • international@oreilly.com

UK, EUROPE, MIDDLE EAST AND AFRICA (EXCEPT FRANCE, GERMANY, AUSTRIA, SWITZERLAND, LUXEMBOURG, AND LIECHTENSTEIN)

INQUIRIES

O'Reilly UK Limited
4 Castle Street
Farnham
Surrey, GU9 7HS
United Kingdom
Telephone: 44-1252-711776
Fax: 44-1252-734211
Email: information@oreilly.co.uk

ORDERS

Wiley Distribution Services Ltd.
1 Oldlands Way
Bognor Regis
West Sussex PO22 9SA
United Kingdom
Telephone: 44-1243-843294
UK Freephone: 0800-243207
Fax: 44-1243-843302 (Europe/EU orders)
or 44-1243-843274 (Middle East/Africa)
Email: cs-books@wiley.co.uk

FRANCE

INQUIRIES & ORDERS

Éditions O'Reilly
18 rue Séguier
75006 Paris, France
Tel: 33-1-40-51-71-89
Fax: 33-1-40-51-72-26
Email: france@oreilly.fr

GERMANY, SWITZERLAND, AUSTRIA, LUXEMBOURG, AND LIECHTENSTEIN

INQUIRIES & ORDERS

O'Reilly Verlag
Balthasarstr. 81
D-50670 Köln, Germany
Telephone: 49-221-973160-91
Fax: 49-221-973160-8
Email: anfragen@oreilly.de (inquiries)
Email: order@oreilly.de (orders)

CANADA (FRENCH LANGUAGE BOOKS)

Les Éditions Flammarion ltée
375, Avenue Laurier Ouest
Montréal (Québec) H2V 2K3
Tel: 1-514-277-8807
Fax: 1-514-278-2085
Email: info@flammarion.qc.ca

HONG KONG

City Discount Subscription Service, Ltd.
Unit A, 6th Floor, Yan's Tower
27 Wong Chuk Hang Road
Aberdeen, Hong Kong
Tel: 852-2580-3539
Fax: 852-2580-6463
Email: citydis@ppn.com.hk

KOREA

Hanbit Media, Inc.
Chungmu Bldg. 210
Yonnam-dong 568-33
Mapo-gu
Seoul, Korea
Tel: 822-325-0397
Fax: 822-325-9697
Email: hant93@chollian.dacom.co.kr

PHILIPPINES

Global Publishing
G/F Benavides Garden
1186 Benavides Street
Manila, Philippines
Tel: 632-254-8949/632-252-2582
Fax: 632-734-5060/632-252-2733
Email: globalp@pacific.net.ph

TAIWAN

O'Reilly Taiwan
1st Floor, No. 21, Lane 295
Section 1, Fu-Shing South Road
Taipei, 106 Taiwan
Tel: 886-2-27099669
Fax: 886-2-27038802
Email: mori@oreilly.com

INDIA

Shroff Publishers & Distributors Pvt. Ltd.
12, "Roseland", 2nd Floor
180, Waterfield Road, Bandra (West)
Mumbai 400 050
Tel: 91-22-641-1800/643-9910
Fax: 91-22-643-2422
Email: spd@vsnl.com

CHINA

O'Reilly Beijing
SIGMA Building, Suite B809
No. 49 Zhichun Road
Haidian District
Beijing, China PR 100080
Tel: 86-10-8809-7475
Fax: 86-10-8809-7463
Email: beijing@oreilly.com

JAPAN

O'Reilly Japan, Inc.
Yotsuya Y's Building
7 Banch 6, Honshio-cho
Shinjuku-ku
Tokyo 160-0003 Japan
Tel: 81-3-3356-5227
Fax: 81-3-3356-5261
Email: japan@oreilly.com

SINGAPORE, INDONESIA, MALAYSIA AND THAILAND

TransQuest Publishers Pte Ltd
30 Old Toh Tuck Road #05-02
Sembawang Kimtrans Logistics Centre
Singapore 597654
Tel: 65-4623112
Fax: 65-4625761
Email: wendiw@transquest.com.sg

ALL OTHER COUNTRIES

O'Reilly & Associates, Inc.
101 Morris Street
Sebastopol, CA 95472 USA
Tel: 707-829-0515
Fax: 707-829-0104
Email: order@oreilly.com

AUSTRALIA

Woodslane Pty., Ltd.
7/5 Vuko Place
Warriewood NSW 2102
Australia
Tel: 61-2-9970-5111
Fax: 61-2-9970-5002
Email: info@woodslane.com.au

NEW ZEALAND

Woodslane New Zealand, Ltd.
21 Cooks Street (P.O. Box 575)
Waganui, New Zealand
Tel: 64-6-347-6543
Fax: 64-6-345-4840
Email: info@woodslane.com.au

ARGENTINA

Distribuidora Cuspide
Suipacha 764
1008 Buenos Aires
Argentina
Phone: 54-11-4322-8868
Fax: 54-11-4322-3456
Email: libros@cuspide.com

O'REILLY®

TO ORDER: **800-998-9938** • **order@oreilly.com** • **http://www.oreilly.com/**
OUR PRODUCTS ARE AVAILABLE AT A BOOKSTORE OR SOFTWARE STORE NEAR YOU.
FOR INFORMATION: **800-998-9938** • **707-829-0515** • **info@oreilly.com**